ARTIFICIAL NEURAL NETWORKS - APPLICATION

Edited by **Chi-Leung Hui**

INTECHOPEN.COM

Artificial Neural Networks - Application

Edited by Chi-Leung Hui

CBS, Edition 2016

Published by InTech

Janeza Trdine 9, 51000 Rijeka, Croatia

Publishing Process Manager Ivana Lorkovic

Technical Editor Teodora Smiljanic

Cover Designer InTech Design Team

Image Copyright Oldrich Barak, 2010. Used under license from Shutterstock.com

Additional hard copies can be obtained from orders@intechopen.com

Artificial Neural Networks- Application, Edited by Chi-Leung Hui
p. cm.
ISBN 978-953-307-188-6

INTECH

open science | open minds

Contents

Preface

This book covers 27 articles in the applications of artificial neural networks (ANN) in various disciplines which includes business, chemical technology, computing, engineering, environmental science, science and nanotechnology. They modeled the ANN with verification in different areas. They demonstrated that the ANN is very useful model and the ANN could be applied in problem solving and machine learning. This book is suitable for all professionals and scientists in understanding how ANN is applied in various areas.

Chi-Leung Hui

Part 1

Application of ANN in Business

World-Level Analysis in Top Level Football Analysis and Simulation of Football Specific Group Tactics by Means of Adaptive Neural Networks

Memmert Daniel[1], Bischof Jürgen[2], Endler Stefan[2], Grunz Andreas[1], Schmid Markus[3], Schmidt Andrea[1] and Perl Jürgen[2]
[1]*Institute of Cognitive and Team/Racket Sport ResearchGerman Sport University Cologne*
[2]*Institute of Computer Science, University of Mainz*
[3]*Institute of Sport and Sport Science, University of Heidelberg*
Germany

1. Introduction

In modern soccer tactical skills play an important role in all age groups and proficiency levels (Memmert & Harvey, 2010; Memmert & König, 2007). Many experts regard tactics as the factor which gets the least attention in the training process (Greco, Memmert & Morales, 2010; Memmert & Roth, 2007). For that reason, the most potential seems to lie in the tactics area. There are a couple of journal articles in the area of group tactics, however, a systematic overview is not available yet. It is even more crucial that there are no empirically validated differentiations of group tactical requirements in soccer. To be more specific: Of course taxonomies of group tactics occur in books sporadically, but it was not shown yet, whether they are actually relevant in amateur or competitive soccer.

Therefore, Memmert (2006) work on those deficits in order to provide a scientifically based analysis of soccer specific group tactics. Building on pilot studies (second division of German Bundesliga), the coaching philosophy of Hansi Flick (current assistant coach of the German national soccer team) was indirectly examined based on 27 3rd division home games of 1899 Hoffenheim in the seasons 2002/2003 and 2003/2004. During the recorded game, he selected important positive and negative behaviours of different position groups without being aware of the fact that their coaching skills were being evaluated. All in all, 585 match situations were judged and commented on by the coaches. The implicit expert knowledge (video sequences and comments) from the single case analysis was solidified with the help of further qualitative content analyses. The resulting offensive and defensive group tactical skills were allocated to superordinate basic categories by means of inductive categorization. Thus, group tactical challenges were identified, which have to be solved through cooperation of several team members (= position groups). Such position groups are, for instance, strikers or midfielders, but also players in certain areas (e.g. left and right wing) or players from different positions, that move across those areas in a particular moment. Based on the analysis, the following group tactical categories were validated empirically (cf. Table 1.1. & Table 1.2).

Defense	
Quick regrouping	□ Group tactical requirement, which demands that position groups prevent their opponent's attacks through quick changes from offense to defense
Pressing	□ Group tactical requirement, which demands that position groups disturb the offense actions of their opponent as early as possible
Man to man marking	□ Group tactical requirement, which demands that the members of a position groups are aware of the marking of their opponents e.g. during corner kicks or man-marking in general
Competing for the second ball	□ Group tactical requirement, which demands that position groups and individual players position themselves adequately in order to win second balls (e.g. after goal-kicks or tacklings)
Communication	□ Group tactical requirement, which demands that position groups keep their orientation on the pitch by making adequate use of previously agreed codewords
Support play	□ Group tactical requirement, which demands that position groups gain ball possession or avoid shots on goal by an appropriate position play

Table 1.1. List of 6 defensive group tactics, which result from inductive category formation and further qualitative evaluation steps (Memmert, 2006)

Offense	
Attacking play	□ Group tactical requirement, which demands that position groups initiate play by systematic actions, e.g. vertical passes
Combination play	□ Group tactical requirement, which demands that position groups keep the ball possession through double passes, short passes or triangular passes
Switch play	□ Group tactical requirement, which demands that position groups create space by passing the ball from one side of the pitch to the other
Creating space	□ Group tactical requirement, which demands that position groups choose adequate paths (e.g. cross-over and dummy runs in order to give each other space
Wing play	□ Group tactical requirement, which demands that position groups pose a goal threat on the wings e.g. by through-balls
Counter attacks	□ Group tactical requirement, which demands that position groups try to intersect the defense quickly, e.g. by playing through balls
Set pieces	□ Group tactical requirement, which demands that position groups create a goal threat through free kicks, corner kicks and throw-ins.
Setting up shots on goal	□ Group tactical requirement, which demands that position groups try to pass to their team mates so that they can score a goal from a long or short distance

Table 1.2. List of 8 offensive group tactics, which result from inductive category formation and further qualitative evaluation steps (Memmert, 2006)

These group tactics constitute the theoretical framework for our project in which evaluation tools are developed for the analysis of group tactics. Therefore, international top level soccer matches (world level analysis) are examined on the basis of position data with reference to the effectiveness of group tactical processes. "Considering the influence of the opponent, how do the players have to play together at which point in time in order to be a goal threat?" or to be more specific: "How can group tactical behaviour patterns in soccer be modeled and summarized to characteristic categories? This question is explored in section 2 of the chapter (step 1). By means of an example, potential problems in the process are illustrated and possible solutions are given. In addition, first preliminary results (step 2) are presented which compare the net based position data related procedure with conventional methods (validation study; Section 3). Section 4 of that Chapter illustrates how behaviour patterns can be evaluated, how one can identify creative behaviour and how the simulation can be used for a prognostic evaluation of the effectiveness (step 3).

2. Modelling and typification of group tactical behavior patterns by means of position data (step 1)

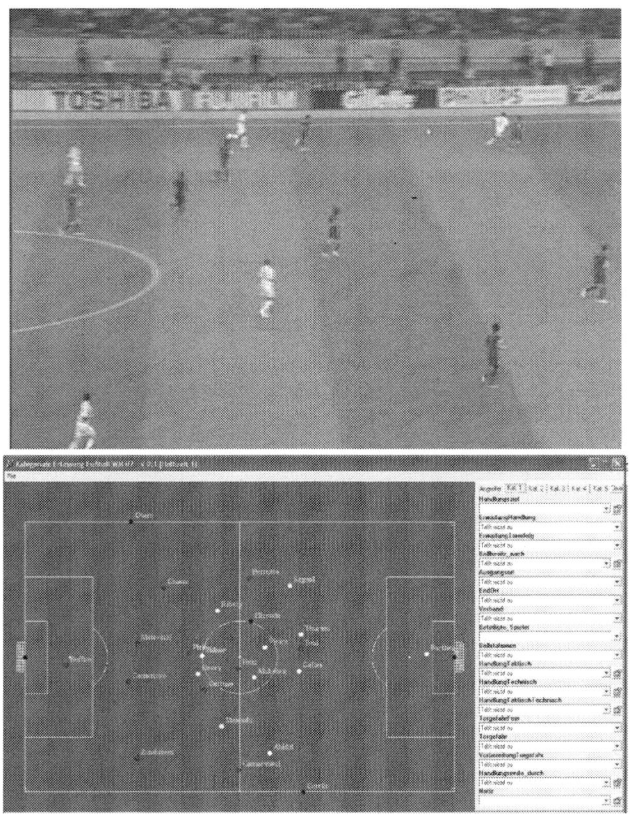

Fig. 1. Display of the in-house developed software system for the conventional analysis (a) and position data-supported analysis (b) of team sports (soccer)

At the moment, a variety of team sports (soccer, handball, basketball, volleyball) are analyzed by means of video sequences (conventional analysis, cf. Figure 1a). Current technical improvements however, allow a complete capture of position data of all 22 players and the ball (cf. Figure 1b) so that one can access the xy coordinates of the players and the ball for the entire 90 minutes. With a sampling rate of 25 frames per second, 135.000 xy data per player are produced. Thus, when looking at all players including the ball, one gets the amount of 23 x 135.000, i.e. 3.105.000 xy data.
With the software system from Figure 1b, individual match sequences can be allocated to different categories. By means of these categories, according position data can be extracted and used to train neural nets (Memmert & Perl, 2005). This process is illustrated through the following example.

Fig. 2. Display of a video sequence of wing play and the schematic representation as it is usually used to display the actions.

In the video sequence, a wing play is identified (cf. Figure 2, above). The according match sequence is thus allocated to the category "wing play" in the software system and the involved players are inputted. By means of the extracted position data, the wing play can be illustrated schematically on a graphic pitch (cf. Figure 2, down right). Figure 2 shows just one possible realization of a wing play. A couple of variations are schematically depicted in Figure 3. The position data of involved players obtained from several wing plays are then used to train a neural net and memorize the pattern "wing play". When looking at the wing plays, their capture through a neural net poses a first problem. The number of the involved players varies, down left in Figure 3 there are three players, in the other ones there are just two. Hence, the xy data set from the position data of the players and the ball contains four xy data for the wing play down left and three for the other ones. A neural net however, has a fixed dimension and thus can only process data of a certain length.

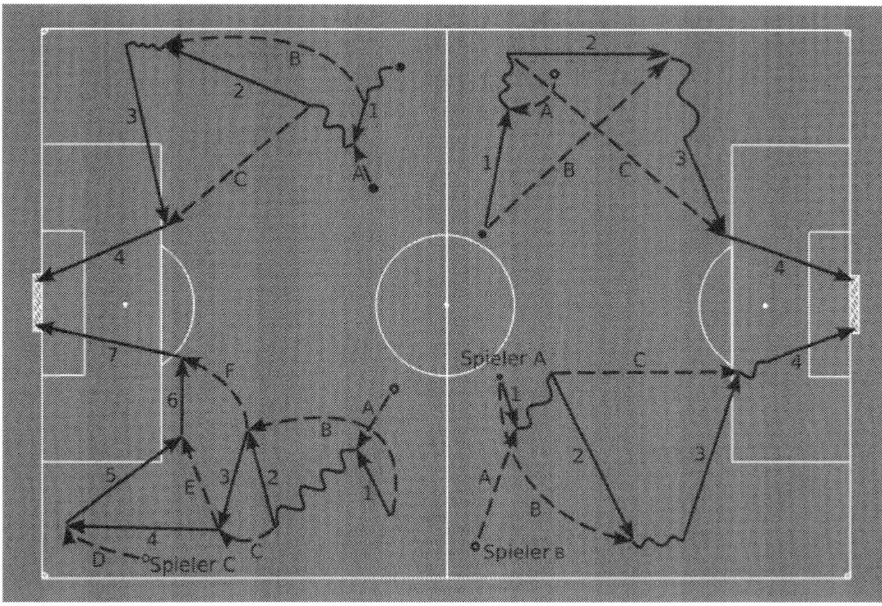

Fig. 3. Display of variations of wing play.

One solution can be to train different nets for different numbers of involved players (which would be one for two players and one for three players with respect to Figure 3). If there are more players involved, further nets would be necessary. A second problem arises due to the fact that areas on neural nets with a lot of information do not have more neurons available than areas with only few information. Thus, the lower information content could be solved

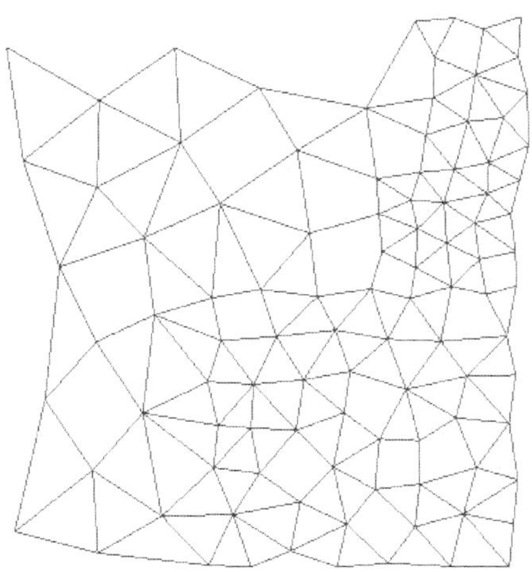

Fig. 4. Exemplary display of a neural net with variable neuron density (Perl, Memmert, Bischof & Gerharz, 2006).

better than the higher information content. With respect to the wing play, for example, this could imply that certain formations of the involved players occur more often than others, and that the more important ones are underrepresented on the net. This problem could, for example be solved with the help of a dynamic generation and administration of nodes. This is illustrated in Figure 4 by means of a two-dimensional neural net: On the left there is an area in which no neurons exist. On the bottom right, on the contrary, one can see a cluster of neurons. Thus, from left to right there is an increase of the neuron density.
When the training of the nets is complete, the movement patterns of individual players, position groups or the whole team can be depicted as trajectories on the net (cf. Figure 5)

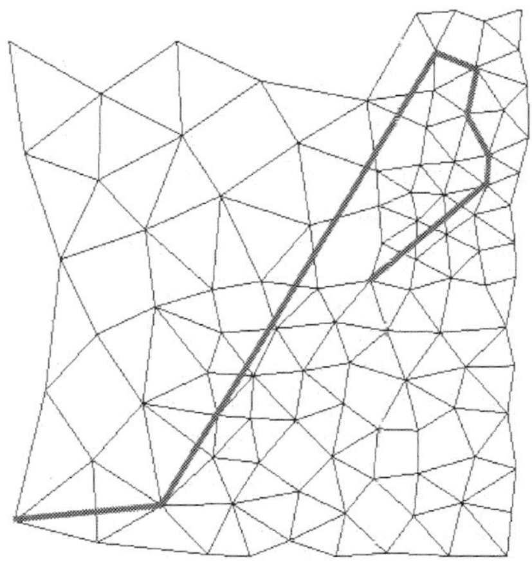

Fig. 5. Exemplary display of a trajectory as an image of a game sequence on a neural net (Perl et al., 2006).

In this process, every data set of a match sequence activates a neuron in the net. Consecutively connected, all activated neurons result in a trajectory. With a superior neural net, groups of similar match sequence patterns shall then be allocated to a mutual neuron or a cluster of adjacent neurons. For instance, all realizations of a wing play shall be identified by a neuron or neuron cluster "wing play". For this purpose, the net must have been trained with a multiplicity of different wing play patterns in advance. From this follows a third problem: For being extracted from recorded matches, there are usually only a limited number of realizations of a pattern available. Thus, it could, for example, happen that there are no position data available for some of the variations of a wing play. One solution could be to schematically draw the variations of a movement pattern onto a graphic display of a pitch, in order to let the software calculate the position data for the training with the help of a Monte Carlo simulation. This approach may seem a bit odd, but it turned out to be remarkably successful and effective due to the special training model (Perl, 2004). When processing the trajectories, the above mentioned problems occur: On the one hand, trajectories can be too long so that high dimensional nets are generated. On the other hand, trajectories can differ in length. When looking at the schematic displays in Figure 3, one can recognize that the distance covered by the involved players and the ball, varies in each example. Consequently, due to the length of the match sequence, longer trajectories are generated if the distance in longer movement patterns is not covered faster. As mentioned before, training specific nets with different lengths is not viable. With the systematic removal of redundant vectors, trajectories which are too long, can be shortened to a standard length. However, this approach is problematic for implicitly accelerating the speed of the actions. A practicable solution is the "sliding window method": from sequences of different lengths, sequences with a constant length are cut out.

3. Validation study (step 2)

For the validation of the trained nets, the results of the traditional game analysis ("golden standard") and the results of the net based position data based procedure have to be compared. Pre-studies showed that almost 80 % of the traditionally identified group tactical match events from Table 1 like playmaking, set pieces (further differentiated into throw-ins, free kicks and corner kicks) and shots on goal were also identified by our nets. At the moment we are working on a further optimization in order to obtain matching rates of more than 90 %.

4. Evaluation, creativity and simulation (step 3)

With the help of trained nets, it is possible to automatically display all match sequences of the above mentioned categories - even for yet uncategorized matches. For example, one wants to have an overview of all wing plays in a soccer match, view all sequences on video and capture them in a database for a comprehensive analysis. For example, the action patterns, which were obtained through the net based typification, can be analyzed statistically. This way, the frequency can be determined, with which a certain pattern occurs, as well as frequency of the transition from one pattern to the other.
Therefore, in a study analyzing the individual creativity (see for a definition: Memmert, 2010) of soccer players, nets were developed and validated in pre-studies, which were able to represent the individual training processes of soccer players including creative behavior (cf. Memmert & Perl, 2009b). Beginning with a red and ending with a yellow square, Figure 6 depicts the particular time steps of the respective process as red edges on all of the individual net representations. In the three steps of the process, the trajectory runs through the colored quality areas (from light green (excellent) to dark violet (poor)). The results (Figure 6) show a very unequal creativity development of 20 soccer players over the time period of 15 training months: In 5 of 20 cases (25%) the performance increased in the beginning, but turned out to be worse than in the middle of the training process eventually (up-down fluctuation process). The opposite results came up for 30 % of the test persons (down-up fluctuation process). In 25 % of the cases the performance increased monotonically, whereas it decreased monotonically in 10 % of the cases. In 10 % of the cases the performance remained (almost) entirely the same.
For the qualitative classification of actions and action types, a rating is required, which normally is not just the result of a team's actions, but rather the result of the interaction with the opponent team. The net based solution for this problem consists of the usage of team specific nets for the actions, which enable the identification and analysis of the interaction types through a hierarchically super-ordinate net. This way, actions and action types can be rated in the context of the respective interaction.
Figure 7 illustrates the used methodology: The sequence of the offense actions of Team A is illustrated in the according offense net (top left) in colored sub-sequence representations, so called phases (phase diagram offense, top), which correspond with the according defense phases of Team B (phase diagram defense, bottom). The corresponding phase sequences are transferred to the interaction net where they deliver the data for interaction and movement analyses.

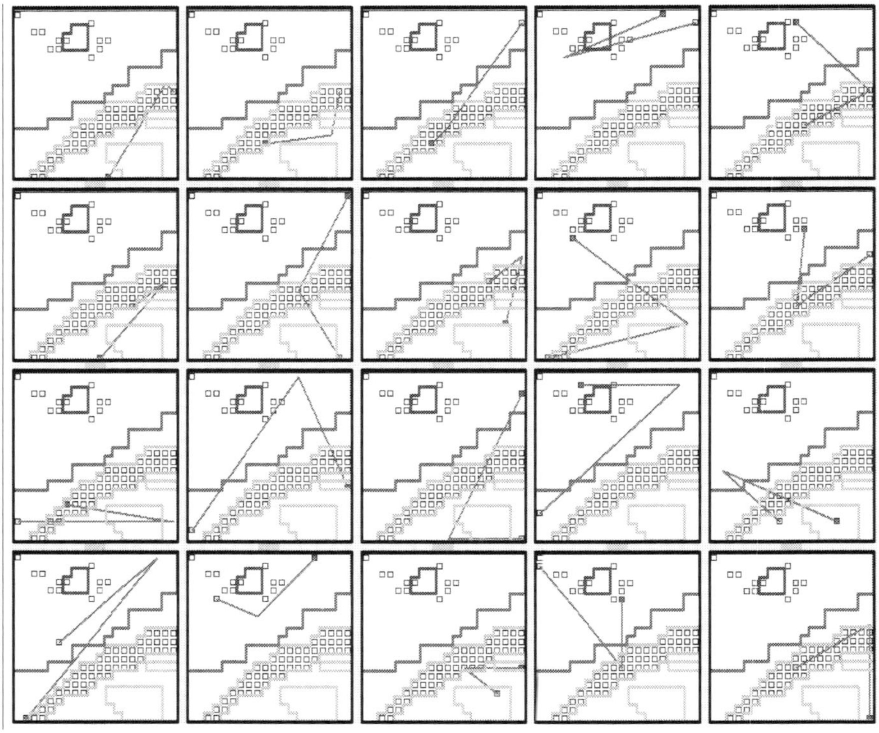

Fig. 6. Representation of intra-individual trajectories of a soccer training. The learning process begins in the red square and ends in the yellow square (cf. Memmert & Perl, 2009b).

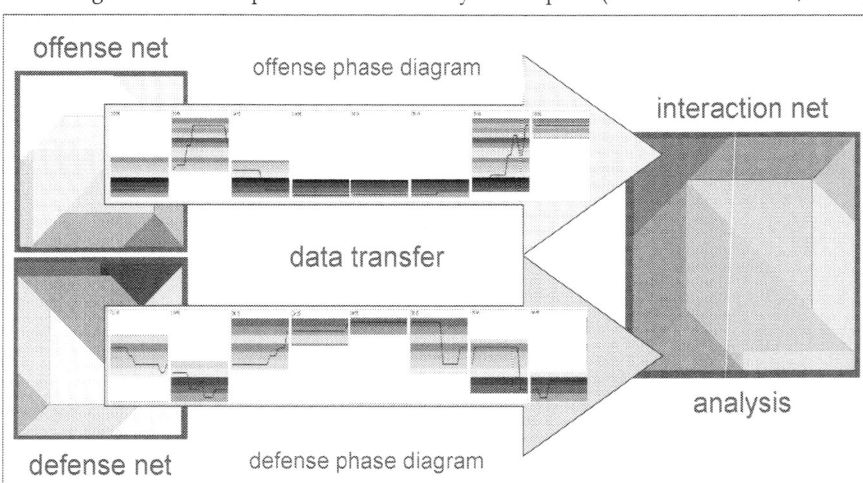

Fig. 7. Hierarchical interaction - and evaluation analysis (Grunz, Memmert & Perl, 2009)

From this approach result two important applications: First, by means of a simulation, the effectiveness of behavior processes can be evaluated prognostically. For that purpose, the game is stopped, and instead of the next action type, another type with a higher rating is chosen for the examined team. Afterwards, the game proceeds and a target performance analysis is conducted in order to determine a possible advantage of the simulated action. This way, tactical options can be tested in simulations and dropped if necessary. Second, creative actions in the sense of relevance (surprising, rare) and adequacy (successful in a particular situation) can be identified and inserted into the simulative analysis process.

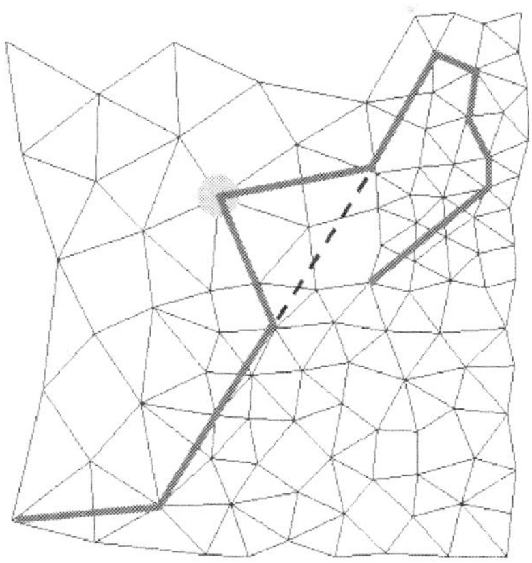

Fig. 8. Exemplary display of creative behavior in the frame of a neural net (cf. figure 5)

Figure 8, as opposed to figure 5, is a schematic depiction of a behavioral process with a new, creative aspect. The progression of the trajectory taken from figure 5 is illustrated by the dashed line. Due to the creative action, a neuron is activated and hence the trajectory deviates from the expected progression. In a longitudinal study, Memmert and Perl (2009a,b) could validate neural nets that are able to identify creative actions. Therefore, special neural nets were constructed, which combined DyCoN's (Dynamically Controlled Networks, see Perl, 2004) and neural gas elements. With their help, it was possible to select not only rare, but also tactically relevant behaviours from a multiplicity of behavior patterns. By the means of these preliminary works (Memmert & Perl, 2009a,b), in a third research episode, it is looked for rare but successful actions in the frame of different group tactics. To be concrete, the important question for practical application is explored, whether there are unusual actions in the set of wing play situations that pose a goal threat.

5. Summary and practical applications in competitive soccer

The developed nets allow a comparison of match scenes of one or more games in order to find out which tactical formations lead to which results on the pitch. The goal is to make the selection of soccer match scenes easier so that it does not have to be done manually (conventional analysis) but automatically with the help of neural nets. Thus, it is made possible to classify extensive data volume according to differences and similarities within a short time period. The analysis system based on neural nets can arrange match situations according to success or failure within seconds and hence find out whether a 4-2-3-1 formation is superior to an opponent's 4-4-2 formation under certain circumstances. With the aid of simulations, the question is followed whether changes in offense and defense (change of formation or replacements of players) have an influence on the probability of success of certain tactical moves. Furthermore, the net based approach helps not only to identify standard match sequences, but also rare and surprising sequences, and evaluates those with respect to success and adequacy in their specific contexts. Often, extraordinary actions or rare goals are discounted as coincidence, which can be identified as spontaneous, creative and non-accidental processes after a closer analysis. This could be extremely helpful for the evaluation of sport-specific training concepts to improve creative behavior (Memmert, 2007; Memmert, Baker & Bertsch, 2010).

Of course, neural nets will still never be able to replace experts. However, they offer the opportunity of an interactive communication (high speed and online) with coaches and provide them with specific data and information that they can interpret and make use of. This way, results are provided in a quick and convenient manner. These results are helpful to study an opponent and they give information about which game formations are more likely to be successful against a certain team with a certain tactic and a certain formation.

6. References

Greco, P.; Memmert, D. & Morales, J. C. P. (2010). The effect of deliberate play on tactical performance in basketball. *Perceptual & Motor Skills, 110,* 849-856. [0.30]

Grunz, A.; Memmert, D. & Perl, J. (2009). Analysis and Simulation of Actions in Games by Means of Special Self-Organizing Maps. *International Journal of Computer Science in Sport, 8,* 22–37.

Memmert, D. (2006). Optimales Taktiktraining im Leistungsfußball [Optimal Training of Group Tactics in Top Level Soccer]. Balingen: Spitta Verlag.

Memmert, D. (2007). Can creativity be improved by an attention-broadening training program? - An Exploratory Study Focusing on Team Sports. *Creativity Research Journal, 19,* 281–292. [0.81]

Memmert, D. (2010, in press). Sports and Creativity. M. Runco & S. Pritzker, Encyclopedia of Creativity, 2nd Edition. Elsevier.

Memmert, D. & Harvey, S. (2010, in press). Identification of Non-Specific Tactical Problems in Invasion Games. *Physical Education and Sport Pedagogy.*

Memmert, D. & König, S. (2007). Teaching Games at Elementary Schools. *International Journal of Physical Education, 44, 54–67.*

Memmert, D. & Perl, J. (2005). Game Intelligence Analysis by Means of a Combination of Variance-Analysis and Neural Networks. *International Journal of Computer Science in Sport, 4,* 29–38.

Memmert, D. & Perl, J. (2009a). Analysis and Simulation of Creativity Learning by Means of Artificial Neural Networks. *Human Movement Science, 28,* 263–282.

Memmert, D. & Perl, J. (2009b). Game Creativity Analysis by Means of Neural Networks. *Journal of Sport Science, 27,* 139–149.

Memmert, D. & Roth, K. (2007). The Effects of Non-Specific and Specific Concepts on Tactical Creativity in Team Ball Sports. *Journal of Sport Science, 25,* 1423–1432. [1.80]

Memmert, D.; Baker, J. & Bertsch, C. (2010). Play and Practice in the Development of Sport-Specific Creativity in Team Ball Sports. *High Ability Studies, 21,* 3-18.

Perl, J. (2004). A Neural Network approach to movement pattern analysis. *Human Movement Science, 23,* 605–620.

Perl, J.; Memmert, D.; Bischof, J. & Gerharz, Ch.(2006). On a First Attempt to Modelling Creativity Learning by Means of Artificial Neural Networks. *International Journal of Computer Science in Sport, 5,* 33–38.

2

Artificial Neural Networks Numerical Forecasting of Economic Time Series

Michael Štencl and Jiří Šťastný
Mendel University in Brno, Faculty of Business and Economics, Dept. of Informatics
Czech Republic

1. Introduction

The current global market is driven by many factors, e.g. by the facts that we live in the information age and that information is distributed in short times, large amounts and by many data channels. It is practically impossible to analyse all kinds of incoming information flows and transform them to data by classical methods. New requirements call for new methods. Artificial neural networks once trained on patterns can be used for forecasting and they are able to work with extremely big datasets in reasonable time. Traditionally, this is solved by means of a statistical analysis - first a time-series model is constructed and then statistical prediction algorithms are applied to it in order to obtain future values. The common point for both methods is the learning process from samples of past data, or learning from the past. From many of the uncommon points the input conditions for the model creation and the length of the time series pattern set could be pointed out. On one hand, very sophisticated statistical methods exist that have strictly defined input conditions for datasets; on the other hand, practically open input conditions of artificial neural networks can be used. Regarding the length of the time series, the main problem of the Czech Republic, short and middle term predictions are valuable datasets. The lengths of selected economic values are not huge enough for quality of prediction or forecasting. Hand-in-hand with typical problems of real datasets (noisiness and/or missing data), there is the issue of the quality of the numerical forecasting. In addition, the strong nonlinearity of the models leads to an unsolvable usage of classical methods or construction of models that are not representing the reality. These are only few of the difficulties related to economic and financial modelling and prediction. Possible problems of numerous types of the artificial neural networks with *n*-setups make the issue even more complicated.

The aim of this chapter is to compare different types of artificial neural networks using short and middle terms predictions of a real-world economic index. A number of papers dealing with artificial neural networks used for particular problems and often for the test do not use real-world economic indexes.

The chapter is divided into four sections. The first simply presents the introduction to the research domain. The second section describes state-of-the-art artificial intelligence approaches to both prediction and forecasting of economic indexes. In the third section, neural network types and learning algorithms dealing with the prediction of time series and learning optimization are presented. In detail, the third section also includes methods of verification and validation of artificial neural networks and description of real-world economic indexes used in the experiments. In addition, the experimental approach including methods and strategies for neural network adaption to real-world data approximation and prediction is included as a subchapter. The last chapter presents a number of prediction experiment results of the real-world economic indexes, including the learning process optimization by different learning algorithms, multithread implementation of artificial neural networks. Evaluating the different artificial neural networks types on short and middle term prediction with commented results is another part of the fourth section. Global conclusions end this chapter and give further perspectives for future development of proposed approaches.

2. Artificial Neural Network approach

Artificial neural networks do not need to know the algorithm to reach forecast as in the statistics methods and this makes the main difference (Novák, 1998; Sarle, 1994; Šnorek & Jiřina, 1998). The forecasting of future values with artificial neural networks is based on learned past pattern sets for a defined length. The principle of artificial neural networks is based on learning values from past periods and then approximating the future values. The accuracy of the prediction is influenced by several attributes such as the topology of the selected artificial neural network, the learning rule, the types of activation function, the number of inputs, the length and also the structure of input time series. Globally, there are two main categories of artificial neural network models - feed-forward networks and recurrent networks. A feed-forward network represents a function of its current input; thus, it has no internal state other than the weights themselves. A recurrent network feeds its outputs back into its own inputs. (Russel & Norvig, 2003) These authors formulate learning as an optimization search in weight space. The definition means the reset of the weights of inputs on each input node. Artificial neural networks use two types of learning - supervised and unsupervised. When supervised learning is used a training set for output validation must be supplied. Training sets are used as inputs for the network and the computed outputs are compared with sample results. Weights of all neurons are adjusted backwards according to the output error. The learning algorithm used defines a specific algorithm of resetting the weights. Both genetic algorithm and back-propagation algorithm were tested as the learning algorithms. Back-propagation seems to yield better results in prediction tasks (Štastný & Škorpil, 2007).

One of the basic but also very powerful types of the network is the Multi Layer Perceptron Network (MLP); it belongs to the group of feed-forward neural networks. The configuration variations of MLP networks including the selection of different learning algorithms are a very complex task. The MLP network with the back-propagation learning algorithm (Štastný & Škorpil, 2005) is also one of the most widely used methods in time series forecasting. Often the MLP model is also combined with statistical models in hybrid systems (Tseng & Tzeng, 2002). The MLP model is one of the basic models but often brings very good results. According to the article (Štastný & Štencl, 2008), there has been wide interest in making the comparison study of the published MLP forecast with other models such as the radial basis function (RBF-NN) or competitive networks. The prediction of economic values has its own specifics. First of all, a large number of variables causes a strong non-linear increase in complexity of its analysis and usually the time series (Mostafa, 2009), especially in the conditions of the Czech Republic, is not very long. Another notable problem is incompleteness of and uncertainty in the datasets. Making the models with statistic methods is often impossible, but certain artificial intelligence methods are able to solve that problem.

3. Methods

This part describes two learning algorithms for training MLP networks. Commonly known Back Propagation learning algorithm and Levenberg-Marquardt algorithm are described. Both were selected during previous research (Štencl & Šťastný, 2009; Štencl & Šťastný, 2010; Šťastný & Škorpil, 2005) focused on learning process optimization and both showed the ability to be used for short and middle term prediction of real-world economic time series. As the second type of the artificial neural network, the Radial Basis Function network was selected (Štencl et al., 2009; Štencl & Šťastný, 2009). At the end of the upcoming Results part of this chapter, the comparison of selected artificial neural network results with genetic algorithm approach is presented (Štencl et al., 2009; Šťastný & Škorpil, 2007).

3.1 Neural Networks learning algorithms

First, and most known, the Back Propagation (BP) learning algorithm is the most common learning algorithm for Multi-layer perceptron networks (MLP NN). The algorithm is based on minimizing the error of neural network output compared to the target value. A more detailed description of BP was published previously (e.g. Bishop, 2000; Šťastný & Škorpil, 2005; Štencl & Šťastný, 2009). Standard BP algorithm could be modified to BP with momentum and variable step learning.

The features and usage of the momentum in BP is described in classical BP algorithm. Basically, the algorithm remembers in a parameter the direction in which the current state in error space was reached. This parameter prevents the algorithm from being stuck in local minima. The momentum is added to the learning rule fitting up to changes in weights which are equal to the sum of the recent changes and new variations calculated using BP. The momentum constant defines the effect of the momentum. If the constant is equal to zero, the momentum is ignored, if it is equal to one, the changes are ignored and weights remain the same.

Variable step learning (η) provides learning acceleration. MLP is learning faster with a bigger learning step. However, when the learning step reaches the maximal value, the learning process becomes unstable. Variable step learning is set up by the maximal (initial) learning step, the minimal (final) learning step and the type of the function.

$$\eta = \eta_{\max} - i^{\exp}\left(\frac{\eta_{\max} - \eta_{\min}}{i_{cel}^{\exp}}\right) \tag{1}$$

At the beginning, the maximal (initial) learning step is set to boost the network learning progress. The network looks first for the rough values of weights. After that, the values are decreasing with each learning step according to the selected type of the function. The curve defined by the type of the function connects the maximal and the minimal step value. The type of the curve can be anything from abscissa, over quadratic function to the cubic function. The exponent value determines the decreasing speed at the beginning of the learning process and at the end of the learning process. The value of learning step in the *i*-th iteration is obtained by formula (1); where exp is representing the exponent of the calculated curve, the i_{cet} is the global amount of iteration, $\eta_{\max}$ and $\eta_{\min}$ is the maximal, resp. minimal, learning step.

The momentum and variable learning steps are some of the optimization methods for the BP algorithm. The set-up of the BP algorithm with a momentum and a variable step is presented at Fig. 1.

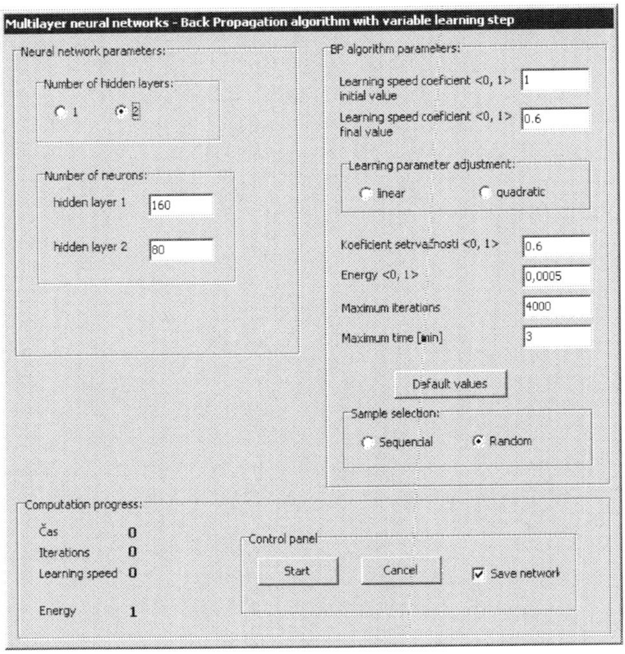

Fig. 1. Set-up window of MLP Network for BP algorithm with a variable learning step

There are also many different techniques including the Levenberg–Marquardt algorithm. The Levenberg–Marquardt method is one of the fastest learning algorithm methods for MLP networks (Hagan & Menhaj, 1999; Sotirov, 2005). The Levenberg-Marquardt (LM) algorithm is an iterative technique that locates the minimum of a multivariate function which is expressed as the sum of squares of non-linear real-valued functions (Sotirov, 2005). It has become a standard technique for non-linear least-squares problems, widely adopted in a broad spectrum of disciplines. LM can be thought of as a combination of steepest descent and the Gauss-Newton method.

As noticed before, the LM algorithm is a variant of the Gauss-Newton method and was designed to approach second-order training speed without having to compute the Hessian matrix (Hagan & Menhaj, 1999). Typically, for the learning of feed-forward neural networks, a sum of squares is used as the performance function. Then the Hessian matrix can be approximated as

$$H = J^T J \tag{2}$$

and the gradient can be computed as

$$g = J^T e \tag{3}$$

where J is the Jacobian matrix (for single neuron shown at (4), where w is vector of the weights, w_0 bias of the neuron, ε error vector) that contains first derivate of the network error with respect to the weights and biases, and e is a vector of network errors (Hagan & Menhaj, 1999; Sotirov, 2005).

$$J = \begin{bmatrix} \frac{\partial \varepsilon_1}{\partial w_1} & \cdots & \frac{\partial \varepsilon_1}{\partial w_n} & \frac{\partial \varepsilon_1}{\partial w_0} \\ \vdots & & \vdots & \vdots \\ \frac{\partial \varepsilon_p}{\partial w_1} & \cdots & \frac{\partial \varepsilon_p}{\partial w_n} & \frac{\partial \varepsilon_p}{\partial w_0} \end{bmatrix} = \begin{bmatrix} x_{1_1} & \cdots & x_{n_1} & 1 \\ \vdots & & \vdots & \vdots \\ x_{1_p} & \cdots & x_{n_p} & 1 \end{bmatrix} \tag{4}$$

The LM algorithm uses the (2) approximation of the Hessian matrix, and the determination of new weight configuration is calculated as follows:

$$w_{k+1} = w_k - \left[J^T J + \mu I\right]^{-1} J^T \varepsilon_k \tag{5}$$

When the scalar μ is zero, the algorithm uses an approximation of the Hessian matrix. When μ is large, this becomes gradient descent with a small step size. Each iteration decreases μ after a successful step, which reduces the performance function and increases μ only when a tentative step would increase the performance function (Hagan & Menhaj, 1999; MathWorks, 2010). Matlab R2010a has an efficient implementation of LM. Because the solution of the matrix equation is a built-in function, its attributes become even more pronounced in a Matlab environment (MathWorks, 2010).

3.2 RBF Neural Networks

Radial Basis Function neural networks (RBF-NN) belong to the feed-forward models of neural networks. RBF-NN consists of three layers of nodes. The first is the input layer that transports the input vector to each of the nodes in the hidden (second) layer. The third layer consists of one node. It sums up the outputs of the hidden layer of nodes to yield the decision value (Wedding & Cios, 1996).

As defined in (Wedding & Cios, 1996; Šíma & Neruda, 1996) the hidden layer of nodes, each node represents a data cluster, which is centred at a particular point and has a given radius and could be named as local unit. As in (Šíma & Neruda, 1996) the local units have the relevant output located at the point in close neighbourhood defined by its parameters. When an input vector goes on each node of hidden layer simultaneously, each node then calculates the distance from the input vector to its own centre (Wedding & Cios, 1996). The MLP nodes, on the other hand, divide the input space into subspaces in which there is a big difference on output.

Radial Basis Functions are used for the approximation and interpolation in numerical mathematics. The approximation process is based on a function. Usually, the linear combination of base functions, here the radial functions, is used. The basis function realizes the transformation of the distance value, calculated from the input vector to its own centre, to the output value of the node. The output value is then multiplied by a weighting value or a constant.

Problems with the creation of RBF-NN consist in the determination of the number of neurons in the hidden layer, the determination of the middles of these neurones and the determination of the neurones width. A powerful method for the determination of the number and quality of neurons of the hidden layer is the algorithm APC-III (Štencl & Šťastný, 2009). This single-pass associating algorithm unlike others uses a constant radial (Ripley, 1996).

```
Algorithm APC-III:
C:      the number of neurons
c_j:    the middle of  j-th  neuron
n_j:    the number of samples in j-th neuron
d_ij:   the distance between  x_i and j-th neuron

{
        C=1; c_1 ← x_1; n_1 = 1;
          for(i = 2; i =< P; i++) // for every pattern from training set
        {
                for(i = 1; i =< C; i++) // for every neuron
                {
                  calculated_ij;
                  if(d_ij=< R_0) // insert x_i into j-th neuron
                  {
                        c_j = (c_jn_j + x_i)/(n_j + 1);
                        n_j = n_j + 1;
                        break;
                        };
                };
                if(x_i is not in any neuron) // create new neuron
                {
                        C = C + 1;
                        c_c ← x_i;
                        n_c= 1;
                };
        };
};
```

Fig. 2. Algorithm APC-III symbolic implementation (Štencl & Šťastný, 2009)

The learning process consists in a precept of the given network to answer correctly to an entire training set. As the hidden layer was in this network represented by so-called areas and the middles of the areas are fast added to it, the learning process oversimplifies only to the setting of scales and thresholds of the output layer. The gradient method and the Least Mean Square (LMS) method were tested for learning of the neuron network.

The gradient method uses relations derived for the outgoing layer for algorithm Back-Propagation (BP). In contrast to the BP method, this method only optimizes scales and thresholds of the outgoing layer.

In the learning stages, the network

1. estimates centres of c_j with $x(t)$,
2. estimates widths b_j,
3. determines the weights w_{sj} of input neurones $(x(t),y(t))$.

At the first stage, centres c_j are determined for each RBF unit. The centres c_j are represented by the weights between the input and the hidden layer. For example, the algorithms for cluster analysis are used. To speed up this stage, non-adaptive methods can also be used such as uniform or random distribution of RBF neuron centres over the input space. The second stage sets up other values of RBF neurons. The setup values of RBF units (b_j) determine the wideness of the area around estimated centres of c_j. The objective of the third stage of learning is to determine the weights of input neurons, for example the least square method or gradient algorithms can be used.

In global view, the RBF-NN learning includes the unsupervised learning at the first stage. At the second stage the setup of RBF units is made. The typically used function for this setup is the Gaussian Radial Basis Function (Šíma & Neruda, 1996) defined as in (6).

$$\varphi(x) = e^{-\left(\frac{\|x-c\|}{b}\right)^2} \quad (6)$$

The RBF unit determines the important output values in the radial zone with the centre in c; b represents the width of φ and determines the size of the radial zone. The setup parameters of RBF units determine the wideness of the controlled area and affect the generalization capability of the network. If the parameters are smaller it means a lower generalization capability; on the other hand, for a wider area the units lost their local mean.
At the last stage, the supervised learning is used. The last stage sets up the weights w_{sj}. The setup is made by mineralization process of typical error function (Šíma & Neruda, 1996).
After the learning process the RBF-NN is ready to approximate training sets and also provide good results for answers outside the training set. Different techniques for regularization have been discussed for a long time. For example, Bishop (1991) works with the same RBF units as training patterns. This technique brings a uniform resolution and wideness of the Gaussian function, provided that the input data have the same time of generation.

4. Results

All of the above described methods are applied to solve the prediction of real numerical time series represented by Czech household consumption expenditures. The tested dataset includes twenty-eight observations between the years 2001 and 2007. The observations are represented by quarterly data and the goal is to predict three future values for the first three quarters of 2008. As the second real-world economic index, the Czech Republic Goods transport indexes were used. The data are originally from the Czech Statistical Office and are measured quarterly. The length of the time series is 32 units and represents quarters of the years 2000 and 2008. The number of data used to train networks and to test network is a representative for the generalization ability testing of each selected method. The predicted values of both experiments are compared with the measured values. In the next step, a comparison of neural network topology efficiency with respect to learning algorithms is made. The used dataset includes all of the previously specified problems of the real-world economic index. Conditions for all the experiments remain defined as following:

- the tests were performed at the same hardware with monitoring of the kernel processes to keep them on the same level
- all the comparison tests were performed in Matlab 2010a environment with the neural Network Toolbox
- the same input, targets, validation and cross-validation datasets are used
- the short and middle term prediction is performed.

The parameters compared are based on previous research and they reflect the objective comparison with other methods. The first of the parameters is the output precision measured with the Mean Square Error and the Normalized Mean Square Error respectively. The second comparison parameter is the absolute comparison of the output value with the absolute value of the specific index.

The results of the experiments identify the main differences in the used neural networks architectures together with numerical forecasting of a real-world economic index. The detected differences are then verified by means of practical comparative examples.
The most important and also difficult part of working with ANN generally is the right architecture setup of selected network. For the multi-layer networks the number of hidden layers and units is one of the most important setups. The number of hidden units and layers estimates the flexibility of the network to approximate nonlinearization in the data. For estimating the "right" number of hidden layers and unit there is no universal approach. Hastie (2001) claims that the choice of the number of hidden layers is guided by background knowledge and experimentation. Typically, the number of hidden units is somewhere in the range of 5 to 100, the number increasing with the number of inputs and number of training cases (Hastie et al., 2001). Kecman (2001) gives a reasonable approach when deciding about the MLP networks architecture. We should specify the cost function for the neural network performance, including the size of the neural network learning time, implement ability in hardware, accuracy achieved, and the like (Kecman, 2001). Based on author's experience, the pseudo system approach has been applied in presented experiments. We covered all areas defined by Kecnam (2001) and used automated implementation of testing different numbers of hidden units and layers. The system approach starts with a huge number (it depends on the number of inputs) of hidden units, decreasing in several steps depending on the generalization capability. The presented architectures brings best setups of selected neural networks models.

4.1 Learning Algorithms comparison

The first set of experiments was performed using our own modification of MLP network with BP learning algorithm tested through Matlab R2010a environment. The second part of the experiment was performed using the MLP network with LM algorithm implementation in Matlab R2010a based on the previously described principles. The dataset was divided into input data and validation data in order to obtain better generalization of the results.
Both networks described in the following section are based on one-hidden-layer architecture. The stopping criterions for learning process were normalized mean square error (MSE), and total amount of epochs set to 2000 epochs. The observed values for comparison are the total amount of learning epochs and the number of neurons in the hidden layer respecting the specified learning algorithm. In order to compare the MLP network using the BP learning algorithm and the MLP network using the LM learning algorithm, the dataset was divided into a training set (70 % of the dataset) and a test set (remaining 30 % of the dataset). The training set was then divided into the training set itself (80 %) and a validation set (20 %). The performance of both experiments was evaluated for the test set. For the purposes of the experiment, the comparison starts at the third quarter of 2002.
The comparison process stops at the fourth quarter of 2007. The prediction is made for the first three quarters of 2008. The computed results of both MLP networks are then compared with real measured values. The hardware used for both experiments was an Intel Core i5, with 2.66 GHz and 4 GB of RAM. The operating system was the UNIX based Mac OS X. Both experiments had the same conditions so that the learning process is not affected.
The first setup is made by the MLP network with the BP learning algorithm. The architecture had twenty neurons in the hidden layer and the learning process ended when the stopping criterion defined by MSE (valued to 0.01) was reached after 890 epochs. The

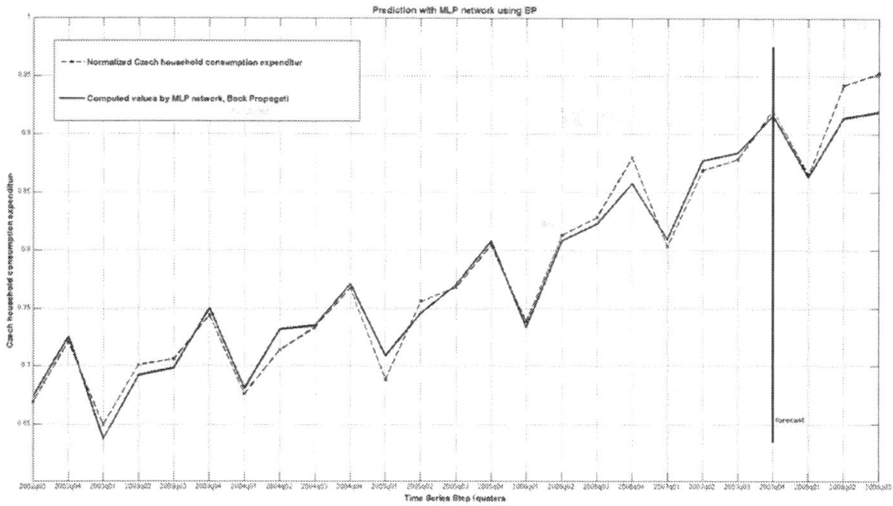

Fig. 3. Prediction with MLP network using BP learning algorithm (Štencl & Šťastný, 2010)

results of the experiment are presented at Figure 3. The dashed line represents the original real input values and the solid line represents the calculated output of the MLP network with the BP learning algorithm. The prediction starts with the first quarter of 2008 (as indicated by the solid line and description forecast). The difference between the calculated value and the real value for the first quarter of 2009 is 0.00169. With the next two values the prediction gains more error.

The second setup works with the MLP network using the LM learning algorithm. The architecture was different because the LM learning algorithm works with smaller networks topologies. The test was performed with more network architectures. The best result, by reaching the stopping criterion of MSE, has been reached by the MLP network with ten (10) neurons in the hidden layer. The performance of the learning and the validation processes is presented at Fig. 4. The plot presents training, validation and test values calculated using mean square errors (MSE). The MLP network reached the stopping criterion on epoch 20 with the best validation performance value of 0.0058 (MSE).

Figure 4 represents the comparison of the values calculated by the MLP network with the LM learning algorithm implemented in Matlab R2010a (by function *trainlm*). Again, the dotted line represents normalized real Czech household consumption expenditure. The solid line represents the calculated values of the MLP network with the LM learning algorithm. Again, the comparison starts at the third quarter of 2002 and ends with the last quarter of 2007. The prediction is made for the first three quarters of 2008. When comparing the real and the calculated values of the MLP network, the main difference is in the first quarter of 2008, where the empirical variance is -0.076. For the next calculated values the empirical value decrease to vales of -0.00047 and 0.00074 respectively.

Both networks ended the learning process on reaching the first stopping criterion defined by normalized mean square error (MSE). The first difference is in the architecture of the MLP networks. When using the LM with twenty neurons in the hidden layer, the network over fits the data. By decreasing the number of neurons in the hidden layer, it brings better

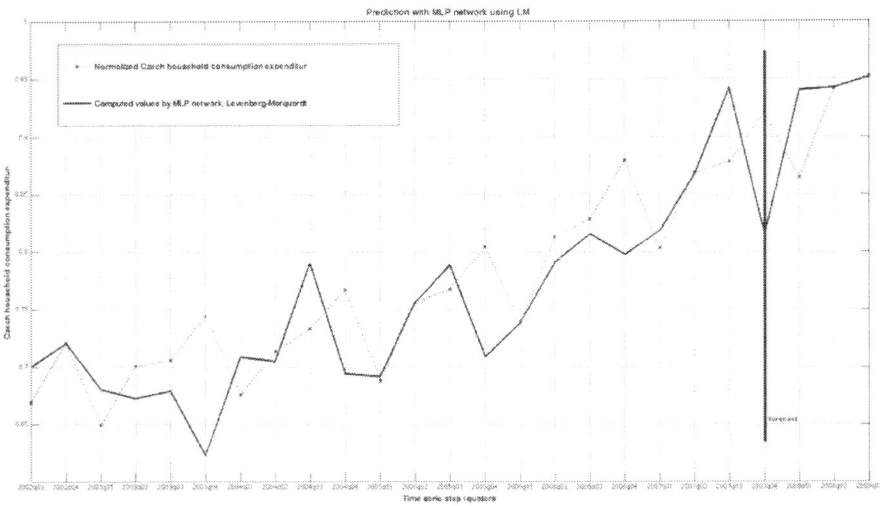

Fig. 4. Prediction with MLP network using LM learning algorithm (Štencl & Šťastný, 2010)

results. With ten neurons in the hidden layer the stopping criterion has been reached. Further decrease in the number of neurons in the hidden layer did not enhance the network error. Another difference is in the learning time. The MLP network with the BP needed 890 epochs to reach the stopping criterion defined by the mean square error. The MLP network with the LM finished the learning process after twenty epochs by reaching the stopping criterion. Regarding just to these two facts the LM algorithm seems to be more effective even on the time series models with limited data.

The MLP network with the BP brings better approximation (as presented at Fig. 2) and with a better prediction for the first quarter of 2008. Then the prediction error increases continually. The MLP network with the LM did not fit with the target data as well as the MLP network with the BP, but it computed better results for the second and the third quarters of 2008.

We can conclude by the fact that it is either possible to retrieve the results in short time (using the LM algorithm), or use the standard learning algorithm to obtain competitive computed values of the used dataset. The prediction results of the LM algorithm for the second and the third quarters of 2008 are definitely positive within the experiments. Both methods generally agree on the future values of the time-series.

4.2 Multithread MLP-NN implementation

This experimented was motivated by the learning process optimization on the computational level. Taking into account the results of the first experiments, we expected a better approximation ability of data. The multi-threaded calculation may allow faster computation (the value is lower than the maximum number of epochs) with a greater range of the network. The expectations of the multi-thread experiment results were defined as the achievement of more accurate values for the middle-term prediction in fewer learning epochs. The total number of epochs was chosen as a criterion because of relativity of time as evaluation criterion. The main evaluation criterion remains the MSE as used within the previous experiments to reach a qualified comparison.

For the multi-thread calculation, the open source Java framework Joone has been used (available at http://sourceforge.net/projects/joone). The chosen Joone function was executed through the Matlab 2010a environment to keep the experiment conditions. The calculation was performed on the workstation with an Intel Core i5 with a frequency of 2.66 GHz and 8 GB memory. The aim of the tests was to identify the key indicators for the optimization of the prediction of multithreaded real data with previously defined expectations. For multithreaded computations it was necessary to choose a greater range of MLP network topology. Based on the cross-validation a network with three layers with 5 neurons in the first hidden layer (linear activation function), 15 neurons in the second hidden layer (sigmoid activation function), 5 neurons in the second hidden layer (sigmoid activation function) and one neuron in output layer was selected for testing. As a training evaluation criteria the overall network error (set to the desired value 0.001) and the maximum number of epochs of network training (1000 epochs) were selected.

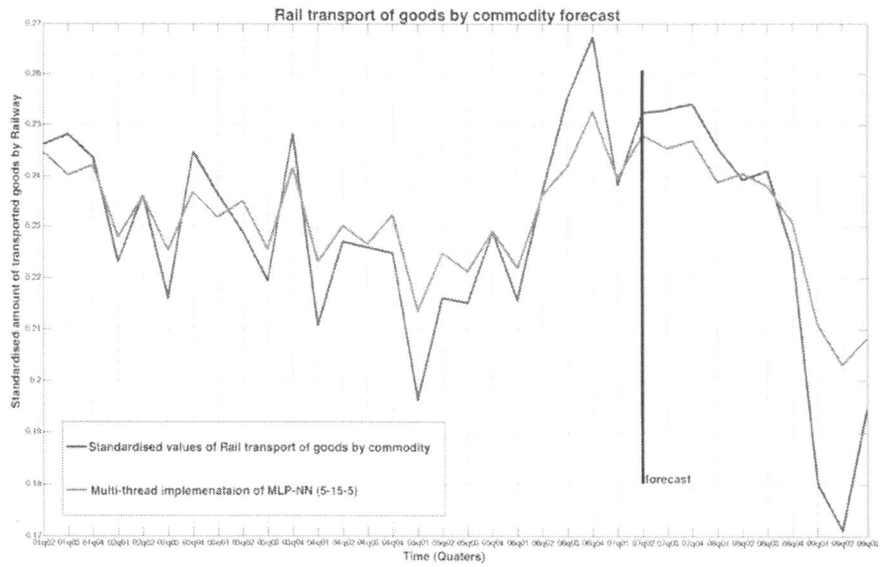

Fig. 5. Multi-thread prediction of standardised amount of transported goods by railway

Experiment Time series consists of goods transported by railway in as long-term trend of individual indicators by months and years as Volume indicators. Experiment dataset contains tons of goods transported by railways in the Czech Republic. The values where standardized to the interval <0, 1> for better adaptation of ANN. The length of the validation set was 35 observations (the last value of the second quarter of 2007). The forecast was set at 5 future values. The resulting values were compared with the real values from upcoming quarters in 2007 and 2008. The training of the ANN ended at 1320 epoch with a total network error (MSE) of 0.00098. The subsequent validation of the real data demonstrates the ability to predict the mean square error of 0.0012, which corresponds to the learning setup.

The validation result of the comparison experiment is shown at Figure 5. The figure includes the comparison of the computed values with the real-values of the selected index. The comparison starts at the second quarter of 2007 (signed as *forecast*). Networks of larger scale have a better capability of approximation for large datasets. A positive benefit of our experiment is the good ability of the trained network to successfully predict the trend of real-world index of a small input dataset.

The resulting total number of epochs in training may be due to the nature of the training dataset. Another positive conclusion is the ability of the network to predict the huge decrease in the future as is shown between the third quarter of 2008 and the second quarter of 2009. In this period the index fell down to the extreme - the global minimum. The trained network was, in spite of the unexpected decrease, able to forecast. The expectations of this experiment were not confirmed. Working with the multi-thread implementation did not optimize the learning process by decreasing the number of epochs with reaching the defined learning error. But the experiment confirmed a better ability of generalization of the multi-layer MLP implementation than the single layer implementation used in previous experiments.

4.3 Radial basis function experiment

The experiment consists of comparison tasks of the RBF NN implementation in Matlab R2007a and MLP NN used in (Štencl & Šťastný, 2008). Figure 6 describes the standard topology of the Matlab RBF NN implantation algorithm. The experiment dataset consists of selected consumption expenditures time series violated by a random constant. The customization of the selected value has been made to get diverse time series model simulating different variations.

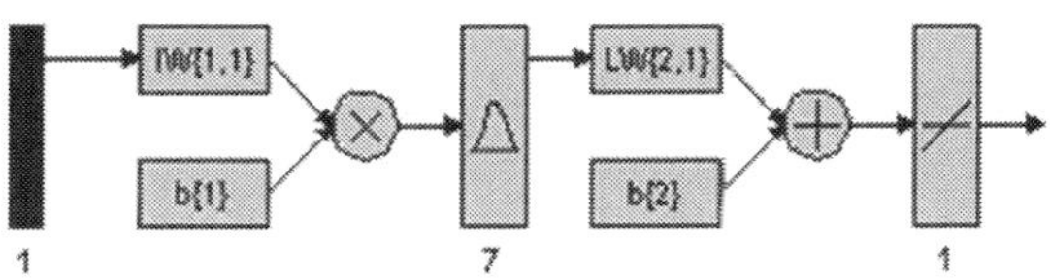

Fig. 6. Matlab RBF-NN topology (Štencl & Šťastný, 2009)

The final model consists of 40 observations representing quarters of the years from 1998 to 2008. The absolute variety in the dataset is 3. The forecast is made for five future periods.

The stopping criterion for learning process was the normalized mean square error (MSE), and the total amount of epochs was set to 2000 epochs. The learning criterions are identical to the previous experiment because of the comparison aspect. The observed values for comparison are the total amount of learning epochs and the number of neurons in the hidden layer with respect to the radial basis neural network learning process. The learning process of the network was much faster than in the case of the MLP network with the Back-propagation algorithm.

The obtained values are not as exact as in the case of the MLP network. Precisely in this case, Matlab implementation does not allow a better configuration of the network. Figure 7 shows the performance progress for the Matlab implementation of RBF NN. The performance value for the MLP NN was 0.23124. The performance value for the Matlab was 0.6973.

Concluding this experiment, the RBF network should be used more for the short-term prediction. For smaller datasets there is a notable huge noisiness in the data computed by

RBF networks. In spite of that, RBF networks produce good results for datasets containing approximately fifty observations. For datasets with fewer observations, RBF networks are unable to approximate the selected data as the MLP networks in our case. As shown at figure 7, both types of ANN have shown a good generalization ability resulting in a better prediction for the MLP NN when reaching a smaller error. The RBF networks confirmed a better endurance for architecture changes than the MLP NN during the experiment and faster learning adoption.

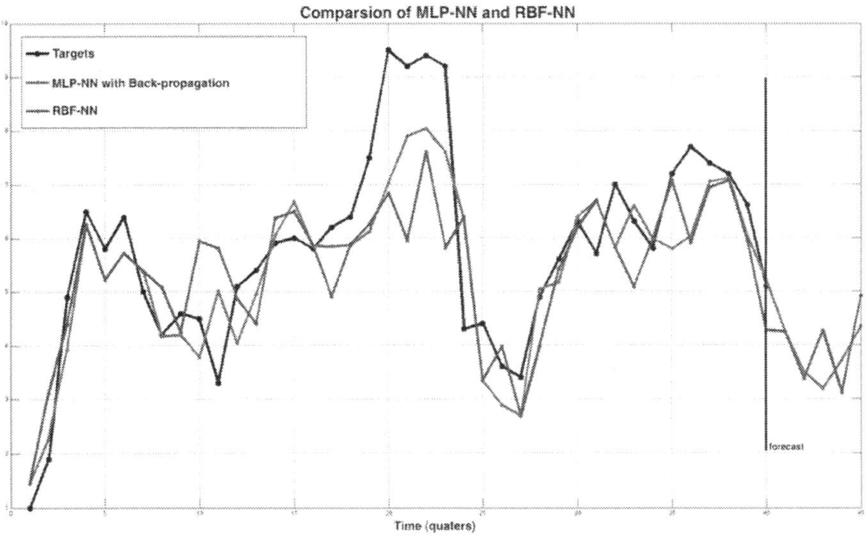

Fig. 7. Comparison of MLP-NN and RBF-NN (Štencl & Štastný, 2009)

4.4 Comparison of RBF NN and two-level grammatical evolution

The experiment was previously published as (Štencl et al., 2009). The sample dataset for experiment consists of 40 observations defined at part 4.3; values lie in interval <1, 9.5>. The first part of the experiment was performed using RBF NN implementation in Matlab R2007a based on the previously described principles. The dataset was divided into input data and validation data in order to obtain better generalization of the results. The second part of the experiment was conducted using our own implementation of two-level grammatical evolution (Popelka, 2007).

Figure 8 shows the input data and two sample runs of both methods. Both methods generally agree on the future values of the time-series. The output of neural network is shown only with the values displayed, the output of the grammatical evolution is both the values displayed and the formula that makes the main difference between both the approaches. But if we focus on the learning time efficiency, the grammatical evolution provides us with more information, but its training would take much more time than training a neural network. In this simple case it would be about 10 generations of the underlying genetic algorithm, which takes about 40 minutes (about 4 times longer) using the same computer.

Fig. 8. Comparison of trained RBF NN and two-level grammatical evolution (Štencl et al., 2009)

Both methods provide comparable results in terms of accuracy. Briefly this could be described that it is either possible to obtain numerical results in a short time, or use a more complicated algorithm to obtain autoregressive formula of the time-series.

5. Conclusion

In this chapter we have presented comparison studies of different artificial neural networks on prediction of the real-world economic index. For this type of tasks the statistical analysis is used. For the statistical prediction, a time-series model must be constructed first and then the prediction is made. The set of input conditions is strictly defined which limits the generalization ability. The resulting forecast is then affected also by the noisiness and the length of the input dataset. The length of economic datasets is the typical problem of Czech conditions. Thus, the length of the input dataset and the noisiness, joined with the strong nonlinearity of the input models lead to an unsolvable usage of classical methods. Some of the mentioned difficulties can be reduced by using selected Artificial Neural Network models.

We evaluated the selected Artificial Neural Networks using different types of networks models by means of a systematic approach. The selection is based on a state-of-the-art analysis and also author's experience. The evaluation of the selected ANN is based on previously published papers with added consequences between them. For the experiments the real-world economic time series has been used. The input datasets include typical problems mentioned before. All the predictions are based on the comparison with real values of selected time-series model. For comparison purposes a few values of the dataset where excluded from the learning process to be compared later with the computed values.

The basic, but also very powerful, type of the ANN is the multi-layer perceptron network (MLP NN). The network architecture is the key element for an effective usage of the MLP

NN, together with the learning method. As we proposed in the text, there is no guaranteed approach to setup the right network architecture. For our experiment we used the systematic approach similar to cross-validation. We also tested different learning algorithms as part of the learning process optimization. The results of the experiments show better approximation of MLP NN with Back-propagation learning rule. The training of the MLP NN with Levenberg-Marquardt learning rule results in overfitting of the data. The comparison of both approaches leads to conclusion that both methods are effective. We also add an experiment with the multithread MLP NN. The expected results were not confirmed because of the maximal number of epochs (which was one of the comparison aspects). The multi-thread implementation provides a better generalization ability than in case of single thread computation.

As the second type of ANN used for prediction, the Radial Basis Function neural networks have been tested. The RBF NN generally provide a good forecasting ability. The RBF NN had a worse approximation ability than the MLP NN. Another interesting point is the endurance of the RBF NN for the architecture changes. The computed values show noisiness in the resulting values. This is probably produced because of the length of the input dataset. The RBF NN typically needs to have more data for better generalization. In the last experiment of this work we have compared the RBF NN with the two-level grammatical evolution. The experiment results confirmed the ability of both approaches with the main difference in time efficiency. We can conclude that the RBF NN are more effective for retrieving the values of the prediction.

Generally, we can conclude that these approaches have a good potential for short and middle term predictions of real-world economic index. We have also confirmed good efficiency of ANN when working with short or missing datasets. When comparing the different type of the ANN, the MLP NN showed the best generalization ability. The RBF NN is better to use with a longer input dataset, but they are more effective for obtaining the numerical values of time-series model as another Artificial Intelligence approach (a genetic algorithm in our case).

In future work we would like to use artificial neural network methods on different real-world data. Newly, the analysis of the business cycle opens a new application area for different types of artificial neural networks. A thorough analysis including the comparison with selected statistical methods shows that possible inconsistencies in the prediction of used methods can be described and quantified. The scope of further research will be also focused on testing of different architectures including the multi-thread implementations which show a very good generalization ability. The research will also include the modelling with Bayesian Networks.

This work has been supported by the Research design of MENDELU in Brno number 116/2101/IG1100791.

6. References

Bishop, C. M. (2000). Neural Networks for Pattern Recognition, *Oxford University press*, ISBN 0-19-853864-2.

Hagan, M.T. & Menhaj, M. (1999). Training feed-forward networks with the Marquardt algorithm, *IEEE Transactions on Neural Networks*, Vol. 5, No. 6, pp. 989-993.

Hastie, T.; Tibshirani, R. & Friedman, J. (2001). The elements of statistical learning; data minig, inference, and prediction, *Springer series in statistics*, ISBN 978-0387-95284-0.

Kecman, V. (2001). Learning and soft computing; support vector machines, neural networks, and fuzzy logic models, *A Bradford Book, The MIT Press*, ISBN 0-262-11255-8.

MathWorks™, Neural Network Toolbox Documentation. [online] Available at <http://www.mathworks.com/access/helpdesk/help/toolbox/nnet/backpro7.html#8119>

Mostafa, M. M. (2009). Consumer credit scoring models with limited data, *Expert Systems with Applications, 36,* DOI: 10.1016/j.eswa.2008.06.016.

Popelka, O. (2007). Two-level Optimization using Parallel Grammatical Evolution and Differential Evolution, *Proceedings of MENDEL'2007,* Prague, Czech Republic, pp. 88-92. 2007. ISBN 978-80-214-3473-8.

Sotirov, S. (2005). A Method of Accelerating Neural Network Learning, *Neural Process. Lett.* 22, 2 (Oct. 2005), 163-169. DOI= http://dx.doi.org/10.1007/s11063-005-3094-9.

Štencl, M.; Popelka, O. & Štastný, J. (2009). Time Series forecasting using machine learning methods, *Proceedings of 12th international Information Society,* pp. 66-69, ISSN 1581-9973, Ljubljana, Slovenia, October 2009, Jožef Stefan Institute, Ljubljana.

Štencl, M. & Štastný, J. (2010). Neural network learning algorithms comparison on numerical prediction of real data, *MENDEL 2010, 16th International Conference on Soft Computing,* pp. 280-285, ISSN 1803-3814, Brno, Czech Republic, Jun 2010, Brno University of Technology.

Štencl, M. & Štastný, J. (2009). Advanced approach to numerical forecasting using artificial neural networks. *Acta Universitatis agriculturae et silviculturae Mendelianae Brunensis,* Vol. 6, No. 2, (09/2010), ISSN 1211-8516.

Štencl, M. & Štastný, J. (2008). Nové metody predikce numerických dat, *Aktuálne manažerske trendy v teórii a praxi,* 1st Edition, Žilina: Žilinská univerzita v Žiline, EDIS, 2008, s. 28-33. ISBN 978-80-8070-966-2.

Štastný, J. & Škorpil, V. (2007). Genetic Algorithm and Neural Network. *WSEAS Applied Informatics & Communications,* ISSN 1790-5117.

Štastný, J. & Škorpil, V. (2005). Neural Networks Learning Methods Comparison. *International Journal WSEAS Transactions on Circuits and Systems,* Vol. 4, No. 4, ISSN 1109-2734.

3

Neural and Bayesian Networks to Fight Crime: the NBNC Meta-Model of Risk Analysis

Gaetano Bruno Ronsivalle
"Sapienza" University of Rome
Italy

1. Introduction

According to a recent study quoted by the Union National Observatory, in 2009 about 50% of European bank robberies took place in Italy. Beyond the reliability of this percentage value, such datum highlights one of the most complex problems security bank officers have to face in order to make all national branches more secure.

Since 2009 ABI (Italian Banking Association) has been trying to solve such problem by using a software to analyze the bank robbery risk. The software is based on a model involving the analysis, description, explanation and estimation of the phenomenon. The last version of the tool, released in May 2010, is the final result of a five-year activity of researches, experimentations and sharing with companies managers.

The latest update of the software supplies an online control panel to analyze the actual state of all Italian branches and scientifically support the robbery risk management in real time. The specific goal of this tool is to provide Italian bank security managers with an operative model able to:

a. "describe" the variables and define the "robbery" phenomenon;
b. "explain" the modalities to calculate (i) the "Exogenous", (ii) the "Endogenous" and (iii) the Global Risk Indexes for each single branch;
c. "predict", by a simulation module, the variations of the compound risk in relation with the different branches security systems.

Thanks to these data resulting from years of experience, I decided to generalize and extend the features of the model in other contexts such as the management of the Cash Risk, energy sources, e-learning courses and so on. Then I developed a meta-model exclusively focused on criminal phenomenology, NBNC (Neural and Bayesian Network to fight Crime). Such meta-model integrates ANN and Bayesian network in order to effectively analyze many kinds of operative risks related to the organized crime, such as anti-terrorism and criminal investigation techniques.

The present chapter includes:

- a premise about the concepts of "complexity" and "risk management" applied to crime phenomenology;
- an analytical presentation of the logic structure and the main features of the NBNC meta-model;
- a brief discussion about the method used in order to derivate a Bayesian network from a database through an ANN;

- a description of a concrete application of this meta-model, that is the ABI model applied to analyze the robbery risk in Italian Banking System.

2. Complex phenomena and risk management in criminality

The NBNC meta-model represents a theoretical framework to design and develop "intelligent models" in order to analyze the Risk in criminality.

This meta-model is based on three elements: a hybrid architecture integrating a database related to the phenomenology we need to analyze, a Bayesian network reproducing the probabilistic conditions between the variables involved, an ANN network system defining the rules that build the Bayesian simulator.

The structure of the NBNC model has been designed according to the complexity of the criminality and the risk analysis techniques: before describing its features, it would be useful to answer some questions:

what is "complex criminality"? Why it's so difficult to analyze and prevent "events" like bank robberies or terrorist attacks? Why is it almost impossible to build an "intelligent model" in order to effectively apply the most advanced criminal investigation techniques? Which are the Risk general features in criminality?

2.1 Definition of "complex phenomenon" in criminality

Let's start from a general definition: the complexity of a phenomenon essentially derives from the "impossibility" of representing its fundamental characteristics and dynamic evolutions through a linear quantitative frame. Such frame can correspond to any polynomial function, as:

$$f(x) = a_0 + a_1 x + a_2 x^2 + ... + a_n x^n \quad (1)$$

where n is the function degree f, coefficients a_i are real numbers entirely independent of each others and a_0 is the constant term.

This "impossibility" depends on several interrelated factors:

- the coefficients of the hypothetical function meant to describe the phenomenon are interdependent;
- the variables composition effects can't be explained through the analysis of each single variable behavior;
- the phenomenon shows a very high number of inhomogeneous variables;
- the initial conditions affect the phenomenon dynamic evolution and show a "chaotic" behavior.

A phenomenon having these characteristics is defined as a "complex phenomenon". For instance, in most cases a "robbery" represents an "unpredictable" phenomenon related to different and interdependent factors (social, economic, psychological, geographical and environmental).

Similarly, a terrorist attack represents the effect of some variables interactions: International Relations, religious views, conflicting interests, social and economic conditions, links with the organized crime.

The same happens in case of many criminal events, in particular murders involving specific investigation techniques. As forensics experts could tell, the phenomenon shows a strong fragmentation and stratification of several factors and initial conditions. That's why the model should take into account the following variables:

- the preliminary investigations results, that are the final outputs of public prosecutor, police, lawyers and defense experts activities;
- the crime scene reconstruction through planimetry, photos, collection of trace evidence, autopsies;
- the identity checks, through several kind of identification techniques (fingerprint, anthropological, vocal, genetic identification, graphology and so on);
- the forensic ballistics results.

2.2 The criminal "risk" analysis

The "criminal" phenomena analysis entails five different and complementary meanings of "risk". Then a risk can be:

1. the probability some conditions B can occur and cause the criminal event A: P(B);
2. the probability that, given some initial conditions B, the criminal event A: P(A | B) can occur;
3. the probability that, given some initial conditions B, the criminal event A can occur with some particular characteristics or specific magnitude $P(A_i \mid B)$;
4. the probability that, given some initial conditions B, the criminal event A can determine some (almost always harmful) effects C while P[C | (A *and* B)] is happening;
5. the probability that, given some initial conditions B, the criminal event A can determine some (almost always harmful) effects D after P{D | [C *and* (A *and* B)]} happened.

Clearly, these five meanings imply different analysis modalities and risk management typologies.

Focusing only on the first and second definition, we could analyze the risk by essentially monitoring the initial conditions in order to avoid the criminal event - robbery, terroristic attack, murder -. In terms of probabilistic conditions, it's necessary to control B so that P(A | B) = 0. In bank robberies this kind of approach could support the defense systems maintenance management or justify the introduction of a new armed security service. Or in the terroristic attack prevention, the initial conditions control could be focused on arms dealers travels in a particular risk area.

According to the third definition, the analysis model could be based on the assumption the criminal event is unavoidable: then, it would be necessary to focus on the initial conditions control in order to determine the criminal event characteristics. If A_i is the particular state describing the criminal event "expected" characteristics (the maximum threshold of magnitude), the goal is monitoring B so that $P(A_i \mid B) = 1$. Therefore, in case of a bank robbery, the risk analysis modality could be translated in a set of indications aimed at dealing some initial conditions (for example timed safes, instructions about cash management for all bank employees and so on) and reducing the robbery duration or the cash stolen amount.

The forth definition is an extension of the second one and suggests a more refined risk analysis model. According to the logical flow B→A→C, if we monitor B and, after that, A we can reduce C effects related to the criminal event. In the bank robbery example, the analysis results could induce the bank to provide all employees with some guidelines: learning

which are the most appropriate behaviors to keep in case of robbery can help avoiding things or people damages.
The fifth definition, a particular version of the third one, includes a risk analysis model aimed at monitoring the logical flow B →A → C → D (representing the criminal event A effects). In the case of a bank robbery, this analysis modality could be translated in some training activities to involve all the employees in the criminal event simulation in order to reduce the post-robbery psychological trauma. Another possibility could be the implementation of a communication plan to assure the customers the robbed bank branch is actually safe.

3. The NBNC meta-model

The NBNC meta-model includes the five "risk" meanings and summarizes them in a unique analysis modality: such approach includes the criminal event prevention, the analysis of possible practices to contain the event and the selection of specific activities to reduce its effects during and after.
In fact, given a **Ω** set of criminal phenomena, the meta-model application to the Ω analysis must guarantee:

1. a "description" of each Ω element state in a particular time interval t_n;
2. an "explanation" of every Ω event e_i in a specific moment t_n, according to the initial conditions set;
3. a definition of a "predictive system" to evaluate/simulate the Ω initial conditions and calculate the probability an event can occur in a specific time interval t_n;

The NBNC meta-model application shows a "descriptive" dimension based on the Ω modeling through the definition of an ontology in order to represent all the potentially occurring events ($\alpha_1, \alpha_2, \alpha_3, \ldots, \alpha_n$) in Ω.
Hence the construction of a relational database describing the "story" of Ω consistently with the defined ontology.
The "explanatory" and "predictive" dimensions are based on a symbolic rules system and the construction of a Bayesian network. The ANN system recurrent training refers to an updated database describing the Ω phenomena story: this will help us building the Bayesian network.

3.1 The "descriptive" dimension

First, the meta-model must provide an exhaustive, quantitative and operative description of the α_i phenomenon in Ω. In other words it has to:

- identify all the different factors affecting and determining the criminal events $\alpha_1, \alpha_2, \alpha_3, \ldots, \alpha_n$ subject of the analysis;
- introduce a measurement system in order to translate the different factors in quantitative terms;
- clearly describe the identified factors characteristics in order to define the measurement different areas;
- adopt a "translator" handbook in order to map all the categories used by the field leading experts (who are the future users of the tool);
- develop a theoretical framework to "tell" the evolution of the phenomenon e_i over time;
- distinguish the dynamic variables defined in state description from the boundary structural variables;
- introduce new categories in order to circumscribe clusters of similar variables;

- define the observation conditions of each variable depending on the measurement system adopted;
- determine the specific factors frequency and the *a priori* probability through descriptive statistics tools;
- map the national and international legislation, in particular the different sanctions for criminal acts, affecting the categories definition;
- develop a relational database structure in order to include all the variables the model introduced.

In brief, it's about defining the system reference ontology and the specific vocabulary to highlight the more relevant aspects of the phenomenon α_i in Ω. The goal is determining a univocal "description" of the different criminal events involved. The identification of the "fundamentals" implies as final output a formalized language to represent every possible phenomenon α_i.

3.2 The transition from the "descriptive" to the "explanatory" dimension

After providing all the information and categories to describe every possible phenomenon, the tool must quantitatively define the involved variables rules and relations.

Therefore the explanatory dimension includes the preparation of a series of assumptions on the set functional rules meant to represent the variables relationships. These rules are essential in order to support the α_i criminal phenomenon "modeling" - which will be complete only when the phenomenon characteristics will be reproduced within a simulation -. A symbolic notation can synthesize the different elements without any loss of information.

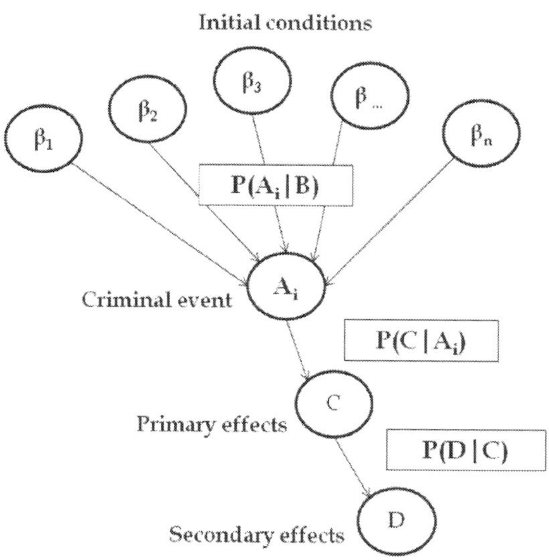

Fig. 1. Representation of simple conditional probabilities

As already mentioned, in case of complex phenomena such as bank robberies, terrorist attacks or murders, it may be useful to adopt the notation of the conditional probabilities calculation. A Bayesian framework can define the possible causal or interdependence

relations between initial conditions B = { β_1, β_2, β_3, … , β_n}, the criminal event A, the primary effects C and the secondary effects D (Fig.1).
Then on a descriptive level, it might be useful to identify a number of intermediate levels in order to define any clusters of variables and possible interactions within each level, as exemplified in the following Bayesian network (Fig. 2):

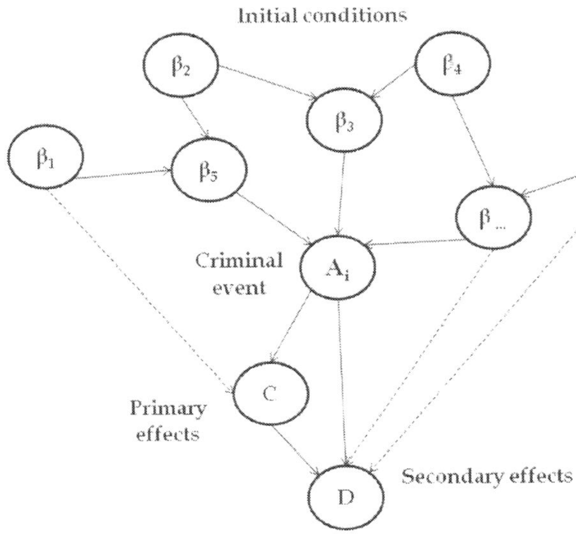

Fig. 2. Representation of complex conditional probabilities

3.3 The "explanatory" and "predictive" dimensions: Bayesian network learning system based on neural networks

The logical structure represented by the Bayesian network is still a hypothesis about general rules managing the phenomenology under observation. In fact, it shows the relationships but doesn't provide any information about the variables weight and the probability distributions values. At this point it is necessary to test the hypothesis derived from historical data and information necessary to effectively build the Bayesian network and turn the model into a powerful tool for risk analysis.
This can be possible by referring to the Motomura and Hara application of the method (Motomura & Hara, 2000). According to the authors we have to create one ANN for each conditional probability, that is each child node.
Let's start, for instance, from an elementary conditional probability: B → A.
According to Motomura and Hara method, we can build the ANN for the conditional probability P(A | B). This ANN has input neurons to represent the parent node B, hidden and output neurons to represent the child node A.
In our case, A and B are discrete variables and the number of ANN neurons input and output depends on the number of states A and B can assume.
In particular, if the child node A can assume a number of discrete values k, then:

$$A = (\alpha_1; \alpha_2; \alpha_3; \dots ; \alpha_k). \quad (2)$$

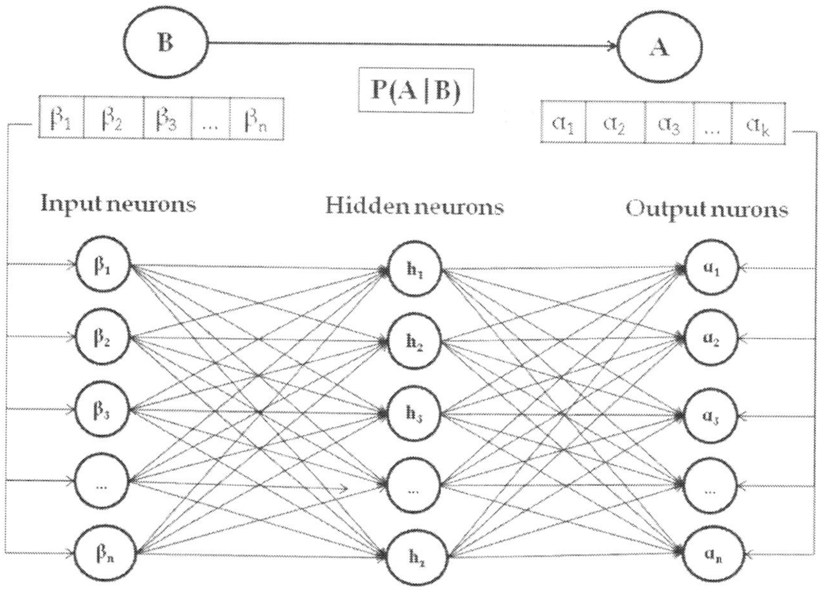

Fig. 3. The ANN representing P(A | B)

k is the neurons output number $P(\alpha_1)$; $P(\alpha_2)$; $P(\alpha_3)$; … ; $P(\alpha_k)$, that is the probability vector of the child node A (Fig. 3).
Then, how can we "neuronally" represent each conditional probability $P(A \mid B = \beta)$ in order to build a Bayesian network?
First, we must analyze all α_k and β possible combinations:

	α_k	*not* α_k
β	α_k *and* β	*not* α_k *and* β
not β	α_k *and not* β	*not* α_k *and not* β

Table 1. Possible combinations of α and β

Secondly, we have to determine the probability of each combination:

	α_k	*not* α_k	*Sum*
β	P(α_k *and* β)	P(*not* α_k *and* β)	**P(β)**
not β	P(α_k *and not* β)	P(*not* α_k *and not* β)	**P(*not* β)**
Sum	**P(α_k)**	**P(*not* α_k)**	1

Table 2. Probabilities of α and β combinations

in the strength of these premises and according to Bayes Theorem,

$$P(\alpha_k \mid \beta) = \frac{P(\alpha_{\mathrm{k}} \text{ and } \beta)}{P(\beta)}. \tag{3}$$

From a neuronal point of view,

- if v, w and b are ANN connection weights,
- and the logistic activation function is

$$g(\beta) = \frac{1}{1 + \exp^{-\beta}} \tag{4}$$

- the Motomura and Hara (Motomura & Hara, 2000) solution will be:

$$f_k(\beta) = g\left(\sum_j v_{jk}\, g\left(\sum_i w_{ij}\beta_i + b_j\right) + b_k\right) \tag{5}$$

$$P(\alpha_k \mid \beta) = \frac{P(\alpha_{\mathrm{k}} \text{ and } \beta)}{P(\beta)} = \frac{f_k(\beta)}{\sum_k f_k(\beta)}. \tag{6}$$

Similarly, in the case of a more complex network that describes the criminal phenomenon A and the related effects, this method allows us assigning step by step all the conditional probabilities values and exactly defining the functional architecture of the Bayesian network (Fig. 4).
In addition, through the ANN training we can indirectly verify the conditional dependency between each child node and its corresponding parent in the network. Indeed, the learning failure shows there isn't a conditional dependency between nodes and the network structure must be updated.

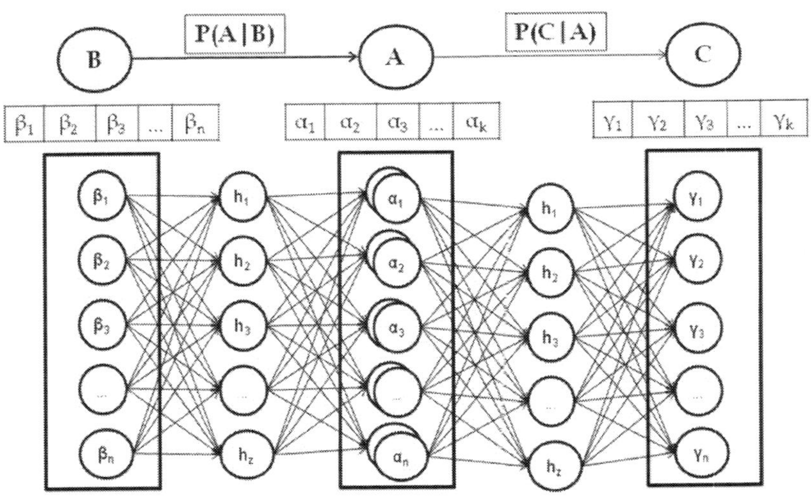

Fig. 4. ANN representing a complex Bayesian network

The final output is a Bayesian probabilistic model: describing, explaining and simulating a certain class of events allows supporting the security officers in the operational management of the different crime risk levels. In order to simulate different scenarios and the corresponding risk levels it will be sufficient to observe the states of the network independent variables and calculate the output values. Instead, in a preventing perspective, it will be necessary to go back to the initial functional values by associating the output to the expected values.

4. A real application of the NBNC meta-model: the ABI model of robbery risk analysis

The ABI robbery risk analysis model is a NBNC meta-model application in the world of crime.
First, the "descriptive" dimension of the model ensues from a compared analysis of different banks institutional data and involves the direct confrontation with the major Italian banking groups security representatives. Secondly, the "explanatory" dimension derives from the generalization of the robbery risk variables relations through the network recurrent training including other artificial neural networks (ANN). At last, the "predictive" dimension is based on the attribution of "weights" to the single internal variables and on the definition of a Bayesian network representing the probabilistic conditions and the variables dependence relations.

4.1 The "descriptive" dimension: the three robbery risk indexes

The first fundamental achievement of ABI research team was to create a univocal vocabulary of variables in order to describe all the basic features, plants and services of a bank branch. From this vocabulary the team elaborated the criteria to define the robbery risk different meanings and identify three Indexes:

1. the Exogenous Risk index,
2. the Endogenous Risk index,
3. the Global Risk Index.

Currently, security officers of the Italian banking system are using the three risk indexes in their analysis and robbery risk management. The integration of Exogenous, Endogenous and Global risk also supports an effective risk management procedure in order to prevent the robberies and mitigate the damages.

4.1.1 The Exogenous Risk index and the "environmental" variables of a bank branch

The Exogenous Risk index is annually calculated for every single Italian municipality and shows the concentration degree of criminal events in a specific area. The analyzed variables include:

- the geographical position,
- the population density,
- the annual crime rate in the area, calculated in relation with:
  - the ratio of robberies number per municipality's inhabitants (N),
  - the ratio of bank robberies number per N,
  - the ratio of thefts number per N,
  - the ratio of murders number per N,
  - the ratio of suicides number per N,

- the ratio of rapes number per N,
- the ratio of extortions number per N,
- the ratio of usury crimes number per N,
- the ratio of substance abuses number per N.

The latest version indicator shows a trend index calculated by the minimum square method and expressed by a geo-referenced probabilistic value. Its aim is defining the specific criminal exposure risk in the branch geographic area.

4.1.2 The Endogenous Risk index and the characteristics of a bank branch

The Endogenous Risk index expresses the single branch exposure degree to robberies apart from the geographic situation and the local crime rate. It consequently derives by the combination of the banking branch characteristics:

- the "basic characteristics": the number of employees, the location, the cash risk and so on.
- the "services": for example, the bank security guards;
- the "plants"': for example, the bandit barriers.

The index is calculated with a complex function of robberies in a single branch, during a unit of time in which every "event" has modified the branch internal order.
For example after a robbery, a bank can decide to put in a video camera directly connected to the police.

4.1.3 The Global Risk Index of a bank robbery

The Global Risk Index defines the actual robbery exposure degree of a specific bank branch, including its intrinsic features and geographic situation. It is calculated by considering the evolution of the suffered robberies in relation with the units of time and expresses a trend value.

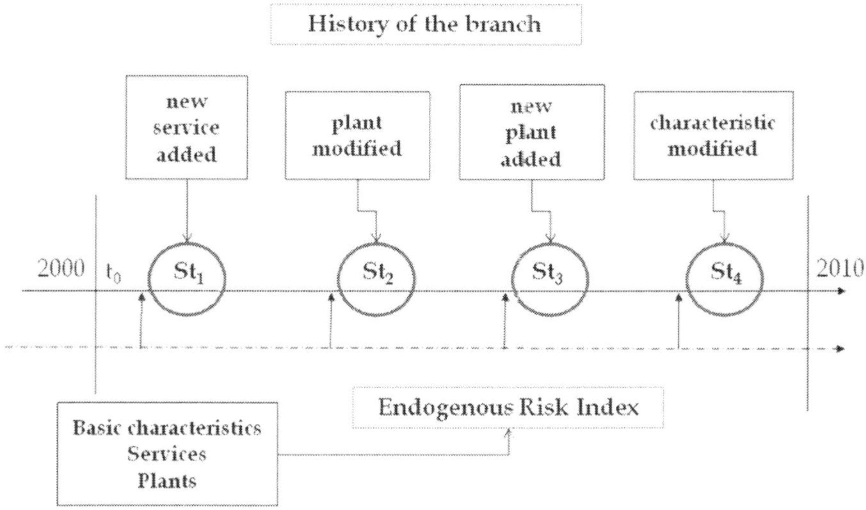

Fig. 5. Graphical representation of the branch states

Therefore the Global Risk Index derives by the non-linear combination of Exogenous and Endogenous Risk and corresponds to the synthesis of the robberies number per month and the number of days the branch is open.
Expressed by a value between 0 and 1, it can be calculated by the minimum square method and represents the trend in relation to the previous values.
But what Global Risk Index means and which is its relationship with the other risk indexes? The model is based on the description of the branch history as a sequence of states (Fig. 5), taking into account every change of its structure (for example, the introduction of a new defending service). In this way we create a direct relation between the branch and the Robbery Global Risk evolutions (Fig. 6).

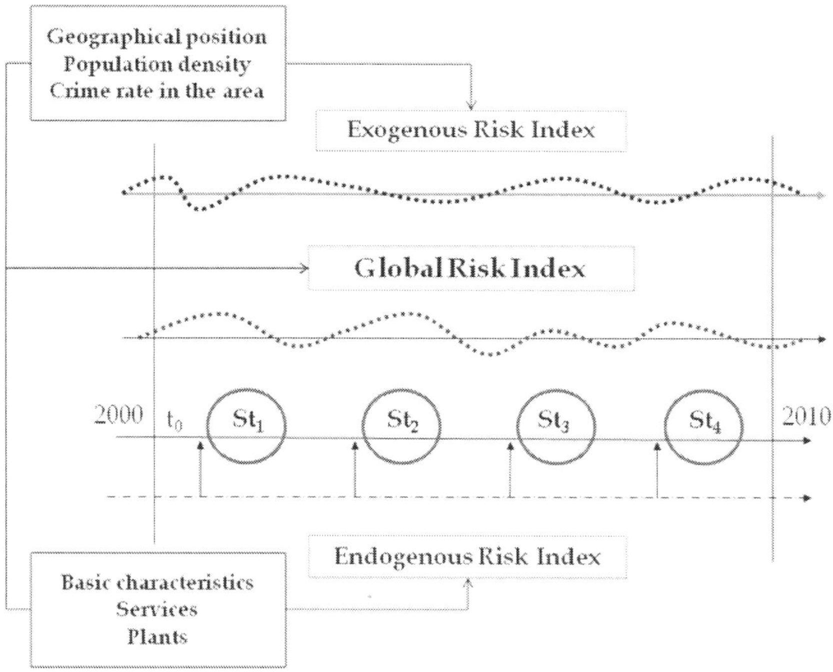

Fig. 6. Graphical representation of the evolution of Robbery Global Risk

To simplify the question, we can use a biological metaphor: the transformation of the branch over time is like a "mutation" of biological organisms populations.
This metaphor allows overcoming a wrong interpretation of the concept of "deterrent".
And the Robbery Global Risk suggests how the "robbery market" replies to the security managers activities.

4.2 A Bayesian simulator for the robbery risk analysis

The recent implementation of a Bayesian network in the simulation module is a significant evolutionary factor in the ABI robbery risk analysis model. Compared to the 2009 release the new version:

i. contributes to make the compound risk predictive system more effective,
ii. allows an exhaustive check and an indirect validation of the ANN training results,
iii. introduces an algorithm that can be easily integrated in many computer system supports,
iv. facilitates the final users (bank security managers) to understand the model functionalities, solving all the skepticisms outcropped in the previous versions.

The analysis of the variables and of the three risk indexes allows defining the logical structure of the probabilistic conditions governing the "bank robbery" phenomenon:

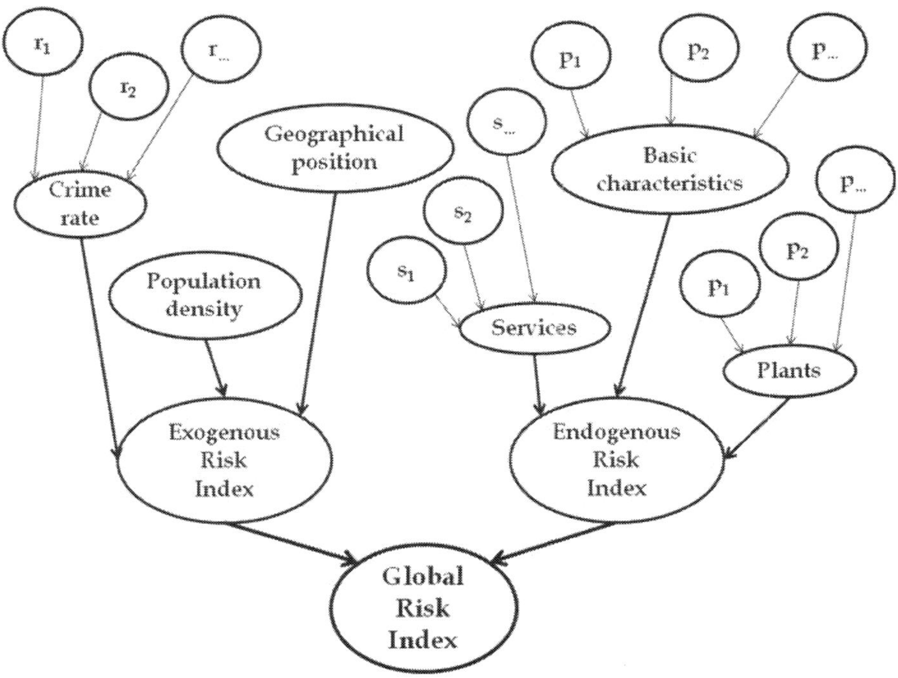

Fig. 7. Bayesian Network of the ABI robbery risk analysis model

The Bayesian Network in Fig. 7 graphically represents the output of the design process: the probabilistic model to analyze the robbery risk. The input values of the simulation software are the elements composing the external and internal risks, whereas the output is defined by the *a priori* calculation of the global risk. The reference database consists of a branches and criminal acts historical archive concerning the time interval 2000-2010.

The creation of the Bayesian Network was articulated in five phases.

1. In the first phase the team revised the database in order to remove possible critical factors.
2. In the second phase all variables connected to the Exogenous and Endogenous Risk were normalized.
3. The third phase was dedicated to design the general structure of the system of ANN and its mathematical properties in relation with the Bayesian network of reference;

4. In the fourth phase we decided to implement a variation of the Back propagation: the "OS.SI.F Quick-propagation" to solve numerical instability and avoid the net permanence in critical situations of local minima.
5. Finally, in the last phase of the process we verified the Bayesian network structure based on ANN. Also some critical nodes were modified in strength of the Exogenous Risk variations according to the population density and the relationship between Endogenous Risk and some new plants.

4.3 The advantages of applying the NBNC meta-model to the robbery risk analysis

The implementation of NBNC to support the Robbery Risk analysis has five fundamental advantages:

- it coherently faces the high complexity degree of the robbery phenomenon;
- it overcomes limited local vision in aid of the Robbery Risk analysis systemic approach;
- it provides a higher degree of accuracy and scientific reliability to define the "risk" and the whole calculation model;
- it ensures the maximum level of flexibility, dynamism and adaptability to contexts and conditions;
- it guarantees an effective integration between a solid calculation model and the security managers professional and human experience.

5. Conclusion

The NBNC meta-model was successfully applied in the creation of the ABI robbery risk analysis tool (currently used in the Italian banking system). Moreover it is a theoretical tool to design "intelligent" systems for the risk analysis in criminal investigations. In fact, it represents an operational framework for the models implementation and takes into account the criminal phenomenology complexity.

In the previous pages I tried to present the meta-model main features, primarily focusing on the importance of the descriptive dimension in the criminal risk analysis tool. In fact, the creation of a formalized language constitutes the foundation to identify some criteria and rigorously analyze the five risk levels. Experience taught me in most cases the community of experts in criminal risk management adopts different words to express the same variables or labels to describe unlike events. This causes ambiguities and misunderstandings that hamper the theoretical framework definition.

Secondly, I reflected on the power of a Bayesian model based on neural networks to adequately describe the complexity of the crime phenomenon. This method allows:

- identifying relevant variables in the mechanism governing the crime phenomenon;
- introducing new variables or redefining the previous ones;
- weighing each variable in relation to the overall structure;
- discarding irrelevant variables;
- falsifying or supporting the same consistency of the assumed logical structure;
- identifying the likely strong causal links between variables;
- defining the values of the Bayesian network probability distributions;
- limiting the reliability of the results expected.

By supporting the activities of prevention, monitoring, control and mitigation of the five risk typologies related to a wide range of phenomena, this method represents a useful contribution to the fight against crime.

6. Acknowledgment

Thanks to Marco Iaconis, Francesco Protani, Fabrizio Capobianco, Giorgio Corito, Giovanni Gioia, Riccardo Campisi, Luigi Rossi, Fausto Ligis and Diego Ronsivalle for the scientific support in the NBNC meta-model development, and to Marisa Orlando and Laura Ferraris for translating the chapter.

7. References

Donato, F. (2006). *Criminalistica e Tecniche investigative,* Editoriale Olimpia, ISBN 88-253-0116-2, Sesto Fiorentino (Firenze), Italy

Einstadter, W.J. & Henry, S. (2006). *Criminological Theory. An analysis of its underlying assumptions,* Rowman & Littlefield Publishers, Inc., ISBN 978-0-7425-4290-7, Lanham, Maryland

Floreano, D. (1996). *Manuale sulle reti neurali,* Il Mulino, ISBN 88323074-4, Bologna, Italy

Iaconis, M. & Corradini, I. (2010) *Guida alla sicurezza per gli operatori di sportello,* Bancaria Editrice, Roma, Italy

Motomura, Y. & Hara, I. (2000). Bayesian Network Learning System based on Neural Networks, *Proceedings of AFSS2000, International Symposium on Theory and Applications of Soft Computing*

Pessa, E. (2004). *Statistica con le reti neurali,* Di Renzo Editore, ISBN 88323074-4, Roma, Italy

Wilson, A.G. & Wilson, G.D. & Olwell, D.H. (2006). *Statistical Methods in Counterterrorism. Game Theory, Modeling Syndromic Surveillance and Biometric Authentication,* Springer Science+Business Media, LLC, ISBN 978-0387-32904-8, New York, USA

Part 2

Application of ANN in Chemical Technology

4

Applications of Neural Networks in Advanced Oxidative Process

Messias Borges Silva, Oswaldo Luiz Cobra Guimarães, Adriano Francisco Siqueira, Hélcio José Izário Filho, Darcy Nunes Villela Filho, Henrique Otávio Queiroz de Aquino, Ivy dos Santos Oliveira and Carlos Roberto de Oliveira Almeida
University of São Paulo – School of Engineering of Lorena
Brazil

1. Introduction

This chapter has the objective of presenting four studies involving neural networks in the area of advanced oxidative process. Advanced Oxidative Processes area based on the generation and reaction of hydroxyl radicals. Because they are not selective and it possesses a high oxidizing power are able to degrade organic contaminants.

Mathematical modeling of chemical process is often addressed in photocatalytic function of some parameters that are inherent in the process, such as the geometry of a reactor or characteristics of the compound to be worked, such as solubility and spectral characteristics of organic compounds. By moving the geometry of the reactor, moves through the proposed model. When they moved the reagents, changes completely the kinetics of the reactions involved and consequently the reactor performance.

The process of decolorization and degradation of organic compounds may involve, according to criteria adopted modeling, a series of reactions kinetics. The photocatalytic process modeling involves the solution to a complex set of equations of energy (radiation), the mass balance, momentum and heat, being a difficult process description. The performance of a photoreactor is strongly influenced by many physical-chemical interaction occurring between these variables. Conventional modeling techniques can produce models not appropriate.

This sense, neural modeling, empirical, presents itself as alternative to the traditional model, because it is based on mathematical equation. Based on the study of behavioral characteristics of the sets of input and output of the process of discoloration and degradation of organic compounds, possessing the ability to "learn" the behavior of linear or nonlinear experimental data. Through this "learning" may provide the optimization of the action of hydroxyl radical oxidation.

Are presented four applications involving neural networks modeling.

a. Neural approximation of the reduction of cod effluents from the manufacturing of polyesters trought photo-fenton procces/ozonization
b. Hybrid neural model for decoloration by UV/H2O2 involving process variables and structural parameters characteristics to azo dyes

c. Optimization of the AZO dyes decoloration process through neural networks: Determination of the H2O2 addition critical point
d. Decoloration process modeling by neural network

2. Artificial Neural Networks

A neural network is formed by processing elements (neurons) interconnected with the bordering neurons through coefficients or weights that stand for the relative influence of the entry neurons on other neurons, in an analogy with the human being brain behavior. There are various types of neural networks and, among them, the feedforward networks make up one of the most utilized classes.
With no further considerations on the physical-chemical processes involved in the transmission of information among the biological neurons, the signal enters the neuron through the dendrites and next it is transmitted to other neurons of the neural network via the axon. The passage of a neuron signal to other neuron dendrites is named synapse, which basically has the function of modulating the signal exchanged through them. In the artificial neuron this signal modulation, or signal intensity, is represented by a ponderation factor, named synaptic weight.
In the feedforward network (Figure 1), the neurons are connected to all the neurons in the posterior layer. The information deriving from a layer undergoes a pondering through weights and is sent to all the neurons in the following layer.

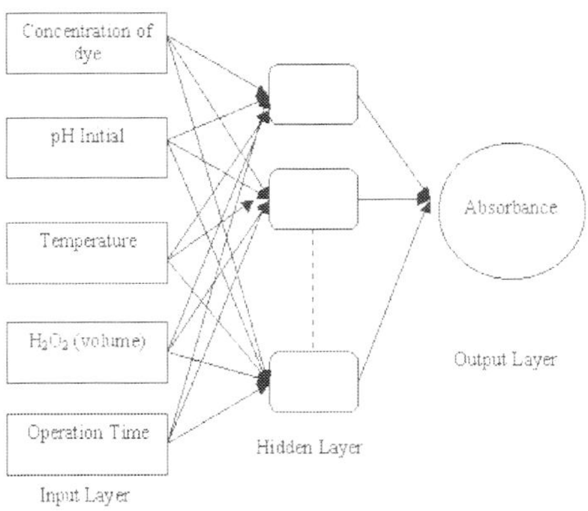

Fig. 1. Example of FeedForward Neural Network Model applied to Oxidative Advanced Process

In the feedforward networks the processing elements of a same layer work in parallel and the process among the layers is sequential.
The Equations that rule the feedforward networks are:

$$s_j^{(k)} = w_{o_j}^{(k)} + \sum_{i=1}^{N_k} w_{ij}^{(k)}.x_i^{(k-1)} \tag{1}$$

$$x_j^{(k)} = f(s_j^{(k)}) \tag{2}$$

In this relation, $s_j^{(k)}$ refers to the output of k layer i element activation function, indicates the weight pondered sum through the inputs and $w_{ij}^{(k)}$ refers to the synaptic connections at k layer j element input, where I is the connection index and N_k is the k layer processing element number.
The feedforward neural network input and output neurons can be related by sigmoidal or linear type functions, given by Equations (3) and (4) respectively.

$$y_j = f(s_j) = \frac{1}{1+e^{-s_j}} \tag{3}$$

$$y_j = f(s_j) = s_j \tag{4}$$

However, other transference functions can be used depending on the characteristics of the problem being studied.
The linear activating function for the output layer is adequate for continuous phenomena, as for instance the oxygen biochemical demand or the absorbance degree in decoloration process. The sigmoidal type transference functions are necessary to introduce non linearities in the network.
Training a network aims to adjust their weight in such a way that the application of a pattern produces an output value, and in this sense the Generalized Delta Rule or any other defined rule intends to reduce the network quadratic error indicated by:

$$\varepsilon = \sum_{j=1}^{m} (d_j - y_j)^2 \tag{5}$$

In Equation (5) d_j stands for the experimental or real value and y_i represents the value predicted from the neural model (Loesch & Sari, 1996).
From a mathematical standpoint, if a network has n processing elements in the input layer and m elements in the output layer, then the network processes the vector $X \in \Re^n$, supplying a vector $Y \in \Re^m$ in such a way that the network works as a function $f : \Re^n \rightarrow \Re^m$
The training algorithm named backpropagation refers to the way the weights are adjusted and this algorithm is also known as Generalized Delta Rule.
In the Generalized Delta Rule, in order to minimize the mean square error the derivatives defined by Euation (6) are estimated.

$$\vec{\nabla}_j^k = \frac{\partial \varepsilon}{\partial W_j^{(k)}} \tag{6}$$

The backpropagation algorithm utilizes this derivative information (gradient) to change the weights according to Equation (7):

$$W_j^{(k)}(n+1) = W_j^{(k)}(n) + \mu\left(-\vec{\nabla} W_j^{(k)}(n)\right) \tag{7}$$

In Equation (7) $\mu > 0$ is the network learning rate that controls the degree in which the gradient affects the weight changes and n represents the current iteration.

The neural network model adopted in this work comprises three layers: input, hidden and output. Some theorems have already been found out relative to the network characteristics:

- if a functions consists of a finite collection of points, then a three layer network is able to learn it;
- in case this function is continuous and defined in a compact dominium, a three layer network is able to learn it, as long as there are enough processing elements in the hidden layer.

The linear activating function for the output layer is adequate for continuous phenomena, as for instance the oxygen biochemical demand or the absorbance degree in decoloration process. The sigmoidal type transference functions are necessary to introduce non linearities in the network.

3. Advanced Oxidatives Process AOP

Advanced Oxidative Processes are methods for water treatment used on substances resistant to conventional processes (Quici *et al.*, 2005) Advanced Oxidative Processes are based on generation of hydroxyl radicals $\left({}^{\bullet}OH\right)$ have been applied to pollutant breakdown due to the radical's high oxidative power (2.8 V).

The Fenton reagent was discovered approximately 100 years ago and its use as an oxidant in the breakdown of organic compounds dates back to 1960 (Neyens & Baeyens, 2003). The Fenton reaction has the advantage of completely breaking down contaminants, producing water, carbon dioxide and non-organic salts through oxidant dissociation and hydroxyl radical production, which acts and destroys organic compounds.

It is characterized as a mix of hydrogen peroxide and iron salts (Lu *et al.*, 2001), generating hydroxyl radicals (Equations 8 and 9) :

$$Fe^{2+} + H_2O_2 \rightarrow Fe^{3+} + OH^{\bullet} + OH^{-} \tag{8}$$

$$OH^{\bullet} + Fe^{2+} \rightarrow OH^{-} + Fe^{3+} \tag{9}$$

The production of hydroxyl radical is potentially increased by the association of the ultraviolet radiation, according to the reaction given by the Equation (10), known as Photo-Fenton Process.

$$[Fe(OH)]^{2+} + hv \rightarrow Fe^{2+} + {}^{\bullet}OH \tag{10}$$

In this work the action of Photo-Fenton processes combined with ozone action has been studied. The beneficient effects of using ozone or oxygen peroxide in UV combined processes are highlighted as related to the individual employment of each one, as the rate of hydroxyl radicals is strongly increased. Ozone is a powerful oxidant (Eo=2.07 V) which is able to react with molecules possessing non-saturated links (C=C, C=N, N=N, etc.) (Cogate & Pandit, 2004). In the presence of ultraviolet radiation, the ozone also can form the radical according to Equations (11) and (12):

$$O_3 + H_2O \xrightarrow{hv} H_2O_2 + O_2 \tag{11}$$

$$H_2O_2 \xrightarrow{hv} 2\ {}^{\bullet}OH \tag{12}$$

4. Results and analysis

4.1 Neural approximation of the reduction of cod effluents from the manufacturing of polyesters trought photo-fenton process/ozonization

For this experiment, a "Pyrex" glass reactor, 1000 mL with an ozone diffusing whirl pooling system was employed. The ultra-violet source (UV) was two 125 W mercury vapor lamps. The thermostatized bath was made with a temperature controller and an ozonizer.
The reagents and solutions used were: Fenton reagent - H_2O_2 at 30% v/v and $FeSO_4.7H_2O$ 0.18 mol L^{-1}; reagents for COD - solution of Ag_2SO_4 conc (98 w/w), $K_2Cr_2O_7$ 1.0 eq L^{-1}, $HgSO_4$ (98 % w/w); for pH control - NaOH 5.0 eq L^{-1} and H_2SO_4 5.0 eq L^{-1}
Iron sulphate was initially added at a concentration of 0.18 mol/L for every trial, and the oxygen peroxide concentration was of 30 % of the total weight. The generation of ozone was performed by the method of electrical discharge via dielectric barriers with the following characteristics: 220 V electrical energy, required power of 60 W, goods with oxygen or dry air, working pressure below 2 bar and production of up to 1.0 g of O_3 per hour. The ozonization occurred with the use of bubbling system through diffusion, with a flow scattering adapted to its outlet. The ozone was given by the conversion of O_2 to O_3 through the Ozone Generator MV 01, which alows a control of variation in its flow.
Table 1 shows the minimum and maximum values of the input variables in the process.

Inlet variables	Minimum	Maximum
T_1	30 min	120 min
$[O_3]$	2 mg/L	4 mg/L
T_2	30 mim	120 min
V_1	2.5 mL	15 mL
pH	2	5
T	25 °C	35 °C
V_2	3 mL	18 mL

Table 1. Input variables and their respective levels

All the neural models were implemented with the use of the software MatLab. The neural model input and output values were normalized in such a way that the average value would be zero and the standard deviation equal to 1. In Table 2 we can see the results

Neurons (Hidden Layer)	Training	Validation	Testing	Epochs
8	0.993	0.980	0.991	6
11	0.994	0.995	0.990	17
12	0.995	0.998	0.996	12
16	0.983	0.970	0.970	8
18	0.993	0.988	0.989	7
21	0.965	0.989	0.991	6
23	0.994	0.987	0.989	11

Table 2. Pearson Correlation Coefficients

calculated through ANN with their linear correlation coefficients, reached during the training and net generalization and verification phase. It can be noticed that the behavior of the created ANN shows an optimal performance.
During the net training process a number of configurations were made with the number of existing neurons in the hidden layer. The best results are shown in Table 3. Among them, we underline the configuration that acted with twelve neurons in the hidden layer, for that was the one that presented best results. The net incorporates 7 neurons in the input layer, corresponding to the 7 input variables; the hidden layer is built with twelve neurons and the net closes with the outcome layer, using 1 neuron referring to the output variable named COD decrease. The charts on Figures 3, 4 and 5portray the best configuration reached, 12 neurons in the hidden layer.
In order to check the neural model, the data total set (2^7 samples) was divided in three sets: training (50 %) validation (25 %) and test (25 %). In Figures 2, 3 and 4 values of the x and y axis represent the decreasing percentage of the Chemical Oxygen Demand.

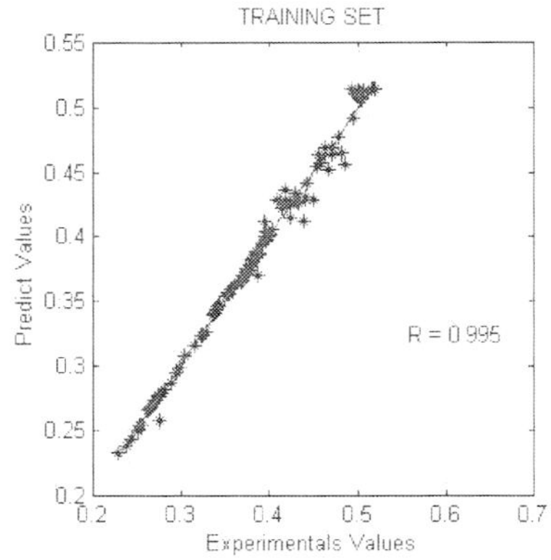

Fig. 2. Adjustment for the Training Set

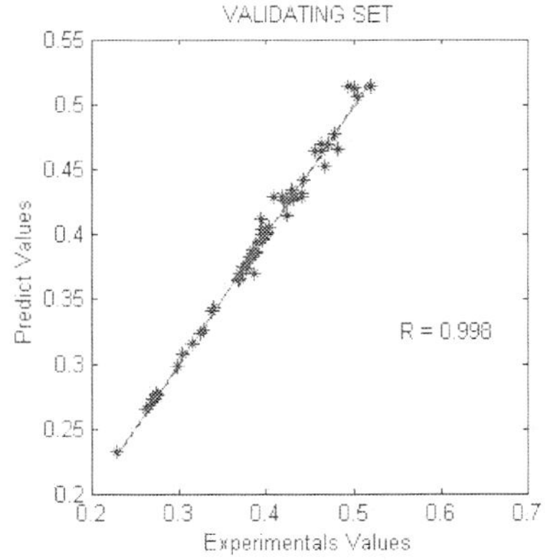

Fig. 3. Adjustment for the Validating Set

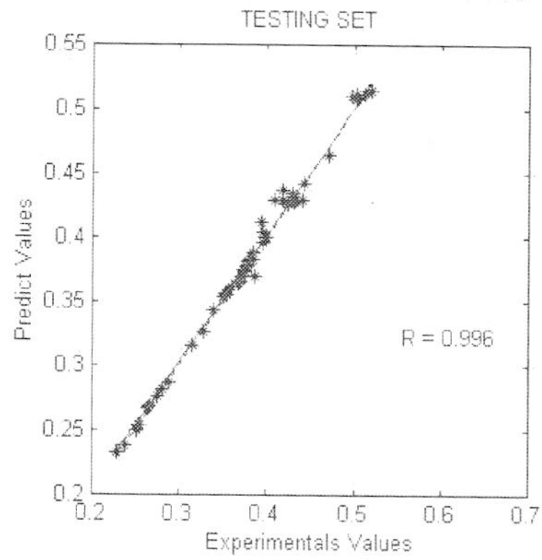

Fig. 4. Adjustment for the Testing Set

Through application of the Disturbance method (Gevrey & Lek, 2003). the relative importance of the input and output variables was evaluated (Figure 5). The Disturbance method consists of attributing isolated noises to every input variable and then observing the quadratic error determination as a function of such variation. Each input neuron passes through an error variation, and its error is compared with quadratic error, not liable to noise.

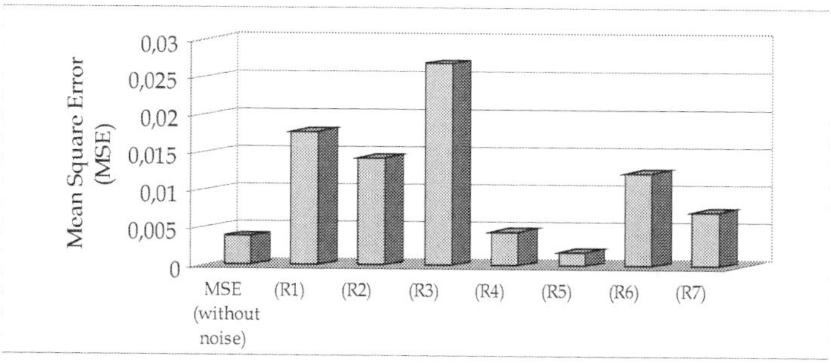

Fig. 5. Chart of MSE with input affected by noise.

We notice in the chart represented by Figure 6 that the 50 % noise provoked on each end every input neuron caused the influence perceived on the MSE value to be larger, in this order, as related to neurons: R3, R1, R2, R6, R7, R4, and R5, which represent, respectively, variables T_2, T_1, $[O_3]$, T, V_2, V_1 and pH. Once the disturbance method indicates only the absolute importance of each neuron or input variable, in order that the aspect of positive or negative influence could be verified, option was made for the study of the effects through Experimental Design. Thus, input variables were as well evaluated according to Experimental Design technology (2^7), where the most important effects can be seen in Figure 6.

Not every independent variable has a strong influence on the process of the reduction of COD as related to the observed output variable (COD), for the predominant ones, in their order, are: T_2, T_1, $[O_3]$, T and V_2, being that the increase in V_1 and pH variables caused a decrease on the yield of COD variation.

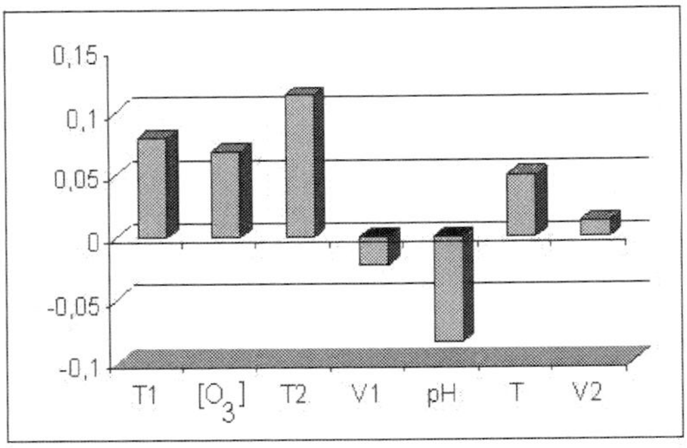

Fig. 6. Influence of Input Variables (Main Effects)

As related to V_1 e pH factors, a negative behavior was observed in the decrease of COD This can be explained as a function of the fact that Fenton Reagent behaves better in a strong acid environment with a pH around 2-3. With respect and a related to the increase of oxygen peroxide amount, it is observed that from a given concentration, it passes to act as a self consumer, of hydroxyl radical, according to the reaction (Equation 13):

$$H_2O_2 + {}^{\bullet}OH \rightarrow H_2O + HO_2^{\bullet} \quad (13)$$

The ozone outflow and ozonization time are important factors to be considered in the reduction of Chemical Oxygen Demand. At this point the influence of ozone for the production of hydroxyl radicals enhance, for they can combine with the $HO_2^{\bullet}$ radical, as per the reaction (Equation 14), and thus, a greater amount of radicals is made liable to attack from organic compounds.

$$O_3 + HO_2^{\bullet} \rightarrow 2O_2 + {}^{\bullet}OH \quad (14)$$

It is pointed out that, from a specific concentration, the hydrogen peroxide works as a hydroxyl radical self-consumer and thus a decrease of the system's oxidizing power happens.

4.2 Hybrid neural model for decoloration by UV/H2O2 involving process variables and structural parameters characteristics to azo dyes

Azodyes are defined as compounds that have in their structure one or more unsaturated groups -N=N- known as chromophore structure, capable of providing color through radiant energy absorbance. Azo class dyes can reach aquatic environments, dissolved or suspended in water, for the conventional treatments can not effectively remove them. The decoloration modeling process, due to the dye complex nature and its dependence on a lot of factors, brings a high level of difficulty to the problem, characterizing itself as a multiple analysis problem.

The polluted water color is reduced when there is cleavage of -C=C- and -N=N- bonds or the cleavage of the aromatic and heterocyclic rings. A lot of f actors may influence the dye chromophore behavior and we have, as example, the dye feature solubility, which is influenced by the change of one substituting in the aromatic ring, with the inclusion of sufonate groups. Hydroxyl radicals (${}^{\bullet}OH$) formed in the H_2O_2 photolysis process under

UV light action and responsible for the organic compound degradation process start, have a short lifetime, in such a way that they can react only where they are formed in a 180 *A* mean distance. This reaction occurs more likely in homogeneous means.
Thus, the proposed model, which relates the azodye structure to the discoloration rate via UV/H_2O_2 process was set in function of the azo bond number (LA) and sulphonate group number (GS) parameters, besides the process operational parameters.
The azodyes and their properties of interest are presented in Table 3.

Name	λ_{max}	Structure	LA	GS
Acid Brown 75	430	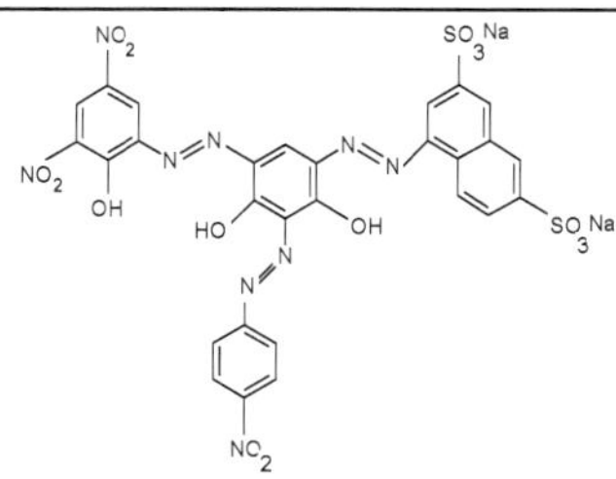	3	2
Acid Orange 10	480	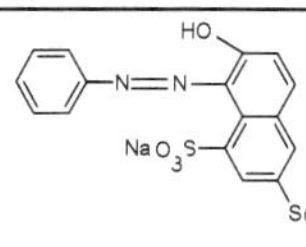	1	2
Acid Orange 52	463	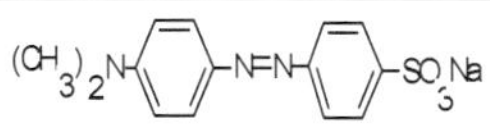	1	1
Direct Red 28	499	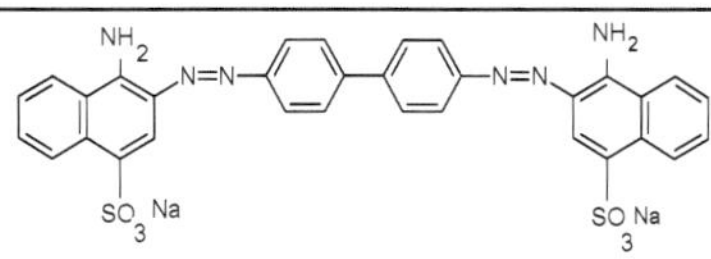	2	2

Table 3. Azodyes Characteristics

Table 4 defines the process operational variant dominium and the Table 3 also defines the dyes structural variant dominium, remarkably in discrete form, being defined by the sets GS={1,2} and LA={1,2,3}.

Parameters	min	max
Operating Time (min)	5	150
Dye Mass (mg)	100	300
H_2O_2 (ml)	2	30
Initial pH	2	11
Temperature (°C)	22	45

Table 4. Operational variant dominium

The decoloration was evaluated in function of the absorbance, measured every 5 minutes via removal of 2 ml of sample, through the Femto 600 spectrophotometer, in the maximum wavelengths raised from the dyes in aqueous solution. The network used in this work was the feedforward backpropagation type implemented at Matlab environment and the sample total kit comprises 498 inlet-outlet values, which were initially normalized. After normalization, the kit of sample data was divided in three sets: training, validation and test for further verification of neural model generalization capacity. Figure 7 presents the network macrostructure utilized in the training process.

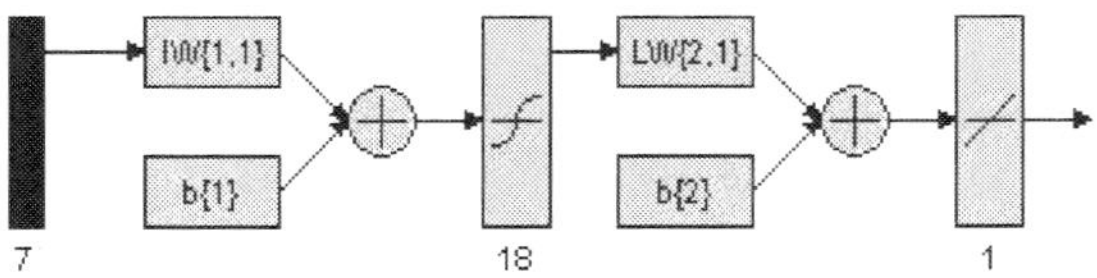

Fig. 7. Neural scheme implemented

As a general feature, in the model proposed the inlet layer is composed of seven independent variants named with azo bond number, sulphonic group number, dye concentration, reaction mean pH, time of operation of the reactor, H_2O_2 volume and temperature. The outlet layer is represented by the absorbance. The hidden layer was composed by a neuron variable number, for each model, in a range from 1 to 25 Neurons, aiming to map a relation of the form A=f(LA, GS, Cc, pH, TO, Vp, T), where A stands for the absorbance, LA is azo bond number, GS the sulphonate group number, Cc the dye concentration, TO is the photo-oxidizing process operation time, Vp is the hydrogen peroxide volume and T the reaction mean temperature.

The Pearson Correlation coefficients higher than 0.9 indicate again the good neural adjustment quality. 16 neurons in the hidden layer was the configuration chosen. Figures 9 to 12 indicate the relation between the real values (T) and the values foreseen by the neural model (A) of the absorbance values.

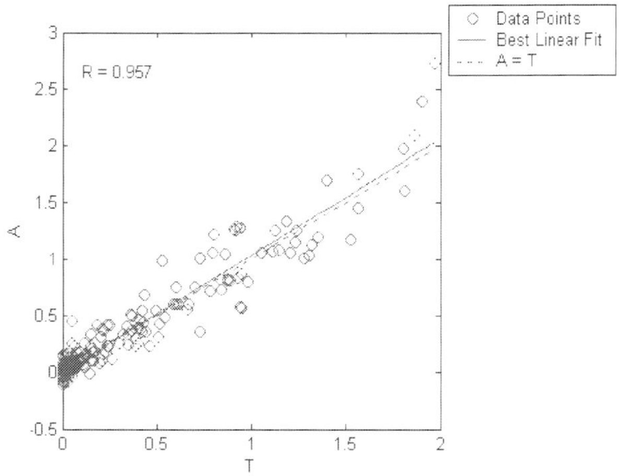

Fig. 8. Training Set Adjustment

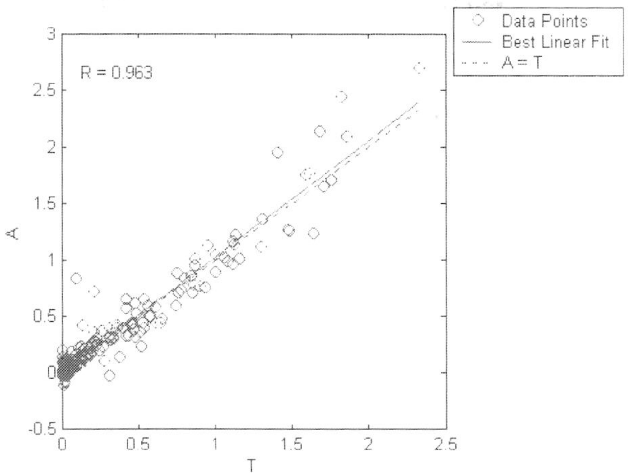

Fig. 9. Validation Set Adjustment

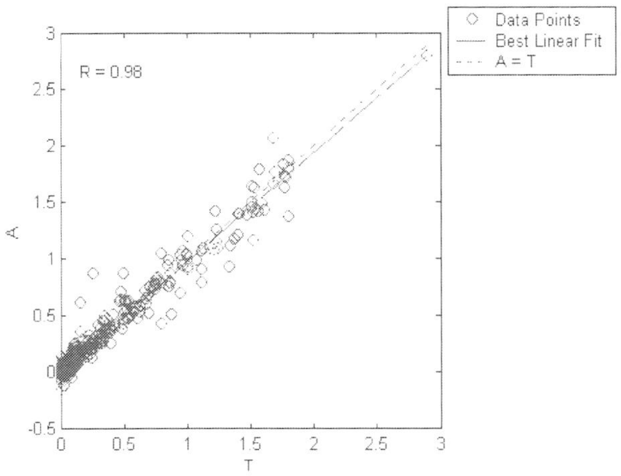

Fig. 10. Test Set Adjustment

The application of the Garson Partition Method reveals a slight predominance of the time of operation in the decoloration process and shows a balance between the structural parameters influence, that is, between the azo bonds and the suphonate groups (Table 5).
The Garson method (Equation 15) and is founded in the partition of the hidden and outlet layer neural weights, in order to determine each network inlet variant relative importance (Garson, 1991), being formulated as shown:

Input Variables	Neuron	Importance (%)
Azo Bond number	1	15.48
Sulphonate group number	2	15.74
Concentration (dye)	3	15.95
Initial pH	4	13.41
Operating Time	5	16.53
H_2O_2 (volume)	6	10.28
Temperature	7	12.61

Table 5. Classification of the Input Variables

$$I_j = \frac{\sum_{m=1}^{N^h}\left(\frac{\left(\left|w_{jm}^{ih}\right|\right)}{\sum_{k=1}^{N^i}\left|w_{km}^{ih}\right|} \times \left|w_{mn}^{h_o}\right|\right)}{\sum_{k=1}^{k=N^i}\left\{\sum_{m=1}^{m=N^h}\left(\frac{\left(\left|w_{km}^{ih}\right|\right)}{\sum_{k=1}^{N^i}\left|w_{km}^{ih}\right|}\right) \times \left|w_{mn}^{h_o}\right|\right\}} \quad (15)$$

The relation I_j above mentioned is the relative importance of the jth input variable on output variable, N^i and N^h are the input and hidden neuron numbers, respectively and w represents the neural weights, and I h and o superscripts refer to the input, hidden and output layers. K, m and n subscripts refer respectively to the input, hidden and output layers.

4.3 Optimization of the AZO dyes decoloration process through neural networks: Determination of the H2O2 addition critical point

In recent years, neural networks have been applied in various areas in the Chemical Engineering and, concerning the Advanced Oxidation Process it can be quoted the work of Pareek *et al.* (2002) in which it was studied the photodegrading of Spent Bayer liquor, with the use of a feedforward-type neural network. Pearson correlation coefficients above 0.99 were obtained in this work.

Slokar *et al.* (1999) utilized Kohonen type neural networks for modeling the Reactive Red 120 dye decoloration process, as a function of the use of H_2O_2/UV.

The present work aimed the determination of an optimum mass relation between the initial amount of hydrogen peroxide and the amount of dye involved in the decoloration process. For the analysis of this relation, was chosen the corante Acid Brown 75, manufactured for industry BASF, widely used in the industries textile and of leathers. It is observed that works related to the degradation or discolouration of this corante had not been found in the bibliography.

The Acid Brown 75 decoloration was evaluated as a function of the absorbance measured every 5 minutes, via Femto 600 spectrophotometer, at the maximum absorbance wavelength (430 nm), optimized from the dye absorbance spectrum in aqueous solution.

The mineralization extents were determined on the basis of total organic carbon content measurements (TOC), performed by using total organic carbon analyzer; TOC- ASI 5000A, Shimadzu.

The photooxidizing process was performed in a Germetec GPJ 463-1 plug-flow reactor, with low pressure radiation source of 21 W, and at the end of each experiment, the system, for washing purposes, was filled with slight acid solution and recirculated.

Table 6 defines the levels of the operational variables utilized in the experiments.

	pH	TO (min)	[dye] mg/L	$V_{H_2O_2}$ (ml)	T (°C)
min (-1)	2	15	30	2	22
max (+1)	11	150	100	22	45

Table 6. Levels of the Operational Variables

An experimental design (2^5) was implemented making up 32 experiments for the dye. The 5 minute interval data collection provided the formation of a neural network input matrix of 528 lines (samples) by 5 columns (process input variables) with the addition of some random experiments. The addition of these randon points was made in central and intermediate points to the extremes of the variables. The output factor of a neural model was constituted of 528 absorbance values in the range of [0, 2].

The sample set deriving from the experiments was divided in training (50%), validation (25%) and test (25%). A scheme for implementing the optimization process by means of "complete" mapping of values simulated by the neural model can be visualized in Figure 11.

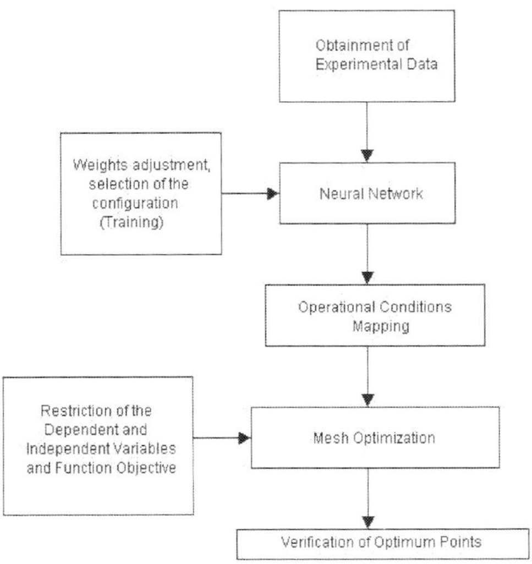

Fig. 11. Implementation of the Optimization Process

After the training and validation phases of the neural model obtained, the mapping of the operational conditions was performed. This phase comprised the discretization of all possible process inlet variables. The multifunctional points discretized and simulated by the neural model generated discretized absorbance values. The discretization period was equal to 0.01 when simulating the neural model obtained.

Once simulated the discretization process to obtain the absorbance values, the linear regression (Time of Operation versus Absorbance) was performed (least square method) for the adjustment of the constant of reaction (k) in a pseudo first order model, mapping the values of this constant through the discretization of the inlet variables, up to the obtainment of its maximum value of this constant.

The following restrictions were imposed during the training phase and complete mapping or discretization.

$$22^oC \leq T_i \leq 45^oC \tag{16}$$

$$30mg / L \leq [dye] \leq 100mg / L \tag{17}$$

$$GD = 0.90 \tag{18}$$

$$2 \leq pH \leq 11 \tag{19}$$

$$15 < TO \leq 150 \text{ mim} \tag{20}$$

$$2\text{ml} \leq V_{H_2O_2} \leq 22\text{ml} \tag{21}$$

Thus, the objective was to determine the process inlet variables values that provided the maximum value of the reaction constant, with the restriction of being reached a decoloration degree imposed as a maximum of 90% for this study.

The photooxidation is supposed to be a reaction of pseudo first order and the kinetics of color degrading can be expressed by:

$$\frac{dC_{dye}}{dt} = -kC_{dye} \tag{22}$$

The integration of this expression produces:

$$\text{Ln}(C_{dye}) = -kt + c_1 \tag{23}$$

From this expression, by linear regression, the values of the constants of reaction kinetics were determined. These values made the composition of the objective function to be mapped in a discretized form by the neural model.

Table 7 present the results of the adjustments for the training (50%), validation (25 %) and test (25 %) sets. The percentages refer to the experimental data total set.

The values of the Pearson Correlation Coefficients above 0.98 for value predicted for absorbance and absorbance real value indicate a good adjustment and prediction capacity for the neural model. The neural model obtained (16 neurons in the hidden layer) mapped a multidimensional space of the form Absorbance=([dye], pH, T, TO, $V_{H_2O_2}$).

Neurons Hidden Layer	R (training)	R (validation)	R (test)
8	0.965	0.954	0.923
12	0.976	0.971	0.963
15	0.982	0.980	0.979
16	0,987	0.981	0.984
20	0.951	0.934	0.921

Table 7. Coefficients of Correlation

The graphic verification of the H_2O_2 addition critical behavior was performed through surface graphs. The k reaction constant maximum value was reached experimentally for values of F in the range of 50 to 60, according to the Equation (24):

$$F = \frac{m_0}{m_1} \tag{24}$$

In the Equation (24), m_o represents the initial hydrogen peroxide mass and m_1 stands for the dye mass.
Figure 12 exemplifies the contour surface graph obtained for experimental values.

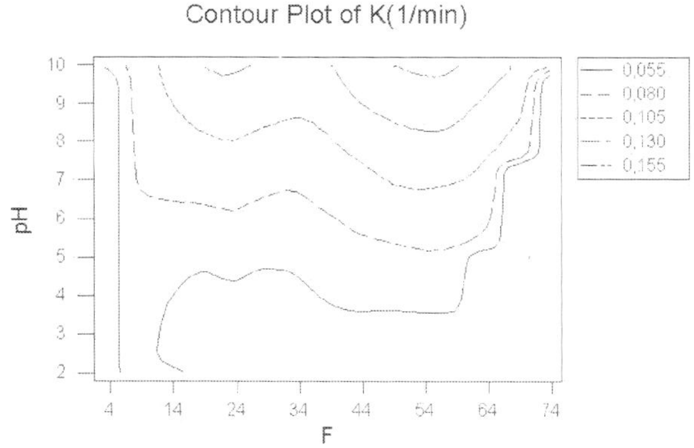

Fig. 12. Contour Surface, ABr 75, T_i=45 °C, 15<TO<150

Table 8 shows some results of the pseudo first order adjustment, where the best performances of the process around a mass relation close to F=50.449 is verified.
In Table 9, some results from contour surfaces graphs (exemplified in Figure 11) are presented, for different operational conditions.

4.4 Discoloration process modelling by Neural Network

Initially a high dye concentration of 170 mg/L and a lesser amount of hydrogen peroxide (1ml) was established for a model experiement. This model experiment was performed up to the point where the absorbance came close to zero value, providing a time of 150 min, that was set as this variable amplitude range maximum value, being characterized a process inspection model. Table 10 presents the levels for which the proposed neural network input variable dominium set was established.

F	K(1/min)	R
3.2450	0.0625	0.9989
9.9990	0.0971	0.9864
16.6650	0.1253	0.9985
26.7170	0.1296	0.9966
33.0330	0.1326	0.9912
50.4490	0.1564	0.9958
53.2216	0.1481	0.9982
56.3206	0.1386	0.9956
73.6900	0.1112	0.9975
100.0900	0.1097	0.9965

Table 8. Constant of Pseudo First Order

pH	m_{dye}	F_{real}	Fpredicted
9.8	100	50<F<60	55.55
10.0	120	50<F<60	51.33
10.5	130	50<F<60	52.22
10.1	140	50<F<60	58.00
9.9	150	50<F<60	50.00
9.6	200	50<F<60	57.89
9.4	250	50<F<60	58.90
10.0	300	50<F<60	53.76

Table 9. Some Results of the Complete Mapping

Variable Level	min	max
H_2O_2 (ml)	2	15
[dye] (mg/L)	3	170
pH	2	12
Temperature (°C)	21	45
Operating Time (minute)	15	150

Table 10. Variables Level

The performance of the method indicated irrelevant results in the reduction of color at absence of peroxide or radiation in isolated processes. The input variable matrixes presented to the neural model are generically shown by:

$$X = \begin{bmatrix} c_1 & pH_1 & t_1 & V_1 & T_1 \\ c_2 & pH_2 & t_2 & V_2 & T_2 \\ . & . & . & . & . \\ . & . & . & . & . \\ . & . & . & . & . \\ c_{218} & pH_{218} & t_{218} & V_{218} & T_{218} \end{bmatrix}. \tag{25}$$

Aiming to verify the existence of this matrix outliers, or solitary points of experiment, and in order to check the homogeneity of the data, each sample "leverage" (Figure 3) was estimated, which is a measurement of how the sample influences the totality of data, and a small value identifies little sample influence over the model building.
Ferreira et al. (1999) indicate that a critical value, or practical rule for the identification of anomalous points, namely, considered points with "leverage" higher than 3k/n, where n is the number of samples (218) and k the number of main components or latent variables, five of them (analysis of components in Matlab environment) for the current work, resulting in a critical value of 0.068807 and, therefore, some samples were discarded from the set to be tested. Matlab prepcap (pn, 0.02) code transforms the input set data matrix already normalized (pn), retaining only the components that contribute with more than 2% in the input data set variance.
There are several methods for picking out the sets to be used as training, validation and test sets. Kanduc *et al.* (2003) establish the random selection, Kennard-Stone and Kohonen maps as some of the possibilities to be employed.
In the present work, the data were worked by following the basic algorithm given by:

1. A clustering was established using K-Means algorithm.
2. After having determined the groups, a statistic test was used to set the training validation and test groups, in such a way that the training, validation and test sets pattern deviation and mean value be equal to less than a value tending to zero.
3. The input variables (in number of 5) and the output variables were processed in such a way that the mean value for each vector containing the dependent and independent variables be zero and the pattern deviation equal to 1, through the pn = (p-meanp)/stdp Matlab environment algorithm, where p is the input or output process matrix or data vector. In Matlab environment, this normalization and the generated set recording were performed by the command:

```
%NORMALIZED SET GENERATION
[pn, meanp, stdp, tn, meant, stdt] = prestd(p', t');
```

The implementation of algorithm K-Means identified 4 clusters, herein named as clusters 1 to 4 (Table 11):

Cluster	Cluster samples number
1	57
2	58
3	51
4	52

Table 11. Cluster Distribution

Table 12 presents the best results with a single hidden layer topology, with the respective linear (R) correlation coefficients. Neural networks with a hidden layer and a sufficiently large number of neurons can interpret any input-output structure and that the hidden layer neuron number is determined in function of the required accuracy.
All the configurations worked with the same 0.01 learning tax and the training performed in 22 epochs.
The functions used in the network training algorithm were tansig and purelin (Matlab language) and the network weight actualization function was the Levenberg-Marquardt backpropagation (trainlm in Matlab language).

Hidden layer neuron number	R_1 (Training Set)	R_2 (Validation set)	R_3 (Test Set)
8	0.988	0.982	0.979
12	0.976	0.971	0.963
15	0.990	0.980	0.979
16	0.991	0.986	0.981
20	0.990	0.984	0.977

Table 12. Correlation Coefficients

The function of error performance was MSE, or mean square error, and the performance learning function utilized was the descending Gradient (learngdm).
Some of the parameters can be visualized in the sequence of commands given by:
net=newff(minmax(pn),[co1{'tansig','purelin'},'trainml');
net.trainParam.epochs = 100; net.trainParam.goal = 0;
net.trainParam.1r = 0.01; % Learning tax
net.trainParam.show = 25; net.trainParam.mc = 0.9;
net.trainParam.1r_inc = 1.05; net.trainParam.1r_dec = 0.7; net.trainParam.max_perf_inc = 1.04;
net.performFcn='MSE';
The diagram of the network implemented may be seen in Figure 13, where 5 input layer neurons related to the 5 network input variables, the 16 layer hidden layer and the input layer with a neuron corresponding to the absorbance output variable.

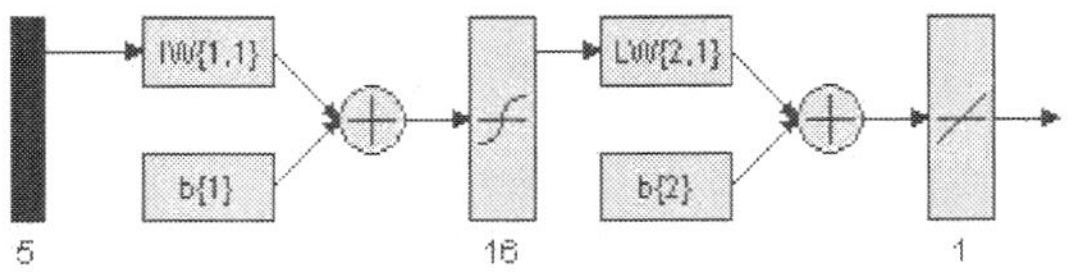

Fig. 13. Diagram of implemented Neural Model

The linear activating function for the output layer is adequate for continuous phenomena, as for instance the oxygen biochemical demand or the absorbance degree in DISCOLORATION process. The sigmoidal type transference functions are necessary to introduce non linearities in the network.
In order to prevent overfitting problem, the training is interrupted if the error for the validation set becomes bigger than the training set error.
In function of the results obtained, hidden layer 16 neuron configuration was chosen. Graphically, the results may be visualized via Figures 14 through 16.
The level of influence of each input variable concerning the modeling problem output variable may be obtained through the neural weight matrix.
As it can be seen in the Table 13, all independent variables strongly influence the absorbances of the discoloration process.
In order to confirm the value importance order classification the pertubation method was applied. Gevrey *et al.* (2003) indicates the perturbation method for input variable analysis. This consists of changes in the form $x_i = x_i + \delta$, where x_i is the selected input variable and δ is the variable change or noise. The method consists of attributing this noise and verifying the changes in the output y_i variable. In this work, the mean square error was used as comparison criterion.

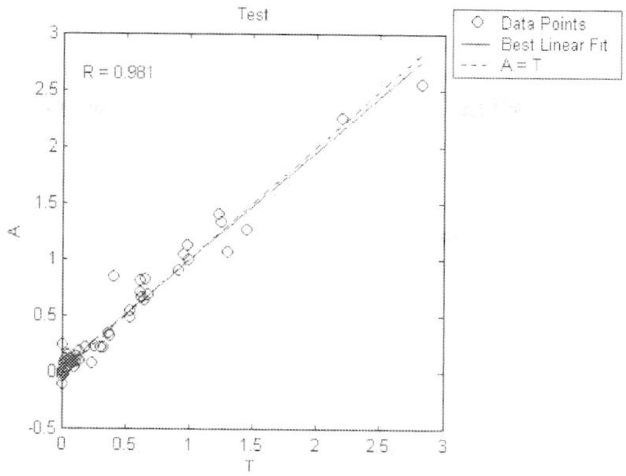

Fig. 14. Linear Regression Test Set

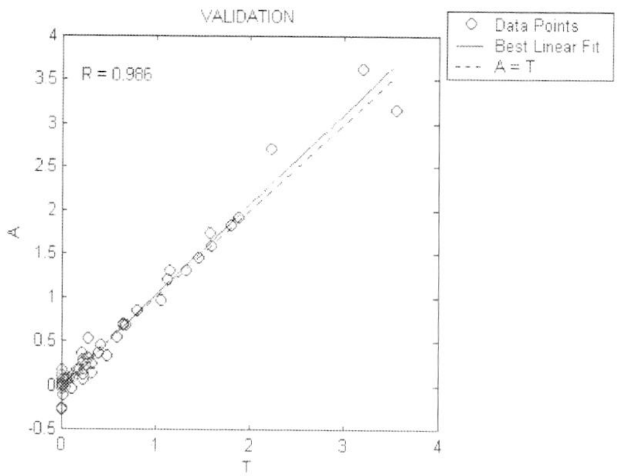

Fig. 15. Linear Regression for validation set

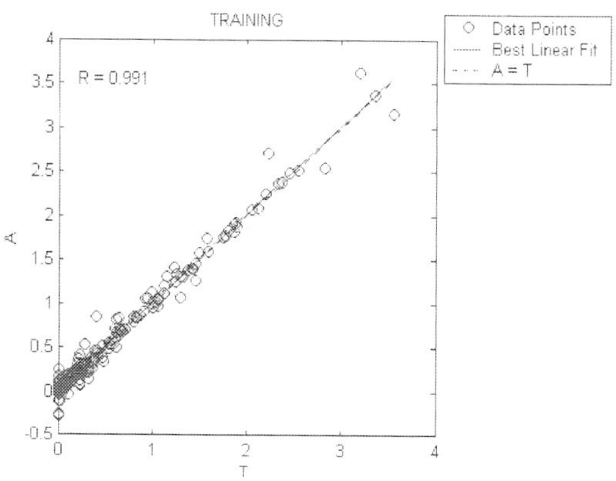

Fig. 16. Linear Regression for Training Set

Variable	Importance(%)
H_2O_2	19.15
[dye]	21.44
pH	21.49
Temperature	16.97
Operating Time	29.95

Table 13. Input Variable Classification

The value δ = 10% attributed in each variable, maintaining the other constants, produced the graph shown in Figure 17, where the major importance of time of operation (t) is visualized, followed by the reaction mean (pH) and hydrogen peroxide volume (V).

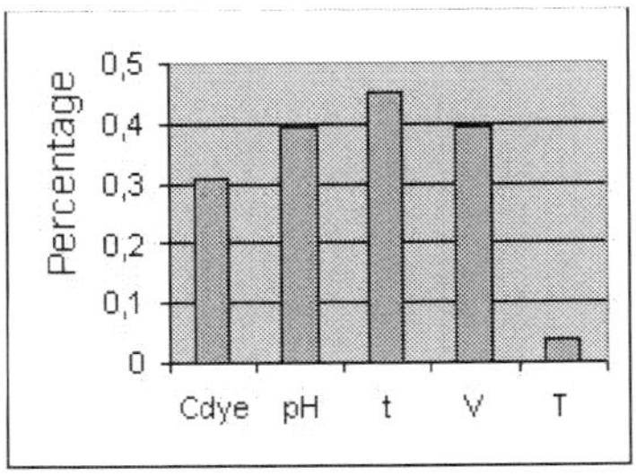

Fig. 17. MSE Variation Percentage

The factors that presented the minor MSE importance were the dye concentration (C_{dye}) and temperature (T), keeping this order of importance. It is noticed the coincidence in the three most important factors in the Garson Partition and Pertubation Methods, namely, time of operation, pH and hydrogen peroxide volume.

In order to verify the stability of the values obtained through Garson Partition and Pertubation methods, the network trainings were repeated 10 times and the average contribution of each variable was calculated.

By comparing the results obtained through Garson Partition and Pertubation methods, an inversion is noticed concerning the dye concentration and temperature variables behavior, but equivalence was observed in the other variables, maintained the levels of importance.

A 10% noise value is attributed to the input data matrix aiming to verify the network capacity to self-adapt and prevent small failures or measurement errors, and Table 14 shows the network adaptation capacity to these noises, with the mean quadratic errors, and the linear correlation coefficients for training set (R_1), validation set (R_2) and test set (R_3).

	R_1	R_2	R_3
Noise (0)%	0.978	0.977	0.947
Noise(10%)	0.974	0.968	0.923

Table 14. Correlation Coefficients under noise in the input variables

5. Conclusion

The employment of a neural model to describe the photo-chemical influence of effluents from polyesters and alcodic resins has shown excellent results, as the model can describe the complex behavior of the process within the experimentation range employed.

The model achieved also allows, for the study of the influence of input variables in the photo-chemical process.

Thus, simulations based on neural nets afford the estimation of the complex behavior of oxidation processes that combine photo-Fenton and ozone agents. Such information is essential for the treatment of industry effluents.

Concerning the efficiency of the oxidizing process utilized, it has to be pointed out the obtainment of the best results close to 55%, values that due to high Chemical Oxygen Demand initial value present the practical feasibility of the oxidizing method proposed for effluents with very high organic charge values.

In relation to case B, This work proposes, via neural networks, a model that involves the process operational and compound structure features to be treated, in such a way that a higher model amplitude occurs. This process has the advantage of working as a database, where new samples, with totally different characteristics, may be added with the need of equationing a new model. Implemented the neural model and analyzed the correlation coefficients (approximately 0.96 for the data total, validation and test sets) it was verified the good model prediction capacity and also the possibility of determining the inlet variable influence degree of the Garson Method. The neural model, because it simply involves the numerical or statistical "behavior analysis", does not troubles about the mathematics involved in the process and, thus, it makes possible the analysis of structural sets that comprise variants of several different spectrums, such as operational and structural ones, opening room for a hybrid and more embracing model. It is pointed out the capacity of application of the herein named hybrid modeling by neural networks, with the possible incorporation of other structural parameters which may foresee different environment values such as oxygen chemical, dissolved organic carbon demand, among other factors of environmental concern. In the present model, the neural model hybrid character was not connected to the fact that the entry variant values be experimental or deriving from certain mathematics models but in these variant nature composition aspect, being of the process operational aspect and structural concerning the dyes.For dyes with the same azo bonds number and sulfonated groups other caracteristics, as label hydrogen number, benzenic and naphthalenic can be incorporated, which will object of further researches.

In relation to the Case "C", The implementation of a neural model and the optimization through complete mapping of the dominium of the independent variables in a process of decoloration by UV/H_2O_2 is presented as a promising technique in the optimization of processes with multiple inlet variables.

The neural model reached good prediction capacity with Pearson Correlation Coefficients above 0.98 for the training, validation and test sets.

From this neural model, the discretization of all process variables could be performed, which made possible the search for the Acid Brown 75 dye decoloration process critical point through the use of UV/H_2O_2. The determination of the critical point, or maximum amount of Hydrogen Peroxide to be added as a function of the dye initial mass, was established in a $50<F<60$ interval, coinciding with the real values obtained in the experiments.

The study of the case "An Acid Orange 52 dye DISCOLORATION neural model", with hydrogen peroxide, activated by UV radiation, was evaluated concerning five factors. The neural network was trained with 218 samples and utilized a configuration with a hidden layer and 16 neurons in this layer, presenting high correlation coefficients for training, validation and test sets (>0.98), verifying the network prediction capacity with high accuracy level. The input layer is formed by five variables: dye concentration, initial pH, time of operation, hydrogen peroxide volume at 30% and temperature. The study of the variable influence level determined that the input variables that influence the Acid Orange 52 DISCOLORATION process are time of operation, initial pH and hydrogen peroxide volume. However, temperature and concentration of the dye should not be neglected, as they also appear to be significant factors.

6. References

Ferreira, M. C. M., Antunes, A.M., Melgo, M.S., Volpe, P.L., Chemometrics I: multivaried calibration, a Tutorial, Química Nova, vol. 22, 1999

Garson, G.D., AI Expert, p.46, 1991;

Gevrey, M., Dimopoulos I., Lek, S., Review and comparison of methods to study the contribution of variables in artificial neural networks models, Ecological Modelling 160, 249-264, 2003.

Gogate, P. R. e Pandit, A. B. A review of imperative technologies for wastewater treatment I: oxidation technologies at ambient conditions, Advances in Environmental Research 8, 501 -551, 2004.

Kanduc, R. K., Zupan, J., Madcen, N., Separation of data on the training and test for modelling: a case study for modelling of five colour properties of a white pigment, Chemometrics and Intelligent Laboratory Systems 65, p. 221-229, 2003;

Loesch C., Sari, S. T., Redes Neurais Artificais Fundamentos e Modelos, Editora da Furb, 1996;

Lu, M.C., Lin, C.J., Liao, C.H., Ting, W.P., Huang, R.Y. *Influence of pH on the dewatering of activated sludge by Fenton's reagent*, Wat. Sci. Technol. 44, 327-332, 2001.

Neyens, E. e Baeyens, J. A review of classic Fenton's peroxidation as an advanced oxidation technique, Journal of Hazardous Materials B98, 33-50, 2003.

Pareek, V. K., Brungs, M. P., Adesina, A. A., Sharma, R. (2002) Artificial neural network modeling of a multiphase photodegradation system. Journal of Photochemistry and Photobiology A: Chemistry 149, 139-146;

Quici, N., Morgada, M. E., Piperata, G., Babay, P., Gettar, R. T., Litter, M. I. Oxalic acid destruction at high concentrations by combined heterogeneous photocatalysis and photo-Fenton processes, Catalysis Today, 2005.

Slokar, Y.M., Zupan, J., Marechal, A. M. (1999) The use of artificial neural network (ANN) for modeling of the H2O2/UV decoloration process: part I. Dyes and Pigments 42, 123-135;

5

Application of Artificial Neural Network for Mineral Potential Mapping

Saro Lee and Hyun-Joo Oh
Geoscience Information Center, Korea Institute of Geoscience and Mineral Resources (KIGAM), 92, Gwahang-no, Yuseong-gu, Daejeon 305-350 Republic of Korea

1. Introduction

Mineral exploration is a multidisciplinary task requiring the simultaneous consideration of numerous disparate geophysical, geological, and geochemical datasets (Knox-Robinson, 2000). The size and complexity of regional exploration data available to geologist are increasing rapidly from a variety of sources such as remote sensing, airbone geophysics, large commercially available geological and geochemical data (Brown et al., 2000). This demands more effective integration and analysis of regional and various of geospatial data with different formats and attributes. In addition, this needs spatial modeling techniques using observations regarding the association of mineral occurrences with various geological features in a qualitative manner.

Geographic Information System (GIS) methods are very useful for processing and combining data within maps in mineral potential mapping. The development of GIS-based methods for integration and analysis of regional exploration datasets has an important role in assisting the decision-making processes for geologists in selection of exploration area (Brown et al., 2000). More recently, the mineral exploration industry has taken this approach further and with the help of spatial data modeling in GIS (Partington, 2010).

The spatial modeling techniques been proposed for mineral potential mapping, such as weights of evidence model (Bonham-Carter et al., 1988, 1989; Agterberg et al., 1990; Xu et al., 1992; Rencz et al., 1994; Pan, 1996; Raines, 1999; Carranza & Hale, 2000; Tangestani & Moore, 2001; Carranza, 2004; Agterberg & Bonham-Carter, 2005; Jianping et al., 2005; Nykanen & Raines, 2006; Porwal et al., 2006; Roy et al., 2006; Nykänen & Ojala, 2007; Raines et al., 2007; Oh & Lee, 2008; Harris et al., 2008; Benomar et al., 2009), Bayesian network classifiers (Porwal et al., 2006), logistic regression (Chung and Agterberg, 1980; Agterberg, 1988; Oh & Lee, 2008), fuzzy logic (An et al., 1991; Bonham-Carter, 1994; Eddy et al., 1995; D'Ercole et al., 2000; Knox-Robinson, 2000; Luo & Dimitrakopoulos, 2003; De Quadros et al., 2006; Carranza et al., 2008; Nykänen, 2008), artificial neural networks (Singer & Kouda, 1996; Harris & Pan, 1999; Brown et al., 2000, 2003; Rigol-Sanchez et al., 2003; Behnia, 2007; Skabar, 2007; Oh & Lee, 2008), and an evidence theory model (Moon, 1990, 1993; An & Moon, 1993; Moon & So, 1995; Porwal et al., 2003; Carranza et al., 2005). Researches using GIS have involved comparison of methods (Harris et al., 2003; Oh & Lee, 2008) and resolutions of spatial data used for mapping mineral potential, development of advanced methods, improvement of prediction accuracy, and case studies for mineral potential mapping. These approaches have been successfully applied to mineral resource appraisal.

Artificial neural network (ANN), one of the spatial modeling methods, has great potential in various fields of application such as pattern recognition, classification, identification, vision, speech, and control systems in solving complex problems. The artificial neural network has advantage compared with statistical methods. Firstly, the artificial neural network method is independent of the statistical distribution of the data and there is no need of specific statistical variables. Compared with the statistical methods, neural networks allow the target classes to be defined with much consideration to their distribution in the corresponding domain of each data source (Zhou, 1999). Mineral potential mapping is an example where ANN method can be applied because the deposit occurrence is usually controlled by numerous interlocking geological features with non-linear relationship. It is difficult to estimate a spatial recognition criteria for appropriate training data in processes of various geological factors to form the deposits on the surface (Nykanen, 2008). It is important to select the training data such as deposit- and non-deposit locations used as input to the ANN's learning algorithm, which is proposed that minimizes some targeted minimal error between the desired and actual outputs of the network (Paola & Schowengerdt, 1995, Skabar, 2005).

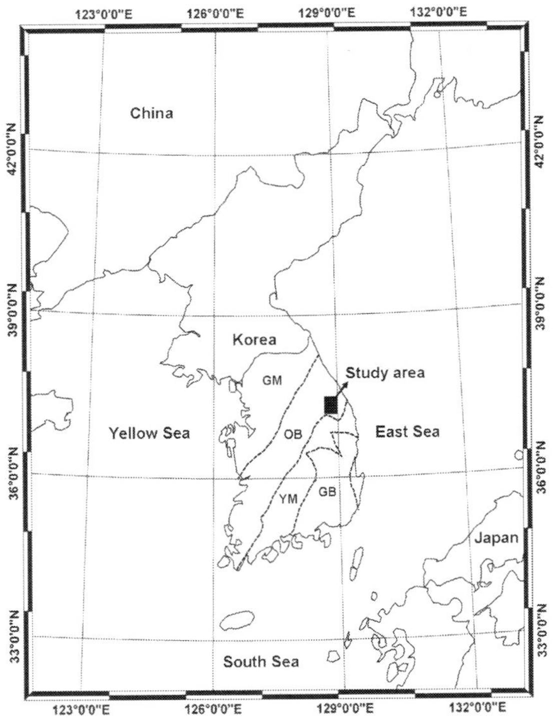

Fig. 1. Study area with tectonic units (GM = Gyeonggi Massif, OB = Ogcheon Belt, YM = Yeongnam Massif, GB = Gyeongsang Basin)

The objective of this study is to set some cases for selection of training data using quantitative mineral potential index by likelihood ratio, weights of evidence and logistic regression models, generate gold-silver potential maps using GIS and ANN to the various training sets, and estimate the predictive accuracy of those potential maps in the Taebaeksan mineralized district, Korea (Fig. 1). The preparation of mineral potential maps using GIS (ArcGIS 9.0) was accomplished in five major steps (Fig. 2): (1) Assembly of a spatial database. A total of 46 gold-silver mineral deposits were used to create a spatial database using GIS. Geological, geochemical and geophysical maps were similarly treated. (2) Processing the data from the database. The known mineral deposits were randomly split 70/30 for training/testing, which used for analyzing and validating mineral potential maps using likelihood ratio, weights of evidence, logistic regression and ANN models (Leite & Souza Filho, 2009). Training locations (deposit and none-deposit occurrence) for ANN analysis were extracted from potential maps based on likelihood ration, weights of evidence and logistic regression models. Training dataset and the factors were analyzed and their weights were determined quantitatively. Especially, the nine cases for selection of training datasets determined from likelihood ratio, weights of evidence and logistic regression models were simulated to evaluate the sensitivity of ANN to training data. (3) Application of weights to generate a mineral potential map. (4) Validation of the potential map using test deposits that were not used directly in the analysis.

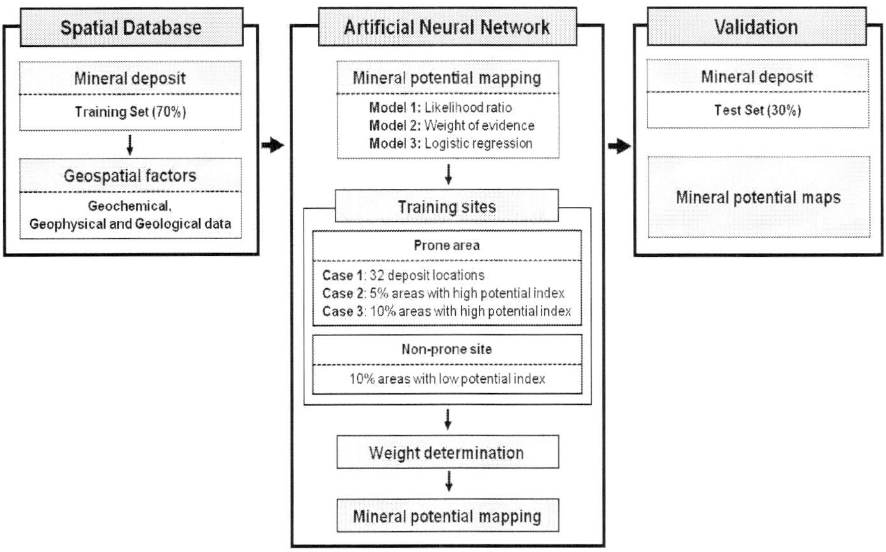

Fig. 2. Study flow for mineral potential mapping

2. Study area

The study area is bounded by latitudes 37°15′24′′–37°30′00′′ N and longitudes 128°30′30′′–129°02′40′′ E and lies in the Taebaeksan mineralized district at central east part of the

Korean Peninsula (Fig. 1). The total study area occupies approximately 1,050 km^2. The study area was chosen as high mineral potential area after regional gold-silver potential analysis in the Taebaeksan mineralized district (Oh & Lee, 2008). This region has many mineral deposits and geological, geochemical and geophysical survey data available.

Geological setting is largely distinguished by five groups of in the study area (Fig. 3). 1) Precambrian metamorphic and metasedimentary rocks (the unit Jugr and PCEt) in the northeastern part. 2) Cambro-Ordovician Joseon System (the unit CEj, CEm, CEp, CEw, Odu, Omg, Od and Oj) largely in the central part. 3) Carboniferous to Early Triassic Pyeongan System (the unit Ch, Ps, TRg, TRn3, TRn2, TRn1 and TRn) in the northwestern and southern parts. 4) Jurassic plutonic rocks (the unit Jigr) in the northern part and around the study area. 5) Cretaceous plutonic rocks (the unit Ksgr) in the southeastern part. Map-scale faults (~20km) trend mostly NNE-SSW and are of Late Cretaceous to Early Paleocene age (Fig. 3).

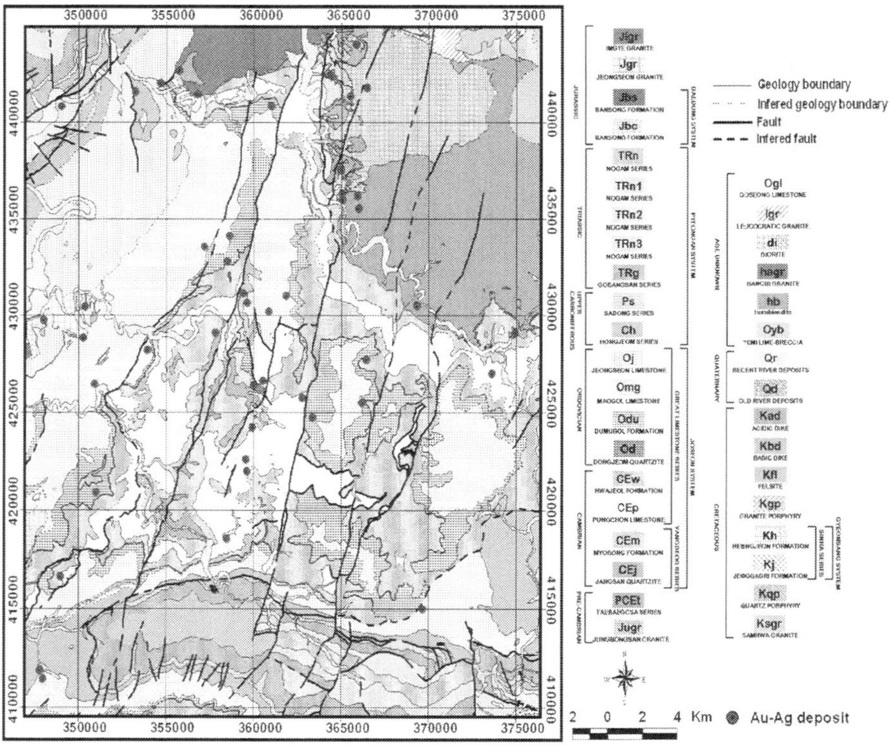

Fig. 3. Geological map with mineral deposits of the study area in Tabaeksan mineralized distract, Korea (combined geological map of Jeongseon, Imgye, Yemi and Homyeong sheets produced by the Korea Institute of Geoscience & Mineral Resources at 1:50,000)

Precambrian metamorphic rocks consist largely of banded gneiss, with lesser amounts of migmatitic gneiss, schist and quartzite. Additionally, there is abundant orthogenic granitic, garnet-bearing granitic, leucocratic and porphyroblastic gneiss incorporated within the complex unit. The Cambro-Ordovician Joseon System is mainly shallow marine in origin and consists predominantly of carbonates with lesser amounts of sandstone and shale, whereas the Carboniferous to Early Triassic Pyeongan System comprises thick clastic successions of marginal marine to non-marine environments. The Jurassic plutonic rock, Imgye Granite, mainly occurs as a large batholith trend NW-SE and as small stocks along the Ogcheon Belt consisting of granite with minor syenite and diorite. The Cretaceous plutonic rock, Samhwa Granite, mainly occurs as small stocks composed of granodiorite andesite, diorite, granite and granite porphyry (Kim et al., 1996, 2001).

Igneous rocks related to gold-silver deposits in the Korean Peninsula are Jurassic and Cretaceous granites. Gold-silver deposits are distributed in and around those granites. The Taebaeksan district is a famous metallogenic area that contains a variety of deposit types, including Cu-Fe-Au, W-Mo and Pb-Zn skarns, Pb-Zn-Ag hydrothermal carbonate replacement ores, Carlne-like, alakite, pegmatite, greisen and gold-silver vein deposits. Gold-silver bearing hydrothermal vein deposits in the study area occur in various host lithologies, consist of multiple generations of quartz and/or carbonates with base metal sulphides, and have NNW, NS or NNE strikes, which seem to be related to NE strike-slip faults. Veins generally comprise quartz, lesser carbonate and polymetallic minerals including pyrite, sphalerite, galena, arsenopyrite, chalcopyrite and pyrrhotite. Electrum is the most common gold bearing ore mineral and the common silver-bearing phases are native silver, argentite, pyrargyrite and polybasite (Park et al., 1988; Lee & Park, 1996; Koh et al., 2003).

3. Spatial database

Data of hydrothermal gold-silver deposits were obtained from mineral deposit maps of the Taebaeksan mineralization with mineral variety and type, which were obtained from the MIRECO (Mine Reclamation Crop.), NHMRG (Natural Hazard Mitigation Research Group) and KIGAM (Korea Institute of Geoscience and Mineral Resources). The available factors related to gold-silver mineral occurrence are geophysical data of magnetic anomaly (Chi et al., 2001), geological data of geology and fault structure, and geochemical data of Al, As, Ba, Ca, Cd, Co, Cr, Cu, Fe, K, Li, Mg, Mn, Na, Ni, Pb, Si, Sr, V, W, Zn, Cl^- and F^- produced by KIGAM (Table 1). All of these factors were used within a spatial database with a pixel size of 30m x 30m. Most of the continuous data was classified into 10 equal-area classes. Categorical data, such as the geology, was set the unique attribute value to the each class. The numbers of rows and columns are, respectively, 986 and 1,183, and the total number of cells in the study area is 1,166,438. The number of mineral deposit occurrences is 46 and the number of factor is 26.

The geological data were derived from 1:50,000 geological maps (Jeongseon, Imgye, Yemi and Homyeong sheets). The geology and distance from fault were registered (Fig. 3). The geochemical maps were made from IDW (Inverse Distance Weighting) interpolation of values of geochemical elements, which were analyzed and collected from a stream water and sediment geochemical survey (Fig. A1a-w, Lee et al., 1998). The geophysical data was acquired through airborne magnetic surveys (Koo et al., 2001) (Fig. A1x).

Category	Factors	Data type	Scale	Remarks
Deposit	Au-Ag	Point	-	46 deposits
Geochemical Data	Al, As, Ba, Ca, Cd, Cl^-, Co, Cr, Cu, F^-, Fe, K, Li, Mg, Mn, Na, Ni, Pb, Si, Sr, V, W, Zn	Point	1:250,000	IDW (Inverse Distance Weight) Interpolation
Geological Data	Geology Distance from fault	Polygon Line	1:50,000	Combination of four geological map sheets
Geophysical Data	Magnetic anomaly	Point	1:250,000	IDW (Inverse Distance Weight) Interpolation

Table 1. Data layer of study area

4. Models

4.1 Artificial neural network model

An artificial neural network is a "computational mechanism able to acquire, represent, and compute a mapping from one multivariate space of information to another, given a set of data representing that mapping" (Garrett, 1994). The purpose of an artificial neural network is to build a model of the data-generating process, so that the network can generalize and predict outputs from inputs that it has not previously seen. The back-propagation is one of the most popular training algorithm used neural network method and is the method used in this study. The back-propagation algorithm trains network layer by layer doing forward and backward computation and is trained using a set of examples of associated input and output values. This learning algorithm is a multi-layered neural network, which consists of three layers; input, hidden and output. The hidden and output layer neurons process their inputs by multiplying each input by a corresponding weight, summing the product, then processing the sum using a log-sigmoid transfer function to produce a result (Fig. 4). An artificial neural network learns by adjusting the weights between the neurons in response to the errors between the actual output values and the target output values. At the end of this training phase, the neural network provides a model that should be able to predict a target value from a given input value (Lee et al., 2007).

There are two stages involved in using neural network for multi-source classification; the training stage, in which the internal weights are adjusted; and the classifying stage. Typically, the back-propagation algorithm trains the network until some targeted minimal error is achieved between the desired and actual output values of the network. Once the training is complete, the network is used as a feed-forward structure to produce a classification for the entire data (Paola & Schowengerdt, 1995).

A neural network consists of a number of interconnected nodes. Each node is a simple processing element that responds to the weighted inputs it received from other nodes. The arrangement of the nodes is referred to as the network architecture (Fig. 4). The receiving node sums the weighted signals from all nodes to which it is connected in the preceding layer. Formally, the input that a single node j receives is weighted according to Eq. (1):

$$net_j = \sum_i w_{ij} \cdot o_i \quad (1)$$

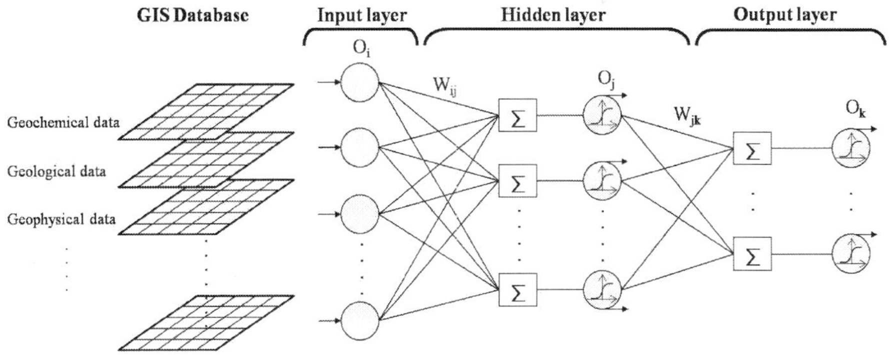

Fig. 4. The architecture of the artificial neural network

where w_{ij} represents the weight between node i and node j, and o_i is the output from node i such as Eq. (2):

$$o_j = f(net_j) \quad (2)$$

The valued produced by hidden node j, o_j, is the activation function, f, evaluated at the sum produced within node j, net_j, net_j, in turn, is a function of the weights between the input and hidden layer, w_{ij}, and the outputs of the input layer nodes, o_i. The function f is usually a non-linear sigmoid function that is applied to the weighted sum of inputs before the signal processes proceeds to the next layer. Advantage of the sigmoid function is that its derivative can be expressed in terms of the function itself such as Eq. (3):

$$f'(net_j) = f(net_j)(1 - f(net_j)) \quad (3)$$

The error, E, for one training pattern for input layer, t, is a function of the desired output vector, d, and the actual output vector, o, given by Eq. (4):

$$E = \frac{1}{2}\sum_k (d_k - o_k) \quad (4)$$

The error back propagated through neural network and the error is minimized by changing the weight between layers. So, the weight can be expressed by Eq. (5):

$$w_{ij}(n+1) = \eta(\delta_j \cdot o_i) + \alpha\Delta w_{ij} \quad (5)$$

where η is the learning rate parameter, δ_j is an index of the rate of change of the error, and α is the momentum parameter. This process of feeding forward signals and back propagating the error is repeated iteratively until the error of the network as a whole is minimized or reaches an acceptable magnitude.

Using the backpropagation, the weight of each factor can be recognized and it can be used to weight determination for mineral potential. Zhou (1999) described the method of determination of the weight using backpropagation. From Eq. (2), the effect of an output o_j from a hidden layer node j on the output o_k from an output layer node k can be represented by the partial derivative of o_k with respect to o_j such as Eq. (6):

$$\frac{\partial o_k}{\partial o_j} = f'(net_k) \cdot \frac{\partial (net_k)}{\partial o_j} = f'(net_k) \cdot w_{jk} \tag{6}$$

The Eq. (6) equation can produce values with both positive and negative signs. If only the magnitude of the effects is of interest, the importance of node j relative to another node jo in the hidden layer can be calculated as the ratio of the absolute values from the Eq. (6):

$$\frac{\left|\partial o_k\right|}{\left|\partial o_j\right|} / \frac{\left|\partial o_k\right|}{\left|\partial o_{j0}\right|} = \frac{\left|f'(net_k) \cdot w_{jk}\right|}{\left|f'(net_k) \cdot w_{j0k}\right|} = \frac{\left|w_{jk}\right|}{\left|w_{j0k}\right|} \tag{7}$$

The Eq. (7) shows that, with respect to a particular node k in the output layer, the relative importance of a node j in the hidden layer is proportional to the absolute value of the weight on its connection to the node k in the output layer. When more than one node in the output layer is concerned, the Eq. (7) equation cannot be used to compare the importance of two nodes in the hidden layer. In other words, the relative importance of a node must somehow normalized to make it more comparable with that of other nodes. One choice is to let, in (7):

$$w_{j0k} = \frac{1}{J} \cdot \sum_{j=1}^{J} \left|w_{jk}\right| \tag{8}$$

to obtain the normalized importance of node j with respect to node k

$$t_{jk} = \frac{\left|w_{jk}\right|}{\frac{1}{J} \cdot \sum_{j=1}^{J} \left|w_{jk}\right|} = \frac{J \cdot \left|w_{jk}\right|}{\sum_{j=1}^{J} \left|w_{jk}\right|} \tag{9}$$

Therefore, with respect to the node k, each node in the hidden layer has a value greater or smaller than one, depending on whether it is more or less important than the average, respectively. With respect to the same node k, all the nodes in the hidden layer have a total importance such as Eq. (10):

$$\sum_{j=1}^{J} t_{jk} = J \tag{10}$$

Consequently, with respect to all nodes in the output layer, to which connected to hidden layer, the overall importance of node j can be calculated as Eq. (11):

$$t_j = \frac{1}{K} \cdot \sum_{k=1}^{K} t_{jk} \tag{11}$$

Similar to Eq. (9), with respect to the node j in the hidden layer, the normalized importance of the node i in the input layer can be defined as Eq. (12):

$$s_{ij} = \frac{|w_{ij}|}{\frac{1}{I} \cdot \sum_{i=1}^{I} |w_{ij}|} = \frac{I \cdot |w_{ij}|}{\sum_{i=1}^{I} |w_{ij}|} \tag{12}$$

With respect to the hidden layer, the overall importance of node i is done by Eq. (13):

$$s_i = \frac{1}{J} \cdot \sum_{j=1}^{J} s_{ij} \tag{13}$$

Correspondingly, the overall importance of the input node i with respect to the output node k is given by Eq. (14):

$$st_i = \frac{1}{J} \cdot \sum_{j=1}^{J} s_{ij} \cdot t_j \tag{14}$$

4.2 Likelihood ratio model

The likelihood ratio is a simple technique for producing a mineral potential map, and it is highly compatible with GIS. The likelihood ratio approach is based on observed relationships between the distribution of mineral deposits and each mineral deposit-related factor and are used to reveal the correlation between mineral deposit locations and factors in the study area. The likelihood ratio is the ratio of occurrence probability to non-occurrence probability for specific attributes.

For a given number of units cells, $N(D)$, containing a mineral deposit, D, and given number of total cells, $N(T)$, the prior probability of an occurrence is expressed by

$$P(D) = \frac{N(D)}{N(T)} \tag{15}$$

Now suppose that a binary predictor pattern, B, occupying $N(B)$ unit cells, occurs in the region, and that a number of known mineral deposits occur preferentially within the pattern, i.e., $N(D \cap B)$, then the probability of locating a deposit given the presence of a predictor(B), and the probability of a deposit occurrence in the absence of a pattern($\overline{B}$) can be expressed by the following conditional probabilities, respectively:

$$P(D \mid B) = \frac{P(D \cap B)}{P(B)} = P(D)\frac{P(B \mid D)}{P(B)} \tag{16}$$

$$P(D|\bar{B}) = \frac{P(D \cap \bar{B})}{P(\bar{B})} = P(D)\frac{P(\bar{B}|D)}{P(\bar{B})} \tag{17}$$

The posterior probability of a deposit occurrence given presence and absence of a favorable predictor pattern are denoted by $P(D|B)$ and $P(D|\bar{B})$, respectively. $P(B|D)$ and $P(\bar{B}|D)$ are the posterior probabilities of being inside and outside the predictor pattern B, respectively, given the presence of a deposit D. $P(B)$ and $P(\bar{B})$ are the prior probabilities of the presence of a predictor pattern B.

The odds, O, is defined as the ration of the probability P that an event will occur to the probability that the event will not occur; i.e. $O = P / \bar{P} = P(1-P)$. Expressed as odds, Eqs. 18 and 19 become:

$$O(D|B) = O(D)\frac{P(B|D)}{P(B|\bar{D})} \tag{18}$$

$$O(D|\bar{B}) = O(D)\frac{P(\bar{B}|D)}{P(\bar{B}|\bar{D})} \tag{19}$$

where $O(D|B)$ and $O(D|\bar{B})$ are the posterior odds of a deposit given the presence and absence of a binary predictor pattern B, respectively, and $O(D)$ is the prior odds of a deposit. The likelihood ratios, which are sufficiency ratio (LS) and necessity ratio (LN), are quire by the following equation:

$$LS = \frac{P(B|D)}{P(B|\bar{D})} \tag{20}$$

$$LN = \frac{P(\bar{B}|D)}{P(\bar{B}|\bar{D})} \tag{21}$$

To calculate the likelihood ratio for the class or type of each factor, all scale factors that consisted of a raster type were reclassified into 10 classes based on equal areas using GIS techniques. The cross tabulation in ArcGIS 9.0 was used to calculate the number of deposit occurrences in the class or type of each factor. The likelihood ratio was used to calculate the ratio of the cell with deposit occurrence in each class for a reclassified factor or categorical factor (i.e., geochemical data and geology), and the ratio was assigned to each factor class again. Finally, the likelihood ratios (Table A1) of each factor type or range were summed to calculate the Mineral Potential Index (MPI) (Fig. 5a), as shown in Eq. (22):

$$MPI_{LR} = Lr_1 + Lr_2 + Lr_3 + \ldots + Lr_n \tag{22}$$

where Lr_n = likelihood ratio of each factor type or range.

The MPI_{LR} represents relative potential of mineral deposit occurrence. The greater the value, the higher the potential of mineral deposit occurrence and the lower the value, the lower the potential of mineral deposit occurrence. The mineral deposit potential map was made using the MPI_{LR} and was used for selecting training sites.

4.3 Weights of evidence model

The following application of Bayesian probability known as the likelihood ratio and weighs of evidence to mineral potential analysis was synthesized from Bonham-Carter (1994) and Bonham-Carter et al. (1989). A detailed description of the formulation of the weights of evidence method is available in Bonham-Carter et al. (1989) and Bonham-Carter (1994). The weights can be defined as shown in Eqs. 23 and 24:

$$W^{+} = \log_{e} LS \tag{23}$$

$$W^{-} = \log_{e} LR \tag{24}$$

$$C = W^{+} - W^{-} \tag{25}$$

$$S(c) = \sqrt{S^{2}(W^{+}) + S^{2}(W^{-})} \tag{26}$$

where W^{+} and W^{-} are the weights of evidence when a binary predictor pattern is present and absent, respectively and also shows the level of positive and negative correlation between the presence and absence of the predictable variable and the deposit occurrence. The difference between the W^{+} and W^{-} weight is known as the weight contrast, C. The C reflects the overall spatial association between the predictable variable and the mineral deposit. The $S^{2}(W^{+})$ and $S^{2}(W^{-})$ are variances of W^{+} and W^{-} and $S(C)$ is the standard deviation of the contrast. The studentized value of C, calculated as the ratio of C to its standard deviation, $C/S(C)$, serves as a guide to the significance of the spatial association, and becomes useful in determining cutoff value to convert multiclass evidential data into binary predictor maps (Bonham-Carter et al., 1989; Carranza, 2004). In this study the cutoff value within which their spatial association with a given pattern is most statistically significant was chosen based on the maximum studentized value of contrast($C/s(C)$).

To calculate the weights of evidence for the class or type of each factor, the same type of input factor as the likelihood ratio is used. The cell number of deposit occurrence in each class of reclassified or categorical factors was also calculated using cross tabulation function in ArcGIS. The binary predictor patterns were also assigned weights (Table A1) and were combined according to Eq. (27). The mineral potential map was shown in Fig. 5b.

$$MPI_{WOE} = Woe_{1} + Woe_{2} + Woe_{3} + \ldots + Woe_{n} \tag{27}$$

where $Woe = W^{+}$ and W^{-} of the binary pattern for a range of each factor values or factor class.

The mineral deposit potential map was made using the MPI_{WOE} and was used for selecting training sites.

4.4 Logistic regression model

The logistic regression, which is one of the multivariate analysis models, is useful for predicting the presence or absence of a characteristic or outcome based on values of a set of spatial variables. The advantage of logistic regression is that, through the addition of an appropriate link a function to a usual linear regression model, the variables may be either continuous or discrete, or any combination of both types (Lee et al, 2007). In this study, the dependent variable is binary representing presence or absence of a mineral deposit and therefore a logistic link function is applicable (Atkinson & Massari 1998). For this study, the dependent variable must be input as either 0 or 1, so the method applies well to mineral potential analysis. Logistic regression coefficients can be used to estimate odds ratios for each of independent variables in the model. The relationship between the occurrence and its dependency on several variables can be expressed as:

$$p = 1/(1+e^{-z}) \tag{28}$$

where p is the probability of the event occurring and z is parameter. In this study, the p is the estimated probability of mineral deposit occurrence. The probability varies from 0 to 1 on an S-shaped curve and z is the linear combination. It follows that logistic regression involves fitting an equation of the following form to the data:

$$z = b_0 + b_1x_1 + b_2x_2 + \ldots + b_nx_n \tag{29}$$

where z is parameter, b_0 is the y-axis intercept, b_i (i = 0, 1, 2, …, n) are the slope coefficients of the logistic regression model and the x_i (i = 0, 1, 2, …, n) are the independent variables. The logistic regression coefficient values are listed in Table A1. The mineral potential map was made using Eqs. (28) and (29) and was used for selecting training sites.

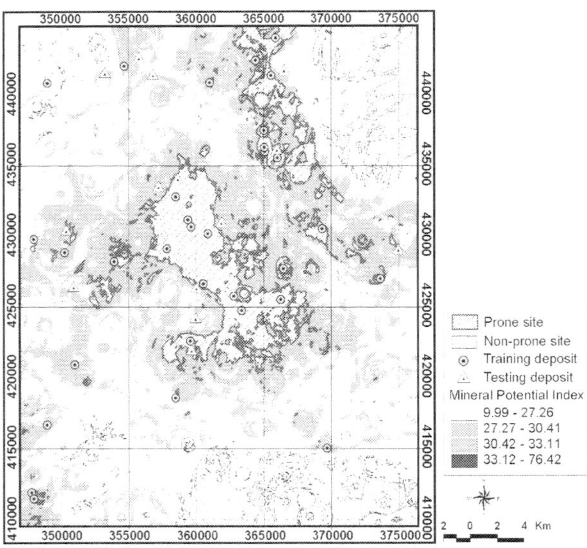

(a)

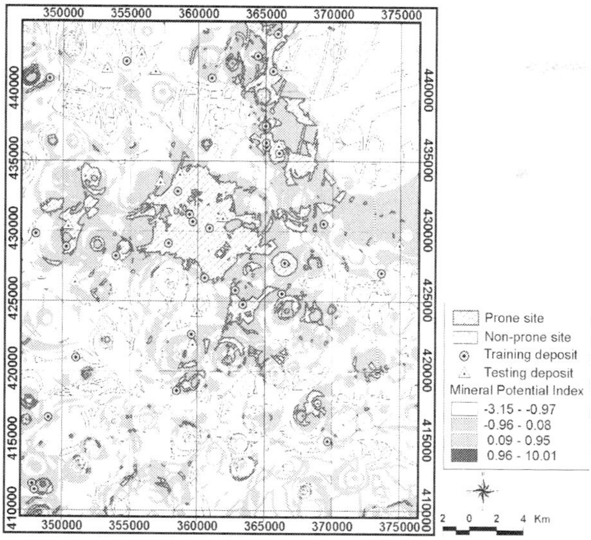

(b)

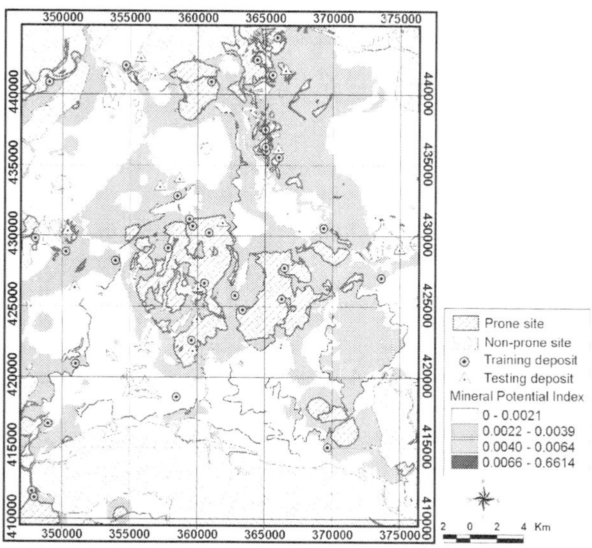

(c)

Fig. 5. Mineral potential maps based on likelihood ratio (a), weights of evidence (b) and logistic regression models (c): reclassification of low 60% (ivory colour), medium 20% (green colour), high 10% (sky blue colour), and very high 10% (blue colour) based on mineral potential index; training sites including "prone" (very high 10%) and "non-prone" (very low 10%) to deposit occurrence

5. Mineral deposit potential analysis using the Artificial Neural Network

The 26 factors were used as the input data. Nine cases of training sites of mineral deposit-prone locations and the locations that were not prone to mineral deposits were made (Table 2). It can be difficult to specifically estimate a criterion for selection of training sites using any predictor map because deposits are formed by various geological factors processes. Classification of location that is prone and non-prone to mineral deposits from expert's experience can also change and be subjective when more information is available. While cells including a known deposit are indubitably mineralized, cells that do not include a known deposit may or may not be mineralized. If small deposit and non-deposit training data are selected from the known deposit cell and the large corpus of non-deposit cell, respectively, the mineral potential map can be highly sensitive to particular choice of deposit and non-deposit training data (Skabar, 2005; Harris et al., 2003). Porwal et al., 2003 and Nykanen (2008) approached the problem of sensitivity of ANN to this non-deposit site training data by selecting training data in low mineral potential area modeled previously using a weights of evidence method. Skabar (2005) used for replicates of deposit locations. For each replicate set, they randomly selected and used 3/4 and 1/4 of the deposit locations for training and testing, respectively.

Models	Case	Prone area	Non-prone area
Likelihood ratio	Case 1	Deposit occurrence	10% areas with low mineral potential index (MPI_{LR})
	Case 2	5% areas with high mineral potential index (MPI_{LR})	10% areas with low mineral potential index (MPI_{LR})
	Case 3	10% areas with high mineral potential index (MPI_{LR})	10% areas with low mineral potential index (MPI_{LR})
Weights of evidence	Case 4	Deposit occurrence	10% areas with low mineral potential index (MPI_{WOE})
	Case 5	5% areas with high mineral potential index (MPI_{WOE})	10% areas with low mineral potential index (MPI_{WOE})
	Case 6	10% areas with high mineral potential index (MPI_{WOE})	10% areas with low mineral potential index (MPI_{LO})
Logistic regression	Case 7	Deposit occurrence	10% areas with low mineral potential index (MPI_{WOE})
	Case 8	5% areas with high mineral potential index (MPI_{LO})	10% areas with low mineral potential index (MPI_{LO})
	Case 9	10% areas with high mineral	10% areas with low mineral

Table 2. Nine different training cases determined from likelihood ratio, weights of evidence and logistic regression models

To select training sites based on scientific and objective criteria, we used values of MPI_{LR}, MPI_{WOE}, MPI_{LO} (Fig. 5) because they represent relationships of deposit- and non-deposit locations with various factors. Pixels from each of the two classes were randomly selected as training pixels, with 32 pixels denoting areas where training mineral deposits occurred.

Factors	Case 1								Case 2								Case 3							
	Run1	Run2	Run3	Run4	Run5	Mean	S.D.	N.V.	Run1	Run2	Run3	Run4	Run5	Mean	S.D.	N.V.	Run1	Run2	Run3	Run4	Run5	Mean	S.D.	N.V.
Al	0.032	0.042	0.037	0.043	0.046	0.040	0.006	1.136	0.037	0.037	0.038	0.041	0.046	0.040	0.004	1.149	0.037	0.038	0.039	0.041	0.038	0.039	0.002	1.148
As	0.034	0.034	0.036	0.036	0.038	0.036	0.002	1.011	0.039	0.034	0.033	0.037	0.038	0.036	0.003	1.045	0.037	0.042	0.034	0.038	0.039	0.038	0.003	1.119
Ba	0.042	0.042	0.037	0.040	0.032	0.038	0.004	1.085	0.038	0.037	0.041	0.037	0.031	0.037	0.004	1.067	0.043	0.037	0.039	0.037	0.040	0.039	0.002	1.165
Ca	0.036	0.035	0.034	0.037	0.038	0.036	0.001	1.019	0.043	0.042	0.036	0.042	0.040	0.040	0.003	1.170	0.037	0.033	0.042	0.042	0.047	0.040	0.005	1.187
Cd	0.034	0.038	0.040	0.040	0.039	0.038	0.002	1.080	0.040	0.036	0.027	0.032	0.038	0.035	0.005	1.000	0.041	0.042	0.044	0.033	0.039	0.040	0.004	1.184
Cl-	0.041	0.036	0.039	0.030	0.033	0.036	0.004	1.014	0.035	0.038	0.037	0.042	0.032	0.037	0.004	1.066	0.045	0.038	0.043	0.044	0.041	0.042	0.003	1.254
Co	0.041	0.034	0.038	0.038	0.039	0.038	0.003	1.068	0.039	0.037	0.035	0.037	0.040	0.038	0.002	1.084	0.040	0.034	0.035	0.036	0.035	0.036	0.002	1.068
Cr	0.040	0.038	0.035	0.035	0.033	0.036	0.003	1.027	0.042	0.044	0.047	0.038	0.035	0.041	0.005	1.190	0.032	0.038	0.033	0.037	0.045	0.037	0.005	1.099
Cu	0.037	0.039	0.041	0.035	0.047	0.040	0.004	1.130	0.038	0.045	0.038	0.035	0.048	0.041	0.005	1.173	0.045	0.033	0.043	0.036	0.044	0.040	0.005	1.195
F-	0.039	0.044	0.044	0.040	0.036	0.041	0.004	1.148	0.031	0.042	0.045	0.041	0.035	0.039	0.006	1.120	0.043	0.036	0.048	0.041	0.031	0.040	0.006	1.183
Fe	0.029	0.038	0.035	0.040	0.037	0.036	0.004	1.010	0.039	0.039	0.034	0.035	0.037	0.037	0.002	1.061	0.037	0.042	0.035	0.035	0.051	0.040	0.007	1.187
K	0.037	0.036	0.036	0.033	0.044	0.037	0.004	1.047	0.035	0.037	0.041	0.036	0.043	0.039	0.003	1.115	0.033	0.031	0.034	0.036	0.035	0.034	0.002	1.000
Li	0.037	0.037	0.036	0.039	0.038	0.037	0.001	1.059	0.042	0.037	0.041	0.048	0.036	0.041	0.005	1.178	0.041	0.038	0.034	0.047	0.038	0.039	0.005	1.170
Mg	0.039	0.042	0.044	0.042	0.042	0.042	0.002	1.191	0.034	0.041	0.035	0.044	0.039	0.038	0.004	1.110	0.036	0.040	0.043	0.044	0.038	0.040	0.003	1.193
Mn	0.033	0.035	0.033	0.043	0.034	0.036	0.004	1.008	0.038	0.041	0.036	0.037	0.035	0.038	0.002	1.086	0.046	0.036	0.035	0.037	0.036	0.038	0.005	1.131
Na	0.041	0.031	0.043	0.033	0.035	0.036	0.005	1.026	0.041	0.038	0.045	0.044	0.036	0.041	0.004	1.176	0.031	0.038	0.042	0.043	0.036	0.038	0.005	1.133
Ni	0.053	0.047	0.039	0.046	0.045	0.046	0.005	1.294	0.050	0.048	0.036	0.040	0.046	0.044	0.006	1.270	0.036	0.042	0.034	0.040	0.036	0.038	0.003	1.114
Pb	0.040	0.035	0.043	0.036	0.040	0.039	0.003	1.101	0.043	0.045	0.036	0.042	0.042	0.042	0.003	1.204	0.037	0.042	0.032	0.042	0.036	0.038	0.004	1.115
Si	0.039	0.039	0.033	0.044	0.040	0.039	0.004	1.101	0.039	0.035	0.038	0.031	0.040	0.037	0.004	1.058	0.039	0.037	0.036	0.031	0.041	0.037	0.004	1.089
Sr	0.033	0.042	0.038	0.037	0.039	0.038	0.003	1.068	0.035	0.035	0.042	0.037	0.040	0.038	0.003	1.101	0.040	0.046	0.038	0.037	0.035	0.039	0.004	1.163
V	0.040	0.040	0.043	0.034	0.044	0.040	0.004	1.137	0.044	0.034	0.049	0.035	0.043	0.041	0.006	1.184	0.035	0.036	0.031	0.036	0.034	0.035	0.002	1.025
W	0.041	0.031	0.045	0.037	0.034	0.038	0.005	1.066	0.031	0.031	0.044	0.035	0.034	0.035	0.005	1.005	0.039	0.046	0.044	0.035	0.040	0.041	0.004	1.207
Zn	0.046	0.039	0.046	0.039	0.034	0.041	0.005	1.154	0.037	0.032	0.041	0.036	0.035	0.036	0.003	1.038	0.039	0.034	0.041	0.036	0.040	0.038	0.003	1.125
Mag.	0.039	0.046	0.037	0.040	0.035	0.039	0.004	1.111	0.034	0.038	0.036	0.043	0.035	0.037	0.004	1.076	0.039	0.044	0.039	0.043	0.036	0.040	0.003	1.196
Fault	0.040	0.045	0.036	0.049	0.043	0.043	0.005	1.205	0.040	0.039	0.034	0.032	0.043	0.037	0.004	1.083	0.036	0.038	0.042	0.032	0.037	0.037	0.004	1.106
Geology	0.038	0.036	0.035	0.035	0.034	0.035	0.002	1.000	0.038	0.039	0.038	0.043	0.034	0.038	0.003	1.109	0.038	0.040	0.043	0.043	0.032	0.039	0.004	1.157

Factors	Case 4								Case 5								Case 6							
	Run1	Run2	Run3	Run4	Run5	Mean	S.D.	N.V.	Run1	Run2	Run3	Run4	Run5	Mean	S.D.	N.V.	Run1	Run2	Run3	Run4	Run5	Mean	S.D.	N.V.
Al	0.031	0.047	0.037	0.033	0.043	0.038	0.007	1.144	0.038	0.031	0.038	0.038	0.042	0.037	0.004	1.078	0.038	0.041	0.034	0.039	0.042	0.039	0.003	1.124
As	0.033	0.043	0.039	0.039	0.044	0.040	0.004	1.186	0.042	0.037	0.033	0.042	0.036	0.038	0.004	1.106	0.042	0.034	0.046	0.040	0.039	0.040	0.005	1.159
Ba	0.041	0.038	0.033	0.037	0.043	0.038	0.004	1.150	0.038	0.036	0.039	0.042	0.039	0.039	0.002	1.118	0.041	0.042	0.039	0.038	0.038	0.040	0.002	1.152
Ca	0.037	0.041	0.040	0.043	0.039	0.040	0.002	1.198	0.036	0.041	0.036	0.039	0.036	0.038	0.003	1.088	0.033	0.037	0.041	0.041	0.035	0.037	0.004	1.078
Cd	0.033	0.037	0.042	0.036	0.034	0.036	0.004	1.090	0.036	0.040	0.039	0.036	0.040	0.038	0.002	1.108	0.038	0.038	0.039	0.042	0.042	0.040	0.002	1.153
Cl-	0.041	0.034	0.041	0.040	0.035	0.038	0.003	1.144	0.033	0.042	0.039	0.042	0.035	0.038	0.004	1.104	0.042	0.035	0.039	0.040	0.043	0.040	0.003	1.148

Co	0.039	0.036	0.039	0.040	0.037	0.038	0.002	1.144	0.037	0.040	0.037	0.033	0.044	0.038	0.004	1.110	0.030	0.034	0.041	0.029	0.049	0.037	0.008	1.060
Cr	0.039	0.039	0.040	0.035	0.042	0.039	0.003	1.168	0.037	0.033	0.034	0.043	0.036	0.036	0.004	1.054	0.038	0.037	0.041	0.040	0.032	0.037	0.003	1.088
Cu	0.036	0.045	0.033	0.039	0.049	0.040	0.007	1.210	0.041	0.034	0.042	0.037	0.034	0.037	0.004	1.085	0.038	0.038	0.034	0.033	0.034	0.035	0.002	1.023
F-	0.038	0.040	0.035	0.043	0.040	0.039	0.003	1.174	0.036	0.039	0.042	0.037	0.035	0.038	0.003	1.096	0.043	0.045	0.036	0.041	0.042	0.041	0.004	1.197
Fe	0.029	0.034	0.033	0.033	0.038	0.033	0.003	1.000	0.044	0.039	0.035	0.035	0.043	0.039	0.004	1.144	0.036	0.038	0.049	0.038	0.036	0.039	0.005	1.141
K	0.037	0.031	0.041	0.043	0.036	0.038	0.005	1.126	0.040	0.034	0.036	0.035	0.037	0.036	0.002	1.053	0.041	0.035	0.042	0.036	0.037	0.038	0.003	1.106
Li	0.038	0.041	0.039	0.034	0.037	0.038	0.003	1.132	0.045	0.038	0.040	0.044	0.037	0.041	0.003	1.182	0.036	0.039	0.033	0.030	0.040	0.035	0.004	1.026
Mg	0.037	0.036	0.043	0.039	0.032	0.037	0.004	1.120	0.041	0.038	0.042	0.037	0.041	0.040	0.002	1.148	0.033	0.039	0.036	0.037	0.038	0.037	0.002	1.062
Mn	0.033	0.044	0.039	0.039	0.041	0.039	0.004	1.174	0.046	0.047	0.033	0.036	0.043	0.041	0.006	1.182	0.043	0.035	0.035	0.043	0.034	0.038	0.004	1.100
Na	0.041	0.037	0.048	0.046	0.041	0.043	0.004	1.275	0.036	0.034	0.042	0.038	0.042	0.038	0.004	1.109	0.045	0.031	0.043	0.040	0.044	0.041	0.005	1.177
Ni	0.053	0.033	0.039	0.042	0.040	0.041	0.007	1.240	0.044	0.035	0.041	0.050	0.040	0.042	0.006	1.212	0.040	0.049	0.037	0.042	0.037	0.041	0.005	1.185
Pb	0.041	0.040	0.038	0.034	0.032	0.037	0.004	1.108	0.042	0.039	0.042	0.031	0.037	0.038	0.004	1.104	0.037	0.035	0.033	0.036	0.032	0.034	0.002	1.000
Si	0.038	0.037	0.031	0.030	0.031	0.033	0.004	1.000	0.028	0.037	0.033	0.036	0.044	0.036	0.006	1.035	0.042	0.039	0.039	0.042	0.036	0.040	0.002	1.150
Sr	0.033	0.037	0.041	0.036	0.035	0.036	0.003	1.090	0.046	0.039	0.037	0.035	0.037	0.039	0.004	1.123	0.036	0.042	0.035	0.041	0.047	0.040	0.005	1.164
V	0.039	0.034	0.036	0.033	0.038	0.036	0.003	1.078	0.037	0.045	0.041	0.043	0.030	0.039	0.006	1.133	0.041	0.041	0.046	0.041	0.031	0.040	0.005	1.159
W	0.045	0.046	0.047	0.047	0.038	0.045	0.004	1.335	0.036	0.039	0.045	0.038	0.037	0.039	0.004	1.129	0.045	0.034	0.034	0.038	0.040	0.038	0.005	1.112
Zn	0.046	0.037	0.031	0.036	0.037	0.037	0.005	1.120	0.034	0.041	0.047	0.039	0.039	0.040	0.005	1.158	0.033	0.039	0.042	0.040	0.040	0.039	0.003	1.130
Mag	0.044	0.037	0.040	0.049	0.043	0.043	0.005	1.275	0.047	0.046	0.038	0.038	0.040	0.042	0.004	1.208	0.040	0.045	0.037	0.041	0.035	0.040	0.004	1.152
Fault	0.039	0.038	0.037	0.035	0.036	0.037	0.002	1.108	0.036	0.038	0.035	0.044	0.040	0.039	0.004	1.117	0.038	0.045	0.037	0.033	0.040	0.039	0.005	1.121
Geology	0.038	0.039	0.037	0.040	0.040	0.039	0.001	1.162	0.030	0.038	0.035	0.033	0.037	0.035	0.003	1.000	0.033	0.035	0.036	0.040	0.040	0.037	0.003	1.071

	Case 7								Case 8								Case 9							
Factors	Run1	Run2	Run3	Run4	Run5	Mean	S.D.	N.V.	Run1	Run2	Run3	Run4	Run5	Mean	S.D.	N.V.	Run1	Run2	Run3	Run4	Run5	Mean	S.D.	N.V.
Al	0.038	0.034	0.040	0.038	0.037	0.037	0.002	1.081	0.034	0.036	0.038	0.041	0.039	0.038	0.002	1.180	0.038	0.033	0.041	0.036	0.035	0.037	0.003	1.128
As	0.035	0.048	0.042	0.042	0.040	0.041	0.005	1.192	0.042	0.042	0.047	0.051	0.042	0.045	0.004	1.413	0.040	0.040	0.040	0.037	0.037	0.039	0.002	1.193
Ba	0.040	0.032	0.033	0.034	0.035	0.035	0.003	1.000	0.038	0.034	0.046	0.037	0.040	0.039	0.004	1.227	0.040	0.041	0.033	0.037	0.037	0.037	0.003	1.152
Ca	0.044	0.039	0.038	0.036	0.041	0.040	0.003	1.144	0.032	0.038	0.034	0.035	0.036	0.035	0.002	1.095	0.033	0.044	0.035	0.035	0.036	0.037	0.004	1.124
Cd	0.036	0.039	0.036	0.039	0.038	0.037	0.002	1.084	0.034	0.034	0.034	0.038	0.039	0.036	0.002	1.133	0.042	0.039	0.038	0.038	0.032	0.038	0.004	1.164
Cl-	0.041	0.038	0.043	0.042	0.036	0.040	0.003	1.150	0.041	0.039	0.038	0.037	0.041	0.039	0.002	1.232	0.041	0.043	0.038	0.044	0.041	0.041	0.002	1.276
Co	0.041	0.042	0.040	0.038	0.037	0.040	0.002	1.150	0.042	0.042	0.044	0.038	0.041	0.041	0.002	1.296	0.037	0.038	0.037	0.035	0.039	0.037	0.001	1.150
Cr	0.040	0.038	0.041	0.042	0.043	0.041	0.002	1.178	0.037	0.036	0.036	0.041	0.036	0.037	0.002	1.168	0.036	0.047	0.041	0.037	0.040	0.040	0.004	1.241
Cu	0.041	0.035	0.037	0.046	0.038	0.039	0.004	1.136	0.035	0.036	0.040	0.039	0.038	0.037	0.002	1.173	0.036	0.026	0.041	0.039	0.037	0.036	0.006	1.098
F-	0.040	0.040	0.040	0.034	0.030	0.037	0.005	1.059	0.042	0.045	0.037	0.041	0.045	0.042	0.003	1.309	0.045	0.031	0.043	0.043	0.042	0.041	0.006	1.262
Fe	0.039	0.036	0.039	0.032	0.040	0.037	0.003	1.073	0.037	0.034	0.036	0.036	0.041	0.037	0.002	1.159	0.039	0.036	0.035	0.034	0.042	0.037	0.003	1.151
K	0.038	0.039	0.032	0.039	0.036	0.037	0.003	1.064	0.038	0.039	0.037	0.036	0.037	0.037	0.001	1.173	0.036	0.041	0.035	0.036	0.038	0.037	0.002	1.142
Li	0.043	0.040	0.040	0.036	0.041	0.040	0.003	1.160	0.041	0.041	0.041	0.031	0.033	0.037	0.005	1.172	0.030	0.036	0.036	0.034	0.043	0.036	0.004	1.099
Mg	0.041	0.037	0.037	0.040	0.034	0.038	0.003	1.093	0.037	0.039	0.041	0.040	0.034	0.038	0.003	1.196	0.037	0.038	0.033	0.042	0.041	0.038	0.004	1.171

Mn	0.037	0.039	0.040	0.039	0.041	0.039	0.001	1.134	0.035	0.036	0.038	0.039	0.040	0.037	0.002	1.176	0.040	0.035	0.035	0.033	0.031	0.035	0.003	1.068
Na	0.042	0.041	0.041	0.040	0.041	0.041	0.001	1.189	0.044	0.043	0.040	0.042	0.037	0.041	0.003	1.298	0.036	0.041	0.043	0.039	0.033	0.038	0.004	1.173
Ni	0.030	0.038	0.038	0.039	0.047	0.038	0.006	1.110	0.044	0.035	0.040	0.038	0.039	0.039	0.003	1.228	0.042	0.036	0.041	0.037	0.038	0.039	0.002	1.198
Pb	0.041	0.034	0.034	0.041	0.044	0.039	0.004	1.120	0.041	0.041	0.041	0.036	0.043	0.041	0.003	1.274	0.042	0.036	0.043	0.042	0.051	0.043	0.005	1.317
Si	0.038	0.041	0.033	0.030	0.038	0.036	0.004	1.039	0.033	0.040	0.037	0.038	0.040	0.038	0.003	1.178	0.038	0.042	0.037	0.035	0.044	0.039	0.003	1.210
Sr	0.040	0.045	0.042	0.039	0.035	0.040	0.004	1.164	0.040	0.047	0.036	0.044	0.049	0.043	0.005	1.354	0.043	0.039	0.040	0.036	0.044	0.040	0.003	1.241
V	0.034	0.034	0.040	0.011	0.044	0.038	0.004	1.112	0.044	0.043	0.039	0.036	0.030	0.038	0.006	1.200	0.042	0.038	0.039	0.041	0.038	0.040	0.002	1.220
W	0.030	0.044	0.033	0.038	0.029	0.035	0.006	1.010	0.043	0.038	0.033	0.033	0.035	0.036	0.004	1.142	0.048	0.039	0.040	0.050	0.035	0.042	0.006	1.304
Zn	0.039	0.040	0.043	0.040	0.039	0.040	0.002	1.161	0.037	0.037	0.027	0.027	0.031	0.032	0.005	1.000	0.037	0.043	0.036	0.044	0.041	0.040	0.004	1.240
Mag.	0.038	0.044	0.035	0.039	0.033	0.038	0.004	1.092	0.034	0.039	0.034	0.038	0.042	0.037	0.003	1.173	0.028	0.033	0.036	0.036	0.030	0.032	0.004	1.000
Fault	0.039	0.033	0.043	0.045	0.045	0.041	0.005	1.182	0.035	0.032	0.044	0.044	0.036	0.038	0.005	1.202	0.034	0.043	0.046	0.039	0.038	0.040	0.005	1.227
Geology	0.036	0.033	0.041	0.032	0.039	0.036	0.004	1.040	0.041	0.034	0.043	0.046	0.037	0.040	0.005	1.258	0.041	0.044	0.039	0.042	0.037	0.040	0.003	1.239

Mag.: Magnetic anomaly
S.D.: Standard deviation
N.V.: Normalized value divided by the minimum average weight

Table 3. Weight of artificial neural network in study area

The back-propagation algorithm was then applied to calculate the weights between the input layer and the hidden layer, and between the hidden layer and the output layer, by modifying the number of hidden node and the learning rate. A three-layered feed-forward network was implemented using the MATLAB software package based on the framework provided by Hines (1997). Here, "feed-forward" denotes that the interconnections between the layers propagate forward to the next layer. The number of hidden layers and the number of nodes in a hidden layer required for a particular classification problem are not easy to deduce. In this study, a 26 x 52 x 2 structure was selected for the network, with input data normalized in the range 0.0-1.0. The nominal and interval class group data were converted to continuous values ranging between 0.0 and 1.0. Therefore, the continuous values were not ordinal data, but nominal data, and the numbers denote the classification of the input data. The learning rate was set to 0.01, and the initial weights were randomly selected to values between 0.1 and 0.3. The weights calculated from 5 test cases were compared to determine whether the variation in the final weights was dependent on the selection of the initial weights (Table 3).

The results show that the initial weights did not have an influence on the final weight under the conditions used. The back-propagation algorithm was used to minimize the error between the predicted output values and the calculated output values. The algorithm propagated the error backwards, and iteratively adjusted the weights. The number of epochs was set to 5,000, and the root mean square error (RMSE) value used for the stopping criterion was set to 0.01. Most of the training data sets met the 0.01 RMSE goal. However, if the RMSE value was not achieved, then the maximum number of iterations was terminated at 5,000 epochs. When the latter case occurred, then the maximum RMSE value was <0.2.

The final weights between layers acquired during training of the neural network and the contribution or importance of each of the 26 factors used to predict mineral deposit potential are shown in Table 3. The results were not the same, as the initial weights were assigned random values. Therefore, in this study, the calculations were repeated 5 times, to allow the results to achieve similar values. For easy interpretation, the average values were calculated, and these values were divided by the average of the weights of the some factor that had a minimum value. For Case 1, the geology value was the minimum value, 1.00, and the Ni was the maximum value, 1.294. For Case 2, the Cd value was the minimum value, 1.00, and the Ni was the maximum value, 1.270. For Case 3, the K value was the minimum value, 1.00, and the Cl- was the maximum value, 1.254. For Case 4, the Fe value was the minimum value, 1.00, and the W was the maximum value, 1.335. For Case 5, the geology value was the minimum value, 1.00, and the Ni was the maximum value, 1.212. For Case 6, the Pb value was the minimum value, 1.00, and the F- was the maximum value, 1.197. For Case 7, the Ba value was the minimum value, 1.00, and the As was the maximum value, 1.192. For Case 8, the Zn value was the minimum value, 1.00, and the As was the maximum value, 1.413. For Case 9, the magnetic value was the minimum value, 1.00, and the Pb was the maximum value, 1.317. The standard deviations of the results for all cases were in the range 0.001–0.008, and therefore, the random sampling did not have a large effect on the results. As the result, the As value was the minimum value, 1.00, and the Si was the maximum value, 1.1829. Finally, the weights were applied to the entire study area, and the mineral deposit potential maps were created for each training cases (Fig. 6).

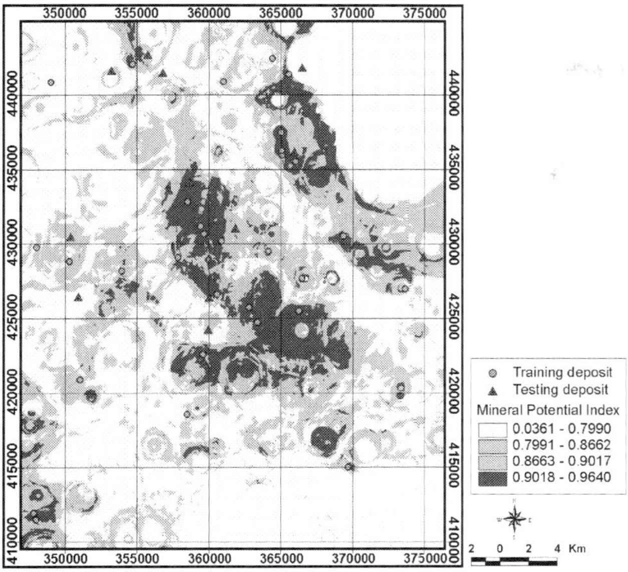

(a) Case 1

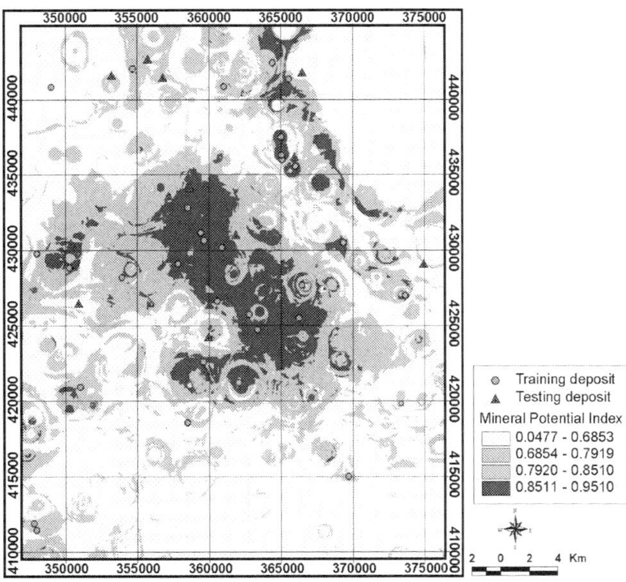

(b) Case 2

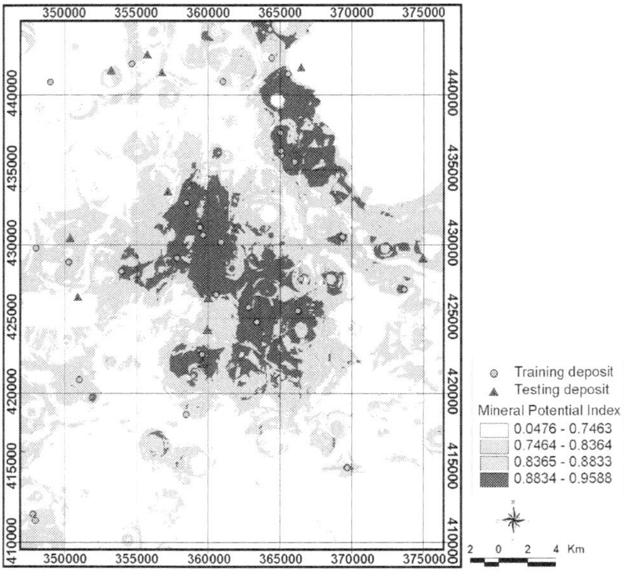

(c) Case 3

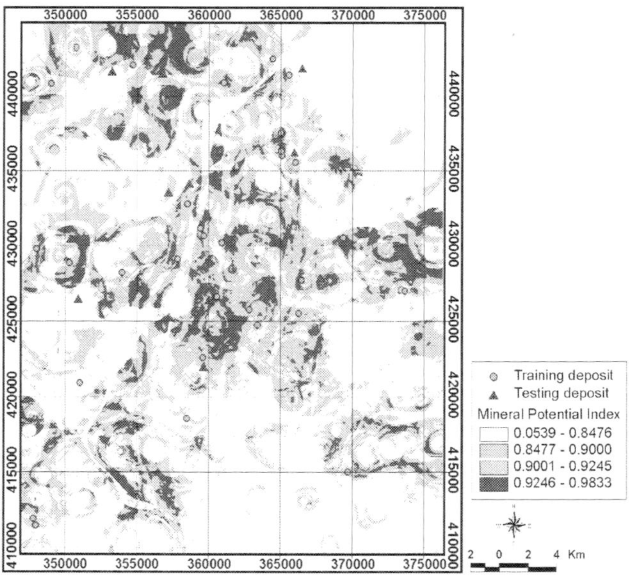

(d) Case 4

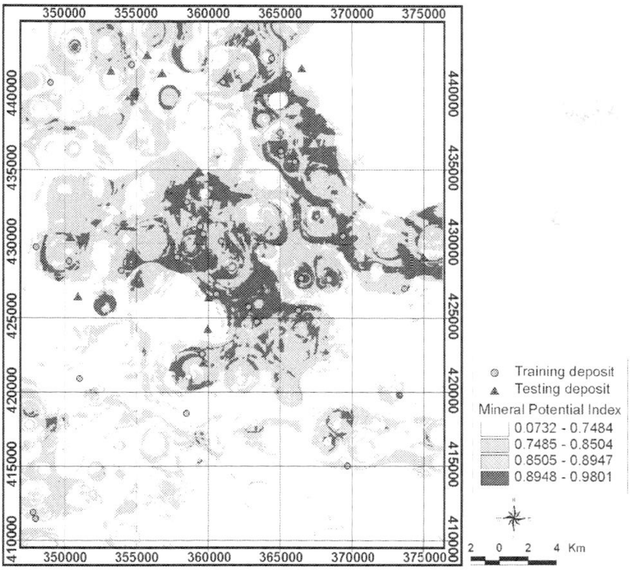

(e) Case 5

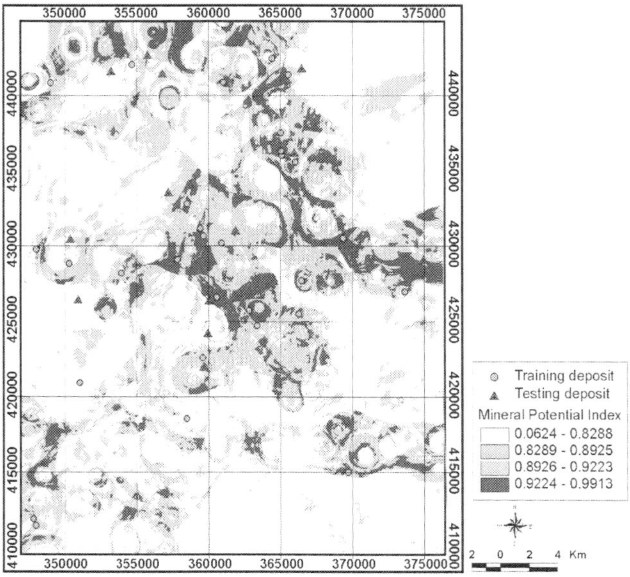

(f) Case 6

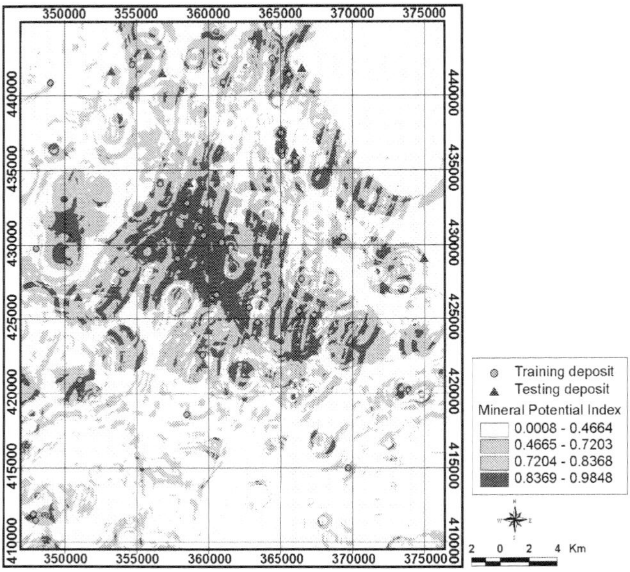

(g) Case 7

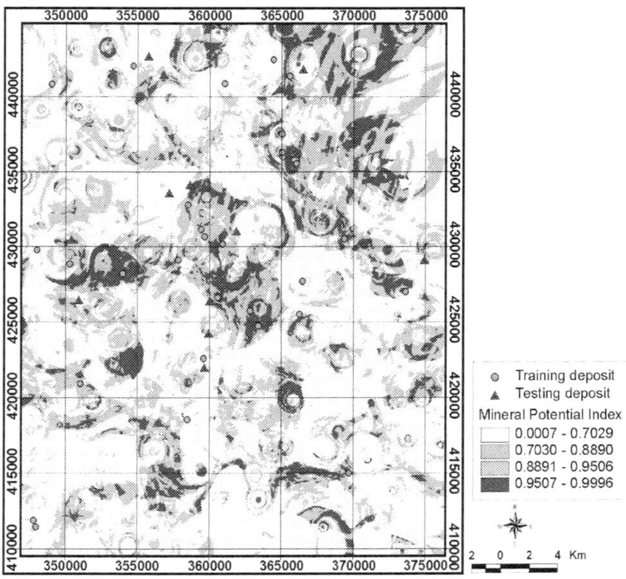

(h) Case 8

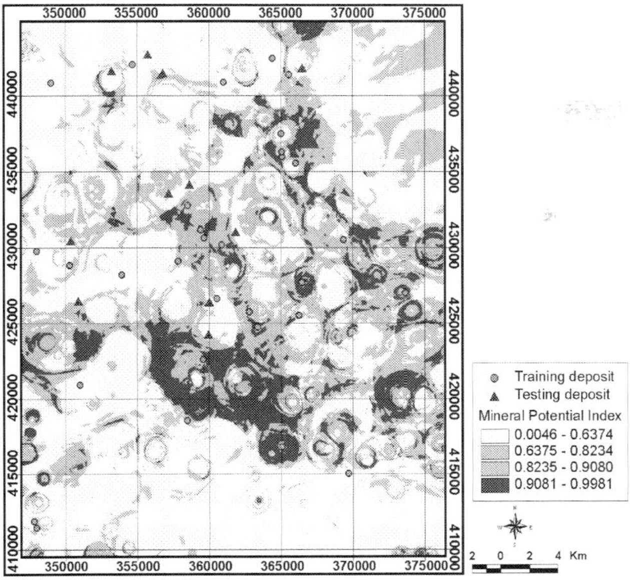

(i) Case 9

Fig. 6. Predictive gold-silver mineral potential map generated by reclassification of low 60% (ivory colour), medium 20% (green colour), high 10% (sky blue colour), and very high 10% (blue colour) based on mineral potential index; Case 1 (a), Case 2 (b), Case 3 (c), Case 4 (d) Case 5 (e), Case 6 (f), Case 7 (g), Case 8 (h) and Case 9 (i)

6. Validation

The mineral potential maps were validated by comparison with known mineral deposit locations (test set: 30% of total deposit) which were not used during the training of the artificial neural network model. For this, the success rate curves were calculated for quantitative prediction and area of under the curves was calculated. The rate shows how well the model and factors predict the mineral deposit occurrence. Thus, the area beneath the curve qualitatively assesses the prediction accuracy. To obtain the relative ranking for each prediction pattern, the calculated index values of all the pixels in the study area were sorted in descending order. The ordered pixel values were then divided into 100 classes with accumulated 1% intervals. The validation rate appears as a graph (Fig. 7).

For Case 1, Case 2, Case 3, Case 4, Case 5, Case 6, Case 7, Case 8 and Case 9, the 80-100% class (20%) in which the mineral potential index had a high rank could explain 56%, 50%, 56%, 56%, 56%, 50%, 44%, 25% and 44% of all the mineral deposit occurrences, respectively. The graphs shown are the best prediction accuracy among the five running.

To compare the result quantitatively, the areas under the curve were re-calculated as if the total area were one, which indicates perfect prediction accuracy. The area beneath a curve can therefore be used to assess the prediction accuracy qualitatively. For Case 1, Case 2, Case 3, Case 4, Case 5, Case 6, Case 7, Case 8 and Case 9, the area ratio was 0.7406, 0.7459,

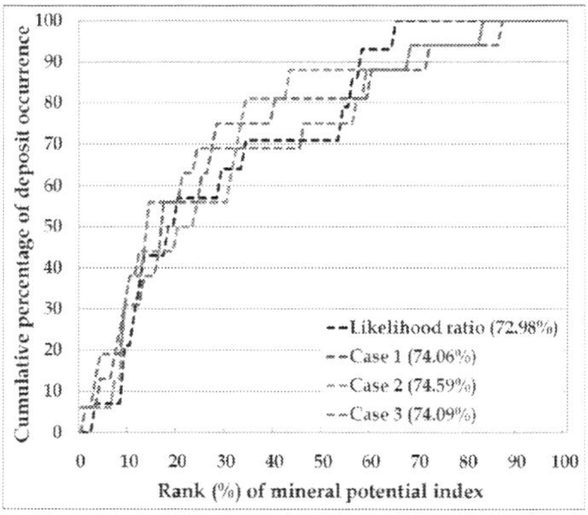

(a)

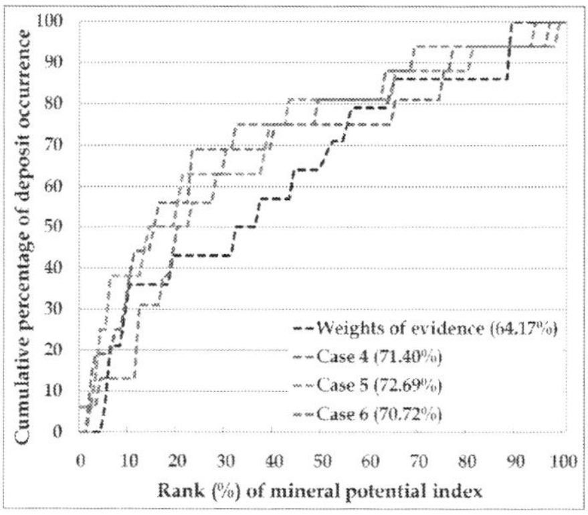

(b)

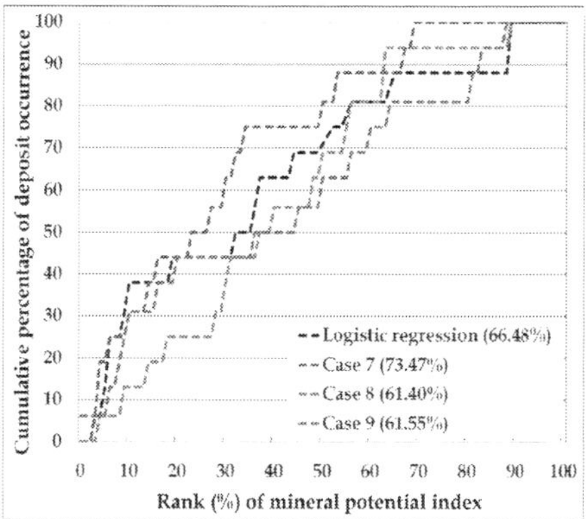

(c)

Fig. 7. Illustration of cumulative frequency diagram showing rank (%) of mineral potential index (x-axis) occurring in cumulative percent of mineral deposit occurrence (y-axis)

0.7409, 0.7140, 0.7269, 0.7072, 0.7347, 0.6140 and 0.6155 meaning a prediction accuracy of 74.06%, 74.59%, 74.09%, 71.40%, 72.69%, 70.72%, 73.47%, 61.40% and 61.55%.

7. Conclusion

Training sites were extracted from mineral potential maps based on likelihood ratio, weights of evidence and logistic regression methods, which showed 72.98%, 64.71% and 66.48% prediction accuracy validated by the test set. In the study, the mineral potential map of gold-silver were made using the artificial neural network and nine cases of training sites, each of which consist of 32 locations randomly selected among known mineral occurrences in 5% and 10% of areas with the high mineral potential index values and 32 non-deposit locations randomly selected in 10% of areas with low mineral potential index. The validation result of Case 1, Case 2, Case 3, Case 4, Case 5, Case 6, Case 7, Case 8 and Case 9 showed, respectively, the 74.06%, 74.59%, 74.09%, 71.40%, 72.69%, 70.72%, 73.47%, 61.40% and 61.55% prediction accuracy using 14 test mineral deposits not used directly for the analysis. All training cases exhibited accuracies of over 70% but Cases 8 and 9, slightly higher or lower than likelihood ratio and very higher than weights of evidence and logistic regression models. Overall, training cases based on likelihood ratio model, gave higher accuracies than training cases based on weights of evidence and logistic regression models. This result shows that some of the testing deposits plotted in non-prone area to deposit occurrence (Figs. 5b and 5c), and the weights of evidence and logistic regression represented the low accuracy among the methods. However, the analysis result of some training sets shows more sensitive to training data by logistic regression than weighs of evidence.

Some researches approached a degree of sensitivity by selecting non-deposit site training data in low-probability area of previously generated potential maps made using weights of evidence or/and logistic regression (Porwal et al., 2003; Behnia, 2007; Nykanen & Salmirinne, 2007; Nykanen, 2008). Using larger training data reduces the variance of initial weight in the ANN and improves accuracy of the resulting potential map (Skabar, 2005; Nykanen, 2008). In the study, 32 deposit and non-deposit cells were represented equally in the training set, although, the network to training data was repeated five times to reduce sensitive to initial weights of factors related to gold-silver mineral.

The resulting map by ANN can be possible to show better prediction accuracy if training dataset are selected from MPM with more high accuracy than MPM by likelihood ratio in the study. A Geographic Information System (GIS), in concert with artificial neural network software was used to compile, manipulate, analyze and visualize a large geological, geochemical and geophysical dataset collected from the Taebaeksan mineralized district of Eastern Korea. The GIS is not only capable of routine display, but also offer great potential by providing a range of tools to query, manipulate, visualize and analyze geological, geochemical and geophysical data in mineral exploration applications. The artificial neural network that was applied to the logistic sigmoid transfer function proved useful for predicting and evaluating the mineral potential map produced in this study. The models are useful for providing a quantitative measure of the weights among the factors for gold-silver prospects. Furthermore, the maps generated by the models, not only predict known areas of gold-silver occurrence, but also identify areas of potential mineralization where no known deposit occurs. Several areas within the study area are identified as having high gold-silver potential. Many of these areas coincide with areas of known deposits.

8. Appendixes

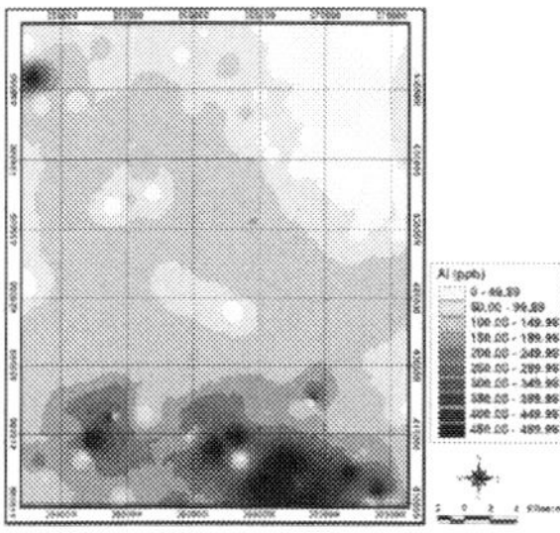
(a) Al

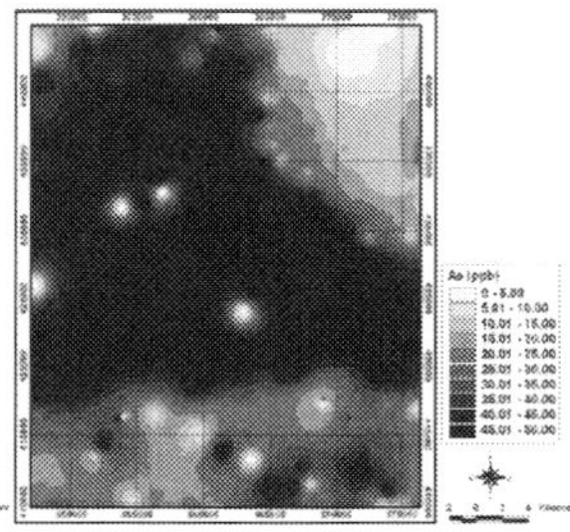
(b) As

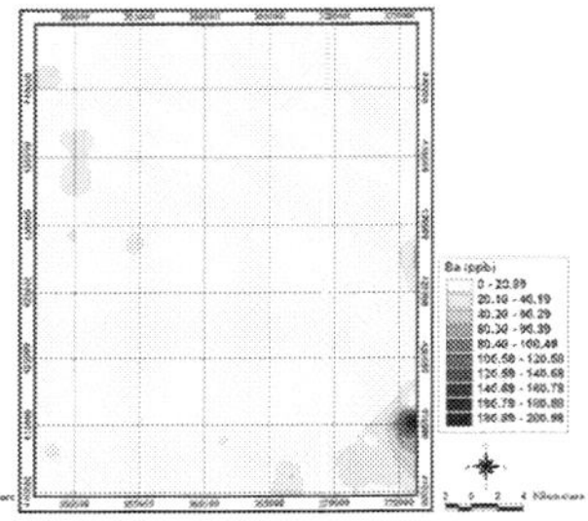
(c) Ba

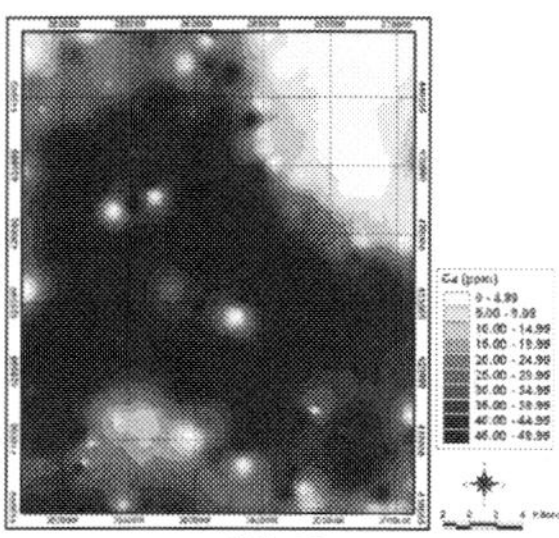
(d) Ca

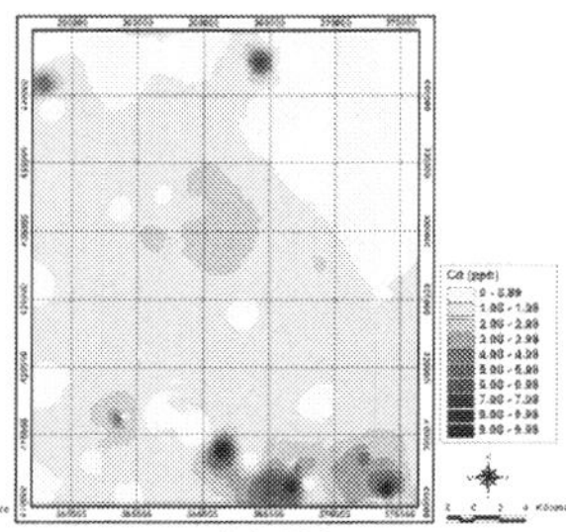
(e) Cd

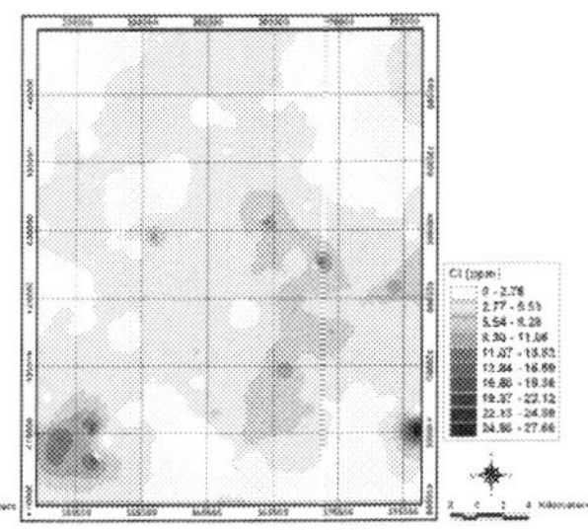
(f) Cl-

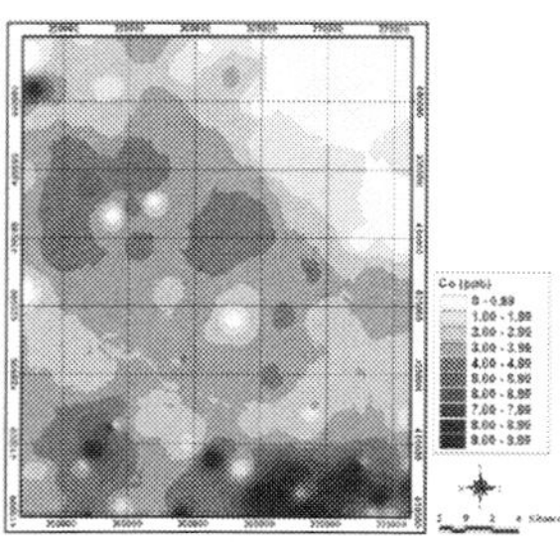
(g) Co

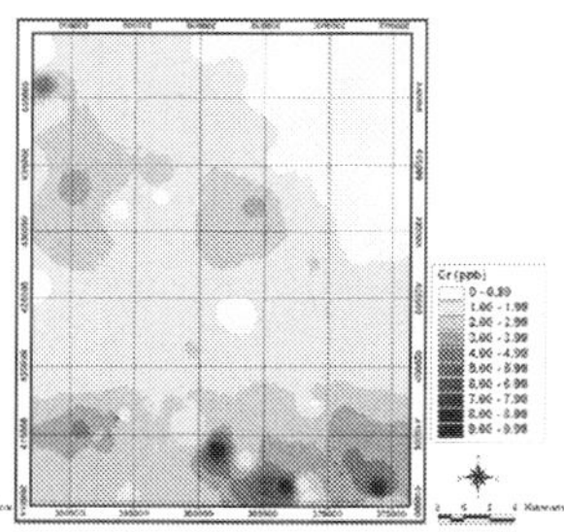
(h) Cr

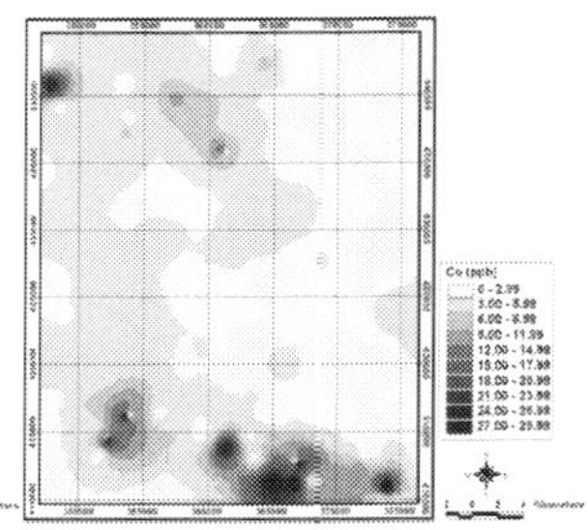
(i) Cu

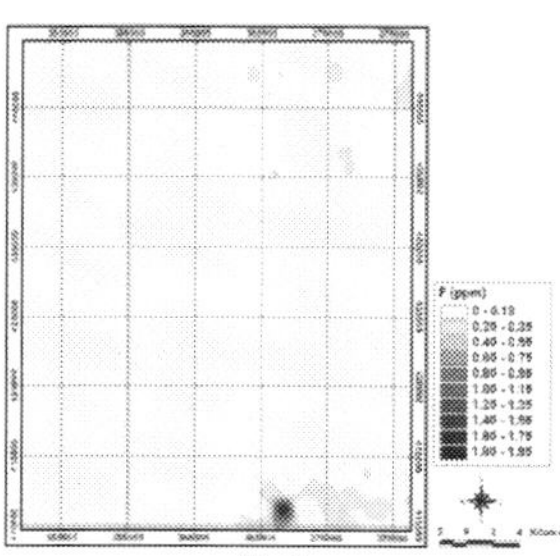
(j) F-

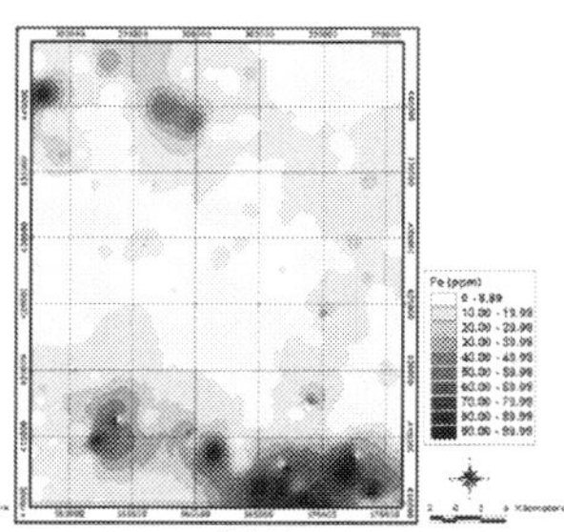
(k) Fe

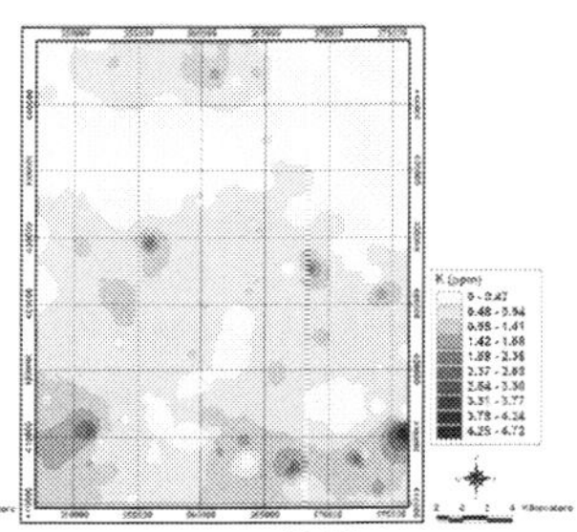
(l) K

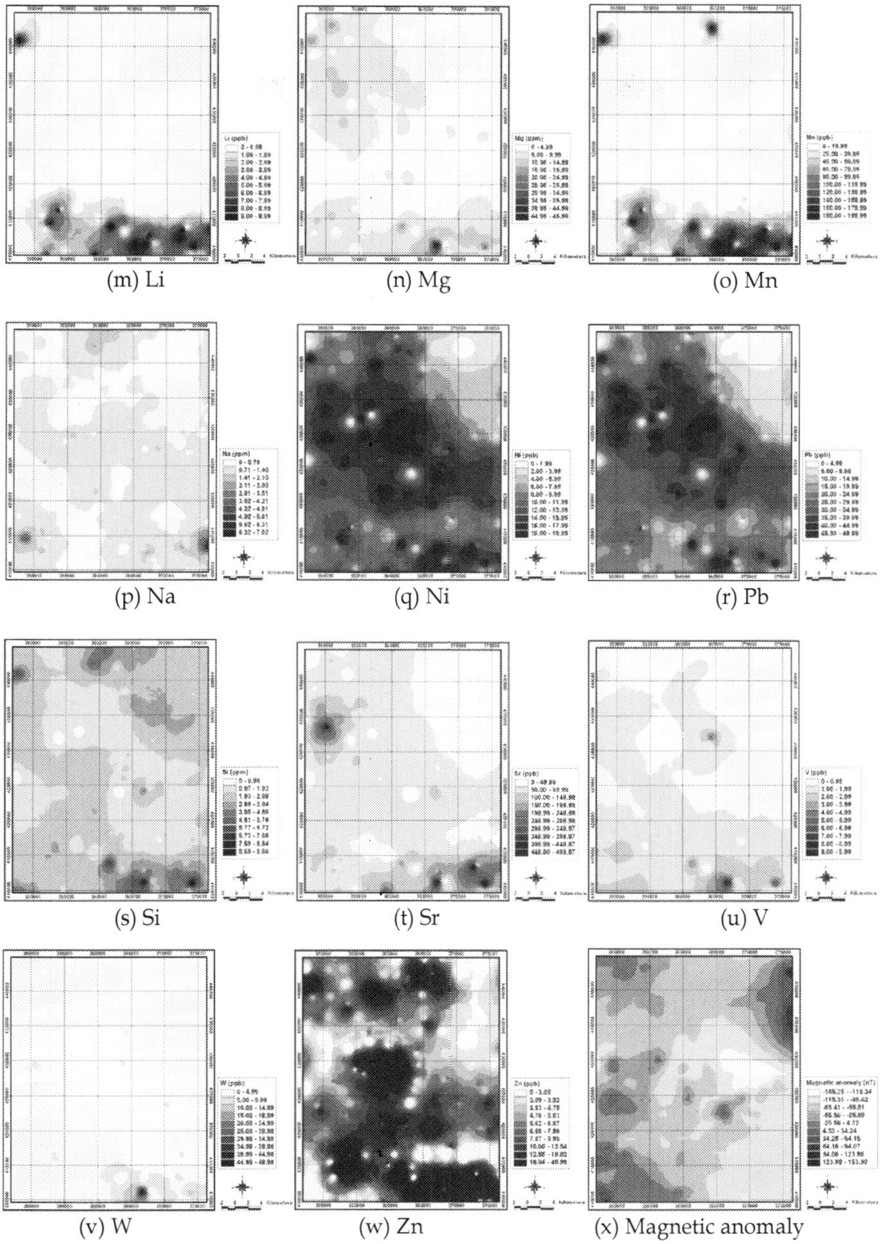

Fig. A1. Geochemical (Lee et al., 1998) and magnetic anomaly (Koo et al., 2001) maps

Factor	Likelihood ratio						Weights of evidence				Logistic regression
	Class [a]	No. of pixels	%Area	Mineral occ.	%occ.	LS [b]	W+	W-	C	C/S(c)	Coefficient [c]
Al (ppb)	26.00-44.15	116666	10.00	3	9.38	0.94	-0.06	0.01	-0.07	-0.12	0.00806
	44.16-84.54	116651	10.00	3	9.38	0.94	-0.06	0.01	-0.07	-0.12	
	84.55-103.39	116737	10.01	4	12.50	1.25	0.22	-0.03	0.25	0.47	
	103.40-112.87	116716	10.01	2	6.25	0.62	-0.47	0.04	-0.51	-0.70	
	112.88-119.29	116695	10.00	7	21.88	2.19	0.78	-0.14	0.92	2.16	
	119.30-124.97	116601	10.00	7	21.88	2.19	0.78	-0.14	0.92	2.16	
	124.98-133.04	116613	10.00	1	3.13	0.31	-1.16	0.07	-1.24	-1.22	
	133.05-164.69	116594	10.00	3	9.38	0.94	-0.06	0.01	-0.07	-0.12	
	164.70-231.11	116586	10.00	2	6.25	0.63	-0.47	0.04	-0.51	-0.70	
	231.12-499.99	116579	9.99	0	0.00	0.00	NaN	0.11	NaN	NaN	
As (ppm)	1.01-14.58	116689	10.00	0	0.00	0.00	NaN	0.11	NaN	NaN	0.03186
	14.59-21.78	116779	10.01	8	25.00	2.50	0.92	-0.18	1.10	2.69	
	21.79-27.56	116734	10.01	0	0.00	0.00	NaN	0.11	NaN	NaN	
	27.57-35.09	116702	10.00	3	9.38	0.94	-0.07	0.01	-0.07	-0.12	
	35.10-43.43	116782	10.01	1	3.13	0.31	-1.16	0.07	-1.24	-1.22	
	43.44-47.59	116901	10.02	4	12.50	1.25	0.22	-0.03	0.25	0.47	
	47.60-49.47	116516	9.99	0	0.00	0.00	NaN	0.11	NaN	NaN	
	49.48-49.99	65606	5.62	3	9.38	1.67	0.51	-0.04	0.55	0.91	
	50.00	283729	24.32	13	40.63	1.67	0.51	-0.24	0.76	2.10	
Ba (ppb)	2.00-3.99	117477	10.07	0	0.00	0.00	NaN	0.11	NaN	NaN	0.04983
	4.00-5.96	116734	10.01	8	25.00	2.50	0.92	-0.18	1.10	0.41	
	5.97-7.04	117258	10.05	2	6.25	0.62	-0.48	0.04	-0.52	0.73	
	7.05-7.86	116532	9.99	3	9.38	0.94	-0.06	0.01	-0.07	0.61	
	7.87-8.55	116787	10.01	5	15.63	1.56	0.45	-0.06	0.51	0.49	
	8.56-9.61	116822	10.02	4	12.50	1.25	0.22	-0.03	0.25	0.53	
	9.62 -10.87	116583	9.99	3	9.38	0.94	-0.06	0.01	-0.07	0.61	
	10.88-13.28	116120	9.96	1	3.13	0.31	-1.16	0.07	-1.23	1.02	
	13.29-17.38	116242	9.97	3	9.38	0.94	-0.06	0.01	-0.07	0.61	
	17.39-200.97	115883	9.93	3	9.38	0.94	-0.06	0.01	-0.06	0.61	
Ca (ppm)	1.53-6.24	116712	10.01	2	6.25	0.62	-0.47	0.04	-0.51	0.73	-0.00001
	6.25-18.99	116637	10.00	5	15.63	1.56	0.45	-0.06	0.51	0.49	
	19.00-28.24	116714	10.01	1	3.13	0.31	-1.16	0.07	-1.24	1.02	
	28.25-35.41	116742	10.01	3	9.38	0.94	-0.07	0.01	-0.07	0.61	
	35.42-40.44	116662	10.00	2	6.25	0.62	-0.47	0.04	-0.51	0.73	
	40.45-43.42	116679	10.00	2	6.25	0.62	-0.47	0.04	-0.51	0.73	
	43.43-46.01	116621	10.00	3	9.38	0.94	-0.06	0.01	-0.07	0.61	
	46.02-48.04	117223	10.05	4	12.50	1.24	0.22	-0.03	0.25	0.53	
	48.05-49.16	116647	10.00	5	15.63	1.56	0.45	-0.06	0.51	0.49	
	49.17-50.00	115801	9.93	5	15.63	1.57	0.45	-0.07	0.52	0.49	
Cd (ppm)	1.0000-1.1008	116740	10.01	3	9.38	0.94	-0.07	0.01	-0.07	0.61	-0.12562
	1.1009-1.2239	116647	10.00	3	9.38	0.94	-0.06	0.01	-0.07	0.61	
	1.2240-1.3473	116690	10.00	2	6.25	0.62	-0.47	0.04	-0.51	0.73	

	1.3474-1.4928	116699	10.00	3	9.38	0.94	-0.07	0.01	-0.07	0.61	
	1.4929-1.6538	116626	10.00	5	15.63	1.56	0.45	-0.06	0.51	0.49	
	1.6539-1.8480	116640	10.00	4	12.50	1.25	0.22	-0.03	0.25	0.53	
	1.8481-1.9829	116621	10.00	2	6.25	0.63	-0.47	0.04	-0.51	0.73	
	1.9830-2.2506	116610	10.00	5	15.63	1.56	0.45	-0.06	0.51	0.49	
	2.2507-3.2164	116585	9.99	1	3.13	0.31	-1.16	0.07	-1.24	1.02	
	3.2165-9.9992	116580	9.99	4	12.50	1.25	0.22	-0.03	0.25	0.53	
	1.0106-2.2074	116644	10.00	1	3.13	0.31	-1.16	0.07	-1.24	1.02	
	2.2075-2.4546	116681	10.00	0	0.00	0.00	NaN	0.11	NaN	NaN	
	2.4547-2.7386	116654	10.00	3	9.38	0.94	-0.06	0.01	-0.07	0.61	
	2.7387-2.9874	116642	10.00	4	12.50	1.25	0.22	-0.03	0.25	0.53	
Cl^-	2.9875-3.2353	116647	10.00	1	3.13	0.31	-1.16	0.07	-1.24	1.02	0.00005
(ppm)	3.2354-3.4804	116642	10.00	7	21.88	2.19	0.78	-0.14	0.92	0.43	
	3.4805-3.8803	116637	10.00	5	15.63	1.56	0.45	-0.06	0.51	0.49	
	3.8804-4.7479	116635	10.00	5	15.63	1.56	0.45	-0.06	0.51	0.49	
	4.7480-5.9843	116628	10.00	2	6.25	0.63	-0.47	0.04	-0.51	0.73	
	5.9844-27.6669	116628	10.00	4	12.50	1.25	0.22	-0.03	0.25	0.53	
	1.0000-1.5665	116648	10.00	4	12.50	1.25	0.22	-0.03	0.25	0.53	
	1.5666-2.5807	116657	10.00	1	3.13	0.31	-1.16	0.07	-1.24	1.02	
	2.5808-1.9789	116722	10.01	6	18.75	1.87	0.63	-0.10	0.73	0.45	
	1.9790-3.1012	116636	10.00	1	3.13	0.31	-1.16	0.07	-1.24	1.02	
Co	3.1013-3.3506	116651	10.00	3	9.38	0.94	-0.06	0.01	-0.07	0.61	-0.51670
(ppb)	3.3507-3.6660	116656	10.00	2	6.25	0.62	-0.47	0.04	-0.51	0.73	
	3.6661-3.9952	116621	10.00	5	15.63	1.56	0.45	-0.06	0.51	0.49	
	3.9953-4.4250	116620	10.00	7	21.88	2.19	0.78	-0.14	0.92	0.43	
	4.4251-5.0758	116620	10.00	2	6.25	0.63	-0.47	0.04	-0.51	0.73	
	5.0759-9.9999	116607	10.00	1	3.13	0.31	-1.16	0.07	-1.24	1.02	
	1.0000-1.1958	116649	10.00	6	18.75	1.87	0.63	-0.10	0.73	0.45	
	1.1959-1.3244	116645	10.00	0	0.00	0.00	NaN	0.11	NaN	NaN	
	1.3245-1.4319	116772	10.01	2	6.25	0.62	-0.47	0.04	-0.51	0.73	
	1.4320-1.5656	116663	10.00	6	18.75	1.87	0.63	-0.10	0.73	0.45	
Cr	1.5657-1.8305	116650	10.00	4	12.50	1.25	0.22	-0.03	0.25	0.53	-0.01601
(ppb)	1.8306-2.0343	116653	10.00	3	9.38	0.94	-0.06	0.01	-0.07	0.61	
	2.0344-2.3185	116625	10.00	4	12.50	1.25	0.22	-0.03	0.25	0.53	
	2.3186-2.7629	116602	10.00	1	3.13	0.31	-1.16	0.07	-1.24	1.02	
	2.7630-3.2865	116601	10.00	6	18.75	1.88	0.63	-0.10	0.73	0.45	
	3.2866-9.9987	116578	9.99	0	0.00	0.00	NaN	0.11	NaN	NaN	
	1.000-2.034	116889	10.02	1	3.13	0.31	-1.17	0.07	-1.24	1.02	
	2.035-2.450	116787	10.01	4	12.50	1.25	0.22	-0.03	0.25	0.53	
	2.451-2.744	116603	10.00	5	15.63	1.56	0.45	-0.06	0.51	0.49	
	2.745-2.994	117174	10.05	6	18.75	1.87	0.62	-0.10	0.73	0.45	
Cu	2.995-3.262	116784	10.01	6	18.75	1.87	0.63	-0.10	0.73	0.45	-0.50809
(ppb)	3.263-3.669	116566	9.99	2	6.25	0.63	-0.47	0.04	-0.51	0.73	
	3.670-3.977	116422	9.98	4	12.50	1.25	0.23	-0.03	0.25	0.53	
	3.978-4.710	116412	9.98	2	6.25	0.63	-0.47	0.04	-0.51	0.73	
	4.711-7.695	116407	9.98	1	3.13	0.31	-1.16	0.07	-1.23	1.02	
	7.696-2.9999	116394	9.98	1	3.13	0.31	-1.16	0.07	-1.23	1.02	

F^- (ppm)	0.03-0.14	117101	10.04	6	18.75	1.87	0.62	-0.10	0.73	0.45	-0.01003
	0.15-0.15	116775	10.01	2	6.25	0.62	-0.47	0.04	-0.51	0.73	
	0.16-0.16	117073	10.04	3	9.38	0.93	-0.07	0.01	-0.08	0.61	
	0.17-0.17	117348	10.06	3	9.38	0.93	-0.07	0.01	-0.08	0.61	
	0.18-0.18	117148	10.04	2	6.25	0.62	-0.47	0.04	-0.52	0.73	
	0.19-0.20	116558	9.99	5	15.63	1.56	0.45	-0.06	0.51	0.49	
	0.21-0.22	116117	9.95	4	12.50	1.26	0.23	-0.03	0.26	0.53	
	0.23-0.24	116151	9.96	3	9.38	0.94	-0.06	0.01	-0.07	0.61	
	0.25-0.28	116321	9.97	3	9.38	0.94	-0.06	0.01	-0.07	0.61	
	0.29-1.99	115846	9.93	1	3.13	0.31	-1.16	0.07	-1.23	1.02	
Fe (ppm)	2.00-6.77	117031	10.03	2	6.25	0.62	-0.47	0.04	-0.51	0.73	0.00002
	6.78-7.86	116771	10.01	5	15.63	1.56	0.45	-0.06	0.51	0.49	
	7.87-8.88	116611	10.00	5	15.63	1.56	0.45	-0.06	0.51	0.49	
	8.89-9.91	117384	10.06	4	12.50	1.24	0.22	-0.03	0.24	0.53	
	9.92-11.12	116592	10.00	6	18.75	1.88	0.63	-0.10	0.73	0.45	
	11.13-12.99	116876	10.02	1	3.13	0.31	-1.17	0.07	-1.24	1.02	
	13.00-15.76	116535	9.99	2	6.25	0.63	-0.47	0.04	-0.51	0.73	
	15.77-21.24	116233	9.96	3	9.38	0.94	-0.06	0.01	-0.07	0.61	
	21.25-35.77	116234	9.96	3	9.38	0.94	-0.06	0.01	-0.07	0.61	
	35.78-99.99	116171	9.96	1	3.13	0.31	-1.16	0.07	-1.23	1.02	
K (ppm)	0.1201-0.3403	116712	10.01	2	6.25	0.62	-0.47	0.04	-0.51	0.73	-0.00053
	0.3404-0.4005	116798	10.01	1	3.13	0.31	-1.16	0.07	-1.24	1.02	
	0.4006-0.4634	116644	10.00	5	15.63	1.56	0.45	-0.06	0.51	0.49	
	0.4635-0.5461	116707	10.01	2	6.25	0.62	-0.47	0.04	-0.51	0.73	
	0.5462-0.6365	116600	10.00	5	15.63	1.56	0.45	-0.06	0.51	0.49	
	0.6366-0.7389	116663	10.00	4	12.50	1.25	0.22	-0.03	0.25	0.53	
	0.7390-0.8133	116604	10.00	5	15.63	1.56	0.45	-0.06	0.51	0.49	
	0.8134-0.9078	116604	10.00	3	9.38	0.94	-0.06	0.01	-0.07	0.61	
	0.9079-1.0807	116575	9.99	2	6.25	0.63	-0.47	0.04	-0.51	0.73	
	10.808-4.7295	116531	9.99	3	9.38	0.94	-0.06	0.01	-0.07	0.61	
Li (ppb)	1.0000-1.0041	116661	10.00	6	18.75	1.87	0.63	-0.10	0.73	0.45	-0.22232
	1.0042-1.1144	116662	10.00	10	31.25	3.12	1.14	-0.27	1.41	0.38	
	1.1145-1.2670	116704	10.01	4	12.50	1.25	0.22	-0.03	0.25	0.53	
	1.2671-1.4984	116661	10.00	0	0.00	0.00	NaN	0.11	NaN	NaN	
	1.4985-1.9352	116631	10.00	2	6.25	0.63	-0.47	0.04	-0.51	0.73	
	1.9353-2.6544	116633	10.00	3	9.38	0.94	-0.06	0.01	-0.07	0.61	
	2.6545-3.5996	116624	10.00	3	9.38	0.94	-0.06	0.01	-0.07	0.61	
	3.5997-4.7935	116622	10.00	2	6.25	0.63	-0.47	0.04	-0.51	0.73	
	4.7936-6.6524	116623	10.00	1	3.13	0.31	-1.16	0.07	-1.24	1.02	
	6.6525-9.9999	116617	10.00	1	3.13	0.31	-1.16	0.07	-1.24	1.02	
Mg (ppm)	0.36-1.12	116873	10.02	0	0.00	0.00	NaN	0.11	NaN	NaN	-0.00001
	1.13-2.50	117756	10.10	8	25.00	2.48	0.91	-0.18	1.09	0.41	
	2.51-3.04	118493	10.16	4	12.50	1.23	0.21	-0.03	0.23	0.53	
	3.05-3.64	117481	10.07	3	9.38	0.93	-0.07	0.01	-0.08	0.61	
	3.65-4.41	116189	9.96	1	3.13	0.31	-1.16	0.07	-1.23	1.02	
	4.42-5.26	116652	10.00	5	15.63	1.56	0.45	-0.06	0.51	0.49	
	5.27-6.18	116279	9.97	4	12.50	1.25	0.23	-0.03	0.25	0.53	

	6.19-7.30	115792	9.93	5	15.63	1.57	0.45	-0.07	0.52	0.49	
	7.31-9.32	115912	9.94	1	3.13	0.31	-1.16	0.07	-1.23	1.02	
	9.33-49.99	115011	9.86	1	3.13	0.32	-1.15	0.07	-1.22	1.02	
	1.00-1.26	118658	10.17	4	12.50	1.23	0.21	-0.03	0.23	0.53	
	1.27-1.60	117500	10.07	2	6.25	0.62	-0.48	0.04	-0.52	0.73	
	1.61-1.90	117854	10.10	7	21.88	2.17	0.77	-0.14	0.91	0.43	
	1.91-2.38	118036	10.12	4	12.50	1.24	0.21	-0.03	0.24	0.53	
Mn	2.39-3.54	115883	9.93	2	6.25	0.63	-0.46	0.04	-0.50	0.73	
(ppb)	3.55-6.19	115970	9.94	5	15.63	1.57	0.45	-0.07	0.52	0.49	0.02688
	6.20-11.26	115651	9.91	1	3.13	0.32	-1.15	0.07	-1.23	1.02	
	11.27-25.24	115647	9.91	2	6.25	0.63	-0.46	0.04	-0.50	0.73	
	25.25-67.60	115630	9.91	4	12.50	1.26	0.23	-0.03	0.26	0.53	
	67.61-199.99	115609	9.91	1	3.13	0.32	-1.15	0.07	-1.23	1.02	
	0.2200-0.5790	116685	10.00	0	0.00	0.00	NaN	0.11	NaN	NaN	
	0.5791-0.6504	116721	10.01	1	3.13	0.31	-1.16	0.07	-1.24	1.02	
	0.6505-0.6959	116839	10.02	3	9.38	0.94	-0.07	0.01	-0.07	0.61	
	0.6960-0.7287	116664	10.00	3	9.38	0.94	-0.06	0.01	-0.07	0.61	
Na	0.7288-0.7844	116629	10.00	8	25.00	2.50	0.92	-0.18	1.10	0.41	
(ppm)	0.7845-0.8366	116622	10.00	2	6.25	0.63	-0.47	0.04	-0.51	0.73	-0.00046
	0.8367-0.8943	116676	10.00	3	9.38	0.94	-0.06	0.01	-0.07	0.61	
	0.8944-0.9611	116614	10.00	5	15.63	1.56	0.45	-0.06	0.51	0.49	
	0.9612-1.1210	116524	9.99	3	9.38	0.94	-0.06	0.01	-0.07	0.61	
	1.1211-4.1488	116464	9.98	4	12.50	1.25	0.22	-0.03	0.25	0.53	
	1.0001-5.3709	116644	10.00	2	6.25	0.62	-0.47	0.04	-0.51	0.73	
	5.3710-8.8292	116646	10.00	4	12.50	1.25	0.22	-0.03	0.25	0.53	
	8.8293-10.4420	116644	10.00	3	9.38	0.94	-0.06	0.01	-0.07	0.61	
	10.4421-11.6711	116651	10.00	6	18.75	1.87	0.63	-0.10	0.73	0.45	
Ni	11.6712-12.7538	116655	10.00	1	3.13	0.31	-1.16	0.07	-1.24	1.02	
(ppb)	12.7539-13.9820	116648	10.00	2	6.25	0.62	-0.47	0.04	-0.51	0.73	-0.63794
	13.9821-14.9556	116644	10.00	1	3.13	0.31	-1.16	0.07	-1.24	1.02	
	14.9557-15.9219	116646	10.00	1	3.13	0.31	-1.16	0.07	-1.24	1.02	
	15.9220-16.7251	116633	10.00	7	21.88	2.19	0.78	-0.14	0.92	0.43	
	16.7252-19.9999	116627	10.00	5	15.63	1.56	0.45	-0.06	0.51	0.49	
	1.00-8.76	116772	10.01	2	6.25	0.62	-0.47	0.04	-0.51	0.73	
	8.77-17.68	116678	10.00	5	15.63	1.56	0.45	-0.06	0.51	0.49	
	17.69-21.65	116889	10.02	0	0.00	0.00	NaN	0.11	NaN	NaN	
	21.66-24.56	117006	10.03	4	12.50	1.25	0.22	-0.03	0.25	0.53	
Pb	24.57-27.30	116743	10.01	4	12.50	1.25	0.22	-0.03	0.25	0.53	
(ppb)	27.31-30.38	116786	10.01	2	6.25	0.62	-0.47	0.04	-0.51	0.73	0.27793
	30.39-33.10	116634	10.00	1	3.13	0.31	-1.16	0.07	-1.24	1.02	
	33.11-36.51	116709	10.01	4	12.50	1.25	0.22	-0.03	0.25	0.53	
	36.52-39.37	116345	9.97	5	15.63	1.57	0.45	-0.06	0.51	0.49	
	39.38-49.99	115876	9.93	5	15.63	1.57	0.45	-0.07	0.52	0.49	
	10.801-16.979	116655	10.00	3	9.38	0.94	-0.06	0.01	-0.07	0.61	
Si	16.980-18.317	116728	10.01	0	0.00	0.00	NaN	0.11	NaN	NaN	
(ppm)	18.318-19.271	116675	10.00	2	6.25	0.62	-0.47	0.04	-0.51	0.73	0.00165
	19.272-20.521	116693	10.00	5	15.63	1.56	0.45	-0.06	0.51	0.49	

	20.522-21.914	116619	10.00	5	15.63	1.56	0.45	-0.06	0.51	0.49	
	21.915-23.443	116686	10.00	3	9.38	0.94	-0.06	0.01	-0.07	0.61	
	23.444-25.021	116607	10.00	1	3.13	0.31	-1.16	0.07	-1.24	1.02	
	25.022-27.559	116627	10.00	4	12.50	1.25	0.22	-0.03	0.25	0.53	
	27.560-31.012	116583	9.99	3	9.38	0.94	-0.06	0.01	-0.07	0.61	
	31.013-96.079	116565	9.99	6	18.75	1.88	0.63	-0.10	0.73	0.45	
Sr (ppb)	8.00-20.48	116702	10.00	3	9.38	0.94	-0.07	0.01	-0.07	0.61	-0.01602
	20.49-42.65	116644	10.00	6	18.75	1.87	0.63	-0.10	0.73	0.45	
	42.66-57.42	116749	10.01	1	3.13	0.31	-1.16	0.07	-1.24	1.02	
	57.43-66.48	116649	10.00	2	6.25	0.62	-0.47	0.04	-0.51	0.73	
	66.49-71.81	116821	10.02	2	6.25	0.62	-0.47	0.04	-0.51	0.73	
	71.82-76.94	116630	10.00	3	9.38	0.94	-0.06	0.01	-0.07	0.61	
	76.95-84.38	116686	10.00	7	21.88	2.19	0.78	-0.14	0.92	0.43	
	84.39-96.47	116540	9.99	4	12.50	1.25	0.22	-0.03	0.25	0.53	
	96.48-134.78	116509	9.99	4	12.50	1.25	0.22	-0.03	0.25	0.53	
	134.79-499.92	116508	9.99	0	0.00	0.00	NaN	0.11	NaN	NaN	
V (ppb)	10.000-10.001	116806	10.01	4	12.50	1.25	0.22	-0.03	0.25	0.53	0.53038
	10.002-10.320	116672	10.00	5	15.63	1.56	0.45	-0.06	0.51	0.49	
	10.321-10.744	116623	10.00	4	12.50	1.25	0.22	-0.03	0.25	0.53	
	10.745-11.616	116648	10.00	1	3.13	0.31	-1.16	0.07	-1.24	1.02	
	11.617-12.435	116656	10.00	4	12.50	1.25	0.22	-0.03	0.25	0.53	
	12.436-14.190	116633	10.00	4	12.50	1.25	0.22	-0.03	0.25	0.53	
	14.191-15.335	116625	10.00	1	3.13	0.31	-1.16	0.07	-1.24	1.02	
	15.336-17.900	116593	10.00	5	15.63	1.56	0.45	-0.06	0.51	0.49	
	17.901-20.623	116598	10.00	4	12.50	1.25	0.22	-0.03	0.25	0.53	
	20.624-99.985	116584	9.99	0	0.00	0.00	NaN	0.11	NaN	NaN	
W (ppb)	1.000-2.152	116858	10.02	1	3.13	0.31	-1.16	0.07	-1.24	1.02	-0.10819
	2.153-2.458	116646	10.00	2	6.25	0.62	-0.47	0.04	-0.51	0.73	
	2.459-2.683	116776	10.01	5	15.63	1.56	0.45	-0.06	0.51	0.49	
	2.684-2.988	116706	10.01	5	15.63	1.56	0.45	-0.06	0.51	0.49	
	2.989-3.363	116762	10.01	0	0.00	0.00	NaN	0.11	NaN	NaN	
	3.364-4.015	116577	9.99	5	15.63	1.56	0.45	-0.06	0.51	0.49	
	4.016-4.478	116788	10.01	4	12.50	1.25	0.22	-0.03	0.25	0.53	
	4.479-4.946	116606	10.00	6	18.75	1.88	0.63	-0.10	0.73	0.45	
	4.947-6.530	116366	9.98	4	12.50	1.25	0.23	-0.03	0.25	0.53	
	6.531-49.994	116353	9.98	0	0.00	0.00	NaN	0.11	NaN	NaN	
Zn (ppb)	1.00-3.28	117143	10.04	4	12.50	1.24	0.22	-0.03	0.25	0.53	0.06175
	3.29-4.34	117519	10.08	3	9.38	0.93	-0.07	0.01	-0.08	0.61	
	4.35-5.21	117200	10.05	1	3.13	0.31	-1.17	0.07	-1.24	1.02	
	5.22-6.13	116683	10.00	3	9.38	0.94	-0.06	0.01	-0.07	0.61	
	6.14-7.22	116931	10.02	3	9.38	0.94	-0.07	0.01	-0.07	0.61	
	7.23-8.81	116420	9.98	3	9.38	0.94	-0.06	0.01	-0.07	0.61	
	8.82-11.02	116562	9.99	2	6.25	0.63	-0.47	0.04	-0.51	0.73	
	11.03-13.62	116052	9.95	3	9.38	0.94	-0.06	0.01	-0.07	0.61	
	13.63-21.96	115998	9.94	4	12.50	1.26	0.23	-0.03	0.26	0.53	
	21.97-49.99	115930	9.94	6	18.75	1.89	0.63	-0.10	0.74	0.45	

Magnetic anomaly (nT)	-145--101	128137	10.99	3	9.38	0.85	-0.16	0.02	-0.18	0.61	-0.00657
	-100--92	121586	10.42	4	12.50	1.20	0.18	-0.02	0.21	0.53	
	-91--83	118890	10.19	6	18.75	1.84	0.61	-0.10	0.71	0.45	
	-82--76	131697	11.29	4	12.50	1.11	0.10	-0.01	0.12	0.53	
	-75--68	118478	10.16	3	9.38	0.92	-0.08	0.01	-0.09	0.61	
	-67--59	115975	9.94	4	12.50	1.26	0.23	-0.03	0.26	0.53	
	-58--49	115502	9.90	0	0.00	0.00	NaN	0.10	NaN	NaN	
	-48--32	110107	9.44	4	12.50	1.32	0.28	-0.03	0.32	0.53	
	-31--9	105926	9.08	2	6.25	0.69	-0.37	0.03	-0.40	0.73	
	-8-153	100140	8.59	2	6.25	0.73	-0.32	0.03	-0.34	0.73	
Distance from fault (m)	0-120	119087	10.21	0	0.00	0.00	NaN	0.11	NaN	NaN	0.00003
	123-256	118526	10.16	4	12.50	1.23	0.21	-0.03	0.23	0.53	
	258-408	118732	10.18	3	9.38	0.92	-0.08	0.01	-0.09	0.61	
	416-577	117138	10.04	7	21.88	2.18	0.78	-0.14	0.92	0.43	
	579-771	115748	9.92	5	15.63	1.57	0.45	-0.07	0.52	0.49	
	774-993	115764	9.92	2	6.25	0.63	-0.46	0.04	-0.50	0.73	
	994-1268	115499	9.90	3	9.38	0.95	-0.05	0.01	-0.06	0.61	
	1271-1632	115411	9.89	6	18.75	1.90	0.64	-0.10	0.74	0.45	
	1633-2292	115313	9.89	0	0.00	0.00	NaN	0.10	NaN	NaN	
	2294-6224	115220	9.88	2	6.25	0.63	-0.46	0.04	-0.50	0.73	
Lithology	Ogl	1064	0.09	0	0.00	0.00	NaN	0.00	NaN	NaN	-1.54617
	lgr	4841	0.42	0	0.00	0.00	NaN	0.00	NaN	NaN	-2.63001
	Di	14	0.00	0	0.00	0.00	NaN	0.00	NaN	NaN	-2.82522
	Hagr	245	0.02	0	0.00	0.00	NaN	0.00	NaN	NaN	-3.00918
	Hb	2281	0.20	2	6.25	31.96	3.46	-0.06	3.53	4.83	10.46756
	Oyb	1022	0.09	0	0.00	0.00	NaN	0.00	NaN	NaN	-1.30763
	Qr	49757	4.27	2	6.25	1.47	0.38	-0.02	0.40	0.55	8.51705
	Qd	533	0.05	0	0.00	0.00	NaN	0.00	NaN	NaN	-0.77791
	Kad	136	0.01	0	0.00	0.00	NaN	0.00	NaN	NaN	-2.43856
	Kbd	881	0.08	1	3.13	41.37	3.72	-0.03	3.75	3.69	12.86849
	Kfl	3	0.00	0	0.00	0.00	NaN	0.00	NaN	NaN	-2.66456
	Kgp	359	0.03	0	0.00	0.00	NaN	0.00	NaN	NaN	-0.74304
	Kh	262	0.02	0	0.00	0.00	NaN	0.00	NaN	NaN	0.00000
	Kj	792	0.07	0	0.00	0.00	NaN	0.00	NaN	NaN	-1.41765
	Kqp	520	0.04	0	0.00	0.00	NaN	0.00	NaN	NaN	-1.78021
	Ksgr	9862	0.85	0	0.00	0.00	NaN	0.01	NaN	NaN	-2.19213
	Jigr	19233	1.65	0	0.00	0.00	NaN	0.02	NaN	NaN	-3.80720
	Jgr	3466	0.30	0	0.00	0.00	NaN	0.00	NaN	NaN	-1.49119
	Jbs	584	0.05	0	0.00	0.00	NaN	0.00	NaN	NaN	-1.66856
	Jbc	3969	0.34	0	0.00	0.00	NaN	0.00	NaN	NaN	-1.74379
	TRn	20281	1.74	0	0.00	0.00	NaN	0.02	NaN	NaN	-0.32642
	TRn1	20837	1.79	0	0.00	0.00	NaN	0.02	NaN	NaN	-1.21220
	TRn2	12158	1.04	0	0.00	0.00	NaN	0.01	NaN	NaN	-0.83909
	TRn3	6944	0.60	0	0.00	0.00	NaN	0.01	NaN	NaN	-1.12328
	TRg	53754	4.61	0	0.00	0.00	NaN	0.05	NaN	NaN	-1.18890
	Ps	18150	1.56	0	0.00	0.00	NaN	0.02	NaN	NaN	-1.79743
	Ch	69942	6.00	0	0.00	0.00	NaN	0.06	NaN	NaN	-2.32484
	Oj	78322	6.71	1	3.13	0.47	-0.76	0.04	-0.80	-0.79	8.10235

	Omg	215666	18.49	8	25.00	1.35	0.30	-0.08	0.38	0.94	9.80276
	Odu	89243	7.65	4	12.50	1.63	0.49	-0.05	0.54	1.02	9.55816
	Od	6794	0.58	0	0.00	0.00	NaN	0.01	NaN	NaN	-1.58241
	CEw	129104	11.07	3	9.38	0.85	-0.17	0.02	-0.18	-0.30	8.72195
	CEp	112818	9.67	5	15.63	1.62	0.48	-0.07	0.55	1.13	8.86861
	CEm	58514	5.02	2	6.25	1.25	0.22	-0.01	0.23	0.32	7.71460
	CEj	17535	1.50	0	0.00	0.00	NaN	0.02	NaN	NaN	-3.25116
	PCEt	103955	8.91	2	6.25	0.70	-0.35	0.03	-0.38	-0.53	7.64571
	Jugr	52597	4.51	2	6.25	1.39	0.33	-0.02	0.34	0.47	7.53975

[a] Using the quantile classification method
[b] Likelihood ratio
[c] Constant value : - 19.07087

Table A1. Spatial relationship between mineral deposits and some related factors

9. References

Agterberg, F.P. & Bonham-Carter, G.F. (2005). Measuring performance of mineral-potential maps. *Natural Resources Research,* Vol. 14, No. 1, 1-17, ISSN 15207439

Agterberg, F.P. (1988). Application of recent developments of regression analysis in regional mineral resource evaluation, In: *Quantitative analysis of mineral and energy resources,* Chung, C.F.; Fabbri, G. & Sinding-Larsen, R. (Ed.), 1-28, D Reidel Publishing, ISBN 9027726353, Dordrecht

Agterberg, F.P.; Bonham-Carter, G.F. & Wright, D.F. (1990). Statistical pattern integration for mineral exploration, In: *Computer Applications in Resource Estimation Prediction and Assessment for Metals and Petroleum,* Gaal, G. & Merriam, D.F. (Ed.), 1-21, Pergamon Press, ISBN 01068667, Oxford

An, P. & Moon, W.M. (1993). An evidential reasoning structure for integrating geophysical, geological and remote sensing data, Proceedings of the International Geoscience and Remote Sensing Symposium (IGARSS), pp. 1359-1361, ISBN 0-7803-1240-6, August, 1993, Tokyo

An, P.; Moon, W.M. & Rencz, A.N. (1991). Application of fuzzy set theory to integrated mineral exploration. *Canadian Journal of Exploration Geophysics,* Vol. 27, No. 1, 1-11, ISSN

Atkinson, P.M. & Massari, R. (1998). Generalized linear modeling of susceptibility to landsliding in the central Apennines Italy. *Computers & Geosciences,* Vol. 24, No. 4, 373-385, ISSN 0098-3004

Behnia, P. (2007). Application of radial basis functional link networks to exploration for proterozoic mineral deposits in central Ira. *Natural Resources Research,* Vol. 16, No. 2, 147- 155, ISSN 15207439

Benomar, T.B.; Hu, G. & Bian, F. (2009). A predictive GIS model for potential mapping of copper, lead, and zinc in langping area, China. Geo-Spatial Information Science, Vol. 12, No. 4, 243-250, ISSN 10095020

Bonham-Carter, G.F. (1994). Geographic Information Systems for Geoscientists: Modeling with GIS, 398, Pergamon Press, ISBN 0 08 041867 8, Netherland

Bonham-Carter, G.F.; Agterberg, F.P. & Wright, D.F. (1988). Integration of geological datasets for gold exploration in Nova Scotia. *Photogrammetic Engineering and Remote Sensing*, Vol. 54, No. 11, 1585-1592, ISSN 00991112

Bonham-Carter, G.F.; Agterberg, F.P. & Wright, D.F. (1989). Weights of evidence modeling: A new approach to mapping mineral potential, In: *Statistical Applications in the Earth Sciences*, Agterberg, F.P. & Bonham-Carter. G.F. (Ed.), 171-183, Geological Survey of Canada 98, ISBN 0660135922, Canadian Government Publishing Centre

Brown, W.; Groves, D. & Gedeon, T. (2003). Use of Fuzzy Membership Input Layers to Combine Subjective Geological Knowledge and Empirical Data in a Neural Network Method for Mineral-Potential Mapping. *Natural Resources Research*, Vol. 12, No. 4, 183-200, ISSN 15207439

Brown, W.M.; Gedeon, T.D.; Groves, D.I. & Barnes, R.G. (2000). Artificial neural networks: a new method for mineral prospectively mapping. *Australian Journal of Earth Sciences*, Vol. 47, No. 4, 757-770, ISSN 08120099

Carranza, E.J.M. & Hale, M. (2000). Geologically constrained probabilistic mapping of gold potential, Baguio district, Philippines. *Natural Resources Research*, Vol. 9, No. 3, 237-253, ISSN 15207439

Carranza, E.J.M. (2004). Weights of evidence modeling of mineral potential: a case study using small number of prospects, Abra, Philippines. *Natural Resources Research*, Vol. 13, No. 3, 173-187, ISSN 15207439

Carranza, E.J.M.; Hale, M. & Faassen, C. (2008). Selection of coherent deposit-type locations and their application in data-driven mineral prospectivity mapping. *Ore geology reviews*, Vol. 33, No. 3-4, 536-558, ISSN 01691368

Carranza, E.J.M.; Woldai, T. & Chikambwe, E.M. (2005). Application of data-driven evidential belief functions to prospectivity mapping for aquamarine-bearing pegmatites, Lundazi District, Zambia. *Natural Resources Research*, Vol. 14, No. 1, 47-63, ISSN 15207439

Chi, K.H.; Lee, J.S.; Jin, M.S.; Chi, S.J. & Park, S.H. (2001). Construction of GIS based geological database of South Korea Area. *Korea Institute of Geoscience and Mineral Resources*, KR-01(T)-08, 210

Chung, C.F. & Agterberg, F.P. (1980). Regression models for estimating mineral resources from geological map data. *Mathematical Geology*, Vol. 12, No. 5, 473-488, ISSN 08828121

D'Ercole, C.; Groves, D.I. & Knox-Robinson, C.M. (2000). Using fuzzy logic in a Geographic Information System environment to enhance conceptually based prospectively analysis of Mississippi Valley-type mineralization. *Australian Journal of Earth Sciences*, Vol. 47, No. 5, 913-927, ISSN 08120099

De Quadros, T.F.P.; Koppe, J.C.; Strieder, A.J. & Costa, J.F.C.L. (2006). Mineral-potential mapping: A comparison of weights-of-evidence and fuzzy methods. *Natural Resources Research*, Vol. 15, No. 1, 49-65, ISSN 15207439

Eddy, B.G.; Bonham-Carter, G.F. & Jefferson, C.W. (1995). Mineral resource assessment of the Parry Islands, high Arctic, Canada: A GIS-base fuzzy logic model, Proceedings of Canadian Conference on GIS, CD ROM session C3, Paper 4, Ottawa

Garrett, J. (1994). Where and why artificial neural networks are applicable in civil engineering. *Journal of Computing in Civil Engineering*, Vol. 8, No. 2, 129-130, ISSN 0887-3801

Harris, D. & Pan, G. (1999). Mineral favorability mapping: A comparison of artificial neural networks, logistic regression, and discriminant analysis. *Natural Resources Research*, Vol. 8, No. 2, 93-109, ISSN 15207439

Harris, D.; Zurcher, L.; Stanley, M.; Marlow, J. & Pan, G. (2003). A comparative analysis of favorability mappings by weights of evidence, probabilistic neural networks, discriminant analysis, and logistic regression. *Natural Resources Research*, Vol. 12, No. 4, 241-256, ISSN 15207439

Harris, J.R.; Lemkow, D.; Jefferson, C.; Wright, D. & Falck, H. (2008). Mineral potential modelling for the greater Nahanni ecosystem using GIS based analytical methods. Natural Resources Research, Vol. 17, No. 2, 51-78, ISSN 15207439

Hines, J.W. (1997). *Fuzzy and neural approaches in engineering*, Wiley, ISBN 978-0471192473, New York

Jianping, C.; Gongwen, W. & Changbo, H. (2005). Quantitative prediction and evaluation of mineral resources based on GIS: A case study in Sanjiang region, southwestern China. *Natural Resources Research*, Vol. 14, No. 4, 285-294, ISSN 15207439

Kim, J.C.; Koh, H.J.; Lee, S.R.; Lee, C.B.; Choi, S.J. & Park, K.H. (2001). Explanatory note the Gangreung-Sokcho Sheet. *Korean Institute of Geoscience and Mineral Resources*, KR-M 25-08 2001, 76

Kim, J.H.; Kee, W.S. & Seo, S.K. (1996). Geological structures of the Yeoryang-Imgye area, northern part of Mt. Taebaek Region, Korea. *The Journal of the Geological Society of Korea*, Vol. 32, No. 1, 1-15, ISSN 0435-4036

Knox-Robinson, C.M. (2000). Vectorial fuzzy logic: a novel technique for enhanced mineral prospectivity mapping, with reference to the orogenic gold mineralisation potential of the Kalgoorlie Terrane, Western Australia. *Australian Journal of Earth Sciences*, Vol. 47, No. 5, 929-941, ISSN 08120099

Koh, S.M.; Kim, S.Y.; Lee, D.J.; Kim, D.O.; Lee, H.Y.; Kim, Y.U.; Yoo, J.H.; Kim, Y.I.; Ryoo, C.R. & Song, M.S. (2003). Construction of the data-base and assessment of domestic mineral resources III (Area of 1:250,000 Seoul and Gangreung Geological Sheets). *Ministry of Commerce, Industry and Energy*, KR-2002-C-14-2003-R, 84

Koo, S.B.; Cho, J.D.; Lee, T.S.; Park, Y.S.; Lim, M.T.; Choi, J.H.; Sung, N.H.; Hwang, H.S. & Koh, I.S. (2001). Regional geophysical exploration. *Korean Institute of Geoscience and Mineral Resources*, KR-2000-R-11-2001-R, 70

Lee, C.H. & Park, H.I. (1996). Epithermal gold-silver mineralization and depositional environment carbonate-hosted replacement type Baegjeon Deposits, Korea. *Economic and Environmental Geology*, Vol. 29, No. 2, 105-117, ISSN 1225-7281

Lee, J.S.; Seo, H.J. & Hwnag, I.H. (1998). Regional geochemical mapping of the Kangneung Sheet (1:250,000). *Korean Institute of Geoscience and Mineral Resources*, KR-98(C)-02, 147

Lee, S.; Ryu, J.H. & Kim, I.S. (2007). Landslide susceptibility analysis and its verification using likelihood ratio, logistic regression, and artificial neural network models: case study of Youngin, Korea. *Landslide*, Vol. 4, No. 4, 327-338, ISSN 1612510X

Leite, E.P. & Souza Filho, C.R. (2009). Artificial neural networks applied to mineral potential mapping for copper-gold mineralizations in the Carajas Mineral Province, Brazil. *Geophysical Prospecting*, Vol. 57, No. 3, 1049-1065, ISSN 00983004

Luo, X. & Dimitrakopoulos, R. (2003). Data-driven fuzzy analysis in quantitative mineral resource assessment. *Computers & Geosciences*, Vol. 29, No. 1, 3-13, ISSN 0098-3004

Moon, W.M. & So, C.S. (1995). Information representation and integration of multiple sets of spatial geoscience data, International Geoscience and Remote Sensing Symposium (IGARSS), pp. 2141-2144, ISBN 0-7803-2567-2, July, 1995, Firenze

Moon, W.M. (1990). Integration of geophysical and geological data using evidence theory function. *IEEE, Transactions on Geoscience and Remote Sensing*, Vol. 28, No. 4, 711-720, ISSN 0196-2892

Moon, W.M. (1993). On mathematical representation and integration of multiple spatial geoscience data sets. *Canadian Journal of Remote Sensing*, Vol. 19, No. 1, 63-67, ISSN 07038992

Nykänen, V. & Ojala, V.J. (2007). Spatial analysis techniques as successful mineral-potential mapping tools for orogenic gold deposits in the northern Fennoscandian shield, Finland. Natural Resources Research, Vol. 16, No. 2, 85-92, ISSN 15207439

Nykanen, V. & Raines, G.L. (2006). Quantitative analysis of scale of aeromagnetic data raises questions about geologic-map scale. *Natural Resources Research*, Vol. 15, No. 4, 213-222, ISSN 15207439

Nykanen, V. & Salmirinne, H. (2007). Prospectivity analysis of gold using regional geophysical and geochemical data from the Central Lapland Greenstone Belt, Finland, In: *Gold in the Central Lapland Greenstone Belt*, Ojala, V.J., (Ed.), 235-253, Geological Survey of Finland, Special Paper 44

Nykanen, V. (2008). Radial Basis Functional Link Nets Used as a Prospectivity Mapping Tool for Orogenic Gold Deposits Within the Central Lapland Greenstone Belt, Northern Fennoscandian Shield. *Natural Resources Research*, Vol. 17, No. 1, 29-47, ISSN 15207439

Oh, H.J. & Lee, S. (2008). Regional Probabilistic and Statistical Mineral Potential, Mapping of Gold - Silver Deposits Using GIS in the Gangreung Area, Korea. *Resource Geology*, Vol. 58, No. 2, 171 - 187, ISSN 13441698

Pan, G.C. (1996). Extended weights of evidence modeling for the pseudo-estimation of metalgrades. *Natural Resources Research*, Vol. 5, No. 1, 53-76, ISSN 15207439

Paola, J.D. & Schowengerdt, R.A. (1995). A review and analysis of backpropagation neural networks for classification of remotely-sensed multi-spectral imagery. *International Journal of Remote Sensing*, Vol. 16, No. 16, 3033-3058, ISSN 01431161

Park, H.I.; Chang, H.W. & Jin, M.S. (1988). K-Ar ages of mineral deposits in the Taebaek Mountain district. *The Journal of Korean Institute of Mining Geology*, Vol. 21, No. 1, 57-67, ISSN 0379-7546

Partington, G. (2010). Developing models using GIS to assess geological and economic risk: An example from VMS copper gold mineral exploration in Oman. *Ore Geology Reviews*, In Press, doi:10.1016/j.oregeorev.2010.02.002

Porwal, A.; Carranza, E.J.M. & Hale, M. (2003). Artificial neural networks for mineral potential mapping: a case study from Aravalli Province, western India. *Natural Resources Research*, Vol. 12, No. 3, 155-177, ISSN 15207439

Porwal, A.; Carranza, E.J.M. & Hale, M. (2006). A hybrid fuzzy weights-of-evidence model for mineral potential mapping. *Natural Resources Research*, Vol. 15, No. 1, 1-14, ISSN 15207439

Raines, G.L. (1999). Evaluation of weights of evidence to predict epithermal-gold deposits in the Great Basin of the Western United States. *Natural Resources Research*, Vol. 8, No. 4, 257-276, ISSN 15207439

Raines, G.L.; Connors, K.A. & Chorlton, L.B. (2007). Porphyry copper deposit tract definition - A global analysis comparing geologic map scales. *Natural Resources Research,* Vol. 16, No. 2, 191-198, ISSN 15207439

Rencz, A.N.; Harris, J.R.; Watson, G.P. & Murphy, B. (1994). Data integration for mineral exploration in the Antigonish Highlands, Nova Scotia: Application of GIS and remote sensing. *Canadian Journal of Remote Sensing,* Vol. 20, No. 3, 257-267, ISSN 07038992

Rigol-Sanchez, J.P.; Chica-Olmo, M. & Abarca-Hernandez, F. (2003). Artificial neural networks as a tool for mineral potential mapping with GIS. *International Journal Remote Sensing,* Vol. 24, No. 5, 1151-1156, ISSN 01431161

Roy, R.; Cassard, D.; Cobbold, P.R.; Rossello, E.A.; Bailly, L. & Lips, A.L.W. (2006). Predictive mapping for copper-gold magmatic-hydrothermal systems in NW Argentina: Use of a regional-scale GIS, application of an expert-guided data-driven approach, and comparison with results from a continental-scale GIS. *Ore Geology Reviews,* Vol. 29, No. 3-4, 260-286, ISSN 01691368

Singer, D.A. & Kouda, R. (1996). Application of a feed forward neural network in the search for Kuroko deposits in the Hokuroku District, Japan. *Mathematical Geology,* Vol. 28, No. 8, 1017-1023, ISSN 08828121

Skabar, A. (2007). Modeling the spatial distribution of mineral deposits using neural networks. *Natural Resource Modeling,* Vol. 20, No. 3, 435-450, ISSN 1939-7445

Skabar, A.A. (2005). Mapping mineralization probabilities using multilayer perceptrons. *Natural Resources Research,* Vol. 14, No. 2, 109-123, ISSN 15207439

Tangestani, M.H. & Moore, F. (2001). Porphyry copper potential mapping using the weights-of-evidence modeling a GIS northern Shahr-e-Babak Iran. *Australian Journal of Earth Sciences,* Vol. 48, No. 5, 913-927, ISSN 08120099

Xu, S.; Cui, Z.K.; Yang, X.L. & Wang, G.J. (1992). A preliminary application of weights of evidence in gold exploration in Xionger mountain region. Henan province. *Mathematical Geology,* Vol. 24, No. 6, 663-674, ISSN 08828121

Zhou, W. (1999). Verification of the nonparametric characteristics of backpropagation neural networks for image classification. *IEEE Transactions on Geoscience and Remote Sensing,* Vol. 37, No. 2, 771-779, ISSN 0196-2892

6

The Use of Artificial Neural Network (ANN) for Modelling, Simulation and Prediction of Advanced Oxidation Process Performance in Recalcitrant Wastewater Treatment

Emad S. Elmolla[1] and Malay Chaudhuri[2]

[1]Dept. of Civil Engineering, Faculty of Engineering, Al-Azhar University, Cairo,
[2]Dept. of Civil Engineering, Universiti Teknologi PETRONAS, Tronoh, Perak,
[1]Egypt
[2]Malaysia

1. Introduction

Treatment of recalcitrant wastewater by advanced oxidation processes (AOPs) is influenced by several factors. Due to complexity of the processes, they are difficult to be modelled and simulated using conventional mathematical modelling. Artificial neural network is used in many areas of science and engineering as a promising tool because of its simplicity in simulation, prediction and modelling of process performance (Prakash et al., 2008). The chapter presents artificial neural network and training of artificial neural network, advanced oxidation processes (AOPs), case studies, conclusions and references.

2. Artificial Neural Network (ANN)

The ANN is an artificial intelligence technique that mimics the human brain's biological neural network in the problem solving processes. As humans solve a new problem based on the past experience, a neural network takes previously solved examples, looks for patterns in these examples, learns these patterns and develops the ability to correctly classify new patterns. In addition, the neural network has the ability to resemble human characteristics in problem solving that is difficult to simulate using the logical, analytical techniques of expert system and standard software technologies (Daosud et al., 2005).

A neural network is defined as a system of simple processing elements called neurons, which are connected to a network by a set of weights. The neuron is a processing element that takes a number of inputs, weighs them, sums them up, adds a bias and uses the outcome as the argument for a singule-valued function (transfer function) which results in the neuron's output (Strik et al., 2005). The network is determined by the architecture of the network, the magnitude of the weights and the processing element's mode of operation. At the start of training, the output of each node tends to be small. Consequently, the derivatives of the transfer function and changes in the connection weights are large with respect to the input. As learning progresses and the network reaches a local minimum in error surface, the node outputs approach stable values. Consequently, the derivatives of the transfer function

with respect to input, as well as changes in the connection weights, are small (Maier and Dandy, 1998).
The different types of neural network based on their incremental complexity are: feedforward, recurrent, stochastic and modular network (Prakash et al., 2008). The chapter will focus on the feedforward network which is widely used in the area of wastewater treatment.

2.1 Feedforward ANN

The feedforward ANN is composed of two or more layers of processing elements which are linked by weighted connections (Figure 1). The information flow is unidirectional, no feedback connections are present and data are presented to input layer, passed on to hidden layer and passed on to output layer.

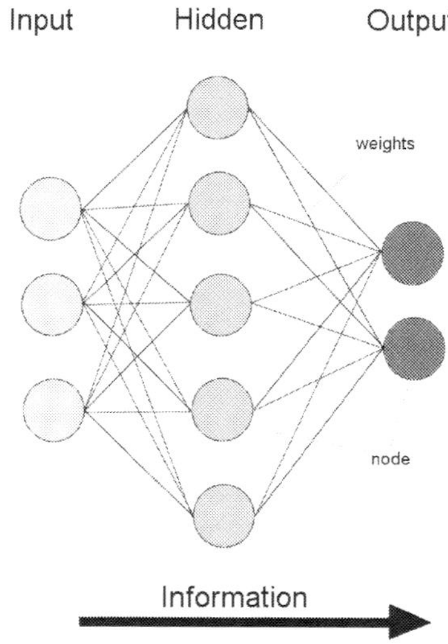

Fig. 1. Feedforward ANN

2.2 Training of Artificial Neural Network

According to Artificial neural network tutorial (2008), the learning situation can be categorized as the following.

Supervised learning

In supervised or associative learning, the network is trained by providing it with input and matching output patterns. Backpropagation is a form of supervised training. Using the actual outputs, the backpropagation training algorithm takes a calculated error and adjusts the weights of the various layers backwards from the output layer to the input layer. It means adjusting the weights in neurons with regard to the difference between the outputs predicted by the model and the actual outputs (Figure 2).

Unsupervised learning

In unsupervised learning or self-organisation, an output unit is trained to respond to clusters of pattern within the input. In this paradigm, the system is supposed to discover statistically salient features of the input population. Unlike the supervised learning paradigm, there is no *a priori* set of categories into which the patterns are to be classified; rather the system must develop its own representation of the input stimuli.

Reinforcement learning

This category of learning may be considered as an intermediate form of the above two types of learning. Here the learning machine does some action on the environment and gets a feedback response from the environment. The learning system grades its action as good (rewarding) or bad (punishable) based on the environmental response and accordingly adjusts its parameters. Generally, parameter adjustment is continued until an equilibrium state occurs, following which there will be no more changes in its parameters. The self organizing neural learning may be categorized under this type of learning.

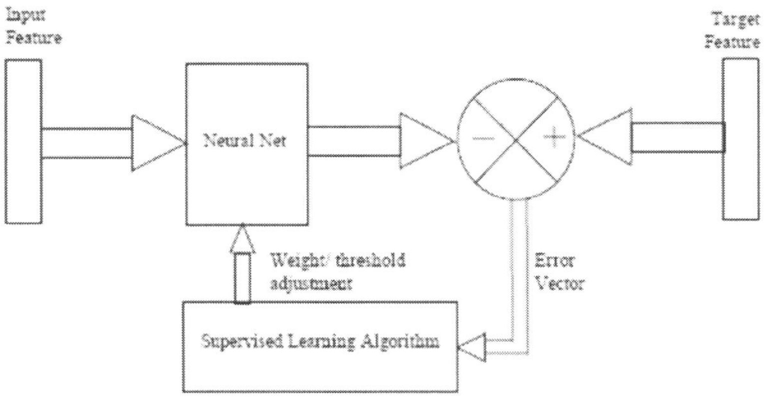

Fig. 2. Supervised learning (Artificial neural network tutorial, 2008)

3. Advanced Oxidation Processes (AOPs)

AOPs are defined by Glaze et al. (1987) as near ambient temperature and pressure water treatment processes which involve the generation of highly reactive radicals (especially, hydroxyl radicals ($OH^{\bullet}$)) in sufficient quantity to effect water purification. These treatment processes are considered very promising methods for the remediation of contaminated water and wastewater containing non-biodegradable organic pollutants. Due to the toxic characteristics of non-biodegradable organic pollutants, e.g. antibiotics, a wastewater containing these pollutants may not suitably be treated by a conventional biological process. In addition, separation technologies such as coagulation-filtration, activated carbon adsorption and reverse osmosis only transfer the pollutants from one phase to another without destroying them. AOPs are promising methods for the remediation of contaminated wastewaters containing non-biodegradable (recalcitrant) organic pollutants. AOPs can be classified by considering the phase where the process takes place, hence homogenous or heterogeneous processes can be differentiated. AOP classification can also consider the different possible ways of hydroxyl radical production. In this way, photochemical and non-photochemical processes can be distinguished. Table 1 shows classification of the most important AOPs into photochemical and non-photochemical processes.

Photochemical process	Non-photochemical process
Photo-Fenton ($UV/Fe^{2+}/H_2O_2$)	Fenton (Fe^{2+}/H_2O_2)
UV/O_3	O_3/H_2O_2
UV/H_2O_2	O_3/Ultrasound
$UV/H_2O_2/O_3$	Ozonation (O_3/OH^-)
Heterogeneous photocatalysis (UV/TiO_2)	H_2O_2/Ultrasound

Table 1. Classification of AOPs as photochemical and non-photochemical processes

The chapter will focus on the Fenton, photo-Fenton, UV/H_2O_2, heterogeneous photocatalysis and ozonation, and these processes are described in the following sections.

3.1 Fenton and photo-Fenton processes

Fenton and photo-Fenton are homogenous advanced oxidation process. The Fundamentals of these processes as well as the main factors affecting the process are described below.

Fundamentals of Fenton Reactions

The Fenton reaction was discovered by Fenton (1894) and forty year later, the reaction mechanism was described by Haber and Weiss (1934). In the Fenton reaction, hydroxyl radicals ($OH^\bullet$) are generated by interaction of H_2O_2 with ferrous salts as in Reaction (1).

$$Fe^{2+} + H_2O_2 \rightarrow Fe^{3+} + OH^\bullet + OH^- \qquad (1)$$

Generated Fe^{3+} can be reduced by reaction with exceeding H_2O_2 to form again ferrous ion and more radicals. This second process is called Fenton-like and it is slower than Fenton reaction as in Reactions 2 and 3 (Sychev and Isaak, 1995).

$$Fe^{3+} + H_2O_2 \rightarrow HO_2^\bullet + Fe^{2+} + H^+ \qquad (2)$$

$$Fe^{3+} + HO_2^\bullet \rightarrow Fe^{2+} + O_2 + H^+ \qquad (3)$$

Other important dark reactions involving ferrous ion and hydrogen peroxide in absence of other interfering ions and organic substances are shown in Reactions 4-6.

$$Fe^{2+} + HO_2^\bullet + H^+ \rightarrow Fe^{3+} + H_2O_2 \qquad (4)$$

$$Fe^{2+} + OH^\bullet \rightarrow Fe^{3+} + OH^- \qquad (5)$$

$$H_2O_2 + OH^\bullet \rightarrow HO_2^\bullet + H_2O \qquad (6)$$

The below listed radical-radical reactions, as well as the auto-decomposition of H_2O_2 are also part of the complex process as shown in Reactions 7-10.

$$2H_2O_2 \rightarrow 2H_2O + O_2 \qquad (7)$$

$$2OH^\bullet \rightarrow H_2O_2 \qquad (8)$$

$$2HO_2^\bullet \rightarrow H_2O_2 + O_2 \qquad (9)$$

$$HO_2^\bullet + OH^\bullet \rightarrow H_2O + O_2 \qquad (10)$$

Fundamentals of Photo-Fenton Reactions

Fenton reaction rate is strongly increased by irradiation with UV/visible light (Kiwi et al., 1994; Huston & Pignatello, 1999). During the reaction, Fe^{3+} ions accumulate in the system and after Fe^{2+} are consumed, the reaction practically stops. Photochemical regeneration (Reaction 11) of Fe^{2+} ions by photoreduction of Fe^{3+} ions was proposed (Huston & Pignatello, 1999). The newly generated ferrous ion reacts with H_2O_2 generating a second $OH^{\bullet}$ radical and Fe^{3+} and the cycle continues.

$$Fe^{3+} + H_2O + h\upsilon \rightarrow Fe^{2+} + OH^{\bullet} \quad (11)$$

The main factors affecting Fenton and photo-Fenton processes are summarized below.

Initial H_2O_2 Concentration

Degradation rate of the organics increases with increase of H_2O_2 concentration. This could be explained by the effect of the additionally produced $OH^{\bullet}$ radicals (Zhao et al., 2004). However, above a certain H_2O_2 concentration, the reaction rate levels off and sometimes is negatively affected by the increase of H_2O_2 concentration. This may be due to scavenging of $OH^{\bullet}$ by H_2O_2 as in Reaction 6 (Kavitha and Palanivelu, 2005). Therefore, H_2O_2 should be added at an optimal concentration to achieve the best degradation. This optimal H_2O_2 concentration depends on the nature and concentration of the pollutants and the iron concentration.

Initial Fe^{2+} Concentration

Degradation rate of the organics increases with increase of iron concentration; however, above a certain iron concentration the efficiency decreases. This may be due to the recombination of $OH^{\bullet}$ radicals or increase of turbidity that hinders the absorption of the UV light required for the photo-Fenton process. Fe^{2+} reacts with $OH^{\bullet}$ radicals as a scavenger (Reaction 5). It is desirable for Fe^{2+} or Fe^{3+} to be as small as possible, so recombination can be avoided and iron complex production reduced (Kwon et al., 1999).

pH

The Fenton and photo-Fenton processes have a maximum activity at about pH 3. The pH value influences the generation of $OH^{\bullet}$ radicals and thus the oxidation efficiency of the process. At higher pH, generation of $OH^{\bullet}$ radicals decreases and this is due to the decrease of dissolved iron as well as dissociation and auto-decomposition of H_2O_2 (Zhao et al., 2004). At low pH, oxidation efficiency is lower due to solvation of hydrogen peroxide in presence of high concentration of H^+ to form stable oxonium ion (H_3O^{2+}), thus reducing substantially its reactivity with ferrous ions (Kwon et al., 1999).

Temperature

Fenton and photo-Fenton processes are generally conducted at ambient temperature. However, temperature is a key parameter that has to be taken into account because thermal Fenton process is accelerated with increasing temperature (Arasasinghan et al., 1989). But high temperature (above 40 °C) may decompose hydrogen peroxide to oxygen and water as in Reaction 7 (Nesheiwat & Swanson, 2000).

3.2 UV/H_2O_2 process

The UV/H_2O_2 system involves the formation of $OH^{\bullet}$ radicals by hydrogen peroxide photolysis and subsequent propagation reactions. The mechanism most commonly accepted for the photolysis of H_2O_2 is the cleavage of the molecule into hydroxyl radicals as in Reaction 12.

$$H_2O_2 + h\upsilon \rightarrow 2OH^{\bullet} \qquad (12)$$

The major drawback of this process is that if the solution presents a strong absorbance, this can compete with hydrogen peroxide for the radiation. Thus, cloudy water or water containing compounds absorbing UV radiation can present problems in treatment by this method.

3.3 Heterogeneous photocatalysis

Heterogeneous photocatalysis is a technology based on the irradiation of a catalyst, usually a semiconductor, which may be photoexcited to form electron-donor sites (reducing sites) and electron-acceptor sites (oxidizing sites) providing great scope as redox reagents. The bands of interest in photocatalysis are the occupied valence band (VB) and the unoccupied conduction band (CB), separated by an energy distance referred to as the band gap (E_{bg}). When the semiconductor is illuminated with light of greater energy than that of the band gap, an electron is promoted from the VB to the CB leaving a positive hole in the valence band as illustrated in Figure 3 (Cardona, 2001). After separation, the electron (e^-) and hole (h^+) pair may recombine generating heat or can become involved in electron transfer reactions with other species in solution.

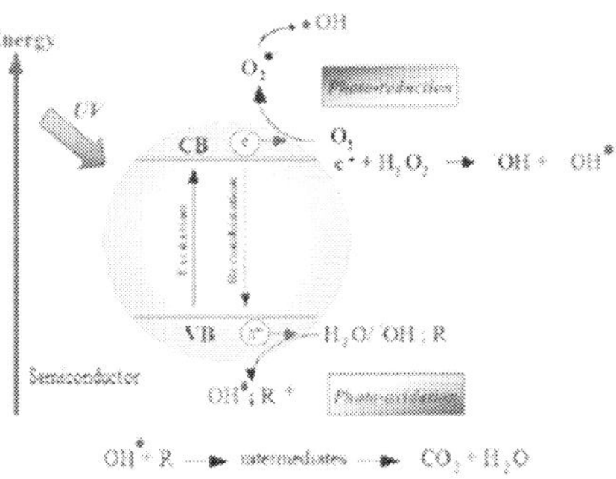

Fig. 3. Mechanism of semiconductor photocatalysis (Cardona, 2001).

Among the semiconductors, titanium dioxide (TiO_2) has proven to be the most suitable for widespread environmental applications. TiO_2 is biologically and chemically inert; it is stable to photo and chemical corrosion, and inexpensive. Furthermore, TiO_2 is of special interest since it can be photoexcited by natural (solar) UV radiation. This is because TiO_2 has an appropriate energetic separation between its valence and conduction bands, which can be surpassed by the energy of a solar photon. The VB and CB energies of the TiO_2 are estimated to be +3.1 and −0.1 eV, respectively, which means that its band gap is 3.2 eV and therefore absorbs in the near UV region (λ<387 nm)

Mechanism of TiO_2 Photocatalysis

Reaction mechanisms of photocatalytic processes have been discussed in the literature (Sadik *et al.*, 2007). When a semiconductor such as TiO_2 is illuminated by photons having an energy level that exceeds their band gap (*hv* > Ebg = 3.2 eV in case of TiO2), electrons (e-) are excited from the valence band to the conduction band and holes (h^+) are produced in the valence band

(Reaction 13). The photogenerated valence band holes react with either water (H_2O) or hydroxyl ions (OH^-) adsorbed on the catalyst surface to generate $OH^•$ radicals which are strong oxidants (Reaction 14 and 15). The hydroxyl radical reacts readily with surface adsorbed organic molecules, either by electron or hydrogen atom abstraction, forming organic radical cations, or by addition reactions to unsaturated bonds (Sadik et al., 2007) (Reaction 16). Since the reaction of the holes on the particle interface is faster than electrons, the particles under illumination contain an excess of electrons. Removal of these excess of electrons is necessary to complete the oxidation reaction, by preventing the recombination of electrons with holes. The most easily available electron acceptor is molecular oxygen and in presence of oxygen the predominant reaction of electrons is that with O_2 to form superoxide ions ($^•O_2^-$) as in Reaction (17). In acidic condition, superoxide ion combines with proton to form a hydroperoxide radical and it reacts with conduction band electron to form hydroperoxide ion. The hydroperoxide ion reacts with proton to form hydrogen peroxide. Cleavage of hydrogen peroxide by the conduction band electrons yields further hydroxyl radicals and hydroxyl ions (Reaction 18). The hydroxyl ions can then react with the valence band holes to form additional hydroxyl radicals. Recombination of the photogenerated electrons and holes may occur and indeed it has been suggested that preadsorption of substrate (organic substance) onto the photocatalyst is a prerequisite for highly efficient degradation.

$$TiO_2 + h\nu \rightarrow TiO_2\,(e^- + h^+) \tag{13}$$

$$h^+ + H_2O \rightarrow H^+ + OH^• \tag{14}$$

$$h^+ + OH^- \rightarrow OH^• \tag{15}$$

$$\text{Organics} + OH^• \rightarrow \text{products} \tag{16}$$

$$e^- + O_2 \rightarrow {}^•O_2^- \tag{17}$$

$$H_2O_2 + e^- \rightarrow OH^• + OH^- \tag{18}$$

Main Factors Affecting Photocatalytic

The main factors affecting photocatalysis reactions are described below.

Catalyst Concentration

The reaction rate is affected by the catalyst concentration; however, above a certain concentration value the reaction rate becomes independent of catalyst concentration. This limit depends on the nature of the pollutant and on the geometry and working conditions of the photoreactor corresponding to the maximum catalyst concentration in which all the particles are totally illuminated. Decrease of reaction rate at higher catalyst concentration may be due to decrease of light penetration or increase of light scattering (Kansal et al., 2007). Agglomeration and sedimentation of catalyst under high catalyst concentration may take place and available catalyst surface for photon absorption may decrease (San et al., 2007).

Temperature and pH

Experimental studies on dependence of the reaction rate of degradation of organic compounds on temperature have been conducted (Evgenidou et al., 2005). Generally, increase in temperature enhances recombination of charge carriers and desorption process of adsorbed reactant species, resulting in decrease of photocatalytic activity.

Nature of the Photocatalyst

A very important parameter influencing the performance of photocatalyst in photocatalytic oxidation is the surface morphology (Dinga et al., 2005). Numerous forms of photocatalyst have been synthesized by different methods to arrive at a photocatalyst exhibiting desirable physical properties, activity and stability for photocatalytic application (Gao & Liu, 2005). Smaller particle size is reported to give higher degradation of organic compounds (Maira et al., 2001).

Light Intensity

Photocatalytic reaction rate depends largely on the radiation absorption of the photocatalyst (Curcó et al., 2002). The increase of degradation rate with increase of light intensity during photocatalytic degradation have been reported (Qamar et al., 2006).

3.4 Ozonation

Ozonation is the oxidation process based on the use of ozone as basic compound. Ozone may be used alone or with other compounds such as UV radiation, hydrogen peroxide, activated carbon, etc. Ozone formation in the upper atmosphere is based on the photolysis of diatomic oxygen as in the following reaction:

$$O_2 + h\upsilon \rightarrow 2O^{\bullet} \tag{19}$$

$$O_2 + 2O^{\bullet} \rightarrow O_3 \tag{20}$$

The first use of ozone was reported at the end of the 19th century as a disinfectant in water treatment plants, hospitals, and research centres such as the University of Paris where the first doctoral thesis on ozonation was presented (Le Paulouë & Langlais 1999). Ozone is known as a very reactive agent in both air and water and its high reactivity is due to its electronic configuration. The half-life of ozone in water is highly dependent on the pH and matrix content of the water. For example, the half-life of ozone in distilled water can vary from about 102 sec at pH 12 to 105 sec at pH 2 or from 10 sec for secondary wastewater effluents to 104 sec for certain ground and surface waters (Hoigné, 1998). The fundamentals of ozonation is beyond the scope of this chapter.

4. Case studies

In this section, eight case studies on use of artificial neural network for modelling, simulation and prediction of advanced oxidation process (Fenton, photo-Fenton, UV/H_2O_2, UV/TiO_2 and Ozonation) performance in recalcitrant wastewater treatment are summarized.

4.1 The use of Artificial Neural Network (ANN) for modeling of COD removal from antibiotic aqueous solution by the Fenton process

Elmolla et al. (2010) reported the implementation of artificial neural networks (ANNs) for the prediction and simulation of antibiotic degradation in aqueous solution by the Fenton process. Experimental data sets (120) were divided into input matrix [p] and target matrix [t]. The input variables were reaction time (t), H_2O_2/COD molar ratio, H_2O_2/Fe^{2+} molar ratio, pH and COD concentration. The corresponding COD removal was used as a target. Principal component analysis (PCA) was performed on input data to filter out uncorrelated

random data. The data sets were divided into training (one half), validation (one fourth) and test (one fourth) subsets, each of which contained 60, 30 and 30 sets, respectively.
A three-layer backpropagation neural network was optimized to predict and simulate the degradation of amoxicillin, ampicillin and cloxacillin in aqueous solution in terms of COD removal. Figure 4 shows the optimized network. It was a three-layer ANN with tangent sigmoid transfer function (tansig) at hidden layer with (1) neurons, linear transfer function

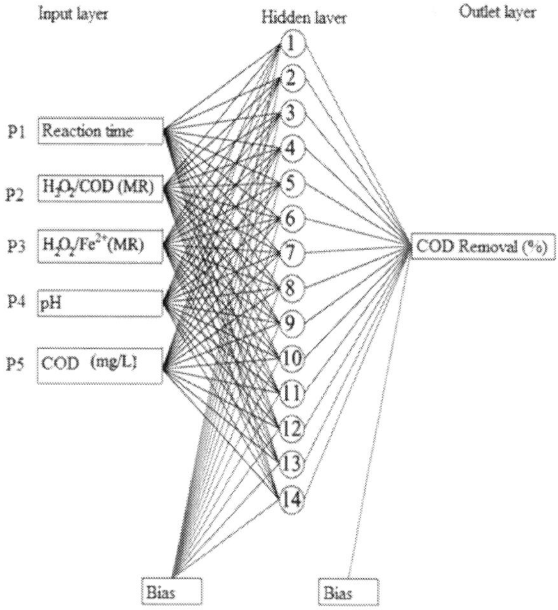

Fig. 4. Artificial neural network optimized structure (Elmolla et al., 2010)

(purelin) at output layer and Levenberg-Marquardt backpropagation training algorithm (LMA). The network was tested and the mean square error was 0.000376. In a comparison between ANN predicted results and the experimental results, the correlation coefficient (R^2) was 0.997 (Figure 5). The sensitivity analysis was conducted using two methods. The first one was based on the neural net weight matrix and Garson equation (Aleboyeh et al., 2008). Garson (1991) proposed an equation based on the partitioning of connection weights

$$I_j = \frac{\sum_{m=1}^{m=Nh}\left(\left(\left|W_{jm}^{\text{ih}}\right| \div \sum_{k=1}^{Ni}\left|W_{km}^{\text{ih}}\right|\right)\times\left|W_{mn}^{\text{ho}}\right|\right)}{\sum_{k=1}^{k=Ni}\left\{\sum_{m=1}^{m=Nh}\left(\left|W_{km}^{\text{ih}}\right| \div \sum_{k=1}^{Ni}\left|W_{km}^{\text{ih}}\right|\right)\times\left|W_{mn}^{\text{ho}}\right|\right\}} \tag{1}$$

where, I_j is the relative importance of the jth input variable on the output variable, N_i and N_h are the numbers of input and hidden neurons, respectively, Ws are connection weights, the superscripts 'i', 'h' and 'o' refer to input, hidden and output layers, respectively, and subscripts '*k*', '*m*' and '*n*' refer to input, hidden and output neurons, respectively. The second evaluation process was based on the possible combination of variables (Yetilmezsoy and Demirel, 2008). Performance of the groups of one, two, three, four, and five variables were examined by the optimum ANN structure. The input variables were reaction time (P_1), H_2O_2/COD molar ratio (P_2), H_2O_2/Fe^{2+} molar ratio (P_3), pH (P_4) and COD concentration (P_5). Table 2 shows the results of the sensitivity analysis for different combination of input variables.

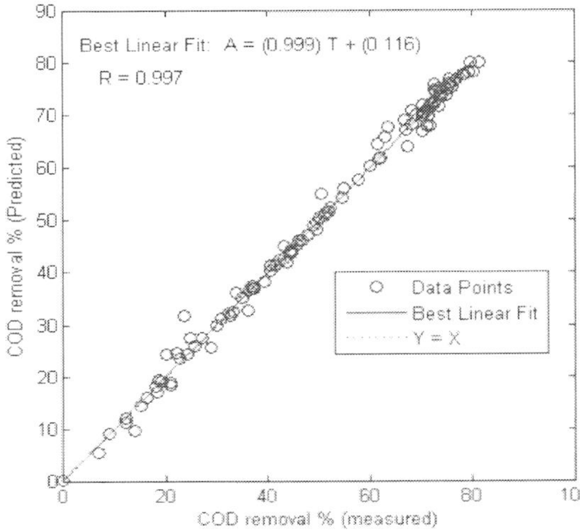

Fig. 5. Comparison between predicted and measured values of the output (Elmolla et al., 2010)

The sensitivity analysis showed that all studied variables (reaction time, H_2O_2/COD molar ratio, H_2O_2/Fe^{2+} molar ratio, pH and COD) have strong effect on antibiotics degradation in terms of COD removal. In addition, H_2O_2/Fe^{2+} molar ratio is the most influential parameter with relative importance of 25.8%. The results showed that neural network modelling could effectively predict and simulate the behaviour of the Fenton process.

4.2 The use of Artificial Neural Network (ANN) with oxidation reduction potential for dosage control of the Fenton process for color removal from textile wastewater

Yu et al. (2009) built a Fenton dosage control strategy that uses oxidation reduction potential (ORP) monitoring and artificial neural network models for removing color from textile wastewater. The input variables were peak value (mV), pH value at the ORP peak, H_2O_2 dose Fe^{2+}, dose and H_2O_2/Fe^{2+} molar ratio. The corresponding decolorization efficiency was used as a target. The data sets (74) were divided into training 46 and testing 24. A three-layer backpropagation neural network was used to predict and simulate the process. The network was tested and the root mean square (RMS) value was 0.053. In a comparison between ANN predicted results and the experimental results, the correlation coefficient (R^2) was 0.97 (Figure 6). Figure 7 shows the proposed Fenton dosage control strategy based on the developed artificial neural network control model.

Combination	Mean square error (MSE)	Epoch	Correlation coefficient (R^2)	Best linear equation
P_1	365.889	6	0.315	y = 3.71X +880
P_2	276.46	8	0.599	y = 7.44X +763
P_3*	270.141	10	0.616	y = 8.93X +689
P_4	378.575	7	0.395	y = 3.15X +991
P_5	404.727	12	0.284	y = 1,7X +953
P_1+P_2	0.500941	7	0.538	y = 0.409X +29.2
P_1+P_3	0.451707	8	0.649	y = 0.452X +25.9
P_1+P_4	0.65364	9	0.451	y = 0.32X +31.8
P_1+P_5	0.714965	6	0.391	y = 0.30X +38
P_2+P_3	0.415012	9	0.742	y = 0.528X +25
P_2+P_4	0.388861	5	0.764	y = 0.528X +24.3
P_2+P_5	0.552496	5	0.636	y = 0.405X +32.1
P_3+P_4*	0.304122	9	0.848	y = 0.701X +16.9
P_3+P_5	0.571864	10	0.646	y = 0.509X +23.5
P_4+P_5	0.755573	5	0.487	y = 0.232X +40.6
$P_1+P_2+P_3$	0.313754	16	0.802	y = 0.642X +18.1
$P_1+P_2+P_4$	0.2901	14	0.825	y = 0.675X +16.4
$P_1+P_2+P_5$	0.453212	10	0.702	y = 0.675X +25.2
$P_1+P_3+P_4$	0.141262	25	0.873	y = 0.873X +6.2
$P_1+P_3+P_5$	0.43797	10	0.69	y = 0.57X +21.1
$P_1+P_4+P_5$	0.583005	16	0.528	y = 0.57X +32.7
$P_2+P_3+P_4$*	0.117252	12	0.936	y = 0.849X +9.37
P_2+P_3+P5	0.379122	47	0.77	y = 0.579X +23.1
$P_3+P_4+P_5$	0.300483	25	0.85	y = 0.695X +17.1
$P_1+P_2+P_3+P_4$*	0.00278282	34	0.995	y = 0.997X +0.402
$P_1+P_2+P_3+P_5$	0.270749/0	25	0.818	y = 0.679X +15.7
$P_1+P_2+P_4+P_5$	0.264695	15	0.832	y = 0.682X +15.8
$P_1+P_3+P_4+P_5$	0.139748	15	0.912	y = 0.87X +6.27
$P_2+P_3+P_4+P_5$	0.113608	36	0.915	y = 0.862X +8.92
$P_1+P_2+P_3+P_4+P_5$*	0.000376	20	0.997	y = 0.999X +0.116

* The best group performances according to number of parameters

Table 2. Evaluation of combination of input variables (Elmolla et al., 2010)

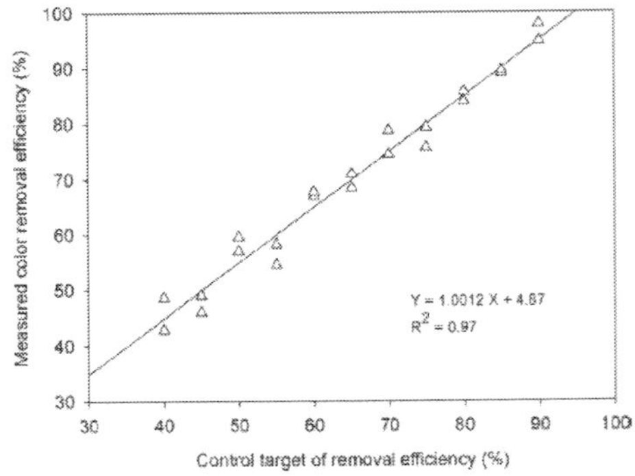

Fig. 6. Correlation of measured color removal efficiency and control target for real textile wastewater (Yu et al., 2009)

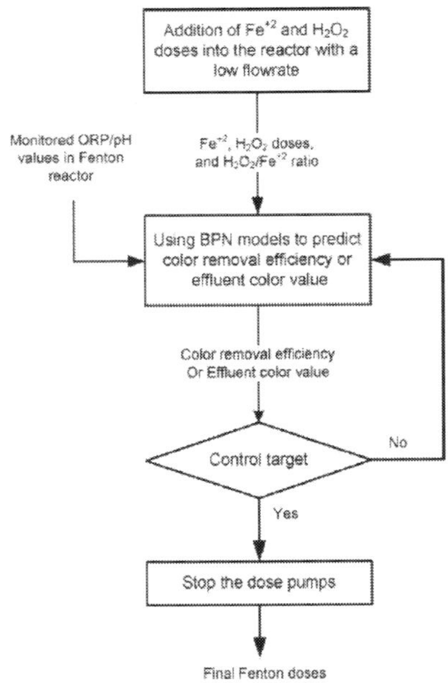

Fig. 7. Proposed Fenton dosage control strategy based on the developed artificial neural network control model (Yu et al., 2009)

4.3 The use of Artificial Neural Network (ANN) for modeling of DOC removal from polyvinyl alcohol aqueous solution by the photo-Fenton process

Giroto et al. (2006) reported the implementation of artificial neural network (ANN) for modelling of DOC removal from polyvinyl alcohol aqueous solution by the photo-Fenton process. Experimental data sets (432) were divided into input matrix [p] and target matrix

[t]. The input variables were reaction time (t), initial DOC, Fe^{2+} and H_2O_2 concentrations. The corresponding DOC removal was used as a target. In a comparison between ANN calculated DOC and the experimental DOC, the correlation coefficient (R^2) was 0.966 (Figure 8).

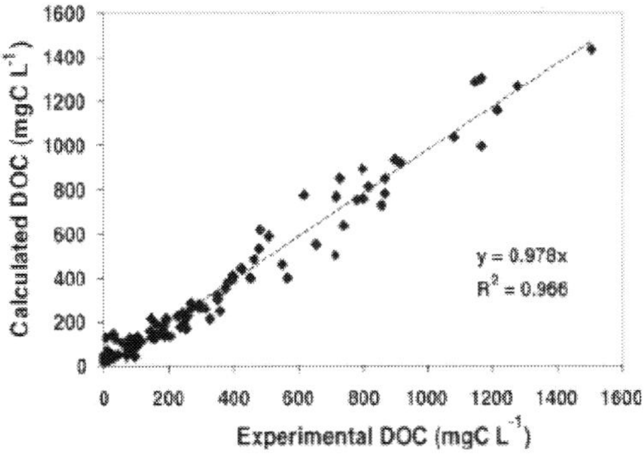

Fig. 8. Comparison between calculated and experimental DOC (Giroto et al., 2006)

4.4 The use of Artificial Neural Network (ANN) for prediction of azo dye decolorization by UV/H_2O_2

Aleboyeh et al. (2008) developed an artificial neural network model for the prediction and simulation of photochemical decolorization of C.I. Acid Orange 7 solution by UV/H_2O_2 process. Experimental data sets were divided into input matrix [p] and target matrix [t]. The input variables were initial concentration of dye and hydrogen peroxide, the pH of the solution and time of UV irradiation. The corresponding decolorization efficiency was used as a target. The data sets (228) were divided into training (one half), validation (one fourth) and test (one fourth) subsets, each of which contained 114, 57 and 57 sets, respectively.

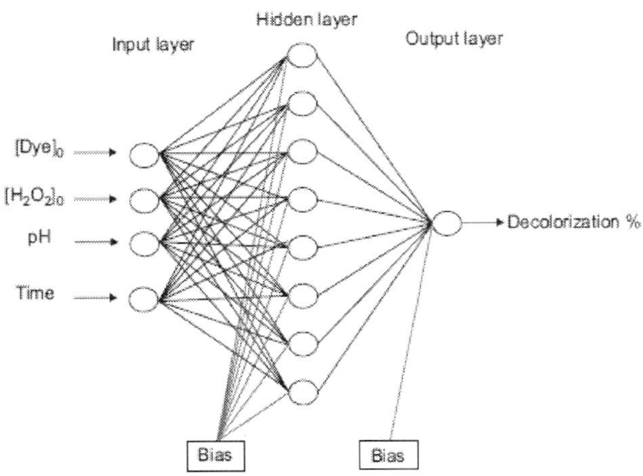

Fig. 9. Comparison between predicted and experimental decolorization (Aleboyeh et al., 2008)

A three-layer backpropagation neural network was used to predict and simulate the process. Figure 9 shows the optimized network. It was a three-layer ANN with tangent sigmoid transfer function (tansig) at hidden layer with 14 neurons, linear transfer function (purelin) at output layer and *scaled conjugate gradient algorithm* training algorithm. The network was tested and the mean square error was 0.004. In a comparison between ANN predicted results and the experimental results, the correlation coefficient (R^2) was 0.996 (Figure 10). The sensitivity analysis was conducted based on Garson equation (Equation 1) and it showed that all studied variables (initial concentration of the dye and H_2O_2, initial pH and reaction time) had considerable effects on decolorization. In addition, the initial concentration of H_2O_2 was the most influential parameter in the decolorization process with relative importance of 48.89%.

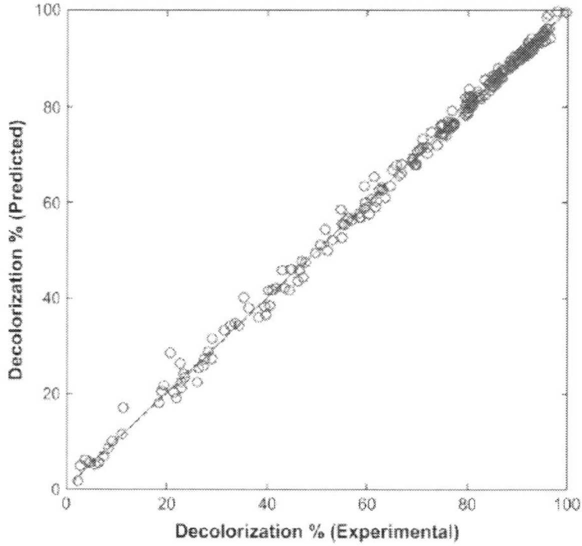

Fig. 10. Comparison between predicted and measured decolorization (Aleboyeh et al., 2008)

4.5 Decolorization process modeling by neural network

Guimarães et al. (2008) developed an artificial neural network model for the prediction and simulation of photochemical decolorization of acid orange 52 dye solution by the UV/H_2O_2 process. The input variables were dye concentration, pH, hydrogen peroxide concentration, temperature and time of operation. The corresponding absorbance was used as a target. A three-layer backpropagation neural network was used to predict and simulate the process. It was a three-layer ANN with tangent sigmoid transfer function (tansig) at hidden layer with 16 neurons, linear transfer function (purelin) at output layer and descending gradient *(learngdm)* training algorithm. The neural network was trained with 218 samples and utilized a configuration with a hidden layer and 16 neurons in the layer, presenting high correlation coefficient of (R^2) 0.991 (Figure 11). The sensitivity analysis using Garson equation (Equation 1) showed that all studied variables (dye concentration, pH, hydrogen peroxide concentration, temperature and time of operation) had considerable effects on the decolorization.

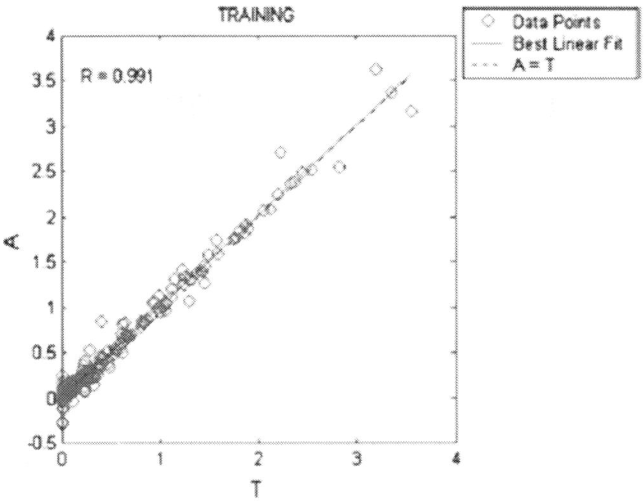

Fig. 11. Comparison between predicted and measured absorbance (Guimarães et al., 2008)

4.6 The use of Artificial Neural Network (ANN) for prediction of Methyl Tert-Butyl Ether (MTBE) degradation by UV/H_2O_2 process

Salari et al. (2005) proposed an artificial neural network model for the prediction and simulation MTBE concentration during irradiation time in optimized conditions of the UV/H_2O_2 process. The input variables were reaction time (t), initial concentration of MTBE, initial concentration of H_2O_2 and pH of the solution. The concentration of MTBE, as a function of reaction time ([MTBE]t), was used as a target. The data sets were divided into training (one half), validation (one fourth) and test (one fourth) subsets, each of which contained 32, 16 and 16 sets, respectively. Figure 12 shows the optimized network. It was a three-layer ANN with tangent sigmoid transfer function (tansig) at hidden layer with 14 neurons and linear transfer function (purelin) at output layer. The network was tested and

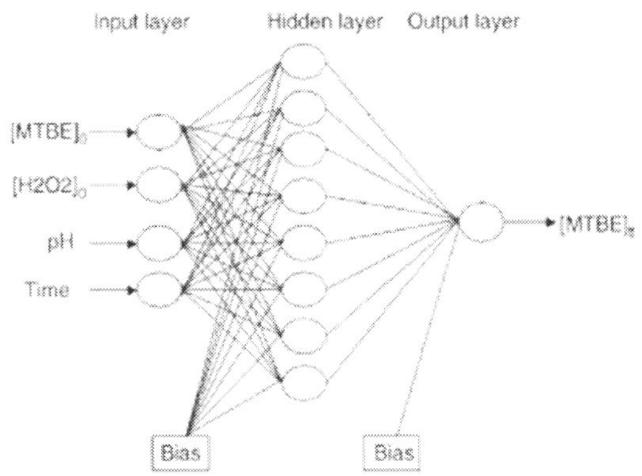

Fig. 12. Artificial neural network optimized structure (Salari et al., 2008)

the mean square error was 0.0004. In a comparison between ANN predicted results and the experimental results, the correlation coefficient (R^2) was 0.998 (Figure 13).

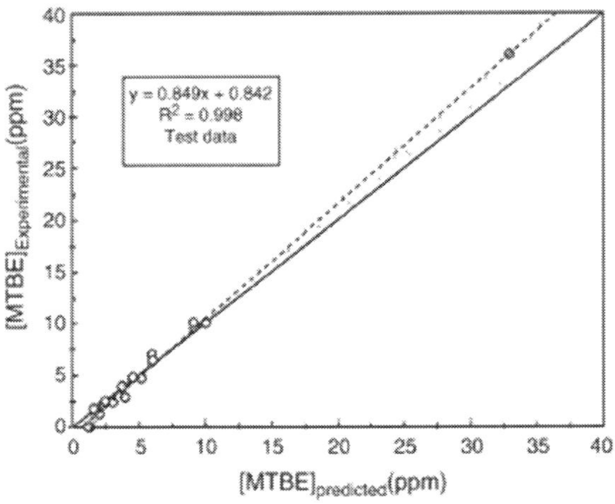

Fig. 13. Comparison between predicted and experimental results (Salari et al., 2008)

4.7 The use of Artificial Neural Network (ANN) for prediction of nitrogen oxides removal efficiency by TiO_2 photocatalysis

Toma et al. (2004) predicted the photocatalytic removal efficiency of nitrogen oxides (NO and NO_x) over a TiO_2 powder (Degussa P25). The network input layer contained three neurons representing powder quantity, irradiation time and surface, respectively. The output layer comprised two neurons representing the photocatalytic efficiency in terms of NO and NO_x. The data of 488 experimental sets were used to feed an ANN structure. Figure 14 shows the optimized ANN structure characterized by three hidden layers containing seven, four and three neurons, respectively. Correlations were learnt from the database with a percentage of 98.57%. The overall optimization error was on average less than 5%.

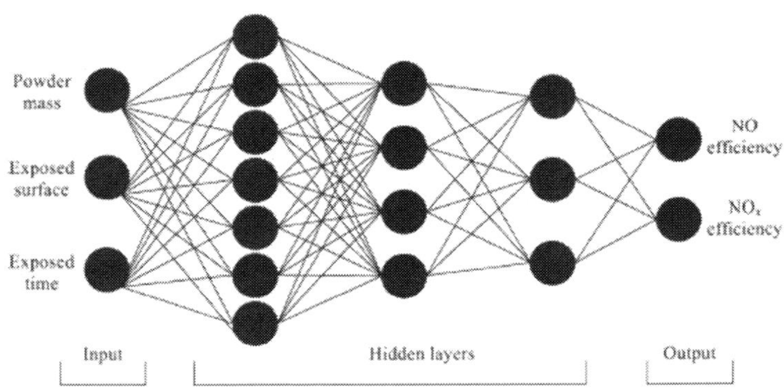

Fig. 14. Artificial neural network optimized structure (Toma et al., 2004)

4.8 The use of Artificial Neural Network (ANN) modeling of humic substance removal from an aqueous solution by ozonation

Oguz et al. (2008) modelled the removal of humic substances from aqueous solution by ozonation. The input variables to the neural network were treatment time (t), initial concentration of humic substance, powdered activated carbon dose (PAC), ozone-air flow rate, ozone generation potential, pH, temperature and HCO_3^- ion concentration. The output variable was humic substance removal. The best result was obtained from the Levenberg-Marquardt algorithm, hyperbolic tangent function in the hidden layer and the linear activation function in the output layer. As shown in Figure 15, the optimized network structure was 8 neurons at the input layer, 1 neuron at the hidden layer and 1 neuron at the output layer. In a comparison between ANN predicted values and the observed values, the correlation coefficient (R^2) was 0.995 with standard deviation ratio 0.065, mean absolute error 4.057 and root mean square error 5.4967 (Figure 16).

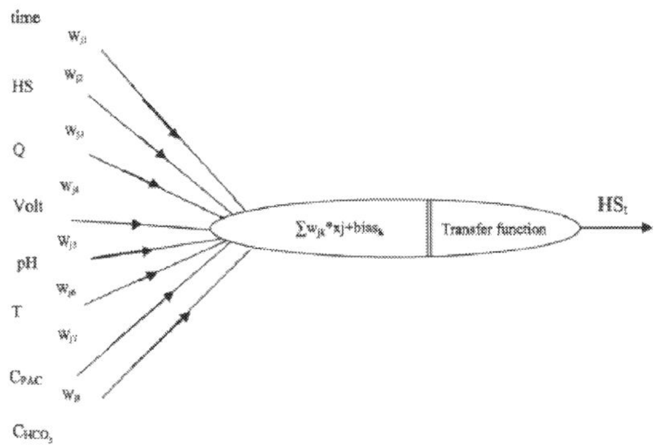

Fig. 15. Artificial neural network optimized structure (Oguz et al., 2008)

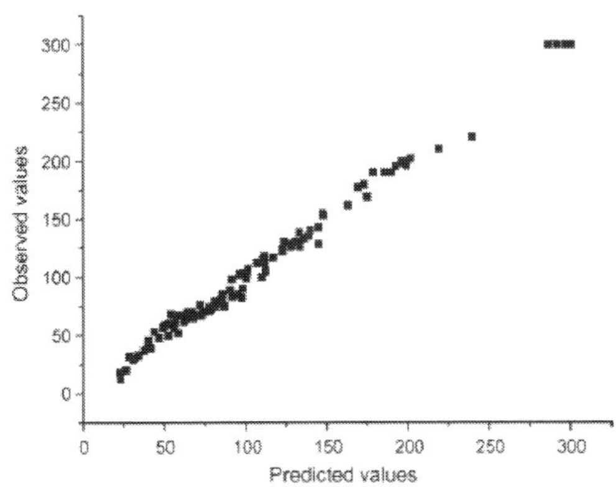

Fig. 16. Comparison between predicted and observed values (Oguz et al., 2008)

5. Conclusions

Artificial neural network is a promising tool for simulation, modelling and prediction of advanced oxidation process (AOP) performance. The output of modelling can be used for sensitivity analysis and to study the dynamic behaviour of the AOP. More research should be done for application of other artificial intelligent technique such as Neuro-fuzzy for prediction as well as control the process.

6. References

Aleboyeh, A.; Kasiri, M.B.; Olya, M.E. & Aleboyeh, H. (2008). Prediction of azo dye decolorization by UV/H_2O_2 using artificial neural networks. *Dyes and Pigments*, 77, 288-294.

Arasasinghan, R.D.; Cornman, C.R. & Balch, A.L. (1989). Detection of alkylperoxo and ferryl, $(FeIV=O)^{2+}$, intermediates during the reaction of tert-butyl hydroperoxide with iron porphyrins in toluene solution. *Journal of the American Chemical Society*, 111, 7800-7805.

Artificial neural network tutorial, 2008, http://www.learnartificialneuralnetworks.com/ access September 2009

Cardona, S.P.P. (2001). Coupling of photocatalytic and biological processes as a contribution to the detoxification of water: catalytic and technological aspects. PhD thesis, Thesis No. 2470, *Institute* of *Environmental Engineering, Department of Rural Engineering,* EPFL, Lausanne, Switzerland.

Curcó, D.; Gimènez, J.; Addardak, A.; Cervera-March, S. & Esplugas, S. (2002). Effects of radiation absorption and catalyst concentration on the photocatalytic degradation of pollutants. *Catalysis Today*, 76,177-188.

Daosud, W.; Thitiyasook, P.; Arpornwichanop, A.; Kittisupakorn, P. & Hussain, M. (2005). Neural network inverse model-based controller for the control of a steel pickling process. *Computers & Chemical Engineering*, 29, 2110–2119.

Dinga, H.; Suna, H. & Shan, Y. (2005). Preparation and characterization of mesoporous SBA-15 supported dye-sensitized TiO_2 photocatalyst. *Journal of Photochemistry and Photobiology A: Chemistry*, 169, 101-107.

Elmolla, E.S. ; Chaudhuri, M. & Eltoukhy, MM. (2010). The use of artificial neural network (ANN) for modeling of COD removal from antibiotics aqueous solution by Fenton process. *Journal of Hazardous Materials*, 179, 127-134.

Evgenidou, E.; Fytianos, K. & Poulios, I. (2005). of dichlorvos in water using TiO_2 and ZnO as catalysts. *Applied Catalysis B: Environmental*, 59, 81-89.

Fenton, H.J.H. (1894). Oxidation of tartaric acid in the presence of iron. *Journal of the Chemical Society*, 65, 899-910.

Gao, Y. & Liu, H. (2005). Preparation and catalytic property study of a novel kind of suspended photocatalyst of TiO_2-activated carbon immobilized on silicone rubber film. *Materials Chemistry and Physics*, 92, 604-608.

Garson, G.D. (1991). Interpreting neural-network connection weights. *AI Expert*, 6, 47-51.

Giroto, J.A.; Guardani, R.; Teixeira, A.C.S.C. & Nascimento, C.A.O. (2006). Study on the photo-Fenton degradation of polyvinyl alcohol in aqueous solution. *Chemical Engineering and Processing*, 45, 523–532.

Glaze, W.H., Kang, J.W. & Chapin, D.H. (1987). The chemistry of water treatment processes involving ozone, hydrogen peroxide and ultraviolet radiation. *Ozone: Science & Engineering*, 9, 335-352.

Guimarães, O.L.C. ; Chagas, M.H.D.R. ; Filho, D.N.V. ; Siqueira, A.F. ; Filho, H.J I. ; Aquino, H.O.Q.D. & Silva, M.B. (2008). Discoloration process modeling by neural network. *Chemical Engineering Journal*, 140, 71–76.

Haber, F. & Weiss, J. (1934). The catalytic decomposition of hydrogen peroxide by iron salts. *Proceedings of the Royal Society of London. Series A, Mathematical and Physical Sciences,* 147, 332-351.

Hoigné , J. (1998). *Chemistry of aqueous ozone and transformation of pollutants by ozonation and advanced oxidation processes.* In: Hrubec, J. ed. The Handbook of Environmental Chemistry. Vol. 5. Part C. Quality and Treatment of Drinking Water II. Berlin: Springer-Verlag.

Huston, P.L. & Pignatello, J. 1999. Degradation of selected pesticide active ingredients and commercial formulations in water by the photo-assisted Fenton reaction. *Water Research,* 33, 1238-1246.

Kansal, S.K.; Singh, M. & Sud, D. (2007). Studies on photodegradation of two commercial dyes in aqueous phase using different photocatalysts. *Journal of Hazardous Materials,* 141, 581-590.

Kavitha, V. & Palanivelu, K. (2005). Destruction of cresols by Fenton oxidation process. *Water Research,* 39, 3062–3072.

Kiwi, J.; Pulgarin C. & Peringer, P. (1994). Effect on Fenton and photo-Fenton reactions on the degradation and biodegradability of 2 and 4-nitrophenols in water treatment. *Applied Catalysis B: Environmental,* 3, 335-350.

Kwon, B.G.; Lee, D.S.; Kang, N. & Yoon, J. (1999). Characteristics of p-chlorophenol oxidation by Fenton's reagent. *Water Research,* 33, 2110–2118.

Le Paulouë, J. & Langlais, B. (1999). State of the art of ozonation in France. *Ozone: Science & Engineering,* 21,153–162.

Maier, H.R. & Dandy, G.C. (1998). Understanding the behavior and optimizing the performance of back-propagation neural networks: an empirical study. *Environmental Modelling & Software,* 13, 179-191

Maira, A.J.; Yeung, K.L.; Soria, J.; Coronado ; Belver ; J.M.C. ; Lee, C.Y. & Augugliaro, V. (2001). Gas-phase photo-oxidation of toluene using nanometer-size TiO_2 catalysts. *Applied Catalysis B: Environmental,* 29, 327-336.

Nesheiwat, F.K. & Swanson, A.G. (2000). Clean contaminated sites using Fenton's reagent. *Chemical Engineering Progress,* 96, 61-66.

Oguz, E. ; Tortum, A. & Keskinler, B. (2008). Determination of the apparent rate constants of the degradation of humic substances by ozonation and modeling of the removal of humic substances from the aqueous solutions with neural network. *Journal of Hazardous Materials,* 157, 455–463.

Prakash, S.N. ; Manikandan, A. ; Govindarajan, L. & Vijayagopal, V. (2008). Prediction of biosorption efficiency for the removal of copper (II) using artificial neural networks. *Journal of Hazardous Materials,* 152, 1268–1275.

Qamar, M. ; Muneer, M. & Bahnemann, D. (2006). Heterogeneous photocatalysed degradation of two selected pesticide derivatives, triclopyr and daminozid in aqueous suspensions of titanium dioxide. *Journal of Environmental Management,* 80, 99-106.

Sadik, W.A. ; Nashed, A.W. & El-Demerdash, A.M. (2007). Photodecolourization of ponceau 4R by heterogeneous photocatalysis. *Journal of Photochemistry and Photobiology A: Chemistry,* 189, 135–140.

Salari, D. ; Daneshvar, N. ; Aghazadeh, F. & Khataee, A.R. (2005). Application of artificial neural networks for modeling of the treatment of wastewater contaminated with methyl tert-butyl ether (MTBE) by UV/H_2O_2 process. *Journal of Hazardous Materials*, B125, 205–210.

San, N. ; Kilic, M.; Tuiebakhova, Z. & Cinar, Z. (2007). Enhancement and modeling of the photocatalytic degradation of benzoic acid. *Journal of Advanced Oxidation Technologies*, 10, 43–50.

Strik, D.P.BT.B. ; Domnanovich, A.M ; Zani, L.; Braun, R. & Holubar, P. (2005). Prediction of trace compounds in biogas from anaerobic digestion using the MATLAB neural network toolbox. *Environmental Modelling & Software*, 20, 803-810.

Sychev, A.Y. & Isaak, V.G. (1995). Iron compounds and the mechanisms of the homogeneous catalysis of the activation of O_2 and H_2O_2 and of the oxidation of organic substrates. *Russian Chemical Reviews Articles*, 64, 1105-1129.

Toma, F.L. ; Guessasma, S. ; Klein, D. ; Montavon, G. ; Bertrand, G. & Coddet C. 2004. Neural computation to predict TiO_2 photocatalytic efficiency for nitrogen oxides removal. *Journal of Photochemistry and Photobiology A: Chemistry*, 165, 91–96.

Yu, R-F. ; Chen, H-W. ; Cheng, W-P. & Hsieh, P-H. (2009). Dosage control of the fenton process for color removal of textile wastewater applying ORP monitoring and artificial neural networks. *Journal of Environmental Engineering*, 135, 325-332.

Zhao, X. ; Yang, G. ; Wang, Y. & Gao, X. (2004). Photochemical degradation of dimethyl phthalate by Fenton reagent. *Journal of Photochemistry and Photobiology A: Chemistry*,161, 215–220.

7

Construction of Optimal Artificial Neural Network Architectures for Application to Chemical Systems: Comparison of Generalized Pattern Search Method and Evolutionary Algorithm

Matthias Ihme
Department of Aerospace Engineering, University of Michigan
Ann Arbor, MI 48109,
USA

1. Introduction

Artificial neural networks (ANNs) are computational models of their biological counterparts. They consists of densely interconnected computing units that work together to solve a specific problem. The information, which is acquired during a learning process, is stored in the synaptic weights of the internodal connections. The main advantage of neural networks is their ability to represent complex functions and the efficient storage of information. ANNs are frequently employed in applications involving data classification, function approximation, and signal processing (Haykin, 1994).

The topology of ANNs consists of an arrangement of neurons, which are equipped with a transfer function and synaptic weights, and the nodal connections. Despite these simple topological elements, the flexible arrangement of neurons and connections allows the generation of ANNs with arbitrary complexity. The resulting topological complexity, however, directly affects the network performance. The performance, or fitness, is a measure of the accuracy of a network in representing an input-output relation. For instance, network topologies with only few neurons and synaptic weights provide only limited flexibility in representing complex functions. They have therefore typically only a poor fitness. On the other side, complex networks that provide large flexibility in representing new data, can lead to poor generalizability and extensive computational costs for training and data retrieval (Yao, 1999). Considering the integration of such networks in large-scale simulations, data retrieval from such large networks can lead to a significant increase in overall computing time. Because of the inherent topological complexity it is apparent that the *a priori* identification of a network topology with near-optimal performance is a challenging task, and is often guided by heuristics or trial-and-error.

The design of a specific network topology with optimal performance can be formulated as an optimization problem. The choice of the method to solve this problem is determined by the inherent properties of the ANN (Miller et al., 1989):

1. The dimension of the architecture space is infinite since the number of neurons and nodal connections is unbounded.

2. Assessing the performance of a particular network topology usually requires the prior training of the network, which in itself is an optimization problem and usually time consuming.
3. The design parameters determining the topology of the network can be both of continuous and categorical type.
4. The objective function that quantifies the network performance with respect to the design variables is noisy and non-differentiable.
5. Different ANN topologies can lead to similar performance, implying that the solution space is multimodal.

Over recent years considerable research has been conducted on the evolution of topological structures of networks using evolutionary strategies (Bornholdt & Graudenz 1992; Fogel & Fogel 1990; Husken et al. 2005; Koza & Rice 1991; Miller et al. 1989; Porto et al. 1995; Tang et al. 1995 and references in Yao 1999). Evolutionary strategies (ESs) are global search algorithms and have frequently been used to find optimal network topologies and nodal transfer functions. ESs can conveniently be implemented in an existing code and do not require gradient information. Despite their popularity, ESs are known to be expensive, typically characterized by slow convergence, and usually lack formal convergence theory. Other methods which have been employed for the automatic design of near-optimal networks are so-called construction and destruction algorithms (Frean, 1990; Mozer & Smolensky, 1989), in which neurons are systematically added or deleted with the objective to improve the network fitness. These methods, however, search only in a restricted subset of possible network architectures (Angeline et al., 1994).

As an alternative to these optimization techniques Ihme et al. (2008) proposed to use a generalized pattern search (GPS) method for the generation of optimal ANNs. They applied the GPS method to the optimization of multi-layer perceptrons (MLPs), and considered the number of neurons, transfer functions, and the nodal connectivity as free parameters in the optimization problem. The GPS algorithm is a derivative-free, mesh-based optimization method and provides robust convergence properties (Audet & Dennis, 2003). To increase the efficiency of the GPS for computationally expensive problems, this method can be complemented by a surrogate representation, which was developed by Serafini (1998) and Booker et al. (1999).

The objective of this work is to utilize the GPS method and an evolutionary strategy for the generation of optimal artificial neural networks (OANNs) to approximate non-linear functions, that are, for instance, encountered in representing chemical systems. These chemical system can be formulated as:

$$\mathcal{D}(\underline{\phi}) = \underline{w}(\underline{\phi}) \,, \tag{1}$$

where $\mathcal{D}$ is a linear operator acting on $\underline{\phi}$ (in the simplest case, $\mathcal{D}$ is the temporal derivative ∂_t), $\underline{\phi} \in \mathbb{R}^{N+1}$ denotes the vector of N chemical species and temperature, and $\underline{w} : \mathbb{R}^{N+1} \to \mathbb{R}^{N+1}$ is a function, representing the chemical source terms and the heat release rate.

Chemical mechanisms often comprise thousands of reactions among hundreds of species. In numerical simulations of combustion systems the direct solution of transport equations for all of these species is usually not feasible. Alternative approaches, such as intrinsic low dimensional manifolds (Maas & Pope, 1992) or computational singular perturbation (Lam & Goussis, 1988) have been developed, in which a part of the chemical species are projected onto a lower dimensional manifold, resulting in a reduced chemical reaction mechanism. However, the necessary introduction of certain assumptions, required for reducing the mechanism, can result in a degradation of the accuracy and generality.

On the other side, tabulation techniques, such as conventional structured look-up tables, are often employed for the parameterization of thermochemical quantities. Since, however, the memory requirement for the tabulation rapidly increases with the number of independent parameters, this method imposes drastic restrictions when more than three or four independent parameters are used. Other tabulation techniques include the in situ adaptive tabulation (ISAT) (Pope, 1997) or solution mapping using piecewise polynomial approximation (PRISM) (Tonse et al., 1999).

Over recent years, ANNs have successfully been employed for the approximation of chemical systems (Blasco, Fueyo, Dopazo & Ballester, 1999; Blasco et al., 2000; Blasco, Fueyo, Larroya, Dopazo & Chen, 1999; Chen et al., 2000; Christo, Masri & Nebot, 1996; Christo, Masri, Nebot & Pope, 1996; Flemming et al., 2005; Ihme et al., 2009; Sen & Menon, 2008; 2010). Important advantages of ANNs over tabulation methods are the modest memory requirement, and cost-effective and smooth function representation. However, in many if not all of these applications *ad hoc* network topologies were used, that were not fully optimized for the particular problem, so that the optimal performance could not be achieved.

Motivated by the chemistry application, the objective of this work is to demonstrate the potential of OANNs for application to chemical reacting flows. To this end, two different chemical systems of increasing complexity are considered. Specifically, the first problem considers an one-step chemical reaction in a homogeneous flow, representing decaying turbulence. The particular advantage of this problem is that it allows us to systematically evaluate different ANN-representations and compare the results against other predictions. The second problem considers the unsteady three-dimensional combustion of a methane/hydrogen-air mixture in a technical-relevant burner system. For this, large-scale simulations are employed and the accuracy of ANNs and conventional tabulation methods are assesses in the context of high-performance computations of turbulent reacting flows.

In order to assess the ANN performance, we consider two metrics, namely the ANN fitness evaluation under static and dynamic conditions. To explain both metrics, we consider Eq. (1), in which the source term is now approximated through an ANN:

$$\mathcal{D}(\underline{\varphi}) = \underline{w}_{\mathcal{A}}(\underline{\varphi}) \,. \tag{2}$$

where $\underline{\varphi} = \underline{\phi} + \underline{\varepsilon}$ and $\underline{w}_{\mathcal{A}}$ is the source-term representation by the ANN. After writing $\underline{w}_{\mathcal{A}}$ as

$$\underline{w}_{\mathcal{A}} = \underline{w} + \underline{\Omega} \,, \tag{3}$$

with $\underline{\Omega}$ denoting the ANN approximation error, Eqs. (1) and (2) can be combined to derive the following expression for the evolution of the error $\underline{\varepsilon}$:

$$\mathcal{D}(\underline{\varepsilon}) = \underline{\Omega}(\underline{\phi}) + \underline{\varepsilon}\, \underline{w}'_{\mathcal{A}}(\underline{\phi}) \,. \tag{4}$$

This expression shows that the ANN-approximation error acts as a spurious source term on the solution $\underline{\phi}$. Depending on the functional form of $\underline{\Omega}$ and $\underline{w}_{\mathcal{A}}$, the error $\underline{\varepsilon}$ can either grow, decay, or cancel.

The static ANN analysis characterizes the ability of the network to accurately represent the function $\underline{w}$. For this, a large set of sample data is used to evaluate the network fitness following the ANN training process. This metric is widely-used and is typically referred to as "testing." As such, the static analysis allows for the assessment of the ANN approximation error $\underline{\Omega}$.

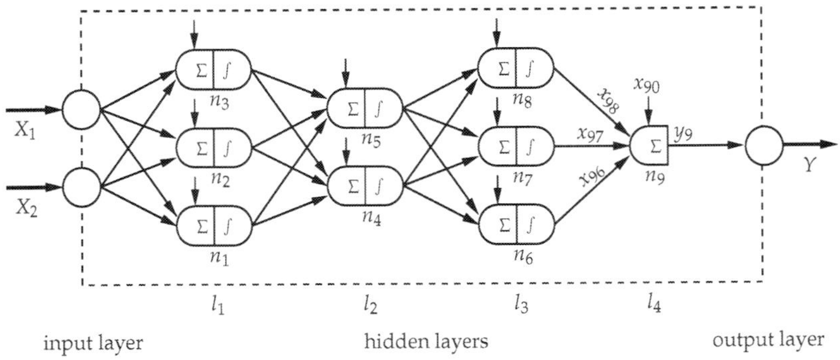

Fig. 1. Architecture of a multilayer perceptron, consisting of an input layer with two input channels X_1 and X_2, one output channel Y, and 4 hidden layers with, respectively, 3, 2, 3, and 1 neurons in each layer. The neurons in the hidden layers are denoted by n_i, with $i = 1, \ldots, 9$, and the number of neurons in this network is $|\underline{N}_N| = 9$.

Since ANNs are integrated into dynamic systems of the form of Eq. (2), a main shortcoming of this static analysis is that it does not account for the feedback on the solution vector $\underline{\varphi}$. In particular, small errors arising from the network approximation could either cancel, or – worse – induce a drift in the solution vector leading to long-time instability issues of the governing equations.

To address this issue, we will also assess the ANN-performance under dynamic conditions. To this end, the temporal evolution of the error $\underline{\varepsilon}$ in Eq. (4) is evaluated in order to assess the dynamic stability of the system. This metric, which we refer to as dynamic ANN performance measure, allows us to directly characterize feedback-effects of ANN-approximation errors on the solution. It will be shown in the second part of this article that this dynamic ANN performance evaluation provides more realistic estimates of the ANN-fitness potential, whereas the static ANN analysis gives typically too optimistic estimates.

The remainder of this article is organized as follows. Section 2 discusses the ANN model and describes the training process. The GPS method and ES are presented in Sec. 3. The performance of OANNs are assesses by considering two combustion-chemical problem of increasing complexity. Specifically, Sec. 4 considers the evolution of a chemical species in decaying homogeneous isotropic turbulence. The combustion process is described by a reversible one-step chemical reaction, in which the mixing and combustion are described by a Lagrangian Fokker-Planck model. In the second problem, OANNs are integrated into a high-fidelity large-eddy simulation to predict the turbulent combustion in a swirl-stabilized burner system of practical relevance. Model formulation, experimental setup and comparisons with experimental data and conventional tabulation methods are presented in Sec. 5, and conclusions are drawn in Sec. 6.

2. Artificial neural networks

In the following, the class of multilayer perceptrons (MLPs) is considered. A MLP, schematically shown in Fig. 1, consists of an input layer with N_I input channels, an output layer having N_O channels, and N_L hidden layers. The number of neurons in each hidden layer is denoted by $\underline{N}_N \in \mathbb{Z}^{N_L}$. The connectivity of the network is denoted by $\underline{\underline{C}}$, corresponding to a binary matrix, in which the element C_{ij} is unity if neurons i and j are connected and zero otherwise. The output y_i of neuron i is computed according to

$$y_i = \psi_i \left(\sum_{j=0}^{N_C} C_{ij} \omega_{ij} x_{ij} \right) , \tag{5}$$

where N_C is the number of connections in the network, ω_{ij} are the synaptic weights, and x_{ij} are the input signals. Note that $x_{i0} = -1$ is a threshold value. The transfer function of the neuron i is denoted by ψ_i. The synaptic weights in the network are adapted during the training process, which in itself represents an optimization problem and can be written as

$$\min_{\omega \in \mathbb{R}^{N_\omega}} E(\omega) , \tag{6}$$

where N_ω denotes the number of synaptic weights in the network, and $E : \mathbb{R}^{N_O \times N_t} \to \mathbb{R}$ is a measure of the error between the actual and desired output of the network. The number of training samples is denoted by N_t. In the following, E is defined as

$$E = \frac{1}{2N_t} \sum_{j=1}^{N_t} e^t(j) , \tag{7}$$

with

$$e^t(j) = \sum_{i=1}^{N_O} \left[Y_i(j) - Y_i^t(j) \right]^2 , \tag{8}$$

and $Y_i^t(j)$ represents the jth training sample of the output signal i.
The topology of a particular network is defined by its neural arrangement, consisting of the number of layers N_L and neurons per layer $\underline{N}_N$, the connectivity $\underline{\underline{C}}$, and the neural transfer functions $\underline{\psi}$. In the following, this network topology is formally written as

$$\mathcal{A} = \mathcal{A}(N_L, \underline{N}_N, \underline{\underline{C}}, \underline{\psi} | N_I, N_O, Y, J) , \tag{9}$$

in which the last four arguments are constrained by the problem and the desired performance of the ANN. The performance – or generalization potential – of a trained network can be characterized by the cost function J, which is evaluated using test samples that typically differ from the training data. Testing – or static ANN performance analysis – is done after training to evaluate the ability of the network in representing untrained samples. In the present work, the following cost function is used:

$$J(\mathcal{A}) = \log_{10} \left(\sqrt{ \frac{1}{N_s} \sum_{j=1}^{N_s} (e^s(j))^2 } \right) , \tag{10}$$

where N_s refers to the number of test samples, and the decadic logarithm is introduced to enlarge the resolution of the cost function.
The objective is to identify a particular network topology $\mathcal{A}$ that minimizes the cost function, or in other words, maximizes the generalizability. In the following, we will restrict our discussion to a multidimensional optimization problem that only includes continuous parameters, i.e., real- or integer-valued variables. For this, a network will be considered, in

which a single neuron in the last hidden layer is used having a linear transfer function,

$$\psi(s) = s\,. \tag{11}$$

A sigmoidal function,

$$\psi(s) = \gamma_1 \tanh(\gamma_2 s)\,, \tag{12}$$

is used for all other neurons in the $N_L - 1$ hidden layers. The parameters γ_1 and γ_2, characterizing the saturation and slope of the transfer function, are considered as free parameters that will be adjusted during the optimization process. Furthermore, the network architecture will be constrained to a fully connected feed-forward network. With this, the resulting optimization problem may be formulated as

$$\begin{aligned} \min_{N_L, \underline{N}_N, \underline{\gamma}} \quad & J(\mathcal{A}) \\ \text{subject to} \quad & N_L = N_L^{\max}\,, \\ & N_{N,i} \in \{0, 1, \ldots, N_N^{\max}\}, \qquad \text{for } i = 1, 2, \ldots, N_{L-1}\,, \\ & N_{N,N_L} = 1\,, \\ & \underline{\gamma} \in \mathcal{G}\,, \end{aligned} \tag{13}$$

where $\underline{\gamma} \in \mathbb{R}^{2\times(|\underline{N}_N|-1)}$, $\mathcal{G}$ denotes the bounded parameter space for the transfer function coefficients, and the number of neurons in all layers is denoted by $|\underline{N}_N|$.

In this context it is important to point out that the herein employed optimization method is not restricted to continuous variables, and can also be applied to the optimization of categorical or discrete variables. This has been discussed by Ihme et al. (2008), in which the connectivity and transfer functions were included in the optimization of the network topology.

3. Topological optimization

3.1 Generalized pattern search method

In the following, a generalized pattern search method is used to solve the optimization problem (13). The GPS method is a derivative-free method, in which a sequence of iterates is generated whose cost function is non-increasing (Audet & Dennis, 2003). All points at which the cost function is evaluated are restricted to lie on a mesh, and the limited point of the sequence of iterates corresponds to a local optimal solution that is defined with respect to a user-specified neighborhood. GPS methods for unbounded problems have been discussed and analyzed by Torczon (1997); they were later extended by Lewis & Torczon (1999; 2000) to bounded and linearly constrained problems.

The GPS algorithm, schematically shown in Fig. 2, proceeds in two steps, namely a search and a poll step. In the search step a finite set of search points are evaluated to facilitate a global exploration of the parameter space. Since the search step is not required for convergence, different strategies can be employed to identify a promising region in the parameter space that potentially results in an improved cost function. For instance, *a priori* knowledge, random sampling using Latin hypercube sampling (LHS) (McKay et al., 1979), or a surrogate can be employed. In the case of a surrogate, the cost function is approximated by a lower-dimensional model, whose evaluation is typically less expensive. This surrogate approximation is continuously updated during the simulation, and is then used to identify a new point with a potentially lower cost function. Kriging is frequently employed as surrogate

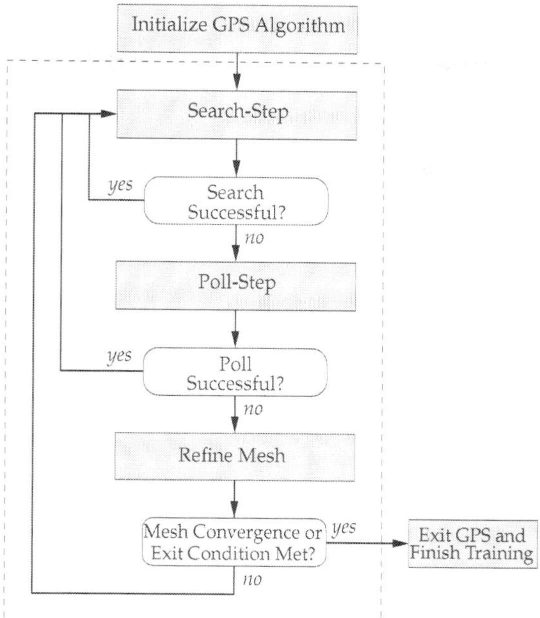

Fig. 2. Schematic diagram of the GPS algorithm.

approximation, and its multidimensional extension makes this method particularly attractive for application to network optimization.

In the case that the search step does not result in an improvement in the cost function, the algorithm continues with a poll step, which guarantees the convergence of the GPS algorithm. The poll step is restricted to a mesh that is constrained by the parameter space, and centered around the incumbent point $\underline{\eta}$. The vector $\underline{\eta}$ is of dimension $N_L - 1 + 2(|\underline{N}_N| - 1)$, and contains information about the number of non-linear neurons and coefficients in its respective non-linear transfer functions. At iteration k the mesh for the poll step is defined by

$$M_k = \left\{ \underline{\eta}_k + \Delta_k \underline{\underline{D}} \right\} \tag{14}$$

where $\Delta_k > 0$ is the mesh size parameter, which is obtained through a successive refinement of the mesh according to

$$\Delta_k = \tau^k \Delta_0 \, , \tag{15}$$

and $\tau = 1/2$ is used in the following application. The discrete directions in the parameter space that are evaluated during a poll step are specified by the matrix $\underline{\underline{D}}$ whose columns form a positive spanning set. That is, if $\underline{\underline{I}}$ denotes the identity matrix and $\underline{i}$ is the vector of ones, then $\underline{\underline{D}}$ is typically chosen as $\underline{\underline{D}} = [\underline{\underline{I}}, -\underline{i}]$ or $\underline{\underline{D}} = [\underline{\underline{I}}, -\underline{\underline{I}}]$ (Audet & Dennis, 2003). During the poll step the cost function is evaluated for these poll candidates. In the case that the poll step is unsuccessful the mesh is refined, and the algorithm continues with a new iteration, starting with a search step (see Fig. 2). This process continues until a convergence criterion is met or Δ_k reaches a minimum mesh size. More details on the algorithm and convergence proofs can be found in Audet & Dennis (2003) and extensions of the algorithm to include categorical parameters are discussed in Audet & Dennis (2000) and Abramson (2004).

3.2 Evolutionary strategy

In addition to the GPS method, an evolutionary strategy is used to solve Eq. (13). Evolutionary strategies have been proposed as simple mutation selection mechanisms by Rechenberg (1973), and were later generalized by Schwefel (1977; 1981). ES belongs to the general category of evolutionary algorithms, and is based on a collective evolution process of individuals in a population. The evolution of this population follows a biologically inspired process, consisting of a sequence of steps, involving mutation, recombination, and selection. In this work, a so-called (μ, λ)-ES is used, in which μ denotes the number of parents and λ corresponds to the number of offsprings in each generation. For completeness, the general form of the ES algorithm (Bäck & Schwefel, 1993) is briefly summarized.

In ES, the independent parameters for each individual network candidate are represented by a joint Gaussian distribution. This distribution is characterized by a zero expectation, a variance for each optimization parameter, and a rotation vector to ensure positive definiteness of the parameter covariance matrix. The mutation of each individual is sampled from the joint Gaussian distribution, which is modified by mutating the standard deviation and the rotation angle. More details on this mutation strategy and the self-adaptation, which are employed in the present work, can be found in Bäck & Schwefel (1993). For the recombination of individuals and strategy parameters, different mechanisms are used. Here, a discrete recombination of individuals is used, in which a new individual is produced from a random sampling of parameter components from two parents. For the recombination of the strategy parameters, i.e., mutation step size and rotation angle, pairwise intermediate recombination is used. Following the recombination and mutation, the ES continues with a deterministic selection step. In the (μ, λ)-ES, the μ-best candidates out of λ offsprings are selected. The best candidates are then used as parents in the subsequent generation. In the following application $\mu = 2$, $\lambda = 12$, and at most 80 iterations were used in the ES algorithm. It was found that the results for the optimal ANN topology showed some sensitivity to the initialization and the choice of the exogenous parameters in the ES algorithm. It is assumed that this sensitivity is mainly attributed to the heterogeneous search space, and the slow convergence of the ES.

4. Combustion in decaying homogeneous isotropic turbulence

4.1 Mathematical model

In the following problem, the mixing and reaction of fuel and oxidizer in decaying homogeneous isotropic turbulence are considered. The corresponding reaction equation can be written as

$$\mathrm{F} + r\mathrm{O} \rightleftarrows (1+r)\mathrm{P} \,. \tag{16}$$

The reaction rate w of this one-step reversible reaction follows an Arrhenius expression

$$\begin{aligned} w(Z,C) = {} & (1+r)A\exp\{-\beta\}\exp\left\{-\frac{\beta(1-C)}{C}\right\} \\ & \times \left[Z_{st}(1-Z_{st})\left(\frac{Z}{Z_{st}} - C\right)\left(\frac{1-Z}{1-Z_{st}} - C\right) - \frac{1}{K}C^2\right] , \end{aligned} \tag{17}$$

in which r is the stoichiometric coefficient, A is the frequency factor, β is the Zeldovich number, Z_{st} is the stoichiometric mixture fraction, and K is the equilibrium constant. Values for these

A	β	K	Z_{st}	r
80,000	4.0	100	0.5	1

Table 1. Parameters used for one-step chemical reaction.

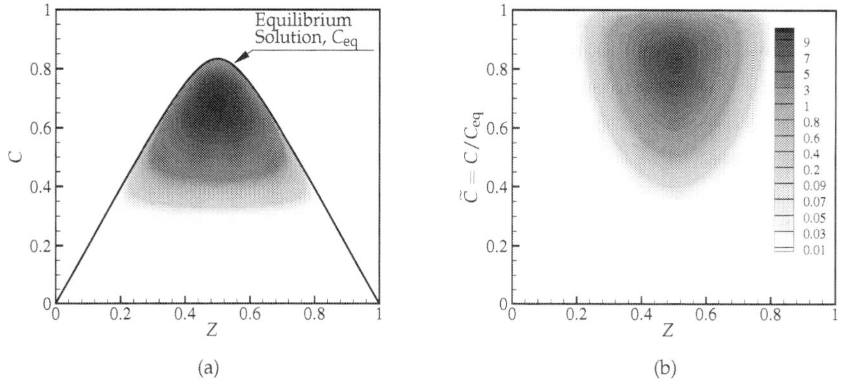

Fig. 3. Chemical reaction rate w as function of mixture fraction and reaction progress variable.

parameters are summarized in Tab. 1, and the interested reader is referred to Sripakagorn et al. (2004) for a more detailed discussion on the chemical reaction and parameter specifications. The chemical reaction rate given in Eq. (17) is only a function of mixture fraction Z and reaction progress variable C, corresponding to the non-dimensional temperature. Here, $Z \in [0,1]$ and $C \in [0, C_{eq}]$, and the reaction rate as function of Z and C is shown in Fig. 3(a). The progress variable at equilibrium, C_{eq}, is a function of Z, and is obtained by solving Eq. (17) for $w = 0$, resulting in:

$$C_{eq} = \frac{25}{24}\left(1 - \sqrt{1 - \frac{96}{25}Z(1-Z)}\right) , \tag{18}$$

in which prescribed values for Z_{st} and K from Tab. 1 are used. Using C_{eq}, a normalized progress variable can be introduced, $\widetilde{C} = C/C_{eq}$, so that $\widetilde{C} \in [0,1]$, and w as function of $\widetilde{C}$ and Z is illustrated in Fig. 3(b). In the following, OANNs are generated for the approximation of the chemical reaction rate as function of Z and $\widetilde{C}$.

The temporal evolution of reactants and products is obtained from the solution of a Lagrangian Fokker-Planck (LFP) model. In this model, the trajectories of individual particles in composition space are described by the solution of a set of stochastic differential equations (SDEs). For the one-step chemical reaction, which is fully characterized by mixture fraction Z and reaction progress variable C, the Fokker-Planck model can be written as (Fox, 2003):

$$\mathrm{d}\begin{pmatrix} Z \\ C \end{pmatrix} = \begin{pmatrix} 0 \\ w(Z,C) \end{pmatrix} \mathrm{d}t - \underline{\underline{A}}\begin{pmatrix} Z - \langle Z \rangle \\ C - \langle C \rangle \end{pmatrix} \mathrm{d}t + \underline{\underline{B}}\,\mathrm{d}\underline{W}(t) . \tag{19}$$

where W is a Wiener process, and the angular brackets denote the mean value which is defined by $\langle \phi \rangle = \int \phi P(\phi) \mathrm{d}\phi$ for $\phi = \{Z, C\}$. The PDF is denoted by P, and the scalar fluctuation ϕ' is computed as $\phi' = \phi - \langle\phi\rangle$. The drift matrix $\underline{\underline{A}}$ is given by

$$\underline{\underline{A}} = \begin{pmatrix} \langle\chi_Z\rangle/\langle Z'^2\rangle & 0 \\ 0 & \langle\chi_Z\rangle/\langle C'^2\rangle \end{pmatrix}, \tag{20}$$

and the diffusion matrix is

$$\underline{\underline{B}} = \begin{pmatrix} \langle\chi_Z\rangle \dfrac{(Z - Z_{\text{eq}}^-)(Z_{\text{eq}}^+ - Z)}{\langle (Z - Z_{\text{eq}}^-)(Z_{\text{eq}}^+ - Z)\rangle} & 0 \\ 0 & \langle\chi_C\rangle \dfrac{C(C_{\text{eq}} - C)}{\langle C(C_{\text{eq}} - C)\rangle} \end{pmatrix}^{1/2}, \tag{21}$$

with

$$Z_{\text{eq}}^{\pm} = \frac{1}{2}\left(1 \pm \sqrt{1 - 2C\left(1 - \frac{12}{25}C\right)}\right) \tag{22}$$

from Eq. (18). $\langle\chi_Z\rangle$ and $\langle\chi_C\rangle$ are the mean scalar dissipation rates for mixture fraction and progress variable, and are modeled by an exponential decay

$$\langle\chi_\phi\rangle = \langle\chi_\phi\rangle_0 \exp\{-t/\tau_\phi\}\ . \tag{23}$$

The initial particle distribution is sampled from a beta distribution with $\langle Z\rangle(t = 0) = \langle Z\rangle_0 = 0.5$ and $\langle Z'^2\rangle(t = 0) = \langle Z'^2\rangle_0 = 0.2$, and the progress variable is set to the equilibrium condition $C_{\text{eq}}(Z)$. The mean lifetime for the decay rates of $\langle\chi_Z\rangle$ and $\langle\chi_C\rangle$ correspond to the averaged decay constant from the direct numerical simulation by Sripakagorn et al. (2004) with $\tau_Z = 1.5$ and $\tau_C = 1.0$. Note that the time in Eq. (19) is non-dimensionalized by the initial large-eddy turnover time (Sripakagorn et al., 2004). Since the evolution of $\langle Z'^2\rangle$ obeys the ODE $d_t\langle Z'^2\rangle = -\langle\chi_Z\rangle$ and $\lim_{t\to\infty}\langle Z'^2\rangle(t) = 0$, the initial condition for $\langle\chi_Z\rangle$ is $\langle\chi_Z\rangle_0 = \langle Z'^2\rangle/\tau_Z$, and $\langle\chi_C\rangle_0$ is set to 0.25. After the initialization of 2×10^6 particles, the LFP model is advanced over $T = 10$ non-dimensional time units with a step size of $dt = 1 \times 10^{-3}$. In order to allow for a direct comparison of the different simulations, the increment in the Wiener process is kept identical for all runs.

4.2 Network optimization

The chemical source term, given in Eq. (17), is approximated by optimal ANNs. For this, GPS and ES are used to identify optimal network topologies that result in the lowest approximation error. For the network optimization the following constraints on the topological parameter space are imposed: The maximum number of hidden layers (including the last linear layer) is $N_L^{\max} = 3$, and the maximum number of non-linear neurons per hidden layer is restricted to $N_L^{\max} = 8$. Only fully connected networks are considered, and sigmoidal transfer functions are used in all non-linear neurons. The free parameters γ_1 and γ_2 in Eq. (12) are adjusted during the optimization process. Since the GPS algorithm is a mesh-based method these parameters are constrained to $0.4 \leq \gamma_1 \leq 1.2$ and $1 \leq \gamma_2 \leq 5$ having a maximum mesh size of $\Delta\gamma_1^{\max} = 0.4$ and $\Delta\gamma_2^{\max} = 1$, respectively, and the minimum mesh size is $\Delta\gamma_1^{\min} = \Delta\gamma_2^{\min} = 10^{-4}$.
To evaluate the fitness of a particular network candidate, the synaptic weights are first adjusted using a supervised learning strategy. In this technique, a set of training data is presented to the network and the weights are adjusted to reproduce the input-output relation. The training set consists of 50,000 randomly chosen samples, and a Levenberg-Marquardt

algorithm (Hagan et al., 1996) is used to iteratively adjust the synaptic weights. Since this training step is computationally expensive only a maximum of 100 iterations in the Levenberg-Marquardt algorithm are used to train each individual network. Although typically more iterations are necessary to ensure that the synaptic weights are fully converged, it was concluded that this number of iterations is sufficient to assess the fitness potential of a particular network architecture. After an optimal network architecture is identified by the optimization algorithm, this ANN is further trained until the synaptic weights are fully converged (see Fig. 2). It was found that the outcome of the training process shows some sensitivity to the initialization of the synaptic weights that are typically sampled from a uniform distribution. To allow for an objective comparison between different optimization methods, this sensitivity is here eliminated by initializing all synaptic weights with $\omega = 0.1$. For the evaluation of the static performance of each network candidate during the GPS, the cost function (10) is evaluated using $N_s = 50{,}000$ test samples.

4.3 Static ANN performance analysis

Results from the GPS and ES network optimization are presented in Tab. 2. The second column in this table lists the network architecture of the optimal ANN. The static network fitness, characterized by the cost-function, is shown in the third column, and the last column presents the memory requirement which is necessary to store the network architecture. In addition to these optimal network structures, results for conventional look-up tables are also presented. For this, the chemical source term, Eq. (17), is tabulated in terms of Z and $\widetilde{C}$ using an equidistant grid.

OANN/Table	Architecture	Cost Function	Iterations	Memory [kB]
GPS-OANN	7-8-1	-3.289/-3.727	876	7
ES-OANN	7-4-1	-3.077/-3.144	960	4
ANN (fixed $\underline{\gamma}$)	7-8-1	-3.480	–	7
Table	50 × 50	-2.023	–	20
Table	100 × 100	-2.624	–	78
Table	200 × 200	-3.228	–	313
Table	300 × 300	-3.579	–	703
Table	400 × 400	-3.831	–	1,250
Table	500 × 500	-4.022	–	1,953

Table 2. Comparison of OANN architecture and performance obtained from GPS and ES with conventional tabulation. Comparisons with conventional tabulation techniques are also summarized, showing results for tables with increasing grid resolution.

The optimal network structure that was returned from the GPS algorithm consists of a 7-8-1 ANN. This architecture was found after 876 function evaluations in the 34-dimensional parameter space. The cost function of this GPS-OANN is $J(\mathcal{A}) = -3.289$, and was further reduced to $J(\mathcal{A}) = -3.727$ during the training following the GPS optimization. The evolution of $J(\mathcal{A})$ for the GPS-OANN is shown in Fig. 4(a). From this figure it can be seen that after a transition phase the cost function decays continuously, and the evaluation of J after 100 iterations is adequate to assess the fitness potential of a particular network structure.

The coefficients in the neural transfer functions for the GPS-OANN are shown in Fig. 4(b). Note that these parameters are typically kept constant for all neurons with values for the saturation $\gamma_1 = 1.075$ and the slope $\gamma_2 = 2.0$ (Haykin, 1994). It is interesting to point out that the transfer function coefficients in the GPS-OANN are considerably different from these

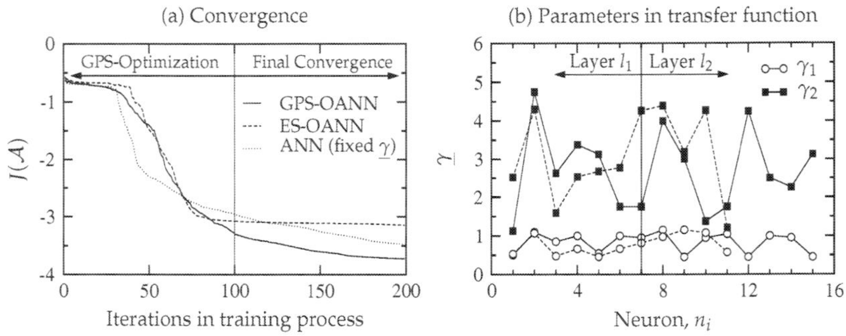

Fig. 4. Performance evolution of the 7-8-1 OANN obtained from the GPS method and optimal coefficients in the neural transfer functions. The dotted line in the left panel shows the fitness for a 7-8-1 ANN having constant transfer function coefficients with $\gamma_1 = 1.075$ and $\gamma_2 = 2.0$ for all neurons.

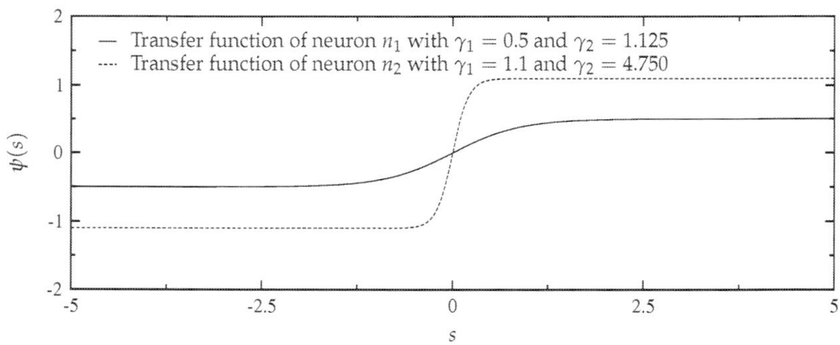

Fig. 5. Transfer function for the first two neurons in the OANN obtained from the GPS algorithm.

values, showing distinct spreading for all neurons. As an example, the transfer functions for the first two neurons are shown in Fig. 5. While γ_1 for the transfer function of the second neuron is generally in good agreement with the frequently employed value of 1.075, the saturation and the slope for the first neuron are considerably different, resulting in a distinctly different neural response characteristics between both neurons. To emphasize the effect of adaptive transfer function coefficients on the network fitness, a 7-8-1 network with constant γ_1 and γ_2 for all neurons is trained resulting in a cost function of $J(\mathcal{A}) = -3.480$. Note, however, that $J(\mathcal{A})$ corresponds to the decadic logarithm of the L_2 error norm. Therefore, this difference of seven percent in the cost function corresponds to an deviation of more than 75 percent in the L_2-norm.

The optimal topology identified by the evolutionary algorithm consists of a 7-4-1 ANN, and was obtained from a total ES population of 960 networks candidates, which have been evolved over 80 generations with two parents and 12 offsprings per generation. The termination of the ES optimization after 80 iterations was mainly motivated by the argument to have comparable computational cost for both GPS and ES optimization. The cost function of the ES-OANN is

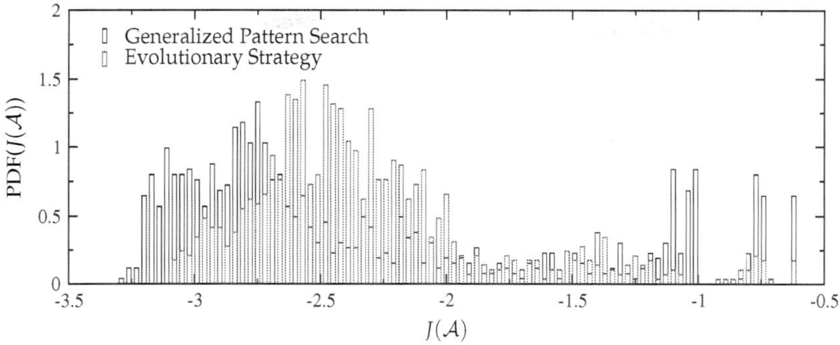

Fig. 6. Probability density function of the cost function evaluated from all network candidates that were evaluated during the GPS and ES optimization.

$J(\mathcal{A}) = -3.144$, and the evolution of $J(\mathcal{A})$ is shown by the dashed line in Fig. 4(a). The initial convergence of the cost function for the ES-OANN is similar to that of the GPS-OANN; however, $J(\mathcal{A})$ decreases only marginally after 80 iterations. This apparent saturation of the fitness can primarily be attributed to the small number of neurons in the second layer. The transfer function coefficients for this network are illustrated in Fig. 4(b). It is interesting to point out that both ES and GPS give similar values for slope and saturation of the neural transfer function in the first hidden layer.

A statistical comparison of the fitness of all network candidates that were evaluated during the GPS and ES optimization is shown in Fig. 6. The distributions of the network performance from both optimization methods is considerably different. For instance, the bimodal PDF from the GPS optimization is strongly skewed towards lower values of $J(\mathcal{A})$. Network candidates with poor fitness were mainly obtained from the random sampling of the parameter space during the search step. In comparison, the PDF from the ES is nearly unimodal and peaks around $J(\mathcal{A}) \approx -2.5$. In this context it is important to point out that the outcome of the ES method is sensitive to the initial conditions and prescribed step size. Therefore, it can be anticipated that a different set of parameters and initial conditions can potentially lead to a different optimal network topology.

In addition to the smooth function representation, a main advantage of ANNs over conventional tabulation techniques is the high knowledge density. This is reflected by the modest memory requirement necessary to store a network architecture. While the ANN-memory demand is nearly independent from the number of input parameters, the storage requirements for look-up tables grows exponentially with the dimensionality of the function. A comparison of the knowledge-density, which is here defined as the ratio between accuracy and memory requirement, is illustrated in Fig. 7. This figure illustrates that ANNs perform significantly better than conventional look-up tables, and for equivalent accuracy the memory savings can be in excess of two orders of magnitude.

4.4 Dynamic ANN Performance Analysis

In the previous section, the fitness of the network architectures obtained from GPS and ES were compared with the conventional tabulation method. It was found that the performance of the GPS-OANN is comparable to that of the tabulation method with a resolution of more than 300 grid points in both Z and $\widetilde{C}$ directions. In this static comparison, a homogeneously

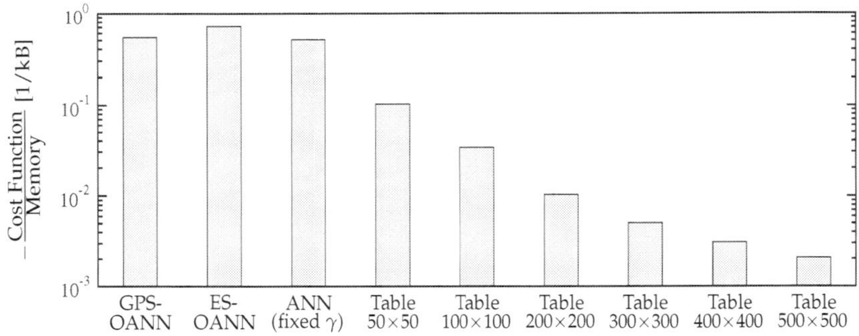

Fig. 7. Comparison of the knowledge-density between ANNs and conventional tabulation techniques. The knowledge density is defined as the ratio between static network fitness and memory requirement.

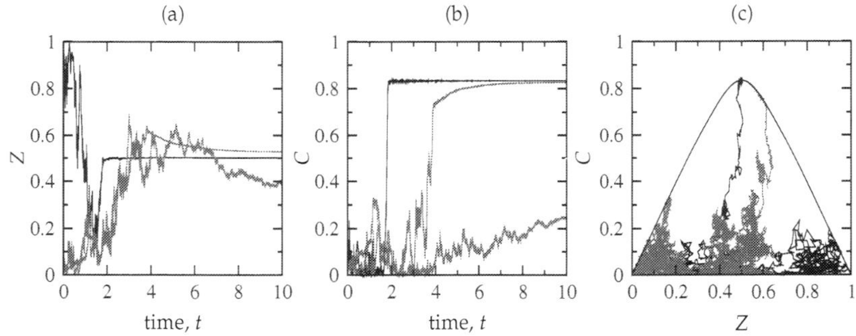

Fig. 8. Evolution of the chemical composition of three representative particles: (a) mixture fraction; (b) reaction progress variable; and (c) corresponding trajectories in composition space.

distributed set of random test samples was used for the performance evaluation. However, the reaction rate which is represented by ANNs and look-up tables corresponds to a source term in a partial differential equation describing the evolution of a chemical system. The primary variable which is of interest in the characterization of this system is the species composition, whose prediction is directly affected by the accurate representation of the chemical source term. This chemical reaction evolves along trajectories that typically occupy only a small region in composition space. This suggests that the static analysis as discussed in the previous section could have only limited relevance for the present application. Therefore, a dynamic OANN performance analysis is conducted in order to assess feedback-effects of ANN approximation errors on the evolution of the dynamic system.

Before analyzing the performance of OANNs and tabulation methods, the evolution of the chemical system as described by the LFP model, Eq. (19), is briefly discussed. The temporal evolutions of the mixture fraction and reaction progress variable for three representative particles are shown in Figs. 8(a) and (b), and the corresponding trajectories in Z-C-composition space are illustrated in Fig. 8(c). Following an initial phase of intense

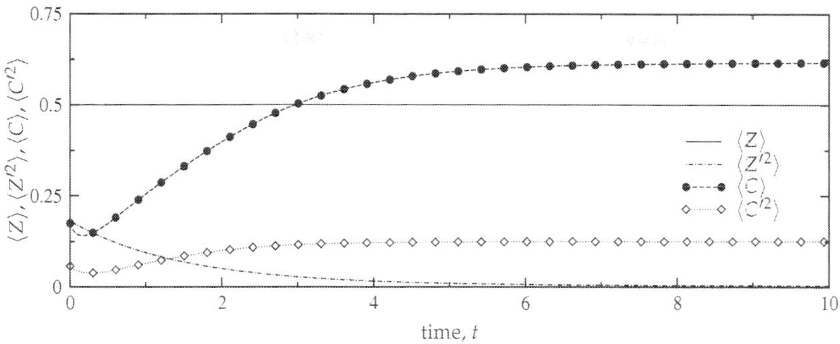

Fig. 9. Statistical evolution of the chemical system.

mixing, the trajectories of the particles, shown by the black and blue lines, converge and reach after approximately two respectively four eddy turn-over times the equilibrium condition. The trajectory of the particle shown by the red line indicates that the particle fails to reach a stably burning state. This can mainly be attributed to the initially large fluctuations in mixture fraction and progress variable.

The statistical evolution of the LFP model is illustrated in Fig. 9, in which the first two moments of mixture fraction and reaction progress variable are shown. From the governing equation for the mean mixture fraction, viz. $\mathrm{d}_t\langle Z\rangle = 0$, follows that $\langle Z\rangle$ is constant and equal to the initial condition, and the mixture fraction variance decays as $\langle Z'^2\rangle(t) = \langle Z'^2\rangle_0 \exp\{-t/\tau_Z\}$. The evolution of the reaction progress variable, which is equal to the normalized temperature, is shown by the dashed line in Fig. 9. Starting from the initial condition, the mixture slowly ignites and with increasing time $\langle C\rangle$ approaches a steady condition. Note that this final state corresponds to the equilibrium condition; however, the maximum temperature $\langle C\rangle = C_{\mathrm{eq}}(\langle Z\rangle) = 5/6$, is not reached, which is also evidenced by the non-vanishing progress variable variance, shown by the dotted line in Fig. 9.

Instead of performing the costly evaluation of the chemical source term from Eq. (17), in the following $w(Z, C)$ is obtained from the GPS-OANN and look-up tables. This comparison allows us to critically assess effects of approximation errors in the source term representation on the evolution of the reaction progress variable. To quantify this error, the following norm is used:

$$L_2^2(\langle C\rangle) = \frac{1}{T}\int_0^T [\langle C\rangle - \langle C\rangle_{\mathrm{ref}}]^2 \mathrm{d}t\,, \tag{24}$$

where the subscript "ref" denotes the solution obtained from the analytical evaluation of the chemical source term, and T corresponds to the simulation time.

Comparisons of the L_2-norm, obtained from the simulations with GPS-OANN and look-up tables, are summarized in Tab. 3. From these results the following observations can be made. First, the solution from the tabulation exhibits a monotonic convergence with quadratic convergence rate. Second, the overall accuracy of the results from the GPS-OANN simulation for this dynamic application is comparable to a tabulation having approximately 80×80 grid point resolution. This is different to the findings from the static analysis of Sec. 4.3. The main reasons for this are the non-linearity in the diffusion matrix $\underline{\underline{B}}$ and the rather strict constraints for $N_{\mathrm{L}}^{\mathrm{max}}$ and $N_{\mathrm{N}}^{\mathrm{max}}$ in Eq. (13). In this ANN optimization, the GPS method was restricted to include only two non-linear hidden layers with a maximum of eight neurons per layer. By

Architecture	$L_2(\langle C\rangle)$
GPS-OANN	4.820×10^{-4}
Table 50×50	1.038×10^{-3}
Table 100×100	2.712×10^{-4}
Table 200×200	6.294×10^{-5}
Table 300×300	2.549×10^{-5}
Table 400×400	1.336×10^{-5}
Table 500×500	5.321×10^{-6}

Table 3. Comparison of the convergence error for the solution of the LFP model.

relaxing these constraints and extending the search space to include a larger number of layers and neurons, the ANN topology becomes more flexible, and will lead to improvements in the ANN performance characteristics. To demonstrate this, an additional GPS optimization was conducted in which four hidden layers with a maximum of eight neurons per non-linear layer were used for the network optimization. For training and performance evaluation of the GPS network candidates respectively 100,000 samples were used, and all synaptic weights were initialized with random numbers. The GPS algorithm returned as optimal topology a 8-8-8-1 network having a cost function of $J(\mathcal{A}) = -4.242$. The application of this larger OANN in the LFP model resulted in an improvement of the L_2 norm by more than 20 % compared to the 7-8-1 GPS-OANN.

To quantify the approximation quality of the ANN and the look-up table, the error surface is compared in Fig. 10. For this, the error Ω is defined as the difference between ANN approximation $w_{\mathcal{A}}(Z, \widetilde{C})$ and the corresponding analytical value (see Eq. (3)). The apparent oscillations in the error surface are an indication for underfitting, and the small differences in the chemical source term representation can lead to incremental deviations in the particle trajectories. The analysis of the ANN function representation suggests that the training of networks with a larger number of samples or a biased distribution of sample points, using for instance an acception-rejection algorithm (Ihme et al., 2008), can lead to a further reduction of this error.

5. Turbulent combustion in a swirl-stabilized burner system

In the previous section, the advantages of optimal ANNs in application to a zero-dimensional combustion problem were discussed. The present section extends this analysis by considering the unsteady turbulent combustion in a technical-relevant burner system. In this application, the large-eddy simulation (LES) technique in combination with a flamelet-based combustion model is employed for predicting the turbulent reacting flow field, heat release, and pollutant formation. These high-fidelity LES computations of turbulent reacting flows are typically performed on massively parallel computing architectures. As such, the utilization of ANNs for chemistry representation and function approximation can provide significant benefits over conventional look-up tables in at least the following three aspects. First, the reduction in storage requirements allows to perform these large-scale combustion simulations on computing architectures with restricted memory. Second, the information retrieval from ANNs amounts to a direct function evaluation which is typically more efficient than table-interpolation. In addition, the smooth function representation of ANNs can result in improved model accuracy and faster convergence.

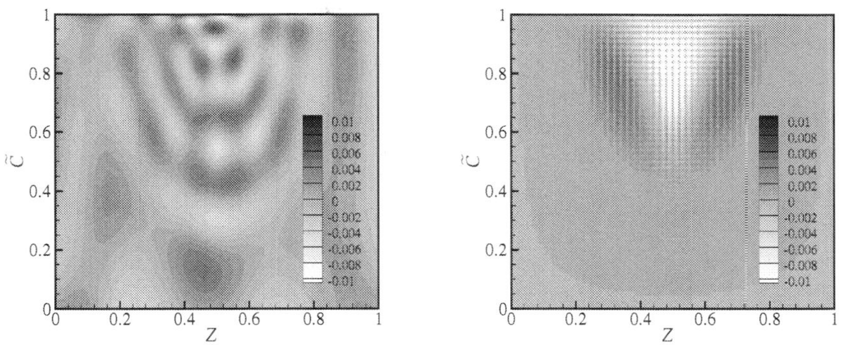

(a) GPS-OANN (b) Table: 100 × 100

Fig. 10. Error surface $\Omega(Z,\widetilde{C})$, showing the difference between the source term approximation from ANN (a) and tabulation (b) and the analytical expression from Eq. (17).

In the following, the potential of ANNs in application to turbulent reacting flows will be assessed, and qualitative comparisons with conventional look-up tables will be presented. The mathematical formulation and governing equations that are solved in the large-eddy simulation are summarized in the next section, and results of the OANN-technique in static and dynamic applications are presented in Secs. 5.3 and 5.4.

5.1 Mathematical formulation and combustion model

The LES technique is based on the separation of large and small scales in a turbulent flow. The decomposition into the different scales is achieved by applying a filtering operator to the field quantities (Sagaut, 1998). Specifically, a Favre-filtered quantity of a scalar ϕ is defined as

$$\widetilde{\phi}(t,\underline{x}) = \frac{1}{\overline{\rho}}\int \rho(t,\underline{y})\phi(t,\underline{y})G(\underline{y},\underline{x};\Delta)\mathrm{d}\underline{y}\,, \tag{25}$$

where ρ is the density, Δ is the filter width and G is the filter-kernel. The time is denoted by t and $\underline{x}$ corresponds to the spatial coordinate. The residual field is then defined as $\phi''(t,\underline{x}) = \phi(t,\underline{x}) - \widetilde{\phi}(t,\underline{x})$, and Favre-filtered quantities are related to Reynolds-filtered quantities by $\overline{\rho}\widetilde{\phi} = \overline{\rho\phi}$.

In the following, the Favre-filtered form of the Navier-Stokes equations are solved in the low-Mach number limit. These equations, describing the conservation of mass and momentum, can be written as

$$\widetilde{\mathcal{D}}_t\overline{\rho} = -\overline{\rho}\nabla\cdot\widetilde{\underline{u}}\,, \tag{26a}$$

$$\overline{\rho}\widetilde{\mathcal{D}}_t\widetilde{\underline{u}} = -\nabla\overline{p} + \nabla\cdot\overline{\underline{\underline{\sigma}}} + \nabla\cdot\overline{\underline{\underline{\sigma}}}^{\mathrm{res}} + \overline{\rho}\underline{g}\,, \tag{26b}$$

where

$$\overline{\underline{\underline{\sigma}}} = 2\overline{\rho}\widetilde{\nu}\left(\widetilde{\underline{\underline{S}}} - \frac{1}{3}(\nabla\cdot\widetilde{\underline{u}})\underline{\underline{I}}\right) \qquad \text{and} \qquad \overline{\underline{\underline{\sigma}}}^{\mathrm{res}} = \overline{\rho}\widetilde{\underline{u}}\widetilde{\underline{u}} - \overline{\rho}\widetilde{\underline{u}\underline{u}} \tag{27}$$

are the filtered viscous stress tensor and the residual stress tensor, respectively. In these equations, $\widetilde{\underline{u}}$ is the filtered velocity vector, $\overline{p}$ is the filtered pressure, $\underline{g}$ is the body force, $\widetilde{\nu}$ is the filtered kinematic viscosity, $\widetilde{\underline{\underline{S}}}$ is the filtered strain rate tensor, and $\widetilde{\mathcal{D}}_t \equiv \partial_t + \widetilde{\underline{u}} \cdot \nabla$ is the substantial derivative. The residual stress tensor, appearing as unclosed term in the momentum equations, is modeled by a dynamic Smagorinsky model (Germano et al., 1991; Lilly, 1992).

In addition to the residual stresses, the filtered density and kinematic viscosity are also unknown and are dependent on the temperature and the species distribution in the flame. To provide information about these quantities, a combustion model is employed which relates the density and all other thermochemical quantities to a reduced set of reaction coordinates.

In the present work, the flamelet/progress variable (FPV) approach (Pierce & Moin, 2004) is used for the prediction of the turbulent reactive flow field. This model is based on the steady laminar flamelet equations (Peters, 1983; 1984), in which all thermochemical quantities are obtained from the solution of the steady flamelet equations. These quantities are parameterized in terms of mixture fraction Z and scalar dissipation rate χ_Z. However, for reasons which are outlined in Pierce & Moin (2004) and Ihme et al. (2005), in the FPV model the scalar dissipation rate is replaced by a reaction progress variable C. This reactive scalar corresponds to a linear combination of major product mass fractions, and is here defined as $C = Y_{CO_2} + Y_{CO} + Y_{H_2O} + Y_{H_2}$. With this, all thermochemical quantities, denoted by $\underline{\phi}$, can then be written as $\underline{\phi} = \underline{\mathcal{G}}_{\phi}(Z, C)$, where $\underline{\mathcal{G}}$ denotes the FPV chemistry library, and $\widetilde{\underline{\phi}}$ is obtained by employing a presumed PDF approach, in which the joint PDF of Z and C is modeled by a beta distribution for the mixture fraction and a mixture fraction-conditioned Dirac function for the progress variable (Pierce & Moin, 2004). The Favre-filtered form of all thermochemical quantities can then be written as $\widetilde{\underline{\phi}} = \widetilde{\underline{\mathcal{G}}}_{\phi}(\widetilde{Z}, \widetilde{Z''^2}, \widetilde{C})$. In addition to the solution of the Favre-filtered Navier-Stokes equations, the FPV model requires also the solution of the Favre-filtered conservation equations for mixture fraction, progress variable, and residual mixture fraction variance, which is denoted by $\widetilde{Z''^2}$. These equations can be written as

$$\overline{\rho}\widetilde{\mathcal{D}}_t\widetilde{Z} = \nabla \cdot (\overline{\rho}\widetilde{\alpha}\nabla\widetilde{Z}) + \nabla \cdot \underline{\tau}_Z^{\text{res}} , \tag{28a}$$

$$\overline{\rho}\widetilde{\mathcal{D}}_t\widetilde{C} = \nabla \cdot (\overline{\rho}\widetilde{\alpha}\nabla\widetilde{C}) + \nabla \cdot \underline{\tau}_C^{\text{res}} + \overline{\rho}\widetilde{\dot{\omega}}_C , \tag{28b}$$

$$\overline{\rho}\widetilde{\mathcal{D}}_t\widetilde{Z''^2} = \nabla \cdot (\overline{\rho}\widetilde{\alpha}\nabla\widetilde{Z''^2}) + \nabla \cdot \underline{\tau}_{\widetilde{Z''^2}}^{\text{res}} - 2\overline{\rho}\widetilde{\underline{u}''Z''} \cdot \nabla\widetilde{Z} - \overline{\rho}\widetilde{\chi}_Z^{\text{res}} , \tag{28c}$$

where $\widetilde{\alpha}$ is the filtered diffusivity, $\widetilde{\dot{\omega}}_C$ is the chemical source term of the progress variable. The residual scalar fluxes $\underline{\tau}_{\psi}^{\text{res.}} = \overline{\rho}\widetilde{\underline{u}}\widetilde{\psi} - \overline{\rho}\widetilde{\underline{u}\psi}$, turbulent scalar transport $\widetilde{\underline{u}''Z''}$, and scalar dissipation rate $\widetilde{\chi}_Z^{\text{res}}$ are modeled using turbulence closure formulations.

In the LES computation, information about the filtered quantities of density $\overline{\rho}$, chemical source term for the progress variable $\widetilde{\dot{\omega}}_C$, kinematic viscosity $\widetilde{\nu}$, and molecular diffusivity $\widetilde{\alpha}$ are required. In addition, for the computation of statistical properties of the flame structure, the filtered temperature $\widetilde{T}$, and mass fractions of CO_2, H_2O and other species are also obtained from the state relation. In order to increase the resolution in the direction of the mixture fraction variance, the unmixedness $\widetilde{S} = \widetilde{Z''^2}/(\widetilde{Z}(1-\widetilde{Z}))$ is introduced and all thermochemical quantities, which are of importance for the numerical simulation, are then parameterized as

$$\widetilde{\underline{\phi}} = \widetilde{\underline{\mathcal{G}}}_{\phi}(\widetilde{Z}, \widetilde{S}, \widetilde{C}) , \tag{29}$$

and $\widetilde{\phi} = (\overline{\rho}, \widetilde{\omega}_C, \widetilde{\nu}, \widetilde{\alpha}, \widetilde{T}, \widetilde{Y}_{CO_2}, \widetilde{Y}_{H_2O})^T$. This information is made accessible during the simulation through a structured look-up table or OANNs.

5.2 Experimental configuration

The SMH1-flame from a series of bluff-body/swirl-stabilized flame experiments is used to analyze the effects due to errors in the table interpolation and in the ANN approximation on the statistical flow field quantities in the context of an LES application.

The burner configuration (see Fig. 11) of this well-characterized flame consists of a central fuel nozzle of 3.6 mm diameter which is surrounded by a bluff body with $D_{ref} = 50$ mm diameter. Swirling air at an axial bulk velocity of $U_s = 42.8$ m/s is supplied through an annulus of 10 mm width. The burner is surrounded by a coflowing air stream with an axial velocity of $U_e = 20$ m/s. The fuel consists of a methane/hydrogen mixture in a volumetric ratio of 1:1. The bulk exit velocity of the fuel stream is $U_J = 140.8$ m/s. The geometric swirl number for this configuration is $S_g = 0.32$. The turbulent flow field of this flame series was measured by Kalt et al. (2002) and Al-Abdeli & Masri (2003), species measurements were performed by Kalt et al. (2002) and Masri et al. (2004), and all experimental results are available from Masri (2006).

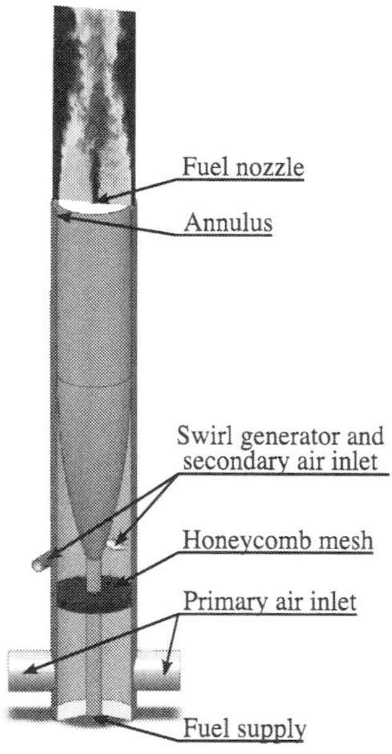

Fig. 11. Schematic of the swirl-stabilized burner (Masri, 2006).

The Favre-filtered transport equations for mass, momentum, mixture fraction, progress variable, and residual mixture fraction variance are solved in cylindrical coordinates (Pierce & Moin, 2004). The computational domain is $5\,D_{ref} \times 3\,D_{ref} \times 2\pi$ in axial, radial, and circumferential directions, respectively. The radial direction is discretized by 230 unevenly spaced grid points concentrated in the shear layer region surrounding the fuel jet and swirling annulus. The grid in axial direction uses 192 points and is stretched in downstream direction while the circumferential direction is equally spaced and uses 64 points.

The turbulent inflow profiles for the fuel nozzle and annulus are computed from a separate pipe flow simulation by enforcing the bulk axial and azimuthal velocity reported in the experiment. The GRI 2.11 mechanism (Bowman et al., 1997) is used for the description of the chemistry, consisting of 279 chemical reactions among 49 species.

5.3 Static ANN performance analysis

The accuracy, memory requirements, and computational cost associated with the table interpolation and the network evaluation are addressed in this section.

In the following, each thermochemical quantity is represented by one network, whose architecture is obtained from the GPS optimization. In this optimization process, the maximum size of the network is restricted to $N_{\mathrm{L}} = 5$ hidden layers, in which the last layer contains only one linear neuron. The maximum number of neurons in the remaining four layers is set to $N_{\mathrm{N}}^{\mathrm{max}} = 8$, having a sigmoidal transfer function. The coefficients in the transfer function, Eq. (12), are kept equal and constant for all neurons with $\gamma_1 = 1.075$ and $\gamma_2 = 2.0$. The training set used for adjusting the synaptic weights consists of 50,000 samples, and 1.2×10^6 data samples are used to evaluate the network fitness, defined in Eq. (10). The optimization of the networks for each thermochemical quantity is performed in parallel and takes approximately three days.

Quantity	OANN Architecture
$\overline{\rho}$	4-8-4-4-1
$\widetilde{\dot{w}}_C$	6-6-8-4-1
$\widetilde{\nu}$	7-8-8-1
$\widetilde{\alpha}$	8-8-8-1
$\widetilde{T}$	8-4-7-8-1
$\widetilde{Y}_{CO_2}$	4-8-8-4-1
$\widetilde{Y}_{H_2O}$	3-8-8-8-1

Table 4. Architecture of the OANNs identified from the GPS algorithm for all thermochemical species in the LES calculation. The connectivity corresponds to a fully-connected feed-forward network with sigmoidal transfer function for all non-linear neurons.

The optimal architectures for the seven networks are summarized in Tab. 4. This table shows that all OANNs except those for $\widetilde{\nu}$ and $\widetilde{\alpha}$ have four non-linear layers and considerably different neural arrangements. These results support the assumption that a separate ANN for each thermochemical quantity provides greater flexibility in obtaining an optimal fitness characteristic.

Table 5 compares the memory requirements and the accuracy between four structured tables and GPS-OANNs. The accuracy of the table increases with increasing resolution. Note, however, that the finest table with 64 million grid points requires 3.4 GB of memory which is typically not available on massively parallel systems. The fitness of all OANNs is comparable to that of a tabulation with a $400 \times 50 \times 400$ resolution. However, the memory requirement to store the network is approximately 5,000 times smaller.

Figure 12 shows regression plots for two structured tables and the optimal ANNs for the temperature and the chemical source term. It is interesting to point out that the scattering for the chemical source term increases with decreasing values in the ANN representation, which might affect the solution of the flame structure in equilibrium-near regions in an LES application.

Table size	Mem. [MB]	Cost function						
		$\overline{\rho}$	$\widetilde{\omega}_C$	$\widetilde{\nu}$	$\widetilde{\alpha}$	$\widetilde{T}$	$\widetilde{Y}_{CO_2}$	$\widetilde{Y}_{H_2O}$
GPS-OANN	0.1	-2.48	-2.67	-2.52	-2.65	-2.49	-1.98	-2.62
100×13×100	7	-1.54	-1.81	-1.84	-1.83	-1.81	-1.61	-1.79
200×25×200	53	-1.86	-2.15	-2.16	-2.17	-2.12	-2.12	-2.10
400×50×400	427	-2.55	-2.78	-2.72	-2.83	-2.66	-2.07	-2.91
800×100×800	3,417	-2.55	-2.98	-2.79	-2.92	-2.74	-2.13	-2.86

Table 5. Comparison of memory requirements and network fitness between tabulation method with increasing resolution and OANNs. Note that a reduction of the table size by a factor of two can be achieved by storing the data in single precision format.

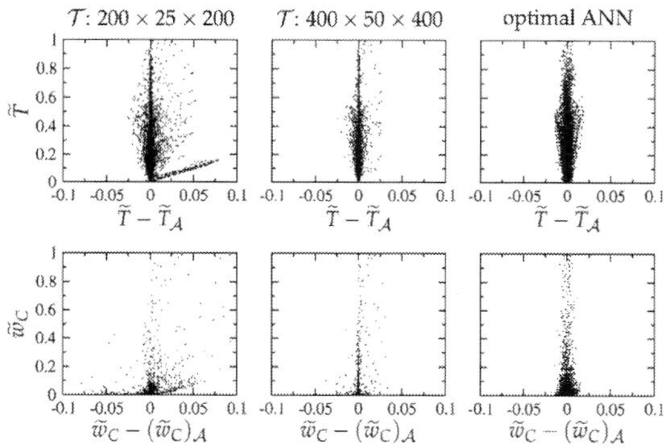

Fig. 12. Regression analysis for the table representation and ANN approximation for the normalized temperature (top) and chemical source term (bottom). The subscript "$\mathcal{A}$" refers to data evaluated from OANNs, and $\widetilde{T}$ and $\widetilde{\omega}_C$ are the sample data.

5.4 Dynamic ANN performance analysis

In this section, results from LES computations employing look-up tables and OANNs for the chemistry representation are presented. Statistical data are collected over four flow-through-times. For reference, the azimuthal and temporal averaged quantity of a scalar ϕ is denoted by $\langle\widetilde{\phi}\rangle$, and the resolved scalar variance is indicated by $\langle\widetilde{\phi''^2_<}\rangle$.

Figure 13 compares the averaged axial velocity field between experiments (left) and ANN simulation (right). The solid line in both figures separates the regions of positive and negative axial velocities. From both figures the decay of the central fuel jet and the contraction of the swirling oxidizer stream after the recirculation bubble are evident.

Radial profiles of the mean and rms mixture fraction are shown in Fig. 14. Both, simulations and experiments predict a region of homogeneous mixture directly behind the bluff body. The location of stoichiometry is aligned with the inner shear layer of the swirling stream. Since the value of the stoichiometric mixture fraction is $Z_{st} = 0.042$, accurate prediction of the shear layer is crucial for the determination of species and temperature distributions. Even though both simulations slightly over-predict the spreading rate of $\langle\widetilde{Z}\rangle$, the computed axial decay rates are in excellent agreement with the experiments.

Radial profiles of mean temperature and CO_2 mass fraction are shown in Fig. 15. The numerical results for $\langle\widetilde{Y}_{CO_2}\rangle$ from the simulations employing the tabulation method are in

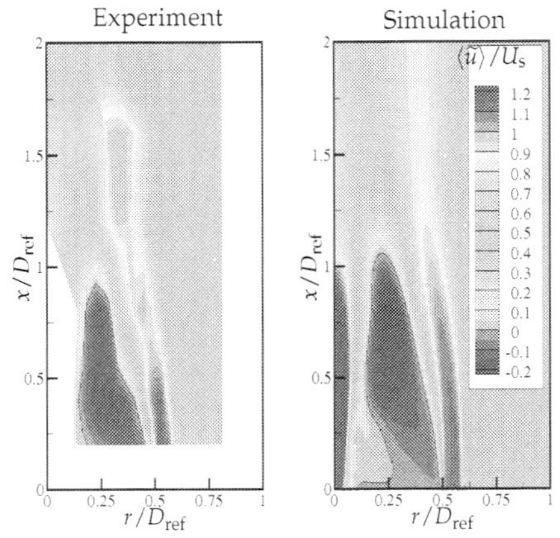

Fig. 13. Comparison of averaged axial velocity fields between experiment (left) and LES calculation employing an OANN chemistry representation (right).

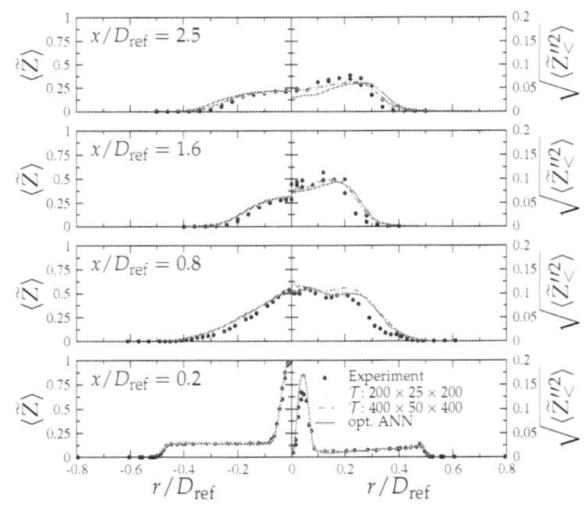

Fig. 14. Comparison of measured and calculated mean and resolved rms statistics of mixture fraction at different axial locations in the Sydney SMH1 flame.

reasonable agreement with experimental data; however, the simulation with ANN chemistry representation under-predicts $\widetilde{Y}_{CO_2}$ on the fuel-rich side of the flame. This is primarily attributed to the poor fitness of the CO_2-OANN. The shift of the profiles for $\langle \widetilde{T} \rangle$ and $\langle \widetilde{Y}_{CO_2} \rangle$ towards the lean side of the flame is due to the slight over-prediction of the mixture fraction in the shear layer surrounding the swirling oxidizer stream. The mean temperature in the region of the bluff body at $x/D_{ref} = 0.2$ is correctly predicted.

In summary, the comparisons of statistical flow field results shows that both methods for the chemistry representation yield similar results. Discrepancies for CO_2-species predictions are primarily attributed to the poor fitness of the ANN, which can be further improved

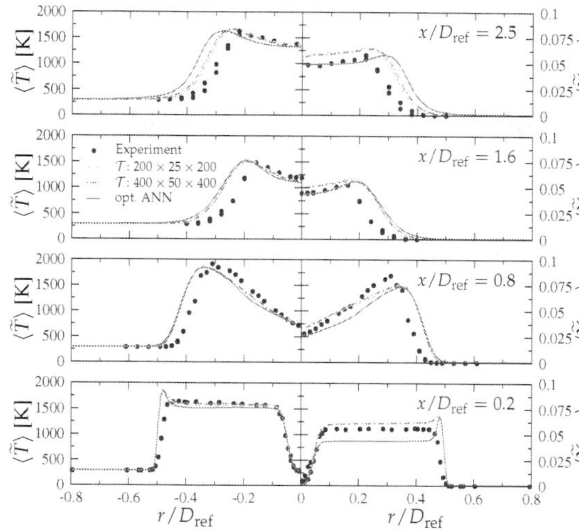

Fig. 15. Comparison of measured and calculated mean temperature and CO_2 mass fraction at different axial locations in the Sydney SMH1 flame.

by considering larger network architectures. These discrepancies emphasize the sensitivity of the flow field structure to the ANN-representation. Furthermore, they demonstrate the significance of evaluating the network performance in dynamic applications, in which the integrated effect of ANN-approximation errors on the system evolution can be assessed.

6. Conclusions

Topological optimization of ANNs for application to chemically reacting flows was conducted. To this end, a generalized pattern search method was presented as attractive alternative to previously employed ANN optimization strategies. This GPS method offers extensive flexibility in the implementation and allows for the consideration of optimization parameters that are of categorical and continuous type. In addition, an evolutionary strategy (ES) was also utilized in order to establish a direct comparison with the GPS method. For the present application, it was shown that, compared to ES, the GPS method is more robust, converges faster, and returns ANN topologies with better performance.

The GPS method was applied to the generation of optimal ANNs to approximate chemical source terms, species mass fractions, and other thermochemical quantities in chemical reacting systems. For this, two different combustion problems with increasing complexity were considered. In the first problem, the combustion of a fuel/air mixture in decaying homogeneous isotropic turbulence was modeled, in which the chemical source term, describing the fuel-conversion rate, was approximated by an optimal ANN. The particularly interesting aspect of this problem is that it allows for a systematic evaluation of ANN approximation errors on the transient evolution of the reacting system. The second problem focused on the unsteady three-dimensional combustion of a methane/hydrogen-air mixture in a technical-relevant burner system. For this, large-scale simulations were employed, and the accuracy of ANNs and conventional tabulation methods were assesses in the context of high-performance computations of turbulent reacting flows.

To enable a comprehensive assessment of the network fitness, two complementary metrics were examined. The first metric considers the static ANN performance analysis, and evaluates the ability of the network to represent untrained samples. A main shortcoming of this metric, which is also referred to as "testing," is that it does not account for feedback-effects of ANN approximation errors on the evolution of the dynamic system. To address this issue, a dynamic ANN performance measure is developed. This metric provides additional diagnostics, and is useful for applications in which ANNs are used as substitutes for complex function-evaluations in dynamic systems. It was shown that this dynamic performance metric provides a practical-relevant assessment of the network fitness, whereas the static ANN analysis gives typically too optimistic estimates.

7. Acknowledgments

The author gratefully acknowledges financial support through ONR under Grant No. N00014-10-1-0717. Helpful discussions with Heinz Pitsch, Christoph Schmitt, and Rodney Fox on the ANN optimization and the LFP model formulation are much appreciated.

8. References

Abramson, M. A. (2004). Mixed variable optimization of a load-bearing thermal insulation system using a filter pattern search algorithm, *Optimization and Engineering* 5(2): 157–177.

Al-Abdeli, Y. A. & Masri, A. R. (2003). Stability characteristics and flowfields of turbulent non-premixed swirling flames, *Comb. Theory Modelling* 7: 731–766.

Angeline, P. J., Saunders, G. M. & Pollack, J. B. (1994). Evolutionary algorithm that constructs recurrent neural networks, *IEEE Trans. Neural Networks* 5: 54–65.

Audet, C. & Dennis, Jr., J. E. (2000). Pattern search algorithms for mixed variable programming, *SIAM J. Optim.* 11(3): 573–594.

Audet, C. & Dennis, Jr., J. E. (2003). Analysis of generalized pattern searches, *SIAM J. Optim.* 13(3): 889–903.

Bäck, T. & Schwefel, H.-P. (1993). An overview of evolutionary algorithms for parameter optimization, *Evolutionary Computation* 1 (1): 1–23.

Blasco, J. A., Fueyo, N., Dopazo, C. & Ballester, J. (1999). Modelling the temporal evolution of a reduced combustion chemical system with an artificial neural network, *Combust. Flame* 113(1-2): 38–52.

Blasco, J. A., Fueyo, N., Dopazo, C. & Chen, J. Y. (2000). A self-organizing-map approach to chemistry representation in combustion applications, *Combust. Theory Modelling* 4(1): 61–76.

Blasco, J. A., Fueyo, N., Larroya, J. C., Dopazo, C. & Chen, J. Y. (1999). Single-step time-integrator of a methane-air chemical system using artificial neural networks, *Computers and Chemical Engineering* 23(9): 1127–1133.

Booker, A. J., Dennis, Jr., J. E., Frank, P. D., Serafini, D. B., Torczon, V. & Trosset, M. W. (1999). A rigorous framework for optimization of expensive functions by surrogates, *Structural Optimization* 17(1): 1–13.

Bornholdt, S. & Graudenz, D. (1992). General asymmetric neural networks and structure design by genetic algorithms, *Neural Networks* 5(2): 327–334.

Bowman, C. T., Hanson, R. K., Davidson, D. F., Gardiner, W. C., Lissianski, V., Smith, G. P., Golden, D. M., Frenklach, M. & Goldenberg, M. (1997). GRI-Mech 2.11. available from `http://www.me.berkeley.edu/gri-mech/`.

Chen, J. Y., Blasco, J. A., Fueyo, N. & Dopazo, C. (2000). An economical strategy for storage of chemical kinetics: Fitting in situ adaptive tabulation with artificial neural networks, *Proc. Comb. Institute* 28: 115–121.

Christo, F. C., Masri, A. R. & Nebot, E. M. (1996). Artificial neural network implementation of chemistry with PDF simulation of H_2/CO_2 flames, *Combust. Flame* 106(4): 406–427.

Christo, F. C., Masri, A. R., Nebot, E. M. & Pope, S. B. (1996). An integrated PDF/neural network approach for simulating turbulent reacting systems, *Proc. Comb. Institute* 26: 43–48.

Flemming, F., Sadiki, A. & Janicka, J. (2005). LES using artificial neural networks for chemistry representation, *Progress in Computational Fluid Dynamics* 5(7): 375–385.

Fogel, D. B. & Fogel, L. J. (1990). Evolving neural networks, *Biological Cybern.* 63(6): 487–493.

Fox, R. O. (2003). *Computational Models for Turbulent Reacting Flows*, Cambridge University Press, Cambridge.

Frean, M. (1990). The upstart algorithm: A method for constructing and training feedforward neural networks, *Neural Computation* 2(2): 198–209.

Germano, M., Piomelli, U., Moin, P. & Cabot, W. H. (1991). A dynamic subgrid-scale eddy viscosity model, *Phys. Fluids A* 3(7): 1760–1765.

Hagan, M. T., Demuth, H. B. & Beale, M. (1996). *Neural Network Design*, PWS Publishing Company, Boston, Massachusetts, USA.

Haykin, S. (1994). *Neural Networks: A Comprehensive Foundation*, Prentice Hall, Upper Saddle River, N.J.

Husken, M., Jin, Y. & Sendhoff, B. (2005). Structure optimization of neural networks for evolutionary design optimization, *Soft Computing* 9(1): 21–28.

Ihme, M., Cha, C. M. & Pitsch, H. (2005). Prediction of local extinction and re-ignition effects in non-premixed turbulent combustion using a flamelet/progress variable approach, *Proc. Combust. Inst.* 30: 793–800.

Ihme, M., Marsden, A. L. & Pitsch, H. (2008). Generation of optimal artificial neural networks using a pattern search algorithm: Application to approximation of chemical systems, *Neural Computation* 20(2): 573–601.

Ihme, M., Schmitt, C. & Pitsch, H. (2009). Optimal artificial neural networks and tabulation methods for chemistry representation in LES of a bluff-body swirl-stabilized flame, *Proc. Combust. Inst.* 32: 1527–1535.

Kalt, P. A. M., Al-Abdeli, Y. A., Masri, A. R. & Barlow, R. S. (2002). Swirling turbulent non-premixed flames of methane: Flow field and compositional structure, *Proc. Combust. Inst.* 29: 1913–1919.

Koza, J. R. & Rice, J. P. (1991). Genetic generation of both the weights and architecture for a neural network, *Proc. IEEE Int. Joint Conf. Neural Networks (IJCNN'91 Seattle)*, pp. 397–404.

Lam, S. H. & Goussis, D. A. (1988). Understanding complex chemical kinetics with computational singular perturbation, *Proc. Comb. Inst.* 22: 931–941.

Lewis, R. M. & Torczon, V. (1999). Pattern search algorithms for bound constrained minimization, *SIAM J. Optim.* 9(4): 1082–1099.

Lewis, R. M. & Torczon, V. (2000). Pattern search methods or linearly constrained minimization, *SIAM J. Optim.* 10(3): 917–941.

Lilly, D. K. (1992). A proposed modification of the Germano subgrid-scale closure method, *Phys. Fluids A* 4(3): 633–635.

Maas, U. & Pope, S. B. (1992). Simplifying chemical kinetics: Intrinsic low-dimensional manifolds in composition space, *Combust. Flame* 88(3-4): 239–264.

Masri, A. R. (2006). Web site for the Sydney swirl flame series http://www.aeromech.usyd.edu.au/thermofluids.

Masri, A. R., Kalt, P. A. M. & Barlow, R. S. (2004). The compositional structure of swirl-stabilised turbulent nonpremixed flames, *Combust. Flame* 137: 1–37.

McKay, M. D., Beckman, R. J. & Conover, W. J. (1979). Comparison of three methods for selecting values of input variables in the analysis of output from a computer code, *Technometrics* 21(2): 239–245.

Miller, G. F., Todd, P. M. & Hegde, S. U. (1989). Designing neural networks using genetic algorithms, *in* J. D. Schaffer (ed.), *Proc. 3rd Int. Conf. Genetic Algorithms and Their Applications*, pp. 379–384.

Mozer, M. C. & Smolensky, P. (1989). Skeletonization: A technique for trimming the fat from a network via relevance assessment, *Connection Sci.* 1(1): 3–26.

Peters, N. (1983). Local quenching due to flame stretch and non-premixed turbulent combustion, *Combust. Sci. Tech.* 30: 1–17.

Peters, N. (1984). Laminar diffusion flamelet models in non-premixed turbulent combustion, *Prog. Energy Combust. Sci.* 10(3): 319–339.

Pierce, C. D. & Moin, P. (2004). Progress-variable approach for large-eddy simulation of non-premixed turbulent combustion, *J. Fluid Mech.* 504: 73–97.

Pope, S. B. (1997). Computationally efficient implementation of combustion chemistry using in situ adaptive tabulation, *Combust. Theory Modelling* 1(1): 41–63.

Porto, V. W., Fogel, D. B. & Fogel, L. J. (1995). Alternative neural network training methods, *IEEE Expert* 10(3): 16–22.

Rechenberg, I. (1973). *Evolutionsstrategie - Optimierung technischer Systeme nach Prinzipien der biologischen Evolution*, PhD thesis, Technical University Berlin, Germany.

Sagaut, P. (1998). *Large Eddy Simulation for Incompressible Flows: An Introduction*, Springer, Berlin.

Schwefel, H.-P. (1977). *Numerische Optimierung von Computer-Modellen mittels der Evolutionsstrategie*, Birkhäuser, Basle, Switzerland.

Schwefel, H.-P. (1981). *Numerical Optimization of Computer Models*, Wiley, Chichester.

Sen, B. A. & Menon, S. (2008). Turbulent premixed flame modeling using artificial neural networks based chemical kinetics, *Proc. Combust. Inst.* 32: 1605–1611.

Sen, B. A. & Menon, S. (2010). Linear eddy mixing based tabulation and artificial neural networks for large eddy simulations of turbulent flames, *Combust. Flame* 157: 62–74.

Serafini, D. B. (1998). *A framework for managing models in nonlinear optimization of computationally expensive functions*, PhD thesis, Rice University, Houston, TX.

Sripakagorn, P., Mitarai, S., Kosály, G. & Pitsch, H. (2004). Extinction and reignition in a diffusion flame: A direct numerical simulation study, *J. Fluid Mech.* 518: 231–259.

Tang, K. S., Chan, C. Y., Man, K. F. & Kwong, S. (1995). Genetic structure for NN topology and weights optimization, *Proc. 1st IEE/IEEE International Conference on Genetic Algorithms in Engineering Systems: Innovations and Applications (GALESIA'95)*, pp. 250–255.

Tonse, S. R., Moriarty, N. W., Brown, N. J. & Frencklach, M. (1999). PRISM: piecewise reusable implementation of solution mapping. An economical strategy for chemical kinetics, *Israel Journal of Chemistry* 39(1): 97–106.

Torczon, V. (1997). On the convergence of pattern search algorithms, *SIAM J. Optim.* 7(1): 1–25.

Yao, X. (1999). Evolving artificial neural networks, *Proc. IEEE* 87(9): 1423–1447.

8

Facile Tool for Prediction of Catalytic Activity - Cu-Lanthanoid Catalyst for Methanol Synthesis

Kohji Omata[1], Tetuo Umegaki[2] and Muneyoshi Yamada[3]
[1]*Tohoku University*
[2]*Nihon University*
[3]*Akita National College of Technology*
Japan

1. Introduction

Methanol (MeOH) and dimethyl ether (DME), which can be easily obtained from MeOH, are superior candidates for clean transportation fuel. A compact and simple process with good economy has been proposed to produce these fuels from dispersed unused carbon resources (Yamada, 2003). The key point of this process is development of a noble catalyst which is active for MeOH synthesis under mild reaction conditions. A number of new catalysts for MeOH synthesis from syngas were discovered and some of them are more active than the conventional Cu/Zn/Al catalyst. Cu-lanthanoid catalyst was reported as one of the alternative catalyst (Andriamasinoro et al., 1993; Nix et al., 1987; Walker et al., 1992). Under mild conditions Cu-Yb showed higher activity than Cu-Zn-Al (Sakata et al., 1998). Prediction of the characteristics of new catalysts or catalyst additives from the physicochemical properties of catalyst components would accelerate catalyst development. In the present study such prediction methodology was developed and applied for MeOH synthesis by Cu-Lanthanoid catalyst.
As reviewed in the introduction of reference(Valero et al., 2009), modeling methodologies were suggested in the research field of catalysis (Baumes et al., 2004; 2007; Farrusseng et al., 2005; Grubert et al., 2003; Holeňa & Baerns, 2003; Serra et al., 2003; Serra, Corma, Valero, Argente & Botti, 2007; Wolf et al., 2000). It was also reported that an artificial neural network, especially a radial basis function network(RBFN),(Omata et al., 2004; Umegaki et al., 2003) was successfully applied for the regression of catalytic phenomena instead of the conventional polynomial equation. Such methodology is effective for integrating the observation(Serna et al., 2008) and the characterization(Barr et al., 2004; Baumes et al., 2009; 2008; Gilmore et al., 2004; Takeuchi et al., 2005). Successful prediction of catalytic properties from the physicochemical properties of the catalyst elements was, however, reported only in few cases (Kito et al., 1992; 1994).
We recently succeeded in identifying an effective additive for Ni/active carbon (AC) catalyst for the carbonylation of methanol based on previous experimental results and the physicochemical properties of the elements (Omata & Yamada, 2004). The physicochemical properties of element X were correlated by means of RBFN to the catalytic selectivity

for vapor-phase carbonylation of methanol with a Ni-X/AC catalyst. Parameters of the RBFN were determined using the experimental results. As a result Sn was predicted and experimentally verified to suppress the methane formation. In the similar way, beryllium was predicted as the most effective additive of Cu/Zn for methanol synthesis from syngas, which was verified experimentally (Omata et al., 2005). In other case, La and Ce, Sc and Nd were predicted to promote the activity of Ni/α-Al_2O_3 for oxidative reforming of methane. The experimentally observed activity of Ni-Sc/α-Al_2O_3 was five times higher than that of unpromoted Ni/α-Al_2O_3 catalyst (Omata et al., 2008).

In the present study, the activity of Cu-lanthanoid catalyst was correlated to the physicochemical properties by means of multiple regression analysis (model 1), RBFN (model 2), and support vector regression (SVR, model 3, 4, and 5). Through the prediction of activity of Cu-Sc and Cu-Pr catalyst, the generalization activity of these methods were compared and then the influential physicochemical properties were determined by the best methodology.

2. Experimental

Ethanol-oxalate method was employed for catalyst preparation. Ethanol solution of nitrates of Cu and lanthanoid was mixed with a given composition (Cu/lanthanoid = 5/1 molar ratio), and then an ethanol solution of oxalic acid was added to precipitate the mixed oxalic salts. The resulting mixed oxalates were washed with ethanol and dried at 353 K for 4 h in vacuo, and then were calcined at 573 K for 4 h into mixed oxide. The catalyst precursor oxide was activated at 403 K, 2.5 h, and 523 K, 1 h in the reaction gas. The reaction gas (syngas) composition was : 60% H_2, 30% CO, 5% CO_2 and 5% Ar (as internal standard). The reaction was conducted at 498 K, 1 MPa, W/F = 1 g·h/mol. Under these conditions, CO conversion is lower than equilibrium limit of methanol synthesis. Activity is shown as a space-time yield (STY, g-MeOH/kg-cat./h). Product gas was analyzed by micro-GC (Agilent, M-200, Molecular Sieve 5A/PoraPLOT U).

3. Prediction method

3.1 Dataset for parameter decision

Experimental results of the activity test are summarized in Fig. 1. The activity of Cu-Sc is much higher than those of Cu-La, Cu-Ce and Cu-Pr which were previously reported. The target of the present study is to predict the activity of Cu-Sc and Cu-Pr (black bars in Fig. 1) based on the experimental result in the figure other than the two catalysts.

As variables of regressions, physicochemical properties of lanthanoid (Periodic Table X , Synergy Creations) such as 1st ionization energy (1I [eV]), 2nd ionization energy (2I [eV]), electro negativity (EN [-]), electric dipole polarizability (ED [Å^3]), boiling point (BP [K]), melting point (MP [K]), specific heat capacity (HC [J/g/K]), heat of fusion (HF [kJ/mol]), heat of vaporization (HV [kJ/mol]), thermal conductivity (TC [W/m/K]), covalent radius (CR [pm]), density (DS [g/cm^3]), ionic radius (IR [pm]), and atomic weight (AW [g/mol]) were used with formation enthalpy of oxide (FE [kJ/mol])(Barin et al., 1993).

These primary properties should affect the secondary properties of catalyst such as surface area, surface composition, metal dispersion, electric state, morphology, thermal stability, and so on. These secondary properties then determine the catalytic activity. Therefore, properties of element should be correlated to the catalytic performance in complicated non-linear manner. Physicochemical properties of lanthanoid used for both the parameter decision and the activity prediction were normalized to 0~1 as shown in Table 1.

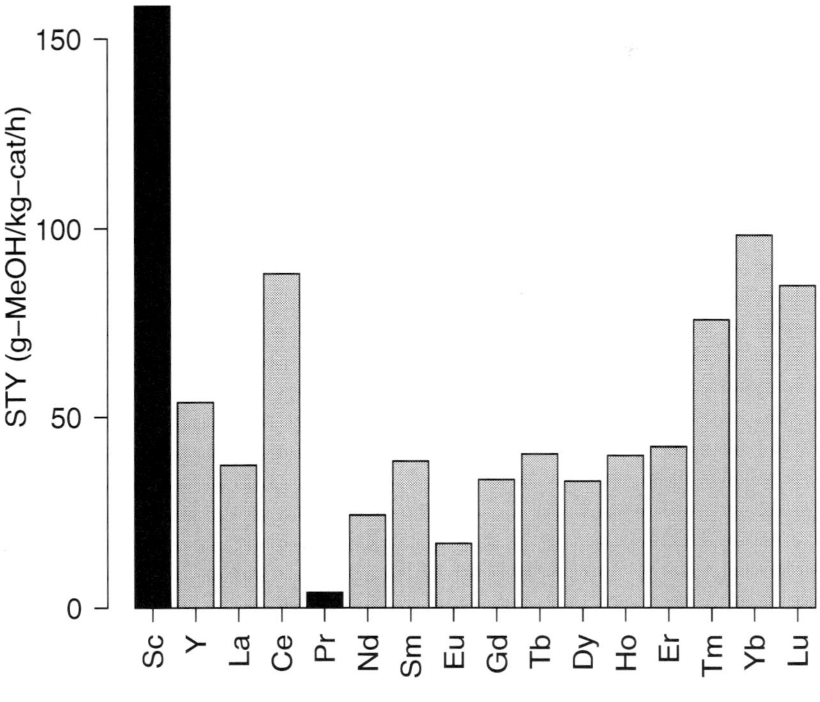

Fig. 1. Activity of Cu-Lanthanoid Catalyst for Methanol Synthesis from Syngas at 1 MPa. Data of black bars were only used for the validation of models.

3.2 Multiple regression analysis (Model 1)

Multiple regression analysis was performed by using statistical language R as model 1. R provides many functions such as $lm()$ and $step()$ available for statistical analysis. Because correlation coefficients of MP to HF, BP to HV, and EN to 2I were over 0.9, respectively, these properties (MP, BP, EN) were eliminated from the analysis to reduce the number of the variables. Then, $step()$ function of R was used to find the influential variables, and HF, 2I, and DS were not included in the final model because of their high AIC (Akaike's Information Criterion (Akaike, 1974)) score. Predicted STYs by the final model are plotted in Fig. 2 and the regression coefficients were determined as shown in Table 2. The activities of Cu-Pr and Cu-Sc were predicted by the regression equation.

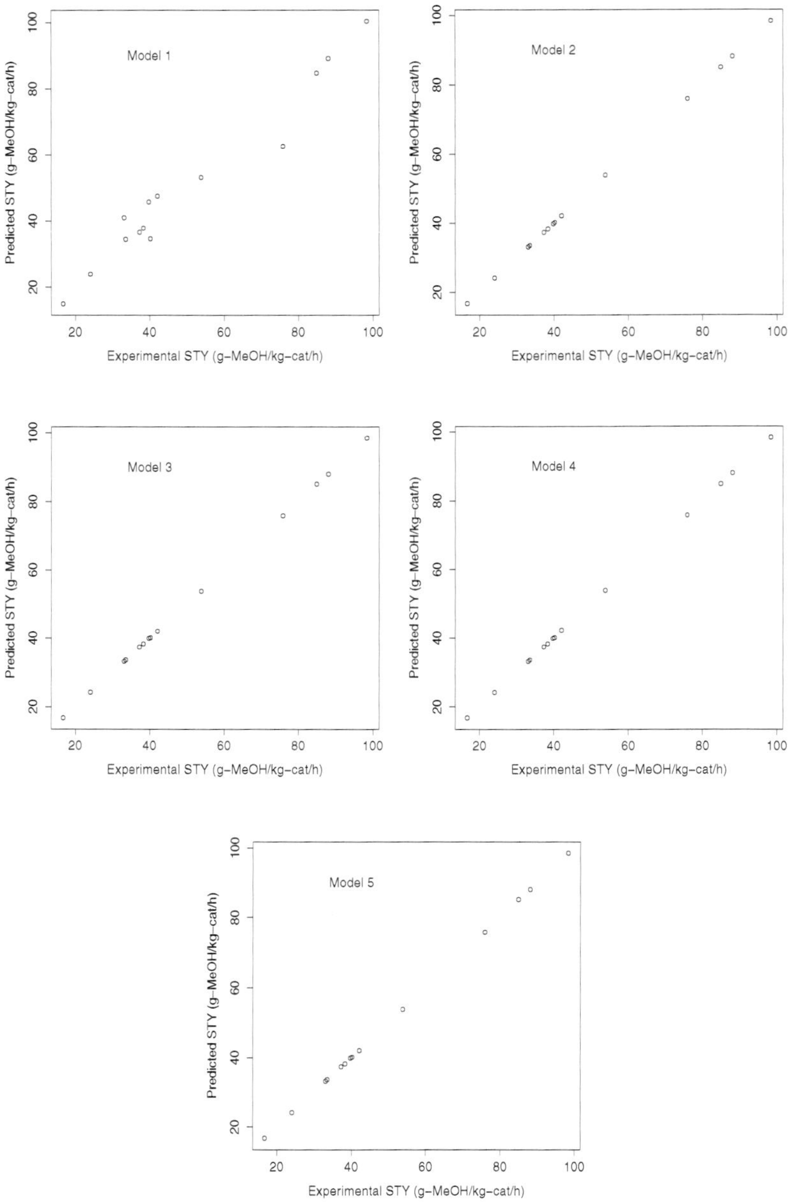

Fig. 2. Predicted STY by optimized model 1–5.

Symbol	AW	MP	BP	HV	HF	HC	CR	IR	EN	1I	2I	ED	DS	TC	FE	response[a)]
Y	0.338	0.842	0.925	0.775	0.835	0.357	0.439	0.590	0.500	0.699	0.504	0.360	0.219	0.272	0.987	53.9
La	0.646	0.141	0.976	0.904	0.242	0.119	0.610	1.000	0.000	0.133	0.152	0.978	0.541	0.119	0.583	37.3
Ce	0.732	0.000	0.963	0.888	0.146	0.095	0.512	0.615	0.000	0.097	0.090	0.868	0.553	0.033	0.000	88.1
Nd	0.764	0.252	0.808	0.628	0.000	0.095	0.488	0.538	0.000	0.088	0.054	1.000	0.585	0.243	0.634	24.1
Sm	0.811	0.317	0.258	0.022	0.313	0.119	0.537	0.718	0.500	0.186	0.155	0.809	0.664	0.111	0.705	38.3
Eu	0.823	0.022	0.174	0.063	0.280	0.071	1.000	0.744	0.000	0.212	0.206	0.728	0.330	0.136	0.108	16.7
Gd	0.864	0.594	0.894	0.528	0.694	0.214	0.415	0.359	0.500	0.637	0.460	0.419	0.715	0.000	0.703	33.5
Tb	0.877	0.646	0.875	0.862	0.760	0.071	0.366	0.256	0.500	0.381	0.290	0.566	0.770	0.021	0.842	40.2
Dy	0.905	0.706	0.590	0.498	0.835	0.048	0.366	0.205	0.500	0.451	0.334	0.493	0.810	0.004	0.834	33.1
Ho	0.923	0.777	0.648	0.535	0.835	0.048	0.341	0.154	0.500	0.522	0.373	0.426	0.848	0.230	0.898	39.8
Er	0.941	0.837	0.720	0.450	0.835	0.048	0.317	0.154	0.500	0.602	0.412	0.360	0.885	0.152	0.960	42.1
Tm	0.954	0.864	0.325	0.327	0.934	0.024	0.293	0.103	0.500	0.664	0.448	0.294	0.925	0.255	0.927	75.9
Yb	0.985	0.030	0.000	0.000	0.173	0.024	0.732	0.769	0.500	0.726	0.487	0.235	0.538	1.000	0.658	98.4
Lu	1.000	1.000	0.950	1.000	1.000	0.000	0.293	0.051	1.000	0.000	1.000	0.301	1.000	0.239	0.889	85.0
Pr	0.738	0.154	1.000	0.736	0.347	0.095	0.512	0.590	0.000	0.027	0.000	0.765	0.551	0.078	0.640	4.1
Sc	0.000	0.857	0.706	0.807	0.727	1.000	0.000	0.000	1.000	1.000	0.672	0.000	0.000	0.214	1.000	158.6

a) STY (g-MeOH/kg-cat/h)

The data in this table was saved in 'table_csv' as csv file and used in the R programs (R Development Core Team, 2009) as below.

```
(zz<-read.csv(table_csv))
(training<-zz[1:14,2:17])
(check<-zz[1:14,2:16])
(prediction<-zz[1:16,2:16])
(symbol<-data.frame(zz[,1]))
```

Table 1. Normalized Physicochemical Properties of Lanthanoid

	Estimate Std.	Error	t value	Pr(> |t|)
(Intercept)	352.9520	83.8388	4.21	0.0136
HV	-11.5397	14.0399	-0.82	0.4573
HC	-166.8569	97.6436	-1.71	0.1627
CR	-257.3117	57.7042	-4.46	0.0112
IR	100.9706	29.2293	3.45	0.0259
X1I	-53.1008	21.2195	-2.50	0.0666
ED	-139.1426	30.6455	-4.54	0.0105
DS	-78.1877	52.0711	-1.50	0.2076
TC	29.8160	24.2563	1.23	0.2864
FE	-82.7350	16.3662	-5.06	0.0072

Residual standard error: 9.319 on 4 degrees of freedom
Multiple R-squared: 0.9596, Adjusted R-squared: 0.8687
F-statistic: 10.55 on 9 and 4 DF, p-value: 0.01837

Table 2. Regression Coefficient of Model 1

3.3 Radial basis function network (Model 2)

Activity of methanol synthesis (response) was expressed by a RBFN as functions of the physicochemical properties in model 2:

$$\text{response} = \sum_{i=1}^{14} w_i \exp\left(-\frac{(\mathbf{x} - \mathbf{c}_i)^2}{2\sigma_i^2}\right) \quad (1)$$

where $\mathbf{c}_i$ is the centers, σ_i is the radii, and w_i is the weights of the radial basis functions and $\mathbf{x}$ is the physicochemical properties. σ_i was defined as the average of the distance to the two nearest-neighbors in the training data, and $\mathbf{c}_i$ was determined as an input vector of the physicochemical properties of elements used as the training data. Of course data of Cu-Sr and Cu-Pr are not included in the training data. The RBFN was coded and constructed by R as below where predicted STY was plotted as shown in Fig. 2 and then the activities of Cu-Pr and Cu-Sc were predicted by the RBFN. The number of nodes in the input layer, in the hidden layer, and in the output layer of the RBFN was 15, 14, and 1 respectively.

```
model2<-function(t,p) {
     p<-as.matrix(p)
     response<-t[,ncol(t)]
     center<-as.matrix(t[,-ncol(t)])
     sigma2<-apply(apply(as.matrix(dist(center))^2,1,sort)[2:3,],2,mean)
     weight<-t(solve(exp(as.matrix(dist(center)^2)/(-2)/sigma2)))%*%response
     pre<-NULL
     tt<-NULL
     for (i in 1:nrow(p)){
          tt<-matrix(data=p[i,],nrow=nrow(center),ncol=ncol(center),byrow=T)
          pre[i]<-exp(apply((tt-center)^2/(-2)/sigma2,1,sum))%*%weight}
     return (pre)}
plot(training$response, model2(training,check))
cbind(symbol,model2(training,prediction))
```

3.4 Support vector regression (Model 3)

Recently support vector machine (SVM) attracts much attention because of its high generalization capability. SVM was first reported in the field of solid catalysis as a classifier (Baumes et al., 2006; Serra, Baumes, Moliner, Serna & Corma, 2007). It can be used also for regression, and by SVM the inputs are mapped into a high-dimensional space in nonlinear manner and then the modified inputs are correlated linearly with the output (Fan et al., 2005; Nandi et al., 2004). These reported results show clearly the superior generalization capability of a SVM and better availability through open source program makes SVM more applicable than an artificial neural network.

In the present study, SVR was performed using *libsvm* library (Fan et al., 2005) through *svm*() function in package e1071 of R. A radial basis function was used as the kernel function and the normalized physicochemical properties and STY in Table 1 other than Cu-Pr and Cu-Sc were used.

In model 3, only cost parameter of SVM (the penalty parameter of the error term) was optimized as below using a trial-and-error method. By increasing cost parameter, the residual sum of squares was decreased as shown in Fig. 3. The predicted STY was in the steady state when cost parameter was larger than 10000. Predicted STY by the final model (cost=10000, gamma=1/15 as default) was plotted in Fig. 2 and then the activities of Cu-Pr and Cu-Sc were predicted by the SVM.

```
library(e1071)
model3<-svm(response~., data=training,cost=10000,scale=F)
(rss<-sum((training$response-fitted(model3))^2))
plot(training$response,fitted(model3))
cbind(symbol,predict(model3,prediction))
```

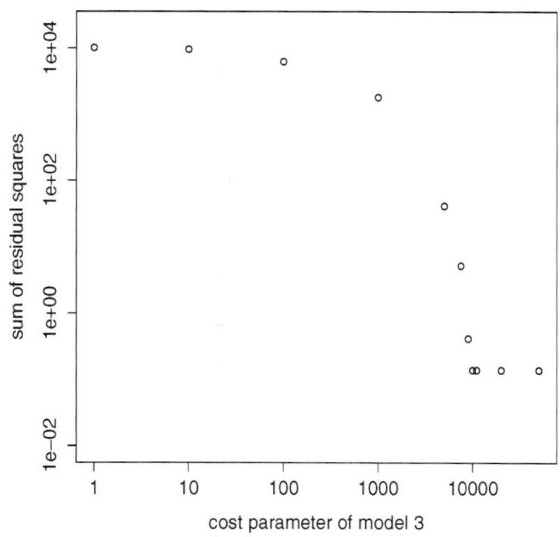

Fig. 3. Optimization of cost parameter of model 3.

3.5 Support vector regression (Model 4)

In model 4, gamma parameters of SVM (the kernel parameter of the RBFs) and cost parameter were optimized simultaneously using a grid search (Fan et al., 2005). *tune.svm*() function was used as below to decrease the sum of squared error between the experimental and the predicted STY other than Cu-Pr and Cu-Sc. The ranges of cost and gamma were gradually narrowed whereas the optimum parameters should not be located at the edge of the range. For example the range of cost parameter was changed from $10^4 \sim 10^{-4}$ to $10^{2.3} \sim 10^{2.4}$ with smaller steps. Predicted STY by the final model was plotted as shown in Fig. 2 and then the activities of Cu-Pr and Cu-Sc were predicted by the SVM.

```
library(e1071)
cost=10^c(seq(2.3,2.4,0.01))
gamma=10^c(seq(-0.3,-0.2,0.01))
model=tune.svm(response~., data=training, gamma=gamma, cost=cost, scale=F,
      tunecontrol=tune.control(sampling="fix"),
      validation.x=training[,-ncol(training)],
      validation.y=training[,ncol(training)])
model4=model$best.model
plot(training$response,fitted(model4))
cbind(symbol,predict(model4,prediction))
```

3.6 Support vector regression (Model 5)

In model 5, leave-one-out method (in this case, 14-fold cross validation) were used instead of the grid search to prevent the over-fitting problem. The ranges of cost and gamma were gradually narrowed as in model 4. Predicted STY by the final model was plotted as shown in Fig. 2 and then the activities of Cu-Pr and Cu-Sc were predicted by the SVM.

```
library(e1071)
cost=10^c(seq(3.85,3.95,0.01))
gamma=10^c(seq(-1.15,-1.05,0.01))
model=tune.svm(response~., data=training, gamma=gamma, cost=cost, scale=F,
      tunecontrol=tune.control(sampling="cross",cross=14))
model5=model$best.model
plot(training$response,fitted(model5))
cbind(symbol,predict(model5,prediction))
```

4. Result and discussion

The activity of Cu-Pr and Cu-Sc were predicted using model 1–5. As mentioned above, activity data of Cu-Sc(159 g-MeOH/kg-cat/h) and Cu-Pr(4.1 g-MeOH/kg-cat/h) were not included in the construction of model 1–5. In Fig. 4 the prediction errors are compared. The activity of Cu-Pr was predicted to be larger than the experimental result in the all model. The precision of the prediction was high as follows: model 5 $>$ model 3 $>$ model 4 $>$ model 2 $\approx$ model 1. Physicochemical properties such as 1I(1st ionization energy) and AW(atomic weight) of lanthanoid are plotted in Fig. 5. Based on the open circles (training data for the regression), activities corresponding to the closed circle (target data) should be predicted. It is understandable that prediction error of Cu-Pr is smaller than that of Cu-Sc because Sc is located far from the training elements. Among the model 1–5, only model 5 is equipped with a mechanism to avoid over-fitting. Using the unevenly distributed training data as shown in Fig. 5, leave-one-out (14-fold cross-validation) was proved to be effective for the precise prediction. Thus, SVM will give the best regression if the parameters are optimized by leave-one-out method.

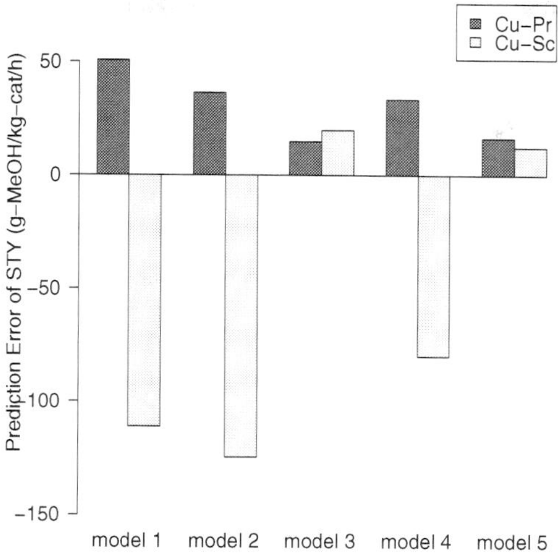

Fig. 4. Comparison of the Prediction Error by Various Regression Method.

In order to find the correlation between the physicochemical properties and the activity of Cu-lanthanoid for methanol synthesis, the best regression model was constructed using the all data in Table 1.

The model 6 was constructed using the SVM of which parameters were optimized by leave-one-out method as same as model 5.

In the model 6, correlation between the physicochemical properties and the activity of methanol synthesis should be unveiled.

The STY of Cu-Sc catalyst is plotted in Fig. 6 as a function of some physicochemical property. Even when the property change is imaginary, the STY change can be predicted by the regression model 6 if one properties is changed. As shown in the figure, effect of TC on the activity of Cu-Sc should be small: even if TC can be changed, the activity of the resulting catalyst is almost same. On the contrary, BP should be influential on the activity. The difference of the maximum and the minimum of such imaginary activity of Cu-Sc was predicted as shown in Fig. 7 for each physicochemical property. In this figure is shown that the five properties are remarkably influential. They can be categorized in two groups:

group 1:EN, 1I

group 2:BP, HV, CR

In methanol synthesis active site of Cu catalyst is not clear yet. However, in Cu/ZnO-based ternary catalysts for methanol synthesis from CO_2 and H_2, Cu^0/Cu^+ ratio influences the activity (Saito et al., 1996). According the results it is natural that the ligand effect of the lanthanoid is influential.

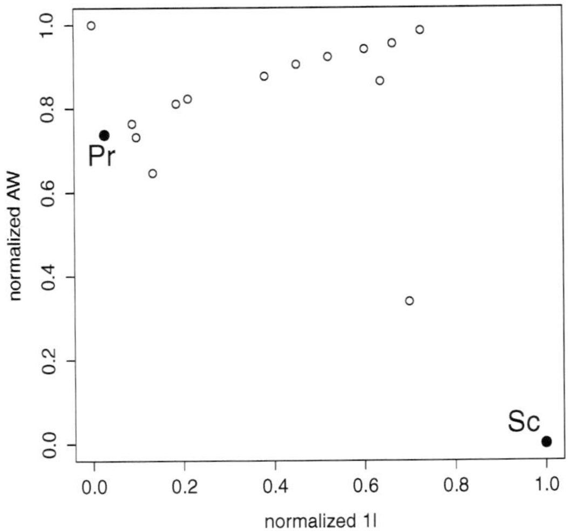

Fig. 5. Distribution of some training data. Open circle = training data.

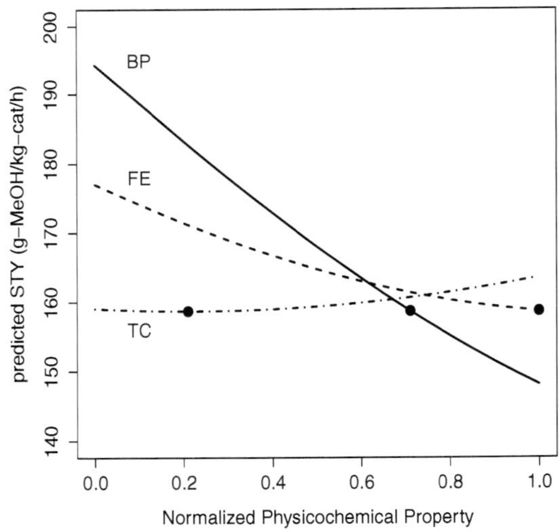

Fig. 6. Predicted Effect of Physicochemical Properties on STY of Cu-Sc Catalyst. Closed circles:experimental result of Cu-Sc.

On the other hand, in the case of metal alloy, metals with higher HV tend to be dominant on the surface. Thus, BP and HV in group 2 probably are the indexes of surface mobility. With Cu-Yb catalyst for hydrogenation, the catalyst morphology is influenced by the pretreatment temperature. Cluster-like ytterbium oxide homogeneously dispersed in copper metal when it is activated at the optimum temperature, and the morphology strongly affects the catalytic performance (Sakata et al., 1999). Because CR is one of the most principal character of the bimetallic catalyst (Cu-lanthanoid), CR can influence the morphology along with the HV or BP, on the surface Cu metal and can influence hydrogenation activity.

Generally, sintering of Cu metal is a serious problem for the stability of Cu catalyst. When highly dispersed and active Cu/Zn/Al catalyst was prepared by ethanol-oxalate method, the cautious start-up was necessary for the appearance of high activity because methanol synthesis is highly exothermic reaction and the facile start-up causes the heat-up and sintering of the catalyst. Thus, thermal-effect-related properties such as TC and HC are potentially the important factor for Cu catalyst. As shown in Fig. 7, however, the effect of TC and HC are negligible on Cu-Sc catalyst. The result brings some insights into the active site of the catalyst.

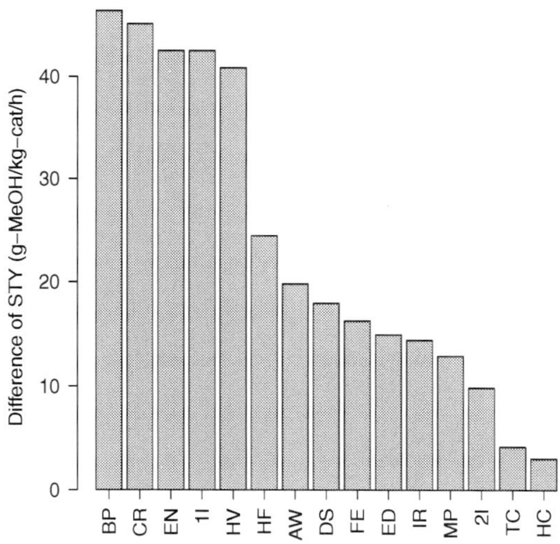

Fig. 7. Effect of Physicochemical Properties on STY Change of Cu-Sc Catalyst.

Thus the influential properties for Cu-lanthanoid catalyst were those for ligand effect (by EN and 1I) and geometric effect (by BP, HV, and CR). Thermal effect (TC and HC) plays a small role in this case.

5. Conclusion

Catalytic activities for methanol synthesis from syngas at 1 MPa and 498 K of Cu-Pr and Cu-Sc were precisely predicted. The activity of Cu-Sc was predicted to be much higher than those of the previous Cu-lanthanoid catalyst and the prediction was confirmed experimentally. For the prediction only the physicochemical properties of lanthanoid elements and the catalytic activity of Cu-lanthanoid other than Cu-Pr and Cu-Sc were necessary. The best regression model was obtained by support vector regression when the parameters of the model was optimized by leave-one-out method. Such optimization method is important to prevent the over-fitting problem. The influential physicochemical properties were those for geometric effect and ligand effect for Cu catalyst, whereas thermal effect plays a small role. Support vector machine can be a robust tool for rapid catalyst development.

6. References

Akaike, H. (1974). A new look at the statistical model identification, *IEEE Transactions on Automatic Control* 19(6): 716–723.

Andriamasinoro, D., Kieffer, R. & Kiennemann, A. (1993). Preparation of stabilized copper-rare earth oxide catalysts for the synthesis of methanol from syngas, *Applied Catalysis. A: General* 106(2): 201–212.

Barin, I., Sauert, F., Schultze-Rhonhof, S. & Sheng, W. (1993). *Thermochemical data of pure substances (2nd ed.)*, VCH, Weinheim.

Barr, G., Dong, W. & Gilmore, C. (2004). High-throughput powder diffraction. II. Applications of clustering methods and multivariate data analysis, *Journal of Applied Crystallography* 37(2): 243–252.

Baumes, L., Farrusseng, D., Lengliz, M. & Mirodatos, C. (2004). Using Artificial Neural Networks to Boost High-throughput Discovery in Heterogeneous Catalysis, *QSAR & Combinatorial Science* 23(9): 767–778.

Baumes, L., Moliner, M. & Corma, A. (2007). Prediction of ITQ-21 zeolite phase crystallinity: Parametric versus non-parametric strategies, *QSAR and Combinatorial Science* 26(2): 255.

Baumes, L., Moliner, M. & Corma, A. (2009). Design of a full-profile matching solution for high-throughput analysis of multi-phases samples through powder x-ray diffraction, *Chemistry-A European Journal* 15(17): 4258–4269.

Baumes, L., Moliner, M., Nicoloyannis, N. & Corma, A. (2008). A reliable methodology for high throughput identification of a mixture of crystallographic phases from powder X-ray diffraction data, *CrystEngComm* 10(10): 1321–1324.

Baumes, L., Serra, J., Serna, P. & Corma, A. (2006). Support vector machines for predictive modeling in heterogeneous catalysis: a comprehensive introduction and overfitting investigation based on two real applications, *Journal of Combinatorial Chemistry* 8(4): 583–596.

Fan, R.-E., Chen, P.-H. & Lin, C.-J. (2005). Working set selection using second order information for training support vector machines, *Journal of Machine Learning Research* 6: 1889–1918.

Farrusseng, D., Klanner, C., Baumes, L., Lengliz, M., Mirodatos, C. & Schüth, F. (2005). Design of discovery libraries for solids based on QSAR models, *QSAR & Combinatorial Science* 24(1): 78–93.

Gilmore, C., Barr, G. & Paisley, J. (2004). High-throughput powder diffraction. I. A new approach to qualitative and quantitative powder diffraction pattern analysis using full pattern profiles, *Journal of Applied Crystallography* 37(2): 231–242.

Grubert, G., Kondratenko, E., Kolf, S., Baerns, M., van Geem, P. & Parton, R. (2003). Fundamental insights into the oxidative dehydrogenation of ethane to ethylene over catalytic materials discovered by an evolutionary approach, *Catalysis Today* 81(3): 337–345.

Holeňa, M. & Baerns, M. (2003). Feedforward neural networks in catalysis A tool for the approximation of the dependency of yield on catalyst composition, and for knowledge extraction, *Catalysis Today* 81(3): 485–494.

Kito, S., Hattori, T. & Murakami, Y. (1992). Estimation of the acid strength of mixed oxides by a neural network, *Industrial & Engineering Chemistry Research* 31(3): 979–981.

Kito, S., Hattori, T. & Murakami, Y. (1994). Estimation of catalytic performance by neural network: product distribution in oxidative dehydrogenation of ethylbenzene, *Applied Catalysis. A: General* 114(2): 173–178.

Nandi, S., Badhe, Y., Lonari, J., Sridevi, U., Rao, B., Tambe, S. & Kulkarni, B. (2004). Hybrid process modeling and optimization strategies integrating neural networks/support vector regression and genetic algorithms: study of benzene isopropylation on Hbeta catalyst, *Chemical Engineering Journal* 97(2-3): 115–129.

Nix, R., Rayment, T., Lambert, R., Jennings, J. & Owen, G. (1987). An in situ X-ray diffraction study on the activation and performance of methanol synthesis catalysts derived from rare earth-copper alloys, *Journal of Catalysis* 106(1): 216–234.

Omata, K., Endo, Y., Ishii, H., Masuda, A. & Yamada, M. (2008). Effective additives of Ni/α-Al_2O_3 catalyst at low methane conversion of oxidative reforming for syngas formation, *Applied Catalysis A: General* 351(1): 54–58.

Omata, K., Hashimoto, M., Sutarto, Ishiguro, G., Watanabe, Y., Umegaki, T. & Yamada, M. (2005). Screening using artificial neural network of additives for Cu-Zn oxide catalyst for methanol synthesis from syngas, *Journal of the Japan Petroleum Institute* 48(3): 145–149.

Omata, K., Watanabe, Y., Hashimoto, M., Umegaki, T. & Yamada, M. (2004). Simultaneous optimization of preparation conditions and composition of the methanol synthesis catalyst by an all-encompassing calculation on an artificial neural network, *Industrial & Engineering Chemistry Research* 43(13): 3282 – 3288.

Omata, K. & Yamada, M. (2004). Prediction of effective additives to a Ni/active carbon catalyst for vapor-phase carbonylation of methanol by an artificial neural network, *Industrial & Engineering Chemistry Research* 43(20): 6622–6625.

R Development Core Team (2009). *R: A Language and Environment for Statistical Computing*, R Foundation for Statistical Computing, Vienna, Austria. ISBN 3-900051-07-0.

Saito, M., Fujitani, T., Takeuchi, M. & Watanabe, T. (1996). Development of copper/zinc oxide-based multicomponent catalysts for methanol synthesis from carbon dioxide and hydrogen, *Applied Catalysis A, General* 138(2): 311–318.

Sakata, Y., Nobukuni, S., Hashimoto, T., Takahashi, F., Imamura, H. & Tsuchiya, S. (1998). Catalytic Activity for Methanol Synthesis over a Copper-Lanthanide Oxide Complex System Prepared from a Copper-Lanthanide Complex Oxide of $Cu_6O_8Yb(NO_3)$, *Chemistry Letters* 27(12): 1211–1212.

Sakata, Y., Nobukuni, S., Kikumoto, E., Tanaka, K., Imamura, H. & Tsuchiya, S. (1999). Preparation and catalytic property of a copper–lanthanide oxide binary system for hydrogenation reaction, *Journal of Molecular Catalysis. A, Chemical* 141(1-3): 269–276.

Serna, P., Baumes, L., Moliner, M. & Corma, A. (2008). Combining high-throughput experimentation, advanced data modeling and fundamental knowledge to develop catalysts for the epoxidation of large olefins and fatty esters, *Journal of Catalysis* 258(1): 25–34.

Serra, J., Chica, A. & Corma, A. (2003). Development of a low temperature light paraffin isomerization catalysts with improved resistance to water and sulphur by combinatorial methods, *Applied Catalysis A, General* 239(1-2): 35–42.

Serra, J., Corma, A., Valero, S., Argente, E. & Botti, V. (2007). Soft computing techniques applied to combinatorial catalysis: A new approach for the discovery and optimization of catalytic materials, *QSAR & Combinatorial Science* 26(1): 11–26.

Serra, M., Baumes, A., Moliner, M., Serna, P. & Corma, A. (2007). Zeolite Synthesis Modelling with Support Vector Machines: A Combinatorial Approach, *Combinatorial Chemistry & High Throughput Screening* 10(1): 13–24.

Takeuchi, I., Long, C., Famodu, O., Murakami, M., Hattrick-Simpers, J., Rubloff, G., Stukowski, M. & Rajan, K. (2005). Data management and visualization of x-ray diffraction spectra from thin film ternary composition spreads, *Review of Scientific Instruments* 76: 062223.

Umegaki, T., Watanabe, Y., Nukui, N., Omata, K. & Yamada, M. (2003). Optimization of catalyst for methanol synthesis by a combinatorial approach using a parallel activity test and genetic algorithm assisted by a neural network, *Energy & Fuels* 17(4): 850 – 856.

Valero, S., Argente, E., Botti, V., Serra, J., Serna, P., Moliner, M. & Corma, A. (2009). DoE framework for catalyst development based on soft computing techniques, *Computers and Chemical Engineering* 33(1): 225–238.

Walker, A., Lambert, R., Nix, R. & Jennings, J. (1992). Methanol synthesis over catalysts derived from $CeCu_2$: transient studies with isotopically labelled reactants, *Journal of Catalysis* 138(2): 694–713.

Wolf, D., Buyevskaya, O. & Baerns, M. (2000). An evolutionary approach in the combinatorial selection and optimization of catalytic materials, *Applied Catalysis A, General* 200(1-2): 63–77.

Yamada, M. (2003). High-quality transportation fuels, *Energy & Fuels* 17(4): 797–798.

Part 3

Application of ANN in Computing

9

Size-Based Software Cost Modelling with Artificial Neural Networks and Genetic Algorithms

Efi Papatheocharous[1] and Andreas S. Andreou[2]
[1]*Department of Computer Science, University of Cyprus*
[2]*Department of Electrical Engineering and Information Technology, Cyprus University of Technology*
Cyprus

1. Introduction

Accurate software cost estimation has always been a major concern especially for people involved in project management, resource control and schedule planning. A high-quality and reliable development effort estimate could provide more efficient planning and control over the whole software process and guide a project to success. As literature shows many researchers proposed a plethora of methods and techniques to model the relationship between software size and the actual development costs (Jørgensen & Shepperd, 2007). However, the track record of IT projects shows that often a large number fails. Most IT experts agree that such failures occur more regularly than they should (Charette, 2005). According to the 10th edition of the annual CHAOS report from the Standish Group that studied over 40,000 projects in 10 years, it seems that success rates increased to 34% and failures declined to 15% of the projects. Even though success rates increased, still, 51% of the projects overrun time/budget, lack critical features and requirements and/or important quality requirements are compromised. Furthermore, average software costs are apparently overrun by 43% (Software Magazine, 2004). One of the main reasons for these figures is failure to estimate the actual effort required to develop a software project.

A reliable software cost estimation model has always been a major challenge and demand for project managers at the initiation phase of the project and also an important asset for the whole process of software development. In addition, there is a large discussion on the discovery of the relationship between cost drivers and effort, especially of one of the most critical cost factors, namely software size (Sommerville, 2007). The aforementioned modelling and estimation problem is further amplified due to the high level of complexity and uniqueness of each project. Estimating software costs, as well as deciding on assessing the appropriate cost drivers, remain difficult issues that need to be addressed. Such issues are constantly at the forefront of the project management's interests from the initiation of the project until the system is delivered. Cost estimates, even for well-planned projects, are hard to make and will probably concern project managers long before the problem is adequately solved.

Over the years software cost estimation has attracted considerable research attention and many techniques have been developed to effectively predict software costs (Briand &

Wieczorek, 2002; Moløkken & Jørgensen, 2003; Jørgensen & Shepperd, 2007). The dominant techniques during the past decades involved Regression since it was applied in well-known software cost estimation models (such as the COnstructive COst MOdel, COCOMO) to capture the relationship between cost drivers and effort. During the last years, analogy-based, expert judgement, decision trees, neural networks, probabilistic and other approaches arose in software cost estimation studies (Jørgensen & Shepperd, 2007). Nevertheless, no single solution has yet been proposed to adequately address the problem. Typically, the amount and complexity of the development effort proportionally drives software costs. However, as other factors, such as technology, team and manager skills, software quality, project size, also affect the development process it becomes even more difficult to assess the actual costs.

A commonly investigated approach is to estimate as accurately as possible some of the fundamental characteristics related to cost, such as effort, usually measured in person-months, through past empirical project examples. In addition, it is also preferable to measure a condensed set of several attributes which can be more informative (descriptive) in regards to effort and then use them to estimate the actual effort. However, previous research identified the lack of standard definitions in software terminology and the presence of inconsistencies in empirical data samples, where it was also concluded that models with too many variables and parameters are very hard to calibrate (Miyazaki et al., 1994). For this reason, building models that focus only on a small set of significant attributes is more practical.

Software size is commonly recognised as one of the most important factors affecting the amount of effort required to complete a project (Fenton & Pfleeger, 1997). Software size in terms of actual code length is considered a fairly subjective metric as it depends on the development language and the code generated by tools or re-used in software development. Also, software size is impractical in providing early effort estimates, that is, at the beginning of a project, mainly because it is unknown until the project's source code is actually written. Therefore, after software specification is finalised, the estimation of software size based on the outline of the project is a fundamental activity. Also, it is very critical to carry out estimation of software size after the initial phases of development and the success of the final effort approximation may probably depend greatly on its value. This chapter looks more closely into the relations of these two most significant parts of software cost estimation.

More specifically, some researchers have investigated various cost models using size to estimate effort (e.g., Wittig & Finnie, 1997; Dolado, 2001) whereas others have directed their efforts towards defining concise methods and measures to estimate software size from the early project phases (e.g., Park, 2005; Albrecht, 1979). The present work is more relevant to the former, aspiring to provide size and effort-based estimations and modelling the relationship between size, as this is expressed in terms of Lines of Code (LOC) or Function Points (FP), and development effort. The size of the programs under development is considered known for a collection of past, historical projects and in some cases their respective effort value is used to train the Artificial Neural Networks (ANN) models proposed. A set of projects is intentionally left out from the training process and is used to verify the generalisation of the models. Therefore, the main target of this investigation is to use the size values of new projects and utilise the robust cost models developed to approximate their effort value. The proposed models also make use of the effort values for the projects employed in the training of the models to investigate accuracy performance. The hypothesis is that once a robust relationship between size and effort is established by means of a model, then it can be used along with the size estimations to predict effort of new projects more accurately. In addition, a Genetic Algorithm (GA) is constructed to calibrate the model's architecture.

Thus, in this work we study the potentials of developing a software cost model using computational intelligence techniques relying only on size and effort data. The core of the model proposed consists of Artificial Neural Networks (ANN). Our principal investigation is to determine which size-related metric between LOC and FP is more descriptive of effort with the aid of ANN. The initial approach builds ANN using size-related input data and the architecture is empirically defined. The second approach investigates a more complicated issue, i.e., which combination of size and/or effort related data of historical projects and which ANN architecture provides better effort approximations for the new projects. Essentially what is investigated in this approach is the size of a sliding-window used to extract inputs and the ANN topology. The experiments conducted suggest that quite promising accuracy results can be obtained and that if we specify the appropriate ANN architecture for each dataset, even more improved effort approximations may be achieved. Therefore, in the third approach the sliding-window length and the ANN architecture are optimised with the use of a Genetic Algorithm (GA). The GA evolves the ANN structure with the appropriate number and type of size-related inputs (i.e., LOC or FP), as well as the optimal internal hidden neuron architecture, to predict effort as accurately as possible. The inputs used to train and test the ANN are in this case: project size measurements (either Lines of Code (LOC) or Function Points (FP)), and/or the associated effort to predict the subsequent in series, unknown project effort. In addition, a Regression cost estimation model is presented as a benchmark to assess the performance of the model materialising estimations of the dependent variable (effort) using the same aforementioned training and testing samples, so that the proposed models are compared to a classic method.

The rest of the paper is organised as follows: Section 2 presents a literature overview of relative research on size-based software cost estimation and especially focuses on machine learning techniques utilising ANN. Section 3 provides a description of the datasets and performance metrics used in the experiments following in Section 4. Section 4 includes the application of an ANN cost estimation model and describes an investigation of further improvements of the model proposing a hybrid algorithm to evaluate the optimal input methods and architectures for the datasets. In addition, this section summarises the results of each respective approach proposed and presents a comparison of the results to a classic Regression. Section 5, concludes with the overall remarks and findings of this work, discusses a few limitations and suggests future research steps.

2. Related work

Several techniques have been investigated for software cost estimation, especially data-driven artificial intelligence techniques, such as neural networks, evolutionary computing, regression trees, rule-based induction as they present several advantages over other, traditional approaches like regression. Most of the relevant studies investigate, among other issues, the identification and realisation of the most important factors that influence software costs. This section focuses on related work mainly of size-based, neural network models proposed for software cost estimation.

To begin with, most size-based models consider either the number of lines written for a project (called Lines of Code (LOC) or thousands of Lines of Code (KLOC)) used in models such as the COCOMO (Boehm, 1981; Boehm et al., 1997), or the number of Function Points

(FP) used in models such as Albrecht's Function Point Analysis (FPA) (Albrecht & Gaffney, 1983). In size-based software cost estimation models essentially, the size of LOC or FP is estimated at the early stages of development. The LOC metric has been primarily used in models such as the COCOMO (Boehm, 1981; Boehm, 1997) and SLIM (Putnam, 1978; Putnam & Myers, 1992; Putnam & Myers, 2003), models first proposed in the previous decades. LOC was considered quite popular because it represents a direct measurement of the length of the software under development. However, the main weakness of the LOC metric is that it cannot be estimated accurately from the beginning of the development phases of a project. Therefore, the FP metric was proposed in order to overcome this limitation (Albrecht, 1979) and estimate software size based on the requirements. FP basically represent a weighted sum of the following five factors: Input Count, Output Count, Logic Files Count, Inquiries Count and Interface Files Count. FP's advantage is that after requirements specification these factors become known and moreover different systems can be compared irrespectively of the technologies and languages used in development. However, there is a lot of discussion regarding the reliability and objectivity of both size metrics as different tools counting LOC depend on the language and definitions used and different practitioners counting FP for the same projects produce different results (Kemerer, 1993).

Many research studies investigate the potential of developing software cost prediction systems using different approaches, datasets and cost factors. Review articles, like the ones of Briand & Wieczorek (2002), Jørgensen & Shepperd (2007), include a detailed description of such studies. In this section we highlight some of the most important relevant studies dealing with size-based estimations.

Wittig and Finnie (1997) estimated effort using the backpropagation algorithm on ANN for the Desharnais and ASMA datasets, mainly using system size to determine it's relationship with effort. The approach yielded promising prediction results indicating, though, that the model required a more systematic development approach to establish the topology and parameter settings so as to obtain better results.

Dolado (2001) searched for the cost estimation equation of the relationship between size and effort by using Genetic Programming tree structures representing several classical equations, like the linear, power, quadratic, etc. The approach reached to moderately good levels of prediction accuracy results by using solely the size attribute and indicated that further improvements can be achieved.

Mittas et al. (2010) proposed the Demming Regression for modelling the relationship between software effort and size on the four datasets, Desharnais, COCOMO, Maxwell and Nasa93 based on the assumption that the observed values of the variables are measurements which coincide with the actual size values. Under this assumption the proposed technique estimated the regression coefficients and showed significant improvements in comparison to the classic Ordinary Least Squares regression.

In summary, the literature thus far, exhibits several research attempts focusing on measuring effort and size and accepting them as the key variables in cost estimation. Many studies indicate that ANN models are quite promising estimators or that they perform at least as well as other approaches. In the rest of this section we investigate such approaches.

Heiat (2002) compared the performance of two cost estimation techniques with respect to the type of language used for developing a range of projects. The finding of this work was that the ANN performed equally well with Regression for the sample projects that were implemented with a third generation programming language (3GL). However, experimenting with a less homogeneous set of projects, that is, projects that were implemented with a third generation programming language (3GL) and others that were implemented with a fourth generation programming language (4GL), ANN outperformed Regression.

Idri et al. (2002) conducted two experiments using a backpropagation trained Multi-Layer Perceptron (MLP) ANN architecture on the COCOMO dataset, the outputs of which were mapped to a fuzzy rule-based system. Results indicated poor accuracy performance, while it is most likely that the experiments suffered from overfitting as an extreme number of iterations (300,000) were executed on just a small set of 63 samples.

Idri et al. (2004) investigated the use and interpretation of Radial Basis Function Networks (RBFN) in software cost estimation by mapping the ANN to a fuzzy rule-based system. Results on the COCOMO dataset indicated that the accuracy of the ANN depended heavily on the parameters of the middle layer and more specifically on the number of hidden neurons and the weight values.

Kumar et al. (2008) used Wavelet Neural Networks (WNN) for software development estimation and compared their effectiveness with MLP, RBFN, Multiple Linear Regression (MLR), Dynamic Evolving Neuro-Fuzzy Inference System (DENFIS) and Support Vector Machines (SVM) in terms of the *Mean Magnitude of Relative Error* (*MMRE*). WNN seemed to outperform all other techniques.

Tronto et al. (2008) investigated the application of ANN and stepwise regression for software effort prediction. The experiments were conducted on the COCOMO dataset employing categorical variables whose impact was identified based on the work of Angelis et al. (2001) forming new categorical values. It was observed that there is a strong relationship between the success of a technique and the size of the learning dataset, the nature of the function for cost and other dataset characteristics (such as existence of outliers, collinearity and number of attributes).

Azzeh et al. (2010) investigated the impact of Grey Relational Analysis (GRA) integrated with Fuzzy set theory in a by-analogy estimation model and also compared it to ANN, CBR and MLR models using several public datasets, i.e., ISBSG, Desharnais, COCOMO, Albrecht and Kemerer. The Fuzzy GRA appeared to produce statistically more significant results than the rest of the models. Moreover, it effectively reduced the uncertainty of attribute measurement between two software projects and improved the way to handle both numerical and categorical data in similarity measurements.

Kaur et al. (2010) proved the effectiveness of ANN models for the NASA dataset compared to the Halstead, Walston-Felix, Bailey-Basili and Doty models, all of which are popular legacy models used in software cost estimation. Backpropagation ANN were used and reported as the most generalised networks currently in use that present good estimation capabilities.

Summarizing some of the findings of the relevant literature, we conclude that many researchers recognise the high prediction accuracy of ANN and their effectiveness in modelling the cost estimation environment. However, a deeper investigation on the topology and configurations of the ANN model, as well as the appropriate inputs required in each case, needs to be carried out, so that the complexity of the technique is not increased proportionally to the number of inputs and the complexity of the sample projects, and still accuracy is driven to better levels.

Subsequently, in this work we firstly aim to examine the potentials of ANN in software cost modelling and secondly to investigate the possibility of providing further improvements for such a model. Our goal is to inspect: (i) whether a suitable ANN model, in terms of input parameters, may be built; (ii) whether we can achieve sufficient estimates of software development effort using only size or function based metrics on different datasets of empirical cost samples; (iii) whether a hybrid computational model, which consists of a combination of ANN and GA, may contribute to devising the ideal ANN architecture and set of inputs that meet some evaluation criteria. Our strategy is to exploit the benefits of computational intelligence in software cost modelling and provide a near to optimal effort predictor for impending new projects.

3. Datasets and performance metrics

A variety of historical software cost data samples coming from different datasets that are popular in software cost estimation empirical research were employed to provide a strong comparative basis with the results reported in other relevant studies. Also, the performance metrics used to assess the ANN's precision accuracy are described in this section.

3.1 Datasets description

The following datasets were selected to demonstrate and test the approach describing historical project data: COCOMO`81 (COC`81), Kemerer`87 (KEM`87), a combination of COCOMO`81 and Kemerer`87 (COKEM`87), Albrecht and Gaffney`83 (ALGAF`83) and finally Desharnais`89 (DESH`89).

The COC`81 (Boehm, 1981) dataset contains information about 63 software projects from different applications. Each project is described by the following 17 cost attributes: reliability, database size, complexity, required reusability, documentation, execution time constraint, main storage constraint, platform volatility, analyst capability, programmer capability, applications experience, platform experience, language & tool experience, personnel continuity, use of software tools, multi-site development and required schedule. Also, for the projects LOC is measured.

The second dataset, named KEM`87 (Kemerer, 1987) contains 15 software project records gathered by a single organisation in the USA, which constitute business applications written mainly in COBOL. The attributes of the dataset are: actual project's effort measured in man-months, duration, KLOC, unadjusted and adjusted FP's count. In addition, a combination of the two previous datasets was created, namely COKEM`87, to allow us to experiment with a larger but rather heterogeneous dataset.

The third dataset ALGAF`83 (Albrecht & Gaffney, 1983) contains information about 24 projects developed by the IBM DP service organisation. The datasets' characteristics correspond to the actual project effort, the KLOC, the number of inputs, the number of outputs, the number of master files, the number of inquiries and the FP's count.

The fourth dataset, DESH`89 (Desharnais, 1989), includes observations for more than 80 systems developed by a Canadian software development house at the end of 1980. The basic characteristics of the dataset account for the following: project name, development effort measured in hours, team's experience, project manager's experience, number of transactions processed, number of entities, unadjusted and adjusted FP, development environment and year of completion.

A major assumption of our work is that the measurements of some attributes provided for the projects in these datasets which are also used in our experiments, like for example the effort and the size-related factors of Lines of Code (LOC) and Function Points (FP), coincide with the actual values of developing the corresponding programs. However, since some of these software project metrics are conceptually subjective and lack standard definitions, they depend on the person counting and the tools used to perform measurements, and thus, this high degree of subjectivity clearly makes the measurement of the software attributes and validation of the prediction systems for the attributes and effort problematic.

3.2 Performance metrics

The performance of the models was evaluated using a combination of common error metrics, namely the *Mean Relative Error* (*MRE*), the *Correlation Coefficient* (*CC*) and the *Normalized Root Mean Squared Error* (*NRMSE*), together with the Prediction at Level (*pred(l)*) and a devised Sign prediction (*Sign*) metric. These error metrics were employed to validate the model's forecasting ability by considering the difference between the actual and the predicted cost samples and their ascendant or descendant progression in relation to the actual values.

The *MRE*, given in equation (1), shows the prediction error focusing on the sample being predicted. $x_{act}(i)$ is the actual effort and $x_{pred}(i)$ the predicted effort of the ith project.

$$MRE(n) = \frac{1}{n}\sum_{i=1}^{n}\left|\frac{x_{act}(i) - x_{pred}(i)}{x_{act}(i)}\right| \tag{1}$$

The *CC* between the actual and predicted series, described by equation (2), measures the ability of the predicted samples to follow the upwards or downwards of the original series as it evolves in the sample prediction sequence. An absolute *CC* value equal or near 1 is interpreted as a perfect follow up of the original series by the forecasted one. A negative *CC* sign indicates that the forecasting series follows the same direction of the original series but with negative mirroring, that is, with a rotation about the time-axis.

$$CC(n) = \frac{\sum_{i=1}^{n}\left[\left(x_{act}(i) - \bar{x}_{act,n}\right)\left(x_{pred}(i) - \bar{x}_{pred,n}\right)\right]}{\sqrt{\left[\sum_{i=1}^{n}\left(x_{act}(i) - \bar{x}_{act,n}\right)^2\right]\left[\sum_{i=1}^{n}\left(x_{pred}(i) - \bar{x}_{pred,n}\right)^2\right]}} \tag{2}$$

The *NRMSE* assesses the quality of predictions and is calculated using the *Root Mean Squared Error* (*RMSE*) as follows:

$$RMSE(n) = \sqrt{\frac{1}{n}\sum_{i=1}^{n}\left[x_{pred}(i) - x_{act}(i)\right]^2} \tag{3}$$

$$NRMSE(n) = \frac{RMSE(n)}{\sigma_{\Delta}} = \frac{RMSE(n)}{\sqrt{\frac{1}{n}\sum_{i=1}^{n}\left[x_{act}(i) - \bar{x}_n\right]^2}} \tag{4}$$

If *NRMSE*=0 then predictions are perfect; if *NRMSE*=1 the prediction is no better than taking x_{pred} equal to the mean value of n samples.

The Prediction Level (*Pred(l)*) defined in equation (5) specifies how many data predictions k out of n (total number of data points predicted) performed well, i.e., below a predefined level specified by the *RE* metric (see equation (6)) is lower than level *l*. In the experiments the parameter *l* was set equal to 0.25.

$$\Pr ed(l) = \frac{k}{n} \tag{5}$$

$$RE(n) = \frac{\left|x_{act}(i) - x_{pred}(i)\right|}{x_{act}(i)} \tag{6}$$

The *Sign Predictor* (*Sign(p)*) metric assesses if there is a positive or a negative transition of the actual and predicted effort trace in the projects used only during the evaluation of the models with the sliding-window technique on unknown test data. With this measure we are not interested in the exact values, but only if the tendency of the next value to the previous is similar. This is expressed in equations (7) and (8).

$$Sign(p) = \frac{\sum_{i=1}^{n} z_i}{n} \tag{7}$$

$$where\ z_i = \begin{cases} 1 \ if((x_{t+1}^{pred} - x_t^{pred}) * (x_{t+1}^{act} - x_t^{act})) > 0 \\ 0 \qquad otherwise. \end{cases} \tag{8}$$

4. Experimental approach

As we have already mentioned, the software cost estimation literature has shown many research attempts focusing on predictions of Artificial Neural Network (ANN) models, which are treated as promising estimators with equal or better performance compared to other popular approaches, like by-analogy or regression-based estimation. Their input variables usually involve numerous internal and external project attributes, typically concerning the actual product under development, the people undertaking the development tasks and the process followed.

In our approach size-based data of various size definitions is used, which have been gathered from industrial projects, either representing software actual lines of code or functionality delivered. We investigate cost estimators in the form of ANN models, that aim to learn and generalise the knowledge embedded in past project samples, so as to estimate the associated development effort as accurately as possible. Consequently, our focus is twofold: Firstly, we will study performance, stability and calibration issues of the proposed models and secondly, identify any present correlations of development effort and size-based attributes.

In this section we provide the detailed experimental process and the results yielded by the models developed: (i) An ANN approach with random holdout samples for validation, (ii) An ANN approach, with varying input method (a random timestamp was given to the data samples which were inputted using a sliding-window technique); (iii) A Hybrid model, coupling ANN with a GA to reach to a near to optimal input method and internal architecture; (iv) A classic Regression model.

4.1 An ANN investigating size-effort relation

The following section presents the ANN model proposed to investigate the relationship between software size (expressed in LOC or FP) and effort, by conducting a series of experiments. We are concerned with inspecting the predictive ability of the ANN with respect to the attribute counting the size of the software developed for each project in each dataset.

4.1.1 Model description

ANN are non-linear, model-free and alternative to traditional statistical methods able to solve complex pattern recognition problems. ANN consist of basic computational elements called neurons organised in groups that form layers. They may be also viewed as directed graphs, composed of nodes and connections, also called weights or synapses, which connect the neurons (Haykin, 1999). Certain types of neurons organised in multiple layers form the Multi-Layer Perceptron (MLP) (McCulloch & Pitts, 1943) which is one of the most popular types of ANN. A simple MLP ANN is shown in Figure 1.

The number of neurons in the input (first) layer is equal to the number of attributes used as independent variables. The last layer is the network output which corresponds to the independent variable (in our case software effort). Each subsequent layer uses the weights coming from the previous layers and adjusts them so that the accuracy error between the actual and predicted values for the dependent variable is diminished. Each neuron uses the respective input vectors, the weights and a momentum coefficient to calculate its output.

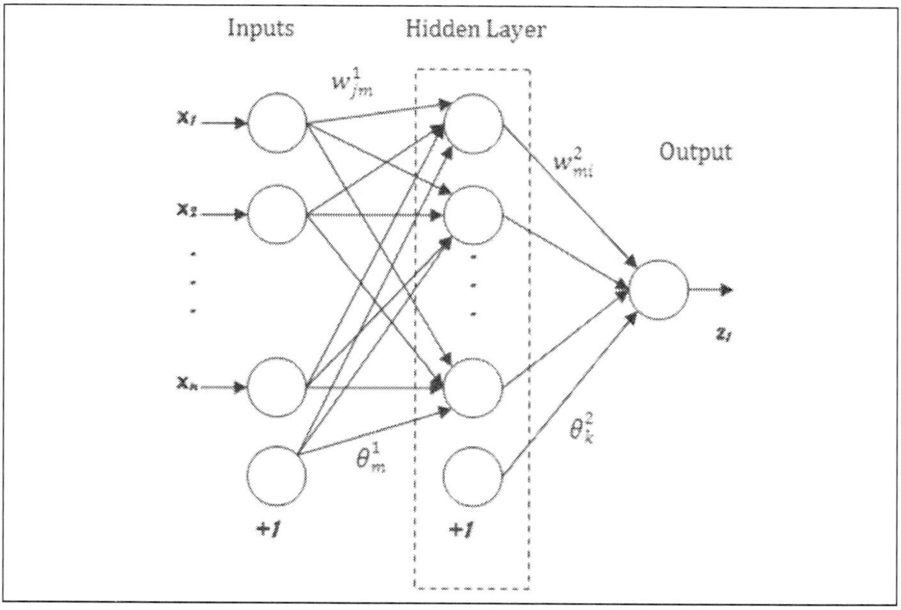

Fig. 1. A feed-forward Multi-Layer Perceptron Neural Network

Equation (9) specifies how the outcome of the first hidden node in the first layer x_1^1 is estimated.

$$x_1^1 = f\left(\sum_{i=1}^{n} x_i w_{i1}^1 + \theta_1^1\right) \tag{9}$$

The networks employed in the present work are single hidden layer networks and MLP networks, which use one hidden layer partitioned into three parallel sub-layers activated by a different function, e.g., the *hyperbolic tangent*, the *Gaussian* and the *Gaussian complement* specified in equations (10), (11) and (12) respectively.

$$f(y) = (1 - \exp(-by)) * (1 + \exp(-by))^{-1} \tag{10}$$

$$f(y) = \exp\left(-x^2\right) \tag{11}$$

$$f(y) = 1 - \exp\left(-x^2\right) \tag{12}$$

The error backpropagation algorithm is one of the most widely used algorithms for training the network and requires data samples in the form of input-output patterns. The backpropagation learning algorithm is used to calculate derivatives of performance of the mean square error with respect to the weight and bias variables. In order to learn efficiently the data fed, the network calculates an error, which is the difference between the desired and the actual response. The error is propagated to the network in a backward manner, so that for each neuron the weights are adjusted to minimise this error iteratively.

Moreover, for the backpropagation algorithm the dataset is randomly divided into three subsets: the training set, the validation set and the testing set. The training set is utilised during the learning process, the validation set is used to ensure that no overfitting occurs in the final result of the learning process and that the network will be able to generalise the knowledge gained. The testing set is an independent subset of the dataset, i.e., does not participate during the learning process and measures how well the network performs with unknown data.

4.1.2 Results

During our experiments we employed a simple, single hidden layer architecture for estimating development effort using LOC or FP from each dataset as input. In case a dataset included both size metrics we developed one ANN model for each metric in order to compare performance results. The number of nodes in the hidden layer was empirically defined for each dataset case due to the simplicity of the models under investigation. For the input layer *netsum* function was used, for the hidden layer the *tansig* function and finally, for the output layer the *purelin* function was used. The models were developed in Matlab R2010b.

Each ANN was trained in a supervised manner, using the backpropagation algorithm and a random selection of 60% of the total projects comprised the training data samples. Also, 20% of the original data samples were used for validation during the training of the ANN and the rest 20% were the holdout samples that were later used for testing the generalisation ability of the best trained model, i.e., the ANN that yielded the lowest *MRE* figure. We randomly initialised the weights and momentum coefficients and re-trained the network 20 times with the backpropagation algorithm. Finally, we utilised the best ANN to proceed to the testing phase.

DATASET	INPUT	TOPO-LOGY	TRAINING PHASE				TESTING PHASE			
			MRE	CC	NRMSE	Pred(.25)	MRE	CC	NRMSE	Pred(.25)
COC`81	LOC	1-4-1	0.888	0.998	0.063	0.333	1.629	0.597	2.890	0.154
KEM`87	FP	1-3-1	0.204	0.966	0.248	0.625	0.282	0.943	0.614	0.333
KEM`87	LOC	1-3-1	0.258	0.861	0.476	0.750	0.257	0.792	0.527	0.333
COKEM`87	LOC	1-2-1	1.335	0.892	0.446	0.132	1.542	0.599	0.971	0.188
ALGAF`83	FP	1-2-1	0.304	0.978	0.213	0.545	0.324	0.987	0.149	0.600
ALGAF`83	LOC	1-4-1	0.301	0.991	0.130	0.364	0.469	0.985	0.691	0.200
DESH`89	FP	1-3-1	0.487	0.697	0.715	0.474	0.348	0.712	0.696	0.400

Table 1. Experimental Results obtained with the ANN-model.

Table 1 summarises the best results obtained with the specific ANN architectures and the various datasets. The first column refers to the dataset used, the second to the type of size metric that was used in the input layer (LOC or FP), the third refers to the ANN topology and the rest of the columns refer to the error metrics during the training and testing phase.
As expected, the degree of accuracy across the datasets varies because accurate and optimum models cannot be developed for every case. However, in some cases the overall performance of the approach is a promising indication that ANN models can reach to quite accurate effort approximations. The datasets whose effort is better approximated is KEM`87, followed by ALGAF`83 using FP as input and then followed by DESH`89. The results of the training phase indicate that the ANN models were able to learn well the training data from all the datasets except COKEM`87, which comprises a concatenation of two different datasets. Therefore, this effect may be attributed to the less homogeneous form of the aforementioned dataset which was merged from two other datasets. The results of the testing phase are also quite successful for KEM`87, ALGAF`83 and DESH`89 datasets but less accurate for the COC`81 and COKEM`87 cases. These figures of effort approximations were considerably easy to achieve, experimenting with only a few internal hidden neurons, i.e., starting from 2 to 5, because we were using one single size attribute as input.
Moreover, for datasets describing both size attributes LOC and FP, i.e., KEM`87 and ALGAF`83, we observe that the ANN models using FP are more accurate in terms of correlation (CC) in the first case, and more accurate in prediction level (*MRE*) in the second case, during the testing phase. This indicates that the proposed model can achieve better approximations using the FP size metric instead of LOC, even though it is worth noting that more thorough investigation needs to be performed with different ANN architectures and coupling LOC and/or FP with effort spent on past projects aiming at improving prediction performance.

4.2 An ANN coupling size-effort

The following section presents an ANN model which investigates the relationship between software size (expressed in LOC or FP) and effort, by conducting a series of experiments coupling size and effort data. We are concerned with inspecting the predictive ability of the ANN according to the architecture utilised and the input method (volume and order of the data fed to the model) per dataset.

4.2.1 Model description

The core architecture of a size-effort coupling ANN was a feedforward MLP (as previously described in Figure 1) connecting each input neuron with hidden layers consisting of parallel slabs activated by different functions. Empirical variations of this architecture were employed regarding the number of inputs and neurons in the internal hidden layers, whereas the difference between the actual and the predicted effort was again manifested at the output layer (forecasting deviation). Again, the ANN were trained in a supervised manner, using the backpropagation algorithm and 70% of the training data samples. Also, 20% of the original data samples were used for validation of the training of the ANN and finally, 10% holdout samples were used for testing the model.

4.2.2 Results

The empirically conducted experiments investigated mainly the appropriate number and type of inputs and internal neurons forming the layers of the ANN. Here, a more complex ANN architecture was used with three different hidden slabs in the internal layers. In addition, in these experiments several ANN parameters were kept constant as some preliminary experiments conducted initially showed that varying the type of the activation function in each layer had no effect on the forecasting quality. More specifically, we employed the following functions: for the input layer the *linear* function [-1, 1], for each respective hidden layer the *Gaussian*, the *tanh*, and the *Gaussian complement* and finally, for the output the *logistic* function.

In addition, for each experiment performed, a sliding-window technique was applied on the randomly generated subsets of training to extract the input vector and feed it to the ANN. Therefore, the selected projects were manifested to the ANN with specific order, so that they would couple size and effort information of past projects developed. Practically, this is expressed in Table 2, covering the following Input Methods (IM) of a varying length (or size i) sliding-window, with $i=1,\ldots,5$:

- IM1-IM2: Using the Lines of Code or the Function Points of the ith projects we estimate the effort of the ith projects;
- IM3-IM4: Using Lines of Code or Function Points with effort of the ith project we estimate the effort required for the next project $(i+1)^{th}$ in the series sequence;
- IM5-IM6: Using Lines of Code or Function Points of the ith and $(i+1)^{th}$ projects and effort of the ith project we estimate the effort required for the $(i+1)^{th}$ project.

In each input method the number of past samples included in the sliding-window, that is, the size i of the window, is specified from 1 to 5 (i index). These combinations enabled us to draw conclusions regarding the dependent variable (effort) for each coupling of input cost drivers and identify its ability to approximate the effort value.

INPUT METHOD	SOFTWARE METRICS*	Output*
IM1	$LOC(t_i)$	$EFF(t_i)$
IM2	$FP(t_i)$	$EFF(t_i)$
IM3	$LOC(t_i)$, $EFF(t_i)$	$EFF(t_{i+1})$
IM4	$FP(t_i)$, $EFF(t_i)$	$EFF(t_{i+1})$
IM5	$LOC(t_i)$, $LOC(t_{i+1})$, $EFF(t_i)$	$EFF(t_{i+1})$
IM6	$FP(t_i)$, $FP(t_{i+1})$, $EFF(t_i)$	$EFF(t_{i+1})$

Table 2. Sliding-window technique to determine the ANN input method (*where $i=1,\ldots,5$)..

The best results obtained with the ANN model and the various datasets are summarised in Table 3. The first column refers to the dataset used, the second to the input method with which the *i* data are fed to the model, the third refers to the ANN topology and the rest of the columns refer to the error metrics during the training and testing phase. The last two columns indicate the number of predicted projects that have the same sign tendency, in the sequence of the effort samples and the total percentage of the successful tendencies during testing.

The figures in Table 3 show that an ANN model deploying a mixture of architectures and input methods yields various accuracy levels. More specifically, the DESH`89 dataset achieves high prediction accuracy, with lowest *MRE* equal to 0.05 and *CC* equal to 1.0. The KEM`87 dataset also performs adequately well with relatively low error figures. The worst prediction performance is obtained with ALGAF`83 and COKEM`87 datasets. These failures may be attributed to the extremely small number of projects involved in the prediction in the first case, and to the use of a heterogeneous dataset in the latter case. Finally, in comparison with the simple ANN models developed previously, the overall prediction accuracy yielded is higher for COC`81, KEM`87 and COKEM`87 datasets, but considerably lower for ALGAF`83 and DESH`89 datasets.

DATASET	INPUT	TOPOLOGY	TRAINING PHASE			TESTING PHASE			Sign (p)	Sign (p) %
			MRE	CC	NRMSE	MRE	CC	NRMSE		
COC`81	IM5	3-15-15-15-1	0.929	0.709	0.716	0.551	0.407	0.952	5/10	50
COC`81	IM1	2-9-9-9-1	0.871	0.696	0.718	0.525	0.447	0.963	7/12	58.33
KEM`87	IM1	1-15-15-15-1	0.494	0.759	0.774	0.256	0.878	0.830	2/3	66.67
KEM`87	IM5	5-20-20-20-1	0.759	0.939	0.384	0.232	0.988	0.503	2/2	100
COKEM`87	IM3	8-20-20-20-1	5.038	0.626	0.781	0.951	0.432	0.948	3/8	37.50
COKEM`87	IM3	4-3-3-3-1	5.052	0.610	0.796	0.768	0.257	1.177	4/8	50
ALGAF`83	IM6	5-3-3-3-1	0.371	0.873	0.527	1.142	0.817	0.649	3/4	75
ALGAF`83	IM2	2-20-20-20-1	0.335	0.975	0.231	1.640	0.936	0.415	2/4	50
DESH`89	IM4	4-9-9-9-1	0.298	0.935	0.355	0.481	0.970	0.247	17/20	85
DESH`89	IM4	6-9-9-9-1	0.031	0.999	0.042	0.051	1.000	0.032	20/20	100

Table 3. Experimental Results obtained with the ANN-model coupling size-effort metrics.

In addition, as the results listed suggest, the COC`81, KEM`87 and DESH`89 datasets achieve adequately fit predictions and thus for some cases, the method is able to approximate the actual development cost. Another observation is that the majority of the best yielded results employ a large number of internal neurons. Therefore, further investigation is needed with respect to different ANN topologies and Input Methods (IM) for the various datasets. To this end, we resorted to using a hybrid scheme, combining ANN with GA, the latter attempting to evolve and reach to the near to optimal network topology and input schema that yields accurate predictions and will have a reasonably small size (i.e., number of neurons) so that the computational cost will not radically increase.

4.3 A hybrid ANN & GA

The rationale behind this attempt was that the performance of ANN obtained thus far highly depended on the size, structure and connectivity of the network and results may be further improved if the right ANN configuration parameters are found. Therefore, we applied a GA to investigate whether we can find the ideal network settings by means of a cycle of generations including candidate solutions that are pruned by the criterion 'survival of the fittest', meaning the best performing ANN in terms of effort prediction accuracy.

4.3.1 Model description

The following steps were employed for the Genetic Algorithm implementation:

1. The initial population of individuals was created randomly containing an encoding of the necessary pieces of information, that is, the number of internal hidden neurons and the Input-Method (IM).
2. From each individual of the generation we extracted the information regarding the network architecture and the structure of the input vector. Then the corresponding network was initialised, trained for a number of epochs and finally, simulated. From the simulation results obtained, all individuals were evaluated and the network state and performance results were stored.
3. Once all individuals of the respective generation have been trained and tested on generalisation, the generation was evaluated as a whole.
4. The top 5% of best individuals were forwarded to the next generation (elitism) and the rest individuals missing to complete the next generation were obtained through reproduction steps applying the selection, crossover and mutation operators. The offsprings produced through these steps replaced their parents in the original population.
5. Steps (2), (3) and (4) were repeated until finally, a predefined number of generations have been reached.

More specifically, the first task for implementing the hybrid model was to determine a type of encoding so as to express the potential solutions. The encoding used was a binary string representing the ANN structure, the internal hidden neurons and the varying input's coupling of effort and size attributes. The inputs were inserted into the ANN models created within the hybrid algorithm following the Input Methods (IM) specified earlier. The number of neurons used in the hidden slabs was restricted not to exceed 20 neurons to avoid building ANN models that would lead to overfitting. The space of all feasible solutions (i.e., the set of solutions among which the desired solution resides) was called the search space. Each point in the search space represents one possible solution. Each possible solution was "marked" by its fitness value, which in our case was expressed by equation (13), minimizing the *MRE* and the overall size of the network, i.e., the total number of internal neurons, to avoid creating overly large and complex networks.

$$fitness = \frac{1}{1 + MRE + size} \tag{13}$$

The GA searches the problem space to locate the best solution among a number of possible solutions. Searching for a solution is then equal to looking for some extreme value (minimum or maximum) in the search space.

The GA developed included three types of operators: selection (roulette wheel), crossover (with crossover rate=0.25) and mutation (with mutation rate=0.01). Selection chooses members from the population of chromosomes proportionally to their fitness and elitism was used to ensure that the best members of each population are always selected for the new population. Crossover adapts the genotype of two parents by exchanging parts of them and creating a new chromosome with a modified genotype. Crossover was performed by selecting a random gene along the length of the chromosomes and swapping all the genes after that point. Finally, the mutation operator simply changes a specific gene of a selected individual in order to create a new chromosome with a different genotype.

4.3.2 Results

In this section we present and discuss the results obtained using the Hybrid model on the various available datasets. The best ANN architectures yielded are listed in the third column of Table 4 with the various error figures obtained both during the training and the testing phase.

The performance of the different ANN architectures constructed with the aid of the GA shows high learning ability. The main observation is that for all of the datasets the hybrid model was able to optimise prediction accuracy. This is remarkably consistent through both the training and the testing error figures reported by the best solutions summarised in Table 4. In fact, for all the datasets investigated, the hybrid model performs adequately well in terms of generalisation ability and prediction accuracy. During training and testing the *MRE* is significantly lowered compared to the results of the experiments conducted with the simple ANN (Table 1) and the empirical coupling ANN (Table 3), the *CC* improves in all cases, whereas the *NRMSE* is also highly improved.

Moreover, it is observed that there is a strong relationship between the success of a particular model and the type of attributes used as inputs. In all datasets, IM1 utilising in each case LOC or FP as inputs, yields the best prediction results compared to IM2 and IM3. Accuracy is usually diminished when adding the effort values in IM2 and in all other cases, except in the dataset DESH`89 case, where IM3 accuracy is considerably improved. This shows that the size metric for all datasets improves effort approximations and that LOC or FP are noticeably highly descriptive factors of effort. We would expect that adding the effort values in the inputs of the ANN models would have improved estimates, but this is not the case due to the existence of some projects outliers in respect to their effort values.

Moreover, it seems that the experiments using KEM`87 showed similar *MRE* and *CC* error figures and an improved *NRMSE* in favor of FP instead of LOC, both during training and testing. The ALGAF`83 dataset showed similar *NRMSE* and *CC* error figures, whereas an improved *MRE* was observed using LOC. Overall, the experiments conducted using one of these two size measures for predicting effort (i.e., in IM1 and IM2) produce superior results consistently throughout all the datasets indicating that both LOC and FP are very good descriptors of effort. Of course this is something that on one hand agrees with what is

DATASET	INPUT	TOPOLOGY	TRAINING PHASE			TESTING PHASE		
			MRE	CC	NRMSE	MRE	CC	NRMSE
COC`81	IM1	1-9-17-10-1	0.004	1.000	0.014	0.003	1.000	0.014
COC`81	IM3	2-20-18-3-1	0.092	0.963	0.270	0.075	0.961	0.278
COC`81	IM5	3-19-20-4-1	0.043	0.990	0.149	0.044	0.981	0.199
KEM`87	IM1	1-17-13-16-1	0.008	1.000	0.015	0.009	1.000	0.019
KEM`87	IM3	2-18-14-18-1	0.246	0.825	0.539	0.211	0.822	0.550
KEM`87	IM5	3-19-15-20-1	0.004	1.000	0.006	0.028	0.997	0.081
ALGAF`83	IM2	1-17-20-11-1	0.006	1.000	0.005	0.009	1.000	0.006
ALGAF`83	IM4	2-19-1520-1	0.041	0.998	0.074	0.062	0.993	0.122
ALGAF`83	IM6	3-19-9-16-1	0.029	0.999	0.045	0.031	0.999	0.051
DESH`89	IM2	1-13-20-6-1	0.002	1.000	0.008	0.005	1.000	0.024
DESH`89	IM4	2-19-20-8-1	0.087	0.990	0.136	0.163	0.977	0.210
DESH`89	IM6	3-19-11-10-1	0.089	0.990	0.139	0.173	0.975	0.218

Table 4. Hybrid model (coupling ANN and GA) results.

already pointed out by numerous studies in literature and on the other suggests that our model behaves as it should. Also, another observation is that the best accuracy is significantly lowered (error rates are higher) when the effort is given as an additional input to the ANN (in the IM3 or IM4 cases), meaning that the model's ability to capture the correlation between size and effort is decreased. This shows that outlying values for the effort of these projects exist and indicates that some sort of filtering could improve the results. Another observation is that ANN could be therefore used in the case of software cost estimation as a filtering process to eliminate outlying project values. We additionally observe that prediction accuracy is significantly and consistently improved when the LOC or FP of the project whose effort is being predicted, is given to the model (in the IM5 or IM6 cases). Heuristically, this is a logical conclusion as the model in the latter case is fed with information regarding the project's LOC or FP and therefore, the prediction accuracy is enhanced by this additional information. Overall, the proposed model seems to work under these assumptions consistently well.

4.4 Regression investigating size-effort relation

In this section we present the results obtained from a simple Regression so as to provide some comparative assessment of the models proposed thus far. Regression assesses how well the regression line approximates the real effort and it is built using the same samples used in the ANN training and testing phase.

Regression analysis is used to capture and explain the relationship between the size and effort of projects in the form of an exponential function which can be represented by a polynomial transformed to linear using the natural logarithm.

4.4.1 Model description

We denote Y as the dependent variable of the total cost for developing software projects (usually expressed as the effort spent) and X the independent variables representing the size of projects (usually in LOC or FP). Each vector $\{(x_1,y_1), \ldots, (x_l,y_l)\}$ represents a sample of projects, where $x_i \in \Re^n$ and $y_i \in \Re$ for each project i and are used in the regression model defined in (14). We assume that the errors ε_i are independent and have a zero mean. The goal is to find the polynomial coefficients β_0 and β_1 representing the constant and the slope of the regression linear function $f(x_i)$ respectively, the latter being defined in (15).

$$y_i = f(x_i) + \varepsilon_i \tag{14}$$

$$f(x_i) = \beta_0 + \beta_1 x_i \tag{15}$$

In case the relationship between the dependent and independent variables is not linear we assume that a simple transformation such as the logarithmic can be used to estimate a model of the form (16).

$$y_i = \beta_0 + \beta_1 x_i + \varepsilon_i \tag{16}$$

The error function the approach is trying to minimise is based on the least-squares form.

4.4.2 Results

Regression is built under the assumption that the dependent variable (effort) is linearly related with the independent variable(s) (size and/or next effort values). The model produces the slope of a line that best fits the data of the training set and then, during the testing phase, we estimate the value of the dependent variable. We utilise the yielded regression coefficients from the training phase to estimate the values of effort for the testing samples. Finally, we compare the estimated effort values to the actual effort using the performance metrics mentioned above.

The Regression approach is tested on all the datasets as they were originally separated into the training and testing subsets and were used by the ANN in the previous experiments. Thus, a comparison with the initial ANN models built is feasible. The results of Regression indicate average performance for all datasets with accuracy staying lower compared to that of the approaches previously proposed in this work (simple and hybrid ANN). This indicates that the form of the problem is considered quite complex and cannot be easily addressed by a simple form of Regression. However, although the ANN approach demonstrated some significant advantages in terms of prediction performance in the experiments of this work, it doesn't mean that it can replace Regression but should be regarded as a promising approach for these certain circumstances.

DATASET	INPUT	TRAINING PHASE				TESTING PHASE			
		MRE	CC	NRMSE	Pred(.25)	MRE	CC	NRMSE	Pred(.25)
COC`81	LOC	0.608	0.834	0.579	0.233	1.022	0.639	1.045	0.154
KEM`87	FP	0.424	0.764	0.663	0.500	0.196	0.974	0.289	0.667
KEM`87	LOC	0.330	0.776	0.627	0.500	0.234	0.825	0.566	0.667
COKEM`87	LOC	1.082	0.893	0.591	0.053	0.999	0.607	0.791	0.188
ALGAF`83	FP	0.354	0.930	0.472	0.364	0.248	0.969	0.453	0.600
ALGAF`83	LOC	0.408	0.837	0.530	0.364	0.397	0.970	0.556	0.200
DESH`89	FP	0.514	0.543	0.848	0.395	0.311	0.708	0.819	0.467

Table 5. Regression Results.

The main problem of the Regression method yielding mediocre results may be attributed mainly to the method's dependence on the distribution and normality of the data points used and its inability to approximate unknown functions, as opposed to the ability demonstrated by the simple ANN model as well as the hybrid approach with the GA. However, we recognise that in order to comparatively assess the results of a range of models statistical tests, like Wilcoxon's, or t-tests need to be performed to investigate the statistical difference between the errors yielded by the comparative models.

5. Conclusions

In this chapter, we considered the problem of reliable and accurate software cost estimations through computational intelligence techniques. Effective modelling of the relationship between software effort and size has always been a challenge, especially for people involved in project resource management, due to the high level of complexity and uniqueness of the software projects developed. The majority of existing estimation models and methods fail to reproduce this relationship so as to yield successful development effort approximations, or have difficulties even to converge to suggesting an explicit, measurable and concise set of factors affecting productivity. Nevertheless, there is a large discussion on the relationship of cost factors and effort and since this relationship is the core of any cost model, it is essential to describe it accurately.

Many studies in the software cost estimation literature encourage the use of Artificial Neural Networks (ANN) as cost predictors showing that they may perform better or at least as well as other approaches. Adopting this position, this chapter involved the investigation of building the relationship of size and effort using ANN. Software size obtained from past historical project data has been proposed as one of the most important attributes affecting effort and has been extensively used to build a variety of cost models.

Essentially, this chapter proposed a modelling approach utilising ANN and the most common size-related factors found in benchmark datasets. These factors refer to software Lines of Code (LOC) and Function Points (FP). The basic assumption of this work was that error-free size measurements are available for a number of software projects obtained from a set of past historical project data which are used as inputs for the ANN cost models created. In addition, a sliding-window of variable length was used to extract size-related sample data from the datasets (i.e., LOC or FP counts) targeting at coupling them with effort subsets from previously completed projects. This coupling was realised in the form of training patterns fed to ANN so as to investigate if a modelling relationship between size and effort may be established. Moreover, a Genetic Algorithm (GA) was implemented to undertake the optimisation of the ANN architecture of the core model to reduce the *Mean Relative Error* (*MRE*). The near-to-optimal ANN topologies and type of inputs selected for each dataset were discussed and compared to Regression models built across the same training and testing data samples.

The results obtained with the ANN models indicated that the performance of such a model mainly depends on its architecture and parameter settings, and relying on empirical rules to determine these settings is not the optimal approach. The problem was thus reduced to finding the ideal ANN architecture to formulate a reliable prediction model for software cost estimation. The first experimental results indicated mediocre prediction success, comparable to the simple Regression, except in a few dataset cases. Also, as the combinations of inputs used in the ANN models increased, we observed that designing an appropriate internal ANN architecture to deal with the complexity in each case (i.e., type of attributes and dataset) was a quite difficult task. Common methods, such as empirical or trial-and-error, often run the risk of overlooking more promising architectures and also, as a result, it was considered particularly hard to further optimise the results yielded by the ANN models. In addition, it became evident that there was need for more extensive exploration of solutions in the search space of various topologies and input methods as the results obtained by the investigated ANN models did not converge to a general solution.

Therefore, this chapter introduced a hybrid model consisting of ANN and Genetic Algorithms (GA). The latter evolved a population of networks to select the optimal architecture and inputs that provided the most accurate software cost predictions. The results of this work showed that the ANN approach combined with a GA yields better estimates than the empirically created ANN and Regression models, something that suggests that the technique is very promising.

The main limitation of this method, as well as any other size-based approach, is that especially LOC size estimates must be known in advance to provide accurate enough effort estimations, which is never the case. Also, there is always the risk that if the same project was counted twice would not give exactly the same size (LOC or FP) or effort measurements, and this basic limitation is usually recognised between practitioners. In addition, these errors in measurements of size and effort should be taken into consideration in any approach used for cost estimation and especially if a large discrepancy between the actual and estimated size is occurring in estimations made in the early project phases.

Another limitation is the lack of a satisfactory volume of homogeneous data, as well as of a clear definition and measurement rules for size units, such as LOC and FP, which result in uncertainty to the estimation process. The software size is also affected by other factors that are not investigated by the models of this chapter, such as the programming language and platform used during development. This means that we have consciously focused only on coding effort, irrespective of the type of software and development method in this work, which accounts for only a percentage of the total effort in software development. Another important limitation related with the technologies used is that the ANNs are considered "black boxes" and so the GA requires an extensive search of the solution space, something which is considered very time-consuming.

In future research steps we will emphasise on other aspects affecting the prediction performance of ANN, i.e., optimising other ANN parameters of different types of ANN, such as activation functions and learning techniques. Also, evolutionary processes on genetic search could help to automate and improve, if not optimise, ANN design required to represent complex behaviours. An evolutionary algorithm thus could be coupled with ANN in other ways, such as: (i) Employing fixed network structures with connection weights under evolutionary control, which includes both supervised learning applications and reinforced learning applications, (ii) Designing the ordering and organisation of the nodes from the input to the output layer of the network, including arrangement of interconnections, (iii) Pre-processing the input types of the training data, which can be also used to reduce the input set by discarding less informative, or descriptive cost drivers for approximating development effort.

Future research steps may also concentrate on ways to improve the performance of the proposed approach, examples of which may be: (i) Study of more factors affecting development effort and their interdependencies, (ii) Further adjustment of the ANN and GA parameter settings, such as modification of the fitness function, (iii) Improvement of the efficiency of the algorithms by testing more homogeneous or clustered data and, (iv) Improvement of the quality of the data to achieve better convergence. Consequently, more experiments and more thorough investigation of the capabilities of the proposed approaches needs to be conducted but there is also the necessity for the consideration of a larger range of cost drivers.

6. References

Albrecht, A. J. (1979). Measuring Application Development Productivity, *Proceedings of the Joint SHARE, GUIDE, and IBM Application Developments Symposium*, pp. 83-92, Monterey CA, October 1979.

Albrecht, A. J., & Gaffney, J. R. (1983). Software Function Source Lines of Code, and Development Effort Prediction: A Software Science Validation, *IEEE Transactions on Software Engineering*, Vol. 9, No. 6, (November 1983), pp. 639-648, ISSN: 0098-5589.

Angelis, L., Stamelos, I., & Morisio, M. (2001). Building A Software Cost Estimation Model Based On Categorical Data, *Proceedings of the 7th International Symposium on Software Metrics*, IEEE Computer Society, ISBN: 0-7695-1043-4, pp. 4-15, London, 4-6 April 2001.

Azzeh, M., Neagu, D., & Cowling, P. I. (2010). Fuzzy Grey Relational Analysis for Software Effort Estimation. *Empirical Software Engineering*, Vol. 15, No. 1, (February 2010), pp. 60-90, ISSN:1382-3256.

Boehm, B. W. (1981). *Software Engineering Economics*, Englewood Cliffs N. J., Prentice-Hall Inc., ISBN: 0130266922. New Jersey.

Boehm, B. W., Abts, C., Clark, B., & Devnani-Chulani, S. (1997). *COCOMO II Model Definition Manual*, Computer Science Department, The University of Southern California, Los Angeles, CA.

Briand, L. C., & Wieczorek, I. (2002). Resource Modeling in Software Engineering, In: *Encyclopedia of Software Engineering* (2nd edition), Editor: J. Marciniak.

Charette, R. N. (2005). Why software fails. *Spectrum IEEE*, Vol. 42, No. 9, September 2005, pp. 42-49, ISSN: 0018-9235.

Desharnais, J. M. (1988). *Analyse Statistique de la Productivite des Projects de Development en Informatique a Partir de la Technique de Points de Fonction*. MSc. Thesis, Montréal (Université du Québec).

Dolado, J. J. (2001). On the Problem of the Software Cost Function, *Information and Software Technology*, Vol. 43, No. 1, January 2001, pp. 61-72.

Fenton, N. E., & Pfleeger, S. L. (1997). *Software Metrics: A Rigorous and Practical Approach*, International Thomson Computer Press.

Haykin, S. (1999). *Neural Networks: A Comprehensive Foundation* (2nd edition), Prentice-Hall, ISBN: 0132-73350-1, New Jersey.

Heiat, A. (2002). Comparison of Artificial Neural Networks and Regression models for Estimating Software Development Effort, *Information and Software Technology*, Vol. 44, No. 15, December 2002, pp. 911-922.

Idri, A., Khoshgoftaar, T. M., & Abran, A.(2002). Can Neural Networks be Easily Interpreted in Software Cost Estimation? Proceedings of the 2002 IEEE International Conference on Fuzzy Systems (FUZZ-IEEE 2002), ISBN: 0-7803-7280-8, Honolulu, HI, USA, 12-17 May 2002, pp. 1162-1167.

Idri, A, Mbarki, S., & Abran, A. (2004). Validating and Understanding Software Cost Estimation Models based on Neural Networks, *Proceedings of the 2004 International Conference on Information and Communication Technologies: From Theory to Applications*, ISBN: 0-7803-8482-2, Damascus Syria, 19-23 April 2004, pp. 433-434.

Jørgensen, M., & Shepperd, M. (2007). A Systematic Review of Software Development Cost Estimation Studies. Software Engineering, *IEEE Transactions on Software Engineering*, Vol. 33, No. 1, January 2007, pp. 33-53, ISSN: 0098-5589.

Kaur, J., Singh, S., Kahlon, K. S., & Bassi, P. (2010). Neural Network - A Novel Technique for Software Effort Estimation. *International Journal of Computer Theory and Engineering*, Vol. 2, No. 1, February 2010, pp. 17-19.

Kemerer, C. F. (1987). An Empirical Validation of Software Cost Estimation Models, *Communications of the ACM*, Vol. 30, No. 5, May 1987, pp. 416-429, ISSN:0001-0782.

Kemerer, C. F. (1993). Reliability of function points measurement: a field experiment. *Communications of the ACM*, Vol. 36, No. 2, February 1993, pp. 85-97, ISSN:0001-0782.

Kumar, K. V., Ravi, V., Carr, M., & Kiran, N. R. (2008). Software Development Cost Estimation using Wavelet Neural Networks. *Journal of Systems and Software*, Vol. 81, No. 11, November 2008, pp. 1853-1867, ISSN: 0164-1212.

McCulloch, W.S., & Pitts, W. (1943) A Logical Calculus of the Ideas Immanent in Nervous Activity. *Bulletin of Mathematical Biophysics*, Vol. 5, pp. 115-133.

Mittas, N., Kosti, M. V., Argyropoulou, V., & Angelis, L. (2010). Modeling the Relationship between Software Effort and Size Using Deming Regression, *Proceedings of the 6th International Conference on Predictive Models in Software Engineering (PROMISE 2010)*, ISBN: 978-1-4503-0404-7, Timisoara Romania, 12-13 September 2010.

Miyazaki, Y. Terakado, Ozaki, K., & Nozaki, H. (1994). Robust Regression for Developing Software Estimation Models. Journal of Systems and Software, Vol. 27, No. 1, October 1994, pp. 3-16, ISSN: 0164-1212.

Moløkken, K., & Jørgensen, M. (2003). A Review of Software Surveys on Software Effort Estimation, *Proceedings of International Symposium on Empirical Software Engineering*, ISBN: 0-7695-2002-2, Rome Italy, 30 September - 1 October 2003, pp. 223–230.

Park, R. E. (1996). Software size measurement: a framework for counting source statements, CMU/SEI-TR-020. *Software Engineering Institute Carnegie Mellon University*. Available from:
http://www.sei.cmu.edu/pub/documents/92.reports/pdf/tr20.92.pdf, Accessed Nov, 2007.

Putnam, L. H. (1978). A General Empirical Solution to the Macro Software Sizing and Estimating Problem. *IEEE Transactions on Software Engineering*, Vol. SE-4, No. 4, July 1978, pp. 345-361, ISSN: 0098-5589.

Putnam, L. H., & Myers, W. (1992). *Measures for Excellence, Reliable Software on Time, Within Budget*, Yourdon Press Computing Series, New Jersey.

Putnam, L. H., & Myers, W. (2003). *Five core metrics: the intelligence behind successful software management*, Dorset House Publishing, ISBN 0-932633-55-2.

Software Magazine (2004) *Standish: Project success rates improved over 10 years*. Available from:
http://www.softwaremag.com/L.cfm?Doc=newsletter/2004-01-15/Standish, Accessed in: November 2007.

Sommerville, I. (2007). *Software Engineering*, Addison-Wesley.

Tronto, I. F. D. B., Silva, J. D. S. D., & Sant'Anna, N. (2008). An Investigation of Artificial Neural Networks based Prediction Systems in Software Project Management, *Journal of Systems and Software*, Vol. 81, No. 3, March 2008, pp. 356-367, ISSN: 0164-1212.

Wittig, G., & Finnie, G. (1997). Estimating software development effort with connectionist models. *Journal of Information and Software Technology*, Vol. 39, No. 7, pp. 469-476.

10

Artificial Neural Network for Cooperative Distributed Environments

Mauricio Paletta
Universidad Nacional Experimental de Guayana (UNEG)
Venezuela

1. Introduction

Distributed systems have become increasingly common because they offer significant computational power and are cost-effective and scalable. Moreover, collaboration between users that are part of these distributed systems improves efficiency and effectiveness for a better utilization of this computational power. Because of this, new specific collaboration/cooperative models for distributive systems are needed for enabling effective collaboration/cooperation between users of these dynamic environments or Cooperative Distributed Environments (CDEs). A CDE is then an environment in which multiple users in remote locations participate in shared activity aiming to achieve a common goal. Most of the CDE work towards providing reliable, customized and QoS guaranteed dynamic computing environments for end-users. The success of achieving this goal in proper time (efficiency) and/or to obtain the higher quality of results (effectiveness) depends on implementing an appropriate collaboration model that should include learning abilities necessary for the use of the previous experience acquired (with situations that occurred in the past) in order to improve new required collaborations.
On the other hand, according to CSCW (Computer Supported Cooperative Work) awareness is a useful concept used to achieve cooperation and collaboration in CDE as it increases communication opportunities (Matsushita & Okada, 1995). A collaborative process is leaded by five processes (Kuwana & Horikawa, 1995) (Malone & Crowston, 1994): 1) co-presence, that gives the feeling that the user is in a shared environment with some other user at the same time; 2) awareness, a process where users recognize each other´s activities on the premise of co-presence, for instance "What are they doing?", "Where are they working?"; 3) communication; 4) collaboration which together with communication permit users to collaborate between each other for accomplishing the tasks and common goals; and 5) coordination which is needed to resolve the conflicts towards effective collaboration.
In the same order of ideas, in CSCL (Computer Supported Collaborative Learning), awareness plays an important role as it promotes collaboration opportunities in a natural and efficient way (Ogata & Yano, 1998) and improves effectiveness of collaborative learning. In this matter, Gutwin et al identified the following types of awareness (Gutwin et al, 1995): social, task, concept, workspace, and knowledge.
Moreover, SMI (Spatial Model of Interaction) (Benford & Fahlén, 1993) is one of the awareness models proposed with the purpose to obtain any knowledge of the immediately closer world in collaborative virtual environments. It is based primarily on the use of a

variety of mechanisms that were defined for this model and to steer the interaction in a virtual environment. These are the concepts of medium, aura, focus, nimbus and awareness. The concept of awareness in this context, more explicitly awareness of interaction, is defined for quantifying the degree, nature and quality of the interaction between the elements of the environment.

This chapter focuses on the use of Artificial Neural Networks (ANNs) as an option to provide learning abilities to a collaborative model to meet goals mentioned above. First, this chapter makes a state of the art on this relationship between CDE and ANN specifically as it relates to the use of ANN to learn to collaborate and/or to improve collaboration. The chapter, then, develops a particular strategy based on the concept of awareness of interaction derived from SMI. The reason for using this strategy is because for cooperative tasks to be successful in CDEs they require from users to be known. Before this process is achieved it is important to know which users are more suitable in the system to cooperate with, as well as which tools are needed to achieve the common goal in the system in a cooperative way. In this regard, awareness allows users to be aware of others' activities each and every moment. Information about others' activities combined with their intentions and purposes could be used to improve cooperation in CDEs.

Finally, this chapter also includes the results of a recent research that was carried out which combine the concepts of awareness of interaction and ANN applied in a particular model known as AMBAR (Awareness-based learning Model for distriButive collAborative enviRonment). Some particular comments related with the ANN used in AMBAR are included in a different section of this chapter.

2. A summary of the state of the art

There are two different categories of works related with ANNs and CDEs: 1) those in which CDE is used to improve the ANN performance; and 2) those where an ANN is used aiming to improve certain processes relative to the CDE. This chapter is more oriented to the second category of researches.

2.1 Improving ANNs by using CDEs

Related with improving the ANN performance by using a CDE, Garcia et al (Garcia et al, 2002 and 2005) proposed a cooperative co-evolutionary model for the evolution of neural network topology and weights. Cooperative co-evolution is a recent paradigm in evolutionary computation that allows the effective modelling of cooperative environments. In a first work, authors proposed MOBNET (Garcia et al, 2002) that evolves subcomponents that must be combined in order to form a network, instead of whole networks. The problem of assigning credit to the subcomponents is approached as a multi-objective optimization task. The subcomponents in a cooperative co-evolutionary model must fulfil different criteria to be useful, these criteria is usually conflicted with each other. In this work authors show how using several objectives for every subcomponent and evaluating its fitness as a multi-objective optimization problem, the performance of the model is highly competitive. MOBNET is compared with several standard methods of classification and with other neural network models showing the best overall performance of all classification methods applied. It also produces smaller networks when compared to other models. Moreover, the basic idea underlying MOBNET is extensible to a more general model of co-evolutionary computation, as none of its features are exclusive of neural networks design.

In a second work of the same authors (Garcia et al, 2005), a general framework is proposed for designing neural network ensembles by means of cooperative co-evolution. The authors state that although theoretically, a single neural network with a sufficient number of neurons in the hidden layer would suffice to solve any problem, in practice many real-world problems are too hard to construct the appropriate network that could solve this problems. In such problems, neural network ensembles are a successful alternative. Nevertheless, the design of neural network ensembles is a complex task. The model proposed in this work has two main objectives: first, the improvement of the combination of the trained individual networks; second, the cooperative evolution of such networks, encouraging collaboration among them, instead of a separate training of each network. Authors concluded that the performance of the model is better than the performance of standard ensembles in terms of generalization error, as well as the size of the obtained ensembles that is also smaller.
On the other hand, another example of improving ANN by using CDE is related with implementing ANNs on a parallel or distributed platform to improve the training performance. Some works related with this subject are (Calbert & Guan, 2005), (Kiran, 2009) and (Wesley-Smith, 2006).

2.2 Improving CDEs by using ANNs

One of the fields where ANN is used aiming to improve some area related with distributed environments has to do with analyzing and monitoring different distributed sources of voluminous data, multiple compute nodes, and distributed user community. So that a data mining technology designed for distributed applications is required. The field of Distributed Data Mining (DDM) deals with this problem mining distributed data by paying careful attention to the distributed resources. A complete bibliography of DDM-related publications can be consulted in (Liu et al, 2006).
Another field to mention in this section is related with cooperative learning systems based on ANNs. In this regard Cristea and Florea (Cristea & Florea, 1999) present a cooperative distance learning system based on the emerging paradigm of intelligent human-computer interaction in which the group of learners is assisted by artificial agents with active role in the learning process. In this research, the tutor in the system may be a human or an artificial agent and the system offers several learning modalities that combine the traditional style of tutorial learning with the "problem based" approach. Moreover, cooperative learning is achieved either by interaction between the student and the tutor or interaction inside the group of learners.
On the other hand, an approach for the optimization of the job scheduling in large distributed systems, based on a self-organizing neural network is presented in (Newman & Legrand, 2000). In this approach, the dynamic scheduling system should be seen as adaptive middle layer software, aware of current available resources and making the scheduling decisions using the past experience. Another example of using neural network in a problem related with collaboration can be consulted in (Blanchard & Frasson, 2002). In this matter, authors present an architecture aiming to address the collaboration in a learning activity to create groups among students. Authors used a neural network algorithm to obtain homogenous groups. In (Yildiz, 2006) author described a load balancing approach by using graph partitioning and ANNs. The aim of this work is to integrate the successful load balancing decisions of graph partitioning algorithms with the efficient decision making mechanism of ANNs. The author affirms that the results obtained by him showed that using ANNs to make efficient load balancing can be very beneficial due to the fact that, once it is trained enough, the ANN may load the balance as good as graph partitioning algorithms or even more efficiently.

An interesting work, different than the others previously mentioned, is the proposal of a complex neural network model of user behaviour in distributed systems (Shelestov et al, 2007). This model reflects both dynamical and statistical features of user behaviour and consists of three components: 1) the on-line model that reflects dynamical features by predicting user actions on the basis of previous ones; 2) the off-line model which is based on the analysis of statistical parameters of user behaviour; and 3) the change detection module which is intended for trends analysis in user behaviour. In both on-line and off-line models neural networks are used to reveal uncharacteristic activity of users.
Regarding the context of awareness and recognizing the current context of a user or device, authors in (Mayrhofer & Radi, 2007) present an approach based on general and heuristic extensions to the growing neural gas algorithm classifier which allow its direct application for context recognition. The authors here used context awareness features for automatically classifying sensor data to recognize user or device context.
Perhaps the most currently related work that discusses the subject of using ANNs to improve some aspect of distributed environments is AMBAR (Awareness-based learning Model for distriButive collAborative enviRonment) (Paletta & Herrero, 2010a), and more specifically in its particular element called CAwANN (Collaborative Distributed Environment by means of an Awareness & Artificial Neural Network strategy) (Paletta & Herrero, 2009f). Both will be explained in detail in this chapter.

3. Cooperative environments by using spatial model of interaction

The aim of this section is to present a proposal to represent cooperative environments based on the SMI.

3.1 Spatial model of interaction (SMI)

SMI is, perhaps, the most well-known awareness model for multi-user environments. This model was developed between 1991 and 1993 by Professor Steve Benford at Nottingham University's School of Computer Science and Information Technology, Lennart E. Fahlén at The Swedish Institute of Computer Science (SICS) and John Bowers at The Royal Institute of Technology (KTH) in Stockholm (Sweden).
Most of the main concepts and ideas of this model emerged from a project, called COMIC, which was a three-year [1992-1995] basic research action to investigate techniques and develop tools for large-scale real-world CSCW application developers (Benford et al, 1994). This project aimed to examine and overcome the practical and theoretical problems limiting effective CSCW product development at that time. One such problem is that simultaneous interaction between all objects is not computationally manageable in any large-scale environment. For this reason, it is important to determine which objects are capable of interacting with other given objects at any given time.
As its name suggests, SMI uses the properties of space as the basis for mediating interaction. It was proposed as a way to control the flow of information in the environment. It allows objects in the environment to govern their interaction through some key concepts: medium, aura (Fahlén & Brown, 1992), awareness, focus, nimbus, adapters (Benford & Fahlén, 1993) and boundaries (Bowers & Rodden, 1993). This model provides a synchronous method of controlling how users and objects make themselves known to the world and how the world is aware of them. It has been driven by a number of objectives (Benford & Fahlén, 1993):

- Scalability: It is based on the concept of aura. Each object has an aura for each medium (visual, audio, text...) in which it can interact, because the aura defines the volume of space within which this interaction is possible. The use of aura facilitates scaling to many users by limiting the number of object interactions that must be considered. This number will be governed by the extent of the object auras and by the population density of the space.
- Interactions: The SMI assumes a space populated by potentially communicating objects. These objects may represent anything: human users or data in a database, for example. The space itself may have any form, for example, a three-dimensional Cartesian space, an abstract higher-dimensional space or a graph. The SMI provides a framework for these objects to manage their interaction, and communication with every pair of objects in the environment. A key component of this management of interaction is the use of the space itself. Thus by controlling their position, orientation, distance, etc., the objects are able to modify their interaction and communication (Greenhalgh, 1994).

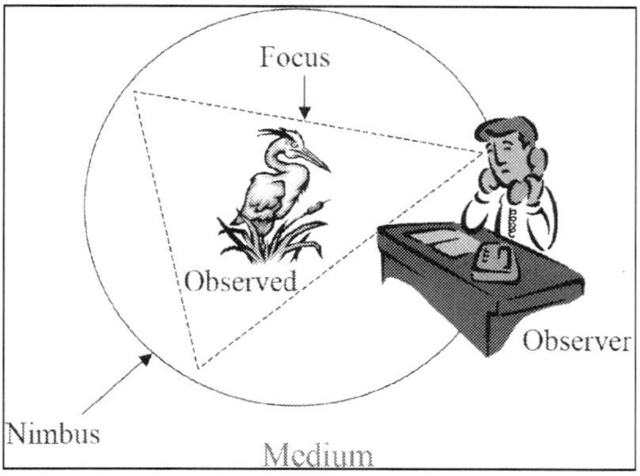

Fig. 1. Key concepts in The Spatial Model of Interaction (Herrero, 2003)

As it was mentioned before, the model itself defines five linked concepts: medium, awareness, aura, focus and nimbus (see Fig. 1 and 2):

- Medium: A prerequisite for useful communications is that two objects have a compatible medium in which both objects can communicate. This medium might include audio, video, graphics and text.
- Awareness: It is the main concept involved in controlling interaction between objects. It quantifies the degree, nature or quality of interaction between two objects. One object's awareness of another object quantifies the subjective importance or relevance of that object. The awareness relationship between every pair of objects is achieved on the basis of quantifiable levels of awareness between them (Benford & Fahlén, 1992) and it is unidirectional and specific to each medium (Benford & Fahlén, 1993).
- Aura: In 1992, Fahlén and Bowers defined aura as the sub-space which effectively bounds the presence of an object within a given medium and which acts as an enabler of potential interaction (Fahlén & Brown, 1992). Once aura has been used to determine the potential for object interactions (see Fig. 2), the objects themselves are subsequently responsible for controlling these interactions. "When two auras collide, interaction between the objects in the medium becomes a possibility" (Benford & Fahlén, 1993).

- Focus: In each particular medium, it is possible to delimit the observing object's interest. This idea was introduced by S. Benford in 1993 as "The more an object is within your focus the more aware you are of it" (Benford & Fahlén, 1993), and it was called Focus.
- Nimbus: similar to what was mentioned above, it is possible to represent the observed object's projection in a particular medium. This area is called Nimbus: "The more an object is within your nimbus the more aware the object is of you".

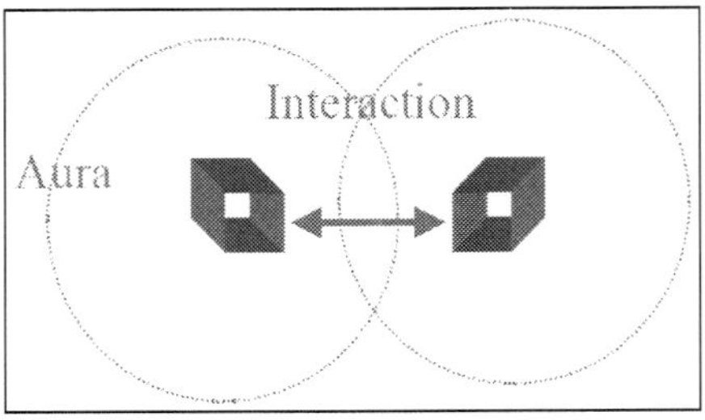

Fig. 2. Collision of two objects' auras (Herrero, 2003)

Therefore, awareness between objects in a given medium is manipulated via Focus and Nimbus, requiring a negotiation process. Considering, for example, A's awareness of B, the negotiation process combines the observer's (A's) focus and the observer's (B's) nimbus. In the words of Benford and Fahlén: "The level of awareness that object A has of object B in medium M is some function of A's focus on B in M and B's nimbus on A in M". For a simple discrete model of focus and nimbus, there are three possible classifications of awareness' values when two objects are negotiating unidirectional awareness (Greenhalgh, 1997):

- Full awareness: The awareness that object A has of object B in a medium M is "full" when object B is inside A's focus and object A is inside B's nimbus (Fig. 3).
- Peripheral awareness: The awareness that object A has of object B in a medium M is "peripheral" when object B is outside A's focus but object A is inside B's nimbus, or object B is inside A's focus but object A is outside B's nimbus (Fig. 4).
- No awareness: An object A has no awareness of object B in a medium M when object B is outside A's focus and object A is outside B's nimbus (Fig. 5).

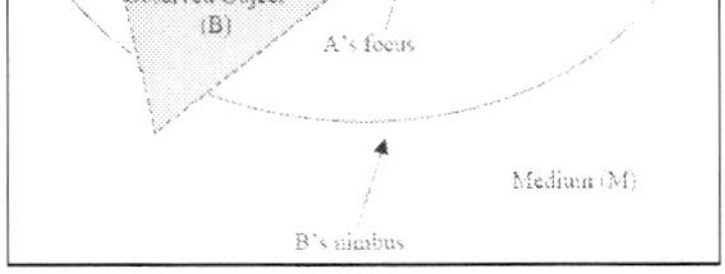

Fig. 3. Full awareness (Herrero, 2003)

In the SMI an object can control its awareness in different ways (Benford & Fahlén, 1993) by modifying its own auras, focus and nimbus:

- Implicitly: By moving and changing direction within the space and hence its aura, focus and nimbus.
- Explicitly: By directly modifying the parameters which define aura, focus and nimbus.

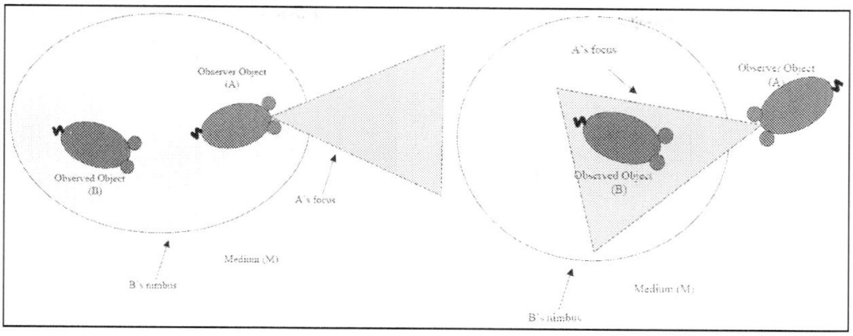

Fig. 4. Peripheral awareness (Herrero, 2003)

Additionally, aura, focus and nimbus may be manipulated through Boundaries in space. Boundaries have more importance in structuring social interaction (Bowers & Rodden, 1993). Boundaries are also a way of structuring space and influencing awareness (Bowers & Rodden, 1993). Therefore, boundaries "divide space into different areas and regions and provide mechanisms for marking territory, controlling movement, and influencing the interactional properties of space" (Benford et al, 1995). It is possible to identify several kinds of boundaries:

- Obstructive: The boundary blocks the property in question (movement, aura, focus, and nimbus).
- Conditionally obstructive: The obstruction can be removed when some condition is obeyed.
- Transforming: The boundary alters the property in some way.
- Non-obstructive: The boundary has no effect on the property.

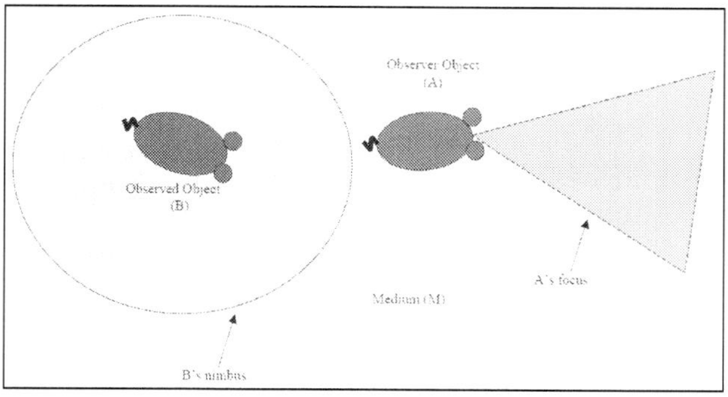

Fig. 5. No awareness (Herrero, 2003)

3.2 Awareness of interaction and artificial neural network

Based on the concepts of the SMI model previously mentioned, Herrero et al proposed an interesting adaptation related with CDEs (Herrero et al, 2007a & 2007b). Some minor changes were then proposed by Paletta & Herrero in (Paletta & Herrero, 2008 & 2009a). A distributed environment E contains a set of n nodes N_i ($1 \le i \le n$) and r different types of resources R_j ($1 \le j \le r$) that nodes can indifferently give. These resources can be shared as a collaborative mechanism among different nodes. The following concepts are defined:

1. $N_i.Focus(R_j)$: It can be interpreted as the subset of the space (distributed environment) on which N_i has focused his attention aiming to interact or collaborate, according to the resource R_j.
2. $N_i.NimbusState(R_j)$: Indicates the current grade of collaboration that N_i can give over R_j. It could have three possible values: *Null*, *Medium* or *Maximum*. If the current grade of collaboration given by N_i about R_j is not high, and this node could collaborate more over this resource, then $N_i.NimbusState(R_j)$ will get the *Maximum* value. If the current grade of collaboration given by N_i about R_j is high but N_i could improve the collaboration over this service, then $N_i.NimbusState(R_j)$ would be *Medium*. Finally, $N_i.NimbusState(R_j)$ will be *Null* if N_i cannot offer R_j or if it cannot collaborate any more with this service.
3. $N_i.NimbusSpace(R_j)$: Represents the subset of the distributed environment where N_i aims to establish the collaboration over R_j.
4. $R_j.AwareInt(N_a, N_b)$: This concept quantifies the degree of collaboration over R_j between a pair of nodes N_a and N_b. It is manipulated via *Focus* and *NimbusSpace*, and and requires a negotiation process. Following the awareness classification introduced by Greenhalgh (Greenhalgh, 1997), values of this concept could be *Full*, *Peripheral* or *Null*. It is calculated using (1).

$$R_j.AwareInt(N_a, N_b) = \begin{cases} N_b \in N_a.Focus(R_j) \wedge N_a \in N_b.NimbusSpace(R_j),\ Full \\ (N_b \in N_a.Focus(R_j) \wedge N_a \notin N_b.NimbusSpace(R_j)) \vee \\ (N_b \notin N_a.Focus(R_j) \wedge N_a \in N_b.NimbusSpace(R_j)),\ Peripheral \\ \text{Otherwise},\ Null \end{cases} \quad (1)$$

5. $N_i.TaskResolution(R_1,\ldots,R_p)$: N_i requires collaboration with all R_j ($1 \le j \le p$) to solve a specific task T.
6. $N_i.CollaborativeScore(R_j)$: Determines the score for R_j to collaborate in N_i. It is represented with a value within [0, 1]. The closer the value is to 0 the hardest it will be for N_i to collaborate with the necessary R_j. The higher the value is (closer to 1) the completer will the willingness to collaborate be.

Trying to use an ANN to learn specific situations of the CDE, and therefore take decisions at the basis of these situations, depends on the ability to represent and inform the ANN about the current state of the CDE. Based on the fact that current CDE conditions could be represented by the concepts of $N_i.Focus(R_j)$, $N_i.NimbusState(R_j)$ and $N_i.NimbusSpace(R_j)$, and from these concepts it is possible to obtain the corresponding $R_j.AwareInt(N_a, N_b)$, it is possible to identify the following variables:

1. A value $Nst \in [0,1]$ representing $N_a.NimbusState(R_j)$ that is further interpreted/ represented in (2).
2. A value $AwI \in [0,1]$ representing $R_j.AwareInt(N_a, N_b)$ that is further interpreted/ represented in (3).
3. A value *Foc* that is equal to 1 if $N_b \in N_a.Focus(R_j)$. If $N_b \notin N_a.Focus(R_j)$ then the entry is 0.

With these variables and depending of the searched goal, it is possible to define parts of a pattern that can be used as an input in an ANN so that the ANN might learn different scenarios related with the current CDE. Some examples can be seen in the case study presented in the next section, specifically in the topic related with the heuristic-based learning strategies.

$$Nst = \begin{cases} 1, N_a.NimbusState(R_j) = Maximum \\ 0.5, N_a.NimbusState(R_j) = Medium \\ 0, N_a.NimbusState(R_j) = Null \end{cases} \quad (2)$$

$$AwI = \begin{cases} 1, R_j.AwareInt(N_a, N_b) = Full \\ 0.5, R_j.AwareInt(N_a, N_b) = Peripheral \\ 0, R_j.AwareInt(N_a, N_b) = Null \end{cases} \quad (3)$$

The next section explains in detail the AMBAR model, as a case study based on the concepts presented in this section.

4. AMBAR: A case study

AMBAR was proposed as a learning collaboration agent-based model for distributed environments endowed with heuristic-based strategies. This was done aiming to take into account the information of awareness' collaborations occurring in the environment for achieving the most appropriate future awareness situations. AMBAR is structured by the following elements (see Fig. 6):

1. The awareness representation and collaborative process.
2. An architecture (SOFIA) used for designing the intelligent agents known as IA-Awareness.
3. A negotiation mechanism to deal with saturated conditions.
4. A mutual exclusion strategy to synchronize the use of critical sections.
5. A load-balancing strategy (CAwaSA).
6. A communication protocol that allows agents to exchange messages and hence interact with each other.
7. Heuristic-based learning strategies (CAwANN).

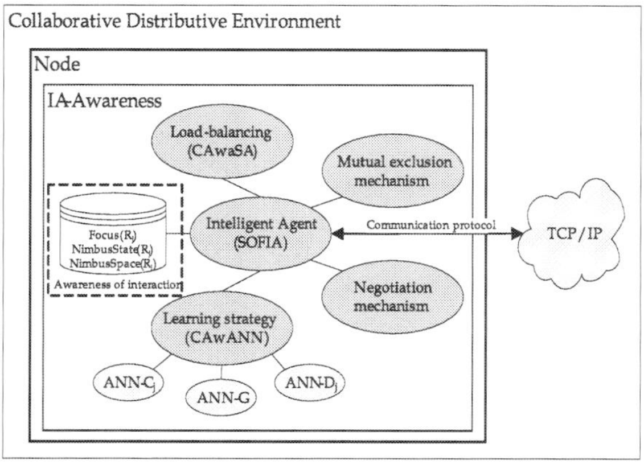

Fig. 6. The AMBAR structure

4.1 Awareness representation and collaboration process

Awareness representation is defined as was explained in Section 3.2. Any node N_a in the distributive environment is endowed with an IA-Awareness agent, that has the corresponding information about *E*, i.e.: $N_a.Focus(R_j)$, $N_a.NimbusState(R_j)$ and $N_a.NimbusSpace(R_j)$ for each R_j. The collaborative process in the system follows these steps:

1. N_b must solve a task *T* by means of a collaborative task-solving process making use of the resources $R_1,\ldots, R_p$, so that, it generates a $N_b.TaskResolution(R_1,\ldots, R_p)$.
2. N_b looks for the current conditions to calculate the values associated to the key concepts of the model (*Focus*, *NimbusState* and *NimbusSpace* related to the other nodes), given by $N_i.Focus(R_j)$, $N_i.NimbusState(R_j)$ and $N_i.NimbusSpace(R_j)$ $\forall i, 1 \leq i \leq n$ and $\forall j, 1 \leq j \leq r$. This information is used to decide the most suitable node with which to collaborate related with any resource R_j (by using the load-balancing strategy CAwaSA). Nodes in this environment respond to requests for information made by N_b. This is done through the exchange of messages between agents (by using the communication protocol). As a final result of this information exchange the model will calculate the current awareness levels given by $R_j.AwareInt(N_i, N_b)$ as well as the collaboration score $N_b.CollaborativeScore(R_j)$.
3. For each resource R_j $(1 \leq j \leq p)$ included in $N_b.TaskResolution(R_1,\ldots, R_p)$, N_b selects the node N_a whose $N_a.CollaborativeScore(R_j)$ is the most suitable to start the collaborative process (greatest score). Then, N_a will be the node in which N_b should collaborate on resource R_j.
4. Once N_a receives a request for cooperation, it updates its *Nimbus* (given by $N_a.NimbusState(R_j)$ and $N_a.NimbusSpace(R_j)$). In like manner, once N_a has finished collaborating with N_b it must update its *Nimbus*.

The IA-Awareness agent, that each node in the system has, is designed to take into account the following considerations/features:

1. While each node may have different agents / processes, the IA-Awareness is the one that handles and manages the collaboration process; moreover, it learns to collaborate. In this sense, any need for cooperation from a source that is currently running on the node needs to communicate through the IA-Awareness service $TaskResolution(R_1,\ldots, R_p)$. In response to this service, IA-Awareness returns a list of *p* nodes, one for each resource R_j, better suited to collaborate with the current node in relation with the corresponding R_j.
2. There are services (abilities) that report on current levels of $Focus(R_j)$, $NimbusState(R_j)$ and $NimbusSpace(R_j)$ for a specific resource R_j.
3. Once all the necessary information is achieved, the search for the most suitable nodes to collaborate related with any R_j is done by using the service $FindSuitableNodes(R_1,\ldots, R_p)$.
4. When conditions on the environment are not appropriated enough to establish a collaboration process ($N_i.NimbusState(R_j) = Null$ for most of the N_i, R_j), the nature of the node N_b ,initiating a collaborative process to answer a $N_b.TaskResolution(R_1,\ldots, R_p)$, can lead to having no options, so that N_b can start a negotiation process that allows for N_b to identify new candidates to collaborate with. The detection of this saturated conditions is accomplished by using the service $IsOverloaded(N, R)$.
5. The initiation and completion of the collaboration associated with the resource *R* is achieved through the implementation of services $StartCollaboration(R)$ and $EndCollaboration(R)$.

4.2 The agent architecture

SOFIA (SOA-based Framework for Intelligent Agents) (Paletta & Herrero, 2009d and 2009e) is the architecture used to design the IA-Awareness agents used in AMBAR. It focuses on the design of a common framework for intelligent agents with the following characteristics: 1) it merges interdisciplinary theories, methods and approaches, 2) it is extensible and open as to be completed with new requirements and necessities, and 3) it highlights the agent´s learning processes within the environment. SOFIA's general architecture contains four main components (see Fig. 7):

1. The Embodied Agent (IA-EA) or the "body": It is a FIPA-based structure (FIPA, 2002b) because it has a Service Directory element which provides a location where specific and correspondent services' descriptions can be registered. The IA-EA encloses the set of services related to the abilities of sensing stimuli from the environment and interacting with it.
2. The Rational Agent (IA-RA) or the "brain": This component represents the agent's intelligent part and therefore, it encloses the set of services used by the agent to implement the process associated with these abilities. It is also a FIPA-based structure.
3. The Integrative/Facilitator Agent (IA-FA) or the "facilitator": It plays the role of simplifying the inclusion of new services into the system as well as the execution of each of them when it is necessary. The basic function of the IA-FA is to coordinate the integration between the IA-SV and the rest of the IA components. This integration is needed when a new service is integrated with the IA and therefore it is registered into the corresponding Service Directory, even when an existing service is executed.
4. The IA Services or "abilities" (IA-SV): It is a collection of individual and independent software components integrated to the system (the IA) which implements any specific ability either to the IA-EA or the IA-RA.

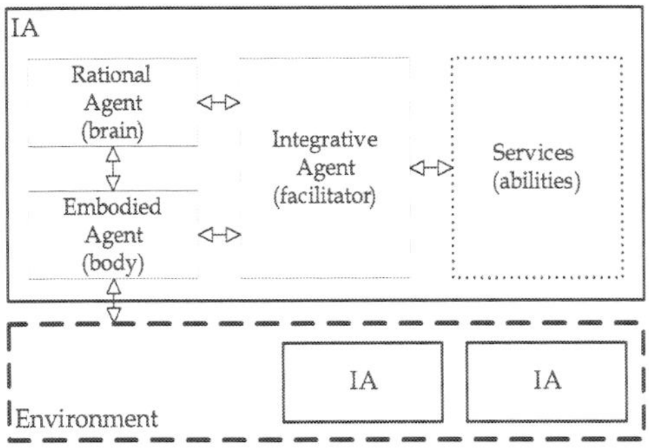

Fig. 7. The SOFIA general architecture

4.3 The negotiation mechanism

The negotiation mechanism included in AMBAR consists of three elements (Paletta & Herrero, 2010b) (see more details below in Section 4.6): 1) a heuristic algorithm used for deciding the most suitable node to initiate negotiation based on current conditions; 2) a

heuristic method to accept/decline a need for collaboration during a negotiation; 3) a protocol for exchanging messages between agents.
The basic idea is to find / identify a node N that might will be a potential candidate to negotiate with, taking into account the possibility of making changes in its *Nimbus* in relation with the resource R. N can then collaborate with this node in relation with R. "Potential" means that N accepts i.e. the negotiation is successful.

4.4 The mutual exclusion mechanism

The nature of a node initiating a collaborative process to answer a $TaskResolution(R_1,\ldots,R_p)$, provokes a change in the conditions of the collaboration levels of the environmental nodes involved in the process. Since this information is required by the process of taking action, the levels of collaboration between the nodes turn into a critical section, so that a mutual exclusion mechanism is required. The strategy used in AMBAR is a variation of the Naimi-Tréhel's token-based algorithm (Naimi et al, 1996). In the AMBAR token-based approach (Paletta & Herrero, 2009b), the token travels with a queue Q which has the nodes that require the exclusive use of the critical section and haven't been able to satisfy that need.

4.5 The load-balancing strategy

Having a set of p resources R_j $(1 \le j \le p)$. For each resource a particular node must identify the most suitable other node in the environment with which to collaborate according to the corresponding resource. "Most suitable" means that it should consider the following assumptions:

1. The node N_b that seeks collaboration should be on the *Focus* of the node N_a that needs to be identified, i.e. $N_b \in N_a.Focus(R_j)$.
2. The score of collaboration given by $N_a.CollaborativeScore(R_j)$ must indicate the full readiness to collaborate on R_j (value equal or close to 1).
3. The selection must be done so that there will be a load-balancing process distributed equally among all possible nodes with which to collaborate. This should take into account the current environment conditions given by $N_i.NimbusState(R_j)$ and $N_i.NimbusSpace(R_j)$ $\forall i,j$ $1 \le i \le n$, $1 \le j \le r$.
4. The answer must be given in a dynamic way and in a reasonable amount of time (preferably at the same time as the request is generated).

The strategy used to solve this problem is based in the Simulated Annealing technique (Kirkpatrick, 1984) (Metropolis et al, 1953) which is a generalization of a Monte Carlo method that searches for a minimum in a more general system forming the basis of an optimization technique to solve combinatorial and other problems. This strategy is called CAwaSA (Collaborative Distributive Environment by means of Awareness and SA) and its results can be found in (Paletta & Herrero, 2009c).

4.6 The communication protocol

Messages for AMBAR-based agent interaction are defined according to the FIPA performative (FIPA, 2002a) and used for: 1) querying the current conditions of each node in the environment given by its Focus/Nimbus; 2) performing the mutual exclusion mechanism; 3) performing the negotiation mechanism; and 4) informing the initiation and completion of the collaboration associated with a particular resource. There are a total of ten different messages.

4.7 The heuristic-based learning strategies

An IA-Awareness has learning abilities and in AMBAR the element that has these abilities are known as CAwANN. This strategy combines Neural-Gas (NGAS) (Martinetz & Schulten, 1991), Radial Based Function Network (RBFN) (Lingireddy & Ormsbee, 1998) (Shahsavand & Ahmadpour, 2005) and Multi-Layer Perceptron (MLP) (Haykin, 1998) ANN-based models aiming to cover different aspects in the learning capabilities of AMBAR: 1) a supervised-based method for learning for learning how to collaborate based on levels of awareness; 2) an unsupervised-based method for selecting a potential candidate to negotiate on saturated conditions; and 3) a supervised-based method to learn the decision whether or not a node must change the information that describes its current conditions related with collaboration.

Just as a quick reminder, NGAS is a Vector Quantization (VQ) (Kohonen et al, 1984) (Makhoul et al, 1985) (Nasrabadi and Feng, 1988) (Nasrabadi & King, 1988) (Naylor & Li, 1988) technique with soft competition between the units. VQ is the process of quantizing n-dimensional input vectors to a limited set of n-dimensional output vectors usually generated by clustering a given set of training vectors. The goal of clustering is to reduce large amounts of raw data by categorizing it in smaller sets of similar items. On the other hand, radial based functions were originally developed to discuss problems involving the adaptation of irregular topographic contours through a series of geographic data. ANN's based on this technique (RBFNs) are among the best choices in models out there as an alternative to achieve excellent results in alignment of data caused either by stochastic or deterministic functions (Jin et al, 2001). Finally, MLP is one of the most used neural models for implementing a variety of problems.

4.7.1 Learning levels of collaboration

This process is about learning the association between the current status of the environment, given by $N_i.Focus(R_j)$, $N_i.NimbusState(R_j)$ and $N_i.NimbusSpace(R_j)$, and the levels of collaboration obtained from that specific situation, given by the $N_i.CollaborativeScore(R_j)$ ($\forall i, 1 \leq i \leq n; \forall j, 1 \leq j \leq r$).

The ANN used in this solution, called ANN-C, has 2 inputs and 1 output (see Fig. 8). The output relates to the learned value of $N_a.CollaborativeScore(R_j)$. The inputs correspond to the following items:

1. *Nst* as is indicated in Section 3.2.
2. *AwI* as is indicated in Section 3.2.

To differentiate one resource from another, given the fact that each node can have a different treatment in the levels of collaboration, the IA-Awareness has a different ANN-C_j element for each resource R_j. This is an important aspect because:

1. Each resource can be trained separately from the rest.
2. The training process is less complex and, therefore, it is expected to obtain a higher quality in the response given by each ANN-C_j.
3. The model is expansible because new ANNs can be added when a new resource has to be incorporated into the environment.
4. Each node has a particular set of ANN-C_j, i.e. IA-Awareness of each node trains and uses certain ANNs according to the particular handling a node wants to give to each resource R_j, making the collaboration model more flexible.

Since each ANN-C_j has two inputs, each of them with three possible values, there is a total of nine possible patterns for training by combining the *Nst* values (0, 0.5, and 1) with the

AwI values (0, 0.5, and 1). Moreover, this strategy is implemented by using the MLP and RBFN models (see Section 5 for details). The basic idea is to train both ANNs and each time the ANNs are consulted about a specific situation, one of them will choose from the two possible responses taking that which originates from the ANN that has achieved a minor error in the training process (it is represented with a "?" in Fig. 8). The ANN-C_j training is performed automatically after new patterns have been stored on the IA-Awareness agent.

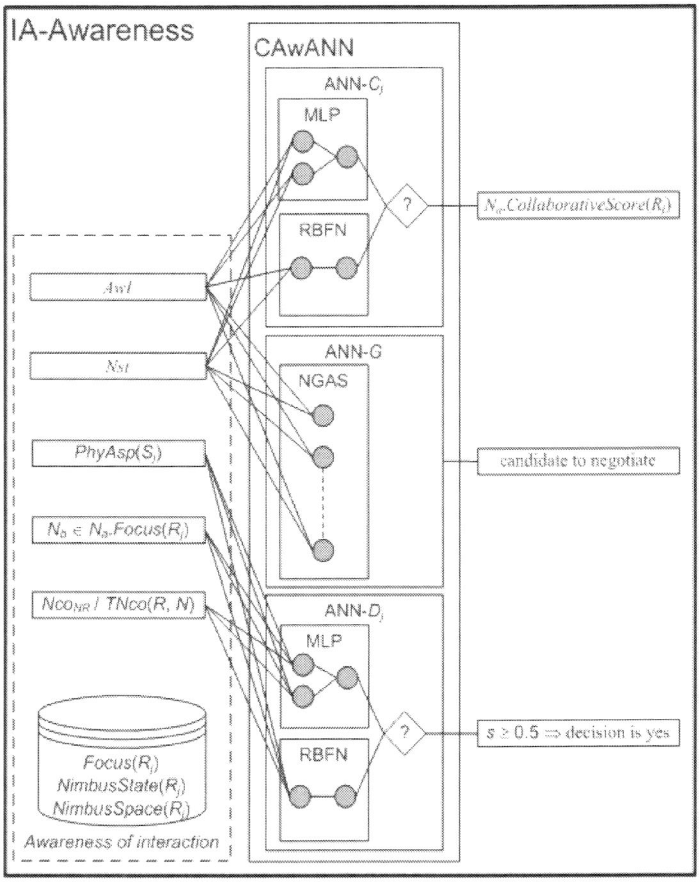

Fig. 8. CAwANN: The AMBAR learning strategy

4.7.2 Learning saturated conditions

The objective in this part of the process is to find / identify a node *N* that might be a potential candidate to negotiate with, taking into account the possibility to make changes in its *NimbusState* and *NimbusSpace* in relation with the resource *R*. *N* can then collaborate with the identified *N* node in relation with *R*. "Potential" means that the negotiation is successful, i.e. that *N* accepts.

To achieve this goal a competitive-learning-based strategy was defined aiming to correlate current information of the nodes in the distributive environment based on clusters. Therefore a NGAS-based algorithm is used. The decision that the node must make consists on identifying the node closest to the hyper-plane defined by the space given by the current environment conditions. In other words, it is necessary to determine the winning unit by testing the NGAS with the environment. The goal of this learning process is 1) to cluster the input data into a set of partitions such as the intra-cluster variance which remains small compared with the inter-cluster variance, and 2) to estimate the probability of the density function. This clustering scheme seems possible as we expect a strong correlation among the awareness information involved.

In CAwANN the NGAS-based ANN used is identified as ANN-G. The input vector is defined as the same as the ANN-C_j (being Nb the node that requires collaboration on a set of services and therefore the one that sends the $N_b.TaskResolution(R_1,\ldots,R_p)$, for each $N_a \neq N_b$):

1. *Nst* as is indicated in Section 3.2.
2. *AwI* as is indicated in Section 3.2.

Therefore, the input vectors for this problem have $2n$ elements, being n the number of nodes in the environment. If $N_a = N_b$ then $Nst = AwI = 0$. Patterns for learning are obtained either by those scenarios that have been stored during the dynamics of the distributed environment, or by an automatic generation, mostly random.

4.7.3 Learning the decision to alter the current condition

The latter case of ANN-based learning strategy is similar to that used with the ANN-C_j. In this case it has one ANN-D_j for each resource R_j. There are three inputs and one output. The output $s \in [0, 1]$ represents the decision i.e. it is accepted if $s \geq 0.5$, and declined otherwise. Inputs are as follows:

1. A value $PhyAsp(S_j) \in [0, 1]$ that indicates the level of physical availability of the resource R_j. This physical aspect is related to the current conditions of the resource and the node's physical ability to actually be able to collaborate on the basis of this resource. For example, the maximum size of a service requests queue, the physical feature of a hardware related with the resource (CPU, memory, communications ports, and others), among others.
2. A value equal to 1 if $N_b \in N_a.Focus(R_j)$, being N_b the node that requires the decision, and N_a the node that should make the decision. If $N_b \notin N_a.Focus(R_j)$ then the entry is 0.
3. A value equal to $NcoNR$ / $TNco(R, N)$ which represents a logical aspect that deals with the relationship that N_b might had had in the past regarding a collaboration process. The idea is to reward those nodes N_b who collaborated in the past with N_a and are now requiring collaboration with N_a. $NcoNR$ is the number of times a node N (node that requires the decision) has collaborated with the current node (node that should make the decision) related to resource R. $TNco(R, N)$ is calculated by following (4).

$$TNco(R,N) = \begin{cases} \sum_{j=1}^{r} Nco_{Nj}, & \sum_{j=1}^{r} Nco_{Nj} \neq 0 \\ \text{random}(Nco_{NR},1), & \text{otherwise} \end{cases} \quad (4)$$

To obtain the information related to the physical aspect associated with the resource, IA-Awareness has the ability to query the corresponding current values. It is represented by a value between [0, 1] which expresses the percentage of current use of the node in relation to R. A value equal to 1 which means that R is being used at its maximum capacity (it is saturated). Furthermore, each node N keeps the nxr matrix Nco whose elements Nco_{ij} matches the number of times the node N_i ($1 \leq i \leq n$) has collaborated with N in relation to the resource R_j ($1 \leq j \leq r$). This information as well as $N.Focus(R_j)$ are used to calculate the logical aspects needed for taking a decision.

The training of the ANN-D_j is performed automatically after a new pattern has been stored on the IA-Awareness agent. An ANN-D_j is considered trained when a proper number of patterns has been stored and used. As happens with the ANN-C_j, the ANN-D_j are trained and used by using both MLPs and RBFNs strategies.

4.7.4 Evaluation

In summary, and as it can be seen in Fig. 8, CAwANN strategy is the combination of the ANN-C_j ($1 \leq j \leq r$), the ANN-G, and the ANN-D_j ($1 \leq j \leq r$) previously explained. It was implemented using Java. Its evaluation was conducted in a TCP/IP-based LAN (Local Area Network) which assumes that each node (PC) can directly communicate with any other node. The experimentation was conducted by simulating different scenarios aiming to rate the capability of the method used for managing the growth of the nodes in the different conditions of the environment. The scenarios were defined by changing the quantity of nodes/PCs n (agents) as well as the number of resources r according to $n \in \{4, 8\}$ and $r \in \{2, 6, 10\}$. Therefore 6 different scenarios were simulated: 1) $n = 4$, $r = 2$; 2) $n = 4$, $r = 6$; 3) $n = 4$, $r = 10$; 4) $n = 8$, $r = 2$; 5) $n = 8$, $r = 6$; and 6) $n = 8$, $r = 10$. Moreover:

1. The hardware platform of the PCs was the same for all the nodes: Intel T2600 (2.16 GHz) with 2 GB RAM.
2. The initial condition of the distributed environment for each scenario ($N_i.Focus(R_j)$, $N_i.NimbusState(R_j)$ and $N_i.NimbusSpace(R_j)$; $1 \leq i \leq n$; $1 \leq j \leq r$) was randomly defined by considering the following: one node belongs to the *Focus* of another node with a probability of 0.75 and to the *Nimbus* with a probability of 0.85.
3. All N_b nodes execute an automatic process that generates $N_b.TaskResolution(R_1,\ldots,R_p)$ by randomly selecting the involved resources from the 50% of the total resources in the scenario.
4. $PhyAsp(R_j)$, $\forall j\ 1 \leq j \leq r$ were randomly initialized.
5. The parameters used for configuring the NGAS-based ANNs (i.e. the ANN-G) are the following: $\varepsilon(0) = 1.58$; $\varepsilon(T) = 0.02$; $\rho(0) = 5.59$; $\rho(T) = 0.07$. In fact, a genetic program was used to find the best configuration to deal with this problem. The network was trained with T = 40.000 signals.
6. The MLP-based ANNs were configured as follows: the transfer function used is the sigmoid; additional to the input and output units the topology has one hidden layer with two units; the learning rate is equal to 0.125; momentum (Phansalkar & Sastry, 1994) is used with a rate equal to 0.9.
7. The RBFN-based ANNs were configured by using a genetic program to find the best configuration to deal with this problem. Especially regard to the range of initialization of the connections' weights and the learning factors. Only one hidden unit is used.

Aiming to measure the effectiveness (θ) and efficiency (ξ) of the learning strategy, expressions (5) and (6) were defined respectively. Note that both measures (θ, ξ) are positive values in [0, 1] where 1 is the maximum effectiveness and efficiency. Where:

- PSC: is the percentage of successful collaborations based on the number of resources in which there was positive response from a node to collaborate with, in relation to the total quantity of resources in which collaboration was required.
- PSN: is the percentage of successful negotiations made in saturated conditions, based on the number of negotiations that receive a positive response from a node requesting to change its current saturated conditions in relation to the total attempts made.
- ATL: is the mean duration in seconds of the learning process.
- ATC: is the average time of collaboration in seconds calculated since $TaskResolution(R_1,\ldots,R_p)$ starts until it ends.

$$\theta = (PSC + PSN)/200 \tag{5}$$

$$\xi = 1 - ATL / ATC \tag{6}$$

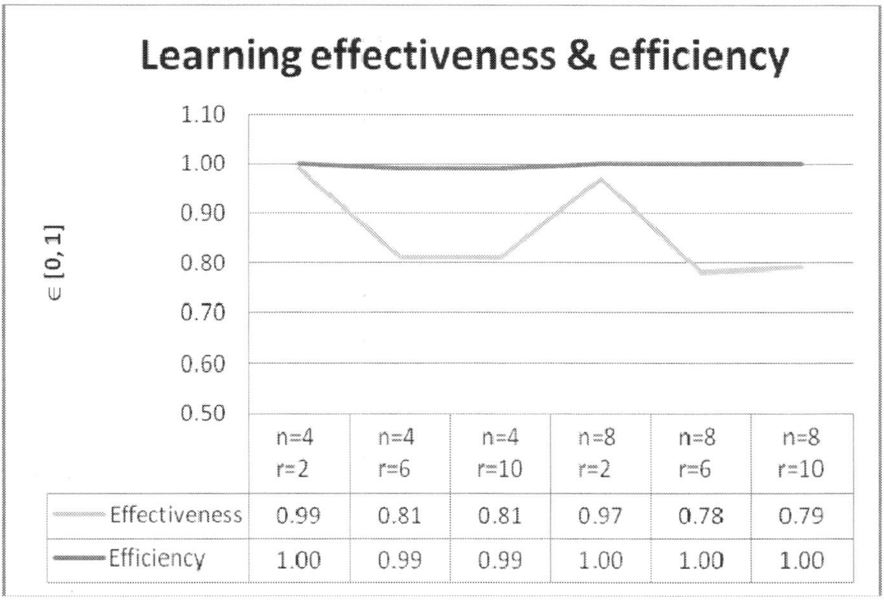

Fig. 9. Effectiveness and efficiency of CAwANN obtained from experimentation

Table 1 shows the measures obtained after a simulation of 120 minutes for each scenario, and Fig. 9 shows the effectiveness and efficiency related with these measures. According to these results it is possible to make the following observations and/or conclusions:

1. The efficiency remains stable at a high value. Therefore the learning process shows to be faster.
2. Both effectiveness and efficiency have a similar trend of behavior.
3. The variation in the number of nodes hasn´t a particular tendency to improve or worsen the effectiveness.
4. The variation in the number of resources has a tendency to undermine the effectiveness.
5. The average effectiveness is 0.86 and the average efficiency is 1.00.

Measure	n=4 r=2	n=4 r=6	n=4 r=10	n=8 r=2	n=8 r=6	n=8 r=10
PSN	100.00	68.13	64.29	93.75	78.13	100.00
PSC	98.96	94.24	97.70	99.89	78.08	57.90
ATT	2.47	5.86	9.58	6.73	167.38	445.15
ATL	0.01	0.02	0.02	0.01	0.03	0.02
θ	0.99	0.81	0.81	0.97	0.78	0.79
ξ	1.00	0.99	0.99	1.00	1.00	1.00

Table 1. Measures obtained from experimentation

It is important to stress that, due to the fact that it is a learning-based mechanism from past situations, it is assumed that, as there is much more to learn, the metrics associated with it must be improved.

4.8 An example

This section follows an example of using AMBAR, and therefore CAwANN in real applications. This example is related with prediction of banking fraud. It represents a distribute system in which financial and national security institutions intervene with the purpose of detecting possible bank frauds during a financial transaction. The main objective of this application is to uncover bank frauds before these occur. This process benefits certain financial institutions, and their respective clients, that are related to transactions that involve money withdrawals and can be susceptible to fraud. For example, assuming that the cashing of a fraudulent check inside a bank when the information presented, included the signature, is false or non valid, goes undetected before the cashing of the check then there will be a loss of money that can put the financial institution and its clients in jeopardy.

According to the experience suffered by financial institutions located in countries where this type of fraud is common, the majority of these fraudulent cases are carried out by the same group of thieves. If this is true then it is possible to try to uncover the fraud through the identification of people that has committed this type of fraud before. It is also known that in the majority of cases thieves won't come back to the same financial institution that was robbed so as not to be identified by the employees that work in the institution or by the surveillance systems employed.

In the same order of ideas, recently people involved in frauds is identified automatically by the use of biometrical techniques and the existence of data bases that associate this person with any other biometrical structure like finger prints, facial features and signature just to name a few. These data bases can be used from public offices of national security (such as police departments and other departments related) and financial institutions that have adopted biometrical techniques as part of their technological solution for banking fraud. By using biometrical techniques this institutions hold biometrical information of all of the financial institution's clients and of the people that, at one time, committed fraud in the institution. With this in mind the following inquires are presented:

- How to have online access to the data bases of national public offices such as police departments?
- How can different financial institutions that cannot stand the biometric technology benefit themselves?

- How different financial institutions can share data bases so that thieves that are registered and identified in a certain community can be easily identified trying to commit the same crime in another community?

To solve these questions and to satisfy the main objective of the problem previously described a distributive collaborative environment is developed designed to be used by financial institutions and national public offices. For this, it is possible to use AMBAR. The collaborative distributive environment E is formed by the nodes N_i that represent the following items:

1. Financial institutions that use biometric technology.
2. Communities that do not possess biometric technology.
3. National and State Public Offices that are in possession of data bases of current thieves.
4. Public institutions that do not manage biometric technology but require it as an activity to satisfy particular objectives.

The resources R_j are equivalent to their own purposes for the usage of the biometrical technology (enroll, identify and certify) that are associated to each one of the technologies (finger print, face and signature). Related to this the next 9 resources are encountered:

- R_1, R_2, R_3: enroll, identify and certify a finger print respectively.
- R_4, R_5, R_6: enroll, identify and certify a face respectively.
- R_7, R_8, R_9: enroll, identify and certify a signature respectively.

It is interesting to mention that if another biometric metric, different from finger print, face or signature, existed it is only necessary to add to the collaborative distributive environment new resources that are able to support the different abilities for enrolling, identifying and certifying the new metrics.

Within the same order of ideas, when it is said that $N_3.Focus(R_2) = \{N_1, N_4\}$ this is really indicating that when the system associated to N_3 has the necessity of identifying a finger print (R_2), N_3 could then ask N_1 and N_4 for collaboration. N_1 and N_4 are supposed to be nodes that possess data bases of finger prints and the abilities to achieve R_2. The expression $N_4.NimbusState(R_2) = Medium$ indicates, not only that N_4 possesses the ability to make R_2, but also, in that specific moment, N_4 is already collaborating in the making of this ability and is able to make it for longer. Speaking of $N_4.NimbusSpace(R_2) = \{N_3\}$ it is essential to make clear that in that specific moment N_4 is working on a process of identification of finger prints (R_2) due to a request of collaboration made by N_3.

Learning capabilities with CAwANN in this particular example means:

1. To learn the better options to ask for collaboration (enroll, identify and certify a finger print, a face, or a signature) needed for doing financial transactions. "Better" in this case means trying to detect and avoid a possible fraud.
2. To learn about better options for selecting a potential candidate to negotiate on saturated conditions and try to avoid delays in the completion of the financial transaction.
3. To learn the decision of whether or not a node (financial institution, society, public institution or office) must change the information that describes its current conditions related with collaboration.

5. Comments related to the ANN

This section was developed aiming to present some aspects related to the way in which the ANN was used in the case study presented in the previous section. One of those aspects deals with the use of both models MLP and RBFN in those cases where a supervised ANN is required. Since not all problems can be treated the same way there is always the question: "what model should be used to treat a particular problem?" the advantage of using both models is to exploit the benefits of both of them to obtain the best results.

The idea related to the previous subject is very simple: There are two ANNs, one of them related to MLP and the other to RBFN. Both ANNs are designed so that the inputs and outputs are the same. Both ANNs are trained at the same time and using the same patterns and the last training error obtained is saved. When an answer is required to a specific situation, both ANNs are consulted with the same input and only that ANN whose last training error is smaller is chosen as the right output.

On the other hand, depending on the problem and specifically on the number of different input patterns, the ANNs can be trained automatically by counting the number of situations that have occurred in the environment related to that problem, every new situation corresponds to a new pattern to be considered for the following training. When the count reached a predetermined number then training is working automatically. For supervised ANN a non ANN-based alternative to obtain the answer it is required to define the training pattern completely.

Finally, and due to the fact that CDE are dynamically continually changing, having multiple small ANNs is better than having only a larger ANN. As a first consequence, the training process is less complex and, therefore, it is expected to obtain a higher quality response. Moreover, changing on the environment can be handled properly by adding / removing the necessary o corresponding ANNs.

6. Conclusion

Collaborative Distributed Environments (CDEs) and Artificial Neural Networks (ANNs) can relate to each order to improve either the ANN performance or any other process relative to the distributed environment. In this regard, theoretical aspects of the Spatial Model of Interaction (SMI), and particularly in the awareness concept are used in this chapter to define an ANN-based learning strategy aiming to improve cooperation/collaboration in CDEs. In fact, the awareness concept quantifies the degree of collaboration needed or occurring over a particular resource between a pair of nodes in the environment. This information, as well as the information related with the CDE current condition, can be used as the input of any ANN defined to deal with a particular situation or problem in the CDE.

As a case study, the chapter presents some details of AMBAR (Awareness-based learning Model for distriButive collAborative enviRonment), and more specifically, the particular element called CAwANN (Collaborative Distributed Environment by means of an Awareness & Artificial Neural Network strategy), which has been designed with the objective to learn from different types of awareness as well as from previous collaborations that were carried out in the environment to foresee future collaborative/cooperative scenarios. The results obtained show that the learning strategy has an average efficiency of 100% and an average effectiveness of 86%.

7. References

Benford, S.D. & Fahlén, L.E. (1992) Focus, Aura and Awareness, *Proceedings of 5th Multi-G Workshop*, KTH, Stockholm, Sweden, December 1992.

Benford, S.D. & Fahlén, L.E. (1993). A Spatial Model of Interaction in Large Virtual Environments, *Proceedings of 3rd European Conference on Computer Supported Cooperative Work*, Kluwer Academic Publishers, pp. 109-124.

Benford, S.D.; Bowers, J.M.; Fahlén, L.E.; Mariani, J. & Rodden, T.R. (1994). Supporting Co-operative Work in Virtual Environments, *The Computer Journal*, Vol. 37, No. 8, Oxford University Press, pp. 653-668.

Benford, S.; Bowers, J.; Fahlen, L.; Grrenhalgh C. & Snowdon D. (1995). User Embodiment in Collaborative Virtual Environments. *Proceedings of ACM Conference on Human Factors in Computing Systems* (CHI'95), Denver, Colorado, USA, pp. 242-249.

Blanchard, E. & Frasson C. (2002) Designing a Multi-agent Architecture based on Clustering for Collaborative Learning Sessions, *Proceedings of International Conference in Intelligent Tutoring Systems*, LNCS, Springer Verlag, Biarritz, France.

Bowers, J. & Rodden, T. (1993). Exploding the Interface: Experiences of a CSCW Network *Proceedings of Conference on Human Factors in Computing Systems: INTERACT '93 and CHI '93*, pp. 255-262, Amsterdam, The Netherlands, April 1993.

Calbert, D. & Guan, J. (2005). Distributed Artificial Neural Network Architectures. *Proceedings of the 19th International Symposium on High Performance Computing Systems and Applications*, IEEE Computer Society, Washington, DC, USA, pp. 2-10.

Cristea, P. & Florea, A. (1999). Artificial Intelligence and Neural Network Tools for Cooperative Learning., *Proceedings of International Workshop on Interactive Computer Aided Learning – Tools and Application* (ICL99), Villach, Austria,

Fahlen, L. & Brown, C. (1992). The Use of a 3D Aura Metaphor for Computer Based Conferencing and Teleworking, *Proceedings of the 4th Multi-G Workshop*, Stockholm, pp. 69-74.

FIPA (2002a) FIPA ACL Message Structure Specification, *Foundation for Intelligent Physical Agents*, SC00061, Geneva, Switzerland. Available on "http://www.fipa.org/specs/fipa00061/index.html"

FIPA (2002b) FIPA Abstract Architecture Specification, *Foundation for Intelligent Physical Agents*, SC00001, Geneva, Switzerland. Available on "http://www.fipa.org/specs/fipa00001/index.html"

Garcia, N.; Hervás, C. & Muñoz, J. (2002). Multi-objective cooperative coevolution of artificial neural networks (multi-objective cooperative networks), *Neural Networks*, Vol. 15, No. 10, Elsevier Science Ltd, pp. 1259-1278.

Garcia, N.; Hervás, C. & Ortiz, D. (2005). Cooperative coevolution of artificial neural network ensembles for pattern classification, *IEEE Transactions on Evolutionary Computation*, Vol. 9, No. 3, pp.271-302.

Greenhalgh, C. (1994). An Experimental Implementation of the Spatial Model, *Comic working paper COMIC-NOTT-4-15*, Department of Computer Science, The University of Nottingham, pp. 53-71.

Greenhalgh, C. (1997). Large Scale Collaborative Virtual Environments, *Doctoral Thesis, University of Nottingham.*

Gutwin, C.; Stark, G. & Greenberg, S. (1995). Support for Workspace Awareness in Educational Groupware, *Proceedings of Computer Supported Collaborative Learning* (CSCL '95), pp. 147-156.

Haykin, S. (1998). Neural Networks: A Comprehensive Foundation; *Prentice Hall*; ISBN: 0-132-73350-1.

Herrero, M.P. (2003). A Human-Like Perceptual Model for Intelligent Virtual Agents, *Doctoral Thesis, Universidad Politécnica de Madrid.*

Herrero, M.P.; Bosque, J.L. & Pérez, M.S. (2007a). Managing dynamic virtual organizations to get effective cooperation in collaborative grid environments, *Proceedings of On the Move to Meaningful Internet Systems 2007*: OTM 2007 Workshops, Lecture Notes in Computer Science, Vol. 4804, Springer, pp. 1435-1452.

Herrero, M.P.; Bosque, J.L. & Pérez, M.S. (2007b). An agents-based cooperative awareness model to cover load balancing delivery in grid environments, *Proceedings of On the Move to Meaningful Internet Systems 2007*: OTM 2007 Workshops, Lecture Notes in Computer Science, Vol. 4805, Springer, pp. 64-74.

Jin, R.; Chen, W. & Simpson, T.W. (2001). Comparative studies of metamodelling techniques under multiple modeling criteria. *Struct Multidiscip Optim*, pp. 1-13.

Kiran, K. (2009). Parallelized Backpropagation Neural Network Algorithm using Distributed System. Master Thesis, *Computer Science and Engineering Department Thapar University*, Patiala, 147004.

Kirkpatrick, S. (1984). Optimization by simulated annealing: Quantitative Studies, *Statistical Phy*, Vol. 34, No. 5-6, pp. 975-986.

Kohonen, T.; Mäkisara, K. & Saramäki, T. (1984). Phonotopic maps- insightful representation of phonological features for speech recognition. *Proceeding of 7th International Conference on Pattern Recognition*, pp. 182-185.

Kuwana, E. & Horikawa, K. (1995). Coordination Process Model - based Design for Synchronous Group Task Support System, *Technical Reports of Information Processing Society of Japan*, Groupware, No. 13, pp. 1-6.

Lingireddy, S. & Ormsbee, L.E. (1998). Neural networks in optimal calibration of water distribution systems. *Artificial Neural Networks for Civil Engineers: Advanced Features and Applications*, pp. 53-76.

Liu, K.; Kargupta, H. & Ryan, J. (2006). Distributed data mining bibliography. Release, pp: 1-7. http://www.biostat.wustl.edu/archives/html/s-news/2003-09/msg00165.html.

Makhoul, J.; Roucos, S. & Gish, H. (1985). Vector quantization in speech coding. *Proceeding of IEEE 73*; IEEE Computer Society, pp. 1551-1588.

Malone, T.W & Crowston, K. (1994). The interdisciplinary study of coordination, *ACM Computing Surveys*, Vol. 26, No. 1, pp. 87-119.

Martinetz, T.M. & Schulten, K.J. (1991). A neural gas network learns topologies. In: Kohonen T, Mäkisara K, Simula O, Kangas J (Eds.). *Artificial Neural Networks*, pp. 397-402.

Matsushita, Y. & Okada, K. (Ed.) (1995). Collaboration and Communication, Distributed collaborative media series 3, Kyoritsu Press.

Mayrhofer, R. & Radi, H. (2007). Extending the Growing Neural Gas Classifier for Context Recognition, *Proceedings of Computer Aided Systems Theory* – EUROCAST'07, pp. 920-927.

Metropolis, N.; Rosenbluth, A.W.; Rosenbluth, M.N.; Teller A.H. & Teller E. (1953). Equations of state calculations by fast computing machines, *J Chem Phy*, Vol. 21, No. 6, pp. 1087-1091.

Naimi, M.; Trehel, M. & Arnold, A. (1996). A log (N) distributed mutual exclusion algorithm based on path reversal, *Parallel Distributed Computing*, Vol. 34, No. 1, pp. 1-13.

Nasrabadi, N.M. & Feng, Y. (1988). Vector quantization of images based upon the Kohonen self-organizing feature maps. *Proceedings of IEEE International Conference on Neural Networks*; IEEE Computer Society, pp. 1101-1108.

Nasrabadi, N.M. & King, R.A. (1988). Image coding using vector quantization: A review. *IEEE Trans Comm*, Vol. 36, No. 8, pp. 957-971.

Naylor, J. & Li, K.P. (1988). Analysis of a Neural Network Algorithm for vector quantization of speech parameters; *Proceedings of First Annual INNS Meeting*, NY; Pergamon Press, pp. 310-315.

Newman, H.B. & Legrand, I.C. (2000). A self-organizing neural network for job scheduling in distributed systems, *Proceedings of Advanced Computing and Analysis Techniques in Physics Research: VII International Workshop* (ACAT 2000). AIP Conference Proceedings, Vol. 583, pp. 113-115.

Ogata, H. & Yano, Y. (1998). Knowledge Awareness: Bridging Learners in a Collaborative Learning Environment, *International Journal of Educational Telecommunications*, Vol. 4, No. 2, pp. 219-236.

Paletta, M. & Herrero, M.P. (2008). Learning cooperation in collaborative grid environments to improve cover load balancing delivery, *Proceedings of IEEE/WIC/ACM Joint Conferences on Web Intelligence and Intelligent Agent Technology*, IEEE Computer Society E3496, pp. 399-402.

Paletta, M. & Herrero, M.P. (2009a). Foreseeing cooperation behaviors in collaborative grid environments, *Proceedings of 7th International Conference on Practical Applications of Agents and Multi-Agent Systems* (PAAMS'09), Vol. 50, Springer, pp. 120-129.

Paletta, M. & Herrero, M.P. (2009b). A Token-Based Mutual Exclusion Approach to Improve Collaboration in Distributed Environments, *Proceedings of 1st International Conference on Computational Collective Intelligence - Semantic Web, Social Networks & Multiagent Systems* (ICCCI 2009), N.T. Nguyen, R. Kowalczyk, S.M. Chen (Eds.); Lecture Notes in Artificial Intelligence Vol. 5796, Springer, pp. 118-127.

Paletta, M. & Herrero, M.P. (2009c). An awareness-based simulated annealing method to cover dynamic load-balancing in collaborative distributed environments, *Proceedings of 2009 IEEE/WIC/ACM International Conference on Intelligence Agent Technology* (IAT 2009); R. Baeza-Yates et al (Eds.), IEEE Computer Society, pp. 371-374.

Paletta, M. & Herrero, M.P. (2009d). Towards fraud detection support using grid technology, *Multiagent and Grid Systems - An International Journal 5*, IOS Press, pp. 311-324.

Paletta, M. & Herrero, M.P. (2009e). Awareness-based learning model to improve cooperation in collaborative distributed environments, *Proceedings of 3rd International KES Symposium on Agents and Multi-agents Systems Technologies and Applications* (KES-AMSTA 2009), A. Håkansson et al. (Eds.), Lecture Notes in Artificial Intelligence, Vol. 5559, Springer, pp. 793-802.

Paletta, M. & Herrero, M.P. (2009f). An awareness-based artificial neural network for cooperative distributed environments, *Proceedings of International Work Conference on Artificial Neural Networks* (IWANN 2009), J. Cabestany et al (Eds.), Lecture Notes in Computer Science Vol. 5517, Springer, pp. 114-121.

Paletta, M. & Herrero, M.P. (2010a). Collaboration in Distributed Systems by means of an Awareness-based Learning Model, *Recent Patents on Computer Science* (CSENG), Vol. 3, No. 2, Bentham Science Publishers, pp. 1-21.

Paletta, M. & Herrero, M.P. (2010b). A MAS-based Negotiation Mechanism to deal with saturated conditions in Distributed Environments, *Proceedings of Second International Conference on Agents and Artificial Intelligence* (ICAART 2010), J. Filipe, A. Fred, B. Sharp (Eds.), INSTICC Press, Vol. 2, pp. 253-256.

Phansalkar, V.V. & Sastry, P.S. (1994). Analysis of the Back-Propagation Algorithm with Momentum, *IEEE Transactions on Neural Networks*, Vol. 5, No. 3, pp. 505-506.

Shahsavand, A. & Ahmadpour, A. (2005). Application of Optimal RBF neural networks for optimization and characterization of porous arterials. *Comput Chem Engineering*, pp. 2134-2143.

Shelestov, A.; Skakun, S. & Kussul O. (2007). Complex Neural Network Model of User Behavior in Distributed Systems. *Proceedings of XIII-th International Conference Knowledge-Dialogue-Solutions*, Varna, Bulgaria, pp. 42-49.

Wesley-Smith, I. (2006). A Parallel Artificial Neural Network Implementation. *Proceedings of The National Conference On Undergraduate Research* (NCUR), Asheville, North Carolina, USA.

Yildiz, A. (2006). Resource-Aware Load Balancing System with Artificial Neural Networks. Master Thesis, *The Graduate School of Natural and Applied Sciences of Middle East Technical University*, Istanbul, Turkey.

11

Applications of Artificial Neural Networks to Facial Image Processing

Thai Hoang Le
Department of Computer Science, HCMC University of Science, HCM City
Vietnam

1. Introduction

During the past 20 years, artificial neural networks was successfully applied for solving signal processing problems. Researchers proposed many different models of artificial neural networks. A challenge is to identify the most appropriate neural network model which can work reliably for solving realistic problem. This chapter provides some basic neural network model and efficiently applying these models in facial image processing problem. In detail, three techniques : a hybrid model of combining AdaBoost and Artificial Neural Network (AANN) to detect human faces, a local texture model based on Multi Layer Perceptron (MLP) for face alignment and a model which combines many Neural Networks applied for facial expression classification are present. This case study demonstrates how to solve face recognition in the neural network paradigm. Each of these techniques is introducted as follows:

Technique 1 - an approach to combine adaBoost and artificial neural network for detecting human faces: The human face image recognition is one of the prominent problems at present. Recognizing human faces correctly will aid some fields such as national defense and person verification. One of the most vital processing of recognizing face images is to detect human faces in the images. Some approaches have been used to detect human faces. However, they still have some limitations. In the research, some popular methods, AdaBoost, Artificial Neural Network (ANN) were considered for detecting human faces. Then, a hybrid model of combining AdaBoost and Artificial Neural Network was applied to solve the process efficiently. The system which was build from the hybrid model has been conducted on database CalTech. The recognition correctness is more than 96%. It shows the feasibility of the proposed model.

Technique 2 - local texture classifiers based on multi layer perceptron for face alignment: Local texture models for face alignment have been proposed by many different authors. One of popular models is Principle Component Analysis (PCA) local texture model in Active Shape Model (ASM). The method uses local 1-D profile texture model to search for a new position for every label point. However, it is not sufficient to distinguish feature points from their neighbours; i.e., the ASM algorithm often faces local minima problem. In the research, a new local texture model based on Multi Layer Perceptron (MLP) was proposed. The model is trained from large databases. The classifier of the model significantly improves accuracy and robustness of local searching on faces with expression variation and ambiguous contours. Achieved experimental results on CalTech database show its practicality.

Technique 3 - facial expression classification based on multi artificial neural network: In recent years, image classification and facial expression classification have received much attention. Many approaches are suggested to solve these problems with aiming to increase efficient classification. One of famous suggestions is described as first step, project the pattern or image to different spaces; second step, in each of these spaces, patterns are classified into responsive class and the last step, combine the above classified results into the final result. The advantages of this approach are to reflect fulfill and multiform of image classified. Based on these advantages, classification system improves its precision. In the research, a model which combines many Neural Networks was developed and applied for the last step. This model evaluates the reliability of each space and gives the final classification conclusion. Our model links many Neural Networks together, so we call it Multi Artificial Neural Network (MANN). The proposal model was applied for 6 basic facial expressions on JAFFE database consisting 213 images posed by 10 Japanese female models.

2. An approach to combine adaBoost and Artificial Neural Network for detecting human faces (Thai et al., 2008)

Face recognition is the problem to search human faces in large image database. In detail, a face recognition system with the input of an arbitrary image will search in database to output people's identification in the input image. The face recognition includes the processing in figure 1.

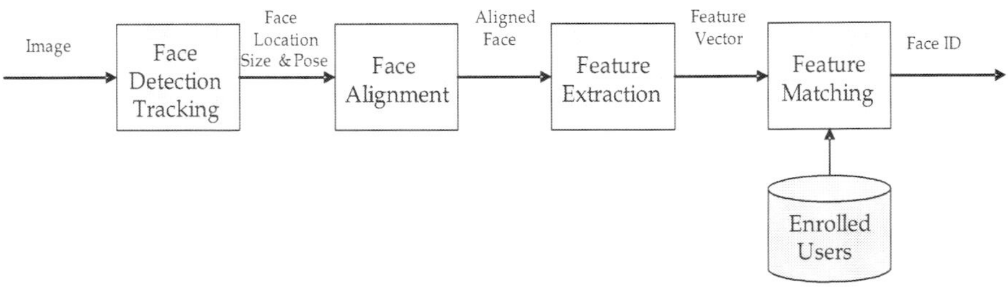

Fig. 1. Structure of a face recognition system

Thus, the face detection processing is the first step of the face recognition system. The step will decide the efficiency of the system, so it is the most important step of the recognition system. Hence, the study only focuses on this step. To carry out it efficiently, many researchers have proposed different approaches. In general, according to Yang et al., 2002, there are four groups of face detecting methods.

Knowledge based methods: these methods are based on sets of rules which have been built from experts on standard face structures. These rules are based on relationships between face features. The methods are mostly used to locate positions of faces. Typical researchers are Kanade et al. , 1973, G.Yang et al. , 1994, and Kotropoulos et al., 1997.

Invariant feature based methods: these methods focus on finding invariant features which always exist in every condition: changes in facial appearance, lighting and expression. Then these features are used only to locate positions of faces. Works which belong in these approaches are K.C.Yow et al., 1997, T.K.Leung et al., 1995.

Template matching based methods: In the approaches, to describe faces or individual face features, face templates would be stored. Detecting faces is based on the correlation between input images and the stored templates. These methods are used both to locate and detect faces. Some typical researchers are Craw et al., 1992 and A.Lanitis et al., 1995.

Machine learning based methods: in contrast to template matching based methods, models of the methods will learn from training sets of image. After that these models will be used to detect faces. These approaches are used only to detect faces. There are some machine learning models based on these methods such as Eigenface (M.Turk et al., 1991), Probability Distribution Based Model (K.Sung et al., 1998), Artificial Neural Network (H.Rowley, 1998), SVM (E.Osuna et al., 1997), Bayes Classification (H. Schneiderman et al., 1998), Hidden Markov Model (A.Rajagopalan et al., 2005), Reinforcement Learning Model: AdaBoost (Viola et al., 2001); FloatBoost (Stan Z.Li et al., 2004).

In the study, machine learning methods is only focused because they eliminate subjective thinking factors from human experience. Moreover, they only depend on training data to make final decisions. Thus if training data is well organized and enough, then these systems will achieve high performance without human factors.

A method of detecting face is to classify the pattern in the sub window as either face or nonface. The classifier is trained by the training set which include face images and nonface images taken under different conditions or extracted in the process of running the program. Face images for training are a part of faces, including left and right eyes, noses and mouths in Figure 2a; nonface images for training do not contain any part of faces in Figure 2b. Training 20x20 images are used for training classifiers. The trained classifiers are able to classify a part of image as face or nonface. In detail, a subwindow 20x20 will be slid on a full image (resized to 120x90). The subwindow is verified by the classifiers to contain a face or not. If the region contains a face, the program will locate it in Figure 3.

(a) Face images

(b) Nonface images

Fig. 2. Images for training classifiers

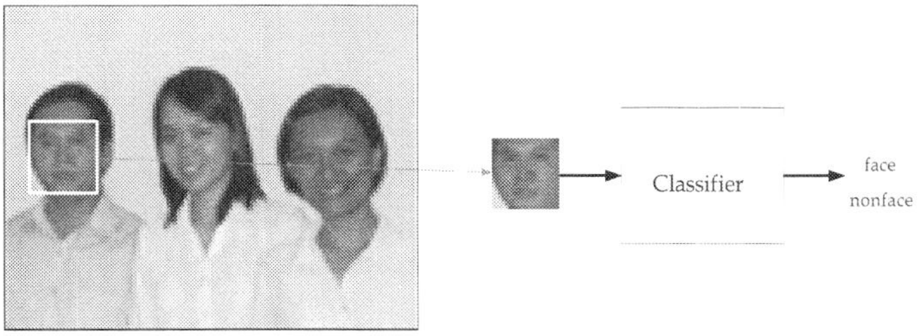

Fig. 3. Classifier 's process for detecting face

Building the classifier is quite feasible because pixels on face images have high correlation to totally describe face structures while ones on nonface images have not the characteristic.
One of the most popular and efficient learning machine based approaches for detecting faces is AdaBoost approach (P. Viola et al., 2001). Viola et al. designed a fast, robust face detection system where AdaBoost learning is used to build nonlinear classifiers. AdaBoost is used to solve the following three fundamental problems: (1) learning effective features from a large feature set; (2) constructing weak classifiers, each of which is based on one of the selected features; and (3) boosting the weak classifiers to construct a strong classifier. Weak classifiers are based on Haar-like features which will be presented in Section 2.1. Viola et al. make use of several techniques for effective computation of a large number of such features under varying scale and location which is important for realtime performance. Moreover, the simple-to-complex cascade of classifiers makes the computation even more efficient, which follows the principles of pattern rejection and coarse-to-fine search. Their system is the first realtime frontal-view face detector, and it runs at about 14 frames per second on a 320×240 image (M. H. Yang et al., 2002). However, to achieve high ratios of detecting faces, we must increase the number of classifiers and Haar-like features. It will cause a significant increase in the performance time. Thus to deal with the issue, we should combine AdaBoost with other machine learning techniques to still achieve both the same face detecting ratios and the minimum performance time. One of the popular methods having the same achievement as well is Artificial Neural Networks (H. A. Rowley et al., 1999).
ANN is the term on the method to solve problems by simulating neuron's activities. In detail, ANNs can be most adequately characterized as 'computational models' with particular properties such as the ability to adapt or learn, to generalize, or to cluster or organize data, and which operation is based on parallel processing. However, many of the previous mentioned properties can be attributed to non-neural models.
In the study, a hybrid approach combining AdaBoost and ANN was suggested to detect faces with the purpose of decreasing the performance time but still achieving the desired faces detecting rate. Section 2.1 is structured as follows. Subsection A will describe in detail on applying AdaBoost and Artificial Neural Network for detecting faces. Subsection B will present the combination model of two previous methods to efficiently solve the face detecting problem and describe experimental result of the proposed system (a software built from the model) conducted on standard databases. Subsection C will give our own evaluations and discussions on the proposed model.

2.1 AdaBoost and ANN model for solving the problem

A. AdaBoost

1. Overview of AdaBoost

AdaBoost is a Boosting algorithm. It originates the PAC learning. It is proved that a combination of weak classifiers will construct a strong classifier. AdaBoost is very efficient because it combines simple statistical learners while reducing significantly not only the training error but also the more vague generalization error.

2. Applying AdaBoost for detecting faces

In detecting faces, AdaBoost based approaches has two main steps. In the first step, strong classifiers will be constructed from weak classifiers. Since then in the second step, the strong classifiers will be combined sequentially to create a cascade of boosted classifier.

a. Building strong classifier

Input: Training data D = n Where $x_k = \left(x_k^1, x_k^2, \ldots, x_k^m\right) \in X$ is a feature vector, $y_k \in Y = \{-1, +1\}$ is a corresponding label (+1 corresponding to face, -1 corresponding to nonface). T weak classifiers h_j: $X \rightarrow \{-1, +1\}$.

We use AdaBoost algorithm to build a strong classifier

Output: The final strong classifier is

$$H(x) = \text{sign}\left(\sum_{j=1}^{j=T} \alpha_j h_j(x)\right) \quad (1)$$

Weak classifiers $h_j(x)$ are simple Haar-like features and a large set of very simple "weak" classifiers that use a single feature to classify the image region as face or nonface.

Each feature is described by the template (shape of the feature), its coordinate relative to the search window origin and the size (scale factor) of the feature. Viola et al. proposed 4 basic templates of scalar features for face detection. Stewart Taylor used 8 different templates and Rainer Lienhart extended to a set of 14 templates (S. Z. Li et al., 2005). Each feature consists of two or three connected "black" and "white" rectangles, either up-right. The Haar-like feature's value is computed as a weighted sum of two components: The pixel sum over the black rectangle and the sum over the whole feature area. The weights of these two components are of opposite signs and for normalization; their absolute values are inversely proportional to the areas. In real classifiers, hundreds of features are used, so direct computation of pixel sums over multiple small rectangles would make the detection very slow. However, Viola et al. suggested a clever method to compute the sums very fast. First, an integral image, Summed Area Table (SAT), is computed over the whole image I, where the pixel sum over a rectangle r = $\{(x,y), x_0 \leq x < x_0+w, y_0 \leq y < y_0+h\}$ can then be computed using SAT by using just the corners of the rectangle regardless of size RecSum(r) = $SAT(x_0+w, y_0+h) - SAT(x_0+w, y_0) - SAT(x_0, y_0+h) + SAT(x_0, y_0)$. This is for up-right rectangles. For rotated rectangles, a separate "rotated" SAT must be used. The computed feature value $x_j = w_{j0}RecSum(r_{j0}) + w_{j1}RecSum(r_{j1})$ is then used as input to a very simple decision tree classifier that usually has just two nodes which are computed in Eq. (2) or three nodes calculated in Eq. (2)

$$h_j = \begin{cases} +1 & x_j \leq \theta_j \\ -1 & x_j > \theta_j \end{cases} \quad (2)$$

$$h_j = \begin{cases} +1 & \theta_{j0} \leq x_j < \theta_{j1} \\ -1 & xj < \theta_{j0} \\ -1 & xj \geq \theta_{j1} \end{cases} \quad (3)$$

Where the response +1 means the face, and −1 means the non-face. Every such classifier, called a weak classifier, is not able to detect a face; rather, it reacts to some simple features in the image that may relate to the face.

However, to achieve good results, an AdaBoost based system need a huge number of features. For example, for a subwindow of size 20x20, there can be tens of thousands of such features for varying shapes, sizes and locations. Since then, this significantly decreases the performance speed of the face detecting system. Moreover, final classifier correctness depends on the correctness of weak classifiers (Haar-like features). Thus the performance effectiveness is not high.

b. Building cascade of boosted classifier

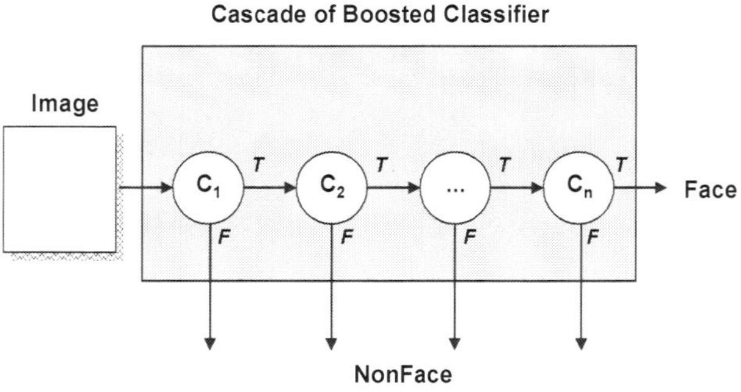

Fig. 4. Structure of cascade of boosted classifier

Most good classifiers need much time to have classification results because they must consider the great number of features of patterns. The cascade structure of strong or boosted classifiers has been suggested in order to reduce performance time, false alarm rates for the classifier (figure 4). The cascade tree has some stages; each stage is a stage classifier. During the detection stage, each pattern is analyzed sequentially by each of the stage classifier they may reject it or let it go through. During the training stage, each stage classifier is trained by false negative patterns of the previous stage. It means that it will learn difficult background patterns. Thus the combination of classifiers in cascade will decrease false alarm rate. With this structure, the classifier can easily recognize background patterns and reject them with first stages. Hence it solves two problems which are complexity and performance time. In summary, the cascade structure has partly improved the performance time, but the detection rate still depends on weak classifiers.

B. ANN

1. Feedforward ANN

There are many prototypes of ANNs. However, this section only concerns feedforward ANN. Feedforward ANN is considered as a mapping between the sets of input and output values. It plays a role of a function f that maps the input set I into the output set O, i.e.: $f : I \rightarrow O$ or $y = f(x)$, where $y \in O$, and $x \in I$.

Each output neuron is real value $\in$ [-1, 1] or [0, 1] depend on the transfer function of ANN. A transfer function which can be linear or nonlinear is used to transform information for each neuron of ANN. Some popular transfer functions are Tanh, Sigmoid and Linear.

Tanh function: $$f(x) = \frac{1 - e^{-x}}{1 + e^{-x}}, f(x) \in [-1,1]$$

Sigmoid function: $$f(x) = \frac{1}{1 + e^{-x}}, f(x) \in [0,1]$$

Linear function: $$f(x)=\begin{cases}1 & \frac{1}{a}<x \\ ax & -\frac{1}{a}\le x\le \frac{1}{a}, f(x)\in[-1,1] \\ -1 & x<-\frac{1}{a}\end{cases}$$

The decision object will belong to the class which has maximum neuron. This network is trained by a back propagation algorithm (C. Bishop et al., 2006).

2. **Applying the network to verify human faces**

In general, human face verifying problem can be defined as following: it is the problem to determine whether a certain image contains any human face or not. Solving the problem is a two-phase process:

Phase 1. Network training phase

- Preparing a sample image set for training. A training sample set must contain two subsets: a subset of human face images and a subset of nonface images.
- Training the system by the sample. After the training phase, the neural network with the new set of weights will be able to verify an image.

Phase 2. Image verifying phase

- Feed the image-to-be-verified to trained neural network. The neural network will return a result: *True* if the image contains a human face or *False* if the image does not contain a human face.

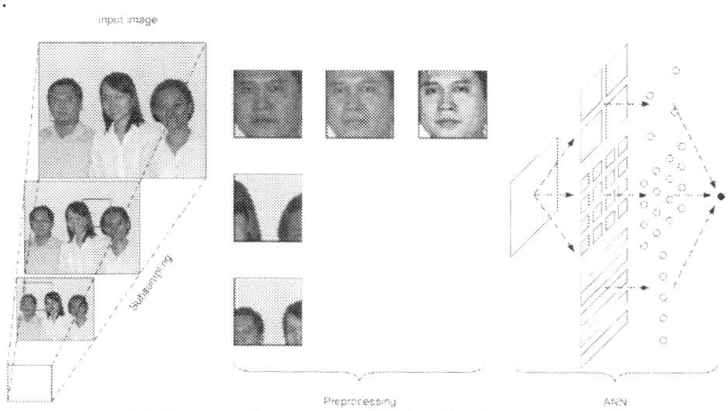

(a) Processing steps of Rowley's system

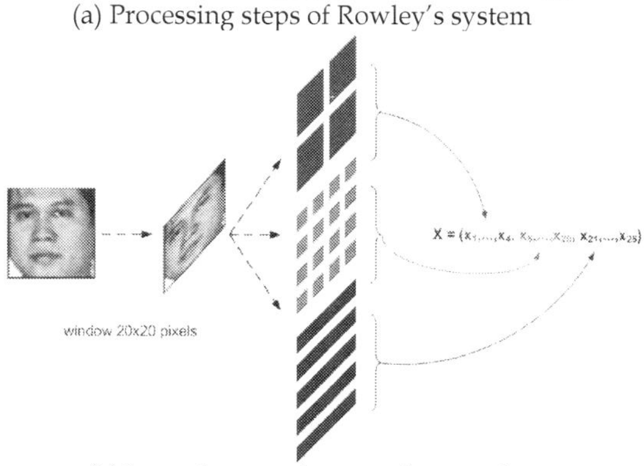

(b) Input features for neural network

Fig. 5. Rowley's system for detecting faces

The selected neural network here is three-layer feedforward neural network with back propagation algorithm. The number of input neurons T is equivalent to the length of extracted feature vector, the number of output neurons is just 1 (C=1), will return *true* if the image contains a human face and *false* if it does not. The number of hidden neurons H will be selected basing on the experiment; it depends on the sample database set of images.

One of the best face verifying system is an ANN based system developed by Rowley (H. A. Rowley et al., 1999).

The input of this first stage is a pre-processed square image (20x20 pixels) and the output of the ANN is a real value between -1 (false) and +1 (true). The preprocessing and ANN steps are illustrated in Figure 5.

The original image is decomposed into a pyramid of images as the following: 4 blocks 10x10 pixels, 16 blocks 5x5 pixels, 5 overlapping blocks 20x6 pixels. Thus the ANN will have 4 + 16 + 5 = 25 input nodes. Its goal is to find out important face features: horizontal blocks to find out mouths and eyes, square blocks to find out each eyes, noses and mouths.

The system uses one hidden layer with 25 nodes to represent local features that characterize faces well. Its activation function is Tanh function with the learning rate $\varepsilon = 0.3$ (H. A. Rowley et al., 1999).

C. Analyses and Evaluations on AdaBoost and ANN

1. Database for experiments

Image set for training: The training database for AdaBoost and ANN has two subsets. One of them contains face images and the other contains nonface images. The database is collected from sources of CMU database and MIT database. The image set containing faces includes 2429 frontal face images. The image set not containing faces includes 4548 images which are landscape, animal images.

Image set for testing: The testing database includes images which have different size, illumination, pose and expression. These images are extracted from testing images of CalTech database. CalTech database have 450 color images.

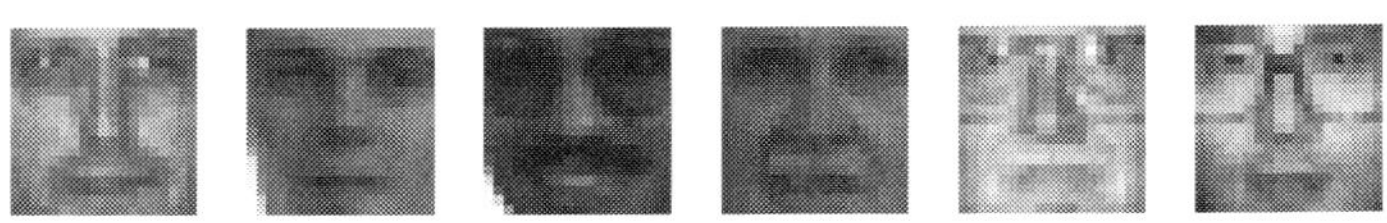

(a) Face images

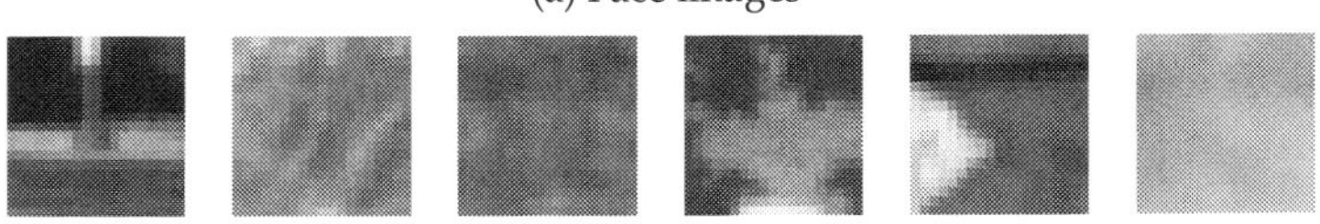

(b) Nonface images

Fig. 6. Some images for training in CMU and MIT database.

Fig. 7. Some images for testing in Caltech database.

2. Experimental results of AdaBoost based system

Database	Number of images	Correct images	Incorrect images		Detecting rate
			False negative	*False positive*	
CalTech	450	389	58	3	86,44%

Table 1. Experimental results by adaboost

The model of cascade of boosted classifiers is used, which is built with Haar-like features. This experimental model is constructed with 25 strong classifiers (n = 25) with 2888 Haar-like features and the search window size is 20 x 20 pixel. CMU and MIT database mentioned in section (2.C.1) are used to train the classifier. After that, CalTech database is used to test the trained classifier and the experimental results are presented in Table 1.

3. Experimental results of ANN based system

Name	Input nodes	Hidden nodes	Output nodes	Learning rate
ANN_FACE	25	25	1	0.3

Table 2. The ann structure for detecting faces

Database	Number of images	Correct images	Incorrect images		Detecting rate
			False negative	False positive	
CalTech	450	380	25	45	84.44%

Table 3. Expermental results by the ann on caltech database

Rowley's ANN model is used for detecting faces presented in the Table II.
Thus a system is implemented by the three-layer feedforward ANN with the Tanh activation function and the back-propagation learning algorithm. The system ran on a PC, CPU 1.8MHz, RAM 512MB. CMU and MIT database mentioned in subsection (2.1.C.1) is used to train the ANN. It took about 8 hours to train the ANN. Then, CalTech database is used to test the trained ANN. The performance is presented in the Table 3.

4. Evaluations on AdaBoost and ANN

The experiments prove that AdaBoost and ANN approaches for detecting faces does not achieve good results of performance time and detecting rate yet. AdaBoost method is one of today's fastest algorithms. However, false face detecting rate is rather high. The cascade of boosted classifier depends on weak classifiers. False images are often false negative. According to the experiments, the ratio between false negative and false positive is 58:3. To solve the drawback, there are two solutions. First, the large number of stage classifiers can be increased in order to achieve desired results. However, increasing the number of both classifiers and features too much will decrease the algorithm speed. Second, AdaBoost with other classification techniques can be combined to reject false negative images in order to increase the correctness of the system. ANN, a strong classification technique, has been used efficiently in problem of detecting faces. In addition, the performance time is not high. Since then, a hybrid model of AdaBoost and ANN is suggested in section 2.2. On the other hand, ANN is appended at the final stage to create a complete hybrid system.

2.2 A hybrid model of AdaBoost and ANN for solving the problem

1. Introduction the hybird model

The hybrid model is named ABANN. This is the model of combining AdaBoost and ANN for detecting faces. In this model, AdaBoost have a role to quickly reject nonface images; then ANN continue filtering false negative images to achieve better results. The final result is face/nonface.

In detail, a model of cascade of classifiers includes many strong classifiers and ANN is combined with the strong classifiers to be a final strong classifier of the system to achieve better results in Figure 8. For example, AB5 includes 5 strong classifiers will be combined with ANN, the sixth strong classifier, to be ABANN5.

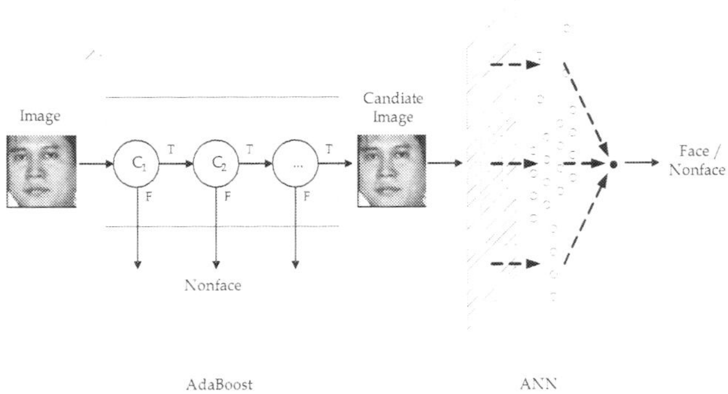

Fig. 8. The process of dectecting faces of ABANN

2. Experimental results

This exerimental also used the databases mentioned in Section (2.1.C). CMU and MIT databases were used for training; CalTech database was used for testing. Two experiments are performed. In the first experiment, AdaBoost classifiers are used with the number of stage classifiers which are 5, 10, 15, 20 or 25. The second experiment implements the AdaBoost classifiers combined with ANN which is Rowley's network with structure like three-layer feedforward neural network with 25 input nodes, 25 hidden nodes, 1 output node and using back-propagation learning algorithm for training (Tanh activation function and learning rate 0.3). These experiments were done on database CalTech. Both of them were trained by database CMU and MIT. The training time for these system is about 22 hours. The results will be showed in Table 4 and 5.

3. Evaluation of experimental results

Name	Number of strong classifiers	Number of Haar-like features to use	correctness rate	Testing time (s) for CalTech
AB5	5	131	55.86%	202
AB10	10	487	66.84%	247
AB15	15	1094	71.27%	270
AB20	20	1905	77.67%	337
AB25	25	2888	86.44%	382

Table 4. Experimental result of casscade of adaboost(AB) without ANN on caltech database (train by CMU and MIT database).

The experimental results showed that system ABs yields low diction rate even though there is a large increase in strong classifiers. For example, with 25 strong classifiers and 2888 Haar-like feature, a system achieved only detection rate 86.44% on database CalTech while system ABANNs (combining AdaBoost and ANN) achieved higher ones even in cases of the number of strong classifier to be low. For instance, ABANN5 (5 strong classifiers + ANN) achieved detection rate 84.44%; ABANN10 (10 strong classifiers + ANN) 86.52% and it got the best result 97% while increasing the number of strong classifiers to 25. The performance time is quite fast and the structure of neural network (Rowley's model) is fair simple. From the achieved results and theoretical analyses presented in Section 2.1.C, the hybrid model of associating AdaBoost with ANN is necessary and can be applied in practicality.

Name	ADABoost structure		ANN structure	Correctness rate	Testing time (s) for CalTech
	Number of strong classifiers	*Number of Haar-like features to use*			
ABANN5	5	131	Rowley's model	84.44%	247
ABANN10	10	487		86.52%	292
ABANN15	15	1094		91.30%	315
ABANN20	20	1905		94.44%	382
ABANN25	25	2888		97.15%	427

Table 5. Experimental result of system associating casscade of adaboost with ANN on caltech database (train by CMU and MIT database).

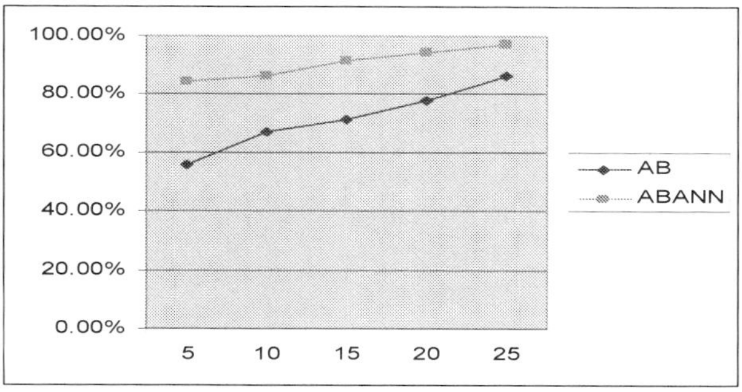

Fig. 9. Experimental resutls

2.3 Conclusions

To the extent of the paper, the two popular methods of detecting faces are presented, AdaBoost and ANN, analyzing, evaluating ones' advantages and disadvantages. From the study, AdaBoost (cascade of boosted AdaBoost) has the fastest performance time; however the correctness rate is not high (because detection results depend on weak classifiers or Haar-like features); and it is proved by the experiments on database CalTech. ANN will reach good verifying results if it has a suitable structure; nevertheless the detection speed is quite slow due to the complexness of ANN. Hence in the experiments we used simple ANN or three-layer feedforward neural network proposed by Rowley.

To improve the performance and eliminate their limitations, the hybrid model of AdaBoost and ANN (ABANN) for detecting faces is used. The system has achieved better results of both correctness rate and performance comparing with individual models (AdaBoost or ANN). For example, ABANN25 achieved the detection result 97.15% comparing to AB25 86.44 % and ANN (based on Rowley's model) 84.44% on database CalTech and the testing time is insignificant. Since then, the hybrid model is very efficient and has a practical meaning in the problem of detecting faces.

3. Local texture classifiers based on multi layer perceptron for face alignment (Thai et al., 2008)

Face recognition is the problem to search human faces in large image database. In detail, a face recognition system with the input of an arbitrary image will search in database to output people's identification in the input image. The face recognition system's stages is illustrated in Figure 1.

The face alignment is one of important stages of the face recognition. Moreover, face alignment is also used for other face processing applications; such as face modeling and synthesis. Its objective is to localize the feature points on face images such as the contour points of eye, nose, mouth and face (illustrated in Figure 10).

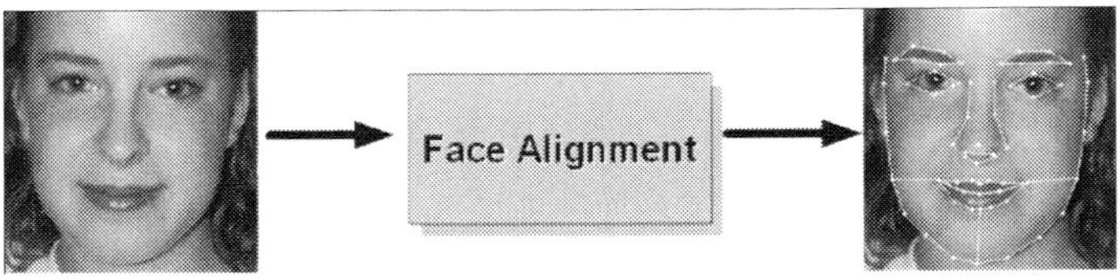

Fig. 10. Face alignment

There have been many face alignment methods. Two popular face alignment methods are Active Shape Model (ASM) and Active Appearance Model (AAM) proposed by Cootes et al (2001).

The two methods use a statistical model to parameterize a face shape with PCA method. However, their feature model and optimization are different. ASM algorithm has a 2-stage loop: in the first stage, given the initial labels, searching for a new position for every label point in its local region which best fits the corresponding local 1-D profile texture model; in the second stage, updating the shape parameters which best fits these new label positions. AAM method uses its global appearance model to directly conduct the optimization of shape parameters. Owing to the different optimization criteria, ASM performs more precisely on shape localization, and is quite more robust to illumination and bad initialization. In the section, the classical ASM method is developed to create a new method named MLP-ASM which has achieved better results.

Because ASM only uses a 1-D profile texture feature, which is not enough to distinguish feature points from their local regions, the ASM algorithm often fell into local minima problem in the local searching stage. A few representative texture features and pattern recognition methods are proposed to reinforce the ASM local searching, e.g. Gabor wavelet (Jiao et al., 2003), Haar wavelet (Zuo et al., 2004), Ranking-Boost (Yan et al, 2003) and FisherBoost (Tu et al., 2004). Nevertheless, an accurate local texture model to large data sets is still unachieved target.

In the section, an ASM method is proposed with a novel local texture model, which use Multi Layer Perceptron (MLP) for ASM local searching. MLP is very sufficient for face detecting (Marcel et al., 2004).
This section is structured as follows: in subsection 3.1, general ASM algorithm is presented; in subsection 3.2, classical local texture model with statistical local searching is discussed; in subsection 3.3, MLP local texture model is proposed for the ASM local searching; in subsection 3.4, the experimental results are presented; in section 3.5, some conclusions about the proposed model is discussed.

3.1 General ASM algorithms

A. Statistical Shape Models

A face shape can be represented by n points $\{(x_i, y_i)\}$ as a 2n-element vector, $X = (x_1, y_1, \ldots, x_n, y_n)^T$. Given s training face images, there are s shape vectors $\{X_i\}$. Before we can perform statistical analysis on these vectors it 0,is important that the shapes represented are in the same coordinate frame. Figure 11 illustrates Shape Model.
In particular, a parameterized model of the form X = **Model**(b) need be found, where b is a vector of parameters of the model. Such a model can be used to generate new vectors, X. If the distribution of parameters, $p_b(b)$ can be model, we can limit them so the generated X's are similar to those in the training set. Similarly, it should be possible to estimate $p_X(X)$ using the model.

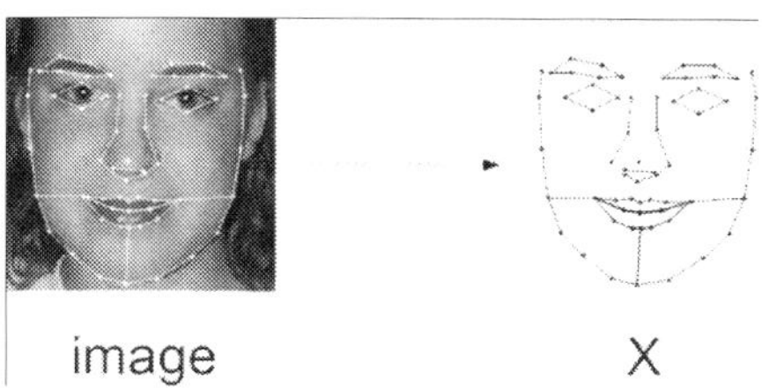

Fig. 11. Shape model of an image

To simplify the problem, we first wish to reduce the dimensionality of the data from 2n to something more manageable. An effective approach is to apply PCA to the data. The data form a cloud of points in the 2n-D space. PCA computes the main axes of this cloud, allowing one to approximate any of the original points using a model with fewer than 2n parameters. The approach is as follows Li et al. 2005.
Step 1 Compute the mean of the data set

$$\overline{X} = \frac{1}{s}\sum_{i=1}^{s} X_i \tag{4}$$

Step 2 Compute the covariance matrix of the data set

$$S = \frac{1}{s-1}\sum_{i=1}^{s}\left(X_i - \overline{X}\right)\left(X_i - \overline{X}\right)^T \tag{5}$$

Step 3 Compute the eigenvectors, p_j and corresponding eigenvalues λ_j of the data set S (sorted so $\lambda_j \geq \lambda_{j+1}$).

Step 4 We can approximate X from the training set

$$X \approx \bar{X} + P_s b_s \tag{6}$$

Where $P_s = (p_1 | p_2 | \ldots | p_t)$ (t, the number of modes, can be chosen to explain a given proportion 98% of the variance in the training data set) and $b_s = (b_1, b_2, \ldots, b_t)$, shape model parameters, given by

$$b_s = P_s^T\left(X - \bar{X}\right), b_i \in \left\{-3\sqrt{\lambda_i}, +3\sqrt{\lambda_i}\right\} \tag{7}$$

A real shape **X** of images can be generated by applying a suitable transformation **T** to the points X: $\mathbf{X} = \mathbf{T}\left(\bar{X} + P_s b_s, x_c, y_c, s_x, s_y, \theta\right)$. This transformation includes a translation (x_c, y_c), a scaling (s_x, s_y) and a rotation (θ).

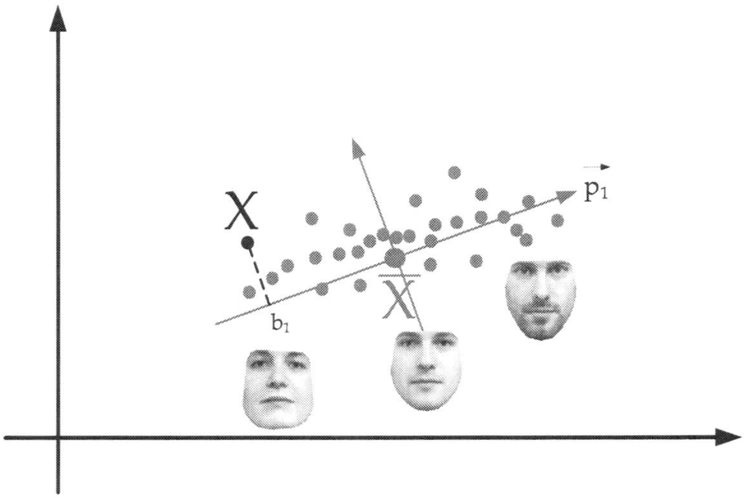

Fig. 12. Using PCA to compute statistical shape model

B. ASM Algorithm

Given a rough starting approximation, the parameters of an instance of a model can be modified to better fit the model to a new image. By choosing a set of shape parameters, b_s, for the model we define the shape of the object in an object centered coordinate frame. We can create an instance X of the model in the image frame by defining the position (x_c, y_c), orientation (θ), and scale (s_x, s_y) parameters. An iterative approach to improve the fit of the instance, $\mathbf{T}\left(\bar{X} + P_s b_s, x_c, y_c, s_x, s_y, \theta\right)$, to an image proceeds as follows.

Step 1 Examine a region of the image around each point of X to find the best nearby match for the points X′. There are some ways to find X′. A popular method, the classical texture model, will be presented in section 3.2, then our method, the MLP local texture model will be presented in subsection 3.3.

Step 2 Repeat until convergence.

Update the parameters (b_s, x_c, y_c, s_x, s_y, θ) to best fit to the new found points X′ to minimize the sum of square distances between corresponding model and image points $E(\mathbf{b}_s, x_c, y_c, s_x, s_y, \theta) = |\mathbf{X}' - T(\bar{X} + \mathbf{P}_s\mathbf{b}_s, x_c, y_c, s_x, s_y, \theta)|^2$

Step 2.1 Fix b_s and find (x_c, y_c, s_x, s_y, θ) to minimize E

Step 2.2 Fix (x_c, y_c, s_x, s_y, θ) and find b_s to minimize E

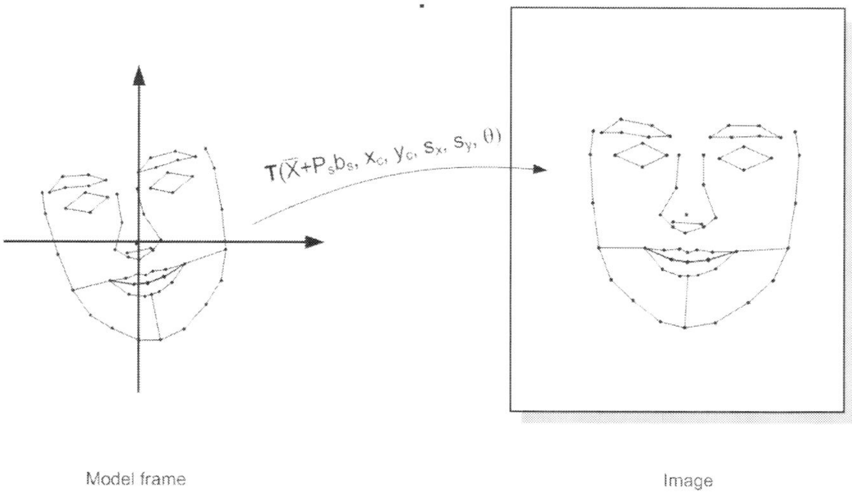

Fig. 13. Transformation model into image

2.2 Classical local texture model

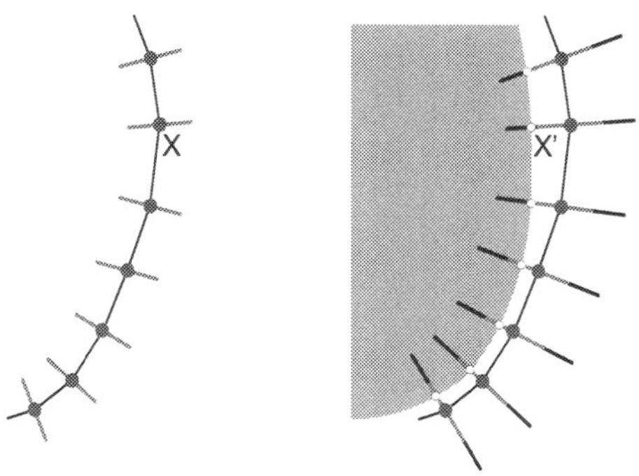

Fig. 14. 1-D profile texture model

Objective is to search for local match for each point (illustrated in figure 14.). The model is assumed to have strongest edge, correlation, statistical model of profile.

Step 1 Computing normal vector at point (x_i, y_i)

Calculating tangent vector t

$$t_x = x_{i+1} - x_{i-1}, \quad t_y = y_{i+1} - y_{i-1} \tag{8}$$

Normalize tangent vector t

$$t_x = t_x / |t|,\ t_y = t_y / |t| \tag{9}$$

Calculate normal vector n

$$n_x = -t_y,\ n_y = t_x \tag{10}$$

***Step* 2** Calculate g(k) by sampling along the 1-D profile of point (x_i, y_i)

$$G(k) = image[x_i + kn_x, y_i + kn_y],\ k \in [\dots, -2, -1, 0, 1, 2, \dots] \tag{11}$$

To noise images, average orthogonal to the 1-D profile

$$g(k) = \frac{1}{4}g_{kl} + \frac{1}{2}g_{kc} + \frac{1}{4}g_{kr} \tag{12}$$

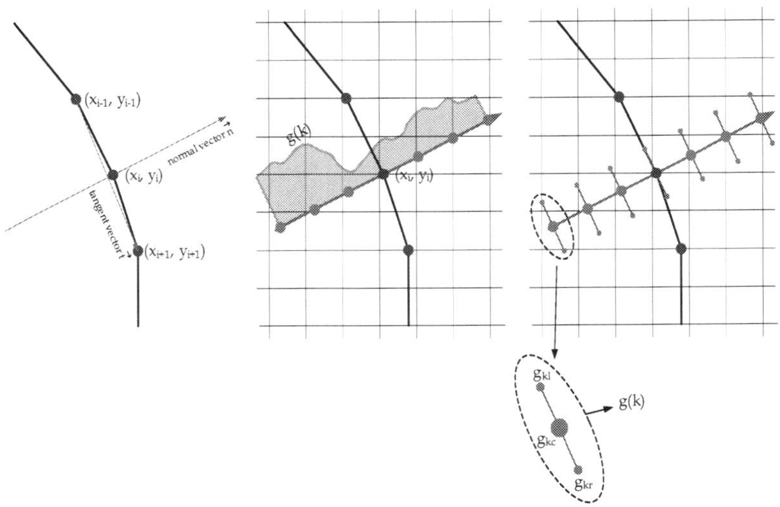

Fig. 15. Computing g(k) function

Making the edges of images clear by image derivation.

We can select the point at the strongest edge. However, sometimes the true point is not at the strongest edge. We use the local probability model to locate the point. For each point, we estimate the probability density function (p.d.f) on the 1-D profile from the training data set to search for the correct point.

The classical ASM method has some weak points, such as, since PCA did not consider discriminative criterions between positive samples (feature points or true points) and negative samples (non-feature points, its neighbors), the result of local searching stage often falls into local minima.

To deal with the problem, distinguishing feature points from non-feature points, which is critical to diminish the effects of local minima problem, we propose the local 2D structure model for each point, which uses MLP trained over a large training set. After training, the model can classify feature points correctly. Multi Layer Perceptron has been proven to be robust and efficient in face detection (Bishop et al., 2006, Marcel et al., 2004).

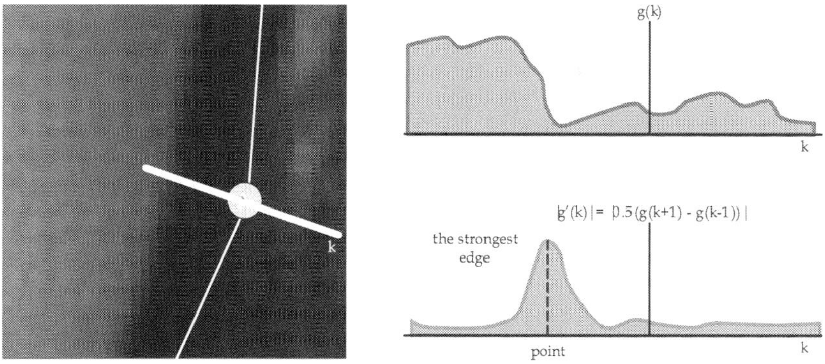

Fig. 16. Selecting the feature point at the strongest edge

3.4 Multi layer perceptron model for local texture classification

A. Structure of Multi Layer Perceptron (Bishop et al., 2006, Marcel et al., 2004)

A Multi Layer Perceptron (MLP) is a function

$$\hat{y} = MLP(x, W),\ with\ x = (x_1, x_2, \ldots, x_n) \text{ and } \hat{y} = (\hat{y}_1, \hat{y}_2, \ldots, \hat{y}_m) \tag{13}$$

W is the set of parameters $\{w_{ij}^L, w_{i0}^L\}, \forall i, j, L$

For each unit i of layer L of the MLP

Integration:

$$s = \sum_j y_j^{L-1} w_{ij}^L + w_{i0}^L \tag{14}$$

Transfer: y_j^L = f(s), where

$$f(x) = \begin{cases} -1 & x \le -\frac{1}{a} \\ a.x & -\frac{1}{a} < x < +\frac{1}{a} \\ 1 & x \ge +\frac{1}{a} \end{cases} \tag{15}$$

On the input layer (L = 0): $y_j^L = x_j$

On the output layer (L = **L**): $y_j^L = \hat{y}_j$

The MLP uses the algorithm of Gradient Back-Propagation for training to update W.

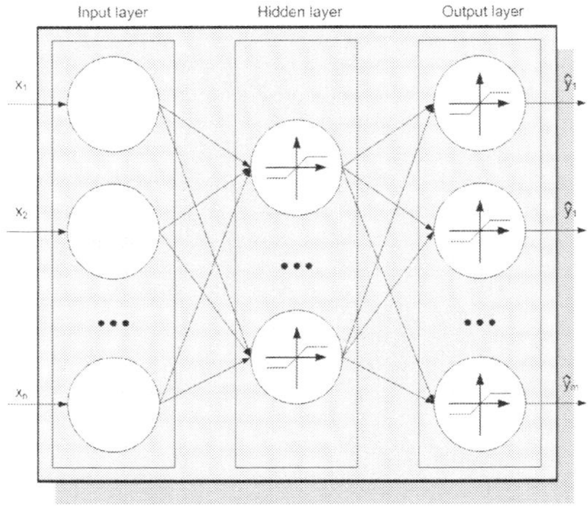

Fig. 17. Multi Layer Perceptron structure

B. Applying the Multi Layer Perceptron for Searching for Feature Points

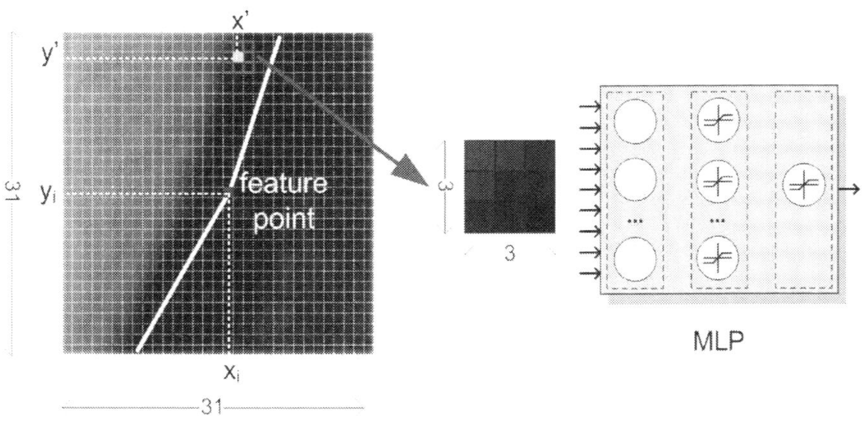

Fig. 18. Multi layer perceptron for searching for feature points

For each feature point, we define the region of a [-15, 15]×[-15, 15] window centered at the feature point. Then, positive samples, feature points, are collected from image points within a [-1, 1]×[-1, 1] sub-window at the center, while negative samples, none feature point are sampled randomly out of the sub-window within the region. Then through learning with Gradient Back-Propagation (Marcel, 2004), W weights of the MLP are updated and it outputs a value which is (+1) corresponding to the feature point or (-1) corresponding to the non-feature point. Figure 18 illustrates MLP for searching for feature points.

The MLP structure for a sub-window has three layers: an input layer, a hidden layer, an output layer. The input layer has 9 units (input values are the first order derivation of pixels in the sub-window); the hidden layer has 9 units and the output layer has one unit (output value $\in \{-1, 1\}$). Such that, the MLP has *(9 inputs + 1 bias)* $\times$ *9 + 9 + 1 bias = 100 parameters*. The

MLP use the transfer function as a linear function with a = 0.5 (equation (12)) (this is the best fit value from the experiments over CalTech database (Weber, 1999)).
A local searching procedure will find around the current feature point to be the new feature position.
Input shape $X\{(x_i, y_i)\}$
Output new shape $X'\{(x_i', y_i')\}$
For each point (x_i, y_i) of shape X
For each sub-window sw′ centered at point (x′, y′) of the window centered at the feature point (x_i, y_i).

- Computing MLP(sw′, W). If the return value is (+1) then point (x′, y′) is at the edge.
- Selecting the nearest point (x′, y′) to the point (x_i, y_i) as the new feature point (x_i', y_i').

3.5 Experiment results

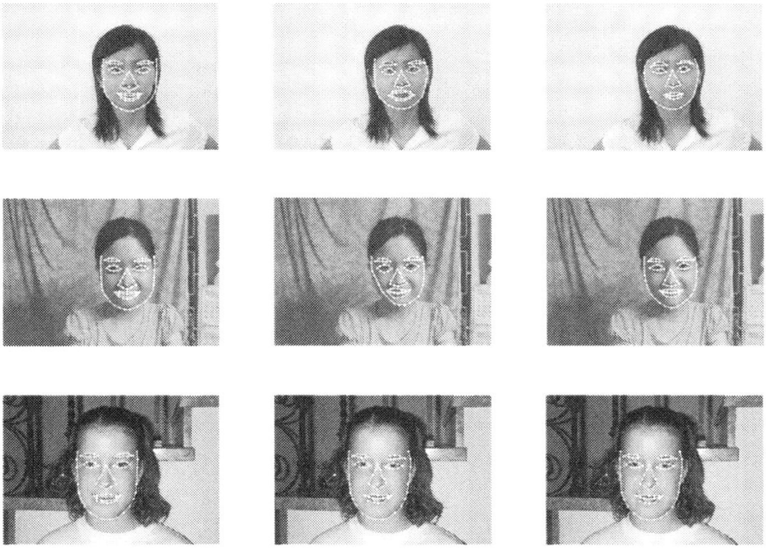

Fig. 19. Experimental results on some images from CalTech database.

We have conducted experiments on a very large data set consisting of 1,000 front face images (450 color images from CalTech data set (Weber, 1999), 550 ones from our data set). They include male and female aging from young to old people, many of which are with exaggerated expressions such as smiles, closed eyes. The average face size is about 320×320 pixels. We randomly chose 600 images for training, and the rest 400 images for testing. The face shape model is made up of 89 feature points, and for each feature point a MLP is trained.
For comparison, classical ASM was also implemented and trained on the same training set.

A. Accuracy

The accuracy is measured with point-point error. The feature points were initialized from the face window which was detected by Ada-Boost (Bradski et al., 2005, Thai et al., 2008). After the alignment procedure, the errors were measured. The average errors of the 89 feature points are compared in Figure 20. The x-axis, which represents the index of feature points, is grouped by organ. It shows that the proposed method outperforms classical ASM; especially, the improvement of the methods is mainly on feature points of mouth and contour.

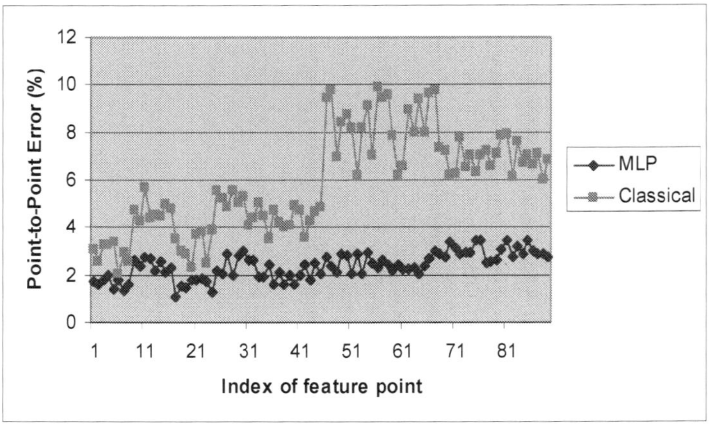

Fig. 20. Comparison of classical ASM and MLP ASM

B. Efficiency

The average performance time is listed in Table 6. All the tests are carried out on a PC with Intel Pentium IV - 2.4G CPU, 1G RAM. The classical ASM is the fastest since its computation of local texture model is very simple. The method is a little slower but is still comparable with the classical ASM.

Algorithm	Classical ASM	MLP ASM
Time per iteration	2ms	56ms

Table 6. The average performance time per iteration (a two-stage process).

3.6 Conclusions

In the section 3, we present a robust face alignment algorithm with a local texture model (MLP ASM). Instead of modeling a local feature by 1-D profile texture, the classifier is learned from its 2-D profile texture patterns against its neighbor ones as a local texture model. The classifier is of great benefit to the local searching of feature points because of its strong discriminative power. The generality and robustness of the MLP method guarantee the performance. Therefore, compared to existing ones achieving their models in relative small training sets, our method shows potential in practical applications.

4. Facial expression classification based on mutil Artificial Neural Network (Thai et al., 2010)

There are many approaches apply for image classification. At the moment, the popular solution for this problem: using K-NN and K-Mean with the different measures, Support Vector Machine (SVM) and Artificial Neural Network (ANN).

K-NN and K-Mean method is very suitable for classification problems, which have small pattern representation space. However, in large pattern representation space, the calculating cost is high.
SVM method applies for pattern classification even with large representation space. In this approach, we need to define the hyper-plane for classification pattern [1]. For example, if we need to classify the pattern into L classes, SVM methods will need to specify 1+ 2+ … + (L-1) = L (L-1) / 2 hyper-plane. Thus, the number of hyper-planes will rate with the number of classification classes. This leads to: the time to create the hyper-plane high in case there are several classes (costs calculation). Besides, in the situation the patterns do not belong to any in the L given classes, SVM methods are not defined (Brown et al., 2005). On the other hand, SVM will classify the pattern in a given class based on the calculation parameters. This is a wrong result classification.
One other approach is popular at present is to use Artificial Neural Network for the pattern classification. Artificial Neural Network will be trained with the patterns to find the weight collection for the classification process (Kiem et al., 2000). This approach overcomes the disadvantage of SVM of using suitable threshold in the classification for outside pattern. If the patterns do not belong any in L given classes, the Artificial Neural Network identify and report results to the outside given classes.
In this section, the Multi Artificial Neural Network (MANN) model is used to apply for pattern and image classification. Firstly, patterns or images are projected to difference spaces. Secondly, in each of these spaces, patterns are classified into responsive class using a Neural Network called Sub Neural Network (SNN) of MANN. Lastly, MANN's global frame (GF) consisting some Component Neural Network (CNN) is used to compose the classified result of all SNN.

4.1 Multi Artificial Neural Network

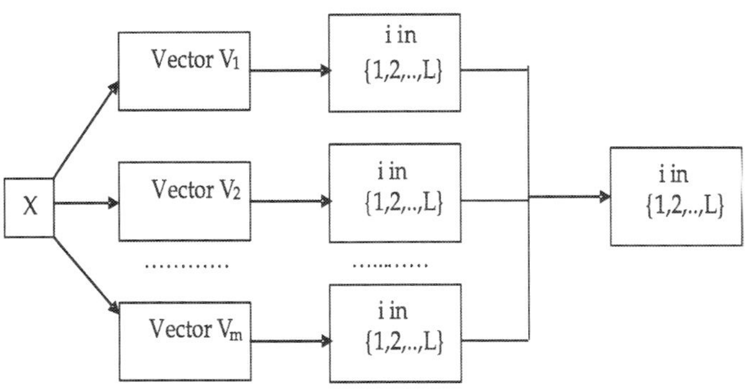

Fig. 21. Image classification

There are a lot of approaches to classify the image featured by m vectors X= $(v_1,v_2,\dots,v_m)$. Each of patterns is needed to classify in one of L classes: $\Omega = \{\Omega i \mid 1 \le i \le L\}$. This is a general image classification problem (Kiem et al., 2000) with parameters (m, L).
A Sub-Neural Network will classify the pattern based on the responsive feature. To compose the classified result, we can use the selection method, average combination method or build the reliability coefficients…

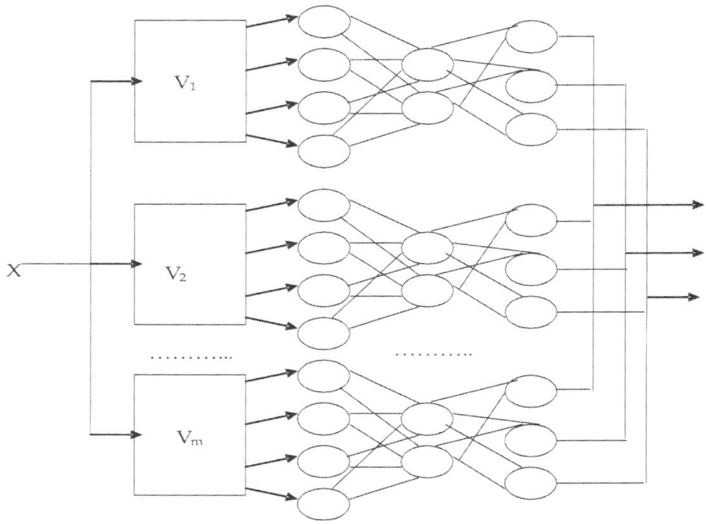

Fig. 22. Processing of Sub neural networks

The selection method will choose only one of the classified results of a SNN to be the whole system's final conclusion:

$$P(\Omega_i \mid X) = P_k(\Omega_i \mid X) \; (k=1..m) \tag{16}$$

Where, $P_k(\Omega_i \mid X)$ is the image X's classified result in the Ω_i class based on a Sub Neural Network, $P(\Omega_i \mid X)$ is the pattern X's final classified result in the Ω_i. Clearly, this method is subjectivity and omitted information.

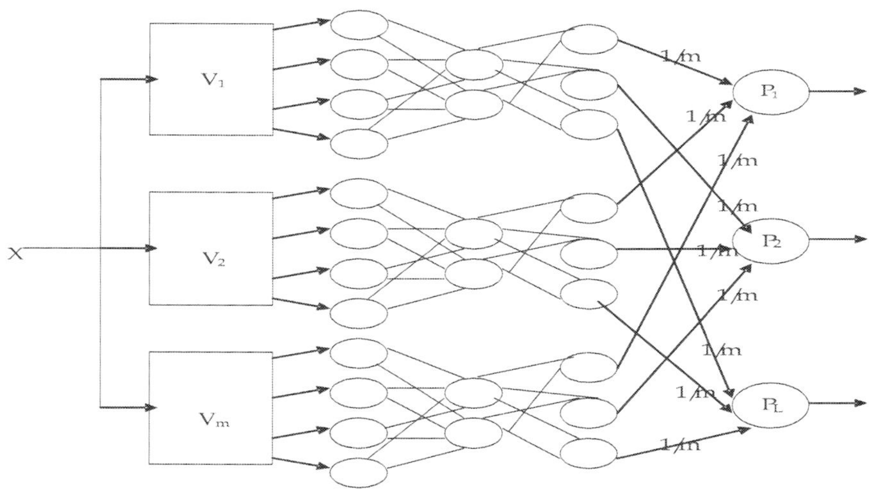

Fig. 23. Average combination method.

The average combination method (Thai et al. 2004) uses the average function for all the classified result of all SNN:

$$P(\Omega_i \mid X) = \sum_{k=1}^{m} \frac{1}{m} P_k(\Omega_i \mid X) \tag{17}$$

This method is not subjectivity but it set equal the importance of all image features.
On the other approach is building the reliability coefficients attached on each SNN's output (Thai, 2004, Bac et al., 2005). The fuzzy logic, SVM, Hidden Markup Model (HMM) (Ghoshal et al., 2005) is used to build these coefficients:

$$P(\Omega_i \mid X) = \sum_{k=1}^{m} r_k P_k(\Omega_i \mid X) \tag{18}$$

Where, r_k is the reliability coefficient of the kth Sub Neural Network. For example, the following model uses Genetics algorithm to create these reliability coefficients.

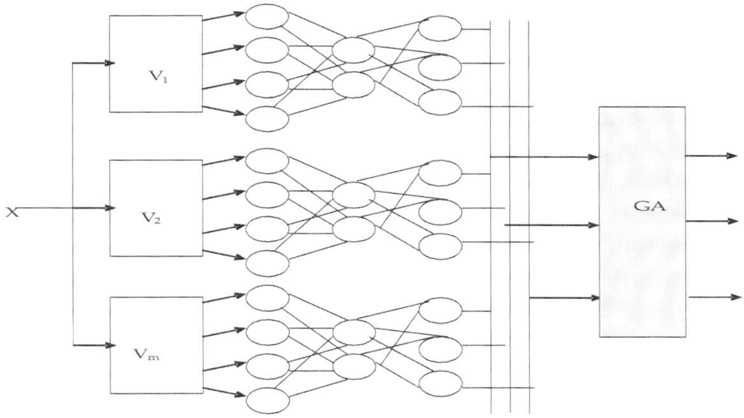

Fig. 24. NN_GA model (Thai, 2004)

In the next section, the Neural Network technique is used. In details, a global frame consisting of some CNN(s) is used. The weights of CNN(s) evaluate the importance of SNN(s) like the reliability coefficients. This model links many Neural Networks together, so it is called Multi Artificial Neural Network (MANN).

4.2 Multi Artificial Neural Network apply for image classification

A. The MANN model

Multi Artificial Neural Network (MANN), applying for pattern or image classification with parameters (m, L), has m Sub-Neural Network (SNN) and a global frame (GF) consisting L Component Neural Network (CNN). In particular, m is the number of feature vectors of image and L is the number of classes.
Definition 1: SNN is a 3 layers (input, hidden, output) Neural Network. The number input nodes of SNN depend on the dimensions of feature vector. SNN has L (the number classes)output nodes. The number of hidden node is experimentally determined. There are

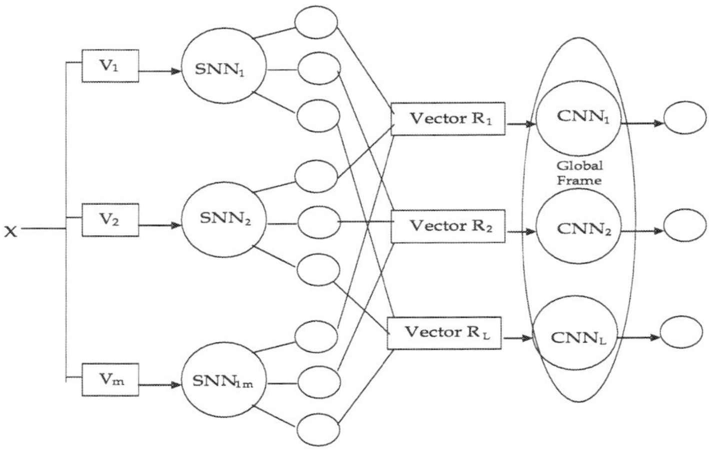

Fig. 25. MANN with parameters (m, L).

m (the number of feature vectors) SNN(s) in MANN model. The input of the ith SNN, symbol is SNN_i, is the feature vector of an image. The output of SNN_i is the classified result based on the ith feature vector of image.

***Definition** 2*: Global frame is frame consisting L Component Neural Network which compose the output of SNN(s).

***Definition** 3*: Collective vector k[th], symbol R_k (k=1..L), is a vector joining the kth output of all SNN. The dimension of collective vector is m (the number of SNN).

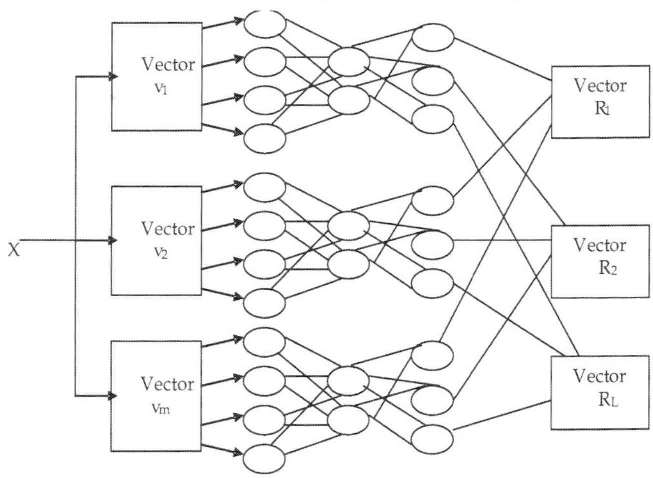

Fig. 26. Create collective vector for CNN(s).

Definition 4: CNN is a 3 layers (input, hidden, output) Neural Network. CNN has m (the number of dimensions of collective vector) input nodes, and 1 (the number classes) output nodes. The number of hidden node is experimentally determined. There are L CNN(s). The output of the jth CNN, symbols is CNN_j, give the probability of X in the jth class.

B. The process of the MANN model

The training process of MANN is separated in two phases. Phase (1) is to train SNN(s) one-by-one called local training. Phase (2) is to train CNN(s) in GF one-by-one called global training. In local training phase, the SNN_1 will be trained first. After that $SNN_2,\ldots,SNN_m$ will be trained.

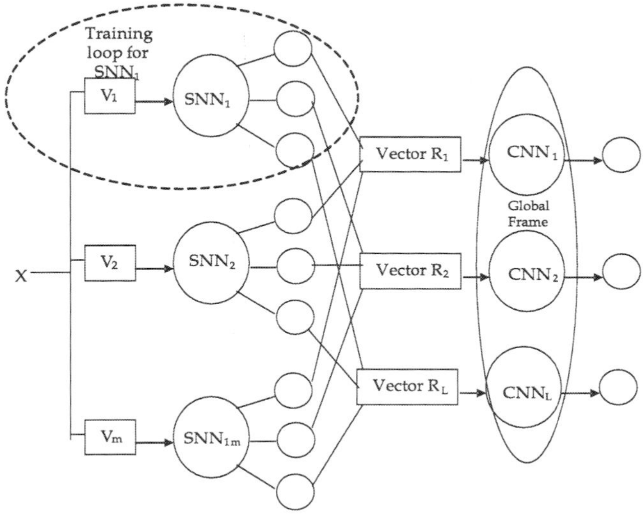

Fig. 27. SNN1 local training

In the global training phase, CNN_1 will be trained. After that $CNN_2,\ldots,CNN_L$ will be trained.

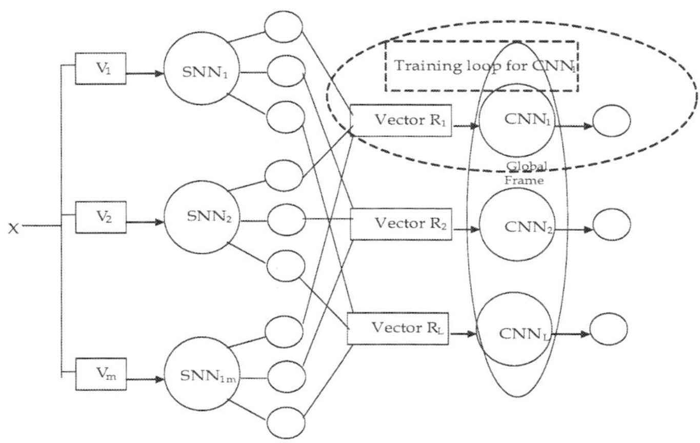

Fig. 28. CNN1 global training.

The classification process of pattern X using MANN is below: firstly, pattern X are extract to m feature vectors. The ith feature vector is the input of SNN_i classifying pattern. Join all the kth output of all SNN to create the kth (k=1..L) collective vector, symbol R_k. R_k is the input of CNN_k. The output of CNN_k is the kth output of MANN. It gives us the probability of X in the kth class. If the kth output is max in all output of MANN and bigger than the threshold. We conclude pattern X in the kth class.

C. Applying the MANN for six basic facial expressions classification

In the above section, the MANN is explained in the general case with parameters (m, L) apply for pattern classification. Now, MANN model is applied for scenery image of regional tourism classification. In fact that this is an experimental setup with (m=4, L=6). The dimensions of input vector of all SNN are not the same. An automatic facial feature extraction system is used, which is able to identify the eye location, the detailed shape of eyes and mouth, chin and inner boundary from facial images (Hung, 2009).

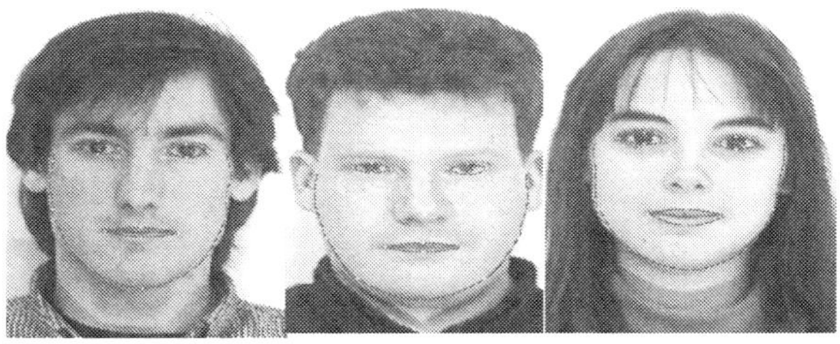

Fig. 29. All Features Extraction (Hung, 2009).

The left eye is the input for SNN_1. The right eye is the input for SNN2. When emotional expression on the face, the left eye and the right eye may not be completely matched each other..The mouth is the input for SNN_3. The inner boundary is the input for SNN_4. All SNN(s) are 6 output nodes matching to 6 basic facial expression (happiness, sadness, surprise, anger, disgust, fear) (Michael et al., 1999). The experimental MANN has 6 CNN(s). They give the probability of the face in six basic facial expressions. It is easy to see that to build MANN model only use Neural Network technology to develop the experimental system.
The proposed model is applied for 6 basic facial expressions on JAFFE database consisting 213 images posed by 10 Japanese female models. The experimental result is presented below:

Comparison	SNN1	SNN2	SNN3	SNN4	Average	MANN
Precision	71%	73%	76%	56%	80%	83%

Table 7. Facial Expression Precision

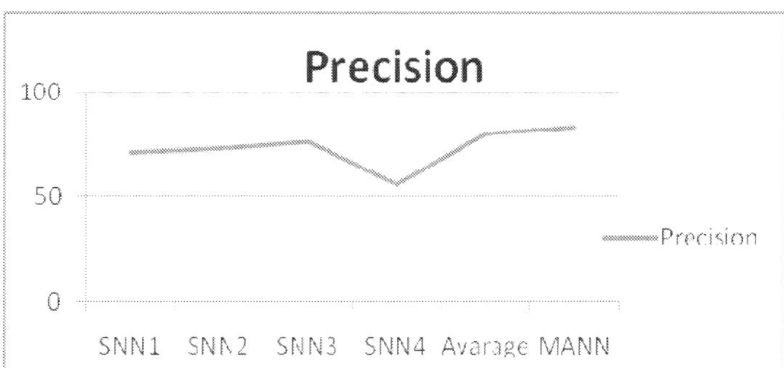

Fig. 30. Facial expression using different methods.

It is a small experimental to check MANN model and need to improve the experimental system. Although the result classification is not high, the improvement of combination result shows that the MANN's feasibility such a new method combines. We need to integrate with another facial feature sequences extraction system to increase the classification precision.

4.3 Conclusion

In this section, the model Multi Artificial Neural Network (MANN) with parameters (m, L) is explained. This model is applied for facial expression or image classification. Include, m is the number of feature vectors of image. L is the number of classes. MANN model has m Sub-Neural Network SNN_i (i=1..m) and a Global Frame (GF) consisting L Components Neural Network CNN_j (j=1..L). Each of SNN uses to process the responsive feature vector. Each of CNN use to combine the responsive element of SNN's output vector. In fact, the weight coefficients in CNN_j are as the reliability coefficients the SNN(s)' the jth output. It means that the importance of the ever feature vector is determined after the training process. On the other hand, it depends on the image database and the desired classification.
To experience the feasibility of MANN model, in this study, we conducted to develop a MANN model with parameters (m=4, L=3) apply for six basic facial expressions on JAFFE database. The experimental result shows that the proposed model improves the classified result compared with the selection and average combination method.

5. Conclusion

This chapter presented some methods for the recognition of human faces using many different modes of artificial neural network and combination models. The proposed techniques are based on the AdaBoost and Artificial Neural Network (AANN) structure, Multi Layer Perceptron (MLP) structure and Multi Artificial Neural Nework (MANN) structure. An implementation example is given to demonstrate the feasibility of each technique for the human face recognition system. The higher recognition rate conventional techniques on the standard database was obtained using these proposed techniques.These show the feasibility of many modes of articial neural network for facial image proceesing.

6. References

C. Bishop (2006), Pattern Recognition and Machine Learning, Springer Press.

H.Schneiderman (2000), A Statistical Approach to 3D Object Detection Applied to Faces and Cars, *CMU.*

S.Z. Li, and A.K. Jain (2005), Handbook of face recognition, Springer Press.

S.Z. Li, and Z. Zhang (2004), FloatBoost learning and statistical face detection, *IEEE Transactions on Pattern Analysis and Machine Intelligence*, pp. 1112-1113.

H.A. Rowley (1999), Neural network Based Face Detection, *Book Neural network Based Face Detection, Series Neural network Based Face Detection*, School of Computer Science, Computer Science Department, Carnegie Mellon University Pittsburgh, PA 15123, 1999

M.A. Turk, and A.P. Pentland (1991), Eigenface for recognition, *Journal of Cognitive Neuroscience*, pp. 76-86.

P. Viola, and M. Jones (2001), Rapid object detection using a boosted cascade of simple features, Proc. Proceedings of IEEE Computer Society Conference on Computer Vision and Pattern Recognition, pp. 511-518.

P. Viola, and M. Jones (2004), Robust real-time face detection, *International Journal of Computer Vision*, pp. 137-154.

M.H. Yang, D.J. Kriegman, and N. Ahuja (2002), Detecting Faces in Images: A Survey, *IEEE Transactions on Pattern Analysis and Machine Intelligence (PAMI)*, pp. 34-47.

Tong, S. and E. Chang (2001), Support vector machine active learning for image retrieval, *Proceedings of the ninth ACM international conference on Multimedia*, p. 107-118.

Brown, R. and B. Pham (2005), Image Mining and Retrieval Using Hierarchical Support Vector Machines, *Proceedings of the 11th International Multimedia Modeling Conference (MMM'05*, p. 446-451.

Hoang Kiem, Le Hoai Bac, Le Hoang Thai (2000), Neural Network and Genetic Algorithm apply for finger recognizes, *the second conference: Informatics Technology Department, Natural Science University*, HCM City, Vietnam.

Le Hoang Thai (2004), Building, Development and Application Some Combination Models of Neural Network (NN), Fuzzy Logic (FL) and Genetics Algorithm (GA), PhD Mathematics Thesis, Natural Science University, HCM City, Vietnam.

Le Hoai Bac, Le Hoang Thai (2004), the GA_NN_FL associated model for authenticating finger printer, *the KES'2004 International Program Committee, Wellington Institute of Technology*, NEW ZEALAND, pp. 708-715.

Ghoshal, A., P. Ircing, and S. Khudanpur (2005), Hidden Markov models for automatic annotation and content-based retrieval of images and video, *Proceedings of the 28th annual international ACM SIGIR conference on Research and development in information retrieval*, p. 544-551.

Chen, Y. and J.Z. Wang (2002), A region-based fuzzy feature matching approach to content-based image retrieval, *Pattern Analysis and Machine Intelligence, IEEE Transactions on*, pp. 1252-1267.

Hoiem, D. et al. (2004), Object-based image retrieval using the statistical structure of images, *Proceedings of the IEEE Computer Society Conference on CVPR 2004*, pp. 490-497 .

Siu-Yeng Cho and Zheru Chi (2005), Genetic Evolution Processing of Data Structure for Image Classification, *IEEE Transaction on Knowledge and Data Engineering*, Vol 17, No 2, pp. 216-231.

Nguyen Viet Hung (2009), Facial Expression Based on Wavelet Transform, *the 2nd International Congress on Image and Signal Processing* (CISP'09), pp. 330-339.

Michael J. Lyons, Julien Budynek, & Shigeru Akamatsu (1999), Automatic Classification of Single Facial Images, *IEEE Transactions on Pattern Analysis and Machine Intelligence 21*, pp. 1357-1362.

Thai Hoang Le, Len Tien Bui (2008), An approach to combine adaboost and artificial neural network for detecting human faces, proceeding of the 2008 IEEE International Conference on System, Man, Cybernetics (SMC 2008), pp. 3411-3415.

Thai Hoang Le, Len Tien Bui (2008), Local texture classifiers based on multi layer perceptron for face alignment, ICTFIT'08, pp. 32-38.

Thai Hoang Le, Hai Son Tran (2010), Facial expression classification based on mutil artificial neural network, proceedings of International Conference on Advanced Computing and Applications (ACOMP), HCM City University of Technology, pp. 125 – 133.

12

Modeling Spammer Behavior: Artificial Neural Network vs. Naïve Bayesian Classifier

Md. Saiful Islam[1] and Md. Rafiqul Islam[2]
[1]*University of Dhaka,*
[2]*Deakin University,*
[1]*Bangladesh*
[2]*Australia*

1. Introduction

The exponential growth of spam emails in recent years is a fact of life. Internet subscribers world-wide are unwittingly paying an estimated €10 billion a year in connection costs just to receive "junk" emails, according to a study undertaken for the European Commission. Though there is no universal definition of spam, unwanted and unsolicited commercial email as a mass mailing to a large number of recipients is basically known as the junk email or spam to the internet community. Spams are considered to be potential threat to Internet Security. Spam's direct effects include the consumption of computer and network resources and the cost in human time and attention of dismissing unwanted messages. More importantly, these ever increasing spams are taking various forms and finding home not only in mailboxes but also in newsgroups, discussion forums etc without the consent of the recipients. Overflowing mailboxes are overwhelming users, causing newsgroups and discussion forums to be flooded with irrelevant or inappropriate messages. As a consequence, users are getting discouraged not to use them anymore though these systems can provide numerous benefits to them.

Combating spam is a difficult job contrast to the spamming. Millions of spammers around the world are engaged in spreading spams with ever changing tricks and tactis to circumvent the filters deployed by the mailbox providers. As spammers are paid per volume for thier job, they invest thier best effort in reaching everyone by all possible ways. No antispamming technique is hundred percent accurate for spam problem. Antispamming techniques try to make a trade-off between rejecting legitimate e-mail vs. not rejecting all spam, and the associated costs in time and effort.

The simplest and most common approaches are to use filters that screen messages based upon the presence of common words or phrases common to junk e-mail. Other simplistic approaches include *blacklisting* and *whitelisting*.

- *Blacklisting* technique automatically rejects messages received from the addresses of known spammers.
- *Whitelisting* accepts messages received from known and trusted correspondents only.

The major flaw in the first two approaches is that it relies upon complacence by the spammers by assuming that they are not likely to change (or forge) their identities or to alter the style and *vocabulary* of their sales pitches. *Whitelisting* risks the possibility that the recipient will miss legitimate e-mail from a known or expected correspondent with a heretofore unknown address, such as correspondence from a long-lost friend, or a purchase confirmation pertaining to a transaction with an online retailer. A detail explanation of these techniques is given in (Islam & Chowdhury, 2005). Ramachandran et al. (2007) propose a new technique called *behavioral blacklisting*, which complements existing blacklists by categorizing spammers based on *how* they send email, rather than the IP address (or address range) from which they are sending it. The intuition behind their idea is that, while IP addresses are ephemeral as identifiers, spam campaigns, spam lists, and spamming techniques are more persistent. If one can identify email-sending patterns that are characteristic of spamming behavior, then she can continue to classify IP addresses as spammers even as spammers change their IP addresses.

Machine learning algorithms namely Naïve Bayesian classifier, Decision Tree induction, Artificial Neural Network and Support Vector Machines, based on keywords or tokens extracted from the e-mail's Subject, Content-Type Header and Message Body, have been used successfully in the past (Aery & Chakravarthy, 2005 ; Drucker et al., 1999; Eichler, 2005; Islam & Chowdhury, 2005). Very soon they fall short to filter out spam emails as the spammer changing themselves in the ways that are very difficult to model by simple keywords or tokens (Stuart et al., 2004). The tactics the spammer uses follow patterns and these behavioral patterns can be modeled to combat spam. Actually the more they try to hide, the easier it is to see them (Stuart et al., 2004). Now the question is:

Ques 1. Are the patterns that the spammers follow common to all?

Ques 2. If the spammers follow patterns to spread spams, is it possible to track those patterns?

Ques 3. If one can track the common spammer patterns, is it possible to model them?

Ques 4. Is it possible to model common spammer patterns by machine learning approaches?

Ques 5. What level of accuracy is possible to achieve if one apply machine learning approaches?

Many researchers observe that spammers follow patterns. These patterns can be discovered from many different places: from email corpus (Stuart et al., 2004) by analysing their contents, network-level behavioral patterns (Ramachandran et al., 2006; Sperotto et al., 2009), transfer pattern during transfer sessions (Zhang et al., 2006), resource usage patterns (Xu et al., 2010) and spammer behavior in terms of the chain of machines they use to deliver their messages (Guerra et al., 2009).

This study investigates the possibilities of modeling spammer behavioral patterns instead of vocabulary as features for spam email categorization and these behavioral patterns are discovered by analysing email corpus *Subject, Content-Type Header* and *Message Body*. The two machine learning algorithms *Naïve Bayesian Classifier* and *Artificial Neural Networks* are experimented to model common spammer patterns and both of them achieve a promising detection rate that can be considered as an improvement of performance compared to the keyword-based contemporary filtering approaches.

2. Methodology

The success of machine learning algorithms in *text categorization* (TC) has led researchers to investigate learning algorithms for filtering spam emails (Sebastiani, 2002). The central purpose of learning is to accurately predict unseen data. There are two types of learning strategy and those are: *supervised* and *unsupervised*. In *supervised learning* both the data objects and their labels are given, but in unsupervised learning only data objects are provided. *Naïve Bayesian classifier*, *Decision Tree induction*, *Artificial Neural Network* and *Support Vector Machines* are *supervised learning* algorithms. Clustering is a good example of *unsupervised learning* algorithm.

To learn the machine both training and test data are needed. Training data are used to build the model and then test data are used to measure the effectiveness of the model. In *n-fold cross validation* technique initial data are divided into *n* subsets. From these *n* subsets, *n*-1 subsets are used to train the model and the remaining subset is used to test the model. This process continues *n* times and average performance is taken to judge the effectiveness of the model.

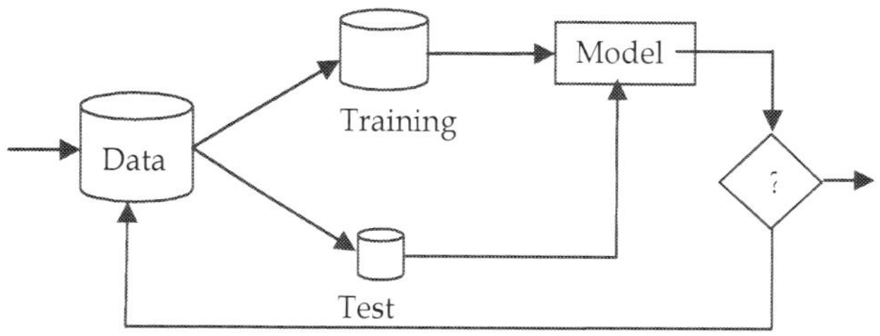

Fig. 1. Learning model

The following two *supervised* machine learning algorithms are exploited to model spammer tricks and techniques in this study.

2.1 Artificial Neural Network

Artificial neural networks (ANN) are non-linear statistical data modeling tools that tries to simulate the functions of biological neural networks. It consists of interconnected collection of simple processing elements or artificial neurons and processes information in a connectionist approach to computation (Han & Kamber, 2001; Stuart et al., 2004). ANN is generally considered to be an adaptive system that changes its structure in response to external or internal information that flows through the network during the learning phase. Fig. 2 shows an example of *multilayer feed forward neural network* (MFFNN).

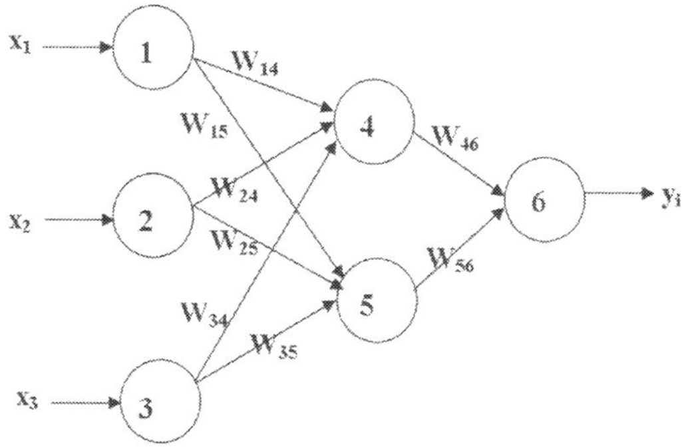

Fig. 2. An example of a multilayer feed-forward artificial neural network

In MFFNN nodes represent neurons are denoted by circle, edges represent connections between neurons are directed edges and labelled with corresponding weight. Nodes in the *input layer* receive inputs (x_i) from external world and nodes in the *output layer* give output (y_i) to the user. Nodes in the *middle layers* (generally called *hidden layers*) receive inputs from the previous layer and deliver it to the next layer. The output of a node in an *artificial neural network* is computed by the equation given below:

$$y_j = \sum_{i=1}^{n} w_{ij} x_i + \theta_j$$

where y_j is the value that will be passed to the next layer from node *j*, *n* is the number of incoming edges to node j, x_i's are the inputs coming from previous layer to node *j* and θ_j is the bias for node *j*.

The *topology* of an artificial neural network is defined by the number of layers in it and the number of nodes that appear in each layer. Once the topology is given of an artificial neural network, the learning task is to assign proper weight in each connection or edge so that it can correctly identify unknown data. This can be done by the most popular method for learning in multilayer networks: *backpropagation*. In *backpropagation* neural network learning algorithm, initially the weights and the biases are assigned randomly in the range [0, 1]. Then one of the example cases is applied to the network and the network produces some output based on the current state of its synaptic weights. This output is compared to the known-good output and a mean-squared error is calculated. The error value is then propagated backwards through the network and changes are made to the weights in each layer. The whole process is repeated for each of the example cases, then back to the first case again, and so on. The cycle is repeated until the overall error value drops below some pre-determined threshold. After then the network assumed to learn the problem well enough. The pseudo code for backpropagation artificial neural network learning algorithm is given below:

```
Step 1: Randomly initialize the weights and the biases in the network
Step 2: For each example e in the training set
            // forward pass
            O = neural-net-output (network, e)
            T = teacher output for e
            Calculate error (T - O ) at the output units

            // backward pass
            Compute delta_wh for all weights from hidden layer to output layer
            Compute delta_wi for all weights from input layer to hidden layer
            Update the weights in the network

Step 3: Continue step 3 until all examples classified correctly or stopping criterion
        satisfied
Step 4: Return the network
```

The detail about *backpropagation* learning can be found in (Han & Kamber, 2001; Rojas, 1996).

2.2 Naïve Bayesian classifier

Bayesian classifier, the simplest and most widely used for filtering spams, is based on the so-called Bayes' theorem. For a training e-mail E, the classifier calculates for each category, the probability that the e-mail should be classified under C_i, where C_i is the ith category, making use of the law of the conditional probability:

$$P(C_i \mid E) = \frac{P(C_i)P(E \mid C_i)}{P(E)}$$

where $P(C_i)$ is the prior probability of hypothesis C_i; $P(E)$ is the prior probability of training data E; $P(C_i \mid E)$ is the probability of C_i given E and $P(E \mid C_i)$ is the probability of E given C_i. Assuming class conditional independence, that is, the probability of each word in an e-mail is independent of the word's context and its position in the e-mail, $P(E \mid C_i)$ can be calculated as the product of each individual word W_j's probabilities appearing in the category C_i (W_j being the jth of l words in the e-mail):

$$P(E \mid C_i) = P(w_1 \mid C_i)P(w_2 \mid C_i)...P(w_l \mid C_i)$$

$$= \prod_{j=1}^{l} P(w_j \mid C_i)$$

The category maximizing $P(C_i \mid E)$ is predicted by the classifier (Han & Kamber, 2001; Eichler, 2005).

Bayesian classifier does not require having lots of observations for each possible combination of the variables and are particularly suitable when the dimensionality of input data is high. The effect of a variable value on a given class in Bayesian Classifier is independent of the values of other variable. This assumption simplifies the computation and despite its simplicity, *Naive Bayesian Classifier* can often outperform more sophisticated classification methods (Caruana & Niculescu-Mizil, 2006) makes it particularly popular in commercial and open-source spam filters (Metsis et al., 2006).

2.3 Spammer behavioral patterns

The keyword-based statistical analyzers mostly depend on tokenization of the email content and extracting feature from tokenized keywords to model spammer behavior. Tokenization can be misguided in many several ways as today's email supports character sets other than ASCII, non-text attachments and bodies with multiple parts. For example, the following HTML tricks can be used to do this:

GET<!-- banana -->V<!-- 45-->I<!-- wumpus -->A<!-- dskfj -->G <!-- adf -- >R<!-- free -->A

Thus above nonsense HTML tags only split the special word "viagra" and disguise the tokenizer though it would be shown as "GET VIAGRA" to email client.

Even a word can be replaced with characters of other languages or like same character. For example, "V1DEO" can be sent instead of "VIDEO" and "Fántástiç" instead of "Fantastic". A combination of special characters can used to produce alphabetical characters. For example, char "V" can be represented as the combination of right slash"\" and left slash "/". A grouping or clustering of these techniques is given Table 1 for quick review.

Table 1 has 30 different tricks and one can easily verify that HTML based tactics cover most of them (70%). It can also be shown that 75% of Cascading Style Sheet (CSS) and 50% of Image-based tricks are also covered by HTML-based tactics. It is evident from table 1 that Java Script and MIME (and/or others) based tricks do not overlap with HTML/CSS based tactics.

In this study, a model has been developed exploiting two machine learning algorithms to capture common spammer patterns instead of keyword analysis. The 21 handy crafted features from each e-mail message extracted from subject header, priority & content-type headers and body shown in Table 2 simulate all possible common spammer tricks. These features have also been optimized in their capability of classifying spam emails. The rationale of these features can be verified by their statistics both in spam and non-spam emails. For example, whether a content-type header appeared within the message headers or whether the content type had been set to "text/html" is a common feature of spam, as our investigation revealed. The corpus that has been used in our experimentation, we observed that 98% spam emails include this feature. Similarly, color element (both CSS and HTML format) is also a frequent feature of spam emails. Colorful images those are generally included in the email for X-rated and unwanted internet marketing groups send to catch users' attention. The use of color elements in non-spam mails is very low. We found that 56% spam emails contain color elements whereas it exists only for 10% non-spam emails. The inclusion of this feature in our classification has improved performance considerably, which shows its practicality. We also added feature 19-21 as in Table 2, which are significant features of recent spams.

	Java Script	Image	CSS	HTML	MIME/Others
Title Case				Y	
Sticky Finger				Y	
Accent					Y
Readable Spell				Y	
Dot Matrix			Y	Y	
Right-to-Left				Y	
HTML Numbers				Y	
Comments				Y	
Styles			Y		
Invisible Ink			Y	Y	
Matrix			Y	Y	
Encoding of MSG					Y
Encrypted Message Bodies	Y				
Copperfield			Y		
Invisible Image		Y			
Zero Image		Y	Y	Y	
Slice and Dice		Y	Y	Y	
Cross Word			Y	Y	
Honorary Title				Y	
Image Chopping		Y			
Cramp				Y	
Framed				Y	
Big Tag				Y	
Fake Text				Y	
Slick Click				Y	
Phishing				Y	
False Click				Y	
Pump & Dump					Y
I'm Feeling Lucky				Y	

Table 1. Common spammer tricks

2.4 Email corpus

Classification based spam filtering systems have two major drawbacks. Firstly, building a perfect data set free from noise or imperfection as noise adversely affect the classifier's performance (Islam et al., 2009). The nature of spam email is very dynamic and the content of email is textually misleading due to obfuscation. This remains a continuous challenge for spam filtering techniques. Secondly, most training models of the classifier have limitations on their operations (Ranawana & Palade, 2006). Classifiers often produce uncorrelated training errors due to the dimension of feature space; a dissimilar output space is generated for changing feature space from small dimension to complex high dimension.

In this work a corpus of 1,000 emails received over a period of several months is used for experimentation. The distribution of both spam and non-spam emails in this collection is equal. The equal distribution is preferred to make the classifier to eliminate the biasness towards a particular category. That is, out of 1,000 emails 500 is spam and 500 is non-spam. The collection of this corpus is selected over a time and latest trend in spamming is kept in mind. Also the author's experience with spam research and statistical selection methodology is applied to the selection, which made this email bank very much representative of current spamming.

Feature	Category 1: Features From the Message Subject Header
1	Binary feature indicating 3 or more repeated characters
2	Number of words with all letters in uppercase
3	Number of words with at least 15 characters
4	Number of words with at least two of letters J, K, Q, X, Z
5	Number of words with no vowels
6	Number of words with non-English characters, special characters such as punctuation, or digits at beginning or middle of word
	Category 2: Features From the Priority and Content-Type Headers
7	Binary feature indicating whether the priority had been set to any level besides normal or medium
8	Binary feature indicating whether a content-type header appeared within the message headers or whether the content type had been set to "text/html"
	Category 3: Features From the Message Body
9	Proportion of alphabetic words with no vowels and at least 7 characters
10	Proportion of alphabetic words with at least two of letters J, K, Q, X, Z
11	Proportion of alphabetic words at least 15 characters long
12	Binary feature indicating whether the strings "From:" and "To:" were both present
13	Number of HTML opening comment tags
14	Number of hyperlinks ("href=")
15	Number of clickable images represented in HTML
16	Binary feature indicating whether a text color was set to white
17	Number of URLs in hyperlinks with digits or "&", "%", or "@"
18	Number of color element (both CSS and HTML format)
19	Binary feature indicating whether JavaScript has been used or not
20	Binary feature indicating whether CSS has been used or not
21	Binary feature indicating opening tag of table

Table 2. Features extracted from each e-mail

2.5 Feature construction

Each email is parsed as text file to identify each header element to distinguish them from the body of the message. Every substring within the subject header and the message body that was delimited by white space was considered to be a token, and an alphabetic word was defined as a token delimited by white space that contains only English alphabetic characters (A-Z, a-z)or apostrophes.

The tokens were evaluated to create a set of 21 hand-crafted features from each e-mail message (Table 2) of which features 1-17 are proposed in (Stuart et al., 2004). In addition of these 17 features this study proposes other four features 18-21. The study investigates the suitability of these 21 features in classifying spam emails. To do this, each email is represented by a vector of dimension 21 in the vector space model (Salton et al., 1975). To learn the neural network the input layer of *Multilayer Perceptron* will have 21 nodes. These nodes receive values from each dimension of the vector representing the email. For Naïve Bayesian Classifier, each dimension corresponds to spammer behavioral pattern instead of keyword.

2.6 Evaluation measures

Estimating classifier accuracy is important since it allows one to evaluate how accurately a given classifier will classify unknown samples on which the classifier has not been trained. The effectiveness of a classifier is usually measured in terms of accuracy, precision and recall (Makhoul et al., 1999). These measures are calculated using the confusion matrix given below:

Category C_i	Correct	
Predicted ↓	YES	NO
YES	TP_i	FP_i
NO	FN_i	TN_i

TP=true positives
FP=false positives
FN=false negatives
TN=true negatives

Table 3. Confusion matrix

Accuracy of a classifier is calculated by dividing the number of correctly classified samples by the total number of test samples and is defined as:

$$Accuracy = \frac{number\ \ of\ \ correctly\ \ classified\ \ samples}{total\ \ number\ \ of\ \ test\ \ samples}$$

$$= \frac{TP + TN}{TP + FP + FN + TN}$$

Precision measures the system's ability to present only relevant items while recall measures system's ability to present all relevant items. These two measures are widely used in TREC evaluation of document retrieval (Makhoul, 1999). Precision is calculated by dividing the number of samples that are true positives by the total number of samples classified as positives and is defined as:

$$\Pr ecision = \frac{number\ \ of\ \ true\ \ positives}{total\ \ number\ \ of\ \ samples\ \ classified\ \ as\ \ positives}$$

$$= \frac{TP}{TP + FP}$$

Analogously, recall is calculated by dividing the number of samples that are true positives by the total number of samples that classifier should classified as positives and is defined as:

$$Recall = \frac{number \quad of \quad true \quad positives}{total \quad number \quad of \quad postive \quad samples}$$

$$= \frac{TP}{TP + FN}$$

3. Experimental results

Table 4 summarizes the comparative results of Naïve Bayesian Classifier and Artificial neural Networks. These algorithms are tested on Weka 3.6.0 suite of machine learning software written in Java, developed at the University of Waikato (Holmes et al., 1994). Before simulating on *Weka Tool* we transform the vectors obtained from our dataset into *Attribute-Relation File Format* (ARFF).

ARFF files have two distinct sections. The first section is the *Header* information, which is followed the *Data* information. The *Header* of the ARFF file contains the name of the relation, a list of the attributes (the columns in the data), and their types. An example header for our dataset is given below:

```
@RELATION Email_Classification

@ATTRIBUTE   feature01    {yes, no}
@ATTRIBUTE   feature02    NUMERIC
@ATTRIBUTE   feature03    NUMERIC
@ATTRIBUTE   feature04    NUMERIC
@ATTRIBUTE   feature05    NUMERIC
@ATTRIBUTE   feature06    NUMERIC
@ATTRIBUTE   feature07    {normal, medium}
@ATTRIBUTE   feature08    {yes, no}
@ATTRIBUTE   feature09    NUMERIC
@ATTRIBUTE   feature10    NUMERIC
@ATTRIBUTE   feature11    NUMERIC
@ATTRIBUTE   feature12    {yes, no}
@ATTRIBUTE   feature13    NUMERIC
@ATTRIBUTE   feature14    NUMERIC
@ATTRIBUTE   feature15    NUMERIC
@ATTRIBUTE   feature16    {yes, no}
@ATTRIBUTE   feature17    NUMERIC
@ATTRIBUTE   feature18    NUMERIC
@ATTRIBUTE   feature19    {yes, no}
@ATTRIBUTE   feature20    {yes, no}
@ATTRIBUTE   feature21    {yes, no}
@ATTRIBUTE   isHam        {yes, no}
```

The last attribute is the class column. The *Data* of the ARFF file looks like the following (only few samples out of 1000 are given here):

no, 0, 0, 0, 1, 2, medium, yes, 2, 0, 118, yes, 1, 13, 0, no, 0, 0, no, yes, no, yes
no, 8, 0, 0, 1, 2, medium, yes, 1, 219, 223, no, 0, 0, 0, no, 0, 0, no, no, no, yes
no, 0, 1, 0, 0, 1, medium, yes, 5, 4, 48, no, 0, 4, 1, no, 2, 0, no, yes, no,yes
no, 0, 0, 0, 0, 1, medium, yes, 3, 0, 144, yes, 1, 69, 0, no, 0, 3, no, yes, no, yes
no, 0, 1, 1, 0, 1, medium, yes, 4, 0, 7, yes, 1, 1, 0, no, 0, 0, no, yes, no,yes
no, 0, 0, 0, 1, 1, medium, yes, 0, 265, 271, no, 0, 0, 0, no, 0, 0, no, no, no, yes
no, 0, 1, 0, 0, 1, medium, no, 0, 0, 0, no, 0, 0, 0, no, 0, 0, no, no, no,yes
no, 0, 0, 0, 1, 0, medium, yes, 0, 0, 1, no, 0, 1, 0, no, 1, 1, no, yes, no,yes
yes, 0, 0, 0, 3, 5, medium, yes, 0, 0, 2, no, 0, 0, 0, no, 0, 0, no, no, no,yes
yes, 0, 0, 0, 3, 6, medium, no, 0, 0, 0, no, 0, 0, 0, no, 0, 0, no, no, no,yes
no, 0, 0, 0, 0, 0, medium, yes, 10, 0, 55, no, 0, 11, 1, yes, 0, 2, no, yes, yes, no
no, 0, 0, 0, 0, 1, medium, yes, 12, 0, 45, no, 0, 0, 1, no, 0, 15, no, yes, yes, no
no, 0, 0, 0, 0, 0, medium, yes, 6, 0, 43, no, 0, 11, 1, no, 0, 0, no, yes, yes, no
no, 0, 0, 0, 0, 1, medium, yes, 2, 0, 3, no, 0, 0, 0, no, 0, 0, no, no, no,no
no, 0, 0, 0, 0, 0, medium, yes, 2, 0, 21, no, 0, 0, 0, no, 0, 2, no, yes, yes, no
no, 0, 0, 0, 0, 1, medium, yes, 8, 0, 12, no, 0, 29, 0, no, 0, 0, no, no, no,no
no, 0, 0, 0, 0, 0, medium, yes, 14, 0, 57, no, 0, 16, 1, yes, 0, 2, no, yes, yes, no
no, 0, 0, 0, 0, 1, medium, yes, 1, 0, 39, no, 0, 14, 1, no, 0, 0, no, yes, yes, no
yes, 1, 0, 0, 4, 6, medium, yes, 2, 0, 17, no, 0, 2, 0, no, 0, 0, no, no, no, no
yes, 4, 0, 0, 4, 5, medium, yes, 3, 0, 8, no, 0, 7, 0, no, 0, 0, no, no, no, no

Features	Naïve Bayesian Classifier (NaiveBayes)			ANN (Multilayer Perceptron)		
	Accuracy	Precision	Recall	Accuracy	Precision	Recall
Category 1 Only	56.5 %	55.7%	56.5%	67.8%	73.1%	67.8%
Category 2 Only	65.2%	75.0%	65.2%	65.2%	75.0%	65.2%
Category 3 Only	88. 7 %	88.7%	88.7%	86.1%	86.1%	86.1%
Category 1+Category 2	66.9 %	67.3%	67.0%	73.1%	77.2%	73.0%
Category 2+ Category3	92.2 %	92.2%	92.2%	87.8%	88.1%	87.8%
Category 1+Category 3	80.8 %	80.9%	80.9%	74.7%	75.4%	74.8%
Category1+ Category 2 + Category 3	86.9 %	87.0%	87.0%	84.3%	85.1%	84.3%

Table 4. Comparison results for Naïve Bayesian classifier and Artificial Neural Network

The highest level of accuracy that can be achieved by Naïve Bayesian classifier is 92.2% (shown in Table 4) using features from category 2 and 3. The accuracy that can be achieved by any learning algorithms using features from category 1 is negligible. Features from category 2 and 3 contribute mostly in classifying spam emails from non-spam emails for all machine learning algorithm experimented in this study.

Highest number of features is always desirable only if their inclusion increase classifier's accuracy significantly. Growing number of features not only hinders multidimensional indexing but also increases overall execution time. So, this study starves to find an optimal number of features that can be effectively used to learn a classifier without degrading the level of accuracy.

Applying best first forward attribute selection method the study gets only 10 features from category 2 and category 3 useful for classifying the spam and non-spam emails without sacrificing the accuracy as shown in Table 5. The set includes features 8, 9, 10, 12, 13, 14, 15, 16, 17, and 18 of which feature 18 is identified in this study. The Naïve Bayesian classifier again outperforms the Artificial Neural Networks. The optimal feature set obtained by applying best first forward attribute selection method for the features proposed in (Stuart et al., 2004) includes only features 8, 9, 10, 12, 13, 14, 15, 16 and 17, a total of 9 features. In this case ANN outperforms than Naïve Bayesian classification algorithm as shown in Table 5.

Features	Naïve Bayesian Classifier(Naïve Bayes)			ANN (Multilayer Perceptron)		
	Accuracy	Precision	Recall	Accuracy	Precision	Recall
Best first: 8, 9, 10, 12, 13, 14, 15, 16, 17, and 18 [This study]	92.2%	92.2%	92.2%	90.4%	90.6%	90.4%
Best first: 8, 9, 10, 12, 13, 14, 15, 16, and 17 (Stuart et al., 2004)	86.1 %	87.4%	86.1%	91.3%	91.4%	91.3%

Table 5. Comparison results for Naïve Bayesian classifier and Artificial Neural Network

The study presented in (Stuart et al., 2004) uses neural network for modeling spammer common patterns and achieved similar performance, but the limitation of neural network is its longer training time and inherent complexity of explaining its derivation (less comprehensibility). On the contrary, Bayesian Classifier has the advantage of incremental inclusion of features and beforehand calculation. Therefore, Naïve Bayes is suitable for adapting itself in modeling new spammer patterns.

4. Conclusion

This research studies the modeling of spammer behavior by Artificial Neural Networks and Naïve Bayesian Classifier algorithms for spam email classification. Based on examining different features and two different learning strategies, the following conclusions can be drawn from the study presented in this study:

Lesson 1. Spammer behavior can be modeled using features extracted from Content-Type header and message Body only.

Lesson 2. The contribution of features extracted from subject header in spam email detection is negligible or insignificant.

Lesson 3. Naïve Bayesian classifier models the spammer behavior best than Artificial Neural Networks.

Lesson 4. It is possible to get an optimal number of features that can be effectively applied to learning algorithms to classify spam emails without sacrificing accuracy

The preliminary result presented in this study seems promising in modeling spammer common behavioral patterns compared to similar research. The contribution of this study is threefold: it shows why keyword based spam email classifier may fail to model spammers' altering tricks, common patterns adopted by spammers and the rationale of using these patterns against them to combat spam; suitability of modeling spammer common patterns using ANN and Naïve Bayes and finally, establishment of the four concluding remarks.

5. References

Aery, M. & Chakravarthy, S. (2005). eMailSift: email classification based on structure and content, *Proceedings of 5th IEEE International Conference on Data Mining*, pp. 1-8, 0-7695-2278-5, Houston, Texas, January 2005, IEEE Computer Society, Los Alamitos, CA

Caruana, R. & Niculescu-Mizil, A. (2006). An empirical comparison of supervised learning algorithms. *Proceedings of the 23rd International Conference on Machine Learning*, pp. 161-168, Pittsburgh, Pennsylvania, 1-59593-383-2, ACM New York, NY, USA

Drucker, H.; Wu, D. & Vapnik, V. N. (1999). Support vector machines for spam categorization, *IEEE Transactions on Neural Networks*, Vol. 10, No. 5, September 1999, pp. 1048-1054, 1045-9227

Eichler, K. (2005). Automatic Classification of Swedish Email Messages, B.A Thesis, Eberhard-Karls-Universitat Tubingen, August 2005

Guerra, P. H. C., Guedes, D., Meira, W., Hoepers, C., Chaves, M. H. P. C., Jessen, K. S. (2009). Spamming chains: a new way of understanding spammer behavior, *Sixth Conference on Email and Anti Spam*, July 1617, 2009, Mountain View, California USA

Han, J. & Kamber, M. (2001). Data Mining Concepts and Techniques, Academic Press, ISBN 81-7867-023-2

Holmes, G; Donkin, A. & Witten, I. H. (1994). Weka: A machine learning workbench, *Proceedings of 2nd Australia and New Zealand Conference on Intelligent Information Systems*, pp. 357-361, 0-7803-2404-8, Brisbane, Australia, November-December 1994

Islam, M. S. & Amin, M. I. (2007). An architecture of active learning SVMs with relevance feedback for classifying E-mail, *Journal of Computer Science*, Vol. 1, No. 1, June 2007, pp. 15-18, 1994-6244

Islam, M. R. & Chowdhury, M. U. (2005). Spam filtering using ML algorithms, *Proceedings of IADIS International Conference on WWW/Internet*, pp. 419-426, 972-8924-02-X, Lisbon, Portugal, October 2005, International Association for Development of the Information Society

Islam, M. R.; Zhou, W.; Xiang, Y. & Gao, M. (2009). An innovative analyser for multi-classifier email classification based on grey list analysis, *The Journal of Network and Computer Applications*, Elsevier, Vol. 32, No. 2, March 2009, pp. 357-366, 1084-8045

Makhoul, J.; Kubala, F.; Schwartz, R. & Weischedel, R. (1999). Performance measures for information extraction, *Proceedings of DARPA Broadcast News Workshop*, pp. 249-252, Herndon, VA, February 1999

Metsis, V., Androutsopoulos, I. & Paliouras, G. (2006). Spam filtering with Naive Bayes - Which Naive Bayes?, *Third Conference on Email and Anti Spam*, July 2728, 2006, Mountain View, California USA

Ramachandran, A. & Feamster, N. (2006), Understanding the network level behavior of spammers, *SIGCOMM'06*, September 1116, 2006, pp., 291-302, Pisa, Italy, ACM New York, NY, USA

Ramachandran, A., Feamster, N. & Vempala, S. (2007). Filtering spam with behavioral blacklisting, *CCS'07*, October 29–November 2, 2007, pp. 342-351, Alexandria, Virginia, USA

Ranawana, R. & Palade, V. (2006). Multi-classifier systems - review and a roadmap for developers, *International Journal of Hybrid Intelligent Systems*, Vol. 3, No. 1, January 2006, pp. 35-61, 1448-5869

Rojas, R. (1996). The backpropagation algorithm, *Neural Networks - A Systematic Introduction*, Chapter 7, ISBN 978-3540605058, Springer-Verlag, Berlin, New-York, 1996

Salton, G.; Wong, A. & Yang, C. S. (1975). A Vector Space Model for Automatic Indexing, *Communications of the ACM*, Vol. 18, No. 11, pp. 613–620

Sebastiani, F. (2002). Machine learning in automated text categorization, *ACM Computing Surveys*, Vol. 34, No. 1, March 2002, pp. 1-47, 0360-0300

Sperotto, A., Vliek, G., Sadre, R. & Pras, A. (2009). Detecting spam at the network level, M. Oliver and S. Sallent (Eds.): *EUNICE 2009*, LNCS 5733, pp. 208–216, Springer-Verlag Berlin Heidelberg 2009

Stuart, J. I.; Cha, S. & Tappert, C. (2004). A neural network classifier for junk E-mail, *Lecture Notes in Computer Science*, Vol. 3163, pp. 442-450, 0302-9743

Xu, K. S., Kliger, M. & Hero, A. O. (2010). Identifying spammers by their resource usage patterns, *Seventh annual Collaboration, Electronic messaging, Anti Abuse and Spam Conference*, July 13-14, 2010, Redmond, Washington, USA

Zhang, X., Liu, J., Zhang, Y. & Wang, C. (2006). Spam behavior recognition based on session layer data mining, *FSKD 2006*, LNAI 4223, pp. 1289–1298, Springer-Verlag Berlin Heidelberg 2006

13

Applying an Artificial Neural Network to Predicting Effort and Errors for Embedded Software Development Projects

Kazunori Iwata[1], Toyoshiro Nakashima[2], Yoshiyuki Anan[3] and Naohiro Ishii[4]

[1]*Dept. of Business Administration, Aichi University*
[2]*Dept. of Culture-Information Studies, Sugiyama Jogakuen University*
[3]*Base Business Division, Omron Software Co., Ltd.*
[4]*Dept. of Information Science, Aichi Institute of Technology*
Japan

1. Introduction

Recently, growth in the information industry has caused a wide range of uses for information devices, and the associated need for more complex embedded software, that provides these devices with the latest performance and function enhancements (Hirayama (2004); Nakamoto et al. (1997)). Consequently, it is increasingly important for embedded software-development corporations to ascertain how to develop software efficiently, whilst guaranteeing delivery time and quality, and keeping development low costs (Boehm (1976); Tamaru (2004); Watanabe (2004)). Hence, companies and divisions involved in the development of such software are focusing on various types of improvement, particularly process improvement. Predicting effort requirements of new projects and guaranteeing quality of software are especially important, because the prediction relates directly to costs, while the quality reflects on the reliability of the corporation Komiyama (2003); N. (2004); Nakashima (2004); Ogasawara & Kojima (2003); Takagi (2003). In the field of embedded software, development techniques, management techniques, tools, testing techniques, reuse techniques, real-time operating systems and so on, have already been studied. However, there is little research on the relationship between the scale of the development and the number of errors, based of data accumulated from past projects. As a result, previously we described the prediction of the total scale using multiple regression analysis (Iwata et al. (2006b); Nakashima et al. (2006)) and collaborative filtering (Iwata et al. (2006a)). In this Chapter we therefore, propose a method for creating effort and errors prediction model using an Artificial Neural Network (ANN) for complementing missing values (Iwata et al. (2006a)). The proposed method calculates the amount of effort and the number of errors by the following 3 steps. The first step, the similarity between the complementary project data, which include missing values, and the complete project data is calculated. Next, applies collaborative filtering using the method Tsunoda et al. (Tsunoda et al. (2005)) to complement missing values in the data and thus produce sufficient amount of data. In the final step, the prediction target project effort (or errors) is calculated

using the model that is derived from the ANN and with this data. However, the ANN has a large margin of errors for some projects. We therefore, propose a method to reduce the margin of errors model. Finally, we also compare the accuracy of the proposed ANN model with that of a multiple regression analysis model using Welch's t-test (Student (1908); Welch (1947)).
The rest of the Chapter is organized as follows. In Section 2, we explain software development management and discuss current problems and the objectives which this study is trying to achieve, and illustrate software development process and selection of data to establish the model in Section 3. Then, Section 4 explains a collaborative filtering to complement missing values. In Section 5 we expound models to predict effort and errors. In section 6 describes evaluation experiment. Section 7 concludes.

2. Software project management and issues

The embedded software for financial institutions developed by "OMRON software Co." is based on the basic software customized for an individual customer's need to install it at various sites. To minimize the customization needed during the development of basic software, parameters are embedded to control the system. This engineering technique assures productivity and quality. This type of approach is actively taken during the process of software development. While using this type of technique, the pressures related to delivery time and quality are more and more intense. This requires improving further the quality and cost during software development. Hence, we have already studied costs of the processes by using analysis(Iwata et al. (2006b); Nakashima et al. (2006)) and collaborative filtering(Iwata et al. (2006a)). To cope with this situation, the tools that can manage the progress status or results in the database are used to improve the quality and productivity. However, the more the volume of software development project increases the more the errors increase. By analyzing the database, we determine the relationship between the volume of software development project and the errors.

3. Software development processes and selection of data

In software development division of "OMRON software Co.", the waterfall model(Boehm (1976)) is used as the basic development-process model. A general description of this model is given in Table 1.
Regarding the data related to project productivity or quality, data for such things as internal effort and size information etc. are recorded as shown in Table 2 and Table 3, for 3 points in time:

1. At the beginning of the project.
2. During the project.
3. At the end of the project.

Before analyzing data, we examined the data and decided which data should be selected to make the model. Table 2 and Table 3 show the latter data and the results of the selection.

3.1 Data sets for creating models

Using the following data, we create models to predict both the planning effort (Eff) and errors (Err).

Eff: "The amount of effort", which needs be predicted.

	Process	Contents of work
1	Conceptual design(CD)	This is so-called "system engineering work". They analyze customer requirements and detail the areas to be addressed as development factors.
2	Design	According to the development factors defined in CD process, designing of software functionality, combining of software modules, and writing of source code are performed.
3	Debugging	Verify the outcome of the design process with the actual machine to see if it is designed according to the design. The same designer in design process is assigned to debug.
4	Test	After finishing debugging, double-check the software to confirm that it satisfies customer's requirements. A different person (not those assigned to design and debug) is assigned to do this.

Table 1. Software Development Process

Items	Data	Selection	Reason
Internal effort	Effort for each planned process and actual performance	Selected	The data are acquired by effort management system. These data are quantitative and accuracy is good.
Project-scale information	Number of lines in new, modified, original and reused software	Selected	These data are quantitative and accuracy is good.
Effort information	Actual effort in each process	Rejected	The data are acquired at the end of the project. Hence, they can not use to predict effort and errors at the beginning of the project.
	Effort for redo in each process	Rejected	The definition of redo is not consistent. The accuracy is poor.

Table 2. Classifications and Selection of Data 1

Items	Data	Selection	Reason
Products information	Product classification and product models	Selected	It is necessary to make characteristics of the products and development process be reflected in the model.
	Customer name and sub project name	Rejected	The data is qualitative and it is difficult to obtain accurate data.
	Development type(new or modification)	Rejected	Because there are only two types, it is not appropriate as parameter for the model.
	Delivery time	Rejected	Because the delivery time is seldom changed, this is not selected.
Outsourcing	The estimation of outsourcing amount and actual situation	Rejected	Because outsourcing amount includes sales aspects, this is not appropriate for actual project error status.
	The estimation of outsourcing effort and actual situation	Rejected	Because this is estimated by outsourcing amount and includes sales aspects, this is not selected.
Quality information	The number of problems in each process	Selected	It is necessary to find relationship between a project and errors. These data consist of "Total Error", "Error in CD and Design", "Error in Debugging" and "Error in Test".

Table 3. Classifications and Selection of Data 2

Err: "The number of errors" in a project.

V_{new}: "Volume of newly added", which denotes the number of steps in the newly generated functions of the target project.

V_{modify}: "Volume of modification", which denotes the number of steps modifying and adding to existing functions to use the target project.

V_{survey}: "Volume of original project", which denotes the original number of steps in the modified functions, and the number of steps deleted from the functions.

V_{reuse}: "Volume of reuse", which denotes the number of steps in functions of which only an external method of has been confirmed and which are applied to the target project design without confirming the internal contents.

4. Collaborative filtering

4.1 Conventional collaborative filtering and complementing values

Collaborative filtering is used as a basic technique in a system (here referred to as a "recommendation system"), that recommends items from a number of available options by matching user preferences (Breese et al. (2000); Tsunoda et al. (2005)). The items are any objects, for which the degree of preference changes according to the user, such as articles, web pages, books, songs, movies, and so on. A recommendation system based on collaborative filtering includes the following two steps:

1. Calculating similarity among users (user evaluation values are used in the calculation).
2. Determining items to be recommended (calculated values for the items are based on similarity). Herein, it is assumed that the preferences of users that are highly similar, will also be similar, and that new items are recommended to users.

This Chapter applies the method of conceptualizing from a recommendation system based on collaborative filtering to complement missing values, and references the effort and errors prediction method proposed by Tsunoda et al., (Tsunoda et al. (2005)). In other words, in this Chapter we calculate missing values based on the assumption that "if a project has any missing values, the values are similar to those of other projects that show striking similarities, because highly similar projects output similar values for each item.". We use metrics to calculate the similarity among projects instead of user evaluation values. However, the range of a metric is different for each class, in contrast to user evaluation values that are all within a fixed range. Hence, the values by each metric are normalized to set its range. Moreover, the values by each metric rely on the scale of the project, and the dispersion of the average values by each metric is extremely large. Because of this, errors will be magnified if the scale of the project is not considered when calculating missing values. Therefore, to calculate missing values, we use revised values corresponding to the scale of the project, and do not use those projects that are too far apart on the scale, even if the similarity is high.

4.2 Complement method for missing value

In this Chapter, the matrix $m \times n$ denotes a data set including missing values. $p_i \in \{p_1, p_2, \ldots, p_m\}$ indicates the ith project, and $m_j \in \{m_1, m_2, \ldots, m_n\}$ indicates the jth metric. $v_{i,j} \in \{v_{1,1}, v_{1,2}, \ldots, v_{m,n}\}$ means the value of the measurement in the jth matrix m_j in the ith project p_i. When $v_{i,j}$ is the missing value, it is denoted as $v_{i,j} = \phi$.

	m_1	m_2	$\cdots$	m_j	$\cdots$	m_b	$\cdots$	m_n
p_1	$v_{1,1}$	$v_{1,2}$	$\cdots$	$v_{1,j}$	$\cdots$	$v_{1,b}$	$\cdots$	$v_{1,n}$
p_2	$v_{2,1}$	$v_{2,2}$	$\cdots$	$v_{2,j}$	$\cdots$	$v_{2,b}$	$\cdots$	$v_{2,n}$
$\cdots$	$\cdots$	$\cdots$		$\cdots$		$\cdots$		$\cdots$
p_i	$v_{i,1}$	$v_{i,2}$	$\cdots$	$v_{i,j}$	$\cdots$	$v_{i,b}$	$\cdots$	$v_{i,n}$
$\cdots$	$\cdots$	$\cdots$		$\cdots$		$\cdots$		$\cdots$
p_a	$v_{a,1}$	$v_{a,2}$	$\cdots$	$v_{a,j}$	$\cdots$	$v_{a,b}$	$\cdots$	$v_{a,n}$
$\cdots$	$\cdots$	$\cdots$		$\cdots$		$\cdots$		$\cdots$
p_m	$v_{m,1}$	$v_{m,2}$	$\cdots$	$v_{m,j}$	$\cdots$	$v_{m,b}$	$\cdots$	$v_{m,n}$

Fig. 1. Matrix $m \times n$ Used in Prediction

Let the value of the bth metric m_b in the ath project p_a be a missing value $v_{a,b} = \phi$ and $\widehat{v}_{a,b}$ mean the prediction value for the metric value $v_{a,b}$.
In calculating $\widehat{v}_{a,b}$ the following three steps are processed.

1. Metric normalization. The range of every metric range is $[0, 1]$ via normalization.
2. Calculation of similarity among projects.
3. Missing value calculation.

4.2.1 Metric normalization

The values of each metric are normalized to set the range for the metric. The range of every metric range is $[0, 1]$ via normalization. The normalized value for a metric of value $v_{i,j}$ is denoted as $f_n(v_{i,j})$, and $f_n(v_{i,j})$ is calculated by the Eq. (1).

$$f_n(v_{i,j}) = \frac{v_{i,j} - min(P_j)}{max(P_j) - min(P_j)} \quad (1)$$

where, P_j is the set of projects able to measure the value of the metric m_j and $max(P_j)$, $min(P_j)$ are the maximum and minimum values of $\{v_{k,j} | p_k \in P_j\}$, respectively.

4.2.2 Calculation of similarity among projects

The similarity between the missing value prediction target project p_a and another project p_i is described as $f_{sim}(p_a, p_i)$. The similarity calculation uses a vector calculation algorithm (Breese et al. (2000)).
The algorithm for calculating similarity is usually used to calculate the similarity between two documents (Salton & MacGill (1983)). In the algorithm, each vectors contain the frequency of words appearing in each document, and similarity is calculated using the cosine of the angles created by the vectors. Breese et al. (Breese et al. (2000)) proposed a recommendation system based on this algorithm, in which they equate a document with a user, the words with items, and the word frequency with the item evaluation value. In this Chapter, we calculate the similarity of projects by equating the user with the project, the item with the metric, and the item prediction value with the metric value similar to the method of Tsunoda et al. (Tsunoda et al. (2005)).
The similarity $f_{sim}(p_a, p_i)$ between the prediction target project p_a and the another project p_i is calculated as in Eq. (2).

$$f_{sim}(p_a, p_i) = \frac{\sum_{j \in M_a \cap M_i} f_n(v_{a,j}) \times f_n(v_{i,j})}{\sqrt{\sum_{j \in M_a \cap M_i} f_n(v_{a,j})^2} \sqrt{\sum_{j \in M_a \cap M_i} f_n(v_{i,j})^2}} \quad (2)$$

where, M_a and M_i are the set of non missing metrics measured in projects p_a and p_i respectively. The value range for the similarity $f_{sim}(p_a, p_i)$ is $[0, 1]$.

4.2.3 Missing value calculation

The prediction value $\widehat{v}_{a,b}$ of a missing value $v_{a,b}$ is calculated using the similarity $f_{sim}(p_a, p_i)$. It is necessary to consider the scale of projects in higher similarity to p_a to calculate $\widehat{v}_{a,b}$, because only the vector angles are used in the similarity calculation and vector size is not taken into account (Tsunoda et al. (2005)). Hence, for the calculation of missing values, the project scale reviser $amplifier : f_{amp}(p_a, p_i)$ is used as a weight. Furthermore, if $f_{amp}(p_a, p_i)$ exceeds the constant value $ampmax$, the project p_i is not used in the calculation of $\widehat{v}_{a,b}$, since the project scale is considered too different even if the similarity is high. $\widehat{v}_{a,b}$ is calculated from Eq. (3).

$$\widehat{v}_{a,b} = \frac{\sum_{i \in knP} v_{i,b} \times f_{amp}(p_a, p_i) \times f_{sim}(p_a, p_i)}{\sum_{i \in knP} f_{sim}(p_a, p_i)} \quad (3)$$

where, knP means a set that has the k projects with a high similarity to project p_a without the value of $amplifier$ exceeding $ampmax$. $f_{amp}(p_a, p_i)$ is calculated from Eq. (4).

$$f_{amp}(p_a, p_i) = \begin{cases} r_n & h = (2n - 1) \\ \frac{r_n + r_{n+1}}{2} & h = 2n \end{cases} \quad (4)$$

where, h is the number of the product set of M_a and $M_i(|M_a \cap M_i|)$, and r_j equals $\frac{f_n(v_{a,j})}{f_n(v_{i,j})}$, that is, the ratio of the values of the metric m_j in projects p_a and p_i.

5. Effort and error prediction models

5.1 An artificial neural network model

Artificial Neural Networks (ANNs) are essentially simple mathematical models defining function.

$$f : X \to Y \quad (5)$$

where $X = \{x_i | 0 \leq x_i \leq 1, i \geq 1\}$ and $Y = \{y_i | 0 \leq y_i \leq 1, i \geq 1\}$.
ANNs are non-linear statistical data modeling tools and that can be used to model complex relationships between inputs and outputs. The basic model is illustrated in Fig. 2, in which the output is calculated as follows.

1. Calculating values for hidden nodes. The value of $Hidden\ Node_j$ is calculated using the following equation:

$$Hidden\ Node_j = f\left(\sum_i (w_{i,j} \times Input_i)\right) \quad (6)$$

where $f(x)$ equals $\frac{1}{1+\exp(-x)}$ and the $w_{i,j}$ is weight calculated by the learning algorithm.

2. Calculating $Output$ using $Hidden\ Node_j$ as follows:

$$Output = f\left(\sum_k (w'_k \times Hidden\ Node_k)\right) \quad (7)$$

where $f(x)$ equals $\frac{1}{1+\exp(-x)}$ and the w'_k is weight calculated by the learning algorithm.

We can use an ANN to create effort and error prediction models.

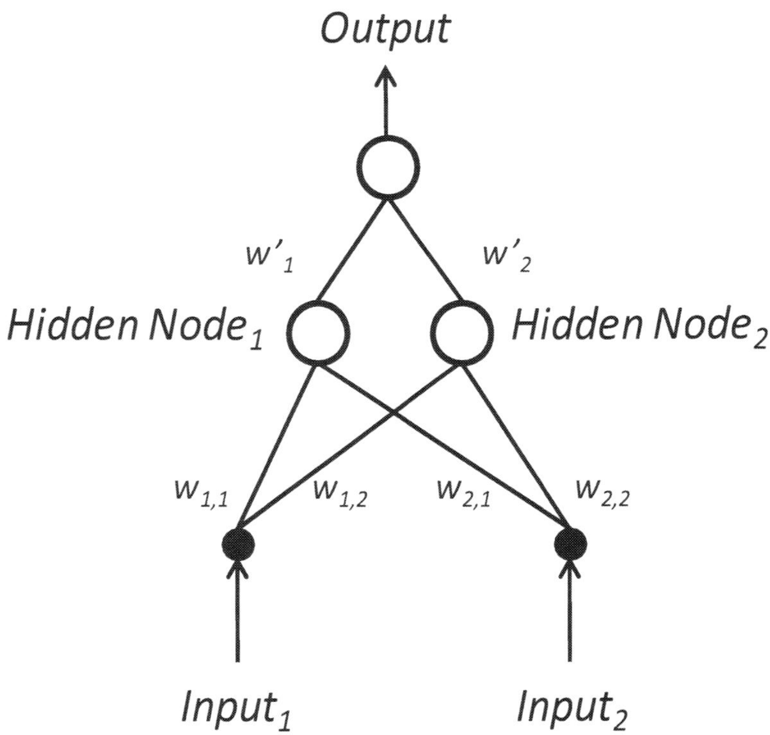

Fig. 2. Basic Artificial Neural Network

5.1.1 Normalization of data

In an ANN, a range of input values or output values is usually less than or equal to 1 and greater than or equal to 0. However, most selected data are grater than 1. Each data range is, therefore, converted to [0, 1] by normalization. The normalized value for t_{kind} is expressed as $f_n(t_{kind})$ (where $kind$ denotes Eff, Err, V_{new}, V_{modify}, V_{survey} and V_{reuse}). The normalized value $f_n(t_{kind})$ is calculated using Eq. (8) , which is the same as Eq. (1).

$$f_n(t_{kind}) = \frac{t_{kind} - min(T_{kind})}{max(T_{kind}) - min(T_{kind})} \tag{8}$$

where T_{kind} denotes the set of t_{kind}, and $max(T_{kind})$ and $min(T_{kind})$ denote the maximum and minimum values, respectively, of T_{kind}.

The normalization is flat and smooth, then, a small change in a normalized value influences a small-scale project to a greater degree than a large scale project.

For example, let $min(T_{Eff})$ equal 10, $max(T_{Eff})$ equal 300, t_{Eff1} equal 15, t_{Eff2} equal 250, predicted value for t_{Eff1} be $\widehat{t_{Eff1}}$ and t_{Eff2} be $\widehat{t_{Eff2}}$. If the prediction model has $+0.01$ error, then $f_{n_l}^{-1}(0.01) = 2.90$. The predicted values result in $\widehat{t_{Eff1}} = 17.90$ and $\widehat{t_{Eff2}} = 252.90$. Both cases has same errors, but their absolute of the relative errors (ARE) are follows:

$$ARE_{Eff1} = \left| \frac{\widehat{t_{Eff1}} - t_{Eff1}}{t_{Eff1}} \right| = \left| \frac{17.90 - 15}{15} \right| = 0.1933$$

$$ARE_{Eff2} = \left| \frac{\widehat{t_{Eff2}} - t_{Eff2}}{t_{Eff2}} \right| = \left| \frac{252.90 - 250}{250} \right| = 0.0116$$

The results indicate the absolute of the relative errors of former is greater than that of the latter. These distributions for the amount of effort and the number of errors indicate the small-scale projects are major and more than the large scale projects. Therefore, in order to improve prediction accuracy, it is important to reconstruct the normalizing way.

5.2 New normalization of data

In order to solve the problem, we adopt new normalizing way in the following equation:

$$f_{n_c}(t) = \sqrt{1 - (f_{n_l}(t) - 1)^2} \tag{9}$$

The comparison between Eq. (8) and Eq. (9) is shown in Figure 3 and 4. The Eq. (9) has a sharp inclination at the lower original data, then a small change at the lower original data get magnified.

Using the same assumption, the predicted values result in $\widehat{t_{Eff1}} = 15.56$ and $\widehat{t_{Eff2}} = 271.11$. Their absolute of the relative errors are in Eq. (10) and Eq. (11).

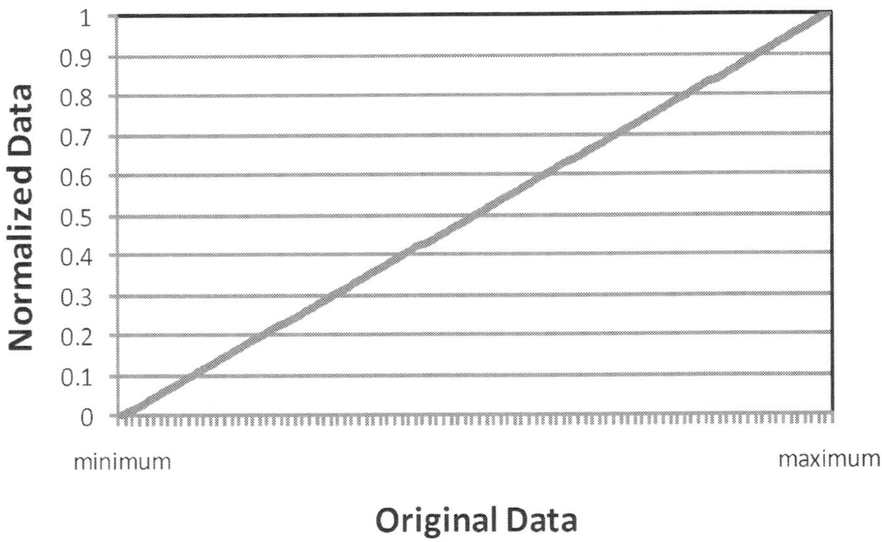

Fig. 3. Normalizing Results using Eq. (8)

$$ARE_{Eff1} = \left| \frac{15.56 - 15}{15} \right| = 0.0373 \quad (10)$$

$$ARE_{Eff2} = \left| \frac{271.11 - 250}{250} \right| = 0.0844 \quad (11)$$

The results show the absolute of the relative errors for the small-scale project is smaller than that of old normalization method and, in contrast, that for the large scale project is slightly larger than that of old normalization method. The more detailed comparison analyses are in Section 6.

5.2.1 Structure of model

In a feed-forward ANN, the information is moved from input nodes, through the hidden nodes to the output nodes. The number of hidden nodes is important, because if the number is too large, the network will over-training. The number of hidden nodes is, generally 2/3 of the number of input nodes or twice the number of input nodes. In this Chapter, we use 8 hidden nodes in our model which is illustrated in Fig. 5.

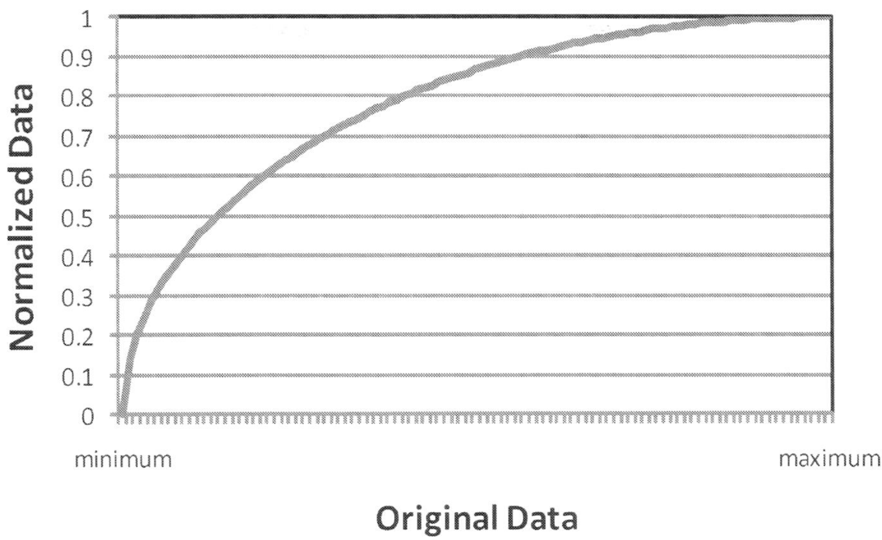

Fig. 4. Normalizing Results using Eq. (9)

5.3 Multiple regression analysis model

The multiple regression analysis (MRA) model is derived from Eq. (12), in which the notation adheres to the meanings defined in Subsection 3.1.

$$D = \alpha_1 \times S^2 + \alpha_2 \times S + \beta \quad (12)$$

where, D indicates Eff or Err, and S is calculated by Eq. (13).

$$S = V_{new} + V_{modify} + \theta_1 \times V_{survey} + \theta_2 \times V_{reuse} \quad (13)$$

where, θ_1 and θ_2 are less than 1, thus Eq. (13) emphasizes V_{new} and V_{modify}.

6. Evaluation experiment

6.1 Evaluation criteria

Equations (14) to (16) are used as evaluation criteria for the effort and errors prediction models. The smaller the value of each evaluation criterion, the higher is the relative accuracy in Eqs. (14) to (16). The accuracy value is expressed as X, and the predicted value as $\widehat{X}$. Also, the number of data is expressed as n.

1. Mean of Absolute Errors (MAE).
2. Standard Deviation of Absolute Errors ($SDAE$).

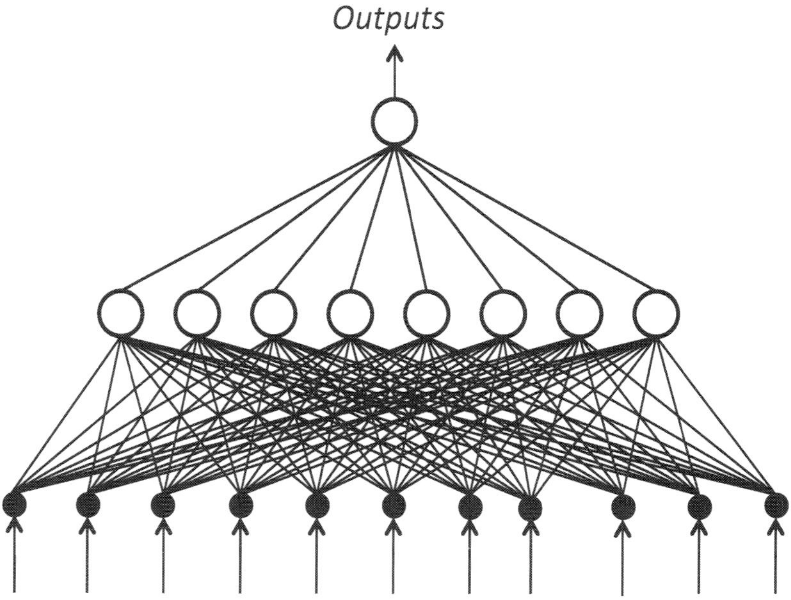

Fig. 5. Structure of Model

3. Mean of Relative Errors (MRE).
4. Standard Deviation of Relative Errors ($SDRE$).

$$MAE = \frac{1}{n}\sum|\hat{X} - X| \quad (14)$$

$$SDAE = \sqrt{\frac{1}{n-1}\sum\left(|\hat{X} - X| - MAE\right)^2} \quad (15)$$

$$MRE = \frac{1}{n}\sum\left|\frac{\hat{X} - X}{X}\right| \quad (16)$$

$$SDRE = \sqrt{\frac{1}{n-1}\sum\left(\left|\frac{\hat{X} - X}{X}\right| - MRE\right)^2} \quad (17)$$

6.2 Data used in evaluation experiment

The evaluation experiment uses the complemented data for projects including missing values by the method described in Subsection 4.2. This complemented project data is divided into two random sets. One of the two sets is used as training data, while the other is test data. The training data is used the generation of the effort (or errors) prediction model generation, which is used to predict the effort (or errors)of the projects in the test data. The prediction criteria presented in Subsection 6.1 are then used to confirm whether the effort were accurately predicted or not by. Both data sets, that is, the training data and test data, are divided into 5 sections and these are used to repeat the experiment 5 times.

6.3 Results and discussion

A total of 73 projects were used in the experiment, of which 53 included missing values. Missing values were added to these 53 projects. For each method, averages of the experiments results for the 5 experiments are shown in Table 5.

	MAE	*SDAE*	*MRE*	*SDRE*
ANN Model	17.440	37.679	0.69892	0.67254
MRA Model	30.825	55.643	0.98884	0.98928

Table 4. Experimental Results for Errors Prediction

	MAE	*SDAE*	*MRE*	*SDRE*
ANN Model	11.345	17.403	0.25536	0.33830
MRA Model	24.962	11.941	0.89056	0.91893

Table 5. Experimental Results for Efforts Prediction

6.3.1 Validation analysis of the accuracy of the models

We compare the accuracy of the ANN model with that of the regression analysis model using Welch's t-test (Welch (1947)). The t-test (called Student's t-test)(Student (1908)) is used as a test of the null hypothesis that the means of two normally distributed populations are equal. Welch's t-test is used when the variances of two samples are assumed to be different to test the null hypothesis that the means of non two normally distributed populations are equal if the two sample sizes are equal (Aoki (n.d.)). The t statistic to test whether the means are different is calculated as follows:

$$t_0 = \frac{|\overline{X} - \overline{Y}|}{\sqrt{\frac{s_x}{n_x} + \frac{s_y}{n_y}}} \tag{18}$$

where $\overline{X}$ and $\overline{Y}$ are the sample means, s_x and s_y are the sample standard deviations and n_x and n_y are the sample sizes. For use in significance testing, the distribution of the test statistic is approximated as an ordinary Student's t-distribution with the following degrees of freedom:

$$\nu = \frac{\left(\frac{s_x}{n_x} + \frac{s_y}{n_y}\right)^2}{\frac{s_x^2}{n_x^2(n_x-1)} + \frac{s_y^2}{n_y^2(n_y-1)}} \tag{19}$$

Thus once the a t-value and degrees of freedom have been determined, a p-value can be found using a table of values from the Student's t-distribution. If the p-value is smaller than or equal

to the significance level, then the null hypothesis is rejected. The significance levels are usually 0.05 and 0.01, are represented by the Greek symbol, α.
The null hypothesis, in these cases, is "there is no difference between the means of the prediction errors for the ANN model and the MRA model". The results of the t-test for absolute errors and relative errors are given in Tables 6 and 7,
are given in Tables 8 and 9, respectively.

	ANN Model	MRA Model
Mean ($\overline{X}$)	17.440	30.825
Standard deviation(s)	37.679	55.643
Sample size (n)	189	189
Degrees of freedom (ν)	362.565	
t value (t_0)	19.0483	
p value	2.2×10^{-16}	

Table 6. Results of t-test for MAE for Effort

	ANN Model	MRA Model
Mean ($\overline{X}$)	0.69892	0.98884
Standard deviation(s)	0.67254	0.98928
Sample size (n)	189	189
Degrees of freedom (ν)	362.82	
t value (t_0)	3.0918	
p value	0.002143	

Table 7. Results of t-test for MRE for Effort

	ANN Model	MRA Model
Mean ($\overline{X}$)	11.345	24.962
Standard deviation(s)	17.403	11.941
Sample size (n)	189	189
Degrees of freedom (ν)	363.409	
t value (t_0)	34.5583	
p value	2.2×10^{-16}	

Table 8. Results of t-test for MAE for Errors

	ANN Model	MRA Model
Mean ($\overline{X}$)	0.25536	0.89056
Standard deviation(s)	0.33830	0.91893
Sample size (n)	189	189
Degrees of freedom (ν)	309.901	
t value (t_0)	7.7881	
p value	1.031×10^{-13}	

Table 9. Results of t-test for MRE for Errors

The results indicate that the means of the absolute (or relative)errors between ANN models and MRA model shows a statistically significant difference, because the p-values are less than 0.01.

7. Conclusion

In this Chapter, we have established effort and errors prediction models using artificial neural networks for complementing missing values. The proposed method calculated the amount of effort and the number of errors by the following 3 steps.

1. Calculating the similarity between the complementary projects data (which include missing values) and the complete project data,
2. Applying collaborative filtering to complement missing values in the data and thus produce sufficient amount of data,
3. Creating models to predict target project effort (or errors) by the ANN and with this data.

In addition, we carried out an evaluation experiment that compared the accuracy of the ANN model with that of the MRA model using Welch's t-test. The results of the comparison indicate that the ANN model is more accurate than the MRA model, because the mean errors of the ANN are statistically significantly lower.
Our future works are the following:

1. In this study, we used a basic artificial neural network. More complex models need to be considered to improve the accuracy by avoiding over-training.
2. We implemented a model to predict the final amount of effort and number of errors in new projects. It is also important to predict effort and errors mid-way in the development process of a project.
3. We used all the data in implementing the model. However, the data include exceptions and there are harmful to the model. Data needs to be clustered in order to to identify these exceptions.
4. Finally, more data needs to be collected from completed projects.

8. References

Aoki, S. (n.d.). In testing whether the means of two populations are different(in Japanese), `http://aoki2.si.gunma-u.ac.jp/lecture/BF/index.html`.

Boehm, B. (1976). Software engineering, *IEEE Trans. Software Eng.* C-25(12): 1226–1241.

Breese, J., Heckerman, D. & Kadie, C. (2000). Empirical analysis of predictive algorithms for collaborative filtering, *Proc. 14th Conf. on Uncertainty in Artificial Intelligence, Wisconsin* pp. 337–386.

Hirayama, M. (2004). Current state of embedded software(in japanese), *Journal of Information Processing Society of Japan(IPSJ)* 45(7): 677–681.

Iwata, K., Anan, Y., Nakashima, T. & Ishii, N. (2006a). Effort prediction model using similarity for embedded software development, *Lecture Notes in Computer Science, Springer* 3981: 40–48.

Iwata, K., Anan, Y., Nakashima, T. & Ishii, N. (2006b). Improving accuracy of multiple regression analysis for effort prediction model, *Proceedings of 5th IEEE/ACIS International Conference on Computer and Information Science – ICIS 2006* pp. 48–55.

Komiyama, T. (2003). Development of foundation for effective and efficient software process improvement(in japanese), *Journal of Information Processing Society of Japan(IPSJ)* 44(4): 341–347.

N., U. (2004). Modeling techniques for designing embedded software (in japanese), *Journal of Information Processing Society of Japan(IPSJ)* 45(7): 682–692.

Nakamoto, Y., Takada, H. & Tamaru, K. (1997). Current state and trend in embedded systems(in japanese), *Journal of Information Processing Society of Japan(IPSJ)* 38(10): 871–878.

Nakashima, S. (2004). Introduction to model-checking of embedded software(in japanese), *Journal of Information Processing Society of Japan(IPSJ)* 45(7): 690–693.

Nakashima, T., Iwata, K., Anan, Y. & Ishii, N. (2006). Studies on project management models for embedded software development projects, *Proceedings of 4th International Conference on Software Engineering Research, Management Applications – SERA 2006* pp. 363–370.

Ogasawara, H. & Kojima, S. (2003). Process improvement activities that put importance on stay power(in japanese), *Journal of Information Processing Society of Japan(IPSJ)* 44(4): 334–340.

Salton, G. & MacGill, M. (1983). *Introduction to Modern Information Retrieval*, Mcgraw-Hill College.

Student (1908). The probable error of a mean, *Biometrika* 6(1): 1–25.

Takagi, Y. (2003). A case study of the success factor in large-scale software system development project(in japanese), *Journal of Information Processing Society of Japan(IPSJ)* 44(4): 348–356.

Tamaru, K. (2004). Trends in software development platform for embedded systems(in japanese), *Journal of Information Processing Society of Japan(IPSJ)* 45(7): 699–703.

Tsunoda, M., Ohsugi, N., Monden, A., Matsumoto, K. & Sato, S. (2005). Software development effort prediction based on collaborative filtering(in japanese), *Journal of Information Processing Society of Japan(IPSJ)* 46(5): 1155–1164.

Watanabe, H. (2004). Product line technology for software development(in japanese), *Journal of Information Processing Society of Japan(IPSJ)* 45(7): 694–698.

Welch, B. L. (1947). The generalization of student's problem when several different population variances are involved, *Biometrika* 34(28).

14

Design of High Speed Neural Networks for Fast Pattern Detection by using Cross Correlation and Matrix Decomposition

Hazem M. El-Bakry
Faculty of Computer Science & Information Systems, Mansoura University, Egypt

1. Introduction

Fast pattern detection and identification is a fundamental problem for many applications of real-time systems (Bruce & Veloso 2003). Its reliability and performance have a major influence in a whole pattern recognition system. Nowadays, neural networks have shown very good results for detecting a certain pattern in a given image (Rowley et al. 1998; Feraud et al. 2000; Anifantis et al. 1999; Lang et al. 1988; El-Bakry 2001). Among other techniques (Schneiderman & Kanade 1998; Zhu et al. 2000; Srisuk & Kurutach 2002; Bao et al. 2006), neural networks are efficient pattern detectors (Rowley et al. 1998; Feraud et al. 2000; El-Bakry 2002,a; El-bakry 2002,b; Essannouni and Ibn Elhaj 2006; Roth et al. 2006; Ramasubramanian & Kannan 2006). But the problem with neural networks is that the computational complexity is very high because the networks have to process many small local windows in the images (Zhu et al. 2000; Srisuk & Kurutach 2002; Yang et al. 2002). The main objective of this paper is to reduce the detection time using neural networks. The idea is to accelerate the operation of neural networks by performing the testing process in the frequency domain instead of spatial domain. Then, cross-correlation between the input image and the weights of neural networks is performed in the frequency domain. This model is called fast neural networks. Compared to conventional neural networks, fast neural networks show a significant reduction in the number of computation steps required to detect a certain pattern in a given image under test. Furthermore, another idea to increase the speed of these fast neural networks through image decomposition is presented. Moreover, the problem of sub-image (local) normalization in the Fourier space which presented in (Feraud et al. 2000) is solved.. The number of computation steps required for weight normalization is proved to be less than that needed for image normalization. Also, the effect of weight normalization on the speed up ratio is theoretically and practically discussed. Mathematical calculations prove that the new idea of weight normalization, instead of image normalization, provides good results and increases the speed up ratio. This is because weight normalization requires fewer computation steps than sub-image normalization. Moreover, for neural networks, normalization of weights can be easily done off line before starting the search process.

In section 2, high speed neural networks for pattern detection are described. The details of conventional neural networks, high speed neural networks, and the speed up ratio of pattern detection are given. A faster searching algorithm for pattern detection which reduces the number of the required computation steps through image decomposition is presented in section 3. Accelerating the new approach using parallel processing techniques is also introduced. Sub-image normalization in the frequency domain through normalization of weights is introduced in section 4. The effect of weight normalization on the speed up ratio is presented in section 5.

2. Fast pattern detection using MLP and FFT

Here, we are interested only in increasing the speed of neural networks during the test phase. By the words "High speed Neural Networks" we mean reducing the number of computation steps required by neural networks in the detection phase. First neural networks are trained to classify face from non face examples and this is done in the spatial domain. In the test phase, each sub-image in the input image (under test) is tested for the presence or absence of the required face/object. At each pixel position in the input image each sub-image is multiplied by a window of weights, which has the same size as the sub-image. This multiplication is done in the spatial domain. The outputs of neurons in the hidden layer are multiplied by the weights of the output layer. When the final output is high this means that the sub-image under test contains the required face/object and vice versa. Thus, we may conclude that this searching problem is cross correlation in the spatial domain between the image under test and the input weights of neural networks.

In this section, a fast algorithm for face/object detection based on two dimensional cross correlations that take place between the tested image and the sliding window (20x20 pixels) is described. Such window is represented by the neural network weights situated between the input unit and the hidden layer. The convolution theorem in mathematical analysis says that a convolution of f with h is identical to the result of the following steps: let F and H be the results of the Fourier transformation of f and h in the frequency domain. Multiply F and H in the frequency domain point by point and then transform this product into spatial domain via the inverse Fourier transform (Klette&Zamperon 1996). As a result, these cross correlations can be represented by a product in the frequency domain. Thus, by using cross correlation in the frequency domain a speed up in an order of magnitude can be achieved during the detection process (El-Bakry2005; El-Bakry 2006; El-Bakry 2007; El-Bakry 2009).

In the detection phase, a sub-image X of size mxn (sliding window) is extracted from the tested image, which has a size PxT, and fed to the neural network. Let W_i be the vector of weights between the input sub-image and the hidden layer. This vector has a size of mxz and can be represented as mxn matrix. The output of hidden neurons h(i) can be calculated as follows:

$$h_i = g\left(\sum_{j=1}^{m}\sum_{k=1}^{z} W_i(j,k)X(j,k) + b_i\right) \quad (1)$$

where g is the activation function and b(i) is the bias of each hidden neuron (i). Eq.1 represents the output of each hidden neuron for a particular sub-image I. It can be computed for the whole image Ψ as follows:

$$h_i(u,v) = g\left(\sum_{j=-m/2}^{m/2}\sum_{k=-z/2}^{z/2} W_i(j,k)\,\Psi(u+j,v+k) + b_i\right) \quad (2)$$

Eq.(2) represents a cross correlation operation. Given any two functions f and g, their cross correlation can be obtained by (Gonzalez & Woods 2002):

$$g(x,y)\otimes f(x,y)=\sum_{m=-\infty}^{\infty}\sum_{z=-\infty}^{\infty} g(m,z)f(x+m,y+z) \tag{3}$$

Therefore, Eq.(2) can be written as follows:

$$h_i = g\left(W_i \otimes \Psi + b_i\right) \tag{4}$$

where h_i is the output of the hidden neuron (i) and h_i (u,v) is the activity of the hidden unit (i) when the sliding window is located at position (u,v) in the input image Ψ and (u,v) $\in$[P-m+1,T-n+1].

Now, the above cross correlation can be expressed in terms of the Fourier Transform:

$$W_i \otimes \Psi = F^{-1}\left(F(\Psi)F^*\left(W_i\right)\right) \tag{5}$$

(*) means the conjugate of the FFT for the weight matrix. Hence, by evaluating this cross correlation, a speed up ratio can be obtained comparable to conventional neural networks. Also, the final output of the neural network can be evaluated as follows:

$$O(u,v) = g\left(\sum_{i=1}^{q} W_o(i)\, h_i(u,v) + b_o\right) \tag{6}$$

where q is the number of neurons in the hidden layer. O(u,v) is the output of the neural network when the sliding window located at the position (u,v) in the input image Ψ. W_o is the weight matrix between hidden and output layer. b_o is the bias of the output neuron.

The complexity of cross correlation in the frequency domain can be analyzed as follows:

1. For a tested image of NxN pixels, the 2D-FFT requires a number equal to $N^2\log_2N^2$ of complex computation steps. Also, the same number of complex computation steps is required for computing the 2D-FFT of the weight matrix for each neuron in the hidden layer.
2. At each neuron in the hidden layer, the inverse 2D-FFT is computed. So, q backward and (1+q) forward transforms have to be computed. Therefore, for an image under test, the total number of the 2D-FFT to compute is $(2q+1)N^2\log_2N^2$.
3. The input image and the weights should be multiplied in the frequency domain. Therefore, a number of complex computation steps equal to qN^2 should be added.
4. The number of computation steps required by the faster neural networks is complex and must be converted into a real version. It is known that the two dimensions Fast Fourier Transform requires $(N^2/2)\log_2N^2$ complex multiplications and $N^2\log_2N^2$ complex additions (Cooley&Tukey 1965). Every complex multiplication is realized by six real floating point operations and every complex addition is implemented by two real floating point operations. So, the total number of computation steps required to obtain the 2D-FFT of an NxN image is:

$$\rho=6((N^2/2)\log_2N^2) + 2(N^2\log_2N^2) \tag{7}$$

which may be simplified to:

$$\rho=5N^2\log_2N^2 \quad (8)$$

Performing complex dot product in the frequency domain also requires $6qN^2$ real operations.

5. In order to perform cross correlation in the frequency domain, the weight matrix must have the same size as the input image. Assume that the input object/face has a size of (nxn) dimensions. So, the search process will be done over sub-images of (nxn) dimensions and the weight matrix will have the same size. Therefore, a number of zeros = (N^2-n^2) must be added to the weight matrix. This requires a total real number of computation steps = $q(N^2-n^2)$ for all neurons. Moreover, after computing the 2D-FFT for the weight matrix, the conjugate of this matrix must be obtained. So, a real number of computation steps $=qN^2$ should be added in order to obtain the conjugate of the weight matrix for all neurons. Also, a number of real computation steps equal to N is required to create butterflies complex numbers $(e^{-jk(2\Pi n/N)})$, where 0<K<L. These (N/2) complex numbers are multiplied by the elements of the input image or by previous complex numbers during the computation of the 2D-FFT. To create a complex number requires two real floating point operations. So, the total number of computation steps required for the high speed neural networks becomes:

$$\sigma=(2q+1)(5N^2\log_2N^2)+6qN^2+q(N^2-n^2)+qN^2+N \quad (9)$$

which can be reformulated as:

$$\sigma=(2q+1)(5N^2\log_2N^2)+q(8N^2-n^2)+N \quad (10)$$

6. Using a sliding window of size nxn for the same image of NxN pixels, $q(2n^2-1)(N-n+1)^2$ computation steps are required when using traditional neural networks for face/object detection process. The theoretical speed up factor η can be evaluated as follows:

$$\eta=\frac{q(2n^2-1)(N-n+1)^2}{(2q+1)(5N^2\log_2N^2)+q(8N^2-n^2)+N} \quad (11)$$

The theoretical speed up ratio (Eq.(11)) with different sizes of the input image and different in size weight matrices is listed in Table 1. Practical speed up ratio for manipulating images of different sizes and different in size weight matrices is listed in Table 2 using 2.7 GHz processor and MATLAB ver 5.3. An interesting property with high speed neural networks is that the number of computation steps does not depend on eith the size of the input sub-image or the size of the weighth matrix (n). The effect of (n) on the the number of computation steps is very small and can be ignored. This is incontrast to conventional networks in which the number of computation steps is increased with the size of both the input sub-image and the weight matrix (n).

In practical implementation, the multiplication process consumes more time than the addition one. The effect of the number of multiplications required for conventional neural networks in the speed up ratio (Eq.(11)) is more than the number of of multiplication steps required by the high speed neural networks. In order to clear this, the following equation (η_m) describes relation between the number of multiplication steps required by conventional and high speed neural networks:

Image size	Speed up ratio (n=20)	Speed up ratio (n=25)	Speed up ratio (n=30)
100x100	3.67	5.04	6.34
200x200	4.01	5.92	8.05
300x300	4.00	6.03	8.37
400x400	3.95	6.01	8.42
500x500	3.89	5.95	8.39
600x600	3.83	5.88	8.33
700x700	3.78	5.82	8.26
800x800	3.73	5.76	8.19
900x900	3.69	5.70	8.12
1000x1000	3.65	5.65	8.05
1100x1100	3.62	5.60	7.99
1200x1200	3.58	5.55	7.93
1300x1300	3.55	5.51	7.93
1400x1400	3.53	5.47	7.82
1500x1500	3.50	5.43	7.77
1600x1600	3.48	5.43	7.72
1700x1700	3.45	5.37	7.68
1800x1800	3.43	5.34	7.64
1900x1900	3.41	5.31	7.60
2000x2000	3.40	5.28	7.56

Table 1. The theoretical speed up ratio for images with different sizes.

Image size	Speed up ratio (n=20)	Speed up ratio (n=25)	Speed up ratio (n=30)
100x100	7.88	10.75	14.69
200x200	6.21	9.19	13.17
300x300	5.54	8.43	12.21
400x400	4.78	7.45	11.41
500x500	4.68	7.13	10.79
600x600	4.46	6.97	10.28
700x700	4.34	6.83	9.81
800x800	4.27	6.68	9.60
900x900	4.31	6.79	9.72
1000x1000	4.19	6.59	9.46
1100x1100	4.24	6.66	9.62
1200x1200	4.20	6.62	9.57
1300x1300	4.17	6.57	9.53
1400x1400	4.13	6.53	9.49
1500x1500	4.10	6.49	9.45
1600x1600	4.07	6.45	9.41
1700x1700	4.03	6.41	9.37
1800x1800	4.00	6.38	9.32
1900x1900	3.97	6.35	9.28
2000x2000	3.94	6.31	9.25

Table 2. Practical speed up ratio for images with different sizes using MATLAB Ver 5.3

.Image size	Conventional Neural Nets	Faster Neural Nets	Speed up ratio (η_m)
100x100	7.8732e+007	2.6117e+007	3.0146
200x200	3.9313e+008	1.1911e+008	3.3007
300x300	9.4753e+008	2.8726e+008	3.2985
400x400	1.7419e+009	5.3498e+008	3.2560
500x500	2.7763e+009	8.6537e+008	3.2083
600x600	4.0507e+009	1.2808e+009	3.1627
700x700	5.5651e+009	1.7832e+009	3.1209
800x800	7.3195e+009	2.3742e+009	3.0830
900x900	9.3139e+009	3.0552e+009	3.0486
1000x1000	1.1548e+010	3.8275e+009	3.0172
1100x1100	1.4023e+010	4.6921e+009	2.9886
1200x1200	1.6737e+010	5.6502e+009	2.9622
1300x1300	1.9692e+010	6.7026e+009	2.9379
1400x1400	2.2886e+010	7.8501e+009	2.9154
1500x1500	2.6320e+010	9.0935e+009	2.8944
1600x1600	2.9995e+010	1.0434e+010	2.8748
1700x1700	3.3909e+010	1.1871e+010	2.8564
1800x1800	3.8064e+010	1.3407e+010	2.8392
1900x1900	4.2458e+010	1.5041e+010	2.8229
2000x2000	7.8732e+007	2.6117e+007	3.0146

Table 3. A Comparison between the number of multiplication steps required for conventional and faster neural nets to manipulate Images with different sizes (n=20, q=30)

$$\eta_m = \frac{qn^2(N-n+1)^2}{(2q+1)(3N^2\log_2 N^2)+6qN^2} \qquad (12)$$

The results listed in Table 3 prove that the effect of the number of multiplication steps in case of conventional neural networks is more than high speed neural networks and this the reason why practical speed up ratio is larger than theoretical speed up ratio.

For general fast cross correlation the speed up ratio (η_g) is in the following form:

$$\eta_g = \frac{q(2n^2-1)N^2}{(2q+1)(5(N+\tau)^2\log_2(N+\tau)^2)+q(8(N+\tau)^2-n^2)+(N+\tau)} \qquad (13)$$

where τ is a small number depends on the size of the weight matrix. General cross correlation means that the process starts from the first element in the input matrix. The theoretical speed up ratio for general fast cross correlation (η_g) defined by Eq.(13) is shown in Table 4. Compared with MATLAB cross correlation function (xcorr2), experimental results show that the proposed algorithm is high speed than this function as shown in Table 5.

(Ben-Yacoub et al. 1999; Fasel 1998; and Ben-Yacoub 1997) have proposed a multilayer perceptron (MLP) algorithm for fast face/object detection. The same authors claimed incorrect equation for cross correlation between the input image and the weights of the neural networks. They introduced formulas for the number of computation steps needed by conventional and high speed neural networks. Then, they established an equation for the

Image size	Speed up ratio (n=20)	Speed up ratio (n=25)	Speed up ratio (n=30)
100x100	5.59	8.73	12.58
200x200	4.89	7.64	11.01
300x300	4.56	7.12	10.26
400x400	4.35	6.80	9.79
500x500	4.20	6.56	9.45
600x600	4.08	6.38	9.20
700x700	3.99	6.24	8.99
800x800	3.91	6.12	8.81
900x900	3.85	6.02	8.67
1000x1000	3.79	5.93	8.54
1100x1100	3.74	5.85	8.43
1200x1200	3.70	5.78	8.33
1300x1300	3.66	5.72	8.24
1400x1400	3.62	5.66	8.16
1500x1500	3.59	5.61	8.08
1600x1600	3.56	5.57	8.02
1700x1700	3.53	5.52	7.95
1800x1800	3.50	5.48	7.89
1900x1900	3.48	5.44	7.84
2000x2000	3.46	5.41	7.79

Table 4. The Theoretical Speed up Ratio for the General Faster Cross Correlation Algorithm

Image size	Speed up ratio (n=20)	Speed up ratio (n=25)	Speed up ratio (n=30)
100x100	10.14	13.05	16.49
200x200	9.17	11.92	14.33
300x300	8.25	10.83	13.41
400x400	7.91	9.62	12.65
500x500	6.77	9.24	11.77
600x600	6.46	8.89	11.19
700x700	5.99	8.47	10.96
800x800	5.48	8.74	10.32
900x900	5.31	8.43	10.66
1000x1000	5.91	8.66	10.51
1100x1100	5.77	8.61	10.46
1200x1200	5.68	8.56	10.40
1300x1300	5.62	8.52	10.35
1400x1400	5.58	8.47	10.31
1500x1500	5.54	8.43	10.26
1600x1600	5.50	8.39	10.22
1700x1700	5.46	8.33	10.18
1800x1800	5.42	8.28	10.14
1900x1900	5.38	8.24	10.10
2000x2000	5.34	8.20	10.06

Table 5. Simulation results of the speed up ratio for the general faster cross correlation compared with the MATLAB cross correlation function (XCORR2)

speed up ratio. Unfortunately, these formulas contain many errors which lead to invalid speed up ratio. Recently, other authors developed their work based on these incorrect equations (Ishak et al. 2004). So, the fact that these equations are not valid must be cleared to all researchers. It is not only very important but also urgent to notify other researchers not to waste their time and effort doing research based on wrong equations.

The authors (Ben-Yacoub et al. 1999; Fasel 1998; and Ben-Yacoub 1997) analyzed their proposed fast neural network as follows: For a tested image of NxN pixels, the 2D-FFT requires $O(N^2(\log_2 N)^2)$ computation steps. For the weight matrix W_i, the 2D-FFT can be computed off line since these are constant parameters of the network independent of the tested image. The 2D-FFT of the tested image must be computed. As a result, q backward and one forward transforms have to be computed. Therefore, for a tested image, the total number of the 2D-FFT to compute is $(q+1)N^2(\log_2 N)^2$ (Ben-Yacoub et al. 1999; Ben-Yacoub 1997). In addition, the input image and the weights should be multiplied in the frequency domain. Therefore, computation steps of (qN^2) should be added. This yields a total of $O((q+1)N^2(\log_2 N)^2+qN^2)$ computation steps for the fast neural network (Ben-Yacoub et al. 1999; Fasel 1998).

Using sliding window of size nxn, for the same image of NxN pixels, qN^2n^2 computation steps are required when using traditional neural networks for the face detection process. They evaluated theoretical speed up factor η as follows (Fasel 1998; Ben-Yacoub 1997):

$$\eta = \frac{qn^2}{(q+1)\log^2 N} \tag{14}$$

The speed up factor introduced in (Ben-Yacoub et al. 1999) and given by Eq.14 is not correct for the following reasons:

a. The number of computation steps required for the 2D-FFT is $O(N^2\log_2 N^2)$ and not $O(N^2\log^2 N)$ as presented in (Fasel 1998; Ben-Yacoub 1997) . Also, this is not a typing error as the curve in Fig.2 in (Ben-Yacoub et al. 1999) realizes Eq.(7), and the curves in Fig.15 in (Fasel 1998) realizes Eq.(31) and Eq.(32) in (Fasel 1998) .
b. Also, the speed up ratio presented in (Ben-Yacoub et al. 1999) not only contains an error but also is not precise. This is because for high speed neural networks, the term $(6qN^2)$ corresponds to complex dot product in the frequency domain must be added. Such term has a great effect on the speed up ratio. Adding only qN^2 as stated in (Fasel 1998) is not correct since a one complex multiplication requires six real computation steps.
c. For conventional neural networks, the number of operations is $(q(2n^2-1)(N-n+1)^2)$ and not (qN^2n^2). The term n^2 is required for multiplication of n^2 elements (in the input window) by n^2 weights which results in another new n^2 elements. Adding these n^2 elements, requires another (n^2-1) steps. So, the total computation steps needed for each window is $(2n^2-1)$. The search operation for a face in the input image uses a window with nxn weights. This operation is done at each pixel in the input image. Therefore, such process is repeated $(N-n+1)^2$ times and not N^2 as stated in (Ben-Yacoub et al. 1999; Ben-Yacoub 1997).
d. Before applying cross correlation, the 2D-FFT of the weight matrix must be computed. Because of the dot product, which is done in the frequency domain, the size of weight matrix should be increased to be the same as the size of the input image. Computing the 2D-FFT of the weight matrix off line as stated in (Ben-Yacoub et al. 1999; Fasel 1998; and Ben-Yacoub 1997) is not practical. In this case, all of the input images must have the

same size. As a result, the input image will have only a one fixed size. This means that, the testing time for an image of size 50x50 pixels will be the same as that image of size 1000x1000 pixels and of course, this is unreliable.

e. It is not valid to compare number of complex computation steps by another of real computation steps directly. The number of computation steps given by pervious authors (Ben-Yacoub et al. 1999; Fasel 1998; and Ben-Yacoub 1997) for conventional neural networks is for real operations while that is required by the high speed neural networks is for complex operations. To obtain the speed up ratio, the authors in (Ben-Yacoub et al. 1999; Fasel 1998; and Ben-Yacoub 1997) have divided the two formulas directly without converting the number of computation steps required by the high speed neural networks into a real version.

f. Furthermore, there are critical errors in the activity of hidden neurons given in section 3.1 in (Ben-Yacoub 1997) and also by Eq.(2) in (Ben-Yacoub et al. 1999). Such activity given by those authors in (Ben-Yacoub et al. 1999; Ben-Yacoub 1997) as follows:

$$h_i = g(\Psi \otimes W_i + b_i) \tag{15}$$

is not correct and should be written as Eq.(4) given here in this chapter. This is because the fact that the operation of cross correlation is not commutative ($W \otimes \Psi \neq \Psi \otimes W$). As a result, Eq.(15) (Eq.(2) in their paper (Ben-Yacoub et al. 1999)) does not give the exact correct results as conventional neural networks. This error leads the researchers who consider the references (Ben-Yacoub et al. 1999; Ben-Yacoub 1997) to think about how to modify the operation of cross correlation so that Eq.(15) (Eq.(2) in their paper (Ben-Yacoub et al. 1999)) can give the exact correct results as conventional neural networks. Therefore, errors in these equations must be cleared to all the researchers. In (El-Bakry 2003), the authors proved that a symmetry condition must be found in input matrices (images and the weights of neural networks) so that fast neural networks can give the same results as conventional neural networks. In case of symmetry $W \otimes \Psi = \Psi \otimes W$, the cross correlation becomes commutative and this is a valuable achievement. In this case, the cross correlation is performed without any constrains on the arrangement of matrices. As presented in (El-Bakry 2003), this symmetry condition is useful for reducing the number of patterns that neural networks will learn. This is because the image is converted into symmetric shape by rotating it down and then the up image and its rotated down version are tested together as one (symmetric) image. If a pattern is detected in the rotated down image, then, this means that this pattern is found at the relative position in the up image. So, if conventional neural networks are trained for up and rotated down examples of the pattern, fast neural networks will be trained only to up examples. As the number of trained examples is reduced, the number of neurons in the hidden layer will be reduced and the neural network will be faster in the test phase compared with conventional neural networks.

g. Moreover, the authors in (Ben-Yacoub et al. 1999; Fasel 1998; and Ben-Yacoub 1997) stated that the activity of each neuron in the hidden layer Eq.(16) (Eq.(4) in their paper (Ben-Yacoub et al. 1999)) can be expressed in terms of convolution between a bank of filter (weights) and the input image. This is not correct because the activity of the hidden neuron is a cross correlation between the input image and the weight matrix. It is known that the result of cross correlation between any two functions is different from their convolution. As we proved in (El-Bakry 2003) the two results will be the same, only when the two matrices are symmetric or at least the weight matrix is symmetric. A practical example which proves that for any two matrices the result of their cross correlation is different from their convolution unless that they are symmetric or at least the second matrix is symmetric as shown in appendix "A".

h. Images are tested for the presence of a face (object) at different scales by building a pyramid of the input image which generates a set of images at different resolutions. The face detector is then applied at each resolution and this process takes much more time as the number of processing steps will be increased. In (Ben-Yacoub et al. 1999; Fasel 1998; and Ben-Yacoub 1997) , the authors stated that the Fourier transforms of the new scales do not need to be computed. This is due to a property of the Fourier transform. If z(x,y) is the original and a(x,y) is the sub-sampled by a factor of 2 in each direction image then:

$$a(x,y) = z(2x,2y) \tag{16}$$

$$Z(u,v) = FT(z(x,y)) \tag{17}$$

$$FT(a(x,y)) = A(u,v) = \frac{1}{4} Z\left(\frac{u}{2}, \frac{v}{2}\right) \tag{18}$$

This implies that we do not need to recompute the Fourier transform of the sub-sampled images, as it can be directly obtained from the original Fourier transform. But experimental results have shown that Eq.(16) is valid only for images shown in the form presented in Eq.(19). In which each block of pixels consists of 4 pixels located beside each other and have the same value as shown in Eq.(19). Certainly, there no guarantee that the input image will be in that form. Of course, it may have another form different from that one presented in Eq.(19).

$$\Psi = \begin{bmatrix} A\ A\ B\ B\ C\ C \ldots\ldots\ldots\ldots \\ A\ A\ B\ B\ C\ C \ldots\ldots\ldots\ldots \\ . \\ . \\ . \\ . \\ S\ S\ X\ X\ Y\ Y \ldots\ldots\ldots\ldots \\ S\ S\ X\ X\ Y\ Y \ldots\ldots\ldots\ldots \end{bmatrix} \tag{19}$$

In (Ben-Yacoub et al. 1999), the author claimed that the processing needs $O((q+2)N^2\log^2 N)$ additional number of computation steps. Thus the speed up ratio will be (Ben-Yacoub et al. 1999):

$$\eta = \frac{qn^2}{(q+2)\log^2 N} \tag{20}$$

Of course this is not correct, because the inverse of the Fourier transform is required to be computed at each neuron in the hidden layer (for the resulted matrix from the dot product between the Fourier matrix in two dimensions of the input image and the Fourier matrix in two dimensions of the weights, the inverse of the Fourier transform must be computed). So, the term (q+2) in Eq.(20) should be (2q+1) because the inverse 2D-FFT in two dimensions must be done at each neuron in the hidden layer. In this case, the number of computation steps required to perform 2D-FFT for the high speed neural networks will be:

$$\varphi=(2q+1)(5N^2\log_2N^2)+(2q)5(N/2)^2\log_2(N/2)^2 \tag{21}$$

In addition, a number of computation steps equal to $6q(N/2)^2+q((N/2)^2-n^2)+q(N/2)^2$ must be added to the number of computation steps required by the high speed neural networks.

3. A new faster algorithm for pattern detection based on image decomposition

In this section, a new faster algorithm for face/object detection is presented. The number of computation steps required for faster neural networks with different image sizes is listed in Tables 6 and 7. From these tables, we may notice that as the image size is increased, the number of computation steps required by high speed neural networks is much increased. For example, the number of computation steps required for an image of size (50x50 pixels) is much less than that needed for an image of size (100x100 pixels). Also, the number of computation steps required for an image of size (500x500 pixels) is much less than that needed for an image of size (1000x1000 pixels). As a result, for example, if an image of size (100x100 pixels) is decomposed into 4 sub-images of size (50x50 pixels) and each sub-image is tested separately, then a speed up factor for face/object detection can be achieved. The number of computation steps required by high speed neural networks to test an image after decomposition can be calculated as follows:

1. Assume that the size of the image under test is (NxN pixels).
2. Such image is decomposed into α (LxL pixels) sub-images. So, α can be computed as:

$$\alpha=(N/L)^2 \tag{22}$$

3. Assume that, the number of computation steps required for testing one (LxL pixels) sub-image is β. So, the total number of computation steps (T) required for testing these sub-images resulting after the decomposition process is:

$$T = \alpha\,\beta \tag{23}$$

The speed up ratio in this case (η_d) can be computed as follows:

$$n_d = \frac{q(2n^2-1)(N-n+1)^2}{(q(\alpha+1)+\alpha)(5N_s^2\log_2 N_s^2)+\alpha q(8N_s^2-n^2)+N_s+\Lambda} \tag{24}$$

where,

N_s: is the size of each small sub-image.

Δ: is a small number of computation steps required to obtain the results at the boundaries between sub-images and depends on the size of the sub-image.

To detect a face/object of size 20x20 pixels in an image of any size by using high speed neural networks after image decomposition into sub-images, the optimal size of these sub-images must be computed. From Table 7, we may conclude that, the most suitable size for

Image size	No. of computation steps in case of using FNN
25x25	1.9085e+006
50x50	9.1949e+006
100x100	4.2916e+007
150x150	1.0460e+008
200x200	1.9610e+008
250x250	3.1868e+008
300x300	4.7335e+008
350x350	6.6091e+008
400x400	8.8203e+008
450x450	1.1373e+009
500x500	1.4273e+009
550x550	1.7524e+009
600x600	2.1130e+009
650x650	2.5096e+009
700x700	2.9426e+009
750x750	3.4121e+009
800x800	3.9186e+009
850x850	4.4622e+009
900x900	5.0434e+009
950x950	5.6623e+009
1000x1000	6.3191e+009

Table 6. The number of computation steps required by faster neural networks (FNN) for images of sizes (25x25 - 1000x1000 pixels), q=30, n=20

Image size	No. of computation steps in case of using FNN
1050x1050	7.0142e+009
1100x1100	7.7476e+009
1150x1150	8.5197e+009
1200x1200	9.3306e+009
1250x1250	1.0180e+010
1300x1300	1.1070e+010
1350x1350	1.1998e+010
1400x1400	1.2966e+010
1450x1450	1.3973e+010
1500x1500	1.5021e+010
1550x1550	1.6108e+010
1600x1600	1.7236e+010
1650x1650	1.8404e+010
1700x1700	1.9612e+010
1750x1750	2.0861e+010
1800x1800	2.2150e+010
1850x1850	2.3480e+010
1900x1900	2.4851e+010
1950x1950	2.6263e+010
2000x2000	2.7716e+010

Table 7. The number of computation steps required by FNN for images of sizes (1050x1050 - 2000x2000 pixels), q=30, n=20

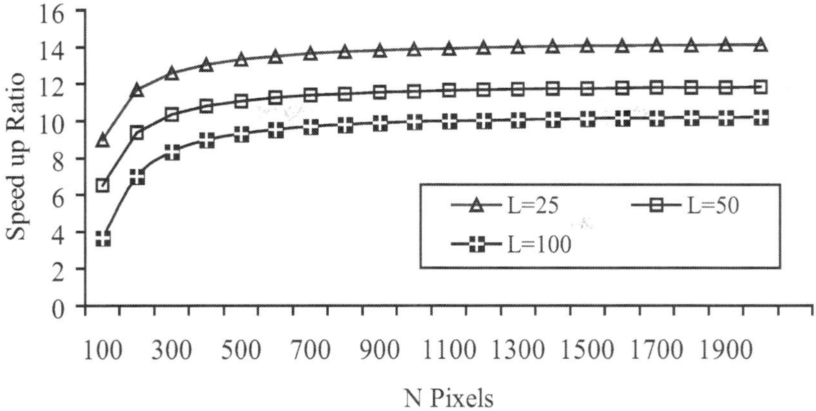

Fig. 1. The speed up ratio for images decomposed into different in size sub-images (L).

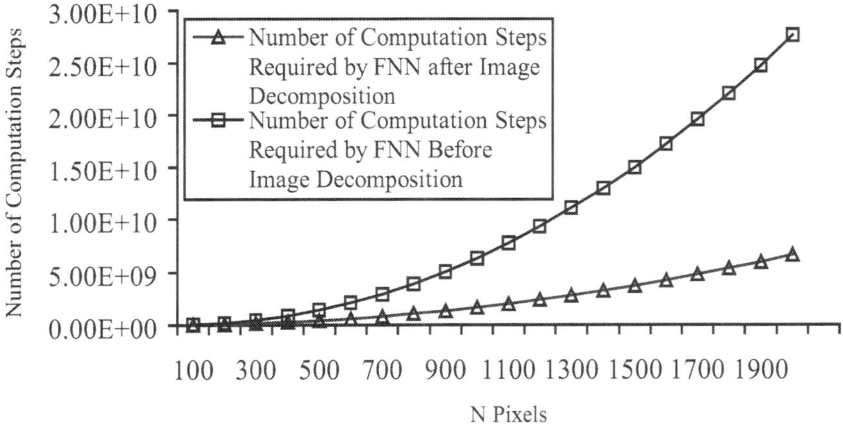

Fig. 2. A comparison between the number of computation steps required by FNN before and after Image decomposition.

the sub-image which requires the smallest number of computation steps is 25x25 pixels. Also, the fastest speed up ratio can be achieved using this sub-image size (25x25) as shown in Figure 1. It is clear that the speed up ratio is reduced when the size of the sub-image (L) is increased. A comparison between the speed up ratio for high speed neural networks and high speed neural networks after image decomposition with different sizes of the tested images is listed in Tables 8 and 9. It is clear that the speed up ratio is increased with the size of the input image when using high speed neural networks and image decomposition. This is in contrast to using only high speed neural networks. As shown in Figure 2, the number of computation steps required by high speed neural networks is increased rapidly with the size of the input image. Therefore the speed up ratio is decreased with the size of the input image. While in case of using high speed neural networks and image decomposition, the

Image size	Speed up ratio in case of using FNN	Speed up ratio in case of using FNN after image decomposition
50x50	2.7568	5.0713
100x100	5.0439	12.4622
150x150	5.6873	15.6601
200x200	5.9190	17.3611
250x250	6.0055	18.4073
300x300	6.0301	19.1136
350x350	6.0254	19.6218
400x400	6.0059	20.0047
450x450	5.9790	20.3034
500x500	5.9483	20.5430
550x550	5.9160	20.7394
600x600	5.8833	20.9032
650x650	5.8509	21.0419
700x700	5.8191	21.1610
750x750	5.7881	21.2642
800x800	5.7581	21.3546
850x850	5.7292	21.4344
900x900	5.7013	21.5054
950x950	5.6744	21.5689
1000x1000	5.6484	21.6260

Table 8. The speed up ratio in case of using FNN and FNN after image decomposition into sub-images (25x25 pixels) for images of different sizes (from N=50 to N=1000, n=25, q=30)

Image size	Speed up ratio in case of using FNN	Speed up ratio in case of using FNN after image decomposition
1050x1050	5.6234	21.6778
1100x1100	5.5994	21.7248
1150x1150	5.5762	21.7678
1200x1200	5.5538	21.8072
1250x1250	5.5322	21.8434
1300x1300	5.5113	21.8769
1350x1350	5.4912	21.9079
1400x1400	5.4717	21.9366
1450x1450	5.4528	21.9634
1500x1500	5.4345	21.9884
1550x1550	5.4168	22.0118
1600x1600	5.3996	22.0338
1650x1650	5.3830	22.0544
1700x1700	5.3668	22.0738
1750x1750	5.3511	22.0921
1800x1800	5.3358	22.1094
1850x1850	5.3209	22.1257
1900x1900	5.3064	22.1412
1950x1950	5.2923	22.1559
2000x2000	5.2786	22.1699

Table 9. The speed up ratio in case of using FNN and FNN after image decomposition into sub-images (25x25 pixels) for images of different sizes (from N=1050 to N=2000, n=25, q=30)

Matrix size	Speed up ratio in case of using FNN	Speed up ratio in case of using FNN after matrix decomposition
100000x100000	3.6109	22.7038
200000x200000	3.4112	22.7092
300000x300000	3.3041	22.7110
400000x400000	3.2320	22.7119
500000x500000	3.1783	22.7125
600000x600000	3.1357	22.7128
700000x700000	3.1005	22.7131
800000x800000	3.0707	22.7133
900000x900000	3.0448	22.7134
1000000x1000000	3.0221	22.7136
1100000x1100000	3.0018	22.7137
1200000x1200000	2.9835	22.7138
1300000x1300000	2.9668	22.7138
1400000x1400000	2.9516	22.7139
1500000x1500000	2.9376	22.7139
1600000x1600000	2.9245	22.7140
1700000x1700000	2.9124	22.7140
1800000x1800000	2.9011	22.7141
1900000x1900000	2.8904	22.7141
2000000x2000000	2.8804	22.7141

Table 10. The speed up ratio in case of using FNN and FNN after matrix decomposition into sub-matrices (25x25 elements) for very large matrices (from N=100000 to N=2000000, n=25, q=30)

number of computation steps required by high speed neural networks is increased smoothly. Thus, the linearity of the computation steps required by high speed neural networks in this case is better. As a result, the speed up ratio is increased. Increasing the speed up ratio with the size of the input image is considered an important achievement. Furthermore, for very large size matrices, while the speed up ratio for high speed neural networks is decreased, the speed up ratio still increase in case of using high speed neural networks and matrix decomposition as listed in Table 10. Moreover, as shown in Figure 3, the speed up ratio in case of high speed neural networks and image decomposition is increased with the size of the weight matrix which has the same size (n) as the input window. For example, it is clear that the speed up ratio is for window size of 30x30 is larger than that of size 20x20. Simulation results for the speed up ratio in case of using fast neural networks and image decomposition is listed in Table 11. It is clear that simulation results confirm the theoretical computations and the practical speed up ratio after image decomposition is faster than using only fast neural networks. In addition, the practical speed up ratio is increased with the size of the input image.

Also, to detect small in size matrices such as 5x5 or 10x10 using only high speed neural networks, the speed ratio becomes less than one as shown in Tables 12,13,14, and 15. On the other hand, from the same tables it is clear that using fast neural and image decomposition, the speed up ratio becomes higher than one and increased with the dimensions of the input image. The dimensions of the new sub-image after image decomposition (L) must not be less than the dimensions of the face/object which is required to be detected and has the same size as the weight matrix. Therefore, the following equation controls the relation between the sub-image and the size of weight matrix (face/object to be detected) in order not to loss any information in the input image.

Image size	Speed up ratio in case of using FNN	Speed up ratio in case of using FNN after image decomposition
100x100	10.75	34.55
200x200	9.19	35.65
300x300	8.43	36.73
400x400	7.45	37.70
500x500	7.13	38.66
600x600	6.97	39.61
700x700	6.83	40.56
800x800	6.68	41.47
900x900	6.79	42.39
1000x1000	6.59	43.28
1100x1100	6.66	44.14
1200x1200	6.62	44.95
1300x1300	6.57	45.71
1400x1400	6.53	46.44
1500x1500	6.49	47.13
1600x1600	6.45	47.70
1700x1700	6.41	48.19
1800x1800	6.38	48.68
1900x1900	6.35	49.09
2000x2000	6.31	49.45

Table 11. The practical speed up ratio in case of using FNN and FNN after image decomposition into sub-images (25x25 pixels) for images of different sizes (from N=100 to N=2000, n=25, q=30)

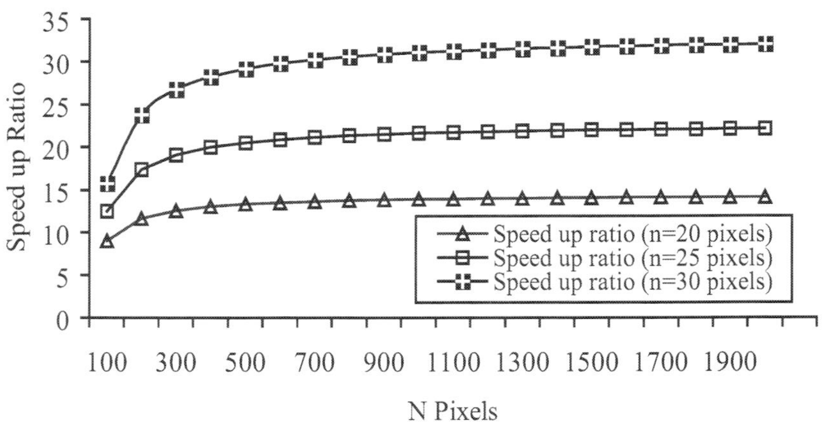

Fig. 3. The speed up ratio in case of image decomposition and different window size (n), (L=25x25).

Image size	Speed up ratio in case of using FNN	Speed up ratio in case of using FNN after image decomposition
50x50	0.3361	1.3282
100x100	0.3141	1.4543
150x150	0.2985	1.4965
200x200	0.2872	1.5177
250x250	0.2785	1.5303
300x300	0.2716	1.5388
350x350	0.2658	1.5448
400x400	0.2610	1.5493
450x450	0.2568	1.5529
500x500	0.2531	1.5557
550x550	0.2498	1.5580
600x600	0.2469	1.5599
650x650	0.2442	1.5615
700x700	0.2418	1.5629
750x750	0.2396	1.5641
800x800	0.2375	1.5652
850x850	0.2356	1.5661
900x900	0.2339	1.5669
950x950	0.2322	1.5677
1000x1000	0.2306	1.5683

Table 12. The speed up ratio in case of using FNN and FNN after image decomposition into Sub-Images (5x5 pixels) for Images of different sizes (from N=50 to N=1000, n=5, q=30)

Image size	Speed up ratio in case of using FNN	Speed up ratio in case of using FNN after image decomposition
1050x1050	0.2292	1.5689
1100x1100	0.2278	1.5695
1150x1150	0.2265	1.5700
1200x1200	0.2253	1.5704
1250x1250	0.2241	1.5709
1300x1300	0.2230	1.5713
1350x1350	0.2219	1.5716
1400x1400	0.2209	1.5720
1450x1450	0.2199	1.5723
1500x1500	0.2189	1.5726
1550x1550	0.2180	1.5728
1600x1600	0.2172	1.5731
1650x1650	0.2163	1.5733
1700x1700	0.2155	1.5735
1750x1750	0.2148	1.5738
1800x1800	0.2140	1.5740
1850x1850	0.2133	1.5742
1900x1900	0.2126	1.5743
1950x1950	0.2119	1.5745
2000x2000	0.2112	1.5747

Table 13. The speed up ratio in case of using FNN and FNN after image decomposition into sub-images (5x5 pixels) for images of different sizes (from N=1050 to N=2000, n=5, q=30)

Image size	Speed up ratio in case of using FNN	Speed up ratio in case of using FNN after image decomposition
50x50	1.1202	3.1369
100x100	1.1503	3.9558
150x150	1.1303	4.2397
200x200	1.1063	4.3829
250x250	1.0842	4.4691
300x300	1.0647	4.5267
350x350	1.0474	4.5678
400x400	1.0321	4.5987
450x450	1.0185	4.6228
500x500	1.0063	4.6420
550x550	0.9952	4.6578
600x600	0.9851	4.6709
650x650	0.9758	4.6820
700x700	0.9672	4.6915
750x750	0.9593	4.6998
800x800	0.9519	4.7070
850x850	0.9451	4.7133
900x900	0.9386	4.7190
950x950	0.9325	4.7241
1000x1000	0.9268	4.7286

Table 14. The speed up ratio in case of using FNN and FNN after Image decomposition into sub-images (5x5 pixels) for images of different sizes (from N=50 to N=1000, n=10, q=30)

Image size	Speed up ratio in case of using FNN	Speed up ratio in case of using FNN after image decomposition
1050x1050	0.9214	4.7328
1100x1100	0.9163	4.7365
1150x1150	0.9114	4.7399
1200x1200	0.9068	4.7431
1250x1250	0.9023	4.7460
1300x1300	0.8981	4.7486
1350x1350	0.8941	4.7511
1400x1400	0.8902	4.7534
1450x1450	0.8865	4.7555
1500x1500	0.8829	4.7575
1550x1550	0.8795	4.7594
1600x1600	0.8762	4.7611
1650x1650	0.8730	4.7628
1700x1700	0.8699	4.7643
1750x1750	0.8669	4.7658
1800x1800	0.8640	4.7672
1850x1850	0.8613	4.7685
1900x1900	0.8586	4.7697
1950x1950	0.8559	4.7709
2000x2000	0.8534	4.7720

Table 15. The speed up ratio in case of using FNN and FNN after image decomposition into sub-images (5x5 pixels) for images of different sizes (from N=1050 to N=2000, n=10, q=30)

$$L \geq n \tag{25}$$

For example, in case of detecting 5x5 pattern, the image must be decomposed into sub-images of size not less than 5x5.

To further reduce the running time as well as increase the speed up ratio of the detection process, a parallel processing technique is used. Each sub-image is tested using a high speed neural network simulated on a single processor or a separated node in a clustered system. The number of operations (ω) performed by each processor / node (sub-images tested by one processor/node) =

$$\omega = \frac{\text{The total number of sub-images}}{\text{Number of processors/nodes}} \tag{26}$$

$$\omega = \frac{\alpha}{Pr} \tag{27}$$

where, P_r is the number of processors or nodes.

The total number of computation steps (γ) required to test an image by using this approach can be calculated as:

$$\gamma = \omega\beta \tag{28}$$

By using this algorithm, the speed up ratio in this case (η_{dp}) can be computed as follows:

$$\eta_{dp} = \frac{q(2n^2 - 1)(N - n + 1)^2}{ceil(((q(\alpha + 1) + \alpha)(5N_s^2 \log_2 N_s^2) + \alpha q(8N_s^2 - n^2) + N_s)/pr)} \tag{29}$$

where, ceil(x) is a MATLAB function rounds the elements of x to the nearest integers towards infinity.

As shown in Tables 16 and 17, using a symmetric multiprocessing system with 16 parallel processors or 16 nodes in either a massively parallel processing system or a clustered system, the speed up ratio (with respect to conventional neural networks) for face/object detection is increased. A further reduction in the computation steps can be obtained by dividing each sub-image into groups. For each group, the neural operation (multiplication by weights and summation) is performed for each group by using a single processor. This operation is done for all of these groups as well as other groups in all of the sub-images at the same time. The best case is achieved when each group consists of only one element. In this case, one operation is needed for multiplication of the one element by its weight and also a small number of operations (ε) is required to obtain the over all summation for each sub-image. If the sub-image has n^2 elements, then the required number of processors to multiply each element in the sub-image matrix by the relevant element in the weight matrix; at the same time; will be n^2. As a result, the number of computation steps will be $\alpha q(1+\varepsilon)$, where ε is a small number depending on the value of n. For example, when n=20, then ε=6 and if n=25, then ε=7. The speed up ratio can be calculated as:

$$\eta = (2n^2-1)(N-n+1)^2/\alpha(1+\varepsilon) \tag{30}$$

Image size	Speed up ratio
50x50	81.1403
100x100	199.3946
150x150	250.5611
200x200	277.7780
250x250	294.5171
300x300	305.8174
350x350	313.9482
400x400	320.0748
450x450	324.8552
500x500	328.6882
550x550	331.8296
600x600	334.4509
650x650	336.6712
700x700	338.5758
750x750	340.2276
800x800	341.6738
850x850	342.9504
900x900	344.0856
950x950	345.1017
1000x1000	346.0164

Table 16. The speed up ratio in case of using FNN after image decomposition into sub-images (25x25 pixels) for images of different sizes (from N=50 to N=1000, n=25, q=30) using 16 parallel processors or 16 nodes

Image size	Speed up ratio
1050x1050	346.8442
1100x1100	347.5970
1150x1150	348.2844
1200x1200	348.9147
1250x1250	349.4946
1300x1300	350.0300
1350x1350	350.5258
1400x1400	350.9862
1450x1450	351.4150
1500x1500	351.8152
1550x1550	352.1896
1600x1600	352.5406
1650x1650	352.8704
1700x1700	353.1808
1750x1750	353.4735
1800x1800	353.7500
1850x1850	354.0115
1900x1900	354.2593
1950x1950	354.4943
2000x2000	354.7177

Table 17. The speed up ratio in case of using FNN after image decomposition into sub-images (25x25 pixels) for images of different sizes (from N=1050 to N=2000, n=25, q=30) using 16 parallel processors or 16 nodes

Moreover, if the number of processors = αn^2, then the number of computation steps will be $q(1+\varepsilon)$, and the speed up ratio becomes:

$$\eta=(2n^2-1)(N-n+1)^2/(1+\varepsilon) \quad (31)$$

Furthermore, if the number of processors = $q\alpha n^2$, then the number of computation steps will be $(1+\varepsilon)$, and the speed up ratio can be calculated as:

$$\eta=q(2n^2-1)(N-n+1)^2/(1+\varepsilon) \quad (32)$$

In this case, as the length of each group is very small, then there is no need to apply cross correlation between the input image and the weights of the neural network in frequency domain.

4. Sub-image centering and normalization in the frequency domain

(Feraud et al. 2000) stated that image normalization to avoid weak or strong illumination could not be done in the frequency space. This is because the image normalization is local and not easily computed in the Fourier space of the whole image. Here, a simple method for image normalization is presented. In (Ben-Yacoub et al. 1999; Fasel 1998; and Ben-Yacoub 1997), the authors stated that centering and normalizing the image can be obtained by centering and normalizing the weights as follows (Ben-Yacoub et al. 1999; Fasel 1998; and Ben-Yacoub 1997) :

Let $\overline{X}_{rc}$ be the zero-mean centered sub-image located at (r,c) in the input image ψ:

$$\overline{X}_{rc} = X_{rc} - \overline{x}_{rc} \quad (33)$$

where, $\overline{x}_{rc}$ is the mean value of the sub-image located at (r,c). We are interested in computing the cross correlation between the sub-image $\overline{X}_{rc}$ and the weights W_i that is:

$$\overline{X}_{rc} \otimes W_i = X_{rc} \otimes W_i - \overline{x}_{rc} \otimes W_i \quad (34)$$

where,

$$\overline{x}_{rc} = \frac{X_{rc}}{n^2} \quad (35)$$

Combining (34) and (35), the following expression can be obtained:

$$\overline{X}_{rc} \otimes W_i = X_{rc} \otimes W_i - \frac{X_{rc}}{n^2} \otimes W_i \quad (36)$$

which is the same as:

$$\overline{X}_{rc} \otimes W_i = X_{rc} \otimes W_i - X_{rc} \otimes \frac{W_i}{n^2} \quad (37)$$

The centered zero mean weights are given by:

$$\overline{W}_i = W_i - \frac{W_i}{n^2} \tag{38}$$

also, Eq. (37) can be written as:

$$\overline{X}_{rc} \otimes W_i = X_{rc} \otimes \left(W_i - \frac{W_i}{n^2} \right) \tag{39}$$

So, it can be concluded that:

$$\overline{X}_{rc} \otimes W_i = X_{rc} \otimes \overline{W}_i \tag{40}$$

which means that cross-correlating a normalized sub-image with the weight matrix is equal to the cross-correlation of the non - normalized sub-image with the normalized weight matrix (Ben-Yacoub et al. 1999; Fasel 1998; and Ben-Yacoub 1997) . However, this proof which presented in (Ben-Yacoub et al. 1999; Fasel 1998; and Ben-Yacoub 1997) is not correct at all because it is proved here mathematically and practically that cross-correlating a normalized sub-image with the weight matrix is not equal to the cross-correlation of the non - centered image with the normalized weight matrix

During the test phase, each sub-image in the input image is multiplied (dot multiplication) by the weight matrix and this operation is repeated for all possible sub-images in the input image. Repeating this process for all sub-images in the input image is equivalent to the cross correlation operation. Therefore, there is no cross correlation between each sub-image and the weight matrix. The cross correlation is done between the weight matrix and the whole input image. Thus, this proves that there is no need to the proof of Eq.(40) (presented in (Ben-Yacoub et al. 1999; Fasel 1998; and Ben-Yacoub 1997)) which is mathematically wrong. The result of Eq.(40) is correct only for the center value which equals to the dot product between the two matrices (sub-image and weight matrices). For all other values except the center value:

$$\overline{X}_{rc} \otimes W_i \neq X_{rc} \otimes \overline{W}_i \tag{41}$$

This fact is true for all types and values of matrices except symmetric matrices and our new technique of image decomposition presented in last section III. A practical example is given in appendix "B".

Furthermore, the definition of the mean value, Eq. (35) presented in (Ben-Yacoub et al. 1999; Fasel 1998; and Ben-Yacoub 1997) is not correct and must be:

$$\bar{x}_{rc} = \frac{\sum_{i=1}^{n} \sum_{j=1}^{n} X_{rc}(i,j)}{n^2} \tag{42}$$

which makes the proof of Eq.(40) (presented in (Ben-Yacoub et al. 1999; Fasel 1998; and Ben-Yacoub 1997)) not correct.

Moreover, the operation performed between the weight matrix and each sub-image is dot multiplication. Our new idea is to normalize each sub-image in the frequency domain by normalizing the weight matrix. The dot product of two matrices is defined as follows:

$$X \bullet W = \sum_{i=1}^{n} \sum_{j=1}^{n} X_{ij} W_{ij} \tag{43}$$

The result of dot product is only one value. We have also the following definitions:

$$1_{nxn} \bullet X = X \bullet 1_{nxn} = \sum_{i,j=1}^{n^2} X_{ij} \tag{44}$$

where, 1_{nxn} is a nxn matrix where every element is 1.

$$1_{nxn} \bullet W = W \bullet 1_{nxn} = \sum_{i,j=1}^{n^2} W_{ij} \tag{45}$$

Lemma : $\overline{w} 1_{nxn} \bullet X = \overline{x} 1_{nxn} \bullet W$

Proof:
From Eqs. 42,43,44,and 45, we can conclude that:

$$\overline{w} 1_{nxn} \bullet X = \overline{w} \sum_{i,j=1}^{n^2} X_{ij} = \frac{1}{n^2} \sum_{i,j=1}^{n^2} W_{ij} \bullet \sum_{i,j=1}^{n^2} X_{ij} \tag{46}$$

which can be reformulated as:

$$\overline{w} 1_{nxn} \bullet X = \frac{1}{n^2} \sum_{i,j=1}^{n^2} W_{ij} \bullet \sum_{i,j=1}^{n^2} X_{ij} \tag{47}$$

also,

$$\overline{x} 1_{nxn} \bullet W = \overline{x} \sum_{i,j=1}^{n^2} W_{ij} = \frac{1}{n^2} \sum_{i,j=1}^{n^2} X_{ij} \bullet \sum_{i,j=1}^{n^2} W_{ij} \tag{48}$$

which is the same as:

$$\overline{x} 1_{nxn} \bullet W = \frac{1}{n^2} \sum_{i,j=1}^{n^2} X_{ij} \bullet \sum_{i,j=1}^{n^2} W_{ij} \tag{49}$$

It is clear that Eq.(47) is the same as Eq.(49), which means:

$$\overline{w} 1_{nxn} \bullet X = \overline{x} 1_{nxn} \bullet W \tag{50}$$

Theorem:

$$\overline{X} \bullet W = \overline{W} \bullet X$$

Proof:

$$\overline{X} \bullet W = (X - \bar{x}1_{nxn}) \bullet W$$

$$= X \bullet W - \bar{x}1_{nxn} \bullet W$$

$$= X \bullet W - X \bullet 1_{nxn}\,\bar{w}$$

$$= X(W - \bar{w} \bullet 1_{nxn})$$

$$= X \bullet \overline{W}$$

So, we may conclude that:

$$\overline{X}_{rc} \bullet W_i = X_{rc} \bullet \overline{W}_i \tag{51}$$

which means that multiplying a normalized sub-image with a non-normalized weight matrix dot multiplication is equal to the dot multiplication between the non - normalized sub-image and the normalized weight matrix. The validation of Eq. (51) and a practical example is given in appendix "C".

As proved in the previous paper (El-Bakry 2002,a), the relation defined by Eq. (40) is true only for the resulting middle value. This is under two conditions. The first is to apply the technique of high speed neural networks and image decomposition. In this case, the cross correlation is performed between each input sub-image and the weight matrix which has the same size as the resulting sub-image after image decomposition. The resulting middle value equals to the dot product between the input sub-image and the weight matrix (the value which we interested in). The second is that the required face/object is completely located in one of these sub-images (not between two sub-images). However applying cross correlation consumes more computation steps than applying dot product which makes Eq. (40) useful less.

5. Effect of weight normalization on the speed up ratio

Normalization of sub-images in the spatial domain (in case of using traditional neural networks) requires $2n^2(N-n+1)^2$ computation steps. On the other hand, normalization of sub-images in the frequency domain through normalizing the weights of the neural networks requires $2qn^2$ operations. This proves that local image normalization in the frequency domain is faster than that in the spatial one. By using weight normalization, the speed up ratio for image normalization Γ can be calculated as:

$$\Gamma = \frac{(N-n+1)^2}{q} \tag{52}$$

The speed up ratio of the normalization process for images of different sizes is listed in Table 18. As a result, we may conclude that:

1. Using this technique, normalization in the frequency domain can be done through normalizing the weights in spatial domain.

Image size	Speed up ratio
100x100	62
200x200	328
300x300	790
400x400	1452
500x500	2314
600x600	3376
700x700	4638
800x800	6100
900x900	7762
1000x1000	9624
1100x1100	11686
1200x1200	13948
1300x1300	16410
1400x1400	19072
1500x1500	21934
1600x1600	24996
1700x1700	28258
1800x1800	31720
1900x1900	35382
2000x2000	39244

Table 18. The speed up ratio of the normalization process for images of different sizes (n =20, q =100)

2. Normalization of an image through normalization of weights is faster than normalization of each sub-image.
3. Normalization of weights can be done off line. So, the speed up ratio in the case of weight normalization can be calculated as follows:

a) For Conventional Neural Networks:

The speed up ratio equals the number of computation steps required by conventional neural networks with image normalization divided by the number of computation steps needed by conventional neural networks with weight normalization, which is done off line. The speed up ratio η_c in this case can be given by:

$$\eta_c = \frac{q(2n^2-1)(N-n+1)^2 + 2n^2(N-n+1)^2}{q(2n^2-1)(N-n+1)^2} \quad (53)$$

which can be simplified to:

$$\eta_c = 1 + \frac{2n^2}{q(2n^2-1)} \quad (54)$$

b) For High speed neural networks:

The over all speed up ratio equals the number of computation steps required by conventional neural networks with image normalization divided by the number of computation steps needed by high speed neural networks with weight normalization, which is done off line. The over all speed up ratio η_o can be given by:

$$\eta_O = \frac{(N-n+1)^2(q(2n^2-1)+2n^2)}{(2q+1)(5N^2\log_2 N^2)+q(8N^2-n^2)+N} \quad (55)$$

The relation between the speed up ratio before (η) and after (η_o) the normalization process can be summed up as:

$$\eta_O = \eta + \frac{2n^2(N-n+1)^2}{(2q+1)(5N^2\log_2 N^2)+q(8N^2-n^2)+N} \quad (56)$$

The overall speed up ratio (Eq. (56)) with images of different sizes and different sizes of windows is listed in Table 19. We can easily note that the speed up ratio in case of image normalization through weight normalization is larger than the speed up ratio (without normalization) listed in Table 1. This means that the search process with normalized high speed neural networks is done faster than conventional neural networks with or without normalization of the input image. The overall practical speed up ratio (Eq. (56)) after normalization of weights off line is listed in Table 20.

Image size	Speed up ratio (n=20)	Speed up ratio (n=25)	Speed up ratio (n=30)
100x100	3.7869	5.2121	6.5532
200x200	4.1382	6.1165	8.3167
300x300	4.1320	6.2313	8.6531
400x400	4.0766	6.2063	8.7031
500x500	4.0152	6.1467	8.6684
600x600	3.9570	6.0796	8.6054
700x700	3.9039	6.0132	8.5334
800x800	3.8557	5.9502	8.4603
900x900	3.8120	5.8915	8.3891
1000x1000	3.7723	5.8369	8.3212
1100x1100	3.7360	5.7862	8.2568
1200x1200	3.7027	5.7391	8.1961
1300x1300	3.6719	5.6952	8.1389
1400x1400	3.6434	5.6542	8.0849
1500x1500	3.6169	5.6158	8.0340
1600x1600	3.5922	5.5798	7.9858
1700x1700	3.5690	5.5458	7.9403
1800x1800	3.5472	5.5138	7.8971
1900x1900	3.5266	5.4835	7.8560
2000x2000	3.5072	5.4547	7.8169

Table 19. Theoretical Results for the Speed up Ratio in case of Image Normalization by Normalizing the Input Weights

Image size	Speed up ratio (n=20)	Speed up ratio (n=25)	Speed up ratio (n=30)
100x100	8.91	12.03	16.74
200x200	7.43	10.42	15.39
300x300	6.72	9.72	14.45
400x400	5.99	8.61	13.59
500x500	5.75	8.32	12.94
600x600	5.61	8.09	11.52
700x700	5.49	7.97	11.04
800x800	5.41	7.83	10.74
900x900	5.32	7.71	10.56
1000x1000	5.29	7.58	10.45
1100x1100	5.41	7.83	10.81
1200x1200	5.36	7.77	10.76
1300x1300	5.32	7.71	10.71
1400x1400	5.28	7.65	10.66
1500x1500	5.24	7.60	10.62
1600x1600	5.21	7.56	10.58
1700x1700	5.18	7.52	10.52
1800x1800	5.14	7.48	10.47
1900x1900	5.11	7.44	10.43
2000x2000	5.08	7.41	10.38

Table 20. The theoretical speed up ratio for images with different sizes

6. Conclusion

Normalized neural networks for fast pattern detection in a given image have been presented. It has been proved mathematically and practically that the speed of the detection process becomes high speed than conventional neural networks. This has been accomplished by applying cross correlation in the frequency domain between the input image and the normalized input weights of the neural networks. A new general formulas for fast cross correlation as well as the speed up ratio have been given. A new high speed neural network approach for pattern detection has been introduced. Such approach has decomposed the input image under test into many small in size sub-images. Furthermore, a simple algorithm for fast pattern detection based on cross correlations in the frequency domain between the sub-images and the weights of the neural net has been presented in order to speed up the execution time. Simulation results have shown that, using a parallel processing technique, large values of speed up ratio could be achieved. In addition, by using high speed neural networks and image decomposition, the speed up ratio has been increased with the size of the input image. Moreover, the problem of local sub-image normalization in the frequency space has been solved. It has been generally proved that the speed up ratio in the case of image normalization through normalization of weights is faster than sub-image normalization in the spatial domain. This speed up ratio is faster than the one obtained without normalization. Simulation results have confirmed theoretical computations by using MATLAB. The proposed approach can be applied to detect the presence/absence of any other object in an image.

Appendix "A"

An Example Proves that the Cross Correlation between any Two Matrices is Different from their Convolution

$$\text{Let}\quad X=\begin{bmatrix}5 & 1\\ 3 & 7\end{bmatrix},\quad \text{and}\quad W=\begin{bmatrix}6 & 5\\ 9 & 8\end{bmatrix},$$

Then, the cross correlation between X and W can be obtained as follows:

$$W\otimes X=\begin{bmatrix}6 & 5\\ 9 & 8\end{bmatrix}\otimes\begin{bmatrix}5 & 1\\ 3 & 7\end{bmatrix}$$

$$=\begin{bmatrix}8\times 5 & 8\times 1+9\times 5 & 9\times 1\\ 5\times 5+8\times 3 & 6\times 5+5\times 1+9\times 3+8\times 7 & 6\times 1+9\times 7\\ 5\times 3 & 6\times 3+5\times 7 & 6\times 7\end{bmatrix}$$

$$=\begin{bmatrix}40 & 53 & 9\\ 49 & 118 & 69\\ 15 & 53 & 42\end{bmatrix}$$

The convolution between W and X can be obtained as follows:

$$W\Diamond X=\begin{bmatrix}8 & 9\\ 5 & 6\end{bmatrix}\Diamond\begin{bmatrix}5 & 1\\ 3 & 7\end{bmatrix}$$

$$=\begin{bmatrix}6\times 5 & 5\times 5+6\times 1 & 5\times 1\\ 9\times 5+6\times 3 & 8\times 5+9\times 1+5\times 3+6\times 7 & 8\times 1+5\times 7\\ 9\times 3 & 8\times 3+9\times 7 & 8\times 7\end{bmatrix}=\begin{bmatrix}30 & 31 & 5\\ 63 & 106 & 43\\ 27 & 87 & 56\end{bmatrix}$$

which proves that $W\otimes X \neq W\Diamond X$.

When the second matrix W is symmetric, the cross correlation between W and X can be computed as follows:

$$W\otimes X=\begin{bmatrix}8 & 9\\ 9 & 8\end{bmatrix}\otimes\begin{bmatrix}5 & 1\\ 3 & 7\end{bmatrix}$$

$$=\begin{bmatrix}8\times 5 & 9\times 5+8\times 1 & 9\times 1\\ 9\times 5+8\times 3 & 8\times 5+9\times 3+9\times 1+8\times 7 & 8\times 1+7\times 9\\ 9\times 3 & 8\times 3+9\times 7 & 8\times 7\end{bmatrix}$$

$$=\begin{bmatrix}40 & 87 & 9\\ 79 & 106 & 71\\ 45 & 53 & 56\end{bmatrix}$$

while the convolution can be between W and X can be obtained as follows:

$$W\Diamond X = \begin{bmatrix} 8 & 9 \\ 9 & 8 \end{bmatrix} \Diamond \begin{bmatrix} 5 & 1 \\ 3 & 7 \end{bmatrix}$$

$$= \begin{bmatrix} 8\times 5 & 9\times 5+8\times 1 & 9\times 1 \\ 9\times 5+8\times 3 & 8\times 5+9\times 3+9\times 1+8\times 7 & 8\times 1+7\times 9 \\ 9\times 3 & 8\times 3+9\times 7 & 8\times 7 \end{bmatrix}$$

$$= \begin{bmatrix} 40 & 87 & 9 \\ 79 & 106 & 71 \\ 45 & 53 & 56 \end{bmatrix}$$

which proves that under the condition that the second matrix is symmetric (or the two matrices are symmetric) the cross correlation between any the two matrices equals to their convolution.

Appendix "B"

A cross correlation Example between a normalized matrix and other non-normalized one and Vise versa

$$\text{Let } X = \begin{bmatrix} 5 & 1 \\ 3 & 7 \end{bmatrix}, \text{ and } W = \begin{bmatrix} 6 & 5 \\ 9 & 8 \end{bmatrix}$$

Then the normalized matrices $\bar{X}$, and $\bar{W}$ can be computed as:

$$\bar{X} = \begin{bmatrix} 1 & -3 \\ -1 & 3 \end{bmatrix}, \text{ and } \bar{W} = \begin{bmatrix} -1 & -2 \\ 2 & 1 \end{bmatrix}$$

Now, the cross correlation between a normalized matrix and the other non-normalized one can be computed as follows:

$$\bar{X} \otimes W = \begin{bmatrix} 1 & -3 \\ -1 & 3 \end{bmatrix} \begin{bmatrix} 6 & 5 \\ 9 & 8 \end{bmatrix} = \begin{bmatrix} 18 & 9 & -5 \\ 9 & 6 & -3 \\ -27 & -15 & 8 \end{bmatrix}$$

$$X \otimes \bar{W} = \begin{bmatrix} 5 & 1 \\ 3 & 7 \end{bmatrix} \begin{bmatrix} -1 & -2 \\ 2 & 1 \end{bmatrix} = \begin{bmatrix} -7 & -17 & -6 \\ 13 & 6 & -7 \\ 2 & 11 & 5 \end{bmatrix}$$

which means that $\overline{X} \otimes W \neq X \otimes \overline{W}$.
However, the two results are equal only at the center element which equals to the dot product between the two matrices. The value of the center element *(2,2)* =6 as shown above and also in appendix "C".

Appendix "C"

A dot product Example between a Normalized Matrix and other Non-Normalized one and Vise Versa

This is to validate the correctness of Eq. (51). The left hand side of Eq. 51 can be expresseded as follows:

$$\overline{X} \bullet W = \begin{bmatrix} X_{1,1} - \overline{X} \ldots\ldots X_{1,n} - \overline{X} \\ \vdots \\ X_{n,1} - \overline{X} \ldots\ldots X_{n,n} - \overline{X} \end{bmatrix} \bullet \begin{bmatrix} W_{1,1} \ldots\ldots W_{1,n} \\ \vdots \\ W_{n,1} \ldots\ldots W_{n,n} \end{bmatrix} \quad (57)$$

and also the right hand side of the same can be repressented as:

$$X \bullet \overline{W} = \begin{bmatrix} X_{1,1} \ldots\ldots X_{1,n} \\ \vdots \\ X_{n,1} \ldots\ldots X_{n,n} \end{bmatrix} \bullet \begin{bmatrix} W_{1,1} - \overline{W} \ldots\ldots W_{1,n} - \overline{W} \\ \vdots \\ W_{n,1} - \overline{W} \ldots\ldots W_{n,n} - \overline{W} \end{bmatrix} \quad (58)$$

$\overline{X}$ and $\overline{W}$ are defined as follows:

$$\overline{X} = \frac{X_{1,1} + X_{1,2} + \ldots\ldots + X_{n,n}}{n^2}$$
$$\overline{W} = \frac{W_{1,1} + W_{1,2} + \ldots\ldots + W_{n,n}}{n^2} \quad (59)$$

By substituting from Eq.(60) in Eq.(58) and Eq.(59), then simplifying the results we can easily conclude that $\overline{X_{rc}} \bullet W_i = X_{rc} \bullet \overline{W_i}$.

Here is also a practical example:

$$\text{Let } X = \begin{bmatrix} 5 & 1 \\ 3 & 7 \end{bmatrix}, \text{ and } W = \begin{bmatrix} 6 & 5 \\ 9 & 8 \end{bmatrix}$$

Then the normalized matrices $\overline{X}$, and $\overline{W}$ can be computed as:

$$\bar{X} = \begin{bmatrix} 1 & -3 \\ -1 & 3 \end{bmatrix}, \text{ and } \bar{W} = \begin{bmatrix} -1 & -2 \\ 2 & 1 \end{bmatrix}$$

Now, the dot product between a normalized matrix and the other non-normalized one can be performed as follows:

$$\bar{X} \bullet W = \begin{bmatrix} 1 & -3 \\ -1 & 3 \end{bmatrix} \begin{bmatrix} 6 & 5 \\ 9 & 8 \end{bmatrix} = 6 - 15 - 9 + 24 = 6$$

$$X \bullet \bar{W} = \begin{bmatrix} 5 & 1 \\ 3 & 7 \end{bmatrix} \begin{bmatrix} -1 & -2 \\ 2 & 1 \end{bmatrix} = -5 - 2 + 6 + 7 = 6$$

which means generally that the dot product between a normalized matrix *X* and non-normalized matrix *W* equals to the dot product between the normalized matrix *W* and non-normalized matrix X. On the other hand, the cross correlation results are different as proved in appendix "C".

7. References

Anifantis D., Dermatas E., Kokkinakis G. (1999) A neural network method for accurate face detection on arbitrary images. In: *Proceedings of 6th IEEE international conference on electronics .Circuits and systems*, Paphos, Cyprus, 5–8 September, pp. 109–112.

Bao J-P, Shen J-Y, Liu H-Y, Liu X-D (2006) A fast document copy detection model. *Soft Comput J* Fusion Found Methodol Appl, vol.10, no. 1, 2006, pp. 41–46.

Ben-Yacoub S. (1997) Fast object detection using MLP and FFT, IDIAP-RR 11, IDIAP.

Ben-Yacoub S., Fasel B., Luettin J. (1999) Fast face detection using MLP and FFT. In: Proceedings of the second international conference on audio and video-based biometric person authentication (AVBPA'99)

Bruce J., Veloso M. (2003) Fast and accurate vision-based pattern detection and identification. In: Proceedings of ICRA'03, the 2003, IEEE International Conference on Robotics and Automation, Taiwan, May 2003, pp. 1-6

El-Bakry HM. (2002,a) Face detection using fast neural networks and image decomposition, *Neurocomputing Journal*, vol. 48, 2002, pp. 1039-1046.

El-Bakry HM. (2002,b) Human Iris Detection Using Fast Cooperative Modular Neural Networks and Image Decomposition," *Machine Graphics & Vision Journal (MG&V)*, Vol. 11, No. 4, 2002, pp. 498-512.

El-Bakry HM. (2003) Comments on Using MLP and FFT for Fast Object/Face Detection, *Proc. of IEEE IJCNN'03*, Portland, Oregon, 20-24 July, 2003, pp. 1284-1288.

El-Bakry HM. (2005) Human Face Detection Using New High Speed Modular Neural Networks, *Lecture Notes in Computer Science,* Springer, Vol. 3696, September 2005, pp. 543-550.

El-Bakry HM. (2006) New Fast Time Delay Neural Networks Using Cross Correlation Performed in the Frequency Domain, *Neurocomputing Journal,* Vol. 69, pp. 2360-2363.

El-Bakry HM. (2007) New Fast Principal Component Analysis for Face Detection, *International Journal of Advanced Computational Intelligence and Intelligent Informatics*, vol.11, no.2, 2007, pp. 195-201.

El-Bakry HM. (2009) New Fast Principal Component Analysis for Real-Time Face Detection, *Machine Graphics & Vision Journal (MG&V)*, vol. 18, no. 4, pp. 405-426.

Essannouni L., Ibn Elhaj E. (2006) Face identification of video sequence. In: *Proceedings of 2006 the second European international symposium on communications, control and signal processing*, 13–15 March 2006, Marrakech, Morocco, 4 p

Fasel B. (1998) Fast multi-scale face detection, IDIAP-Com 98-04

Feraud R., Bernier O., Viallet JE. & Collobert M. (2000) A fast and accurate face detector for indexation of face images. In: *Proceedings of the fourth IEEE international conference on automatic face and gesture recognition*, Grenoble, France, pp. 28–30, March 2000.

Gonzalez RC. & Woods RE. (2002) *Digital image processing*. Prentice-Hall, USA

Ishak KA, Samad SA, Hussian A, Majlis BY (2004) A fast and robust face detection using neural networks. In: *Proceedings of the international symposium on information and communication technologies*. Multimedia University, Putrajaya, Malaysia, Vol 2, 7–8 October, pp 5–8

Cooley JW. & Tukey JW. (1965) An algorithm for the machine calculation of complex Fourier series, *Math. Comput.* 19, 297–301.

Klette R. & Zamperon P. (1996) Handbook of image processing operators. Wiley, New York

Lewis JP (1988) Fast Normalized Cross Correlation. Available from, http://www.idiom.com/*zilla/Papers/nvisionInterface/nip.html

Lang KJ, Hinton GE (1988) The development of time-delay neural network architecture for speech recognition, *Technical Report CMU-CS-88-152*. Carnegie-Mellon University, Pittsburgh, PA

Ramasubramanian P. & Kannan A. (2006) A genetic-algorithm based neural network short-term forecasting framework for database intrusion prediction system. Soft Comput J Fusion Found Methodol Appl, Vol. 10, No. 8, 2006, pp. 699-714.

Roth S., Gepperth A. & Igel C. (2006) Multi-objective neural network optimization for visual object detection, Vol 16. Springer, Berlin

Rowley HA., Baluja S. & Kanade T. (1998) Neural network-based face detection. *IEEE Trans Pattern Anal Mach Intell*, Vol. 20, No.1, 1998, pp.23–38.

Schneiderman H. & Kanade T. (1998) Probabilistic modeling of local appearance and spatial relationships for object recognition, In IEEE Conference on Computer Vision and Pattern Recognition (CVPR), Santa Barbara, CA, pp 45–51.

Srisuk S. & Kurutach W. (2002) A new robust face detection in color images In: *Proceedings of IEEE Computer Society International Conference on Automatic Face and Gesture Recognition*, Washington DC, USA, 20–21 May, 2002, pp 306–311.

Yang M., Kriegman DJ. & Huja N. (2002) Detecting faces in images: a survey. *IEEE Trans Pattern Anal Mach Intell* 24(1):34–58.

Zhu Y., Schwartz S. & Orchard M. (2000) Fast face detection using subspace discriminate wavelet features, *Proceedings of IEEE Computer Society International Conference on Computer Vision and Pattern Recognition (CVPR'00)*, South Carolina, Vol. 1, 13–15 June, pp 1636–1643.

Part 4

Application of ANN in Engineering

15

Study for Application of Artificial Neural Networks in Geotechnical Problems

Hyun Il Park
Samsung C&T
Korea of Republic

1. Introduction

The geotechnical engineering properties of soil exhibit varied and uncertain behaviour due to the complex and imprecise physical processes associated with the formation of these materials (Jaksa, 1995). This is in contrast to most other civil engineering materials, such as steel, concrete and timber, which exhibit far greater homogeneity and isotropy. In order to cope with the complexity of geotechnical behaviour, and the spatial variability of these materials, traditional forms of engineering design models are justifiably simplified. Moreover, geotechnical engineers face a great amount of uncertainties. Some sources of uncertainty are inherent soil variability, loading effects, time effects, construction effects, human error, and errors in soil boring, sampling, in-situ and laboratory testing, and characterization of the shear strength and stiffness of soils.

Although developing an analytical or empirical model is feasible in some simplified situations, most manufacturing processes are complex, and therefore, models that are less general, more practical, and less expensive than the analytical models are of interest. An important advantage of using Artificial Neural Network (ANN) over regression in process modeling is its capacity in dealing with multiple outputs or responses while each regression model is able to deal with only one response. Another major advantage for developing NN process models is that they do not depend on simplified assumptions such as linear behavior or production heuristics. Neural networks possess a number of attractive properties for modeling a complex mechanical behavior or a system: universal function approximation capability, resistance to noisy or missing data, accommodation of multiple nonlinear variables for unknown interactions, and good generalization capability.

Since the early 1990s, ANN has been increasingly employed as an effective tool in geotechnical engineering, including: **constitutive modelling** (Agrawal et al., 1994; Gribb & Gribb, 1994; Penumadu et al., 1994; Ellis et al., 1995; Millar & Calderbank, 1995; Ghaboussi & Sidarta 1998; Zhu et al., 1998; Sidarta & Ghaboussi, 1998; Najjar & Ali, 1999; Penumadu & Zhao, 1999); **geo-material properities** (Goh, 1995; Ellis et al., 1995; Najjar et al., 1996; Najjar and Basheer, 1996; Romero & Pamukcu, 1996; Ozer et al., 2008; Park et al., 2009; Park & Kim, 2010; Park & Lee, 2010; **Bearing capacity of pile** (Chan et al., 1995; Goh, 1996; Bea et al., 1999; Goh et al., 2005; Teh et al., 1997; Lee & Lee, 1996; Abu-Kiefa, 1998; Nawari et al., 1999; Das & Basudhar, 2006, Park & Cho, 2010); **slope stability** (Ni et al., 1995; Neaupane and Achet, 2004; Ferentinou & Sakellariou, 2007; Zhao, 2007; Cho, 2009); **liquefaction** (Agrawal et al., 1997; Ali & Najjar, 1998; Najjar & Ali, 1998; Ural & Saka, 1998; Juang and Chen, 1999; Goh, 2002; Javadi et al., 2006; Kim & Kim, 2006); **shallow foundations** (Sivakugan et al., 1998; Provenzano et al., 2004; Shahin et al., 2005); and **tunnels and underground openings** (Lee & Sterling, 1992; Moon et al., 1995; Shi, 2000; Yoo & Kim, 2007). For example, the behavior of pile foundations installed in soils is considerably complicated, uncertain, and not yet entirely understood (Baik, 2002). This fact has encouraged many researchers to apply the ANN technique to the prediction of the behavior of foundations such as, modeling the axial and lateral load capacities of deep foundations. Constitutive modeling of soil behavior plays an important role in dealing with issues related to soil mechanics and foundation engineering. Over the past three decades many researchers devoted enormous effort collectively to model soil behavior. However, proposed constitutive models based on elasticity and plasticity theories have limited capability to simulate properly the behavior of soils. This is attributed to reasons associated with the formulation complexity, idealization of soil behavior, and excessive empirical parameters. In this regard, many ANNs have been proposed as a reliable and practical alternative to model the constitutive behavior of soils. Geotechnical properties soils are controlled by factors such as mineralogy; stress history; void ratio; pore water pressure, and the interactions of these factors are difficult to establish solely by traditional statistical methods due to their interdependence. Based on the application of ANNs, methodologies have been developed for estimating several soil properties, including the compression index, shear strength, permeability, soil compaction, lateral earth pressure, and others.

The performance and computational complexity of NNs are mainly based on network architecture, which generally depends on the determination of input, output and hidden layers and number of neurons in each layer. The number of layers and neurons in each layer affect the complexity of NN architecture. NN architectures are discussed at length in several research works (Hecht-Nelson,1987; Bounds et al., 1988; Lawrence & Fredrickson, 1988; Cybenko, 1989; Marchandani & Cao, 1989; Fahlman & Lebiere, 1990; Lawrence, 1994; Goh, 1995; Swingler, 1996; Öztütk, 2003). Nevertheless, there is no clear framework to select the optimum NN architecture and its parameters. Structural design of NN involves the determination of layers and neurons in each layer and selection of training algorithm. In general, parameters of NN architecture are determined by trial and error approach such that the number of neurons in input layer, number of hidden layers, number of neurons in hidden layers and number of neurons in output layer are found using several repeated runs of the system.

The main objective of this chapter is to provide a brief overview of the operation of ANN models, the area, the areas of geotechnical engineering to which ANNs have been applied, and highlights and discusses four important issues which require further attention in the future. The chapter is divided into seven major parts. The first part reviews the background for application of ANN methodology to getechnical engineering. In the second part, an introduction to basic neural network architectures is followed. In the third part, methodologies for designing appropriate network architectures and practical guidelines on finding optimum structure of neural network are shortly discussed. The forth part is the application section, which summarizes the completed applicable work in geotechnical engineering problems and mathematical calculation of an ANN model is illustrated in the fifth part. In the sixth part of this chapter, in order to investigate further research directions of ANNs in geotechnical engineering, author's latest issues of researches related to ANNs are reviewed and then the conclusion is followed in the seventh part.

2. Oververw of the Artificial Neural Network

2.1 The concept of artificial neuron

Much is still unknown about how the brain trains itself to process information, so theories abound. In the human brain, a typical neuron collects signals from others through a host of fine structures called *dendrites* (See Fig. 1). The neuron sends out spikes of electrical activity through a long, thin stand known as an *axon*, which splits into thousands of branches. At the end of each branch, a structure called a *synapse* converts the activity from the axon into electrical effects that inhibit or excite activity from the axon into electrical effects that inhibit or excite activity in the connected neurones. When a neuron receives excitatory input that is sufficiently large compared with its inhibitory input, it sends a spike of electrical activity down its axon. Learning occurs by changing the effectiveness of the synapses so that the influence of one neuron on another changes. An artificial neuron is a device with many inputs and one output. The neuron has two modes of operation; the training mode and the using mode. In the training mode, the neuron can be trained to fire (or not), for particular input patterns. In the using mode, when a taught input pattern is detected at the input, its associated output becomes the current output. If the input pattern does not belong in the taught list of input patterns, the firing rule is used to determine whether to fire or not.

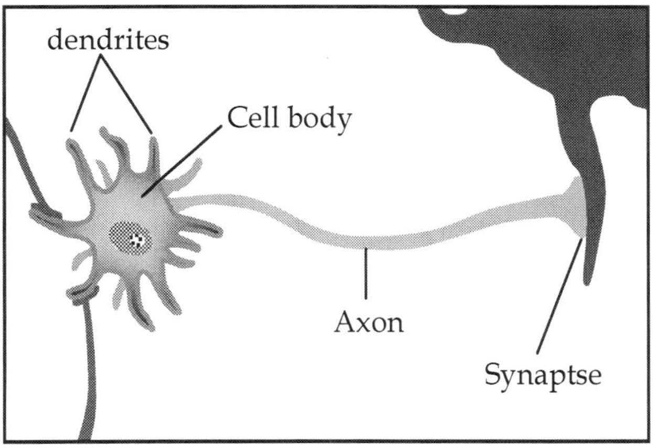

Fig. 1. Biological neuron

2.2 Mathematical modeling of artificial neuron

A *neuron* is an information-processing unit that is fundamental to the peration of a neural network. As shown in Fig. 2, we may identify three basic elements of the neuron model. A set of *synapses*, each of which is characterized by a *weight* or *strength* of its own. Specifically, a signal x_j at the input of synapse *j* connected to neuron *k* is multiplied by the synaptic weight w_{kj}. It is important to make a note of the manner in which the subscripts of the synaptic weight w_{kj} are written. The first subscript refers to the neuron in question and the second subscript refers to the input end of the synapse to which the weight refers. The weight w_{kj} is positive if the associated synapse is excitatory; it is negative if the synapse is inhibitory. An *adder* for summing the input signals, weighted by the respective synapses of the neuron. An *activation function* for limiting the amplitude of the output of a neuron. The activation function is also referred to in the literature as a *squashing function* in that it squashes (limits) the permissible amplitude range of the output signal to some finite value. Typically, the normalized amplitude range of the output of a neuron is written as the closed unit interval [0, 1] or alternatively [-1, 1]. The model of a neuron also includes an externally applied bias (threshold) $w_{k0} = b_k$ that has the effect of lowering or increasing the net input of the activation function. In matrix form, we may describe a neuron *k* by writing the following matrix.

$$v_k = \begin{bmatrix} w_{k0} & w_{k1} & \cdots & w_{kp} \end{bmatrix} \begin{bmatrix} x_0 \\ x_1 \\ \vdots \\ x_p \end{bmatrix} = w_k^T x \quad (1)$$

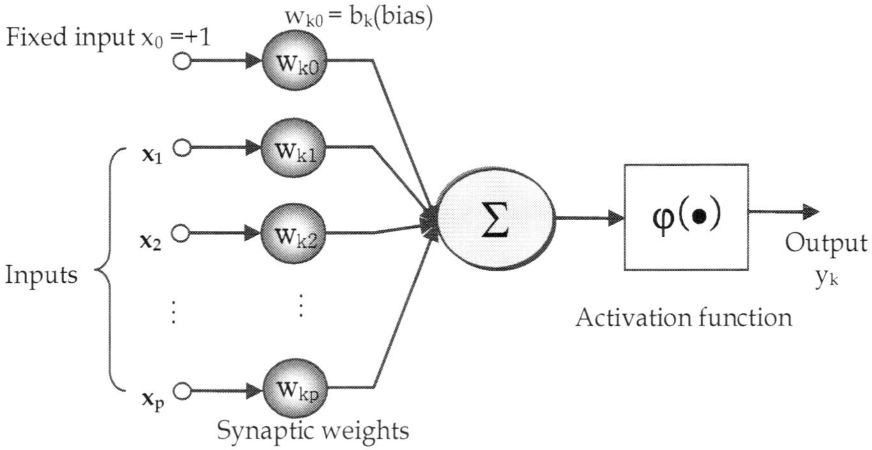

Fig. 2. Basic elements of an artificial neuron

2.3 Activation function

In this section, three of the most common activation functions are presented. An activation function performs a mathematical operation on the output. More sophisticated activation functions can also be utilized depending upon the type of problem to be solved by the network. As is known, a linear function satisfies the superposition concept. The function is shown in Fig. 3(a). The mathematical equation for the above linear function can be written as

$$Y = f(u) = \alpha.u \quad (2)$$

where α is the slope of the linear function. If the slope α is 1, then the linear activation function is called the identity function. The output (y) of identity function is equal to input function (u). Although this function might appear to be a trivial case, nevertheless it is very useful in some cases such as the last stage of a multilayer neural network.

As shown Fig. 3(b), sigmoidal(S shape) function is the most common nonlinear type of the activation used to construct the neural networks. It is mathematically well behaved, differentiable and strictly increasing function. A sigmoidal transfer function can be written in the following form:

$$f(x) = \frac{1}{1+e^{-\alpha x}} \ , 0 \le f(x) \le 1 \tag{3}$$

where α is the shape parameter of the sigmoid function. By varying this parameter, different shapes of the function can be obtained as illustrated in Fig. 3(b). This function is continuous and differentiable.
Tangent sigmoidal function is described by the following mathematical form:

$$f(x) = \frac{2}{1+e^{-\alpha x}} - 1 \ , -1 \le f(x) \le +1 \tag{4}$$

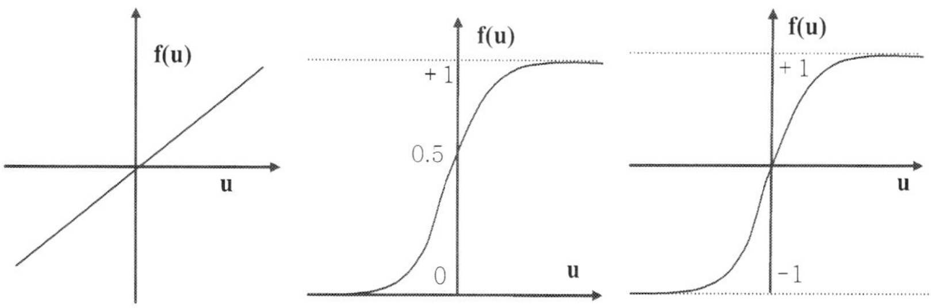

(a) (b) (c)

Fig. 3. Activation Function.

2.4 Multilayered Neural Network

The source nodes in the *input layer* of the network supply respective elements of the activation pattern (input vector), which constitute the input signals applied to the neurons (computation nodes) in the second layer (i.e. the first *hidden layer*). The output signals of the second layer are used as inputs to the third layer, and so on for the rest of the network. Typically, the neurons in each layer of the network have as their inputs the output signals of the preceding layer only. The set of output signals of the neurons in the *output layer* of the network constitutes the overall response of the network to the activation pattern supplied by the source nodes in the input layer. The commonest type of artificial neural network consists of three groups, or layers, of units: a layer of "input" units is connected to a layer of "hidden" units, which is connected to a layer of "output" units (see Fig. 4). The activity of the input units represents the raw information that is fed into the network. The activity of each hidden unit is determined by the activities of the input units and the weights on the connections between the input and the hidden units. The behaviour of the output units depends on the activity of the hidden units and the weights between the hidden and output units.

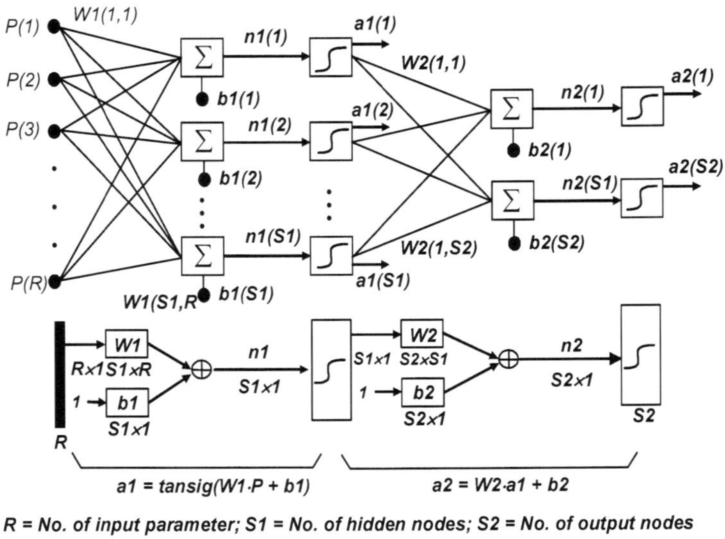

Fig. 4. Example of Multilayer neural network

2.4 Back-propagation

Backpropagation algorithm (BP) is the most widely used search technique for training neural networks. Information in an ANN is stored in the connection weights which can be thought of as the memory of the system. The purpose of BP training is to change iteratively the weights between the neurons in a direction that minimizes the error E, defined as the squared difference between the desired and the actual outcomes of the output nodes, summed over training patterns (training dataset) and the output neurons. The algorithm uses a sample-by-sample updating rule for adjusting connection weights in the network. In one algorithm iteration, a training sample is presented to the network. The signal is then fed in a forward manner through the network until the network output is obtained. The error between the actual and desired network outputs is calculated and used to adjust the connection weights. Basically, the adjustment procedure, derived from a gradient descent method, is used to reduce the error magnitude. The procedure is firstly applied to the connection weights in the output layer, followed by the connection weights in the hidden layer next to output layer. This adjustment is continued backward through to network until connection weights in the first hidden layer are reached. The iteration is completed after all connection weights in the network have been adjusted. Rumelhart, Hinton, and Williams (1986) popularized the use of BP for learning internal representation in neural networks. Despite their popularity, BP has the drawback of converging to an optimal solution slowly when the gradient search technique is applied. That is, a BP using the gradient search technique has two serious disadvantages: the gradient search technique converges to an optimal solution with inconsistent and unpredictable performance for some applications and when trapped into some local areas, the gradient search technique performs poorly in getting a globally optimal solution. The most major problem during the training process of the neural network is the possible overfitting of training data. That is, during a certain training period, the network no longer improves its ability to solve the problem. In this case, the training stopped in a local minimum, leading to ineffective results and indicating a poor fit of the model. In order to attempt to prevent these disadvantages, researchers have modified the basic algorithm to try to escape local optima and find the global solution. Numerous modifications have been implemented in order to overcome this problem.

Over-fitting problem or poor generalization capability happens when a neural network over learns during the training period. As a result, such a too well-trained model may not perform well on unseen data set due to its lack of generalization capability. Several approaches have been suggested in literature to overcome this problem. The first method is an early learning stopping mechanism in which the training process is concluded as soon as the overtraining signal appears. The signal can be observed when the prediction accuracy of the trained network applied to a test set, at that stage of training period, gets worsened. The second approach is the Bayesian Regularization. This approach minimizes the over-fitting problem by taking into account the goodness-of-fit as well as the network architecture. Early stopping approach requires the data set to be divided into three subsets: training, test, and verification sets. The training and the verification sets are the norm in all model training processes. The test set is used to test the trend of the prediction accuracy of the model trained at some stages of the training process. At much later stages of training process, the prediction accuracy of the model may start worsening for the test set. This is the stage when the model should cease to be trained to overcome the over-fitting problem. The Bayesian Regularization approach involves modifying the usually used objective function, such as the mean sum of squared network errors (MSE) The modification aims to improve the model's generalization capability. The objective function in Eq. (5) is expanded with the addition of a term, w E which is the sum of squares of the network weights:

$$F=\beta Ed+\alpha Ew \tag{5}$$

where the α and β are parameters which are to be optimized in Bayesian framework of MacKay (1992a; 1992b). It is assumed that the weights and biases of the network are random variables following Gaussian distributions and the parameters are related to the unknown variances associated with these distributions.

3. Designing the structure of Artificial Neural Network

Structural design of NN involves the determination of layers and neurons in each layer and selection of training algorithm. The selection of only effective input parameters to the NN is one of the most difficult processes since: (1) there may be interdependencies and redundancies between parameters, (2) sometimes it is better to omit some parameters to reduce the total number of input parameters, and therefore computational complexity of the problem and topology of the network, and (3) NN is usually applied to problems where there is no strong knowledge about the relations between input and output, and therefore it is not clear which of the input parameters are most useful. Moreover, other design parameters of NN architecture, such as the number of neurons in input layer, number of hidden layers, number of neurons in hidden layers and number of neurons in output layer, are found using several repeated runs of the system based on trial and error method. There is no clear framework to select the optimum NN architecture and its parameters (Chung and Kusiak, 1994; Kusiak and Lee, 1996). Nevertheless, some research work has contributed to determine the number of hidden layers, the number of neurons in each layer, selecting the learning rate parameter, and others.

3.1 Determining the number of hidden layers

Determining the number of hidden layers and the number of neurons in each hidden layer is a considerable task. The number of hidden layers is usually determined first and is a critical step. The number of hidden layers required depends on the complexity of the relationship between the input parameters and the output value. Most problems only require one hidden layer, and if relationship between the inputs and output is linear the network does not need a additional hidden layer at all. It is unlikely that any practical problem will require more than two hidden layers(THL). Cybenko (1989) and Bounds et al. (1988) suggested that one hidden layer (OHL) is enough to classify input patterns into different group.

Chester (1990) argued that a THL should perform better than an OHL network. More than one hidden layer can be useful in certain architectures, such as cascade correlation (Fahlman & Lebiere, 1990) and others. A simple explanation for why larger networks can sometimes provide improved training and lower generalization error is that the extra degrees of freedom can aid convergence; that is, the addition of extra parameters can decrease the chance of becoming stuck in local minima or on "plateaus". The most commonly used training methods for back-propagation networks are based on gradient descent; that is, error is reduced until a minimum is reached, whether it be a global or local minimum. However, there isn't clear theory to tell how many hidden units are needed to approximate any given function. If only one input availavle, one sees no advantages in using more than one hidden layer. But things get much more complicated when two or more inputs are given. The rule of thumb in deciding the number of hidden layers is normally to start with OHL (Lawrence, 1994). If OHL does not train well, then try to increase the number of neurons. Adding more hidden layers should be the last option.

3.2 Determining the number of hidden neurons

The choice of hidden neuron size is problem-dependent. For example, any network that requires data compression must have a hidden layer smaller than the input layer (Swingler, 1996). A conservative approach is to select a number between the number of input neurons and the number of output neurons. It can be seen that the general wisdom concerning selection of initial number of hidden neurons is somewhat conflicting. A good rule

Formula	Comments
$h = 2i + 1$	Hecht-Nelson (1987) used Kolmogorov's theorem which any function of I variavles may be represented by the superposition of set of 2i+1 univariate functions-to derive the upper bound for the required number of hidden neurons.
$h = (i + o) / 2$ $\frac{N}{10} - i - o \leq h \leq \frac{N}{2} - i - o$	Lawrence and Fredrickson (1988) suggested that a best estimation for the number of hidden neurons is to half the sum of inputs and outputs. Moreover, they proposed the range of number of hidden neurons.
$h = i \log_2 P$	Marchandani and Cao (1989) proposed a equation for best number of hidden neurons

*. h = the number of hidden neurons, i = the number of input neurons, o = the number of output neurons.

Table 1. Rule of thumbs to select the number of neurons in hidden layer of thumb is to start with the number of hidden neurons equal to half of the number of input neurons and then either add neurons if the training error remains above the training error tolerance, or reduce neurons if the training error quickly drops to the training error tolerance.

3.3 Determining the number of training data

In order to train the neural network well, the number of data set must be carefully decided. An over fitted model could approximate the training data well but generalize poorly to the validation data set. On the other hand, an underfitted model would generalize to the validation data set well but approximate the training data poorly. To avoid over fitting and underfitting is to determine the best number of training observations. No general guidelines are available to achieve this. However, Lawrence and Fredrickson (1988) suggested the following rule of thumb.

$$2\,(i + h + o) \leq N \leq 10((i + h + o) \tag{6}$$

4. ANN applications in geotechnical engineering

4.1 Constitutive Modelling of geo-materials

During the past decades, increasing interest has been shown in the development of a satisfactory formulation for the stress-strain relationships of geo-materials that incorporates a concise statement of nonlinearity, inelasticity and stress dependency based on a set of assumptions and proposed failure criteria. In spite of the considerable complexities of these constitutive models, and due to an inadequate understanding of the mechanisms and all factors involved, it is not possible to capture the complete material response along all complex stress paths and densities. Furthermore, the degree of complexity of these constitutive models (in many cases) inhibits their incorporation into general purpose numerical codes, thus restricting their usefulness in engineering practice (Shin and Pande, 2000). On the other hands, for the convenience of practical in engineering, the model seems to be established simple enough. In the process of establishing the model, the conventional method oversimplifies the soil mechanic behavior. When simplifying the model, parameters have been artificially lessened and only a few of them could be applied in setting up the soil constitutive model while the remaining large number of test data is neglected. Eventually, the model will be poor.

Unlike conventional constitutive models, it needs no prior knowledge, or any constants and/or assumptions about the deformation characteristics of the geo-materials. Other powerful attributes of ANN models are their flexibility and adaptivity, which play an important role in material modeling (Ghaboussi & Sidarta 1998). When a new set of experimental results cannot be reproduced by conventional models, a new constitutive model or a set of new constitutive equations, needs to be developed. However, trained ANN models can be further trained with the new data set to gain the required additional information needed to reproduce the new experimental results. These features ascertain the ANN model to be an objective model that can truly represent natural neural connections among variables, rather than a subjective model, which assumes variables obeying a set of predefined relations (Zhu et al., 1998). So far, ANNs have been applied to the constitutive modeling of rocks, clays, sands, gravels and other geo-materials (Zhu et al., 1998; Millar & Calderbank, 1995; Penumadu et al., 1994; Ellis et al., 1995; Penumadu & Zhao, 1999; Najjar & Ali, 1999)

Ghaboussi and co-workers originally proposed an NN-based framework for constitutive modeling in geomechanics (Ghaboussi & Sidarta, 1998; Sidarta & Ghaboussi, 1998). They introduced a concept of nested adaptive NNs, which considers the nested structure of the material test data, e.g. dimensionality, stress path dependency or drainage conditions. By means of the finite element (FE) method and the autoprogressive training algorithm proposed in (Ghaboussi et al., 1998), they trained NNs with experimental nonuniform triaxial test data, in order to capture and reproduce the non-linear response of the soil without conventional concepts of the theory of plasticity. In addition, further research proved that the NN-constitutive models can be successfully embedded within the FE codes to compute the consistent tangent stiffness matrix (Shin and Pande, 2000; Hashash et al., 2004). Hashash et al. (2004) demonstrated that a tangent stiffness matrix can be derived from the NN-based material models, using the explicit formulation represented by network parameters. However, the main drawback of the NN-constitutive models is that it is valid only for a specific material for which a new NN has to be adopted each time. Moreover, a material model loses its 'flexibility', which is inherent in the case of conventional models and which is controlled by parameters explicitly describing concepts of plasticity, such as yield surface, flow rule and hardening law.

4.2 Properties of geo-materials

In geotechnical engineering, empirical relationships are often used to estimate certain engineering properties of soils. Using data from extensive laboratory or field testing, these correlations are usually derived with the aid of statistical methods. The relationships between soil parameters are clearly complex, but the degree of interaction enables a degree of statistical correlation to be established, suggesting the promise of a potential for estimation. Developing engineering correlations between various soil parameters is an issue discussed by Goh (1995). Goh used neural networks to model the correlation between the relative density and the cone resistance from cone penetration test (CPT), for both normally consolidated and over-consolidated sands. Laboratory data, based on calibration chamber tests, were used to successfully train and test the neural network model.

The neural network model used soil parameters as inputs and the compression index as a single output(Ozer et al., 2008; Park & Lee, 2010). The ANN models was found to give higher coefficients of correlation than empirical equations for the training and testing data, respectively, which indicated that the neural network was successful in modelling the complex relationship between the compression index and the other soil parameters. Many other studies have successfully used ANNs for modelling soil properties. Ellis et al. (1995) developed an ANN model for sands based on grain size distribution and stress history. Najjar et al. (1996) showed that neural network-based models can be used to accurately assess soil swelling, and that neural network models can provide significant improvements in prediction accuracy over statistical models. Romero and Pamukcu (1996) showed that neural networks are able to effectively characterise and estimate the shear modulus of granular materials. Agrawal et al. (1994); Gribb and Gribb (1994) and Najjar and Basheer (1996) all used neural network approaches for estimating the permeability of clay liners. Park et al. (2010) used ANN models to develop an empirical model for the resilient modulus of subgrade soils and subbase materials from basic material properties and in-situ conditions related to stresses.

Park and Kim (2010a) proposed an ANN model to predict the unconfined compressive strength of reinforced lightweight soil (RLS). RLS consisting of dredged soil, cement, air-foam, and waste fishing net is considered to be an eco-friendly backfilling material in construction because it provides a means to recycle both dredged soil and waste fishing net.

Several series of laboratory tests were performed to investigate the unconfined compressive strength of RLS in various mixing ratios. It may be difficult to find an optimum mixing ratio of RLS considering the design criteria and the construction's situation using the limited test results because the unconfined compressive strength is complicatedly influenced by various mixing ratios of admixtures. As a result, in order to expedite the field application of reinforced lightweight soil, an appropriate prediction method is needed. However, since the strength of RLS is strongly influenced by the mixing ratio of each admixture (i.e., cement, water, air foam, and waste fishing net), it is difficult to empirically formulate a mathematical relationship between the strength and the admixture content of the composite materials. An ANN model that predict the strength of RLS at a given mixing ratio was developed using experimental test results performed on various mixing admixture contents.

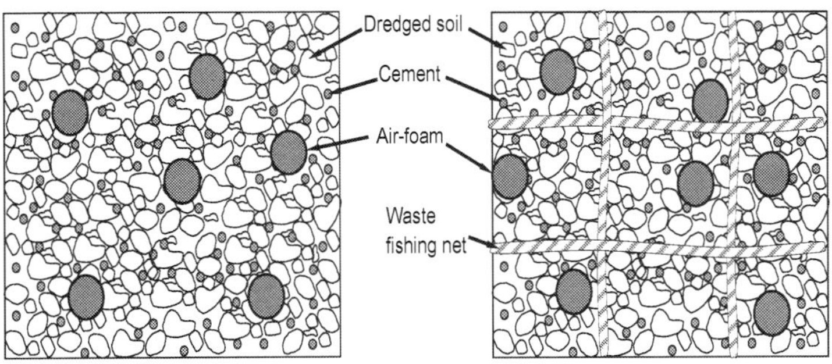

Fig. 5. Schematic diagram of (a) unreinforced and (b) reinforced light-weight soil (Park & Kim, 2010)

As shown in Fig.6(a) the proposed NN model has four nodes in the input layer, four nodes in the hidden layer, and one node in the output layer Fig. 6(a). Fig. 6(b) shows the relationship between the output targets (measured values) and predicted values obtained through the training and testing process. the model shows very good correlation to the

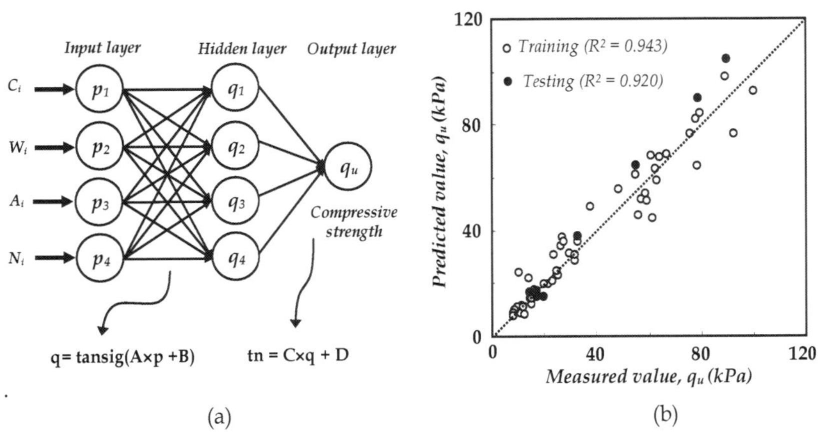

Fig. 6. Architecture for the developed artificial neural network (Park & Kim, 2010)

training and testing data. As shown in Fig. 7, the developed ANN model is able to obtain the complex behaviors between the compressive strength of RLS and the mixing ratios of admixitures. It has been proven that NN is well suited to modeling the complex behavior of most geo-materials which, by their very nature, exhibit extreme variability.

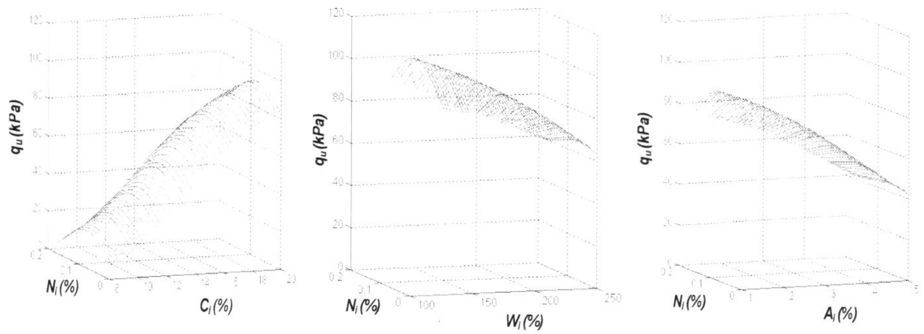

(a) (b) (c)

Fig. 7. The unconfined compressive strength with variation of input parameters (Park & Kim, 2010)

4.3 Pile capacity

Design of axial loaded pile can be done be solving equations of static equilibrium whereas design of lateral loaded piles requires solution of nonlinear differential equations (Poulos & Davis, 1980). Other semi-empirical methods used for lateral load capacity of piles are due to Hansen (1961), Broms (1964) and Meyerhof (1976). Although numerous investigations have been performed over the years to predict the behavior and capacity of piles, the mechanisms are not yet entirely understood. Predicting pile capacity is a difficult task because there are a large number of parameters affecting the capacity which have complex relationships with each other. It is extremely difficult to develop appropriate relationships between various essential parameters, including the soil condition, pile type, driving condition, time effect, and others. Baik (2002) illustrated that these factors include the soil condition (type of soil, density, shear strength, etc.), information related to the piles' shape (diameter, penetration depth, whether the tip of pile is open-ended or closed-ended, etc.), and other information (driving method, driving energy, set-up effect, etc.). Although many methods predicting pile resistance have been presented, they did not appropriately consider the various parameters that affect pile resistance. The main criticism of these methods is that they oversimplify the complicated mechanism of pile resistance, and the soil characteristics, type of pile, and information on driving conditions are not properly taken into account.

Hence, ANN models could be an alternate approach for the above case. Goh (1995) used back propagation neural network (BPNN) to predict the skin friction of pile in clay. Goh (1995; 1996) observed that ultimate load capacity of driven timber, pre-cast concrete and steel piles in cohesionless soils using ANN was found to outperform the methods like Engineering News formula, the Hiley formula and the Janbu formula. Chan et al. (1995) and Teh et al. (1997) found that the static pile capacity predicted by using neural network have

excellent agreement with the same obtained by using the commercially available computer code CAPWAP (GRL, 1972). Lee and Lee (1996) used neural networks to predict the ultimate bearing capacity of piles based on model and in situ pile load test results. Abu-Kiefa (1998) used a generalized regression neural network (GRNN), which is a type of probabilistic neural network to predict the pile load capacity considering separately the tip, the shaft and total load capacity of piles driven in cohesionless soils. Nawari et al. (1999) have used neural networks for prediction of axial load capacity of steel H-piles, steel piles and pre-stressed and reinforced concrete piles using both BPNN and GRNN. They also predicted the top settlement of drill shaft due to lateral load based on in situ testing.
Park and Cho (2010) applied an artificial neural network (ANN) to predict the resistance of driven piles in dynamic load tests. They collected 165 data sets for driven piles at various construction sites in Korea. Predictions on the tip, shaft, and total pile resistance were made for piles with available corresponding measurements of such values. The results indicate that the ANN model serves as a reliable and simple predictive tool to appropriately consider various essential parameters for predicting the resistance of driven piles. The proposed neural network model has seven nodes in the input layer, eight nodes in the hidden layer, and three nodes in the output layer (Fig. 8). In order to find an appropriate combination of transfer functions providing good correlation in training and testing stage, various combinations using log-sigmoid, tan-sigmoid and linear was applied to hidden layer and output layer. The combination of transfer functions applied to the hidden layer and output layer neurons are tan-sigmoid ($2/(1+e^{-2n})-1$) and linear, respectively.

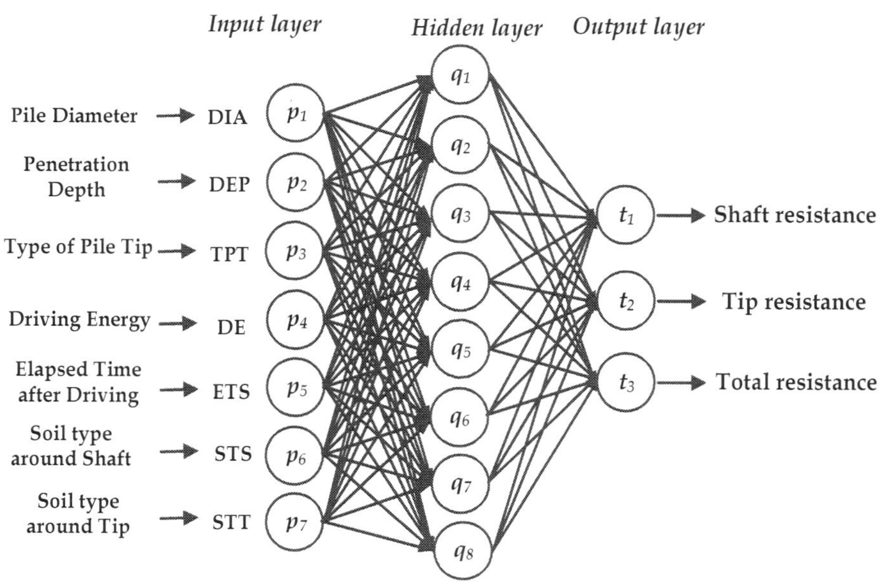

Fig. 8. Architecture of the artificial neural network model (Park & Cho, 2010)

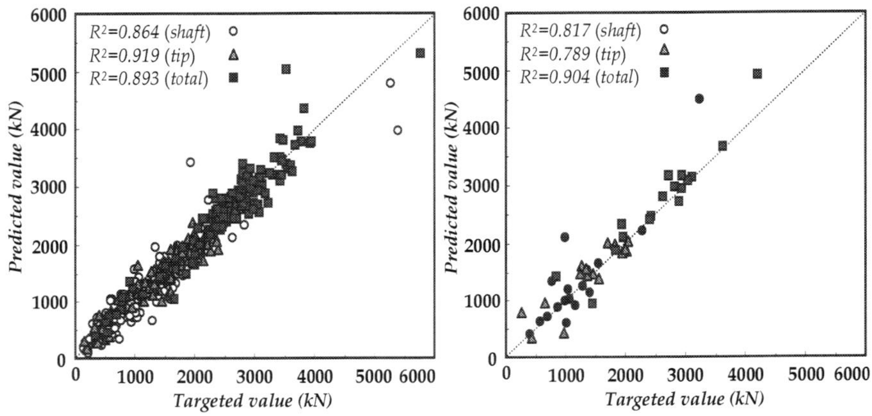

Fig. 9. Comparison of predicted and measured pile resistance (Park and Cho, 2010)

4.4 Slope stability

Slope stability is important because slope failures or landslides can lead to the loss of life and property. Slope failures are complex natural phenomena that constitute a serious natural hazard in many countries. Limited data and unclearly defined problems often complicate the study of landslides (Nieuwenhuis 1991). To prevent or mitigate the landslide damage, slope-stability analyses and stabilization require an understanding and evaluation of the processes that govern the behavior of the slopes. The factor of safety based on an appropriate geotechnical model as an index of stability, is required in order to evaluate slope stability. Black-box models, based on the Artificial Neural Networks (ANNs), currently attract many researchers studying slope instability, owing to their successful performance in modeling non-linear multivariate problems (Ni et al., 1995; Neaupane & Achet, 2004; Sakellariou & Ferentinou, 2005; Cho, 2009; Wang et al., 2005). Many variables are involved in slope stability evaluation and the calculation of the factor of safety requires geometrical data, physical data on the geologic materials and their shear-strength parameters (cohesion and angle of internal friction), information on pore-water pressures, etc. To evaluate slope instability, the complexity of the slope system requires employment of new methods that are efficient in predicting this nonlinear characteristic of natural landslides.

5. Practical mathematical formulation of ANN

5.1 Mathematical formulation

Training a neural network is conducted by presenting a series of example patterns for associated input and output values. Initially, when a network is created, the connection weights and biases are set to random values. The performance of an ANN model is measured in terms of an error criterion between the target output and the calculated output. The output calculated at the end of each feed-forward computation is compared with the target output to estimate the mean-squared error, as shown in Eq. (7)

$$E = \sum_{i=1}^{Num} (T_i - t_i)^2 \tag{7}$$

where, Num = number of target data, T_i = i^{th} target output, t_i = i^{th} calculated output, respectively.

An algorithm called back-propagation is then used to adjust the weights and biases until the mean-squared error is minimized. The network is trained by repeating this process several times. Once the ANN is trained, the prediction mode simply consists of propagating the data through the network, giving immediate results. In this study, the training data sets (inputs and target outputs) were normalized according to Eq. (8). Processing of the training data was performed so that the processed data were in the range of -1 to +1. The output of the network was trained to produce outputs in the range of -1 to +1, and we converted these outputs back into the same units used for the original targets.

$$\mathbf{pn} = 2\,(\,\mathbf{p} - \min \mathbf{p}\,) \,/\, (\,\max \mathbf{p} - \min \mathbf{p}\,) - 1\,,\ \mathbf{tn} = 2\,(\,\mathbf{t} - \min \mathbf{t}\,) \,/\, (\,\max \mathbf{t} - \min \mathbf{t}\,) - 1 \tag{8}$$

where **p** = a matrix of input vectors; **t** = a matrix of target output vectors; **pn** = a matrix of normalized input vectors; **tn** = a matrix of normalized target output vectors; **max p** = a vector containing the maximum values of the original input; **min p** = a vector containing the minimum value of the original input; **max t** = a vector containing the maximum value of the target output; and **min t** = a vector containing the minimum value of the target output. The normalized data were then used to train the neural network to obtain the final connection weights. The data from the output neuron have to be post-processed to convert it back into non-normalized units as shown in Eq. (9).

$$\mathbf{t} = 0.5\cdot(\mathbf{tn} + 1)\cdot(\max \mathbf{t} - \min \mathbf{t}) + \min \mathbf{t} \tag{9}$$

The normalized output is then obtained by propagating the normalized input vector through the network as follows:

$$\mathbf{tn} = \mathbf{W2} \times \log sig\,(\mathbf{W1} \times \mathbf{pn} + \mathbf{B1}) + \mathbf{B2} \tag{10}$$

where **W1** = a weight matrix representing connection weights between the input layer neurons and the hidden layer; **B1** = a weight matrix representing connection weights between the hidden layer neurons and the output neuron; **W2** = a bias vector for the hidden layer neurons; and **B2** = a bias for the output neuron. The log-sigmoid function log *sig* is defined in Eq. (3).

The output **t** is then obtained using Eq. (9) and (10):

$$\mathbf{t} = 0.5\cdot(\,\mathbf{W2} \times \log sig\,(\,\mathbf{W1} \times \mathbf{pn} + \mathbf{B1}\,) + \mathbf{B2} + 1\,)\cdot(\max \mathbf{t} - \min \mathbf{t}\,) + \min \mathbf{t} \tag{11}$$

where the transfer function in the hidden layer is the log-sigmoid activation function $a=1/(1 - e^{-n})$, and the transfer function in the output layer is the linear function a=n.

5.2 Example calculating pile resistance using ANN model(Park and Cho, 2010)

The proposed neural network model has seven nodes in the input layer, eight nodes in the hidden layer, and three nodes in the output layer (Fig. 8). In this study, the soil types near the tip and shaft of pile were classified as shown in Table 2. Weight matrix and bias vector used in the ANN model are summarized in Table 3.

Classification of soil	Value
Clay	1
Silt - Clay	2
Silt	3
Sand - Clay	4
Sand - Silt	5
Fine Sand	6
Sand	7
Sand - Gravel	8

Table 2. Classification according to soil types near the shaft and the tip of pile

W1	0.910	-1.070	-3.323	1.594	0.376	-1.196	-2.252		B1	1.189
	-0.785	0.189	-1.658	-0.106	0.133	1.922	-0.266			0.169
	2.505	0.625	-1.354	-0.422	-4.459	-0.615	1.252			-1.676
	2.871	2.612	-1.622	-0.413	-4.854	0.259	0.277			-0.712
	1.397	2.235	0.354	-0.972	0.194	-1.625	-2.250			-0.889
	0.227	4.302	-2.049	-0.753	0.391	1.649	-1.787			2.777
	-0.153	-0.506	-0.284	-3.868	-0.795	-1.434	1.386			-3.926
	0.058	-4.905	-0.370	0.882	-0.158	-0.712	-3.116			1.408
W2	1.510	-0.472	-3.371	3.190	0.110	-1.474	-0.079	-1.192	B2	0.598
	-0.417	-3.524	3.203	-2.910	-3.145	3.588	-0.768	1.880		-0.899
	1.230	-2.128	-1.662	1.631	-1.397	0.317	-0.441	-0.231		0.543

*. Matrix W1 (8×7), B1 (8×1), W2 (3×8), and B2 (3×1) is used in Eq. (9).

Table 3. Weight matrix and bias vector for ANN Model

The input vector **p** is selected obtained given as follows:

$$p = \begin{bmatrix} DIA \\ DEP \\ TPT \\ DE \\ ETS \\ STS \\ STT \end{bmatrix} = \begin{bmatrix} 0.508 \\ 9.6 \\ 0 \\ 36.3 \\ 31 \\ 3 \\ 3 \end{bmatrix}$$

The normalized input vector **pn** could be calculated using eq. (8) and **min p** and **max p** vectors are given in Table 4.

$$pn = \begin{bmatrix} 0.396 \\ -1.0 \\ -1.0 \\ -0.473 \\ 0.442 \\ 0 \\ -0.429 \end{bmatrix}$$

	Input parameters							Output values		
	DIA (m)	DEP (m)	TPT	DE (kN·m)	ETS (day)	STS	STT	Shaft (kN)	Tip (kN)	Total (kN)
Max.	0.273	0	9.6	1.3	0	1	1	154	158	360
Min	0.610	1	42.8	102.0	43	5	8	5401	2742	6126

*. For the type of pile tip(TPT), 0 represents a closed-ended tip and 1 represents an open-ended one.

Table 4. Maxiimum and minimum values of input parameters and output values

The normalized output could be calculated by propagating the normalized input vector as follows.

$$A \times pn + B = \begin{bmatrix} 0.910 & -1.07 & -3.323 & 1.594 & 0.376 & -1.196 & -2.252 \\ -0.785 & -0.189 & -1.658 & -0.106 & 0.133 & 1.922 & -0.266 \\ 2.505 & 0.625 & -1.354 & -0.422 & -4.459 & -0.615 & 1.252 \\ 2.871 & 2.612 & -1.622 & -0.413 & -4.854 & 0.259 & 0.277 \\ 1.397 & 2.235 & 0.354 & -0.972 & 0.194 & -1.625 & -2.250 \\ 0.227 & 4.302 & -2.049 & -0.753 & 0.391 & 1.649 & -1.787 \\ -0.153 & -0.506 & -0.284 & -3.868 & -0.795 & -1.434 & 1.386 \\ 0.058 & -4.905 & -0.370 & 0.882 & -0.158 & -0.712 & -3.116 \end{bmatrix} \times \begin{bmatrix} 0.396 \\ -1.0 \\ -1.0 \\ -0.473 \\ 0.442 \\ 0 \\ -0.429 \end{bmatrix} + \begin{bmatrix} 1.189 \\ 0.169 \\ -1.676 \\ -0.712 \\ -0.889 \\ 2.777 \\ -3.926 \\ 1.408 \end{bmatrix} = \begin{bmatrix} 6.321 \\ 1.550 \\ -2.262 \\ -2.633 \\ -1.415 \\ 1.908 \\ -2.314 \\ 7.554 \end{bmatrix}$$

$$\log sig(A \times pn + B) = \begin{bmatrix} 0.998 \\ 0.825 \\ 0.094 \\ 0.067 \\ 0.196 \\ 0.871 \\ 0.090 \\ 1.000 \end{bmatrix}$$

$$tn = C \times \log sig(A \times pn + B) + D = \begin{bmatrix} 1.510 & -0.472 & -3.371 & 3.190 & 0.110 & -1.474 & -0.079 & -1.192 \\ -0.417 & -3.524 & 3.203 & -2.910 & -3.145 & 3.588 & -0.768 & 1.880 \\ 1.230 & -2.128 & -1.662 & 1.631 & -1.397 & 0.317 & -0.441 & -0.231 \end{bmatrix} \times \begin{bmatrix} 0.998 \\ 0.825 \\ 0.094 \\ 0.067 \\ 0.196 \\ 0.871 \\ 0.090 \\ 1.000 \end{bmatrix} + \begin{bmatrix} 0.598 \\ -0.899 \\ 0.543 \end{bmatrix} = \begin{bmatrix} -0.848 \\ 0.205 \\ -0.299 \end{bmatrix}$$

The normalized output **tn** could be translated to real Pile resistance values using Eq. (9).
t=0.5·(tn+1)·(max t–min t)+min t=

$$0.5 \cdot \left(\begin{bmatrix} -0.848 \\ 0.205 \\ -0.299 \end{bmatrix} + \begin{bmatrix} 1 \\ 1 \\ 1 \end{bmatrix} \right) \times \left(\begin{bmatrix} 5401 \\ 2742 \\ 6126 \end{bmatrix} - \begin{bmatrix} 154 \\ 158 \\ 360 \end{bmatrix} \right) + \begin{bmatrix} 154 \\ 158 \\ 360 \end{bmatrix} = \begin{bmatrix} 543.7 \\ 1715.1 \\ 2258.8 \end{bmatrix}$$

Measured values for shaft, tip and total resistance of pile are 529.7, 1785.4 and 2315.2 kN and predicted values using ANN model are 543.7, 1715.1 and 2258.8 kN, respectively

6. Advances in ANN technology

6.1 Automatic design of ANN structure

6.1.1 Overviews

Neural network (NN), also called artificial neural system, is an information processing technique which is developed to simulate the functions of a human brain. Although ANN is an effective algorithm for solving complex engineering problems, only few approaches are available to design the network and most of them rely on iterative procedures. The design of network architecture mainly consists of the network layers, number of neurons of each layer, the transfer functions between layers, and the appropriate selections of a training algorithm. Especially, there are some kinds of input variables and values in which some of them may not carry important information to define the relationship between the input and output. These values can be ignored for the sake of solution convergence and efficiency, even sometimes at the cost of losing some input information. This provides smaller network models, which may be more desirable because of computational resource requirements and generalization capability. Therefore, the present study applies GA to select only effective inputs of network to decrease the time required to design smaller network and to reduce the computational complexity of problems. GA is used to find the best combination of only effective input parameters to provide a solution with less computational process.

To make an ANN more efficient, the computational complexity of ANN should be reduced. The computational complexity of network are generally affected by the number of neurons in each layer. And the network performs poorly as the model become larger and more complex. Although the design methodology of structure of ANN was described in the chapter three, the structure of ANN have to be designed by the trial and error approach, which runs repeatedly to find the network architecture. There is no general framework for the selection of the optimum ANN architecture and its parameters.

Genetic Algorithm (GA) is a very effective approach in solving problems from a wide range of applications, which is difficult to solve with traditional techniques. GA works by repeatedly modifying a population of artificial structures through the application of genetic operators (Goldberg, 1989). There have been a large number of applications of the GA for the NN especially for the evaluation of the weights and the architecture as a search engine to improve the convergence speed of network. Yu and Liang (2001) presented a hybrid approach involving ANN and GA to solve job-shop scheduling problem. The computational ability of the hybrid approach, ANN's computability and GA's searching efficiency, is strong enough to deal with complex scheduling problems.

Park & Kim (2011) proposed the hybrid design method based on ANN and GA. In their approach, a trained NN was employed to model the complex relationships among the parameters related to the geotechnical problems, whereas GA was applied to determine a set of optimal architecture of NN including input parameters, number of hidden layer and each layer's neuron, combination of transfer function between layers. The hybrid approach involving ANN and GA was developed and implemented. It consists of two unit: an NN prediction unit and a GA optimization unit. As shown in Fig. 10, their procedure can be summarized as follows:

1. First, an initial population, which contains a number of sets including information about the structure of ANN, is randomly generated. Then the individuals stored in it are fed into a NN-based prediction unit.
2. The predicted quality measures, which related to objective function, are used to indicate the fitness of the individuals. Evaluate the fitness of each individual according to the rank-based fitness.
3. Based on the fitness, select individuals and place them in the mating pool according to the rank-based fitness assignment and stochastic universal sampling.
4. Do crossover and mutation to the current population to create new individuals.
5. Insert a number of new random individuals replacing old individuals in the current population randomly. Make sure that the inserted individuals did not replace the best individual in the population.
6. Evaluate the fitness of each individual.
7. Steps 3–6 are called a generation, and they are repeated until a certain stop criterion is met. Typical stop criteria in a genetic algorithm run include a predefined maximum number of generations or an error smaller than a predefined value. In our genetic algorithm, maximum number of generations is used.

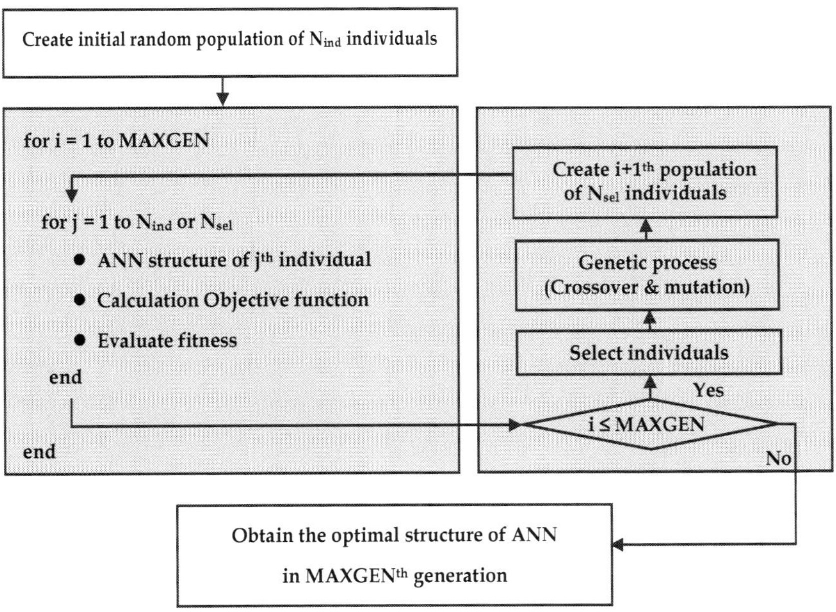

Fig. 10. Schematic flow chart of determination of optimal structure of ANN (Park & Kim, 2011)

6.1.2 Creation of initial population

The hybrid ANN-GA approach starts with the generation of an initial population, which contains a predefined number of chromosomes (strings). Each chromosome is composed of binary strings that include the design information of ANN's structure. For example, in case of design condition given in Table 5, a chromosome created is presented in Fig. 11.

parameters	values
Total number of input variables, N_{ini}	7
Maximum number of hidden layer, N_{HL}	2
Maximum node number in hidden layer, N_{HN} = 15	15
Transfer functions which can be used between layers	linear function, sigmoid function, tangent-sigmoid function

Table 5. An Example of design information to determine the structure of ANN

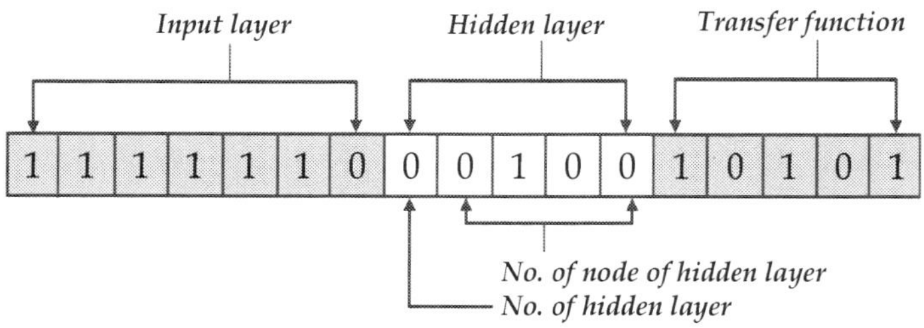

- Node number of input layer, $N_{in} = 6$
- Number of hidden layer, $N_{hl} = 1$(in case of 0, $N_{hl} = 1$ and in case of 1, $N_{hl} = 2$)
- Number of Node of hidden layer, $N_{hn} = 2^3\times0+2^2\times1+2^1\times0+2^0\times1=5$
- Information of transfer function : Determination of the combination of transfer functions using five binary strings

Fig. 11. Design information about the structure of ANN included in chromosome (Park & Kim, 2011)

This chromosome is composed of the eighteen binary strings. First seven binary strings in the chromosome include the information about the selection of input parameters. Six binary strings deal with the input variables used for the network architecture, with the 0 code indicating that a variable that cannot be used and with the 1 code indicating that a variable can be used. There are seven input variables, in this chromosome; seven binary strings present that the first six inputs should be kept, and the last two inputs removed. One Hidden layer was selected and five node was applied to the hidden layer. The information about transfer function is included in the other five binary strings. For example, a population of q individuals can be created as follows:

$$
\begin{array}{lcccccccccccccccc}
P^1 & = & 1 & 0 & 1 & 1 & 0 & 1 & 0 & 0 & 1 & 1 & 1 & 0 & 1 & 0 & 1 \\
P^2 & = & 0 & 1 & 0 & 0 & 1 & 1 & 1 & 0 & 1 & 0 & 1 & 1 & 0 & 0 & 1 \\
\vdots & = & & & & \vdots & & & & \vdots & & \vdots & & & & & \\
P^q & = & 1 & 1 & 1 & 0 & 1 & 0 & 0 & 1 & 0 & 0 & 1 & 1 & 0 & 1 & 0
\end{array}
\tag{11}
$$

6.1.3 Genetic operation

GA is an optimization procedure that operates on sets of design variables. Each set is called a string and it defines a potential. Each string consists of a series of characters representing the values of the discrete design variables for a particular solution. The fitness of each string is the measurement of the performance of the design variables as defined by the objective function.

In its simplest form, a genetic algorithm consists of three operations: (1) reproduction, (2) crossover, and (3) mutation (Goldberg, 1989). Each of these operations is described below.
The reproduction operation is the basic engine of Darwinian natural selection by the survival of the fittest. The reproduction process promotes the information stored in strings with good fitness values to survive into the next generation. The next generation of offspring strings is developed from the selected pairs of parent strings exposed to the application of explorative operators such as crossover and mutation.
Crossover is a procedure in which a selected parent string is broken into segments, some of which are exchanged with corresponding segments of another parent string. In this manner, the crossover operation creates variations in the solutions population by producing new solution strings that consist of parts taken from a selected parent string.

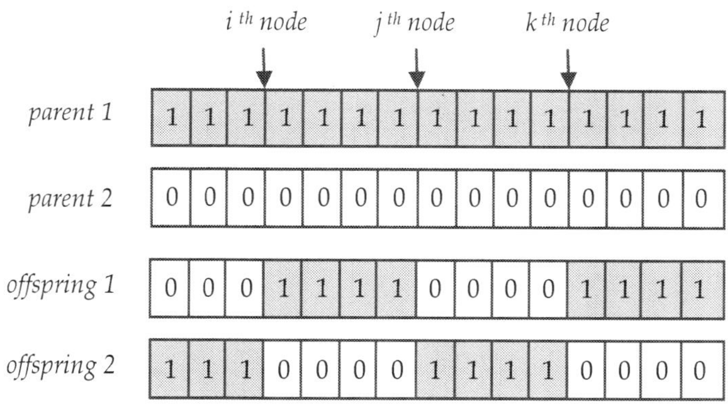

Fig. 12. Genetic process using crossover (Park & Kim, 2011)

The mutation operation is introduced as an insurance policy to enforce diversity in a population. It introduces random changes in the solution population by exploring the possibility of creating and passing features that are nonexistent in both parent strings to the offsprings. Without an operator of this type, some possibly important regions of the search space may never be explored.

6.1.4 Definition of objective function

The objective function for each individual is computed by Eq. 12. The objective function of the ith individual, ObjV(i) is composed of the error function, E_i, calculated as the difference between measured values and predicted values, and the penalty function, P_i , calculated on the basis of the complexity of structure of ANN. The complex structure of an ANN model increases the probability that the value of the error function will decrease, but generality is more likely to decrease due to overfitting. Therefore, the penalty function, P_i, is included in the objective function to control the decrease of generality.

$$ObjV(i) = E_i + P = \left(\sum_{k=1}^{N_{mea}} \frac{|T_k - t_k|}{T_{\max}} \right) / N_{mea} + \alpha \cdot \left(\frac{N_n^i / N_{\max} + CW^i / CW_{\max}}{2} \right) \qquad (12)$$

where $\alpha = 0.01$;N_{mea} = the total number of measured data; T_{max} = the maximum value among measured values; T_k = k^{th} measured value; and t_k = kth predicted value; N^i_n = total number of nodes used in the ith chromosome; N_{max}= the maximum number of nodes that can be applied to the structure of ANN in this study; CW^i= total number of connections used in the ith chromosome; and CW_{max}= the maximum number of connections that can be applied to the structure of ANN in this study.

6.2 Example analysis

The developed methodology was estimated through it's application to the geotechnical problem which ANN was used. The optimal ANN model obtained through opmization process based the developed GA-NN method was compared with the ANN model obtained in basis of researcher's experiance. Rahman et al. (2001) develoved an ANN model to predict the uplift capacity of suction caissons which are frequently used for the anchorage of large compliant offshore structures. The uplift capacity of the suction caissons is a critical issue in these applications. the developed neural network model has five nodes in the input layer, ten nodes in the hidden layer, and one nodes in the output layer. The five input parameters to the neural network model are the aspect ration of caisson (L/d), the undrained shear strength of the caly soil in which the caisson is installed (s_u), the relative depth of the lug to which the caisson forces is applied (D/L), the angle that the chain force makes with the horizontal (θ), and the loading rate defined with respect ot the soil permeability (T_k). the transfer functions applied to the hidden layer and output layer neurons are tan-sigmoid and log-sigmoid functions, respectively.

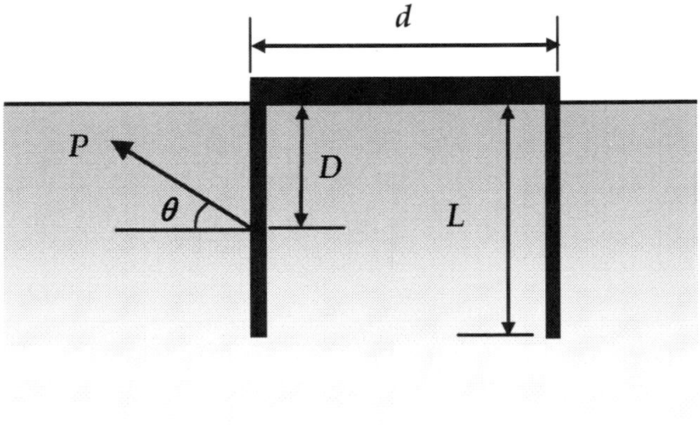

Fig. 13. Description for suction cassion

Design information for the application of GA-NN method is given in Table 6. Through the optimization process using the developed method, the optimal structure of ANN model is obtained in Table 7. Three input variables, D/L, T_k, and θ was removed through the optimization based GA-NN method. The optimized number of hidden node was decreased compared with Rahman et al. (2001)'s model. the transfer functions of the hidden layer and output layer were obtained as tan-sigmoid and linear functions, respectively.

Parameters		Values
GA paraemters	Number of initial population, N_{ind}	400
	Number of maximum generation, MAXGEN	40
	Number of seleced individuals for genetic process, N_{sel}	400×0.9 = 360
	Probability of mutation, P_{mut}	0.005
NN parameters	Maximum number of input node, IL_{max}	11
	Maximum number of hidden layer, HLmax	2
	Maximum node number in each hiddlayer, NH_{max}	16

Table 6. Design condition for application of the developed GA-NN method

Method	No of input node	No. of hidden node	Transfer function		R^2	
			I-H	H-O	Training	Testing
Traditional method	5	10	tansig	logsig	0.970	0.997
GA-NN	2	7	tansig	linear	0.984	0.982

*. I-H means transfer function connecting input layer to hidden layer, H-O means transfer function connecting hidden layer to output layer. Tansig and logsig means tangent-sigmoid and log-sigmoid function, respectively.

Table 7. Parameters of structure of ANN model obtained by each methods

In Fig. 14, the predictied uplift capacity of ANN model obtained by GA-NN method was compared with those of Rahman et al. (2001)'s ANN model. Even though three input variables were ommited in the prediction and also number of hidden node was decreased, it gave almost same correlation in traing and testing stage. the same the ANN model. It means that three input variable ommitted in input layer couldn't affect to output value, uplift capacity in the data sets given by Rahman et al. (2001).

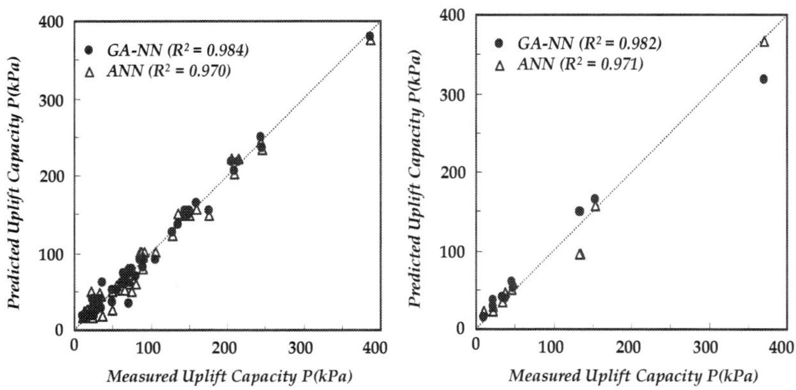

(a) training stage (b) testing stage

Fig. 14. Comparison of the uplift capacity predicted by each methods (Park & Kim, 2011)

In Fig. 15, the values of correlation coefficient, R^2 were obtained with variations of number of hidden node and transfer functions in the ANN model obtained by GA-NN method. The R^2 increased with the number of hidden nodes and then converged to a value after exceeding about seven node. In Eq. 11, Even though the value of error function doesn't decrease any more, the value of complexity fuction should be continually increased with increasing hidden node after seven node. It implies that if seven hidden node gives the minimum value of objective function in comparison of other hidden nodes.
Park & Kim (2011) suggested a hybrid NN/GA approach which is able to design optimal structure of ANN. The proposed approach combines the characteristics of GA and NN to overcome the shortcomings of NN structure design. The results of the proposed approach show that GA may enable the researchers to use NN more effectively and as an efficient tool for the solution of complex problems and reduces the risk of over designing the network architecture. The results of example showed that the performance of NN can be easily guaranteed with GA by selecting the optimal combination of input variables, number of hidden layer, node number of each hidden layer, and transfer functions between layers. GA reduces the complexity and over design of the network structure, as it helps to design smaller network architecture. Processing time of hybrid NN/GA for grouping parts can be decreased nearly to half of the preliminary NN-based approach. In summary, it is seen that GA enables to consider NN as an effective and efficient technique for the computationally complex type problems since it simultaneously reduces the computational complexity and enhances the prediction performance.

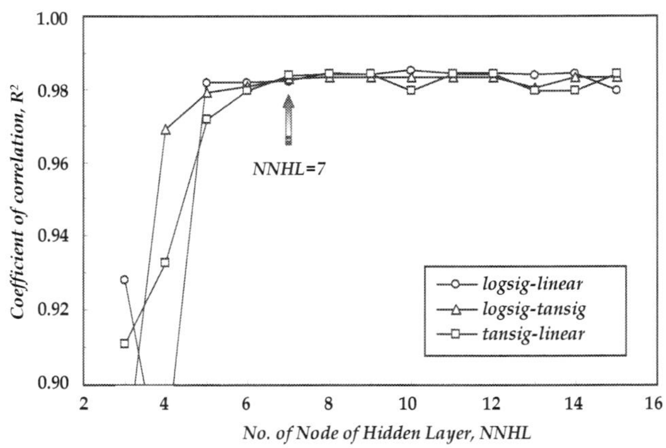

Fig. 15. The values of correlation coefficient with varing the design parameters of ANN model obtained by GA-NN method (Park & Kim, 2011)

6.2 Generalization of Neural Network using committee methodology

6.2.1 Generaliability of Neural Network

Over-training is the most serious problem in neural network training. The drawback is that such a network is quickly over-trained which means that the network error is driven to a small value for the training samples but will become large when new input is presented. This indicates that the network has memorized the training samples but is not able to generalize to give reasonable answers on unseen input parameter combinations. As a result, such a too well-trained model may not perform well on unseen data set due to its lack of generalization capability. In this section, we focus on one particular problem with learning which is typical for neural networks: their generalization capabilities. Generalization is the ability to train with one data set and then successfully classify independent test sets. Although continued training will increase the training set accuracy, the danger exists that test set accuracy decreases after a certain point.

Approaches considered overcoming the over-fitting problems are early stopping, Bayesian Regularization approach, and others (Hirschen & Schäfer, 2006). One approach is to use early stopping, where the algorithm which minimizes the error function prevent it from doing so by stopping the algorithm at some point. In early stopping the available data is divided into a training, a validation and a test subset. The training set is used for training the network and updating the network weights. The validation subset is not used for training, yet the performance function indicates how the trained network responds to these samples. The validation error will normally decrease during the initial phase of training, as does the training set error. When the network begins to overfit the data, the error on the validation set will typically begin to increase. The test set is not used during the training, but utilized to compare different networks. If the response on the test set is too weak one may decide to restart the network training with a different division of data sets. The second approach is the Bayesian Regularization(MacKay, 1992a). This approach minimizes the over-fitting problem by taking into account the goodness-of-fit as well as the network architecture. The following is the short description about the Bayesian regularization. Typically, training aims to reduce the sum of squared errors $F = E_D$. However, regularization adds an additional term; i.e. the objective function becomes $F=\alpha \cdot E_D+\beta \cdot E_W$, where E_W is the sum of squares of the network weights, and α and β are objective function parameters. The relative size of the objective function parameters dictates the emphasis for training. If $\alpha << \beta$, then the training algorithm will drive the errors smaller. If $\alpha << \beta$ training will emphasize weight size reduction at the expense of network errors, thus producing a smoother network response (Foresee & Hagan, 1997).

Single multilayer perceptrons (MLPs), consisting of an input layer, a hidden layer and an output layer, trained by a back-propagation algorithm (e.g. Levengerg-Marquardt, see Hagan, Demuth & Beale 1996, pp. 12-19), have been the conventional method of choice for most practical applications over the last decade. However, single MLP, when repeatedly trained on the same patterns, tends to reach different minima of the objective function each time and hence give a different set of neuron weights, because the solution is not unique for noisy data, as in most geotechnical problems. Therefore, a common approach is to train many nets, and then select the one that yields the best generalization performance. Nevertheless, selecting the single best neural network is likely to result in loss of information. While one network reproduces the main patterns, the others may provide the details lost by the first. The aim should be to exploit, rather than lose, the information contained in a set of imperfect generalizers. This is the motivation for the committee neural network approach, where a number of individually trained networks are combined to improve accuracy and increase robustness. Reddy & Buch (2003), Das et al. (2001), Gopinath & Reddy (2000), and Reddy et al. (1995) developed the concept of committee neural networks in which a large number of networks are trained. Based on initial testing with data obtained from subjects not used in training, a few networks are recruited into a committee. A final evaluation of the committee is conducted with data obtained from subjects not used in training or in initial testing.

6.2.2 Overviews of Committee Neural Network (CNN)

The committee technique for neural networks has been used for engineering problems (Reddy & Buch, 2003; Das et al., 2001; Gopinath & Reddy, 2000; Reddy et al., 1995). It was observed that the committee provided good estimates by means of averaging the results of individual networks in the committee, when the individual errors are uncorrelated. In the committee technique, several multiple neural networks (Fig. 16) are constructed and each individual neural network is trained independently with different initial synaptic weights using the training patterns as

$$TP_1 = \{(x_1, t_1)\},\ TP_2 = \{(x_2, t_2)\},\ \ldots,\ TP_N = \{(x_N, t_N)\} \tag{13}$$

where TP_i is a training patterns for the ith networks, and x_i and t_i are an input vector and target vector for the ith networks, respectively.

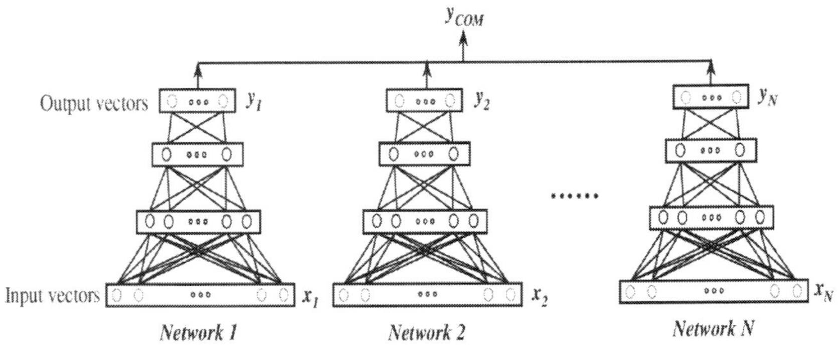

Fig. 16. Illustration of committee of networks (Kim & Park, 2011)

In Fig. 16, y_i is an output vector calculated from the ith networks. A mapping function $f_i(x_i)$ is determined from the ith networks based on the training patterns TP_i, and the error of this function can be calculated as

$$e_i(x_i) = d_i(x_i) - f_i(x_i) \tag{14}$$

where $d_i(x_i)$ is a desired function for the ith networks and is represented as $d_i(x_i) = E[t_i \mid x_i]$
The desired function for the committee of networks is determined as

$$d(x) = E[T \mid X] \tag{15}$$

where $X=\{(x_1, x_2, \ldots, x_N)\}$ and $T=\{(t_1, t_2, \ldots, t_N)\}$.
The committee mapping function can be represented as

$$f_{com}(X) = \sum_{i=1}^{N} \alpha_i f_i = \sum_{i=1}^{N} \alpha_i (d_i - e_i) = \sum_{i=1}^{N} \alpha_i d_i - \sum_{i=1}^{N} \alpha_i e_i = d - \sum_{i=1}^{N} \alpha_i e_i \tag{16}$$

where, α_i is a weighting factor for the ith networks, and $\Sigma\alpha_i=1$. Therefore, the committee output can be calculated as Eq. (17), where the outputs from different neural networks were averaged as

$$y_{com} = \sum_{i=1}^{N} \alpha_i y_i \tag{17}$$

The mean square error (MSE) of f_{com} can be calculated as

$$e\left[f_{COM}\right] = E\left[\left(d - f_{COM}\right)^2\right] = E\left[\left(\sum_{i=1}^{N} \alpha_i e_i\right)^2\right] = E\left[\sum_{i,j}^{N} \alpha_i \alpha_j e_i e_j\right] = \sum_{i,j}^{N} \alpha_i \alpha_j C_{ij} \tag{18}$$

where C_{ij} is a correlation matrix as $C_{ij}=E[e_i e_j]$.
The local minima in determining the synaptic weights of a single MLP and the non-uniqueness of the solution due to the noise and a limited number of measurements may be resolved by employing the committee technique, which is a statistical approach averaging the outputs in the functional space.

6.2.3 Case study for CNN

Kim and Park (2010) examined the feasibility of committee neural network theory for the improvement of accuracy and consistency of the neural network model on the estimation of preconsolidation pressure from the field piezocone measurements. The validity of the committee technique was also examined through the comparison with a single NN model, an empirical and a theoretical model.
The case records from Chen (1994) are evaluated using neural network. A total of 119 case records are used for the training phase and 28 (randomly selected) for the testing phase. The proposed neural network model has four nodes in the input layer, seven nodes in the hidden layer, and one node in the output layer. In input layer, the total and effective overburden pressures σ_{vo}, σ'_{vo}, the cone tip resistance q_T, and pore pressure measurement behind the cone tip u_2 were selected as input variables.
In their study, twenty single neural networks were trained from the different initial weights and biases but with the same training patterns. Fig. 17(a) and (b) show the coefficients of determination between measured and predicted preconsolidation pressure using the piezocone test result from each of the 20 single NNs for the training data and testing data, respectively. As shown in Fig. 17(a), coefficients of determination for training data from each NN model show very similar accuracy i.e., coefficients of determination R2 are almost around 0.93. However, the prediction results for testing data from each NN model aren't as accurate as those of the training data. They significantly fluctuates i.e., they range from 0.84 to 0.94, even though they have the same structural characteristics. Therefore, if a single NN is to be used, the best model must be selected which gives the relatively highest coefficient of determination among various models, e.g., second NN among 20 neural networks, which gives the coefficients of determination of 0.93 and 0.94 in the training and testing phase, respectively. However, in reality, it is quite difficult to choose the best model among a number of candidate NNs.
Several committees of 20 NNs were constructed by changing the accumulated number n of NN in the committee to the equal weighting factor ($\alpha_i=1/n$). Prediction results of each committee are plotted in Fig. 18(a) and 18 (b) with respect to the increase of the accumulated number of NN for training data and testing data, respectively. As can be seen in Fig. 18 (a), the coefficients of determination of the committee neural network still increase with an increase of the number of accumulated NN in the committee for training data. Furthermore,

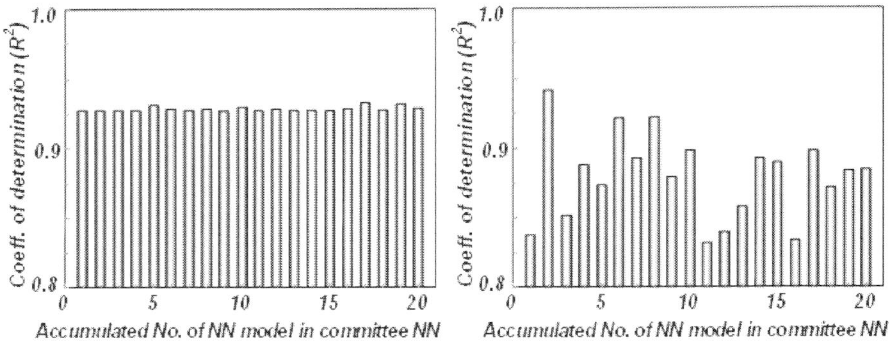

(a) training stage (b) testing stage

Fig. 17. Prediction performance of 20 MLPs which are optimized with different initial weights and biases by trial-and-error method (Kim & Park, 2010)

as shown in Fig. 18 (b) for testing data, even though the R^2 value of each single NN model shows severe variation, the R^2 values of CNNs don't show such a dramatic variation after accumulating two NN models in the committee. From these figures, it can be concluded that any single NN model still cannot avoid the variation on the prediction due to initial dependency of weight and bias. However, such variation can be eliminated by connecting those NNs with an appropriate weighting factor α_i as a committee neural network. Besides, by introducing Committee methodology, the conventional trial-and-error method for the optimization of the structure of a neural network can be used without any consideration of initial weight dependency and structural optimization. The authors observed that a committee neural network system is able to provide improved performance compared with a single optimal neural network. The committee technique has been found to be a very effective technique to improve the accuracy of the estimation of the preconsolidation pressure σ'_p.

The performance of NN has suffered because of its variation on the prediction of target value due to the localization of weight and bias during the optimization process on the structure. To overcome such problems of the single NN, in this study, structural optimization was carefully carried out by the trial-and-error method. Nevertheless, a single MLP, although it has successfully optimized structures, still cannot avoid the large variation on the prediction of preconsolidation pressure due to its initial weight dependency. Therefore, CNN is introduced to overcome the initial weight dependency of the single neural network model. Various committees of the single MLP were tested. It was found that if 8 single NNs, which have the same structure but have been trained with a different initial weight and bias, are accumulated in the committee with the same weighting factor α_i, any variation on the prediction of the preconsolidation pressure from the piezocone test result can be simply and successfully eliminated. A comparison of the prediction results of CNN with the theoretical and empirical method shows that CNN is significantly more precise and consistent than conventional statistical and theoretical methods.

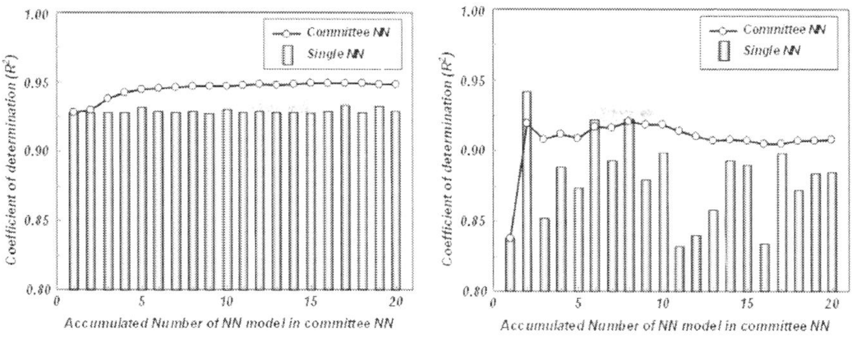

(a) training stage (b) testing stage

Fig. 18. Improvement of estimation accuracy by accumulating the optimized single NNs in the committee (Kim & Park, 2010)

7. Conclusions

Artificial neural networks (ANNs) have been applied to various problem in geotechnical engineering. This include dams, earth retaining structures, environmental geotechnics, ground anchors, liquefaction, pile foundations, shallow foundations, slope stability, soil properties and behavior, site characterization, tunnels, underground openings, and other areas. In mathematical modeling to solve problem of above the geotechnical engineering area, the lack of understanding for complicated physical behavior is easily supplemented by either over-simplifying the problem or incorporating several assumptions into the model. Consequently, many mathematical models are apt to fail to simulate the complex behavior of geotechnical problems. In contrast, ANN methodology is based on the data alone in which the model can be trained on data sets to find the relationship between inputs and out values. There is no need to simplify the problem nor incorporate an any assumption. As geotechnical engineering exhibits extreme variability, ANNs are particularly amenable to modelling the complex behaviour of these materials and have generally demonstrated superior predictive performance when compared with traditional methods.

In science and engineering problems, there is still no clear procedure to design NN architecture. Therefore, this often causes over design or inefficient network structures especially in the case of complex problems. Although considerable research has been accounted in NN and GA applications, their use in optimal NN design is quite recent. Nevertheless, it is seen that GA enables to consider NN as an effective and efficient technique for the computationally complex type problems since it reduces the computational complexity and enhances the search performance.

In training of ANN model, over-fitting problem or poor generalization capability happens frequently when a neural network over learns during the training period. As a result, such a too well-trained model may not perform well on unseen data set due to its lack of generalization capability. Several approaches have been suggested in literature to overcome this problem. The author introduced the feasibility of committee neural network theory for the improvement of accuracy and consistency of the neural network model on the geotechnical probleme.

8. References

Abu-Kiefa, M. A. (1998). General regression neural networks for driven piles in cohesionless soils. *J. Geotech. Geoenv. Engrg., ASCE,* Vol.123, No.12, (December 1998), pp. 1177-1185, ISSN 1090-0241

Agrawal, G.; Weeraratne, S. & Khilnani, K. (1994). Estimating clay liner and cover permeability using computational neural networks, *Proc., First Congress on Computing in Civil Engrg.*, pp. 20-22, Washington, USA.

Agrawal, G.; Chameau, J.A. & Bourdeau, P.L. (1997). Assessing the liquefaction susceptibility at a site based on information from penetration testing. In *Artificial neural networks for civil engineers: fundamentals and applications,* N. Kartam, I. Flood, J.H. Garrett, (Ed.), 185-214, ASCE, ISBN 0784402256, New York, USA

Ali, H.E. & Najjar, Y.M. (1998). Neuronet-based approach for assessing liquefaction potential of soils, *Transportation Research Record,* No. 1633, (January 1998), pp. 3-8, ISSN 0361-1981.

Baik, K. (2002). Optimum Driving Method for Steel Pipe Piles in Sands, *J. of Civil Engineering,* Vol.22, No.1-C, pp. 45-55.

Bea, R.G.; Jin, Z.; Valle, C. & Ramos, R. (1999). "Evaluation of reliability of platform pile foundations." *J. Geotech. Geoenviron. Eng., ASCE,* Vol.125, No.8, (August 1999), pp. 696-704, ISSN 1090-0241

Bounds, D.G.; Lloyd, PJ.; Mathew, B.; and Waddell, G. (1988). A multilayer perceptron network for the diagnosis of low back pain, *Proc. of 2nd IEEE Annual Int'l Conf. on Neural Networks*, pp. 481-489, San Diego, NJ, USA, June 21-24, 1988,

Broms, B.B. (1964). Lateral resistance of piles in cohesive soils, *J. of Soil Mech. Found. Eng., ASCE,* Vol.90, No.2, (March 1964), pp. 27-63, ISSN 0038-0741

Chan, W.T.; Chow, Y.K. & Liu, L.F. (1995). Neural network: an alternative to pile driving formulas. *Comput Geotech,* Vol.17, No.2, pp. 135-156, ISSN 0266-352X

Chester, D.L. (1990). Why two hidden layers are better than one, *Proc. of 4th IEEE Annual Int'l Conf. on Neural Networks*, pp. 1.265-1.268, Washington, DC, NJ, USA, Jan. 15-19.

Cho, S.E. (2009). Probabilistic stability analyses of slopes using the ANN-based response surface, *Computers and Geotechnics*, Vol.36, pp. 787-797, ISSN 0266-352X

Chung, Y. & Kusiak, A. (1994). Grouping parts with a neural network, *Journal of Manufacturing Systems*, Vol.13, No.4, pp. 262-75

Cybenko, G. (1989). Approximation by superpositions of a sigmoidal function, *Mathematics of Control Signals and Systems*, Vol.2, No.4, pp. 303-314.

Das, A.; Reddy, N. P. & Narayanan, J. (2001). Hybrid Fuzzy Logic Committee Neural Networks for Recognition of Swallow Acceleration Signals, *Computer Methods and Programs in Biomedicine*, Vol.64, pp. 87-99.

Das, S.K. & Basudhar, P.K. (2006). Undrained lateral load capacity of piles in clay using artificial neural network, *Computers and Geotechnics*, Vol.33, pp. 454-459.

Ellis G.W.; Yao, C; Zha,o R. & Penumadu, D. (1995). Stress-strain modeling of sands using artificial neural networks, *J Geotech Eng*, Vol.121, No.5, pp. 429-435, ISSN 1089-3032.

Fahlman, S.E. & Lebiere, C. (1990). The cascade correlation learning architecture, In: *Advances in Neural Information Processing Systems*, H, D.S. Tounetzky, (Ed.), Morgan Kaufmann , San Mateo, CA, USA

Ferentinou, M.D. & Sakellariou, M.G. (2007). Computational intelligence tools for the prediction of slope performance, *Computers and Geotechnics*, Vol.34, No.5, pp. 362-384, ISSN 0266-352X

Foresee, F.D. & Hagan, M.T. (1997). Gauss-Newton approximation to Bayesian learning, *Proceedings of the International Joint Conference on Neural Networks,* Vol.3, pp. 1930–1935.

Ghaboussi J. & Sidarta, D.E. (1998). New nested adaptive neural networks (NANN) for constitutive modeling, *Computers and Geotechnics,* Vol.22, No.1, pp. 29–52, ISSN 0266-352X

Ghaboussi J.; Pecknold, D.A.; Zhang, M. & Haj-Ali, R.M. (1998). Autoprogressive training of neural network constitutive models, *International Journal for Numerical Methods in Engineering,* Vol. 42, pp. 105–126, ISSN 0029-5981

Goh, A.T.C. (1996). Pile driving records reanalyzed using neural networks, *J Geotech Engrg,* ASCE, Vol.122, No.6, pp. 492–495, ISSN 1938-6362

Goh, A.T.C. (2002). Probabilistic neural network for evaluating seismic liquefaction potential, Canadian Geotechnical Journal, Vol.39, pp. 219-232, ISSN 0008-3674.

Goh,A.T.C. (1995). Modeling soil correlations using neural networks. *J. Comput. Civil Engrg.,* ASCE, Vol.9, No.4, pp. 275–278, ISSN 1598-2351

Goh, A.T.C.; Kulhawy, F.H. & Chua, C.G. (2005). Bayesian neural network analysis of undrained side resistance of drilled shafts, *Journal of Geotechnical and Geoenvironmental Engineering,* Vol.131, No.1, pp. 84-93.

Goldberg, D.E. (1989). Genetic Algorithms in Search, Optimisation and Machine Learning, Addison-Wesley, USA.

Gopinath, P. & Reddy, N.P. (2000). Toward Intelligent Web Monitoring Performance of Single Vs Committee Neural Networks, *2000 IEEE EMBS Conference on Information Technology Application in Biomedicine Proceedings,* pp. 179-182.

Gribb, M. M. & Gribb, G. W. (1994). Use of neural networks for hydraulic conductivity determination in unsaturated soil." *Proc., 2nd Int. Conf. Ground Water Ecology,* , Water Resources Assoc., pp. 155-163

GRL Associates, Inc. (1996). CAPWAP User Manual.

Hagan, M.T.; Demuth, B.H. & Beale, M. (1996). Neural Network Design, PWS Pub., USA

Hansen, B. (1961). The ultimate resistance of rigid piles against transversal force, Copenhagen: Danish Geotechnical Institute; 1961. Bulletin No. 12. p. 5–9.

Hashash, Y.M.; Jung, S. & Ghaboussi, J. (2004). Numerical implementation of a neural network based material model in finite element analysis, *International Journal for Numerical Methods in Engineering,* Vol.59, pp. 989–1005

Hecht-Nelson, R. (1987). Kolmogorov's mapping neural network existence theorem, *Proc. of 1st IEEE Annual Int'l Conf. on Neural Networks,* pp. III.11-111.14, San Diego, NJ, USA, June 21-24

Jaksa, M.B. (1995). The influence of spatial variability on the geotechncial design properties of a stiff, overconsolidated clay, PhD thesis, The University of Adelaide, Adelaide.

Javadi, A.A.; Rezania, M. & Mousavi Nezhad, M. (2006). Evaluation of liquefaction induced lateral displacements using genetic programming, *Computers and Geotechnics,* Vol. 33, 222-233, ISSN 0266-352X

Juang, C.H. & Chen, C.J. (1999). CPT-based liquefaction evaluation using artificial neural networks, Computer-Aided Civil and Infrastructure Engineering, 14(3), 221-229.

Hirschen, K. & Sch[illegible]fer, M. (2006) Bayesian regularization neural networks for optimizing fluid flow processes, *Comput. Methods Appl. Mech. Engrg.* Vol.195, pp. 481–500

Kim, Y.S. & Park, H.I. (2011). Committee Neural Network for Estimating Preconsolidation Pressure from Piezocone Test Result, *Engineering Computations,* Submitted

Kim, Y.S. & Kim, B.K. (2006). Use of artificial neural networks in the prediction of liquefaction resistance of sands, *Journal of Geotechnical and Geoenvironmental Engineering*, Vol.132, No.11, pp. 1502-1504.

Kusiak, A. & Lee, H. (1996). Neural computing based design of components for cellular manufacturing, *International Journal of Production Research*, Vol.34, No.7, pp. 1777-1790

Lawrence, J. (1994). *Introduction to Neural Networks: Design, Theory, and Applications*, 6th ed. Nevada City, CA: California Scientific Software.

Lawrence, J. & Fredrickson, J. (1998). *BrainMaker User's Guide and Reference Manual*, 7th Ed., Nevada City, CA: California Scientific Software.

Lee, C. & Sterling, R. (1992). Identifying probable failure modes for underground openings using a neural network, *Int. Journal of Rock Mechanics and Mining Science & Geomechanics Abstracts*, Vol.29, No. 1, pp. 49-67

Lee, I.M. & Lee, J.H. (1996). Prediction of pile bearing capacity using artificial neural networks, *Comput Geotech*, Vo.18, No.3, pp. 189–200, ISSN 0266-352X

MacKay, D.J.C. (1992a). Bayesian Interpolation, *Neural Computation*, Vol.4, No.3, pp. 415-447

MacKay DJC. (1992b). A practical bayesian framework for backpropagation networks. *Neural Computation*, Vol.4, No.3, pp. 448–472.

Marchandani, G. & Cao, W. (1989). On hidden nodes for neural nets, *IEEE Trans. on Circuits and Systems*, Vol.36, No.5, pp. 661-664

Meyerhof, G.G. (1976). Bearing capacity and settlement of pile foundations, *J Geotech Engrg*, ASCE, Vol.102, No.3, pp. 196–228.

Millar, D.L. & Calderbank, P.A. (1995). On the investigation of a multi-layer feedforward neural network model of rock deformability behavior, *International congress on rock mechanics*, pp. 933–938, Tokyo, Japan.

Moon, H.K.; Na, S.M. & Lee, C.W. (1995). Artificial neural-network integrated with expert-system for preliminary design of tunnels and slopes, *Proc. 8th Int. Congress on Rock Mechanics*, pp. 901-905, Balkema.

Najjar, Y.M.; Basheer, I.A. & McReynolds, R. (1996). Neural modeling of Kansan soil swelling, *Transportation Research Record No. 1526*, pp. 14-19

Najjar, Y.M. & Basheer, I.A. (1996). Utilizing computational neural networks for evaluating the permeability of compacted clay liners, *Geotechnical and Geological Engineering*, Vol.14, pp. 193-221.

Najjar, Y.M. & Ali, H.E. (1998). CPT-based liquefaction potential assessment: A neuronet approach, *Geotechnical Special Publication*, ASCE, Vol.1, pp. 542-553.

Najjar, Y.M. & Ali, H.E. (1999). On the use of neuronets for simulating the stress-strain behavior of soils, *7th International symposium on numerical models in geomechanics*, pp. 657-662, Austria

Nawari N.O.; Liang, R. & Nusairat, J. (1999). Artificial intelligence techniques for the design and analysis of deep foundations, *Electron. J. Geotech. Eng.*, http://geotech.civeng.okstate.edu/ejge/ppr9909/ index.html.

Neaupane, K.M. & Achet, S.H. (2004). Use of backpropagation neural network for landslide monitoring: a case study in the higher Himalaya, *Engineering Geology*, Vol.74, pp. 213- 226

Ni, S.H.; Lu, P.C. & Juang, C.H. (1995). A fuzzy neural network approach to evaluation of slope failure potential, *Journal of Microcomputers in Civil Engineering*, Vol.11, pp. 59- 66.

Ozer, M.; Isik, N.S. & Orhan, M. (2008). Statistical and neural network assessment of the compression index of clay-bearing soils, *Bull Eng Geol Environ*, Vol.67, pp. 537–545

ϵrzt★rk, N. (2003). Use of genetic algorithm to design optimal neural network structure, *Engineering Computations*, Vol.20, No.8, pp. 979-997

Park, H.I. (2010). Development of neural network model to estimate the permeability coefficient of soils, *Marine Geosources and Geotechnology*, Accepted

Park, H.I.; Keon, G.C. & Lee, S.R. (2009). Prediction of Resilient Modulus of Granular Subgrade Soils and Subbase Materials Based on Artificial Neural Network, *Road Materials and Pavement Design*, Vol.10, No. 3, pp. 647- 665.

Park, H.I. & Cho, C.H. (2010). Neural Network Model for Predicting the Resistance of Driven Piles *Marine Geosources and Geotechnology*, In Press

Park, H.I. & Lee, S.R. (2010). Evaluation of the compression index of soils using an artificial neural network *Computers and Geotechnics*, Submitted

Park, H.I. & Kim, Y.T. (2010). Prediction of Strength of Reinforced Lightweight Soil Using an Artificial Neural Network, Engineering Computation, In press

Park, H.I. & Kim, Y.S. (2011). Evaluation of Geotechnical Parameters Based on Design of Optimal Neural Network Structure, *Computers and Geotechnics*, Submitted

Penumadu, D. & Zhao, R. (1999). Triaxial compression behavior of sand and gravel using artificial neural networks (ANN), *Comput Geotech*, Vol.24, pp. 207–30, ISSN 0266-352X

Penumadu, D.; Jin-Nan, L.; Chameau, J.L.; Arumugam, S. (1994). Rate dependent behavior of clays using neural networks, *Proceedings of the 13th conference of international society of soil mechanics and foundation engineering*, pp. 1445–1448, New Delhi

Poulos, H.G. & Davis, E.H. (1999). *Pile foundation analysis and design*, Wiley, New York

Provenzano, P.; Ferlisi, S. & Musso, A. (2004). Interpretation of a model footing response through an adaptive neural fuzzy inference system, *Computers and Geotechnics*, Vol.31, pp. 251-266

Rahman, M. S.; Wang, J.; Deng, W. & Carter, J. P. (2001). A Neural Network Model for the Uplift Capacity of Suction Caissions, *Computers and Geotechnics*, Vol.39, pp. 337-356.

Reddy, N. P.; Prabhu, D.; Palreddy, S.; Gupta, V.; Suryanarayanan, S., & Canilang, E.P. (1995), Redundant Neural Networks for Medical Diagnosis Diagnosis of Dysphagia, *Intelligent Systems through Artificial Neural Networks*, Vol.5, pp. 699-704.

Reddy, N.P. & Buch, O. (2003). Committee Neural Networks for Speaker Verification, *Computer Methods and Programs in Biomedicine*, Vol.72, pp. 109-115.

Romero, S. & Pamukcu, S. (1996). Characterization of granular meterial by low strain dynamic excitation and ANN, *Geotechnical Special Publication*, ASTM-ASCE, Vol.58, No.2, pp. 1134-1148.

Rumelhart, D.E.; Hinton, G. & Williams, R. (1986). Learning representation by back- 462 propagation errors. *Nature*, Vol.32, No.9, pp. 533–536.

Sakellariou, M.G. & Ferentinou, M.D. (2005). A study of slope stability prediction using neural networks, *Geotechnical and Geological Engineering* Vol.23, pp. 419–445

Shahin, M.A.; Jaksa, M.B. & Maier, H.R. (2005). Stochastic simulation of settlement prediction of shallow foundations based on a deterministic artificial neural network model, Proc. *Int. Congress on Modelling and Simulation*, MODSIM 2005, pp. 73-78, Melbourne (Australia)

Shi, J.J. (2000). Reducing prediciton error by transforming input data for neural networks, *Journal of Computing in Civil Engineering*, Vol.14, No.2, pp. 109-116.

Shin, H.S. & Pande, G.N. (2000). On self-learning finite element codes based on monitored response of structures, *Computers and Geotechnics*, Vol.27, pp. 161–178, ISSN 0266-352X

Sidarta, D.E. & Ghaboussi, J. (1998). Constitutive modeling of geomaterials from non-uniform material tests, *Computers and Geotechnics*, Vol.22, No.1, pp. 53–71, ISSN 0266-352X

Sivakugan, N.; Eckersley, J.D. & Li, H. (1998). Settlement predictions using neural networks, *Australian Civil Engineering Transactions*, CE40, pp. 49-52.

Swingler, K. (1996). *Applying Neural Networks: A Practical Guide*. San Francisco: Morgan Kaufmann Publishers.

Teh, C.I.; Wong, K.S.; Goh, A.T.C. & Jaritngam, S. (1997). Prediction of pile capacity using neural networks, *J Comput Civil Eng.*, ASCE, Vol.11, No.2, pp. 129–38

Ural, D.N. & Saka, H. (1998). Liquefaction assessment by neural networks, *Electronic Journal of Geotechnical Engineering*, http://geotech.civen.okstate.edu/ejge/ppr9803/index.html.

Wang, H.B.; Xu, W.Y. & Xu, R.C. (2005) Slope stability evaluation using Back Propagation Neural Networks, *Engineering Geology*, Vol.80, pp. 302– 315, ISSN 0013-7952

Yoo, C. & Kim, J.-M. (2007). Tunneling performance prediction using an integrated GIS and neural network, *Computers and Geotechnics*, Vol.34, pp. 19-30, ISSN 0266-352X

Yu, H. & Liang, W. (2001). Neural network and genetic algorithm based hybrid approach to expanded job-shop scheduling, *Computers and Industrial Engineering*, Vol. 39, pp. 337-356.

Zhao, H.-B. (2007). Slope reliability analysis using a support vector machine, *Computers and Geotechnics*, in press.

Zhu, J.H.; Zaman, M.M. & Anderson, A.A. (1998). Modeling of shearingbehavior of residual soil with recurrent neural network, *Int J Numer Anal Meth Geomech*, Vol.22, pp. 671–87

16

Confidence Intervals for Neural Networks and Applications to Modeling Engineering Materials

Shouling He[1] and Jiang Li[2]
[1]*Department of Engineering Technology, University of Pittsburgh at Johnstown PA 15904,*
[2]*Department of Civil Engineering, Morgan State University, Baltimore MD 21251, USA*

1. Introduction

Feedforward neural networks have been theoretically proved to be able to approximate a nonlinear function to any degree of accuracy as long as enough nodes exist in the hidden layer(s) (Hornik et. al. 1989). However, when feedforward neural networks are applied to modeling physical systems in the real world, people care more about their prediction capabilities than accurate modeling abilities. If a neural network is trained with noisy data measured from an experiment, what is the predictive performance of the neural network when unseen input data is fed into it? In this chapter, the confidence interval and prediction interval of a neural network model will be discussed. In particular, how the nonlinear structure of a feedforward neural network, impacts the confidence interval will be analyzed. Then, as an application, the measure of confidence to estimate nonlinear elastic behavior of reinforced soil is demonstrated.

This chapter starts with a description of the structure of feedforward neural networks and basic learning algorithms. Then, nonlinear regression and its implementation within the nonlinear structure like a feedforward neural network will be discussed. The presentation will show confidence intervals and prediction intervals as well as applying them to a one-hidden-layer feedforward neural network with one, two or more hidden node(s). Next, it is proceeded to apply the concepts of confidence intervals to solving a practical problem, prediction of the constitutive parameters of reinforced soil that is considered as composite material mixed with soil, geofiber and lime powder. Prediction intervals for the practical case is examined so that more quality information on the performance of reinforced soil for better decision-making and continuous improvement of construction material designs can be provided. Finally, the neural network-based parameter sensitivities will be analyzed.

In order to clearly present the algorithms discussed in this chapter, some notations are declared as follows: matrices and vectors are written in boldface letters, and scalars in italics. Vectors are defined in column vectors. The superscript T of a matrix (or vector) denotes the transpose of the matrix (or vector).

2. Neural network architecture and learning algorithms

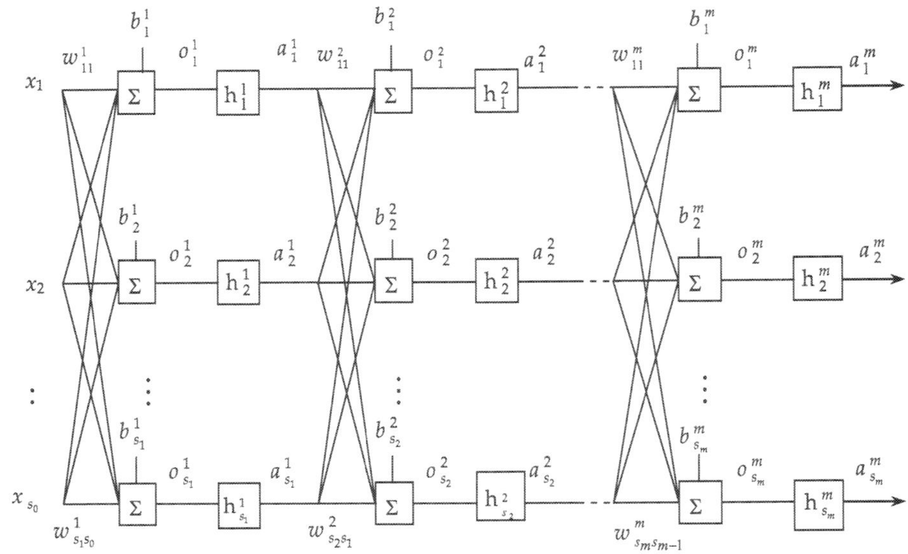

Fig. 1.1a. An m-layer feedforward neural network

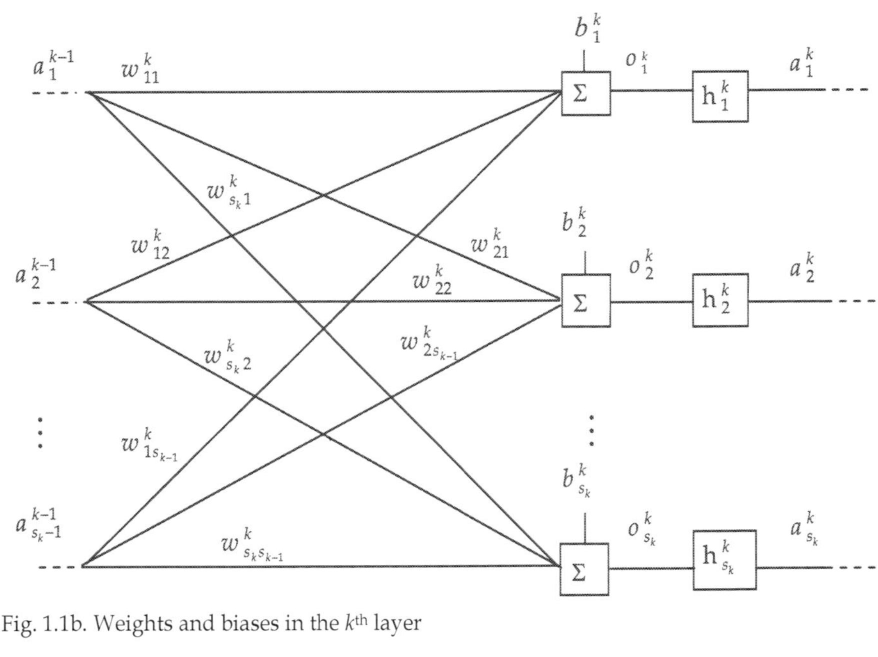

Fig. 1.1b. Weights and biases in the kth layer

2.1 Architecture of feedforward neural networks

A feedforward neural network is a massive net consisting of a number of similar computing units, which are called nodes. The morphology of a neural network can change depending on the way the nodes are interconnected and the operations performed at each node. As shown in Figs. 1.1a and 1.1b, in an m-layer feedforward neural network, the nodes are arranged in layers. All nodes in a layer are fully connected to the nodes in adjacent layers by weights, adjustable parameters to represent the strength of connections. The summation of weighted inputs to a node will be mapped by a nonlinear activation function, $h[.]$. There are no connections between nodes in the same layer. Data information is passed through the network in such a manner that the outputs of the nodes in the first layer become the inputs of the nodes in the second layer and so on.

Mathematically, an m-layer feedforward neural network can be expressed as follows,

$$\mathbf{o}^k = \mathbf{w}^k \mathbf{a}^{k-1} + \mathbf{b}^k \quad \text{and} \quad \mathbf{a}^k = \mathbf{h}^k(\mathbf{o}^k) \qquad (k = 1, \cdots, m) \tag{1}$$

where $\mathbf{a}^0 = \mathbf{x} = [x_1 \ \cdots \ x_{s_0}]^{\mathrm{T}}$ is the input vector; $\mathbf{o}^k = [o_1^k \ \cdots \ o_{s_k}^k]^{\mathrm{T}}$, $\mathbf{h}^k = [h_1^k \ \cdots \ h_{s_k}^k]^{\mathrm{T}}$ and $\mathbf{a}^k = [a_1^k \ \cdots \ a_{s_k}^k]^{\mathrm{T}}$ are the linear output vector of the summation, the activation function vector and the output vector in the kth layer, respectively; s_k is the number of nodes in the kth layer; $\mathbf{w}^k$ and $\mathbf{b}^k$ represent the weight matrix and the bias vector in the kth layer (see Fig. 1.1b), which can be respectively expressed by

$$\mathbf{w}^k = \begin{bmatrix} w_{11}^k & \cdots & w_{1s_{k-1}}^k \\ \vdots & \ddots & \vdots \\ w_{s_k 1}^k & \cdots & w_{s_k s_{k-1}}^k \end{bmatrix} \quad \text{and} \quad \mathbf{b}^k = \begin{bmatrix} b_1^k \\ \vdots \\ b_{s_k}^k \end{bmatrix}, \tag{2}$$

in which the jth row of $\mathbf{w}^k$ is defined by $\mathbf{w}_j^k = [w_{j1}^k \ w_{j2}^k \ \cdots \ w_{js_{k-1}}^k]$ (j=1, ..., s_k).

2.2 Learning algorithms

2.2.1 Standard backpropagation

Given a set of s_0-dimensional input vector, $\mathbf{x}_i$, $(i = 1,...,Q)$, and the corresponding s_m-dimensional output vector, $\mathbf{t}_{i}, (i= 1,...,Q)$, the weights and biases of a feedforward neural network are adjusted such that the following performance index is minimum,

$$E = \sum_{i=1}^{Q} E_i \quad \text{with} \quad E_i = \frac{1}{2}(\mathbf{t}_i - \mathbf{a}_i^m)^{\mathrm{T}}(\mathbf{t}_i - \mathbf{a}_i^m) \tag{3}$$

where $\mathbf{a}_i^m = \mathbf{a}_i^m(\mathbf{x}_i)$ is the output of the feedforward neural network with input $\mathbf{x}_i$ and Q is the number of samples. Since the structure of a feedforward neural network is the same for all samples, for simplicity, the subscript i will be dropped in the derivation of the backpropagation algorithm.

For a single input/output sample, Equation (3) is denoted by E_i. According to the gradient descent algorithm, the weight matrix and bias vector of the kth layer will be updated according to the following equations so that E_i can be minimized,

$$\Delta\mathbf{w}^k = -\eta(\partial E_i / \partial \mathbf{w}^k), \qquad \Delta\mathbf{b}^k = -\eta(\partial E_i / \partial \mathbf{b}^k)^{\mathrm{T}} \tag{4}$$

where η is the learning rate ($\eta > 0$).

By defining the gradient of E_i with respect to the linear output vector $\mathbf{o}^k$ of the kth layer as

$$\boldsymbol{\delta}^k := \nabla_{\mathbf{o}^k} E_i = [\delta_1^k \quad \delta_2^k \quad \cdots \quad \delta_{s_k}^k]^{\mathrm{T}}, \qquad (k = 1, \cdots, m), \tag{5}$$

the differentiation of E_i with respect to the weight matrix and bias vector is presented as follows, (See Appendix for application of the chain rule to the differentiation of a scalar function with respect to a matrix.)

$$\frac{\partial E_i}{\partial \mathbf{w}^k} = \sum_{j=1}^{s_k} \frac{\partial E_i}{\partial o_j^k} \frac{\partial o_j^k}{\partial \mathbf{w}^k} = \delta_1^k \begin{bmatrix} (\mathbf{a}^{k-1})^{\mathrm{T}} \\ \mathbf{0}_{(n-1)\times n} \end{bmatrix} + \cdots + \delta_{s_k}^k \begin{bmatrix} \mathbf{0}_{(n-1)\times n} \\ (\mathbf{a}^{k-1})^{\mathrm{T}} \end{bmatrix} = \boldsymbol{\delta}^k \cdot (\mathbf{a}^{k-1})^{\mathrm{T}}, \tag{6}$$

$$\frac{\partial E_i}{\partial \mathbf{b}^k} = \frac{\partial E_i}{\partial \mathbf{o}^k} \frac{\partial \mathbf{o}^k}{\partial \mathbf{b}^k} = (\boldsymbol{\delta}^k)^{\mathrm{T}},$$

where $o_j^k = \mathbf{w}_j^k \mathbf{a}^{k-1} + b_j^k \ (j = 1, \cdots, s_k)$.

From Equations (1) and (3), it can be seen that E_i is a function of the vector $\mathbf{o}^{k+1}$ and $\mathbf{a}^k$ is also a function of the vector $\mathbf{o}^k$. Using the general chain rule (See Appendix), therefore, it leads to the following relation,

$$\partial E_i / \partial \mathbf{o}^k = (\partial E_i / \partial \mathbf{o}^{k+1})(\partial \mathbf{o}^{k+1} / \partial \mathbf{a}^k)(\partial \mathbf{a}^k / \partial \mathbf{o}^k). \tag{7}$$

Again, by applying the general chain rule and the definition (5) of $\boldsymbol{\delta}^k$, the recurrence relation of the gradient term $\boldsymbol{\delta}^k$ can be written by

$$\begin{aligned} \boldsymbol{\delta}^k &= \nabla_{\mathbf{o}^k} E_i = \nabla_{\mathbf{o}^k} \mathbf{a}^k \cdot \nabla_{\mathbf{a}^k} \mathbf{o}^{k+1} \cdot \nabla_{\mathbf{o}^{k+1}} E_i \\ &= \nabla_{\mathbf{o}^k} \mathbf{a}^k \cdot \nabla_{\mathbf{a}^k} \mathbf{o}^{k+1} \cdot \boldsymbol{\delta}^{k+1} = \dot{\mathbf{H}}^k(\mathbf{o}^k) \cdot (\mathbf{w}^{k+1})^{\mathrm{T}} \cdot \boldsymbol{\delta}^{k+1}, \qquad (k = 1, \cdots, m-1), \end{aligned} \tag{8}$$

where

$$\nabla_{\mathbf{a}^k} \mathbf{o}^{k+1} = (\partial \mathbf{o}^{k+1} / \partial \mathbf{a}^k)^{\mathrm{T}} = (\mathbf{w}^{k+1})^{\mathrm{T}}; \tag{9}$$

$$\nabla_{\mathbf{o}^k} \mathbf{a}^k = (\partial \mathbf{a}^k / \partial \mathbf{o}^k)^{\mathrm{T}} = \dot{\mathbf{H}}^k(\mathbf{o}^k) = \begin{bmatrix} \dot{h}_1^k(o_1^k) & \cdots & 0 \\ \vdots & \ddots & \vdots \\ 0 & \cdots & \dot{h}_{s_k}^k(o_{s_k}^k) \end{bmatrix}; \ (\dot{h}_j^k(o_j^k) = dh_j^k(o_j^k)/do_j^k, \ j=1,\ldots,s_k. \tag{10}$$

This recurrence computation is initialized at the final layer, i.e. the mth layer. According to the general chain rule, $\boldsymbol{\delta}^m$ will be

$$\boldsymbol{\delta}^m = \nabla_{\mathbf{o}^m} E_i = \nabla_{\mathbf{o}^m} \mathbf{a}^m \cdot \nabla_{\mathbf{a}^m} E_i = -\dot{\mathbf{H}}^m(\mathbf{o}^m) \cdot (\mathbf{t}_i - \mathbf{a}_i^m). \tag{11}$$

The learning algorithm of the standard backpropagation proceeds as follows: first, using Equation (1) to calculate the output of each layer $\mathbf{a}^k$ (k=1,…,m); Then, using Equations (11) and (8), the gradient terms $\boldsymbol{\delta}^k$ (k=m,…,1) is computed backward from the mth layer to the 1st layer; Next, the increments of weights and biases are calculated using Equations (6) for k=1,...,m; Finally, the weights and biases are updated using Equations (4) with a chosen learning rate η (k=1,..., m).

2.2.2 Levenberg-Marquardt backpropagation algorithm

The standard backpropagation algorithm has been widely applied in neural network learning. However, due to the low speed of convergence, considerable research works have been done to improve it. A lately developed algorithm, the Levenberg-Marquardt backpropagation, has been used to train feedforward neural networks since it can yield a speed-up of large factors via limited modifications of the standard backpropagation algorithm.

Consider the feedforward neural network (1) as a nonlinear least squares problem, the performance index (3) can be written as below,

$$E(\mathbf{w}) = \frac{1}{2}\sum_{i=1}^{Q}(\mathbf{t}_i - \mathbf{a}_i^m)^{\mathrm{T}}(\mathbf{t}_i - \mathbf{a}_i^m) = \frac{1}{2}(\mathbf{t}-\mathbf{a})^{\mathrm{T}}(\mathbf{t}-\mathbf{a}) \tag{12}$$

where $\mathbf{t} = [\mathbf{t}_1^{\mathrm{T}}\ \ \mathbf{t}_2^{\mathrm{T}}\ \ \cdots\ \ \mathbf{t}_Q^{\mathrm{T}}]^{\mathrm{T}}$ and $\mathbf{a} = [(\mathbf{a}_1^m)^{\mathrm{T}}\ \ (\mathbf{a}_2^m)^{\mathrm{T}}\ \ \cdots\ \ (\mathbf{a}_Q^m)^{\mathrm{T}}]^{\mathrm{T}}$ respectively.

The n-element vector of weights and biases of an m-layer neural network can be written as

$$\begin{aligned}\mathbf{w} &= [w_{11}^1\ \ w_{12}^1\ \ \cdots\ \ w_{s_1}^1\ \ b_1^1\ \ \cdots\ \ b_{s_1}^1\ \ w_{11}^2\ \ w_{12}^2\ \ \cdots]^{\mathrm{T}} \\ &= [w_1\ \ w_2\ \ \cdots\ \ w_n]^{\mathrm{T}}\end{aligned}\ . \tag{13}$$

With the Newton method, the increment $\Delta\mathbf{w}$, by minimization of E with respect to the parameter vector $\mathbf{w}$, is

$$\Delta\mathbf{w} = -\,(\nabla^2 E(\mathbf{w}))^{-1}\nabla E(\mathbf{w})\,, \tag{14}$$

where $\nabla^2 E(\mathbf{w})$ is the Hessian matrix of $E(\mathbf{w})$ and $\nabla E(\mathbf{w})$ is the gradient of $E(\mathbf{w})$.

Given the performance index (12), the gradient and the Hessian matrix of $E(\mathbf{w})$ can be written as

$$\nabla E(\mathbf{w}) = -\mathbf{J}^{\mathrm{T}}(\mathbf{w})\cdot(\mathbf{t}-\mathbf{a}(\mathbf{w}))$$

$$\nabla^2 E(\mathbf{w}) = \mathbf{J}^{\mathrm{T}}(\mathbf{w})\cdot\mathbf{J}(\mathbf{w}) + \sum_{i=1}^{Q}(\mathbf{t}_i - \mathbf{a}_i^m)\nabla^2(\mathbf{t}_i - \mathbf{a}_i^m) \tag{15}$$

where $\mathbf{J}(\mathbf{w})$ is the Jacobian matrix of $\mathbf{a}(\mathbf{w})$ with respect to the vector $\mathbf{w}$,

$$\mathbf{J}(\mathbf{w}) = \partial\mathbf{a}(\mathbf{w})/\partial\mathbf{w} = \begin{bmatrix}\partial\mathbf{a}_1^m/\partial w_1 & \cdots & \partial\mathbf{a}_1^m/\partial w_n \\ \vdots & \ddots & \vdots \\ \partial\mathbf{a}_Q^m/\partial w_1 & \cdots & \partial\mathbf{a}_Q^m/\partial w_n\end{bmatrix}. \tag{16}$$

Since the second term on the right-hand side of Equation (15) is difficult to obtain, the Levenberg-Marquardt method is introduced to approximate the function as follows,

$$\Delta\mathbf{w} = -(\mathbf{J}^{\mathrm{T}}(\mathbf{w})\cdot\mathbf{J}(\mathbf{w}) + \mu\mathbf{I})^{-1}\cdot\mathbf{J}^{\mathrm{T}}(\mathbf{w})\cdot(\mathbf{t}-\mathbf{a}(\mathbf{w})) \tag{17}$$

where $\boldsymbol{I}$ is the identity matrix and μ is an adaptive factor ($\mu > 0$). μ is multiplied by a positive parameter γ (normally chosen as 10) whenever a step results in a decreased $E(\mathbf{w})$ in

Equation (12). Otherwise, μ is divided by γ. Note that when μ is sufficiently large, the algorithm becomes the steepest gradient descent. For a small value of μ, the algorithm becomes the Gauss-Newton algorithm.

In order to apply the backpropagation technique to solving the Jacobian matrix (16), the research work reported by Hagan and Menhaj (Hagan & Menhaj, 1994) provided a detailed algorithm with which the elements of the Jacobian matrix (16) can be calculated backward layer-by-layer, and therefore, the weights of a neural network can be updated simultaneously.

3. Parameter estimates with confidence intervals

The purpose to train a neural network is not solely to get an exact representation of the training data, but to build a satisfactory model that can exhibit intrinsic relationship between input data and output data. Therefore, the trained neural network model is expected to make good predictions for unseen input data. Hence, the performance evaluation of a neural network with unseen data has been intensively studied in the area of applied neural computations.

Traditionally, the performance of generalization of a neural network is examined by testing data, i.e. a set of data is separated into two subsets, training data and testing data, respectively. The neural network trained using the training data should also result in small sum of squared errors (3) when the testing data is fed into it. The method can detect whether a neural network overfits noisy data, but it does not provide quantitative metric to show "how good" the predicted output is.

On the other hand, as far as empirical modeling is concerned, regression analysis is a widely used statistical technique in many practical cases. Since a neural network can be considered as a special nonlinear structure, neural network modeling can be categorized into a nonlinear regression problem.

When a neural network model is used for prediction with a set of inputs that are different from the training patterns, the accuracy of estimation can be represented by a best guess of predicted outcomes plus a range of likely future outcomes around the best guess. Such a range is commonly referred to as a confidence interval with certain confidence level, which provides information indicating where the output is likely to be and how much percent of chances the output is probably to be with the estimates. Hence, solving the neural network regression problem consists of two parts - developing a nonlinear regression model and computing the range of likely future outputs. The range of possible outputs will quantitatively provide how large difference between the real output and the best guess from a statistical point of view when unseen data are fed into the model. Moreover, as discussed below, the confidence interval varies with the structure of a neural network, which provides a practical reference for people to select the structure of a neural network. In this section, the concepts of neural network regression, confidence intervals and prediction intervals will be presented. Then, how a prediction interval changes with the structure of a neural network will be demonstrated through an example.

3.1 Prediction interval for neural network regression

From Equation (1), it is assumed that the true output of an m-layer neural network is $\mathbf{a}_i^m(\mathbf{x},\mathbf{w}^*)$, where $\mathbf{x}$ is the input vector, and $\mathbf{w}^*$ represents the true values of the weight vector from the weight value space $\mathbf{\Omega}$. For simplicity, $\mathbf{a}_i^m$ is replaced by $\mathbf{a}_i$ for future derivation. In addition, the output of the neural network will be considered as a one-dimensional vector, i.e. $\mathbf{a}_i=a_i$. The error, ε_i, associated with the function in modeling is supposed to be independently and identically distributed with variance, σ^2, where the distribution has the form $N(0,\sigma^2)$, i.e. normal distribution with the mean of zero and the variance of σ^2. With each of Q experimental data, the output of the function is represented by

$$a_i = a_i(\mathbf{x}_i,\hat{\mathbf{w}}) + \varepsilon_i\,, \quad {\scriptstyle i=1,2,..,Q;} \qquad \hat{\mathbf{w}} \in \Omega \tag{18}$$

The estimated vector, $\hat{\mathbf{w}}$, is obtained by minimizing the performance index (12) using training data. However, due to many factors, e.g. noisy training patterns or limited number of nodes, the vector, $\hat{\mathbf{w}}$, can be a good estimation of, or say close to, the true value, $\mathbf{w}^*$, of the weight parameters but not equal to them. Considering a neural network as a nonlinear regression model, the linear approximation to this nonlinear regression model can be obtained via the Taylor series expansion of the function to the first order (Seber et al., 1989). Therefore, an estimated value, $\hat{a}_i$, under the input vector, $\mathbf{x}_i$, is

$$\hat{a}_i = a_i(\mathbf{x}_i,\hat{\mathbf{w}}) = a_i(\mathbf{x}_i,\mathbf{w}^*) + \nabla_{\mathbf{w}}^{\mathrm{T}} a_i \,|_{w^*} (\hat{\mathbf{w}} - \mathbf{w}^*) \tag{19}$$

where $\nabla_{\mathbf{w}}^{\mathrm{T}} a_i \,|_{w^*}$ denotes the gradient of the function a_i with respect to the weight vector at the true values, $\mathbf{w}^*$. The error between the input/output pairs and the estimated value from the neural network model yields

$$\begin{aligned} t_i - \hat{a}_i &= t_i - a_i(\mathbf{x}_i,\mathbf{w}^*) - \nabla_{\mathbf{w}}^{\mathrm{T}} a_i \,|_{w^*} (\hat{\mathbf{w}} - \mathbf{w}^*) \\ &= \varepsilon_i - \nabla_{\mathbf{w}}^{\mathrm{T}} a_i \,|_{w^*} (\hat{\mathbf{w}} - \mathbf{w}^*). \end{aligned} \tag{20}$$

The expected value and variance of the difference will be

$$\text{mean}\left[t_i - \hat{a}_i\right] = \text{mean}[\varepsilon_i] - \nabla_{\mathbf{w}}^{\mathrm{T}} a_i \,|_{\mathbf{w}^*} \times \text{mean}(\hat{\mathbf{w}} - \mathbf{w}^*) \approx 0$$

$$\text{var}\left[t_i - \hat{a}_i\right] = \text{var}[\varepsilon_i] - \text{var}[\nabla_{\mathbf{w}}^{\mathrm{T}} a_i \,|_{\mathbf{w}^*} (\hat{\mathbf{w}} - \mathbf{w}^*)] \tag{21}$$

Note that the assumptions that a_i is continuously differentiable and that the matrix $\mathbf{J}^{\mathrm{T}}(\mathbf{w})\mathbf{J}(\mathbf{w})$ (with $\mathbf{J}(\mathbf{w}) = \left[\nabla_{\mathbf{w}} a_1 \;\; \nabla_{\mathbf{w}} a_2 \;\; \cdots \;\; \nabla_{\mathbf{w}} a_Q\right]^{\mathrm{T}}$) is nonsingular are essential in the statistical evaluation. The distribution of $\hat{\mathbf{w}} - \mathbf{w}^*$ can be approximated with the distribution, $N_Q\,(0, \sigma^2[\mathbf{J}^{\mathrm{T}}(\mathbf{w})\mathbf{J}(\mathbf{w})]^{-1})$, where $\mathbf{J}(\mathbf{w})$ is also the Jacobian matrix (16). In fact, given a large value of Q, ε_i being the random numbers with independent and identical distribution and the parameter space of the weights, Ω, being a compact subset of n dimensional real number space, the values of the weight vector, $\hat{\mathbf{w}}$, are certain to be within a small neighborhood of the true value vector, $\mathbf{w}^*$. Therefore, in late calculation, the weight vector, $\hat{\mathbf{w}}$, is used to replace $\mathbf{w}^*$ and is written as $\mathbf{w}$.

With the number of samples, Q, and the number of estimated parameters, n, the unbiased estimator of σ^2 is

$$s^2 = \frac{\sum_{i=1}^{Q} (t_i - a_i(\mathbf{x}_i,\mathbf{w}))^2}{Q-n}\,. \tag{22}$$

Hence, the confidence interval $100\times(1-\alpha)$ for the estimated value, $\hat{a}_i$, will be

$$\hat{a}_i \pm t_{\alpha/2,Q-n} \times s \times (1+\nabla_{\mathbf{w}}^{\mathrm{T}} a_i \{\mathbf{J}^{\mathrm{T}}(\mathbf{w})\mathbf{J}(\mathbf{w})\}^{-1} \nabla_{\mathbf{w}} a_i)^{1/2} \tag{23}$$

where the parameter, α, denotes the level of significance and $t_{\alpha/2,Q-n}$ is the $(1-\alpha/2)$ quartile of a t - distribution with Q-n degrees of freedom.

In order to use the above equation to estimate the likely range of a system output, the model errors should be independently and normally distributed with zero means (Chryssolouris et al., 1996) which can be generally satisfied by practical cases. However, it is also indicated that the confidence bound estimation method is asymptotically valid when a large set of training data is available (Hwang & Ding, 1997). With a small set of training data and relatively large set of parameters, the matrix $\mathbf{J}^{\mathrm{T}}(\mathbf{w})\mathbf{J}(\mathbf{w})$ can be singular. In this case, the estimated confidence intervals are unreliable. According to Yang et. al (Yang et al., 2002), the performance index can be changed into the following,

$$E(\mathbf{w}) = \sum_{i=1}^{Q} (t_i - a_i(\mathbf{x}_i, \mathbf{w}))^2 + \lambda \sum_{i=1}^{n} w_i^2 , \tag{24}$$

where $\lambda > 0$ is a decay parameter. The confidence interval for feedforward neural networks trained by weight decay is

$$\hat{a}_i \pm t_{\alpha/2,Q-n} \times s \times (1+\nabla_{\mathbf{w}}^{\mathrm{T}} a_i \{\mathbf{J}^{\mathrm{T}}(\mathbf{w})\mathbf{J}(\mathbf{w})+\lambda\mathbf{I}\}^{-1} \mathbf{J}^{\mathrm{T}}(\mathbf{w})\mathbf{J}(\mathbf{w}) \{\mathbf{J}^{\mathrm{T}}(\mathbf{w})\mathbf{J}(\mathbf{w})+\lambda\mathbf{I}\}^{-1} \nabla_{\mathbf{w}} a_i)^{1/2} \tag{25}$$

3.2 An example of neural network regression

In order to illustrate how a neural network regression model works, an example is taken below. Consider the following function,

$$f(x) = 0.5 + 0.4\sin(2\pi x) + \varepsilon , \tag{26}$$

where ε is the random noise normally distributed with the mean of zero and the standard deviation of 0.05. A data set of 21 points with equal intervals between 0 and 1 is chosen as inputs to the function.

For convenience of discussion, the feedforward neural network is chosen as one hidden layer and linear nodes in the output layer. Hence, it can be mathematically represented by the following equation,

$$a_i(x_i) = \mathbf{w}^2\mathbf{h}^1(\mathbf{o}^1) + b^2 ; \quad \mathbf{o}^1 = \mathbf{w}^1 x_i + \mathbf{b}^1 ; \quad i=1,\ldots,21 \tag{27}$$

where x_i and a_i, as defined previously, denote input and output, respectively; $\mathbf{w}^k$ and $\mathbf{b}^k$ $_{(k=1,2)}$, as the same as in Equation (2), are the weights and biases of the network with $\mathbf{w}^2 \in \Re^{1\times s_1}$, $\mathbf{w}^1 \in \Re^{s_1\times 1}$, $\mathbf{b}^2 \in \Re, \mathbf{b}^1 \in \Re^{s_1}$ where s_1 is the number of hidden nodes; $h^1(.)$ is the activation function vector in the hidden layer. The activation function $\mathbf{h}^1(\mathbf{o}^1)$ is chosen as a hyperbolic tangent sigmoid function and can be alternatively written by $\mathbf{h}^1(\mathbf{o}^1) = \begin{bmatrix} h_1^1(o_1) & h_2^1(o_2) & \cdots & h_{s^2}^1(o_{s^2}) \end{bmatrix}^{\mathrm{T}}$ with $h_i^1(o_i) = \tanh(o_i) = (e^{o_i} - e^{-o_i}) / (e^{o_i} + e^{-o_i})$.

In order to train the neural network, the initial weights and biases are random numbers uniformly distributed between -1 and 1. The Levenberg-Marquardt backpropagation algorithm is used to train the neural network. The initial value of μ is chosen as 0.001. The parameter γ is chosen as 10. The number of epochs is 1000. Equation (25) is used to calculate the prediction interval, where the parameter, λ, is chosen as 0.0001. And 95% confidence level is used for the simulation.

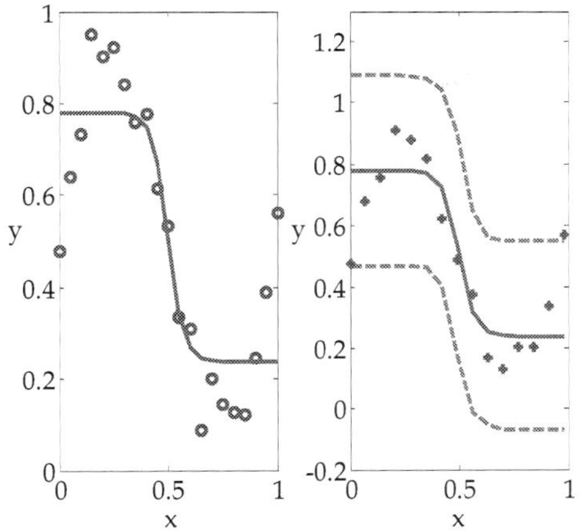

Fig. 2. Neural model of $f(x)$ with one hidden node. Left figure: circles - training data; solid line - neural network output. Right figure: asterisks - testing data; solid line - neural network output; dashed lines - 95% confidence interval

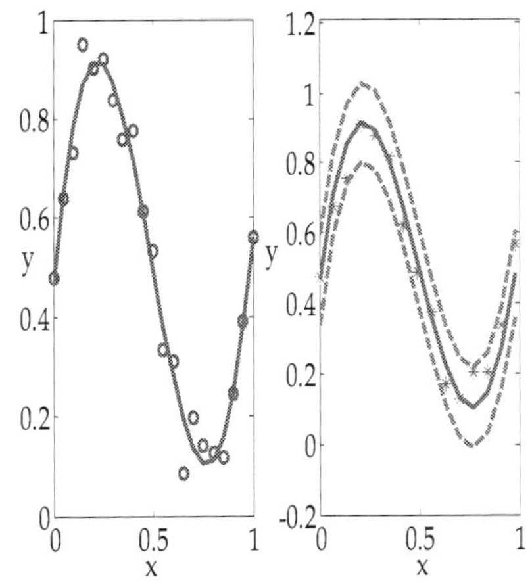

Fig. 3. Neural model of $f(x)$ with two hidden nodes. Left figure: circles - training data; solid line - neural network output. Right figure: asterisks - testing data; solid line - neural network output; dashed lines - 95% confidence interval

Fig. 2 shows the training data points and the neural network output with one hidden node (left figure). After training, the neural network model is used to predict the output of 15 unseen inputs which are corrupted with normally distributed noise of $N(0, 0.05^2)$. The right side of Fig. 2 provides the predicted output of the neural network, which is drawn in solid line, the testing data (in asterisk symbol) and the confidence interval (in dashed line) with 95% confidence level. As can be seen, the neural network model provides a wide prediction range as a consequence of limited capability of the neural network with only one hidden node.

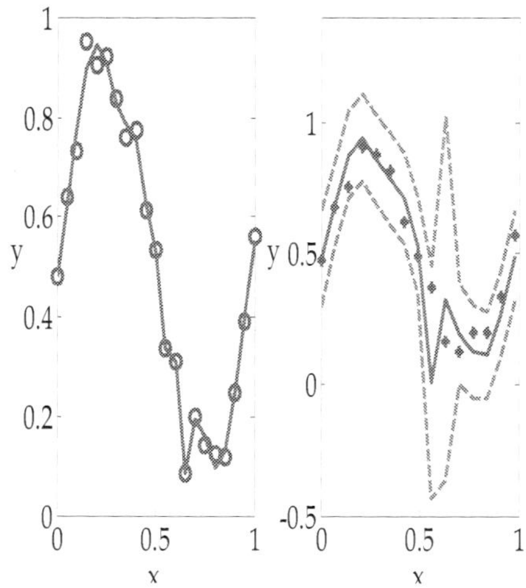

Fig. 4. Neural model of $f(x)$ with five hidden nodes. Left figure: circles - training data; solid line - neural network output. Right figure: asterisks - testing data; solid line - neural network output; dashed lines - 95% confidence interval.

The simulation was repeated 100 times. After each simulation, the maximal predicted interval of 15 points was recorded. The average of the maximal predicted intervals for 100 times of simulations is 0.7524. By comparing to the range of the function $f(x)$, which is between 0 and 1, the predicted interval is found to be too wide. A better fit and prediction ability of the neural network can be obtained by increasing the number of hidden nodes.

Fig. 3 shows the neural network output with two hidden nodes, which gives a much better approximation to $f(x)$. The average of maximal predicted intervals over 100 times of simulations is 0.2889. However, if the number of hidden nodes is too large, then, the error due to approximation to the underlying function becomes worse. Fig. 4 shows the result of fitting the function $f(x)$ using the neural network that contains five hidden nodes. Since the neural network has fitted the data by developing some dramatic oscillations, it eventually provides a poor prediction of $f(x)$ with wide confidence interval at some points, where the neural network fitting to noisy data points can be seen.

In order to examine how the number of hidden nodes impacts the prediction interval, the number of hidden nodes was chosen to be one, two, three, four and five. For each case, the simulation was repeated 100 times, and the average of the maximal prediction intervals were calculated accordingly. The results are shown in Table 1. From Table 1, it can be observed, that, for this example, the neural network with two hidden nodes provides the best prediction. When the number of hidden nodes increases, redundant nodes exist in the neural network, which lead the neural network to overfit some noisy data. Consequently, a wide confidence interval at some points indicates imprecise prediction.

Number of hidden nodes	1	2	3	4	5
Average of maximal prediction intervals by 100 times simulations	0.7524	0.2889	0.3117	0.3149	5.3223

Table 1. Average of maximal prediction intervals versus the number of hidden nodes

4. Modeling and prediction of nonlinear elastic behavior of reinforced soil

In this section, a practical application of feedforward neural networks to modeling of nonlinear behavior of composite materials will be presented. In particular, soil reinforced with geofiber and lime powder is taken as a composite material to be investigated as an example of such an application.

Mechanical behavior of soil under static and dynamic loading plays an important role in performance of infrastructures such as durability of pavement and road beds, and stability of slopes and bridge foundations, etc. To improve engineering properties, soil reinforced with other materials becomes widely applied in geotechnical engineering (Michalowiski & Zhao, 1995, and Li & Ding, 2002). Although the performance can be significantly improved when soil is reinforced with short fiber and stabilized with lime powder, quantitative evaluation of enhancement of soil mechanical behavior is still difficult since the stress-strain relation is highly nonlinear and sensitive to various factors such as lime and fiber contents, confining pressures, sample curing periods mixed with lime, etc. (Li & Zhang, 2003).

Traditionally, modeling of engineering materials was conducted by taking the following three steps. First, a constitutive model (e.g., a nonlinear elastic model) needs to be established. Second, constitutive parameters are identified and calibrated with experimental data using a conventional method (e.g. linear regression). Third, the constitutive model needs to be validated using experimental data from a laboratory or field (e.g., shearing tests). Since the constitutive parameters are nonlinear functions of multiple variables, a traditional approach cannot calibrate the parameters accurately and efficiently. In particular, when soil is mixed with lime powder and fibers, the constitutive parameters become a function of many interrelated variables. Under the circumstance, the coupling effects among different variables may significantly impact on the relationship of stress and strain. The coupling effects, however, cannot be practically described in a traditional model due to their intrigued nature and significant amount of experimental work. In this section, it is proposed that the nonlinear elastic behavior of composite soils is to be modeled using a feedforward neural network.

Applying neural network regression to modeling of reinforced soil is a new research topic. Till now, very few discussions of the potential application of neural networks in civil engineering have been found, for instance, modeling of shear strength of reinforced concrete beams (Rajasekaran & Amalraj, 2002) and estimation of resilient modulus of aggregate base using a feedforward neural network (Issa & Zamam, 1999). Therefore, relatively detailed description of the necessary knowledge regarding experimental investigation and data acquisition is provided in this section. Then, neural network training as well as the prediction using a neural network regression model with unseen inputs will be presented, which provides statistical justification for the case analysis and decision making in construction using the neural network model. Finally, the parameter sensitivities to the inputs such as fiber and lime contents, confining pressure, sample aging period are analyzed based on the neural network regression model (He & Li, 2008 and 2006).

4.1 Problem background and experiment setup

4.1.1 Shear stress-strain relation

The nonlinear elastic behavior exhibited by soil mixed with short fiber and lime powder can be affected by many factors. The shear stress-strain relation of soil skeleton in terms of the second invariants of deviatoric tensors in a three-dimensional space can be expressed by

$$\sigma^s = E\varepsilon^s \tag{28}$$

where ε^s denotes a shear strain invariant related to the second invariant of a deviatoric stress tensor; σ^s denotes a shear strain invariant associated with the second invariant of a deviatoric strain tensor. E is the shear modulus and a function of mechanical properties of the reinforced soil such as the initial shear modulus and strength of reinforced soil.

Since the objective of experiment under the investigation aims to understand the mechanical behavior of subgrade soil reinforced with short fiber and stabilized with lime, consequently, the shear modulus, E, is assumed to be a function of multi-variables, such as shear strain, confining stress, fiber and lime contents. Moreover, when the soil samples are mixed with lime powder, the curing time (or aging period) before a shearing test will be an auxiliary variable with lime content.

For convenience of experimental investigations using a conventional triaxial apparatus, it is necessary to simplify the stress-strain relation (28) from a true three-dimensional space to an expression in a quasi three-dimensional space. In the simplified space, the stress-strain relation in Equation (28) reduces to

$$\sigma_a = E\ (\sigma_0, \varepsilon_a, \beta_F, \beta_L, t)\ \varepsilon_a \tag{29}$$

where σ_0 is confining pressure; σ_a and ε_a denote the principal stresses and strains in three-dimension that are individually simplified from the invariants of the deviatoric stress and strain tensors; β_F and β_L are contents of fiber and lime, respectively; t is the curing time of soil sample before shear testing. For conventional triaxial shearing tests, σ_a and ε_a can simply represent the axial stress and strain respectively. To provide the input data for training and validating a feedforward neural network model, experimental tests need to be conducted in laboratory first so that the stress-strain relationship in Equation (29) can be determined.

4.1.2 Experiment and testing data

In laboratory, nine groups of unsaturated and reinforced soil samples were subjected to triaxial shearing tests. The tested soil has the following physical properties: the wet unit weight γ_{wet} = 16.66 kN/m^3; plastic limit PL = 5%; the soil classification (AASHTO) is A4. The specimen is cylindrical with a dimension of 6.86 cm in diameter and 13.72 cm in height. The sample preparation and testing followed the AASHTO code T297 (or ASTM D4767) with special consideration for the procedure of mixing short geofiber (5 cm) with soil. Nine groups of soil specimens were prepared with β_F = 0%, 0.2% and 0.5%; β_L = 0% and 5%; and t =1, 7, 14 and 28 days before shearing tests. Unsaturated specimens were tested under a consolidated-undrained condition using a conventional triaxial apparatus. The controlled shear loading rate was 0.006 min^{-1}. Four different confining pressures (σ_0 = 50, 100, 150, and 200 kPa) were applied to specimens in each group. The combination of selected fiber contents, lime contents, confining pressures and aging periods of soil specimens generates thirty four sets of experimental setup which is listed in Table 2.

Testing results from 34 shear tests were collected and processed through a data acquisition system. For purpose of demonstration, testing curves of 30 stress-strain (σ_a -ε_a) relations are

Set No.	Test No.	β_F(%)	β_L(%)	σ_0 (kPa)	t(day)
1	S11	0	0	50.0	1
2*	S12	0	0	100.0	1
3	S13	0	0	150.0	1.0
4	S14	0	0	200.0	1.0
5	F5	0.2	0	50.0	1.0
6	F6	0.2	0	100.0	1.0
7	F7	0.2	0	150.0	1.0
8	F8	0.2	0	200.0	1.0
9	F5-5	0.5	0	50.0	1.0
10	F5-6	0.5	0	100.0	1.0
11	F5-7	0.5	0	150.0	1.0
12	F5-8	0.5	0	200.0	1.0
13	Slf2	0.2	5.0	50.0	7.0
14	Slf1,11, 9	0.2	5.0	100.0	7.0
15	Slf6,17	0.2	5.0	150.0	7.0
16	Slf3,15	0.2	5.0	200.0	7.0
17	Slf5,12,16	0.2	5.0	50.0	14.0
18	Slf4	0.2	5.0	100.0	14.0
19	Slf7,8	0.2	5.0	150.0	14.0
20	Slf14	0.2	5.0	50.0	28.0
21*	Slf13	0.2	5.0	100.0	28.0
22	Slf18,19,20	0.2	5.0	150.0	28.0
23*	Slf5-1	0.5	5.0	50.0	7.0
24	Slf5-2	0.5	5.0	100.0	7.0
25	Slf5-4,5-10	0.5	5.0	150.0	7.0
26	Slf5-6,5-12	0.5	5.0	200.0	7.0
27	Slf5-3	0.5	5.0	50.0	14.0
28	Slf5-5	0.5	5.0	100.0	14.0
29	Slf5-7, 5-11	0.5	5.0	150.0	14.0
30	Slf5-8	0.5	5.0	200.0	14.0
31	Slf5-16	0.5	5.0	50.0	28.0
32	Slf5-13	0.5	5.0	100.0	28.0
33	Slf5-14	0.5	5.0	150.0	28.0
34*	Slf5-15	0.5	5.0	200.0	28.0

Table 2. Experimental Conditions

drawn in Fig. 5. In the figure, solid squares, down-triangles, asterisks and five-point stars represent experimental data with confining pressures, σ_0, of 50, 100, 150 and 200 kPa, individually. In each subfigure of Fig. 5, the chosen fiber content β_F, lime content β_L, as well as the curing period of soil sample t, are provided at the bottom of each subfigure. From the subfigures, it can be seen that the strength of reinforced soil can be improved by increasing the fiber content, β_F, without adding lime powder ($\beta_L = 0\%$) and holding the aging period of 1 day. If the fiber content changes from 0% to 0.5%, the maximum value of axial stress, σ_a, can vary from 280 kPa to 500 kPa (see subfigures 1~3 of Fig. 5). Furthermore, by adding lime and prolonging the aging period, the axial stress (soils strength) can be notably enhanced

(see subfigures 4~6 of Fig. 5). Similarly, soil elastic modulus and strength are also evidently improved with increasing the fiber content β_F (see subfigures 7~9 of Fig. 5).
Testing results in Fig. 5 indicate high nonlinearity between the axial stress and axial strain affected by four variables. To describe such mechanical behavior, a feedforward neural network model is used to predict the nonlinear relationship between multiple inputs and the output.

4.2 Modeling and predicting nonlinear elastic behavior of reinforced soil

As indicated in Equation (28), the axial stress, σ_a, is a nonlinear function of variables σ_0, β_F, β_L, t and the axial strain, ε_a. The function is to be approximated using a feedforward neural netowork. To validate the results of neural network regression, the prediction confidence of soil deformation using the feedforward neural network is analyzed.

4.2.1 Modeling of the reinforced soil

To train the feedforward neural network, the variables of fiber content β_F, lime content β_L, confining pressure σ_0 , sample curing period *t* and axial strain ε_a are applied as inputs to the

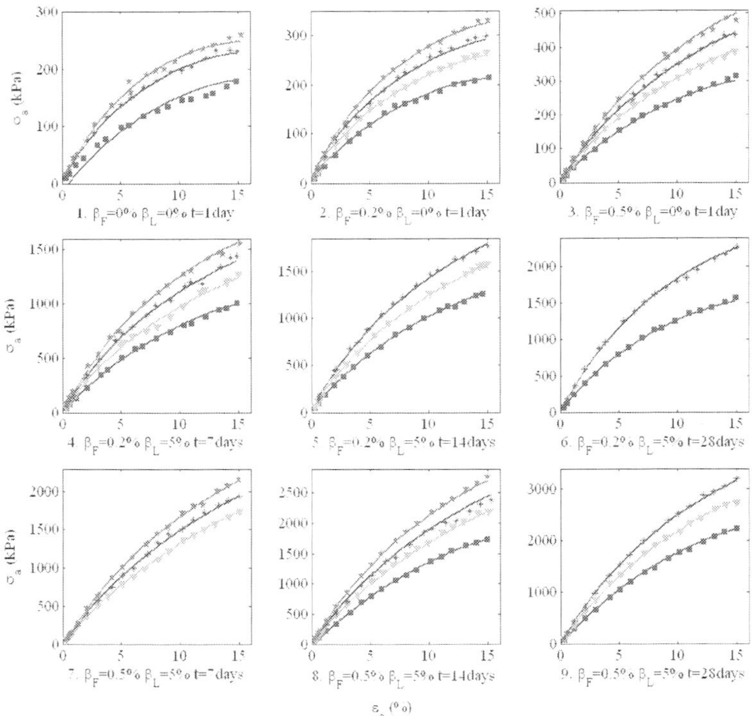

Fig. 5. Relationship of σ_a vs. ε_a with different confining pressures (CP) (Experiment data: Symbols with CP values: ■50 kPa, ▼100 kPa, ✱150 kPa,★200 kPa; The outputs of the neural network are in solid lines)

neural network while the corresponding axial shear stress, σ_a, is designated as the output. Thirty four sets of data in Table 2 (Seventeen axial strain values in each set within a range from 0.3% to 15.25%) generate 578 (=34×17) input patterns. Accordingly, 578 measured values of the axial shear stress are the targets for neural network to learn and test. As presented in Fig. 5, thirty sets of data which produces 510 input/output patterns (30×17=510) are used to train the neural network, whereas the remaining 68 input/output patterns (4 sets) marked with the asterisk sign, *, in Table 2 are applied to test the neural network model. The testing data are chosen to represent low, median and high nonlinearity of soil mechanical behavior.

Without loss of generality, one-hidden-layer feedforward neural network with linear output layer is chosen. In addition, in order to make the neural network converge quickly, the scaling factors 0.01, 10, 1.0, 0.1 and 0.1 are used for the inputs σ_0 (kPa), β_F (%), β_L (%), t (day) and ε_a (kPa), respectively. Similarly, the axial shear stress, σ_a, is scaled by a factor of 0.0001. Thus, the input vector for training the neural network is $x = [0.01\sigma_0, 10\beta_F, \beta_L, 0.1t, 0.1\varepsilon_a]^T$ and the desired output is $0.0001\sigma_a$. With the input, $\mathbf{x}$ and the output, $N\sigma_a$, the neural network model is defined as follows,

$$N\sigma_a(\mathbf{x}_i) = \mathbf{w}^2\mathbf{h}^1(\mathbf{o}^1) + b^2; \quad \mathbf{o}^1 = \mathbf{w}^1\mathbf{x}_i + \mathbf{b}^1; \quad i=1,\ldots,510 \tag{30}$$

As discussed in Section 3, the number of hidden nodes should be chosen so that the neural network model will not overfit the noisy data. After several times of pretraining and prediction capability analysis, the number of hidden nodes has been accordingly chosen as 6. The Levenberg Marquardt backpropagation training algorithm is chosen to train the neural network. The parameters are chosen as follows: the weights and biases are initialized with the random numbers uniformly distributed between -1 and 1; the maximal number of training epochs is 1,500; the error goal is that the sum of squared errors (SSE) is less than or equal to 0.002. The adaptive factor, μ, is initialized as 0.0001 and the update factor, γ, is assumed to be 10. After 702 epochs, the sum of squared errors (SSE) monotonically decreases to 0.00199. After the training, the outputs from the neural network are plotted in Fig. 5 in solid lines along with testing data.

4.2.2 Approximation error and prediction performance

As aforementioned, the most important criterion to evaluate a neural network model is its capacities of generalization and prediction. The prediction intervals for the trained neural network (30) are calculated and analyzed.

Before Equation (30) is used to predict the axial stress, σ_a, with unseen values of the variables σ_0, β_F, β_L, t and ε_a, the modeling errors between the experimental data and the neural network regression model are computed. The errors are sorted with the interval of 20 (i.e., -120, -100, ...,-20, 0, 20, ...,100, 120) and depicted in Fig. 6. The mean value of the errors is 0.05 kPa. Compared to the shear stress values of the experiment, which are between 11.2 kPa and 3667.8 kPa, the mean value is small enough to be considered as zero. The standard deviation of the normal distribution is 19.8 kPa. The unbiased estimator, s, is 20.69 kPa.

With the trained weights, when the testing input patterns are fed into the neural network, the corresponding outputs are predicted. The mean value and standard deviation of errors between experimental data and the outputs of the neural network are 12.2 kPa and 39.5 kPa, respectively, which is relatively larger than the errors provided by training data.

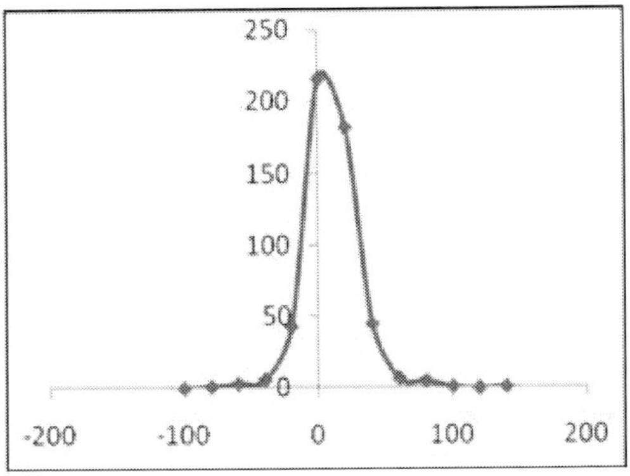

Fig. 6. Distribution of the errors between desired outputs (from 510 experimental data) and corresponding neural network outputs

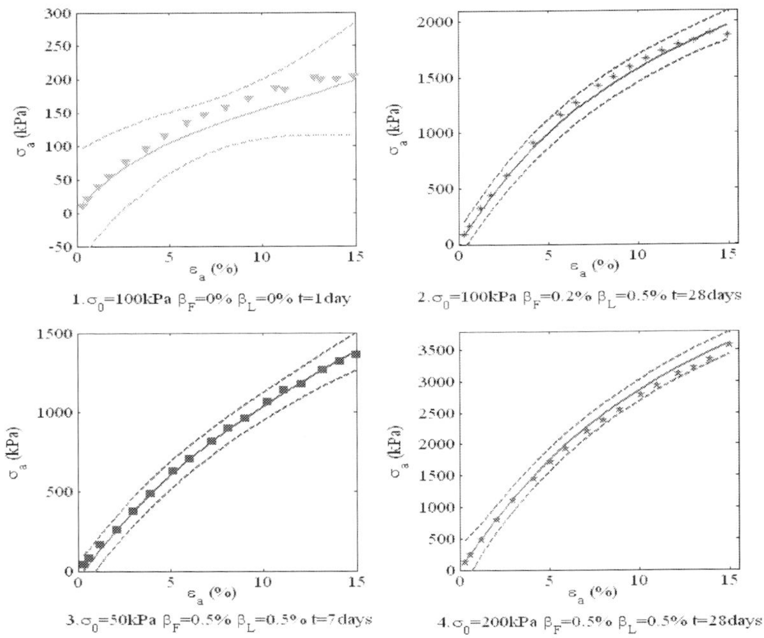

Fig. 7. Testing data with 95% confidence intervals (Experimental data are drawn with the inverse triangle, asterisks, solid squares and five-point stars; the outputs of the neural network are drawn in solid lines. The confidence levels are drawn in dashed lines.)

According to Equation (23), the confidence intervals (with 95% confidence level) are calculated. Dashed lines in Fig. 7 show the envelope of confidence intervals of predicted outputs along the increase of axial shear strain for four sets of data. Actual experimental data are filled in the figure with down-triangles, asterisks and five-point stars and solid squares, respectively. Although some points are close to certain lower bound values, e.g., the outputs of the neural network around 3,000 kPa in subfigure 4 of Fig. 7, all testing data are within its upper and lower bound values. The confidence intervals provide the envelope for prediction of a shear stress output.

4.2.3 Sensitivity analysis of neural network-based parameters

In opposition to the conventional model-based nonlinear technique, a neural network generalizes a model by learning from experimental data, which is particularly important when the underlying relationships of a researched object are unknown. Using the trained neural network model, soil mechanical behavior can be quantitatively analyzed with limited experimental data.

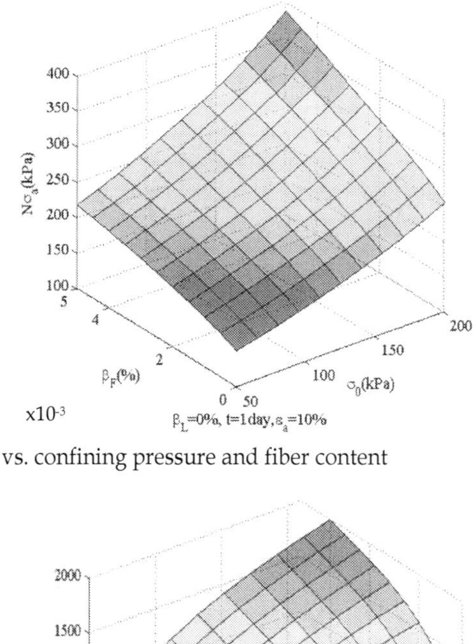

Fig. 8. Axial stress vs. confining pressure and fiber content

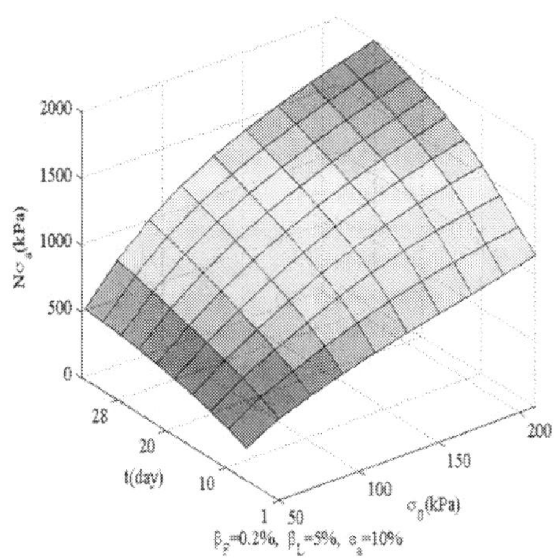

Fig. 9. Axial stress vs. confining pressure and sample aging period

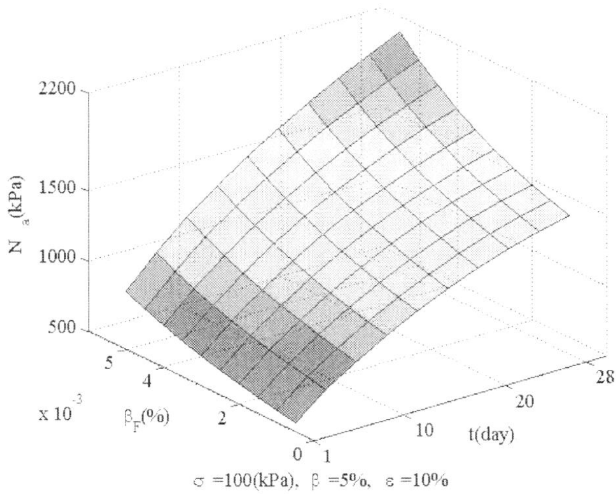

Fig. 10. Axial stress vs. fiber content and sample aging period

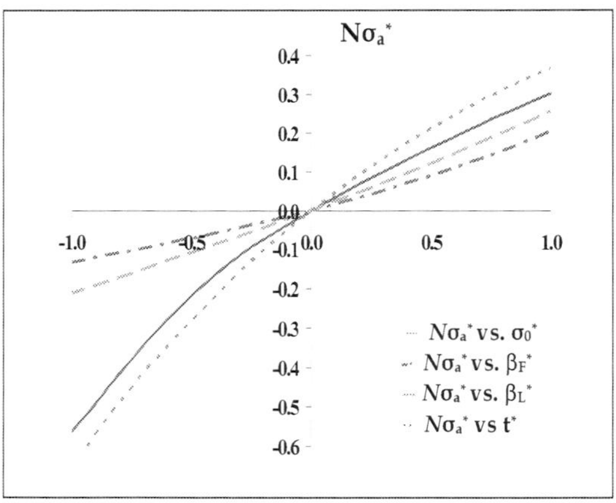

Fig. 11. Sensitivity analysis with dimensionless relations between the axial shear stress and variables (σ_0^*, β_F^*, β_L^*, t^*)

1. Soil mechanical behavior in response to variable coupling effects

The diagrams in Figs. 5 and 7 provide a set of $\sigma_a \sim \varepsilon_a$ relations. Beyond the relations, one may be interested in how the variables like fiber content and lime content as well as aging period co-influence the strength of reinforced soil. In order to investigate parameter coupling effects, the axial strain at 10% is assumed for convenience of analysis. Based on the assumption, joined impacts of multiple variables on axial shear stress are calculated and illustrated by Figs. 8, 9 and 10, respectively.

Firstly, in Fig. 8, a joined impact of confining pressure, σ_0, and fiber content, β_F, on the estimated axial shear stress (i.e. $N\sigma_a$ in Fig. 8) is presented for given lime content (β_L= 0%) and sample curing period t (1 day). According to Fig. 8, if no fiber is added to the soil sample (i.e. β_F = 0%), the axial stress appears linearly increased when the confining pressure changes from 50 kPa to 200 kPa. However, it can be observed that when 0.5% short fiber is mixed with the soil, the axial stress increases exponentially with the change of the confining pressure. This suggests that the stress-strain relation is more sensitively in response to the fiber content than to the confining pressure though both of the two variables have significant impact in soil mechanical behavior.

Secondly, the joined impact of confining pressure, σ_0, and, aging period, t, on soil stress, σ_a, due to adding lime (β_L=5%) is examined. Fig. 9 presents the increase of estimated stress value verse curing time of the lime mixed soil and confining pressure (with fiber content of 0.2%). Again it can be noted that the estimated stress curve, $N\sigma_a$, is nonlinearly changed with the variations of aging period and confining pressure. When aging period is short, e.g. 1 day, adding lime powder seems to have less influence on axial shear stress. The value of axial shear stress will be increased about 290 kPa (from 480 kPa to 770 kPa) with confining pressure raising from 50 kPa to 200 kPa. However, when aging period is extended to 28 days, the variation of the axial stress along with the same range of confining pressure raises to 960 kPa (from 1,130 kPa to 1,990 kPa). This indicates that soil strength can be largely improved by prolonging aging period. In addition, compared to Fig. 8, where the range of axial shear stress is between 100 kPa and 400 kPa, the value of axial shear stress in Fig. 9 can be increased from 500 kPa to 2,000 kPa. This implies that axial resistance between soil granular particles has been substantially enhanced by the extra bonding force due to chemical stabilization because of adding lime powder.

Although Fig. 9 exhibits a significant contribution of lime powder with a longer aging period to the strength of the reinforced soil, it can also be observed that the axial stress is increased logarithmically along the aging period.

Finally, Fig. 10 is used to illustrate the combined impact of the fiber contents and 5% lime content with different aging periods on nonlinear soil stress-strain relations. For given lime content β_L = 5 % and confining pressures σ_0 = 100 kPa, the change of axial shear stress along with different curing periods and fiber contents is shown in the figure. Besides highly nonlinear relation between axial shear stress and aging period and fiber content, it can be clearly observed that the values of axial stress increase exponentially with the increase of fiber content, whereas it increases logarithmically with the increase of aging period. This indicates the short fiber with additional tensile and shear resistance may play a more important role on further improvement of strength of the soil since an exponential function can increase much faster than a logarithmic function with same amount of input.

The results presented in Figs. 8, 9 and 10 indicate: 1) the axial shear stress is a nonlinear function of multiple variables σ_0, β_F, β_L, t and σ_a; 2) the strength of soil can be improved significantly by adding short fiber and lime powder with an aging period; 3) the axial shear stress increases exponentially with the increase of fiber content and logarithmically with a prolonging aging period when mixed with lime powder.

2. Soil mechanical behavior in response to an individual variable

In above section, the coupling effect among confining pressure, fiber content and lime content as well as aging period are qualitatively analyzed and tendencies of parameter changes are depicted. Furthermore, sensitivity of axial shear stress to each of the variables can be quantitatively analyzed. To present the work clearly, the neural network based axial stress-strain relation and relative variables are defined as follows,

$$N\sigma_a = N\sigma_a(\sigma_0, \beta_F, \beta_L, t, \varepsilon_a) . \tag{31}$$

where $N\sigma_a$ represents the axial shear stress predicted by the feedforward neural network to distinguish the notations of the axial stress σ_a in early sections. For purpose of investigation, the axial strain at failure is assumed (ε_a =10%) and the initial values of other variables in (31) are individually chosen as σ_{0i} =100 kPa, β_{Fi}=0.25%, β_{Li} =2.5% and t_i =14 days where the subscript i denotes the initial value. Also for convenience of sensitivity analysis, the normalized deviations from initial input values and the corresponding outputs defined as the following form: $X^* = (X - X_i)/X_i = \Delta X/X_i$ and $Y^* = (Y - Y_i)/Y_i = Y/Y_i - 1$ where X and Y represent the inputs (i.e., σ_0, β_F, β_L or t) and the output [i.e., $N\sigma_a(\sigma_0, \beta_F, \beta_L, t)$]; X_i and Y_i stand for the initial values of X and Y. The normalized deviation of input variables can be alternatively written by $X^* = \Delta X/X_i$ that changes from -1 to +1 when the incremental value ΔX (i.e. $\Delta\sigma_0$, $\Delta\beta_F$, $\Delta\beta_L$ or Δt) varies from $-X_i$ to $+X_i$ as the range chosen for sensitivity analysis. The dimensionless relation below exemplifies how the axial shear stress responds to the confining pressure:

$$N\sigma_a^*(\sigma_0^*) = \frac{N\sigma_a(\sigma_{0i}(1+\sigma_0^*), \beta_{Fi}, \beta_{Li}, t_i, \varepsilon_a)}{N\sigma_a(\sigma_{0i}, \beta_{Fi}, \beta_{Li}, t_i, \varepsilon_a)} - 1 \tag{31}$$

$$\sigma_0^*(\sigma_0) = (\sigma_0 - \sigma_{0i}) / \sigma_{0i} = \Delta\sigma_0 / \sigma_{0i} \tag{32}$$

The relation $N\sigma_a^*(\sigma_0^*)$ in (31) against σ_0^* in (32) is graphically drawn in a solid blue line in Fig. 11. Similar to (31) and (32), the dimensionless relation Y^* vs. X^* for other variables such as $N\sigma_a^*(\beta_F^*) \sim \beta_F^*$, $N\sigma_a^*(\beta_L^*) \sim \beta_L^*$, and $N\sigma_a^*(t^*) \sim t^*$ can be found accordingly and plotted in the same figure.

The results in Fig. 11 display how sensitive the axial shear stress is when changing confining pressure, fiber content, lime content or aging period. In comparison of the relations $N\sigma_a^* \sim \beta_L^*$ (in a dash line) and $N\sigma_a^* \sim t^*$ (in a dot line) with $N\sigma_a^* \sim \beta_F^*$(in a dash-dot line), it can be observed that the soil axial shear stress is more responsive to the lime content than to the fiber content, and most sensitive to the soil-lime curing period among the four input variables. For instance, for the given axial strain and initial values (σ_{0i} = 100 kPa, β_{Fi} = 0.25%, β_{Li} = 2.5% and σ_a = 10%), if β_F^*, β_L^*, and t^* increase by 100% (X^* = 1.0) from their initial values, the soil axial strength is improved by 20%, 25% and 35%, respectively. The quantitative results in Fig. 11 are consistent with the coupling effects shown in Figs. 8, 9 and 10. The fact that confining pressure substantially affects soil strength can be also observed in Fig. 11.

5. Summaries and conclusions

In this chapter, the standard backpropagation algorithm and the Levenberg-Marquardt backpropagation algorithm were derived in vector forms. Then, the confidence intervals and prediction intervals for the nonlinear structure like feedforward neural networks were discussed. Particularly, the impact of neural network structure, i.e. the number of hidden nodes, to confidence intervals was analyzed and demonstrated via a simple example. Finally, modeling of nonlinear elastic behavior of the reinforced soil using a feedforward neural network was conducted. As an application, the sensitivity of the strength of reinforced soil to the constitutive parameters was analyzed using the neural network-based model. From the work presented in this chapter, the following conclusions can be drawn:

1. The standard backpropagation algorithm and the Levenberg-Marquardt backpropagation algorithm were derived in vector forms. The vector forms of the backpropagation algorithms make training neural networks and computing confidence intervals more efficient and less error prone.
2. Confidence intervals and prediction intervals for neural network regressions were presented. Especially, when the Levenberg-Marquardt backpropagation algorithm is used to train a neural network, since the Jacobian matrix has been calculated to update the weights and biases of the neural network, the confidence interval with a confidence level can be easily computed to evaluate the predictive capability of the neural network which the unseen data is fed into. A demonstrated example shows that too many hidden nodes in a neural network may result in a poor prediction, i.e. the prediction interval will be too wide since the trained neural network overfits noisy data. Meanwhile, not enough hidden nodes will also lead a poor prediction since the nonlinearity of a model cannot be fully identified.
3. Modeling of nonlinear elastic behavior of the soil reinforced with short fiber and stabilized with lime powder using a feedforward neural network was performed. This is the first attempt to model the nonlinear elastic behavior of fiber-lime reinforced soil under multi-axial shear loading using a neural network. The results of modeling reinforced soil are satisfactory. From the experimental data, neural network model and prediction intervals calculation, the following three points can be summarized and concluded,

a. Testing results indicate that the axial stress-strain relation is a nonlinear function of multiple variables, such as confining pressure, fiber content, lime content and sample curing time. To simulate such a nonlinear stress-strain relationship, a feedforward neural network is a good tool. The adopted neural network has one hidden layer with six nodes in it. Five variables are designated as inputs to model nonlinear elastic behavior of the soil. To train and test the neural network, thirty sets of data from conventional triaxial shear tests are selected to train the neural network and four sets of unseen data are adopted to evaluate the trained neural network. Using the derived approximate confidence interval equation (23), all predicted values of axial shear stress by the neural network model are within the envelope of the confidence interval with confidence level of 95%.
b. Parameters sensitivity and coupling effect were analyzed using the neural network based model. The sensitivity analysis of soil mechanical property to the model inputs such as the fiber content, the lime content, confining pressure and the sample curing period was conducted. The quantitative results show that the soil mechanical property is more sensitive to the lime content than to the fiber content. The mechanical property of the soil-lime mixture can be substantially improved with a prolonging curing period,

particularly within a duration from 0 to 28 days. From the analysis of coupling effect, the axial shear stress of composite soil increases exponentially with the increase of fiber content and logarithmically with an increasing aging period for the soil mixed with lime powder. Sample curing time plays a more significant role than other factors.

c. The neural network model provides a convenient and useful tool for analysis of mechanical behavior of composite soil and for applications to various engineering designs. With the confidence interval evaluation, the neural network model can be further applied to the stress-strain relation for large soil deformation

6. Appendix

Neural networks derive their advantages from their special structures - the massive interconnection of simple processing units. If the weights and biases of a neural network are considered as elements of matrices, the matrix calculus will become very useful for developing new algorithms for training neural networks. This appendix provides two basic chain rules for matrix derivatives. Detailed information can be found in the books authored by Cichocki and Unbehauen (Cichocki and Unbehauen, 1993) and Lewis (Lewis, 1995).

1. **The general chain rule**

Theorem 1 Let $\mathbf{f}: D \rightarrow \Re^m$ *be a differentiable real vector on an open r-dimensional set* $D \subset \Re^r$, *and let* $\mathbf{u}: S \rightarrow D$ *be differentiable on an open set n-dimensional* $S \subset \Re^n$. *Then, the composite vector function* $\mathbf{F}(\mathrm{x})=\mathbf{f}(\mathrm{u}(\mathrm{x}))$ *is differentiable on the open set S. The general chain rule of the differentiation of the vector function F(x) is*

$$\partial \mathbf{F} / \partial \mathbf{x} = \mathbf{J_F}(\mathbf{x}) = \mathbf{J_f}(\mathbf{u}(\mathbf{x}))\mathbf{J_u}(\mathbf{x}) \tag{A.1}$$

and the gradient matrix $\nabla_{\mathbf{x}}\mathbf{F}$ *is*

$$\nabla_{\mathbf{x}}\mathbf{F} = \nabla_{\mathbf{x}}\mathbf{u}\ \nabla_{\mathbf{u}}\mathbf{f} \tag{A.2}$$

Proof is omitted.

2. **The chain rule for differentiation of a scalar function with respect to a matrix**

Theorem 2 *Let* $F = h(\mathbf{f})$ *be a differentiable real-valued scalar function of a real vector f, h:* $\Re^m \rightarrow \Re$ *and let* $\mathbf{f}(\mathbf{w}) = [f_1(\mathbf{w}) \quad f_2(\mathbf{w}) \quad \cdots \quad f_m(\mathbf{w})]^T$ *be a differentiable vector function of the matrix w with*

$$\mathbf{w} = \begin{bmatrix} w_{11} & w_{12} & \cdots & w_{1l} \\ w_{21} & w_{22} & \cdots & w_{2l} \\ \vdots & \vdots & \ddots & \vdots \\ w_{n1} & w_{n2} & \cdots & w_{nl} \end{bmatrix}.$$

Then, the chain rule for the differentiation of the scalar function F with respect to the matrix $\mathbf{w}$ *yields*

$$\frac{\partial F(\mathbf{w})}{\partial \mathbf{w}} = \sum_{k=1}^{m} \frac{\partial h}{\partial f_k(\mathbf{w})} \frac{\partial f_k(\mathbf{w})}{\partial \mathbf{w}} \tag{A.3}$$

Proof: from the derivative of the scale function with respect to a variable matrix, one has

$$\frac{\partial f(\mathbf{w})}{\partial \mathbf{w}} = \begin{bmatrix} \frac{\partial f}{\partial w_{11}} & \frac{\partial f}{\partial w_{12}} & \cdots & \frac{\partial f}{\partial w_{1l}} \\ \frac{\partial f}{\partial w_{21}} & \frac{\partial f}{\partial w_{22}} & \cdots & \frac{\partial f}{\partial w_{2l}} \\ \vdots & \vdots & \ddots & \vdots \\ \frac{\partial f}{\partial w_{n1}} & \frac{\partial f}{\partial w_{n2}} & \cdots & \frac{\partial f}{\partial w_{nl}} \end{bmatrix} \tag{A.4}$$

For each element of Equation (A.4), use the general chain rule to reach $\nabla_{w_{ij}} F = \nabla_{\mathbf{f}} F \, \nabla_{w_{ij}} \mathbf{f}$, which can be alternatively expressed by:

$$\frac{\partial F(\mathbf{w})}{\partial w_{ij}} = \frac{\partial h}{\partial \mathbf{f}(\mathbf{w})} \frac{\partial \mathbf{f}(\mathbf{w})}{\partial w_{ij}} \tag{A.5}$$

For $\frac{\partial h(\mathbf{f})}{\partial \mathbf{f}} = \begin{bmatrix} \frac{\partial h}{\partial f_1} & \frac{\partial h}{\partial f_2} & \cdots & \frac{\partial h}{\partial f_m} \end{bmatrix}$ and $\frac{\partial \mathbf{f}(\mathbf{w})}{\partial w_{ij}} = [\frac{\partial f_1}{\partial w_{ij}} \quad \frac{\partial f_2}{\partial w_{ij}} \quad \cdots \quad \frac{\partial f_m}{\partial w_{ij}}]^{\mathrm{T}}$, Expression (A.5) becomes

$$\frac{\partial F(\mathbf{w})}{\partial w_{ij}} = \sum_{k=1}^{m} \frac{\partial h}{\partial f_k(\mathbf{w})} \frac{\partial f_k(\mathbf{w})}{\partial w_{ij}} . \tag{A.6}$$

When $i = 1,\ldots,n; j=1,\ldots,l$, (A.6) becomes:

$$\frac{\partial F(\mathbf{w})}{\partial \mathbf{w}} = \sum_{k=1}^{m} \frac{\partial h}{\partial f_k(\mathbf{w})} \frac{\partial f_k(\mathbf{w})}{\partial \mathbf{w}} . \tag{A.7}$$

7. References

Cichocki, A. & Unbehauen, R. (1993). *Neural Networks for Optimisation and Signal Processing*, New York: John Willey and Sons.

Chryssoloiuris, G., Lee, M., and Ramsey, A., (1996), Confidence Interval Prediction for Neural Network Models, *IEEE Trans. Neur. Networks*, 1, 229-232

Hagan, M.T. & Menhaj, M.B. (1994). Training feedforward networks with the Marquardt Algorithm, *IEEE Trans. Neur. Networks*, 5, 989-993

He. S & Li, J. (2008). Modeling Nonlinear Elastic Behavior of Reinforced Soil Using Artificial Neural Networks, *Applied Soft Computing*, 9(3), 954-961.

He. S & Li, J. (2006). Parameter Estimation of Reinforced Soil Based on Neural Networks, in: Proc. Int. Conf. on Computational Intelligence for Modeling, Control and Automation Sydney, Australia, 137-143.

Hornik, K., Stinchcombe, M. & White, H. (1989). Multilayer feedforward networks are universal approximations, *Neur. Networks*, 2, 359-366.

Hwang, J.T.G. & Ding, A. A. (1997) Prediction intervals for artificial neural networks. J. American Statistical Association 92(438), 748-757.

Issa, R. & Zaman, M. (1999). Estimating resilient modulus of aggregate base by backpropagation neural network model, in: *Proc. 4th Int. Conf. on Constitutive Laws for Engineering Materials*, New York, July, 493-496.

Li, J. & Ding, D. W. (2002). Nonlinear elastic behavior of fiber-reinforced soil under cycle loading, *J. of Soil Dynamics and Earthquake Engineering*, 22 (9) (2002) 265-271.

Li, J. & Zhang, L.J. (2003). Nonlinear elastic behavior of soil reinforced with fiber and lime, in: Proc. 12th Pan-American Conf. on Soil Mechanics and Geotechnical Engineering (eds. P. J. Culligan,, H. H. Einstein, and A. J. Whittle), 610-618.

Lewis, F. L. (1995). *Optimal Control*, New York: Wiley-Interscience.

Michalowiski, R. L. & Zhao, A. (1995). Continuum versus structural approach to stability of reinforced soil, *J. of Geotechnical Engineering ASCE*, 121 (2) 152-162.

Rajasekaran, S. & Amalraj, R. (2002). Prediction of design parameter in civil engineering problems using SLNN with a single hidden RBF neuron, *Computers & Structure*, 80 (31) 2495-2505.

Seber, G.A.F. & Wild, C.J. (1989). *Nonlinear Regression*, New York, John Wiley and Sons.

Yang, L., Kavli, T., Carlin, M., Clausen, S, & Groot, P. (2002). An evaluation of confidence bound estimation methods for neural networks, in *Advances in Computational Intelligence and Learning: Methods and Applications*, Kluwer Academic Publishers.

Landslide Susceptibility Mapping: an Assessment of the Use of an Advanced Neural Network Model with Five Different Training Strategies

Dr. Biswajeet Pradha, Shattri Mansor and Saied Pirasteh
Institute of Advanced Technology, Spatial & Numerical Modelling Laboratory
University Putra Malaysia
Serdang, 43400, Selangor Darul Ehsan
Malaysia

1. Introduction

Landslide presents a significant constraint to development in many parts of Malaysia which experiences frequent landslides, with the most recent occurring in 2000, 2001, 2004, 2007 and 2008. Damages and losses are regularly incurred because; historically there has been too little consideration of the potential problems in land use planning and slope stability analysis. Landslides are mostly occurred in Malaysia mainly due to heavy tropical rainfall. In recent years greater awareness of landslide problems has led to significant changes in the control of development on unstable land. So far, few attempts have been made to predict these landslides or preventing the damage caused by them. In last few years, landslide susceptibility analysis using GIS and data mining such as fuzzy logic, and artificial neural network methods have been applied by researchers in different countries (Akgun et al., 2008; Ercanoglu & Gokceoglu 2002; Gomez & Kavzoglu, 2005; Pistocchi et al. 2002; Lee et al. 2003a, 2003b, 2004a, 2004b). But their result output can not be directly used in the Malaysian landslide susceptibility analysis. This is due to the changes in the geographical environment set up, litho types and different climatic conditions. The local geographical settings cause different landslide types based on completely different mechanisms and are absolute incomparable. Through scientific analysis of landslides, we can assess and predict landslide-susceptible areas, and thus decrease landslide damage through proper preparation. To achieve this aim, landslide susceptibility analysis techniques have been applied, and validated in the study area using five different training strategies with the aid of artificial neural network.

In landslide literature, there have been many studies carried out on landslide susceptibility and hazard mapping using GIS. There are number of different approaches for the measurement of landslide hazard, including direct and indirect heuristic approaches, and deterministic, probabilistic, statistical and data mining approaches. Recently, there have been studies on landslide susceptibility mapping using GIS, and many of these studies have applied probabilistic models (Baeza and Corominas, 2001; Clerici et al., 2002; Dahal et al., 2008; Dai et al., 2001; Lee & Dan, 2005; Lee & Lee, 2006; Lee & Min, 2001; Lee & Sambath,

2006; Lee, 2004; Lee et al., 2002a, 2002b; Gokceoglu et al., 2000; Lee & Choi, 2003; Lee & Pradhan, 2006, 2007; Nefeslioglu et al., 2008; Santacana et al., 2003; Pradhan et al., 2006; Youssef et al., 2009). One of the multivariate models available, the logistic regression models, has also been applied to landslide susceptibility mapping (Chau & Chan, 2005; Dai & Lee, 2003; Lee, 2005, 2007a; Pradhan, 2010a; 2010c; Pradhan et al., 2008; Pradhan & Lee, 2010a; Pradhan et al., 2010a; Pradhan & Youssef, 2010; Ohlmacher & Davis, 2003; Suzen & Doyuran, 2004a, 2004b). In last few years, a new approach to landslide hazard evaluation using GIS, data mining using fuzzy logic, and artificial neural network, neuro-fuzzy models have been applied (Catani et al., 2005; Caniani et al., 2008; Chang & Chao, 2006; Ercanoglu and Gokceoglu, 2002; Ercanoglu et al., 2004; Ermini et al., 2005; Kanungo et al., 2006; Lee, 2007b; Lee & Evangelista, 2006; Lee et al., 2006, 2007; Neaupane & Achet, 2004; Pradhan, 2010b, 2010d; 2010c; Pradhan et al., 2009; Pradhan et al., 2010a, b, c, d; Pradhan & Buchroithner, 2010; Pradhan & Lee, 2007, 2009, 2010a, 2010b, 2010c; Pradhan & Pirasteh, 2010; Tangestani, 2004; Yesilncar & Topal, 2005).

In recent years, Lee & Pradhan (2006), Lee & Pradhan (2007), and Pradhan & Lee (2010a) investigated the landslide susceptibility in Malaysia. Pradhan & Lee (2010a) evaluated three models for landslide susceptibility analysis using frequency ratio, logistic regression and artificial neural network model. Pradhan & Lee (2010a) analyzed the rainfall precipitation in the Penang area using back-propagation neural networks. However, they could not have a detail landslide hazard analysis due to lack of rainfall intensity data. Slope stability and rainfall intensity is very important factors causing most of the landslides in Malaysia. Besides these two important factors of rainfall and slope, soil weight and distance to drainage are also important factors in some regions. Pradhan et al., (2009) investigated the landslide susceptibility using fuzzy model at Penang Island and they pointed out some important factors, such as topographic slope, topographic aspect, topographic curvature, distance to drainage, lithology, distance to faults, soil texture, landcover, vegetation index and accumulated rainfall intensity.

The objective and motivation of this study is to demonstrate artificial neural network model with five different training strategies for landslide susceptibility mapping with the aid of GIS. In order to get a stable and reliable result, in this paper, nine geological and geomorphological factors including, topographic slope, topographic aspect, topographic curvature, stream power index (spi), distance from drainage;, flow length, flow accumulation, topographic wetness index, distance to road, lithology, distance to the fault lines, soil types, land cover, and ndvi were used to predict landslide susceptible areas. These fourteen factors constructed an ANN using the back propagation algorithm for landslide susceptibility mapping. To meet the objectives, firstly the ANN model was trained using training sites which can be directly utilized for the landslide susceptibility analysis as long as the recorded nine factors are fed into an ANN model. Five different training samples were selected to train the ANN in order to avoid bias effect in the final results. Finally, the results of the landslide susceptibility maps were validated using the existing landslide location data with the aid of receiver operating characteristics (ROC) approaches.

2. Study area characteristics

In this research, a landslide-prone area in the Cameron Highlands in Peninsular Malaysia (Fig. 1) was selected for landslide susceptibility assessment using ANN model. The study area (Fig. 1) falls in the districts of Cameron Highlands which seeing a rapid development with land clearing for housing estate, hotel /apartment causing erosion and landslides. Cameron Highland is a district of Pahang state which is one of the 13 states of the Federation of Malaysia. The District of Cameron Highlands is located in western Pahang bordering the states of Perak and Kelantan. The Pahang - Perak boundary runs approximately in a north - south direction along a sharp divide with numerous high peaks that rise over 1500m above the mean sea level. From north to south along this divide, the following peaks, Gunung Pass (1587m), two unnamed peaks (1501m and 1796m), Gunung Irau (2110m), Gunung Brinchang (2031m), Gunung Ruil (1718m), Gunung Jasar (1704m), Gunung Dungun (1576m) and Gunung Duri (1530m) are present. At Gunung Duri, the divide turns eastwards for about 10km before turning towards the south and southeasterly (Pradhan and Lee, 2010b). The study area covers an area of 285 km^2 and is located near the northern central part of peninsular Malaysia. It is bounded to the north by Kelantan, west by Perak. Annual rainfall is very high averaging between 2,500 mm to 3,000 mm per year. Two pronounced wet seasons from September to December and February to May. Rainfall peaks between November to December and March to May. The geomorphology of the area consists of undulating plateau stretching about 12 km. The geomorphology of the area is characterized by a rugged topography with the hill ranges varying from 600 m.s.l to over 4800 m. The geology of the Cameron Highlands consists of mostly two types of litho types: igneous and metamorphic rocks. Post-Triassic- Mesozoic granite comprises of most of the granite rocks where as there are few patches of metamorphic rocks mostly comprising of Silurian-Ordovician Schist, phyllite, limestone and sandstone. Several field observations have been carried out in the month of April/June/September 2006 and 2007 for collecting ground data.

The landuse in the study area is mainly peat swamp forest, plantation forest, inland forest, scrub, grassland and ex-mining area. The slope angle of the area ranges from 0 degrees to as much as 86 degrees. The relief of the study area varies between 860- 2110 m.s.l.

The annual rainfall of Cameron Highlands, like in all tropical hilly regions, is very high, averaging between 2,500 and 3,000 mm per annum. There are two pronounced wet seasons from September to December and from February to May each year. Rainfall in Cameron

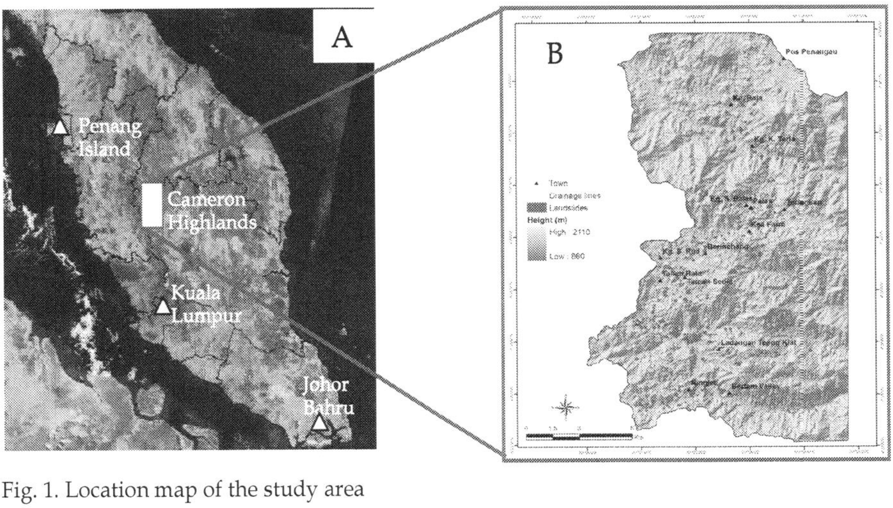

Fig. 1. Location map of the study area

Highlands peaks between March and May and also from November to December. The single-day rainfall high that had been recorded ranged from 87 to 100 mm. It is during such times that many streams and rivers in the Cameron Highlands may overflow, flooding the surrounding areas, and landslides such as debris flow may occur along the river valleys. The intensity of the rain is another factor that affects the fill slopes, causing severe sheet, rill, and gully erosion. During such times, many of the natural and man-made slopes are marginally stable.

3. GIS data used

For the landslide-susceptibility mapping, the main steps were data collection and construction of a spatial database from which the relevant landslide conditioning factors are extracted, followed by assessment of the landslide susceptibility using the relationship between landslide and landslide-conditioning factors, and validation of the results. In the first step, landslides were detected in the study area by interpretation of aerial photographs and extensive field surveys. A landslide inventory map was compiled from 1:10,000 - 1:50,000 scale aerial photographs, and was used to evaluate the frequency and distribution of shallow landslides in the area. In addition, all historical landslide reports, newspaper records, and archived data have been assembled for the period under examination. The source material varies in quality with respect to the precise location of the landslide event. Based on the site description, archived database, and aerial photo interpretation, the locations of the individual landslides were drawn on 1:25, 000 maps, and the location was plotted as close as possible based on the classification scheme proposed by Varnes (1984). Field observations were used to confirm the fresh landslide locations (scars) and types. In the aerial photographs, historical landslides could be observed as breaks in the forest canopy, bare soil, or geomorphological features, like head- and side scarps, flow tracks, and soil- and debris deposits below a scar. These landslides were then classified and sorted out based on their modes of occurrence. The landslide inventory map was very helpful in understanding different triggering factors that control different slope movement types (Cruden & Varnes, 1996). Most of the landslides are shallow rotational, and there are a few translational and flow types. However, during the analyses that were performed in the present study, only the rotational failures are considered, and the other types of failures were eliminated because the occurrence of the other types of failures is rare and ignorable. Consequently, the susceptibility maps that are produced in this paper are valid for the shallow rotational failures. To assemble a database to assess the surface area and number of landslides in the study area, a total of 48 shallow rotational failures were mapped in the study area. The landslide inventory map that was compiled in the present study is shown in Fig. 1b.

In order to develop a method for the assessment of landslide susceptibility, determination of the conditioning factors for the landslides is crucial (Ercanoglu & Gokceoglu, 2002). In fact, the regional landslide assessments should be practical and applicable for the study area. For the first requirement for this statement, the input parameters should be representative, reliable and obtained easily. In this study, we selected the input parameters considering field observations performed on the actual landslides. There were a total of seven landslide conditioning factors considered in the analyses performed. The basic landslide conditioning factors such as altitude, slope angle, plan curvature, distance to drainage, soil texture and stream power index were employed. As a result of the field observations, it was observed that the landslides have a close relation with the distance from the roads. For this reason, the

distance to the road was considered as a landslide conditioning factor for the study area, in addition to the basic landslide conditioning factors. All of the factors that were employed in this paper were transformed into a grid-type spatial database using the GIS (Fig. 2).
Topography, soil, and road transport databases were constructed for the analysis (Fig. 2) (Table 1). Maps relevant to landslide occurrences were constructed from a vector-type spatial database using Arc/Info GIS software (ESRI). These included 1:25,000 scale topographic maps (National Mapping Agency, Malaysia) and 1:100,000 scale soil maps (Department of Irrigation and Drainage, Malaysia). For the digital elevation model (DEM) creation, 20-m interval contours, spot heights and survey base points showing the elevation values were extracted from the 1:25, 000-scale topographic maps. This is used to generate the DEM with 10-m pixel size and triangulated irregular network from which the altitude, slope angle, aspect, curvature and stream power index are derived [Fig. 2(a)-(d)]. The accuracy of the DEM was quantitatively accessed based on the several field-surveyed points using GPS and total station points (Pradhan et al., 2010d). A total of 130 GPS check points were used are used to evaluate the vertical accuracy of the DEM. As a quality assurance of DEM, the vertical accuracy of a set of terrain points is first determined by its root mean square error (RMSE), the square root of the average of the set of squared differences between two points. The RMSE between the "true" values and estimated values is defined as in Eq. (1):

$$RMSE = \sqrt{\frac{\sum_{i=1}^{n}\left(Z_{fieldi} - Z_{DEMi}\right)^2}{n}} \tag{1}$$

where n is the number of field reference points, Z_{field} is the terrain height of points measured by GPS, Z_{DEM} is the height obtained from the DEM. In addition, the height differences between the DEM for the surveyed-check points were analyzed using standard statistical mean and standard deviation to determine the error. The analysis results (Table 2) revealed that the RMSE error for the obtained DEM was ± 2.39 m which is within the acceptable limit (Toz & Erdogan, 2008). Validation results of DEM revealed that, significant differences were not observed from the RMSE values which only differ slightly on each checking locations.

Classification	Sub-Classification	GIS Data Type	Scale
Geological Hazard	Landslide	Polygon coverage	1:25,000
Basic Map	Topographic Map	Point, Line and Polygon coverage	1:25,000
	Geological Map	Polygon coverage	1:63,300
	Drainage	Line coverage	1: 25,000
	Land Cover	GRID	2.50 m × 2.5 m
	Soil Map	GRID	1:100,000
	Normalised Differentiated Vegetation Index (ndvi)	GRID	2.5 m × 2.5 m

Table 1. List of data used in this study

In the present study, substantial attention has been given for slope conditions, because there is a physical relation between the landslide occurrence and slope gradient. Increase in slope gradient results in increase of driving forces. For this reason, slope configuration and steepness plays an important role on the susceptibility of a slope to landsliding. This makes slope an important factor in preparing the landslide susceptibility map. The slope map was reclassified into four classes following the standard classification scheme set by the Ministry of Science, Technology and Environment Malaysia for hill land: (1) < 15 degrees, (2) 16 - 25 degrees, (3) 26 - 35 degrees, and (4) > 35 degrees (Fig. 2a) (Pradhan & Lee, 2010c). In the case of aspect layer, eight directions are shown for the different direction of slope (Fig. 2b).

Average error (m.)	1.58 m
Absolute average error (m.)	1.81 m
RMSE (m.)	± 2.39 m

Table 2. Errors of the DEM for the study area

The term curvature is generally defined as the curvature of a line formed by intersection of a random plane with the terrain surface (Ercanoglu & Gokceoglu, 2002). The influence of plan curvature on the land degradation processes is the convergence or divergence of water during downhill flow. In addition, this parameter constitutes one of the main factors controlling the geometry of the terrain surface where landslides occur (Ercanoglu & Gokceoglu, 2002). In the case of the curvature negative curvatures represent concave, zero curvature represent flat and positive curvatures represents convex surface. The plan curvature map was prepared using the avenue routine in ArcView 3.2 (Fig. 2c).

The fourth parameter considered in the present study is stream power index (SPI) and is shown in Fig. 2d. According to the Moore et al., (1991), SPI is a measure of erosive power of water flow based on the assumption that discharge (q) is proportional to specific catchment area A_s (Equation 2).

$$SPI = A_s \tan\beta \tag{2}$$

where A_s is the specific catchment area (m2m-1) while β is the slope gradient in degree.

In addition, the distance from drainage was calculated using the topographic database. The drainage buffer was calculated based on Euclidean distance method at 50 m intervals as shown in Fig. 2e. The sixth and seventh parameters used in the study are flow length and flow accumulation which were derived from the digital elevation model in ArcGIS (Fig. 2f, 2g). Road-cuts are usually sites of anthropologically instability. A given road segment may act as a barrier, a net source, a net sink or a corridor for water flow, and depending on its location in the area (Ercanoglu & Gokceolgu, 2002). It usually, serves as a source of landslides. The road map is derived from the topography map. From the field observation, it has been noticed that most of the landslides have occurred along the cut-slopes and roads. The distance to road buffer is selected based on the occurrence of landslides to the proximity of the road. Therefore, a 50 m buffer zone is calculated based on the Euclidean distance method in ArcGIS 9.0 (Fig. 2h). Subsequently, the topographic wetness index map was prepared in the ArcGIS (Fig. 2i). The lithology map was prepared from the hardcopy geology map (Fig. 2j). The proximity to major fault lines is calculated based on Euclidean distance method in ArcGIS 9.0 (Fig. 2k). The soil texture map was prepared from a

1:100,000-scale soil map (Fig. 2l), which is the only existing soil map for the studied area. The landcover map was extracted from the Spot 5 satellite images using supervised classification techniques (Fig. 2m). Finally, the normalised difference vegetation index map (ndvi) was also prepared from the Spot 5 satellite image (Fig. 2n).

All the fourteen landslide conditioning factors were converted to a raster grid with 10 m × 10 m cells with 2418 rows by 1490 columns for the application of the ANN model. GIS ArcGIS 9.0 version software package and MATLAB was used as the basic analysis tools for spatial management and data manipulation.

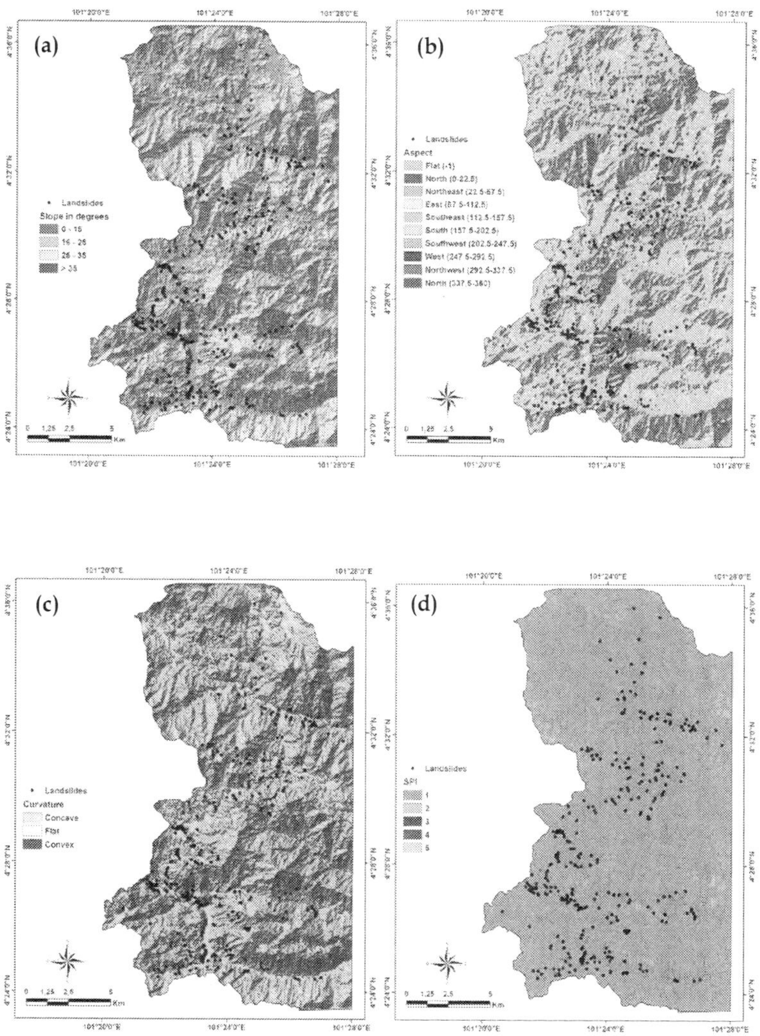

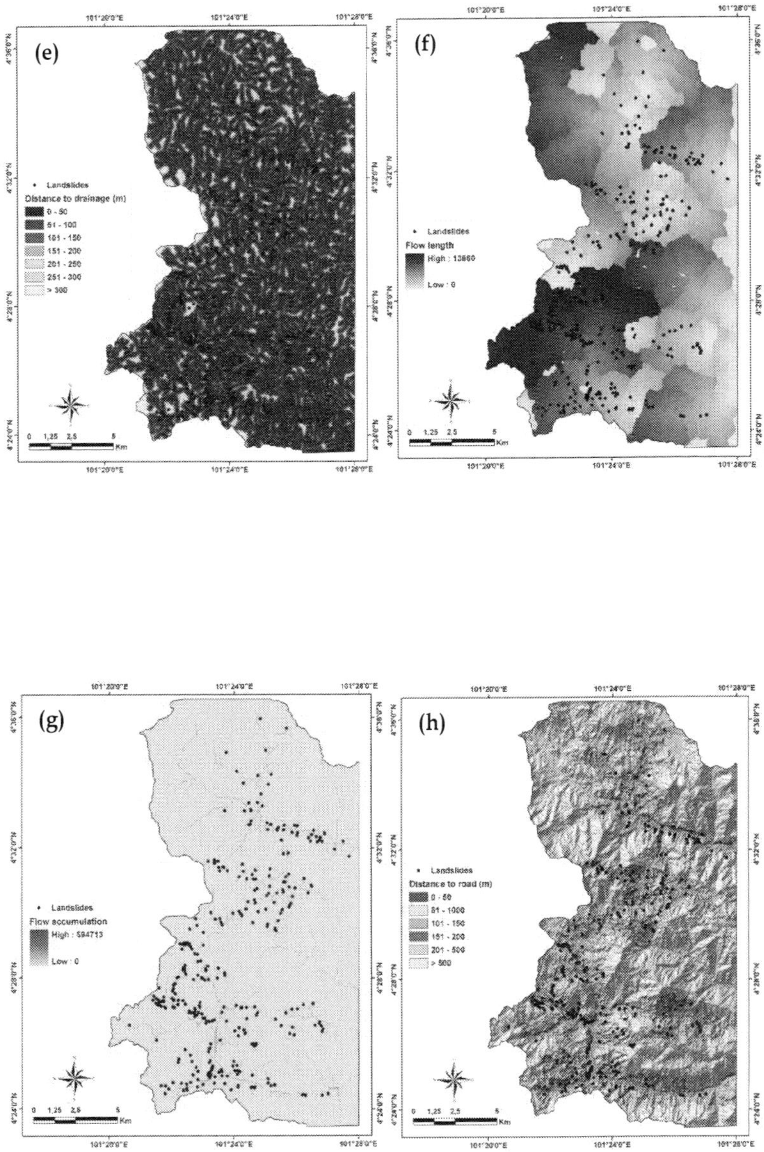
(e)
Landslides
Distance to drainage (m)
0 - 50
51 - 100
101 - 150
151 - 200
201 - 250
251 - 300
> 300
(f)
Landslides
Flow length
High : 13860
Low : 0
(g)
Landslides
Flow accumulation
High : 594713
Low : 0
(h)
Landslides
Distance to road (m)
0 - 50
51 - 1000
101 - 150
151 - 200
201 - 500
> 500

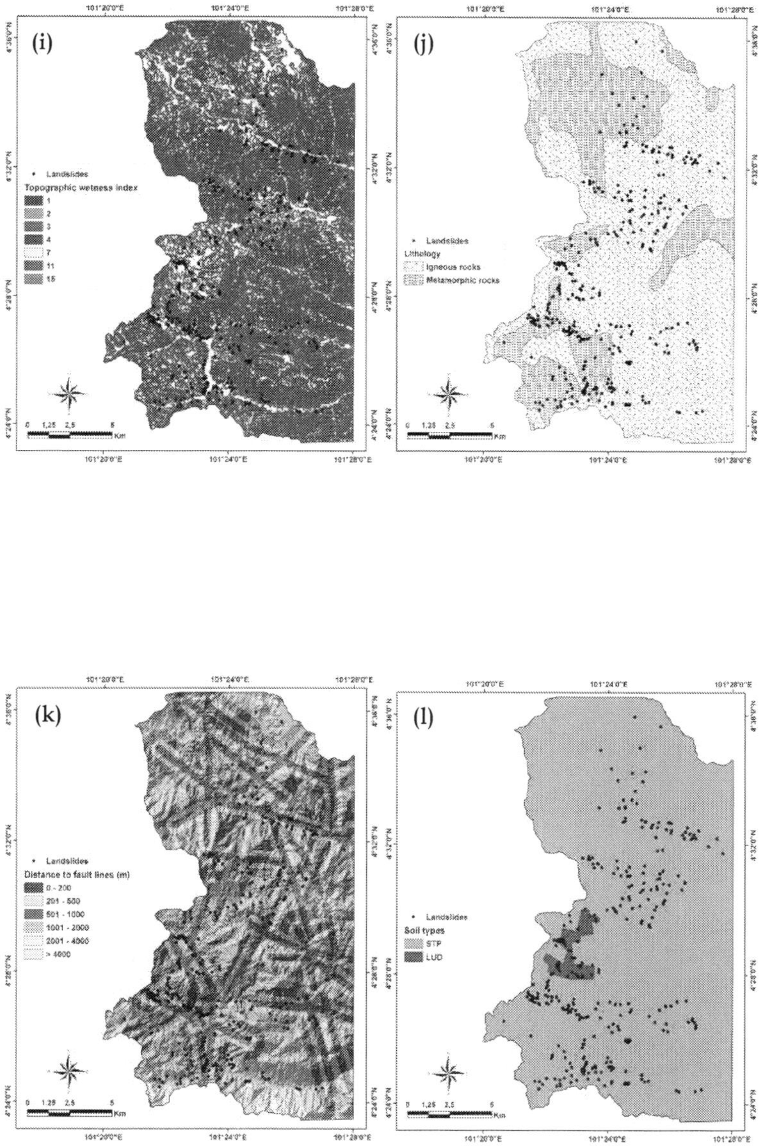
(i)
Landslides
Topographic wetness index
1
2
3
4
7
11
15
(j)
Landslides
Lithology
Igneous rocks
Metamorphic rocks
(k)
Landslides
Distance to fault lines (m)
0 - 200
201 - 500
501 - 1000
1001 - 2000
2001 - 4000
> 4000
(l)
Landslides
Soil types
STP
LUD

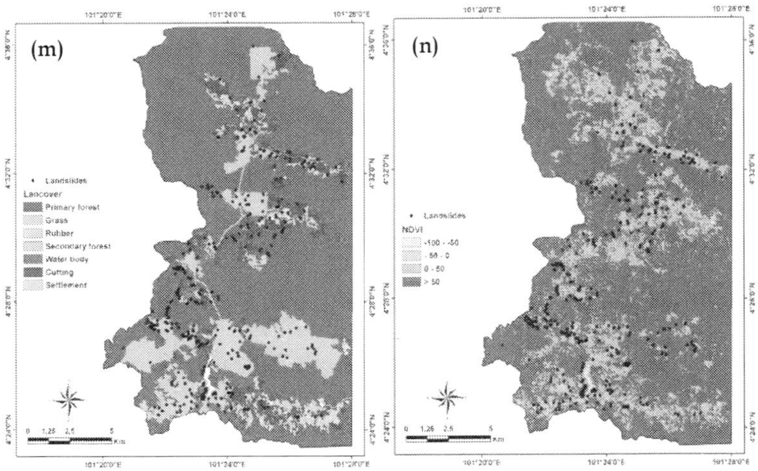

Fig. 2. Input data layers (a) Slope; (b) Aspect; (c) Curvature; (d) Stream power index (spi); (e) Distance from drainage; (f) Flow length; (g) Flow accumulation; (h) Topographic wetness index; (i) Distance to road; (j) Lithology; (k) Distance to the fault lines; (l) Soil types; (m) Land cover; and (n) Vegetation index (NDVI)

4. Artificial Neural Network model: preview

The artificial neural network approach has many advantages compared with other statistical methods (Basheer & Hajmeer, 2000). Firstly, the artificial neural network method is independent of the statistical distribution of the data and there is no need for specific statistical variables. Neural networks allow the target classes to be defined in relation to their distribution in the corresponding domain of each data source (Zhou, 1999), and therefore integration of remote sensing data or GIS data is convenient. An artificial neural network is a "computational mechanism able to acquire, represent, and compute a mapping from one multivariate space of information to another, given a set of data representing that mapping" (Atkinson & Tatnall, 1997). Most ANN models share a number of characteristics. These will be identified before proceeding to describe particular models (Moody & Katz, 2003). First, unlike expert systems, ANNs are not initialized with any external rule base. Rather the goal of the ANN is to internally identify a set of rules for matching input data to output conclusions. An ANN is composed of a set of nodes and a number of interconnected processing elements. ANN uses learning algorithms to model knowledge and save this knowledge in weighted connections, mimicking the function of a human brain (Turban & Aronson, 2001; Schalkoff, 1997). One of the most commonly used ANN models is the feed-forward back-propagation ANN. This is a supervised, pattern recognition model that needs to be trained using a data set for which both the input values (x) for a set of predictors and the correct output values (y) are known for a set of examples. The architecture of this ANN is based on a structure known as the Multi-Layer Perceptron (MLP). The MLP, as the name implies, consists of a set of layers, each of which is composed of a set of nodes (alternatively referred to as "processing elements", "units", "processing units", or "neurons"). The MLP with the back-propagation algorithm is trained using a set of examples of associated input and output values (Hines, 1997). The purpose of an artificial neural network is to build a model of the data-generating process, so that the network can generalize and predict outputs from inputs that it has not previously seen. This learning MLP algorithm is trained with the "Back-Propagation algorithm", which consists of an input layer, hidden layer, and an output layer.

The first layer of the network, or input layer, contains a node for each of l input variables (Fig. 3). The l input variables are analogous to the independent variables in multiple regressions. When a given set of l input values for one of the n samples in the training data set is presented to the input nodes, we say that the network is presented with an input pattern ($x_{i,l}p = x_{i,1}, x_{i,2}, \ldots\ldots, x_{i,3}$, where $i=1$ to n). The superscript indicates terms that consists of or refer to a given pattern of values (Moody & Katz, 2003).

The last layer of the network, or output layer, contains nodes, one for each output type (Fig. 3). In this case, there are nine input nodes (one each for slope, aspect, curvature, stream power index (spi), distance from drainage;, flow length, flow accumulation, topographic wetness index, distance to road, lithology, distance to the fault lines, soil types, land cover, and ndvi). Sandwiched between the input and output layers is one "hidden" layer which will allow complexities to develop in the mapping functions. In this case, a three tired ANN architecture model is used. The hidden layer, like the input and output layer, consists of nodes.

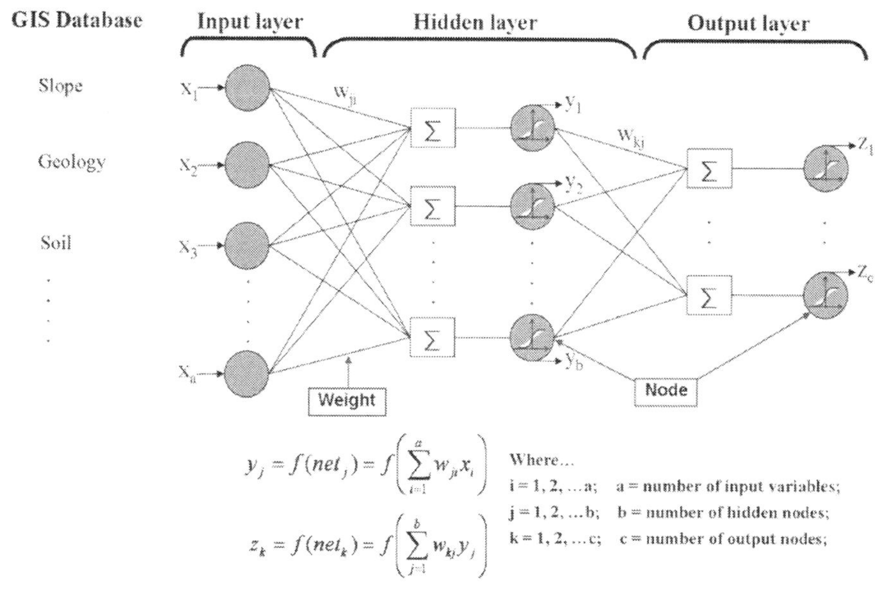

Fig. 2. Three tiered architecture of feed-forward, back-propagation neural network (multilayer perception).

The hidden and output layer neurons process their inputs by multiplying each input by a corresponding weight, summing the product, and then processing the sum using a nonlinear transfer function to produce a result. An artificial neural network "learns" by adjusting the weights between the neurons in response to the errors between the actual output values and the target output values. At the end of this training phase, the neural network provides a model that should be able to predict a target value from a given input value.

There are two stages involved in using neural networks for multi-source classification: the training stage, in which the internal weights are adjusted; and the classifying stage. Typically, the back-propagation algorithm trains the multi-layered until some targeted minimal error is achieved between the desired and actual output values of the network. Once the training is complete, the network is used as a feed-forward structure to produce a classification for the entire data (Paola & Schwengerdt, 1995; Swingler, 1996). For this study, the neural networks were simulated in the neural network module of Mathworks MATLAB (The MathWorks Inc. 1999). The back propagation multilayer perceptron (MLP) is a commonly used and widely available neural network structure in geospatial analysis and was used in this study.

5. Landslide susceptibility mapping using the Artificial Neural Network model

5.1 Application of frequency ratio model

Frequency ratio approaches are based on the observed relationships between distribution of landslides and each landslide-related factor, to reveal the correlation between landslide locations and the factors in the study area. Using the frequency ratio model, the spatial relationships between landslide-occurrence location and each factors contributing landslide occurrence were derived. The frequency is calculated from analysis of the relation between landslides and the attribute factors (Lee & Pradhan, 2006). In the relation analysis, the ratio is that of the area where landslides occurred to the total area, so that a value of 1 is an average value. If the value is greater than 1, it means a higher correlation, and value lower than 1 means lower correlation.

To calculate the Landslide Susceptibility Index (HSI), each factor's frequency ratio values were summed to the training area as in equation (3). The landslide susceptible value represents the relative susceptibility to landslide occurrence. So the greater the value, the higher the susceptible to landslide occurrence and the lower the value, the lower the susceptible to landslide occurrence.

$$HSI = Fr1 + Fr2 + \ldots\ldots + Frn \tag{3}$$

(HSI: Landslide Susceptibility Index; Fr: Rating of each factors' type or range)

5.2 Application of logistic regression model

Logistic regression allows one to form a multivariate regression relation between a dependent variable and several independent variables. Logistic regression, which is one of the multivariate analysis models, is useful for predicting the presence or absence of a characteristic or outcome based on values of a set of predictor variables. The advantage of logistic regression is that, through the addition of an appropriate link function to the usual linear regression model, the variables may be either continuous or discrete, or any combination of both types and they do not necessarily have normal distributions. In the case of multi-regression analysis, the factors must be numerical, and in the case of a similar statistical model, discriminant analysis, the variables must have a normal distribution. In the present situation, the dependent variable is a binary variable representing presence or absence of landslide. Where the dependent variable is binary, the logistic link function is applicable (Atkinson & Massari, 1998). For the present study, the dependent variable must be input as either 0 or 1, so the model applies well to landslide possibility analysis. Logistic regression coefficients can be used to estimate ratios for each of the independent variables in the model.

Quantitatively, the relationship between the occurrence and its dependency on several variables can be expressed as:

$$p = 1 / (1 + e\text{-}z) \quad (4)$$

where p is the probability of an event occurring. In the present situation, the value p is the estimated probability of landslide occurrence. The probability varies from 0 to 1 on an S-shaped curve and z is the linear combination. It follows that logistic regression involves fitting an equation of the following form to the data:

$$z = b0 + b1x1 + b2x2 + \ldots + bnxn \quad (5)$$

where b0 is the intercept of the model, the bi (i = 0, 1, 2, ..., n) are the slope coefficients of the logistic regression model, and the xi (i = 0, 1, 2, ..., n) are the independent variables. The linear model formed is then a logistic regression of presence or absence of landslides (present conditions) on the independent variables (pre-failure conditions).

Using the logistic regression model, the spatial relationship between landslide-occurrence and factors influencing landslides was assessed. The spatial databases of each factor were converted to ASCII format files for use in the statistical package, and the correlations between landslide and each factor were calculated. Though there were two cases, in the first case only one factor was used. Besides, logistic regression mathematical equations were formulated for each case. Finally, the probability that predicts the possibility of landslide-occurrence was calculated using the spatial database, equations (4) and (5). However, in the second case all factors were used logistic regression mathematical equations were formulated as shown in equations (4) and (5) for each case. Using formula (4) and (5), the landslide susceptibility index was calculated.

6. Landslide susceptibility mapping using Artificial Neural Network model

The probabilities of occurrence of landslides were calculated based on (a) the various input attributes that have been listed in table 1 and their cumulative influence (weightage values were derived from ground-based information) and (b) knowledge based classification. Before running the artificial neural network program, the training site should be selected. So, the landslide-prone (occurrence) area and the landslide-not-prone area were selected as training sites. Pixels from each of the two classes were randomly selected as training pixels, with 327 pixels denoting areas where landslide not occurred or occurred. First, areas where the landslide was not occurred were classified as "areas not prone to landslide" and areas where landslide was known to exist were assigned to an "areas prone to landslide" training set. Training sites were selected based on landslide location as prone training site and with a varying slope values as non-prone training site and then the MLP trained back propagation algorithm was computed. Five different training sites were selected randomly to produce five susceptibility maps.

The MLP trained with the Back-Propagation algorithm was then applied to the input attribute layers by modifying the number of hidden nodes and the learning rate. Distribution of hidden layers and entire training dataset is shown in Fig. 3. Hidden layers were selected two times of input attribute layers. So obviously, the output will have both "existing" and "non-existing" landslide areas. Some of the input attributes layers are continuous and others categorical in nature. Therefore, these data were converted to raster grid in order to apply the ANN model. Three-layered feed-forward network was implemented using the MATLAB software package. Here, "feed-forward" denotes that the interconnections between the layers propagate forward to the next layer. The number of hidden layers and the number of nodes in a hidden layer required for a particular classification problem are not easy to deduce. In this study, a 9 x 19 x 2 structure was selected for the network, with input data normalized in the range 0.1-0.9. The nominal and interval class group data were converted to continuous values ranging between 0.1 and 0.9. Therefore, all the layers were normalized in the range 0.1- 0.9. The categorical data and their interval class group were converted to a continuous values ranging 0.1 - 0.9. In this way, the continuous values became nominal for back propagation modeling.

The learning rate was set to 0.01, and the initial weights were randomly selected between 0.1 and 0.3. The MLP trained back-propagation algorithm was used to minimize the error between the predicted output values and the calculated output values. The algorithm

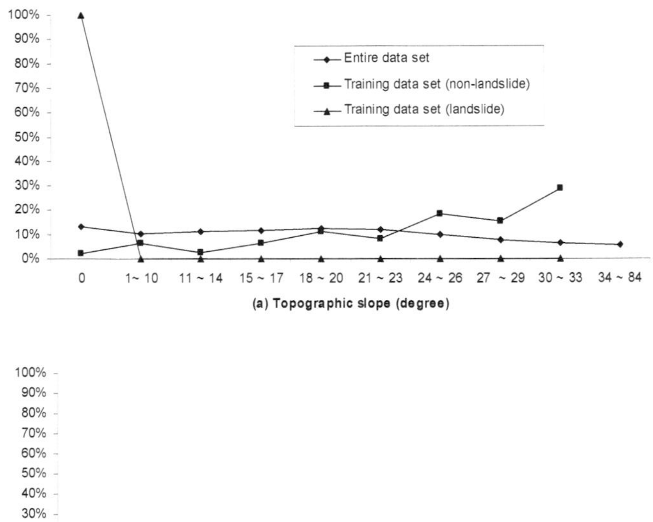

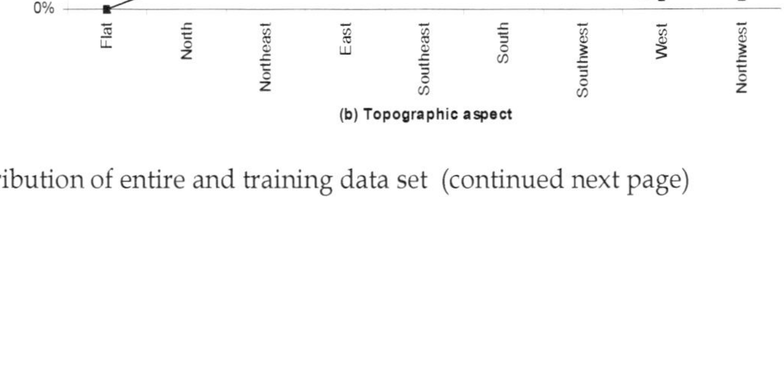

Fig. 3. Distribution of entire and training data set (continued next page)

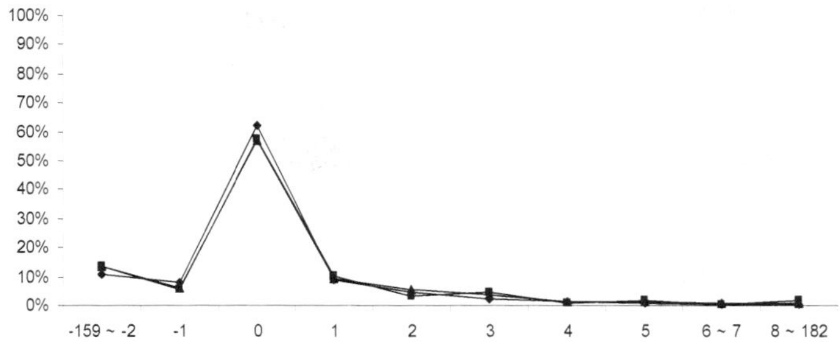

(c) Topographic curvature

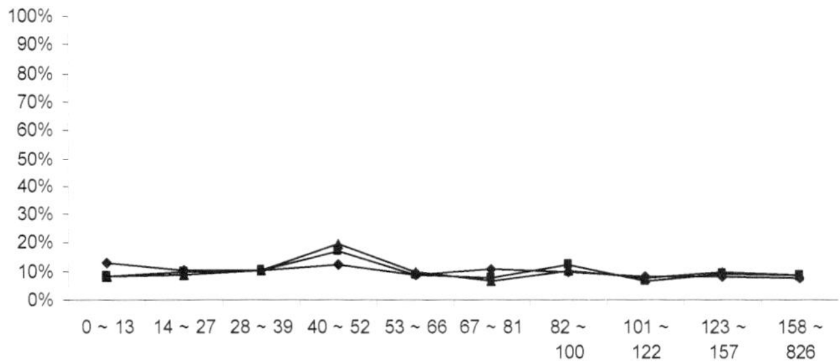

(d) Distance from drainage (m)

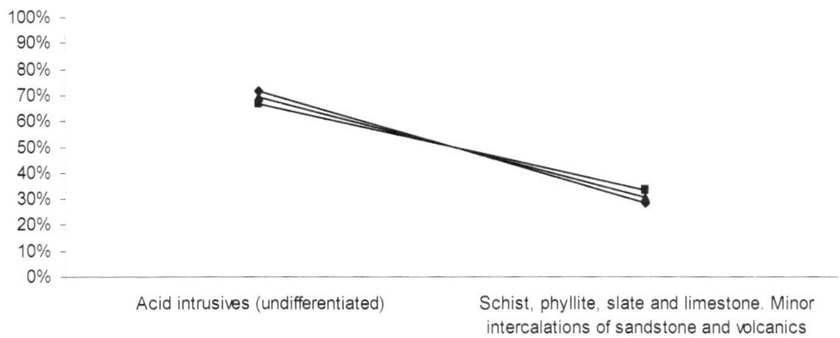

(e) Lithology (types)

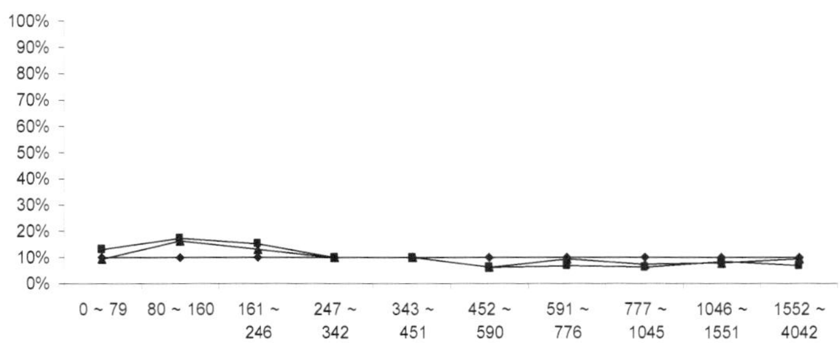

(f) Distance from lineaments (m)

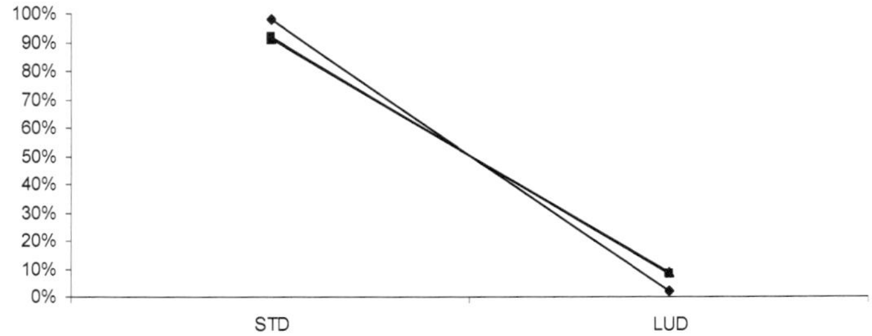

(g) Soil types

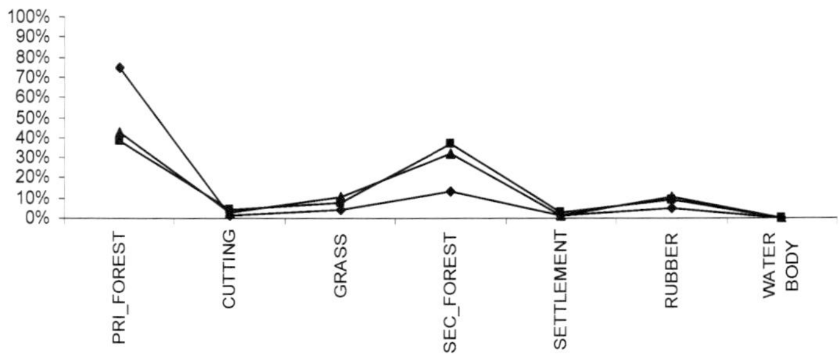

(h) Landcover types

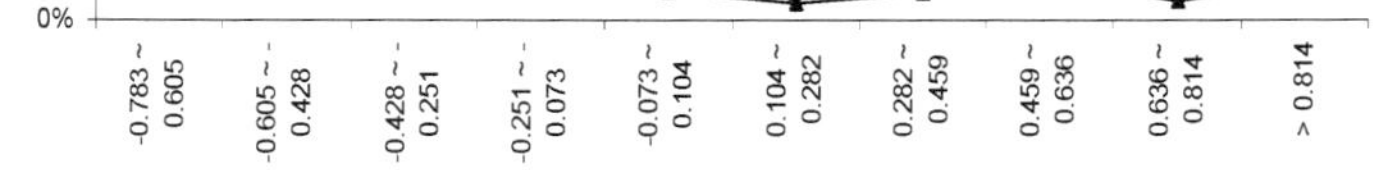

(i) NDVI values

propagated the error backwards iteratively by adjusting the weights. The number of epochs was set to 2,500, and the root mean square error (RMSE) value used for the stopping criterion was set to 0.01. Most of the training datasets met the 0.01 RMSE goal. The results of the learning rate for the training datasets are shown in Figure 3. However, if the RMSE value was not achieved, then the maximum number of iterations was terminated at 2,000 epochs. When the latter case occurred, then the maximum RMSE value was 0.213. Finally, the landslide susceptibility maps were generated using the five training sites (Fig. 4- 8). The values were classified by equal areas and grouped into four classes (highest 10%, second 10%, third 20% and reminding 60%) based on equal area classification for visual interpretation.

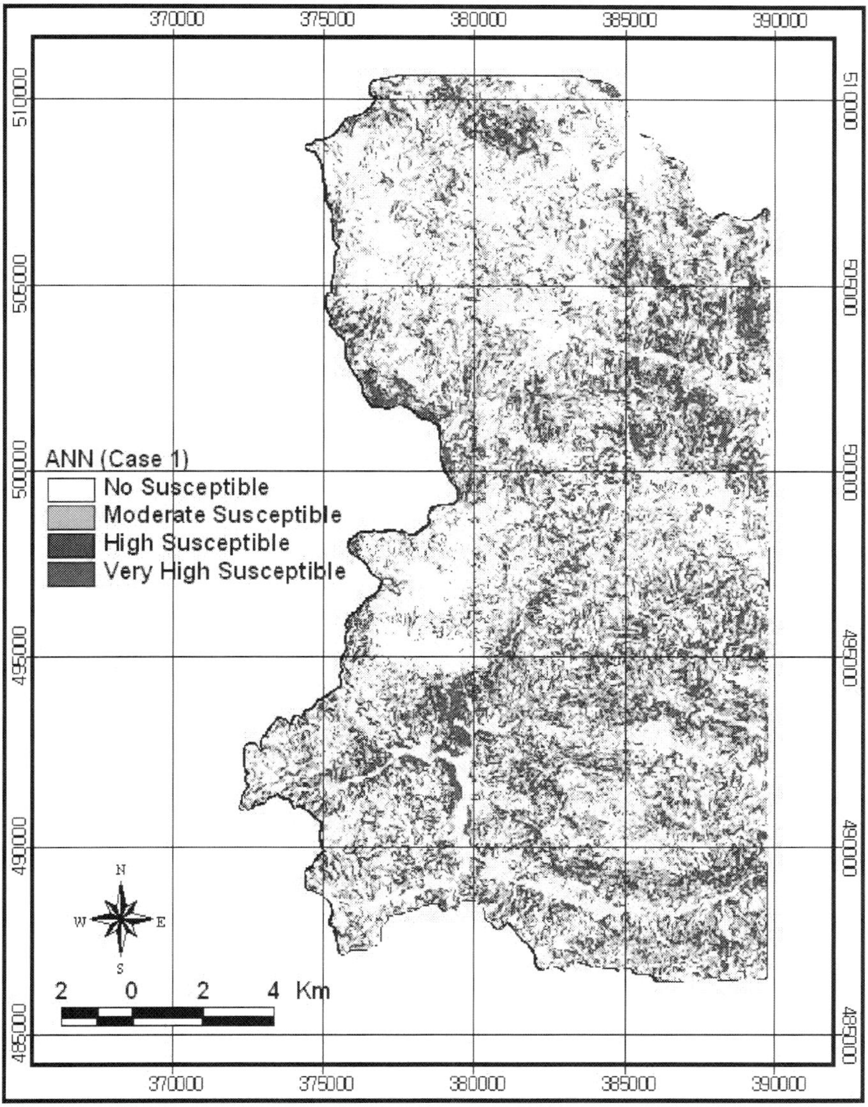

Fig. 4. Landslide susceptibility map using Case 1: Use of landslide location as prone training site and slope is 0 as non-prone training site

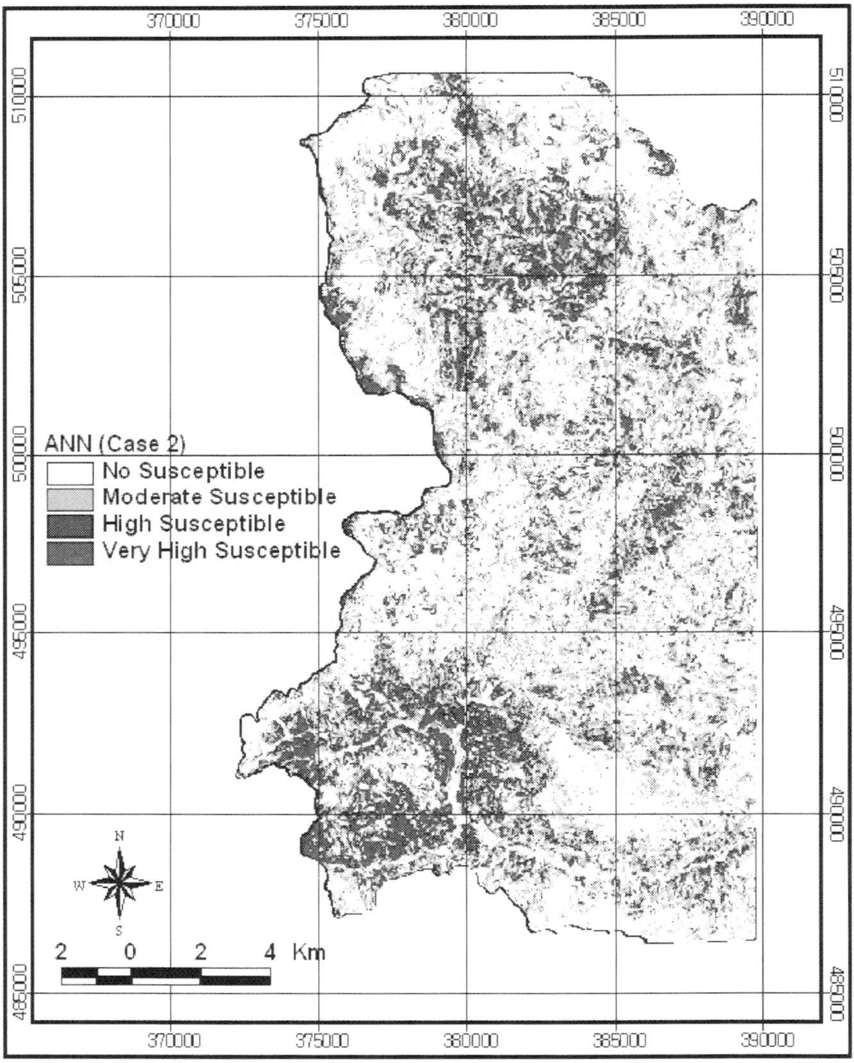

Fig. 5. Landslide susceptibility map using case 2: use of landslide location as prone training site and result from likelihood ratio as non- prone training site

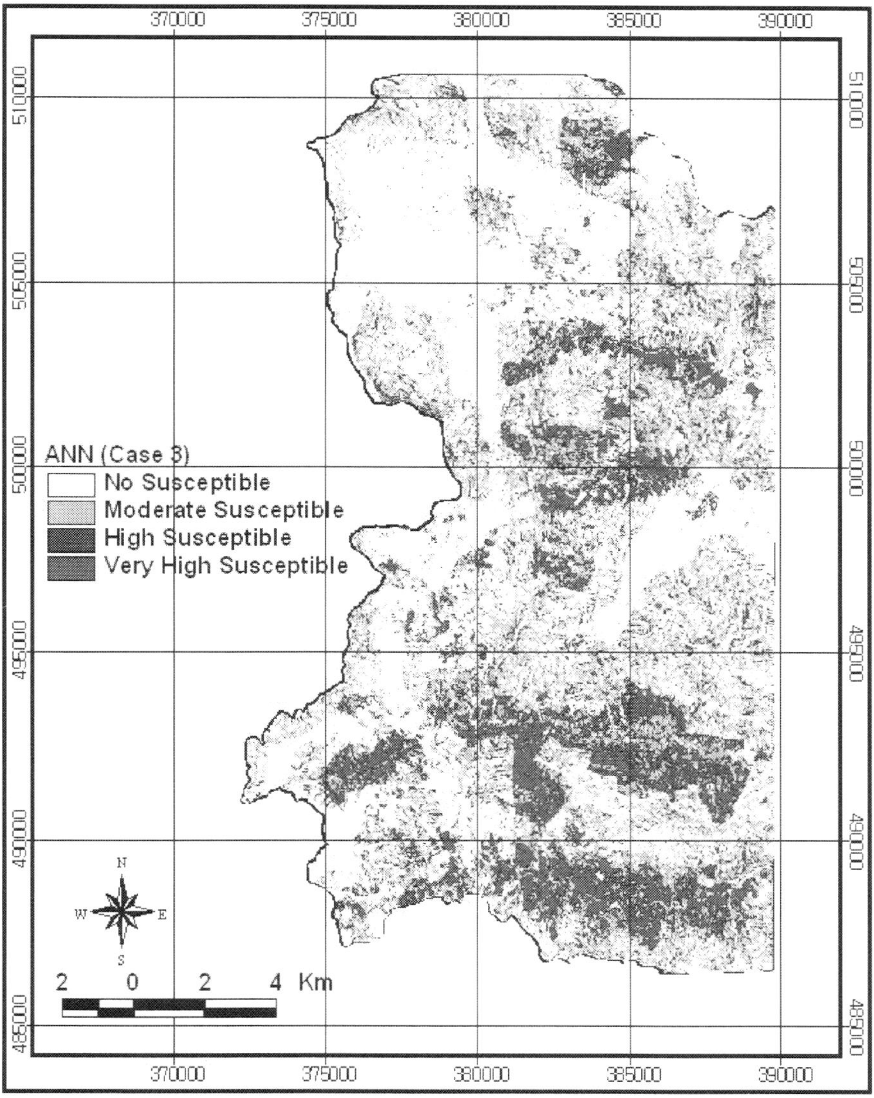

Fig. 6. Landslide susceptibility map using case 3: use of landslide location as prone training site and result from logistic regression as non- prone training site

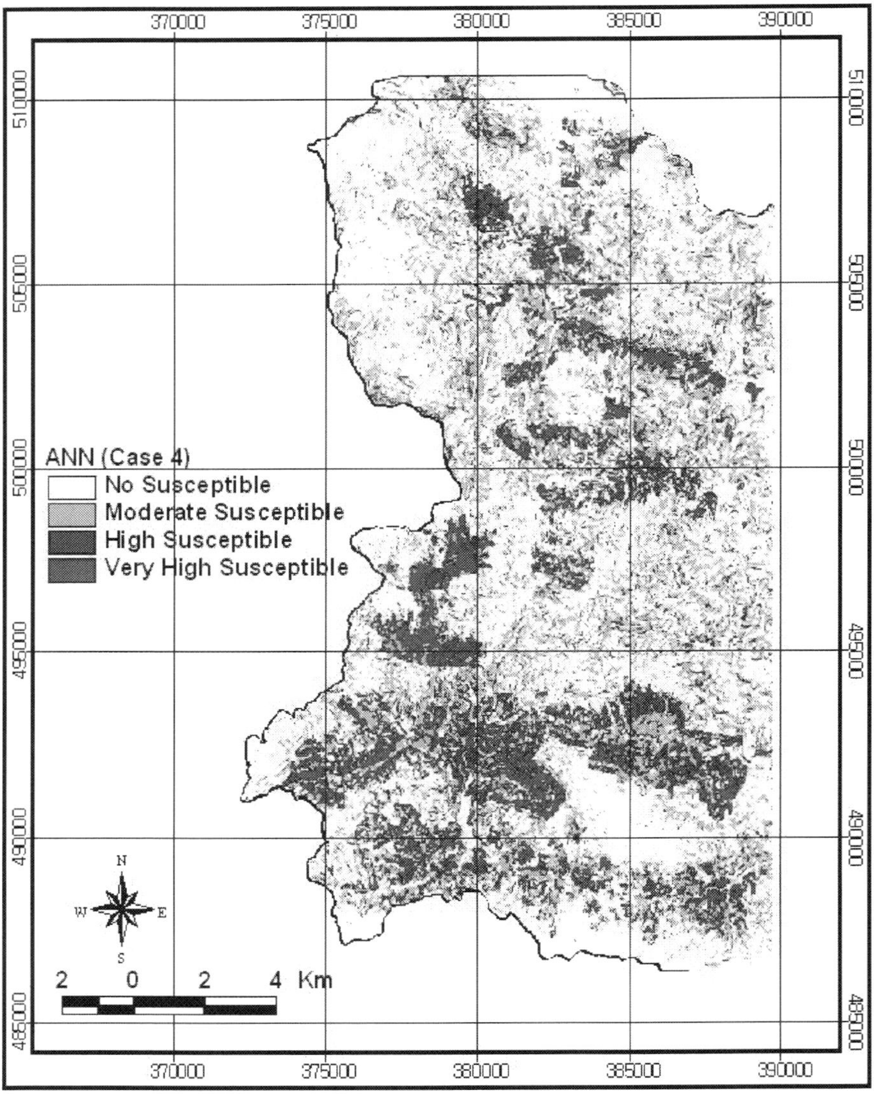

Fig. 7. Landslide susceptibility map using case 4: use of result from likelihood ratio as prone training site and result from likelihood ratio as non-prone training site

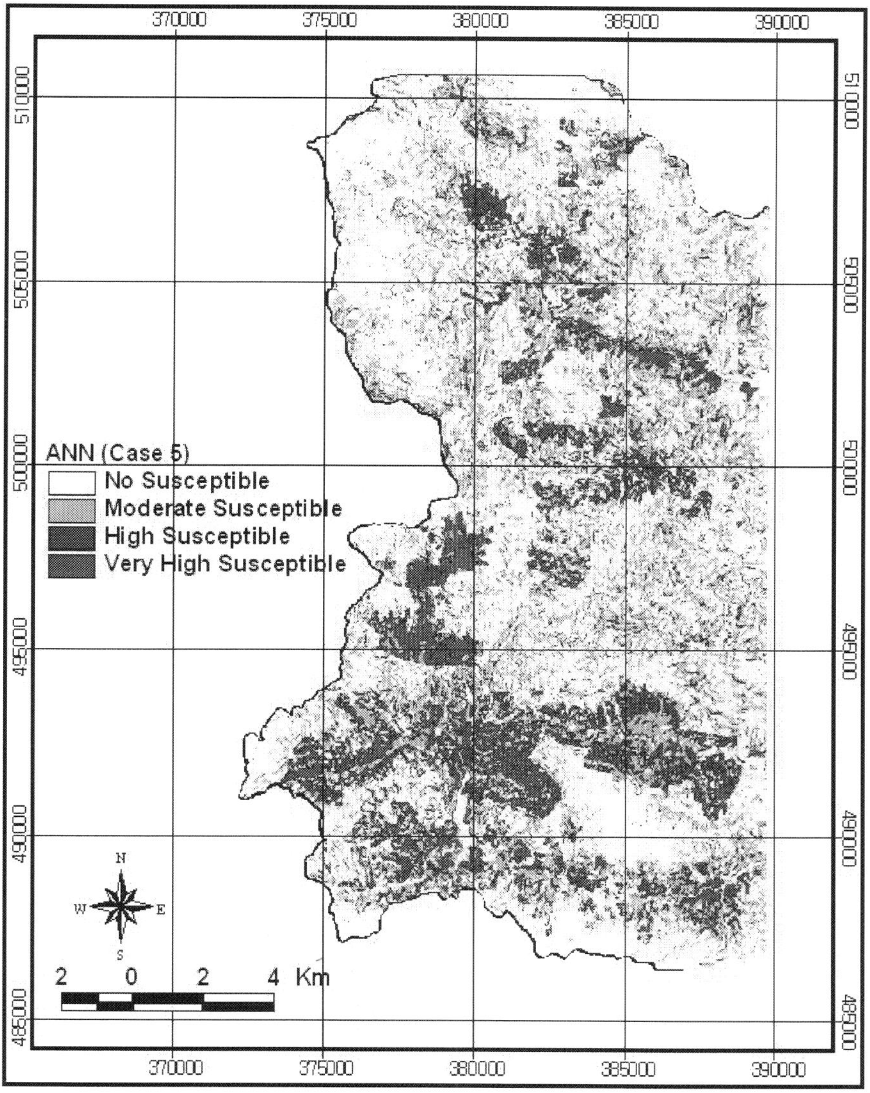

Fig. 8. Landslide susceptibility map using case 5: use of result from logistic regression as prone training site of result from logistic regression as non-prone training site

7. Accuracy assessment and comparison of susceptibility maps

The landslide susceptibility analysis result was verified using landslide test locations which were not used during the modelling process. Global Positioning System data for landslide locations has been collected for various parts of study area. 32 active landslides have been recorded and added to the inventory to be used for the validation of the neural network model output. The rate curves were created and its areas of the under curve were calculated for all cases. The rate explains how well the model and factor predict the landslide. So, the area under curve can assess the prediction accuracy qualitatively. To obtain the relative ranks for each prediction pattern, the calculated index values of all cells in the study area were sorted in descending order. Then the ordered cell values were divided into 100 classes, with accumulated 1% intervals. The rate verification results appear as a line in Fig. 9. For example, in the case of all factor used, 90 to 100% (10%) class of the study area where the landslide susceptibility index had a higher rank could explain 35% of all the landslides. In addition, the 80 to 100% (20%) class of the study area where the landslide susceptibility index had a higher rank could explain 58% of the landslides. To compare the result quantitative, the areas under the curve were re-calculated as the total area is 1 which means perfect prediction accuracy. So, the area under a curve can be used to assess the prediction accuracy qualitatively.

Validation results show that in the training site 1 (case 1) where slope equal to "zero" used for susceptibility map, the area ratio was 0.6935 and the prediction accuracy was 69%. In the training site 2 (case 2) for high frequency ratio values, the area ratio was 0.7465 and the prediction accuracy was 75%. In the training site 3 (case 3) for low frequency ratio values, the area ratio was 0.7030 and the prediction accuracy was 80%. In the training site 4 (case 4) for high logistic regression values, the area ratio was 0.8345 and the prediction accuracy was 83%. In the training site 5 (case 5) for low logistic regression values, the area ratio was 0.8670 and the prediction accuracy was 87%. So from the prediction accuracy graphs (Fig 9), it is quite evident that, training site 5 shows the best prediction accuracy of 87%, where as training site 1 shows the least prediction accuracy of 69% with difference is about 18%. Therefore, one can conclude that the selection of training site is very important for the landslide susceptibility mapping.

8. Concluding remarks

Landslides present a significant constraint to development in Malaysia, notably through the inadvertent reactivation of ancient inland landslides. A series of Government funded research projects has provided much background information and identified suitable methods for the use of landslide susceptibility information in land use planning. However, a number of significant problems remain over the use of this information. In this study, a neural network approach with weights derived from frequency ratio and logistic regression model to estimating the susceptible area of landslides using GIS and remote sensing is presented.

An artificial neural network approach has been used to estimate areas susceptible to landslides using a spatial database for a Cameron Highland. Five different sampling strategies employing different training sites were used for comparison purposes. The results using result from logistic regression as prone training site and result from logistic regression as non-prone training site (Case 5) and result from likelihood ratio as prone training site and result from likelihood ratio as non-prone training site (Case 4) were better than the other three estimation cases, with the results using of landslide location as prone training site and result from likelihood ratio as non- prone training site being the worst.

The back-propagation training algorithm presents difficulties when trying to follow the internal processes of the procedure. The method also involves a long execution time, has a heavy computing load, and there is the need to convert the database to another format. However, landslide susceptibility can be analyzed qualitatively. In addition to using a multi-faceted approach to a solution, they enable the extraction of reliable results for a complex problem, and for continuous and discrete data processing.

Decision making under uncertainty is closely related to susceptibility analysis. Landslide susceptibility map will help for decision making for planners. These decisions are usually in the form of technical countermeasures, regulatory management or combinations of the two. Classic examples of regulatory management are zoning maps which, for instance, exclude some areas from habitation. Regulatory management is often quite intricate in prescribing different permit procedures which may include detailed evaluations and additional exploration or even go so far to prescribing particular slope designs (slope grades e.g.). The latter is actually a combination of regulatory and technical management. Technical mitigating measures range from a variety of stabilizing measures to protective measures such as rock fall galleries to warning devices. One of the most important steps of developing a hazard mitigation plan is assessing risks, or estimating potential losses to the people and properties within the landslide prone area.

9. Acknowledgements

The first author would like to thank the Alexander von Humboldt Foundation (AvH) for awarding a visiting scientist position to carry out research at Dresden University of Technology, Germany. The authors would like to thank the Malaysian Remote Sensing Agency for providing various datasets used in this analysis.

10. References

Akgun, A.; Dag, S. & Bulut, F. (2008). Landslide susceptibility mapping for a landslide-prone area (Findikli, NE of Turkey) by likelihood-frequency ratio and weighted linear combination models. *Environmental Geology*, Vol. 54, 1127-1143

Atkinson, P.M. & Tatnall, A.R.L. (1997). Neural networks in remote sensing. *International Journal of Remote Sensing*, Vol. 18, 699-709

Atkinson, P.M. & Massari, R. (1998). Generalized linear modeling of susceptibility to landsliding in the central Apennines, Italy. *Computer & Geosciences*, Vol. 24, 373-385

Ayalew, L.; Yamagishi, H.; Marui, H. & Kanno, T. (2005). Landslides in Sado Island of Japan Part II. GIS-based susceptibility mapping with comparisions of results from two methods and verifications. Engineering Geology, Vol. 81, 432-445

Baeza, C. & Corominas, J. (2001). Assessment of shallow landslide susceptibility by means of multivariate statistical techniques. Earth Surface Processes & Landforms, Vol. 26, 251-1263

Basheer, I.A. & Hajmeer, M. (2000). Artificial neural networks: fundamentals, computing, design, and application. Journal of Microbiological Methods, Vol. 43, 3-31

Caniani, D.; Pascale, S.; Sdao, F. & Sole, A. (2008). Neural networks and landslide susceptibility: a case study of the urban area of Potenza. Natural Hazards, Vol. 45, 55-72

Catani, F.; Casagli, N.; Ermini, L.; Righini, G. & Menduni, G. (2005). Landslide hazard and risk mapping at catchment scale in the Arno River Basin. Landslides, Vol. 2, No. 4, 329-343

Chang, T.C.; Chao, R.J. (2006). Application of back-propagation networks in debris flow prediction. Engineering Geology, Vol. 85, 270-280

Chau, K.T. & Chan, J.E. (2005). Regional bias of landslide data in generating susceptibility maps using logistic regression: Case of Hong Kong Island. Landslides, Vol. 2, 280-290

Clerici, A., Perego, S., Tellini, C. & Vescovi, P. (2002). A procedure for landslide susceptibility zonation by the conditional analysis method. Geomorphology, Vol. 48, 349-364

Cruden, D.M. & Varnes, D.J. (1996). Landslide types and processes, In: A. K. Turner and R. L. Schuster (eds), Landslides: Investigation and Mitigation, TRB Special Report, 247, National Academy Press, Washington, pp. 36–75

Dahal, R.K.; Hasegawa, S.; Nonomura, S.; Yamanaka, M.; Masuda, T. & Nishino, K. (2008). GIS-based weights-of-evidence modelling of rainfall-induced landslides in small catchments for landslide susceptibility mapping. Environmental Geology, Vol. 54, 311-324

Dai, F.C. & Lee, C.F. (2003). Landslide characteristics and slope instability modeling using GIS, Lantau Island. Hong Kong. Geomorphology, Vol. 42, 213-228

Dai, F.C.; Lee, C.F.; Li, J. & Xu, Z.W. (2001). Assessment of landslide susceptibility on the natural terrain of Lantau Island, Hong Kong. Environmental Geology, Vol. 40, 381-391

Ercanoglu, M & Gokceoglu, C. (2002). Assessment of landslide susceptibility for a landslide-prone area (north of Yenice, NW Turkye) by fuzzy approach. Environmental Geology, Vol. 41, 720-730

Ercanoglu, M.; Gokceoglu, C. & Van Asch, T.W.J. (2004). Landslide susceptibility zoning north of Yenice (NW Turkey) by multivariate statistical techniques. Natural Hazards, Vol. 32, 1–23

Ermini, L.; Catani, F. & Casagli, N. (2005). Artificial neural networks applied to landslide susceptibility assessment. Geomorphology, Vol. 66 No. 1-4, 327-343

Gokceoglu, C.; Sonmez, H. & Ercanoglu, M. (2000). Discontinuity controlled probabilistic slope failure risk maps of the Altindag (settlement) region in Turkey. Engineering Geology, Vol. 55, 277–296

Gomez, H. & Kavzoglu, T. (2005). Assessment of shallow landslide susceptibility using artificial neural networks in Jabonosa River Basin, Venezuela. Engineering Geology, Vol. 78, No. 1-2, 11-27

Hines, J.W. (1997). Fuzzy and neural approaches in engineering. Wiley, New York.

Kanungo, D.P.; Arora, M.K.; Sarkar, S. Gupta, R.P. (2006). A comparative study of conventional, ANN black box, fuzzy and combined neural and fuzzy weighting procedures for landslide susceptibility zonation in Darjeeling Himalayas. Engineering Geology, Vol. 85, 347-366

Lee, S. (2004). Application of likelihood ratio and logistic regression models to landslide susceptibility mapping using GIS. Environmental Management, Vol. 34, No. 2, 223-232

Lee, S. (2005). Application of logistic regression model and its validation for landslide susceptibility mapping using GIS and remote sensing data. International Journal of Remote Sensing, Vol. 26, No. 7, 477-1491

Lee, S. (2007a). Comparison of landslide susceptibility maps generated through multiple logistic regression for three test areas in Korea. Earth Surface Processes and Landf orms, Vol. 32, 2133-2148

Lee, S. (2007b). Application and verification of fuzzy algebraic operators to landslide susceptibility mapping. Environmental Geology, Vol. 52, 615-623

Lee, S. & Dan, N.T. (2005). Probabilistic landslide susceptibility mapping in the Lai Chau province of Vietnam: focus on the relationship between tectonic fractures and landslides. Environmental Geology, Vol. 48, 778–787

Lee, S. & Evangelista, D.G. (2006). Earthquake induced landslide susceptibility mapping using an artificial neural network. Natural Hazards & Earth System Sciences, Vol. 6, 687-695

Lee, S. & Lee, M.J. (2006). Detecting landslide location using KOMPSAT 1 and its application to landslide-susceptibility mapping at the Gangneung area, Korea. Advances in Space Research, Vol. 38, 2261–2271

Lee, S. & Min, K. (2001). Statistical analysis of landslide susceptibility at Yongin, Korea, Environmental Geology, Vol. 40, 1095-1113

Lee, S.; Chwae, U. & Min, K. (2002a). Landslide susceptibility mapping by correlation between topography and geological structure: the Janghung area, Korea. Geomorphology, Vol. 46, 49-162

Lee, S.; Choi, J. & Min, K. (2002b). Landslide susceptibility analysis and verification using the Bayesian probability model. Environmental Geology, Vol. 43, 120-131

Lee, S. & Choi, U. (2003). Development of GIS-based geological hazard information system and its application for landslide analysis in Korea. Geosciences Journal, Vol. 7, 243-252

Lee, S. & Pradhan, B. (2007). Landslide hazard mapping at Selangor, Malaysia using frequency ratio and logistic regression models. Landslides, Vol. 4, 33-41

Lee, S. & Pradhan, B. (2006). Probabilistic landslide risk mapping at Penang Island, Malaysia. Journal of Earth System Sciences, Vol. 115, No. 6, 1-12

Lee, S. & Sambath, T. (2006). Landslide susceptibility mapping in the Damrei Romel area, Cambodia using frequency ratio and logistic regression models. Environmental Geology, Vol. 50, 847–855

Lee, S.; Ryu, J.H.; Min, K. & Won, J.S. (2003a). Landslide susceptibility analysis using GIS and artificial neural network. Earth Surface Processes & Landforms, Vol. 27, 1361-1376

Lee, S.; Ryu, J.H.; Min, K. & Won, J.S. (2003b). Landslide susceptibility analysis using artificial neural network at Boun, Korea. Environmental Geology, Vol. 44, 820-833

Lee, S.; Ryu, J.H.; Min, K. & Won, J.S. (2006). The application of neural networks to landslide susceptibility mapping at Janghung, Korea. Mathematical Geology, Vol. 38, No. 2, 199-220

Lee, S.; Choi, J. & Min, K. (2004a). Probabilistic landslide hazard mapping using GIS and remote sensing data at Boun, Korea. International Journal of Remote Sensing, Vol. 25, 2037-2052

Lee, S.; Ryu, J.H.; Won, J.S. & Park, H.J. (2004b). Determination and application of the weights for landslide susceptibility mapping using an artificial neural network. Engineering Geology, Vol. 71, 289-302

Lee, S.; Ryu, J.H. & Kim, I.S. (2007). Landslide susceptibility analysis and its verification using likelihood ratio, logistic regression, and artificial neural network models: case study of Youngin, Korea. Landslides, Vol. 4, No. 4, 327-338

Moody, A.; & Katz, D.B. (2003). Artificial intelligence in the study of mountain landscapes. In Bishop, M. P. and Shorder, J. F. (Editors), Geographic Information Science and Mountain Geomorphology: Springer, Berlin, pp. 219–249

Neaupane, K.M. & Achet, S.H. (2004). Use of backpropagation neural network for landslide monitoring: a case study in the higher Himalaya. Engineering Geology, Vol. 74, No. 3-4, 213-226

Nefeslioglu, H.A.; Gokceoglu, C. & Sonmez, H. (2008). An assessment on the use of logistic regression and artificial neural networks with different sampling strategies for the preparation of landslide susceptibility maps. Engineering Geology, Vol. 97, 171-171

Santacana, N.; Baeza, B.; Corominas, J.; Paz, A.D. Marturiá, J. (2003). A GIS-based multivariate statistical analysis for shallow landslide susceptibility mapping in La Pobla de Lillet Area (Eastern Pyrenees, Spain). Natural Hazards, Vol. 30, 281–295

Ohlmacher, G.C. &, Davis, J.C. (2003). Using multiple logistic regression and GIS technology to predict landslide hazard in northeast Kansa, USA. Engineering Geology, Vol. 69, 331-343

Paola, J.D. & Schowengerdt, R.A. (1995). A review and analysis of back propagation neural networks for classification of remotely sensed multi-spectral imagery. International Journal of Remote Sensing, Vol. 16, No. 16, 3033-3058

Pistocchi, A.; Luzi, L. & Napolitano, P. (2002). The use of predictive modeling techniques for optimal exploitation of spatial databases: a case study in landslide hazard mapping with expert system-like methods. Environmental Geology, Vol. 41, 765–775

Pradhan, B. (2010a). Remote sensing and GIS-based landslide hazard analysis and cross-validation using multivariate logistic regression model on three test areas in Malaysia. Advances in Space Research, Vol. 45, No. 10, 1244-1256

Pradhan, B. (2010b). Use of GIS-based fuzzy logic relations and its cross application to produce landslide susceptibility maps in three test areas in Malaysia. Environmental Earth Sciences (article on-line first available) DOI 10.1007/s12665-010-0705-1

Pradhan, B. (2010c). Manifestation of an advanced fuzzy logic model coupled with Geo-information techniques to landslide susceptibility mapping and their comparison with logistic regression modelling. Environmental & Ecological Statistics (article on-line first available) DOI 10.1007/s10651-010-0147-7

Pradhan, B. (2010d). Application of an advanced fuzzy logic model for landslide susceptibility analysis. International Journal of Computational Intelligence Systems, Vol.3, No. 3 (September, 2010), 370-381

Pradhan, B. & Buchroithner, M.F. (2010). Comparison and validation of landslide susceptibility maps using an artificial neural network model for three test areas in Malaysia. Environmental & Engineering Geoscience, Vol. 16, No. 2, 107-126

Pradhan, B. & Lee, S. (2010a). Delineation of landslide hazard areas using frequency ratio, logistic regression and artificial neural network model at Penang Island, Malaysia. Environmental Earth Sciences, Vol. 60, 1037 - 1054

Pradhan, B. & Lee, S. (2010b). Regional landslide susceptibility analysis using backpropagation neural network model at Cameron Highland, Malaysia. Landslides, Vol. 7, 13-30

Pradhan, B. & Lee, S. (2010c). Landslide susceptibility assessment and factor effect analysis: backpropagation artificial neural networks and their comparison with frequency ratio and bivariate logistic regression modeling. Environmental Modelling & Software, Vol. 25, 747-759

Pradhan, B. & Lee, S. (2009). Landslide risk analysis using artificial neural network model focusing on different training sites. International Journal of Physical Science, Vol. 3. No. 11, 1-15

Pradhan, B. & Lee, S. (2007). Utilization of optical remote sensing data and GIS tools for regional landslide hazard analysis by using an artificial neural network model. Earth Science Frontier, Vol. 14, No. 6, 143-152

Pradhan, B.; Lee, S. & Buchroithner, M.F. (2010a). Remote sensing and GIS-based landslide susceptibility analysis and its cross-validation in three test areas using a frequency ratio model. Photogrammetrie, Fernerkundung, Geoinformation, Vol. 1, No. 1, 17-32

Pradhan, B.; Lee, S. & Buchroithner, M.F. (2010b). A GIS-based back-propagation neural network model and its cross application and validation for landslide susceptibility analyses. Computer Environment & Urban Systems, Vol. 34, No. 216-235

Pradhan, B.; Lee, S. & Buchroithner, M.F. (2009). Use of geospatial data for the development of fuzzy algebraic operators to landslide hazard mapping: a case study in Malaysia. Applied Geomatics, Vol. 1, 3–15

Pradhan, B.; Lee. S.; Mansor, S.; Buchroithner, M.F.; Jallaluddin, N. & Khujaimah, Z. (2008) Utilization of optical remote sensing data and geographic information system tools for regional landslide hazard analysis by using binomial logistic regression model. Journal of Applied Remote Sensing, Vol. 2, 1–11 DOI:10.1117/12.821511

Pradhan, B.; Oh, J.J. & Buchroithner, M.F. (2010c). Weight-of-evidence model applied to landslide susceptibility mapping in a tropical hilly area. Geomatics, Natural Hazards & Risk 1(3):199-223 doi:10.1080/19475705.2010.498151

Pradhan, B. & Pirasteh, S. (2010). Comparison between prediction capabilities of neural network and fuzzy logic techniques for landslide susceptibility mapping. Disaster Advances, Vol. 3, No. 3, 26-34

Pradhan, B.; Sezer, E.; Gokceoglu, C. & Buchroithner, M.F. (2010d). Landslide susceptibility mapping by neuro-fuzzy approach in a landslide prone area (Cameron Highland, Malaysia). IEEE Transactions on Geoscience & Remote Sensing, Vol. 48, No. 10 (article on-line first available) doi:10.1109/TGRS.2010.2050328

Pradhan, B. & Youssef, A.M. (2010). Manifestation of remote sensing data and GIS on landslide hazard analysis using spatial-based statistical models. Arabian Journal of Geosciences, Vol. 3, No. 3, 319-326

Pradhan, B.; Singh, R.P. & Buchroithner, M.F. (2006). Estimation of stress and its use in evaluation of landslide prone regions using remote sensing data. Advances in Space Research, Vol. 37, 698 -709

Schalkoff, R.J. (1997) Artificial neural networks, New York, NY: Wiley

Suzen, M.L. & Doyuran, V. (2004a). Data driven bivariate landslide susceptibility assessment using geographical information systems: a method and application to Asarsuyu catchment, Turkey. Engineering Geology, Vol. 71, 303–321

Suzen, M.L. & Doyuran, V. (2004b). A comparison of the GIS based landslide susceptibility assessment methods: multivariate versus bivariate. Environmental Geology, Vol. 45, 665–679

Swingler, K. (1996). Applying Neural Networks: A practical guide. Academic Press, New York.

Tangestani, M.H. (2004. Landslide susceptibility mapping using the fuzzy gamma approach in a GIS, Kakan catchment area, southwest Iran. Austrian Journal of Earth Sciences, Vol. 51, 439–450

Varnes, D.J. IAEG Commission on Landslides (1984) Landslide hazard zonation - a review of principles and practice. UNESCO, Paris 63

Yesilncar, E. & Topal, T. (2005) Landslide susceptibility mapping: A Comparison of logistic regression and artificial neural networks methods in a medium scale study, Hendek region (Turkey). Engineering Geology, Vol. 79, 251-266

Youssef, A.M.; Pradhan, B.; Gaber, A.F.D. & Buchroithner, M.F. (2009) Geomorphological hazard analysis along the Egyptian red sea coast between Safaga and Quseir. Natural Hazards & Earth System Sciences, 751-766

Zhou, W. (1999). Verification of nonparametric characteristics of backpropagation neural networks for image classification. IEEE Transactions on Geosciences & Remote Sensing, Vol. 37, 771-779

Part 5

Application of ANN in Environmental Science

18

Dynamic Fuzzy Neural-Network Model for Estimating Heavy Metal Concentration in Rice Using Spectral Indices and Environmental Parameters

Xiangnan Liu and Meiling Liu
School of Information Engineering, China University of Geosciences
China

1. Introduction

1.1 Predictors of heavy metal concentrations in rice

Several spectral indices and environmental parameters were analyzed in order to determine heavy metal concentrations in rice. Excessive heavy metal concentrations in rice affect its chlorophyll content and cell structure(Huang et al., 2007;Liu et al., 2010b), which can be reflected by hyperspectral reflectance(Yoder and Pettigrew-Crosby 1995; Blackburn 1998; Curran et al., 2001). So, it is feasible to estimate the heavy metal concentrations in plants using hyperspectral data. That is to say, spectral indices deriving from hyperspectral reflectance were utilized to examine rice's physiological responses to heavy metal contamination in paddy fields. Whereas environmental parameters including those relating to soil and weather were important factors for determining heavy metal diffusion in rice. They were selected as input variables on the basis of two important reasons. On the one hand, the involvement of environmental parameters facilitates the application of GDFNN model in different environmental conditions and thus increases the ability of model to be used extensively. On the other hand, the involvement of environmental parameters can improve the accuracy of prediction of heavy metal concentrations in rice leaves. Therefore, in this research, predictors of heavy metal concentrations in rice are composed of spectral indices and environmental parameters.

1.2 Spectral parameters

A number of studies have demonstrated that the variation in spectra curve of plant induced by heavy metal pollution occurred in both the visible and the near-infrared (NIR) part of the spectrum (Kooistra et al., 2004). In order to improve the accuracy for estimating heavy metal concentrations in rice, spectral indices sensitive to heavy metal concentrations in rice were selected according to previous studies. Five spectral parameters including red edge position (REP), optimized soil adjusted vegetation index (OSAVI), ratio vegetation index (RVI), normalized difference vegetation index (NDVI) and difference vegetation index (DVI) were selected in this study (Table 1).

Spectral indices	Wavebands (nm)	Formula	Reference
REP	between 680 and 760 nm	$D_{\lambda_i} = \frac{R(\lambda_{i+1}) - R(\lambda_{i-1})}{\lambda_{i+1} - \lambda_{i-1}}$, when D_{λ_i} is maximum value	Chang and Colllins, 1983
OSAVI[670,800]	670,800	$OSAVI = (1 + 0.5)(R_{800} - R_{670}) / (R_{800} + R_{670} + 0.5)$	Huete et al., 1988
RVI[700,750]	700,750	$RVI = R_{750} / R_{700}$	Schuerger et al., 2003
NDVI[695,760]	695,760	$NDVI = \frac{R_{760} - R_{695}}{R_{760} + R_{695}}$	Schuerger et al., 2003
DVI[682,734]	682,734	$DVI = R_{734} - R_{682}$	Kooistra et al., 2004

Note: R_i is the reflectance of band i.

Table 1. Five spectral indices used as input variables of GDFNN model

1.3 Soil parameters

The physical and chemical properties of soil, such as pH, soil texture, organic matter (OM), colloid type and granularity, etc. have great influence on the transfer of heavy metals from soil to crop (Jackson and Alloway, 1992; De Vries et al., 2005).That is to say, the mobility and bioavailability of heavy metals are influenced by various soil properties. But different researchers drew different conclusions. But most researchers agreed that, of all physical and chemical properties of soil, soil pH and organic matter in soil have the greatest effect on the bioavailability of heavy metals, especially for soil pH. Since the extent of soil contamination can also be evaluated by comparing the maximum allowable concentrations (MAC) (National Environmental Protection Agency of China, 2006) of the metals in agricultural land. As soil pH partially governs the speciation and bioavailability of heavy metals, MAC values are adjusted according to soil pH (Fu et al., 2008). Liao et al.(2008) demonstrated that the contents of Cr, Cu, Pb, Hg, Ni and Cd etc. represent an obvious negative correlation with pH and the content of As represents a positive correlation with pH; that the contents of Cd, Cr, Cu, Pb and Hg, etc. are positively correlated with OM; the contents of Ni and As are negatively correlated with OM by conducting a correlation analysis on seven kinds of heavy metal in soil pH and OM in the study area. Likely, other researchers investigated that phytotoxicity and availability of heavy metal is strongly influenced by the pH and OM of soil (Foy et al., 1978; Fernandes and Henriques, 1991; Das et al., 1997).. Jung and Thornton (1997) investigation of relatively high metal concentrations in rice found it to occur under conditions of decreased pH and increasing OM in soil. Other studies also showed that heavy metal concentrations in rice have a significant negative correlation with soil pH and are positively correlated with OM (Fu et al., 2008; Liao et al., 2008; Hang et al., 2009).

1.4 Meteorological parameters

Since meteorological conditions have influence on the metabolism, transpiration and absorption capabilities of plant roots, they affect the diffusion and translocation of heavy metals in plants (Reber, 1989; Kádár, 1995). Some researchers have investigated meteorological factors, such as air temperature, relative humidity, sunlight, precipitation, etc., and have seen that they have important influence on the diffusion of metals in plants (Cui et al., 2004; Pan et al., 2007). The most important factors affecting metal bioavailability in paddy soil are temperature, sunlight and precipitation (Jung and Thornton, 1997; Cheng et al., 2005). So, temperature, sunlight and precipitation can belong to the set of possible predictors of heavy metal concentrations in rice. In this analysis, values for temperature (T; mean month temperature), sunlight (S; month accumulative sunlight) and precipitation (P; month accumulative precipitation) during rice growing seasons from July to October in 2008 were measured.

2. Models for estimating of heavy metal concentrations in rice

2.1 Model architecture

In this paper, a generalized dynamic fuzzy neural network (GDFNN) model was constructed to obtain heavy metal concentrations in rice leaves. GDFNN is a hybrid system that combines the fuzzy logic interference and theories of neural networks. 'Dynamic' indicates the network structure of fuzzy neural network is not predetermined. Namely, the system starts with no rules. Then, rules can be recruited or deleted according to the significance of each rule on output parameters of the structure in existing fuzzy neural network so that not only can the parameters but also the structure can be self-adaptive. GDFNN is a four-layer hybrid neural network with the ability to self-organize its own neurons in the learning process (Wu et al., 2001). The structure of the GDFNN is also shown in Fig. 1.

The layered operation of the GDFNN is as follows:

Layer 1: The input layer—Each neuron in this layer represents an input variable, x_i, i=1; 2, ..., r.

Layer 2: The EBF layer—Each neuron in the EBF layer represents an if-part of a fuzzy rule. The outputs of EBF neurons are computed by products of grades of member function (MF). In this layer physical variables are converted into fuzzy variables. Each MF is in the form of a Gaussian function:

$$\mu_{ij}(x_i) = \exp[\frac{-(x_i - c_{ij})}{\sigma^2_{ij}}] \quad (i=1,\cdots,r; j=1,\cdots,u) \tag{1}$$

where μ_{ij} is the ith membership function in the jth neuron, c_{ij} is the centre of the ith membership function in the jth neuron, σ_{ij} is the width of the ith membership function in the jth neuron, r is the number of input variables, u is the number of neurons and also represents the numbers of fuzzy rules.

Layer 3: The then-part of a fuzzy rule for the fuzzy model—The output of the jth neuron in this layer is

$$\phi_j = \exp[-\sum_{i=1}^{r} \frac{(x_i - c_{ij})}{\sigma^2_{ij}}] \quad (j=1,\cdots,u) \tag{2}$$

Layer 4: The output layer—Each neuron in this layer represents an output variable as the summation of incoming signals. In this GDFNN a unique output variable is considered: heavy metal concentrations in rice .The output of a neuron in this layer is

$$y(x_1, x_2, \cdots, x_r) = \sum_{j=1}^{u} w_j \cdot \phi_j \quad (3)$$

Here, W_j the weight of jth rule in neural network.

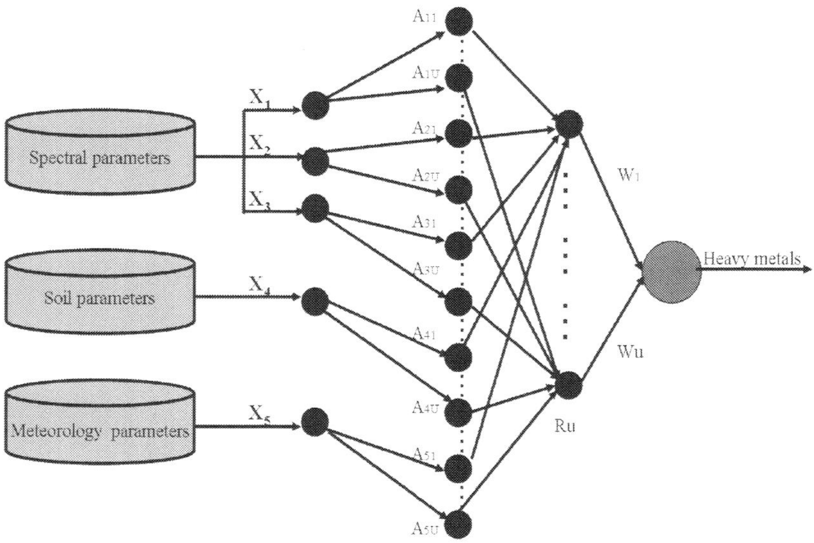

Fig. 1. A simple structure of GDFNN model

2.2 Model algorithms

GDFNN is based on ellipsoidal basis function (EBF) and is functionally equivalent to a Takagi-Sugeno-kang fuzzy system (Wu et al., 2001; Leng et al., 2005). Fig. 2 shows the process for learning algorithm in GDFNN.

As seen in Fig. 2, the GDFNN can extract fuzzy rules from the training data without predefined fuzzy rules. In addition, fuzzy rules can be generated automatically according to the systematic error (e_k) and ε -completeness of fuzzy rules. A new rule is created in the case where $md_{\min}^{k} > k_d$ and $e_k > k_e$. Whereas, if the conditions $md_{\min}^{k} < k_d$ and $e_k > k_e$ are satisfied, the width of Gaussian function in each rule are adjusted. Else only the consequent parameters are modified under other conditions. However, whether or not an existing rule should be deleted according to the error reduction ratio of each EBF neuron and fuzzy rules to the system performance. If $\eta_j < k_{err}$, then the rule is deleted. Namely, the less important EBF neurons will be deleted. Based on the learning algorithm in GDFNN, the methods of the structure and parameter learning are based on new adding and pruning techniques and a gradient descent learning algorithm, so GDFNN has high accuracy with a compact structure.

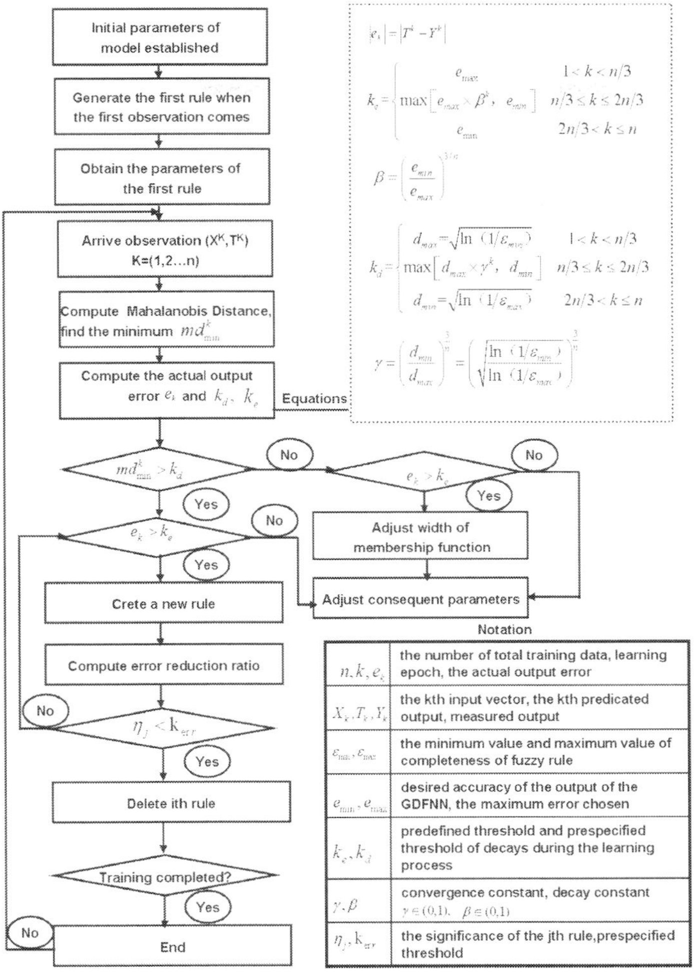

Fig. 2. The process flow chart for the learning algorithm of GDFNN model

2.3 Model evaluation

Generally, the root mean square error (RMSE) and absolute percent error (APE) have been used to measure the performance of DFNN (Jang, 1993; Pai et al., 2009). In this study, the parameters were: (i) RMSE ; (ii) APE; and (iii) the correlation coefficient (R^2). The three parameters were computed by:

$$APE = \frac{1}{N}\sum_{i=1}^{N}\frac{|y_{ai} - y_{mi}|}{|y_{ai}|} \tag{4}$$

where y_{ai}, y_{mi}, APE are the real-valued output variable, measured output variable, absolute percent error respectively; N is the sample number. APE provides information on the accuracy that the model can yield using a given data set. The nearer the value approaches 0, the better the performance of the model.

$$RMSE = \sqrt{\frac{\sum_{i=1}^{N}(y_{ai} - y_{mi})^2}{N-1}} \tag{5}$$

Here, RMSE is root mean square error between real-valued output variable and measured output variable. The lower RMSE, the better the performance of the model.

$$R^2 = \frac{\left[\sum_{i=1}^{N}(y_{ai} - \overline{y_a})\sum_{i=1}^{N}(y_{mi} - \overline{y_m})\right]^2}{\sum_{i=1}^{N}(y_{ai} - \overline{y_a})^2 \sum_{i=1}^{N}(y_{mi} - \overline{y_m})^2} \tag{6}$$

Here, R^2, $\overline{y_m}$ and $\overline{y_a}$ are the correlation coefficient, the average measured output variable and the average real-valued output variable, respectively. R^2 represents the correlation between predicted and measured variables. It is assumed that the predicted and measured variables follow a normal distribution. Its value ranges from 0 to 1. The higher the value of the correlation, the stronger the indication of existing linear relations between the actual and predicted variables.

With the exception of the above three evaluation indicators, a fuzzy rule (labelled u) was also taken into consideration in this analysis. This is due to the fact that the degree of complexity of the network largely depends on the number of fuzzy rules in the GDFNN model. With sufficiently high accuracy, fewer fuzzy rules are generated in model and the performance of the model improves. Hence, the model has a compact structure as well as a high accuracy.

3. Methodology

The crucial procedures for estimating heavy metal concentrations in rice were the selection of input variables and the establishment of a data retrieval model (Fig.3). Firstly, spectral parameters, soil parameters and meteorological parameters were taken into consideration as input variables for the model. The reasons were follows: spectral parameters were selected to examine rice physiological responses to heavy metal contamination, while soil parameters and meteorological parameters were regarded as important factors influencing rice uptake of heavy metal. Moreover, to be useful for practical simulations, specific parameters were needed to satisfy the following requirements: (1) dominant principle: the parameters should be significantly correlated to heavy metal concentrations in crops; (2) ready availability: the parameters could be obtained quickly and at a large scale. Secondly, GDFNN was developed to integrate spectral parameters, soil parameters and meteorological parameters in order to estimate heavy metal concentrations in rice. This model consisted of an input layer, an output layer and several hidden layers, with the hidden layers belonging to fuzzy interference system by carrying out fuzzy reasoning using the structure of neural network.

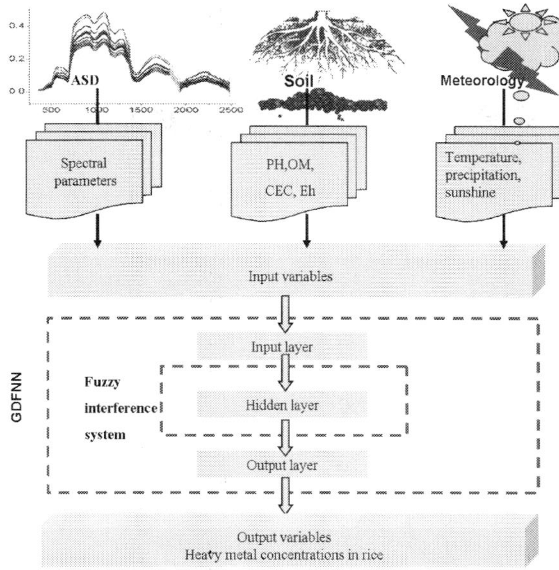

Fig. 3. The general flow chart for estimating heavy metal concentrations in rice

4. Examples

4.1 Site description

The city of Changchun, Jilin Province in China is an important industrial and agricultural location. Some areas have been contaminated by industrial pollutants, particularly by heavy metals. Suburban farms have soil with copper (Cu) and cadmium (Cd) at higher

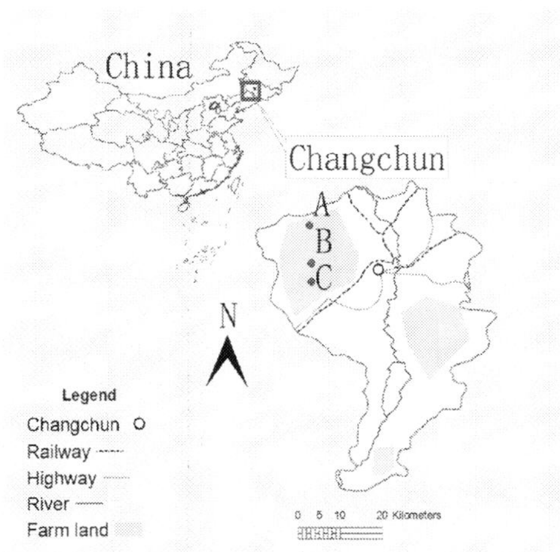

Fig. 4. Location map for experimental sites in Changchun, Jilin Province, China

concentrations than what is considered to be normal for the area. Three field experiments (43° 51' 34.8" N–43° 51' 37.0" N, 125° 09' 07.2" E–125° 10' 25.3" E) adjacent to the important industrial district (i.e., the contamination source) in Changchun were selected (Fig. 4). Heavy metal contamination stress levels in the soil of the three field experiments (labeled A, B, and C) varied. The soil and the stress rates were determined according to a soil sample analysis (Table 2) to be at a safe level, level I pollution and level II pollution, respectively. The site is within the temperate continental climate zone with a mean annual rainfall of 522-615 mm, where the land is predominantly black soil, with a pH of 6.5-7.3 and 2-4% of sufficient organic matter. The crop selected in this site was rice which is one of the most important staples in China.

Site	Geographical location	Copper Content ($mgkg^{-1}$)	Cadmium Content ($mgkg^{-1}$)	Pollution level	Soil quality standard* ($mgkg^{-1}$)
A	43° 52.2' N, 125° 10.2' E	68.2±2.86	0.465±0.002	II	II (50≤Cu≤400; 0.3≤Cd≤1.0)
B	43° 54.6' N, 125° 10.4' E	45.5±2.44	0.182±0.002	I	I (35≤Cu <50; 0.2≤Cd <0.3)
C	44° 06.3' N, 125° 10.2 E	20.4±2.44	0.093±0.002	Safe	Safe (Cu <20.8; Cd <0.097)

Note: * Soil quality standard according to the Environment Monitoring Centre of China

Table 2. The location and heavy metal concentrations of the experiment sites

4.2 Data collecting

The data collection was carried out in sunny days during a typical rice growth season: 8 July, 4 August, 29 August, 18 September 2008, which corresponded to the seeding, tillering, booting and mature growth stages of rice. All spectral measurements were taken under cloudless or near cloudless conditions between 10:00 and 14:00, using an ASD FieldSpec Pro spectrometer (Analytical Spectral Devices, Boulder, CO. USA). The spectrometer was fitted with 10° field of view fibre optics, operated in the 350-2500 nm spectral region with sampling intervals of 2 nm. A $BaSO_4$ calibration panel was used for determining the black and baseline reflectance. A panel radiance measurement was taken before and after rice measurement using two scans each time. Rice radiance measurements were made at 30-40 sites in each plot and every measurement was recorded as the average of 10 consecutively acquired spectra in order to reduce the noise level. Five spectral indices derived from hyperspectral reflectance were calculated in Table 3.

The measurement of soil property and heavy metal concentrations in rice and soil were taken almost synchronously with rice spectral reflectance measurements. In this context, soil pH was determined in a paste with a ratio of 1:2.5 soils to water using a pH meter (Model PHS-3C, Shanghai Precision and Scientific Instrument Co. Ltd.). Soil organic matter was analyzed according to Chinese CRM/RM information center (http://www.gbw114.org). The metal content was analyzed at the Chinese Academy of Agricultural Sciences, Beijing, China. Soil and rice total heavy metals (Cu, Zn, Pb, Cd, Cr, As) were determined by flame atomic absorption spectrometry (AAS), after nitric-perchloric acid (2:1) digestion. Soil extractable metals were extracted with 5 mM diethylenetriaminepentaacetic acid (DTPA)/10 mM $CaCl_2$/100 mM triethanolamine at pH 7.3 (Lindsay and Norvell, 1978). The measured meteorological data for the Changchun station were obtained from the CMA (http://cdc.cma.gov.cn/).Soil parameters and meteorological data were also summarized in Table 3.

Variables	Abbreviation	Unit	Min	Max	Medium	Mean	SD
Red edge position	REP	nm	694	730	695	699	10
Optimized soil adjusted vegetation index	OSAVI	-	0.24	0.56	0.39	0.38	0.07
Normalized difference vegetation index	NDVI	-	0.19	0.68	0.39	0.40	0.13
Ratio vegetation index	RVI	-	1.30	3.68	1.87	2.06	0.72
Difference vegetation index	DVI	-	0.08	0.36	0.18	0.19	0.06
pH	pH	-	6.5	7.0	6.8	6.8	0.1
Organic matter	OM	%	2.4	3.2	2.7	2.8	0.15
Sunlight	S	hours	149.3	261.3	-	-	-
Temperature	T	°	9.5	23.5	-	-	-
Precipitation	P	mm	17	199.8	-	-	-
Cu concentration in rice leaves	Cu	$mgkg^{-1}$	18.77	31.12	23.34	24.29	2.87
Cd concentration in rice leaves	Cd	$mgkg^{-1}$	0.036	0.042	0.039	0.039	0.001

Notes: values for T (mean month temperature), S (month accumulative sunlight) and P(month accumulative precipitation).SD, Standard deviation

Table 3. Basic statistics of the measured spectral indices and environmental parameters in field experimental sites

4.3 Data processing

In this study, to avoid data saturation, the input variables in this model were normalized, based on their possible ranges using the following equation:

$$x_{norm}=\frac{x_i - x_{min}}{x_{max} - x_{min}} \tag{7}$$

where x_i, x_{min}, x_{max} and x_{norm} are the real-valued input variable, the minimum input variable, maximum input variable and its normalized value respectively. The output from the GDFNN model is an indexed value that corresponds to the input variable. To get the real-predicted value, the indexed output value needs to be de-normalized according to the following equation:

$$y_{ai} = y_{min}+y_{norm}(y_{max} - y_{min}) \tag{8}$$

Where y_{ai}, y_{min}, y_{max} and y_{norm} are the real-predicted value, the minimum and maximum values of the real-valued output, and the indexed output value from the GDFNN model respectively.

5. Results and discussions

Since the maximal absolute value of the difference of heavy metal concentrations in rice leaves from different contaminated levels occurred at the tillering growth stage, this indicates the best stage for estimating heavy metal concentrations is at that stage (Liu et al., 2010a). Therefore, in this research, 138 training data sets and 69 test data sets from the tillering growth stage of rice were obtained for different levels of heavy metal pollution. Considering that spectral parameters were considered as dominant input variables and environmental parameters as complementary input variables of GDFNN model. In GDFNN, five parameters were taken as input variables, i.e., three spectral parameters, one soil parameter and one meteorological parameter, while the individual concentrations of Cu and Cd in rice served as output variables. By trying different combinations of input data sets (three selected from the five spectral parameters, the fourth was taken from the two soil parameters, and the fifth came from the three meteorological parameters). 60 groups ($C_5^3 \times C_3^1 \times C_2^1 = 60$) different input parameters were developed (Table 4). Fuzzy rules (u), APE, R^2 and RMSE of all groups for estimating Cu concentration and Cd concentration are shown (Fig. 5). From Fig. 5, regardless of the group for Cu and Cd, fewer u were achieved in GDFNN, with u ranging from 2 to 14. Additionally, the more u in the developed model, the lower value APE. When it comes to R^2 and RMSE, R^2 of all groups, the values were over 0.6 and the RMSE of all models were below 2.5. According to the parameters for assessing the performance of GDFNN, the optimal group should have a low RMSE and APE, and an R^2 value close to 1. Four groups of optimal combined parameters for estimating Cd concentration are displayed in Fig. 6. Their input variables were NDVI-RVI-DVI-OM-P, NDVI-RVI-DVI-OM-S, NDVI-RVI-DVI-pH-P and NDVI-RVI-DVI-pH-S. All four groups were highly accurate and had compact architectures. Specifically, u was nearly 10, while R^2 was over 0.9, and APE was below 1.0%. With respect to combined parameters, the three best spectral parameters (NDVI, RVI and DVI) and soil parameters (pH and OM) were found as the main factors controlling the availability and concentration of Cd in rice. Meanwhile, precipitation (P) and sunlight (S) were shown to be chief factors affecting Cd concentration in rice. However, temperature (T) was determined to be a negligible factor influencing Cd concentration in rice. Similarly, four groups of optimal combined parameters for estimating Cu concentration are displayed in Fig.7. Their input variables were OSAVI-NDVI-DVI-OM-P, REP-NDVI-DVI-OM-T, OSAVI-RVI-DVI-pH-P and REP-OSAVI-NDVI-pH-T. All four groups were highly accurate and had compact architectures. Specifically, u was nearly 10, R^2 was over 0.9, APE was below 1.5%.Concerning combined parameters, it was observed that spectral parameters differed with respect to soil parameters and meteorological parameters. The main factors controlling the availability of Cu were pH and OM in soil, and this affected the Cu concentration in rice. Precipitation (P) and temperature (T) mainly affectd Cu concentration in rice. However, sunlight (S) was merely a negligible factor in influencing Cu concentration in rice.

To examine whether combined parameters can improve the performance of predictions for heavy metal concentrations in rice, a comparison between the application of GDFNN with combined parameters (including spectral parameters, soil parameters and meteorological parameters) and simply with spectral parameters alone was made (Fig.8). The linear fitting equation between predicted heavy metal concentrations and measured heavy metal concentrations gave the following results through the application of these two methods with the different respective input variables:

1. Five spectral parameters including REP, OSAVI, NDVI, DVI and RVI for estimating Cu and Cd concentration in rice are:

$$y_{aicu} = 0.8353\, y_{micu} + 3.9194 \quad (9)$$

$$y_{aicd} = 0.8150\, y_{micd} + 7.2685 \quad (10)$$

Here, R^2= 0.7848 and 0.8235 respectively. Values for y_{aicu} and y_{aicd} predicted Cu and Cd concentration respectively, while y_{micu} y_{micd} are measured for Cu and Cd concentration respectively.

2. The best model of combined parameters for estimating Cu and Cd concentration in rice are:

$$y_{aicu} = 0.9921\, y_{micu} + 0.1924 \quad (11)$$

$$y_{aicd} = 0.9967\, y_{micd} + 0.1278 \quad (12)$$

Here, R^2= 0.9929 and 0.9921 respectively. Values for y_{aicu} and y_{aicd} predicted Cu and Cd concentration respectively, while y_{micu} y_{micd} are measured Cu and Cd concentration respectively.

Group	Parameters	Group	Parameters
1	REP, OSAVI, NDVI, OM, P	31	REP, OSAVI, NDVI, pH, P
2	REP, OSAVI, RVI, OM, P	32	REP, OSAVI, RVI, pH, P
3	REP, OSAVI, DVI, OM, P	33	REP, OSAVI, DVI, pH, P
4	REP, NDVI, RVI, OM, P	34	REP, NDVI, RVI, pH, P
5	REP, NDVI, DVI, OM, P	35	REP, NDVI, DVI, pH, P
6	REP, RVI, DVI, OM, P	36	REP, RVI, DVI, pH, P
7	OSAVI, NDVI, RVI, OM, P	37	OSAVI, NDVI, RVI, pH, P
8	OSAVI, NDVI, DVI, OM, P	38	OSAVI, NDVI, DVI, pH, P
9	OSAVI, RVI, DVI, OM, P	39	OSAVI, RVI, DVI, pH, P
10	NDVI, RVI, DVI, OM, P	40	NDVI, RVI, DVI, pH, P
11	REP, OSAVI, NDVI, OM, S	41	REP, OSAVI, NDVI, pH, S
12	REP, OSAVI, RVI, OM, S	42	REP, OSAVI, RVI, pH, S
13	REP, OSAVI, DVI, OM, S	43	REP, OSAVI, DVI, pH, S
14	REP, NDVI, RVI, OM, S	44	REP, NDVI, RVI, pH, S
15	REP, NDVI, DVI, OM, S	45	REP, NDVI, DVI, pH, S
16	REP, RVI, DVI, OM, S	46	REP, RVI, DVI, pH, S
17	OSAVI, NDVI, RVI, OM, S	47	OSAVI, NDVI, RVI, pH, S
18	OSAVI, NDVI, DVI, OM, S	48	OSAVI, NDVI, DVI, pH, S
19	OSAVI, RVI, DVI, OM, S	49	OSAVI, RVI, DVI, pH, S
20	NDVI, RVI, DVI, OM, S	50	NDVI, RVI, DVI, pH, S
21	REP, OSAVI, NDVI, OM, T	51	REP, OSAVI, NDVI, pH, T
22	REP, OSAVI, RVI, OM, T	52	REP, OSAVI, RVI, pH, T
23	REP, OSAVI, DVI, OM, T	53	REP, OSAVI, DVI, pH, T
24	REP, NDVI, RVI, OM, T	54	REP, NDVI, RVI, pH, T
25	REP, NDVI, DVI, OM, T	55	REP, NDVI, DVI, pH, T
26	REP, RVI, DVI, OM, T	56	REP, RVI, DVI, pH, T
27	OSAVI, NDVI, RVI, OM, T	57	OSAVI, NDVI, RVI, pH, T
28	OSAVI, NDVI, DVI, OM, T	58	OSAVI, NDVI, DVI, pH, T
29	OSAVI, RVI, DVI, OM, T	59	OSAVI, RVI, DVI, pH, T
30	NDVI, RVI, DVI, OM, T	60	NDVI, RVI, DVI, pH, T

Note: REP-red edge position, OSAVI-optimized soil-adjusted vegetation index, ratio RVI-vegetation index, NDVI-normalized difference vegetation index, DVI-difference vegetation index), pH, OM-organism matter for soil, T-temperature, S-sunlight, P- precipitation

Table 4. Sixty groups of combined parameters as input variables for GDFNN

Based on the above analysis, the GDFNN model using combined parameters as input variables showed better prediction performance than that with only five spectral parameters. It confirmed that soil parameters and meteorological parameters had improved the accuracy in estimating Cu and Cd concentration in rice. Yet it should be noted that three different experiment sites are adjacent, consequently the difference in the physical and chemical properties of soil, and meteorological condition are subtle. A GDFNN model using combined parameters requires testing under different environmental conditions. In the current study, we focused on proposing a new methodology and developing ideas for estimating heavy metal concentrations in crop by using spectral parameters and environmental parameters as input variables of GDFNN.

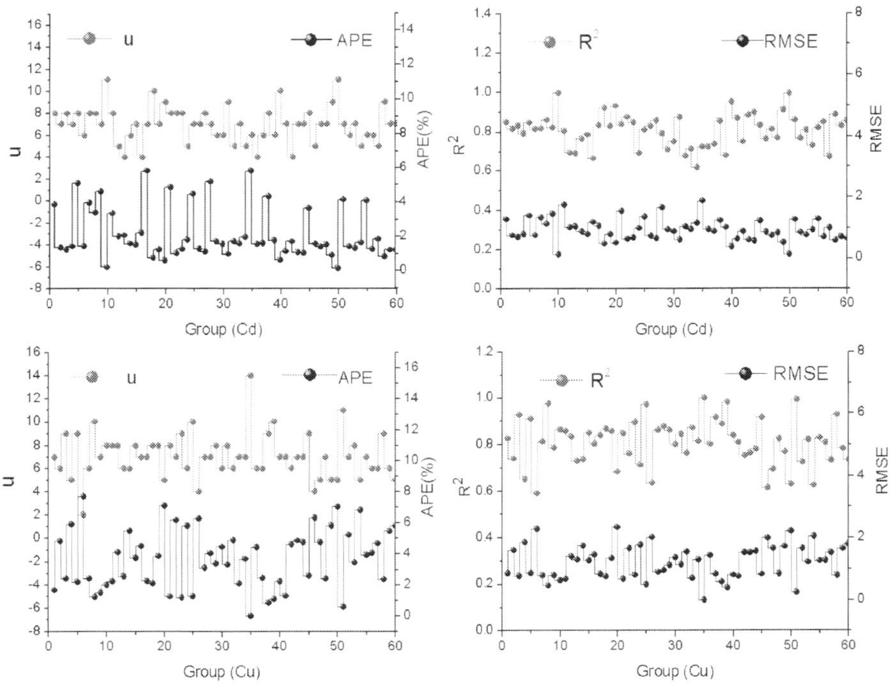

Fig. 5. The four evaluation parameters (u, APE, R^2 and RMSE) results for sixty groups of combined parameters as input variables for estimating Cu and Cd concentration in rice leaves. Each group consists of parameters according to Table 4.

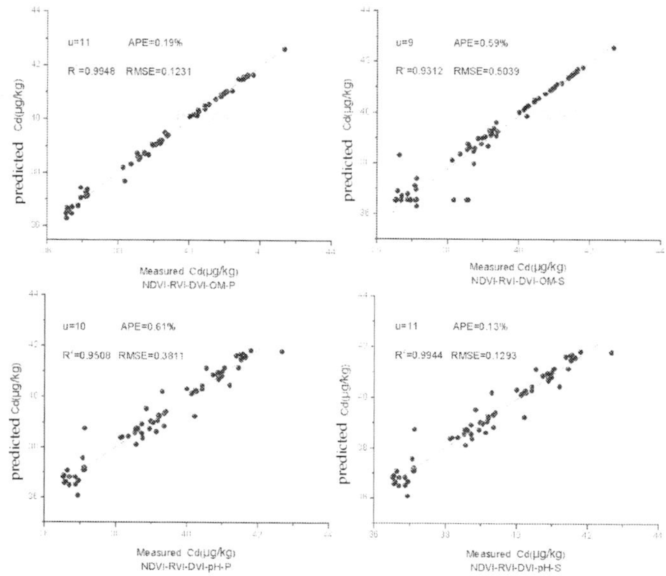

Fig. 6. Measured and predicted Cd concentration in rice leaves for four groups of optimal combined parameters using GDFNN

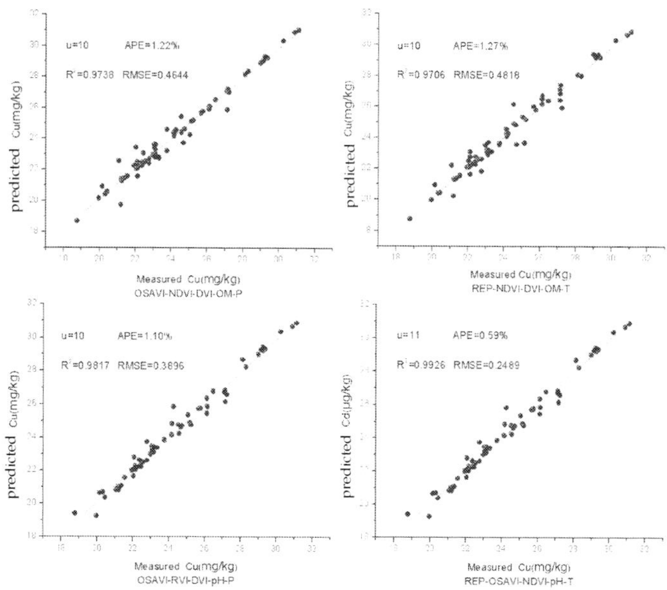

Fig. 7. Measured and predicted Cu concentration in rice leaves for four groups of optimal combined parameters using GDFNN

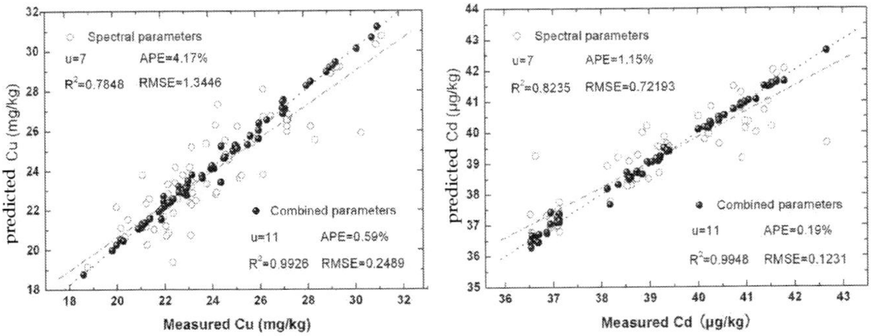

Fig. 8. Comparison of predicted Cu and Cd concentration in rice leaves using spectral parameters and combined parameters as input variables for GDFNN

6. Conclusions

The aim of this study is to develop a GDFNN model based on fuzzy theory and neural network theory to predict heavy metal concentrations in rice. Spectral indices and environmental parameters were integrated as input variables. Spectral indices were utilized to examine rice's physiological responses to heavy metal contaminations (Cu and Cd) in paddy fields, while environmental parameters including those relating to soil and weather were important factors for determining heavy metal diffusion in rice. Five parameters, three of which were selected from the five spectral parameters (REP, OSAVI, NDVI, DVI, RVI), one of which came from the two soil parameters (pH, OM), with the final one coming from the three meteorological parameters (T, S, P) were used as input variables in GDFNN. Additionally, different combined parameters were treated as input variables in order to achieve the best GDFNN prediction for heavy metal concentrations in rice. The analysis revealed that the best input variables in predicting Cu concentrations in rice were the REP, OSAVI, NDVI, pH and T, where this model had u, APE, R^2 and RMSE values of 11, 0.59%, 0.9926 and 0.2489 respectively. While the best input variables in predicting Cu concentrations in rice were the NDVI, RVI, DVI, OM and P, which had respective u, APE, and R^2 values of 11, 0.19%, 0.9948 and 0.1231. It indicated that the GDFNN developed in this study had a high accuracy as well as a compact structure (i.e. fewer fuzzy rules: u=11, R^2 was over 0.99 nearly 1). Compared with only spectral parameters as input variables of GDFNN, the use of combined parameters as input variables showed slightly better performance in estimating Cu and Cd concentrations in rice. After testing a trial set, our results showed that the GDFNN developed using fewer input variables can accurately estimate heavy metal concentrations in rice, thus aiding the assessment of pollution levels of heavy metals in soil. It can be concluded that by using a GDFNN model, hyperspectral parameters and environmental parameters can provide sufficient information to detect the level of pollutants in field operations efficiently.

7. Reference

Blackburn, G.A. (1998). Quantifying chlorophylls and caroteniods at leaf and canopy scales: An evaluation of some hyperspectral approaches. Remote Sensing of Environment, 66, 273-285.

Chang, S. H., &Colllins, W.(1983). Confirmation of the airborne biogeophysica mineral exploration technique using laboratory methods. Economic Geology, 78, 723-736.

Cheng, W.D., Zhang, G.P., Yao, H.G., &Tang, M.L.(2005). Effect of grain position within a panicle and variety on As, Cd, Cr, Ni, Pb concentrations in japonica rice. Rice Science, 12: 48-56(in Chinese).

Cui, Y.J., Zhu, Y.G., Zhai, R.H., Chen, D.Y., Huang, Y.Z., Qiu, Y., & Liang, J.Z. (2004). Transfer of metals from soil to vegetables in an area near a smelter in Nanning, China. Environment International, 30, 785-791.

Curran, P.J., Dungan, J.L., & Peterson, D.L. (2001). Estimating the foliar biochemical concentration of leaves with reflectance spectrometry testing the Kokaly and Clark methodologies. Remote Sensing of Environment, 76, 349-359.

Das, P., Samantaray, S., & Rout, G.R. (1997). Studies on cadmium toxicity in plants: A review. Environmental Pollution, 98, 29-36.

De Vries, W., Curlik, J., Muranyi, A., Alloway, B., & Groenenberg, B.J. (2005). Assessment of relationships between total and reactive concentrations of cadmium, copper, lead and zinc in Hungarian and Slovakian soils. Ekologia-Bratislava, 24, 152-169.

Fernandes, J. C. &Henriques, F. S. (1991). Biochemical, physiological, and structural effects of excess copper in plants. The Botanical Reivew, 57, 246–266.

Foy, C. D., Chancy, R. L. & White, M. C. (1978) The physiology of metal toxicity in plants. Annual Review of Plant Physiology, 29, 511-566.

Fu, J.J., Zhou, Q.F., Liu, J.M., Liu, W., Wang, T., Zhang, Q.H., & Jiang, G.B. (2008). High levels of heavy metals in rice (Oryza sativa L.) from a typical E-waste recycling area in southeast China and its potential risk to human health. Chemosphere, 71, 1269-1275.

Hang, X.S., Wang, H.Y., Zhou, J.M., Ma, C.L., Du, C.W., & Chen, X.Q. (2009). Risk assessment of potentially toxic element pollution in soils and rice (Oryza sativa) in a typical area of the Yangtze River Delta. Environmental Pollution, 157, 2542-2549.

Huang, S.S., Liao, Q.L., Hua, M., Wu, X.M., Bi, K.S., Yan, C.Y., Chen, B., & Zhang, X.Y. (2007). Survey of heavy metal pollution and assessment of agricultural soil in Yangzhong district, Jiangsu Province, China. Chemosphere, 67, 2148-2155.

Huete, A. R. (1988). A soil vegetation adjusted index (SAVI). Remote Sensing of Environment, 25,295-309.

Jackson, A.P., &Alloway, B.J.(1992). The transfer of cadmium from agricultural soils to the human food chain. In: D.C. Adriano Ed.., Biogeochemistry of Trace Metals. Lewis, Boca Raton, FL, pp. 109–158.

Jang J.S.R.(1993). ANFIS: adaptive-network-based fuzzy inference system. IEEE Transactions on Systems Man and Cybernetics, 23, 665–684.

Jung, M.C., & Thornton, I. (1997). Environmental contamination and seasonal variation of metals in soils, plants and waters in the paddy fields around a Pb-Zn mine in Korea. Science of the Total Environment, 198, 105-121.

Kádár, I.(1995). Effect of heavy metal load on soil and crop.Acta Agronomica Hungarica, 43, 3–9.

Kooistra, L., Salas, E.A.L., Clevers, J., Wehrens, R., Leuven, R., Nienhuis, P.H., &Buydens, L.M.C.(2004). Exploring field vegetation reflectance as an indicator of soil contamination in river floodplains. Environmental Pollution, 127, 281-290.

Leng, G., McGinnity, T.M., &Prasad, G.(2005). An approach for on-line extraction of fuzzy rules using a self-organising fuzzy neural network. Fuzzy Sets and Systems, 150, 211-243.

Liao, F.Q., Zhou, S.L., Zhang, H.F., Wu, S.H., & Zhao, Q.G. (2008). Spatial distribution and changes of heavy metals of agricultural lands in typical pregrading coast in Dongtai City, Jiangsu Province, China. Chinese Geographical Science, 18, 276-283.

Lindsay,W. L.,&Norvell, W. A.(1978). Development of a DTPA soil test for zinc, iron, manganese, and copper. Soil Science Society of America Journal, 42, 421-428.

Liu,M. L., Liu ,X. N.,Li,M., Fang, M. H., &Chi,W. X.(2010a). Neural-network model for estimating leaf chlorophyll concentration in rice under stress from heavy metals using four spectral indices. Biosystems Engineering, 6, 223-233.

Liu,Y.,Chen,H.,Wu,G.F., &Wu,X.G.(2010b). Feasibility of estimating heavy metal concentrations in Phragmites australis using laboratory-based hyperspectral data—A case study along Le'an River, China. International Journal of Applied Earth Observation and Geoinformation (in press). http://doi:10.1016/j.jag.2010.01.003

National Environmental Protection Agency of China, 2006. Farmland environmental quality evaluation standards for edible agriculture products.. State Environmental Protection Administration, China. HJ332-2006.

Pai, T.Y., Wan, T.J., Hsu, S.T., Chang, T.C., Tsai, Y.P., Lin, C.Y., Su, H.C., & Yu, L.F. (2009). Using fuzzy inference system to improve neural network for predicting hospital wastewater treatment plant effluent. Computers & Chemical Engineering, 33, 1272-1278.

Pan,W.J.,Jiang,C.Y.,Tang,Y.J.,Li, J.X. &Huang,J.G(2007). Effect of environment on Cadmium and lead content in tobacco. Soil, 39 (3): 369–374(in Chinese).

Reber, H. H.(1989). Threshold levels of cadmium for soil respiration and growth of spring wheat (Triticum aestivumL.),and difficulties with their determination. Biology and Fertility of Soils, 7,152–157.

Schuerger, A.C., Capelle, G.A., Di Benedetto, J.A., Mao, C.Y., Thai, C.N., Evans, M.D., Richards, J.T., Blank, T.A., & Stryjewski, E.C. (2003). Comparison of two hyperspectral imaging and two laser-induced fluorescence instruments for the detection of zinc stress and chlorophyll concentration in bahia grass (Paspalum notatum Flugge.). Remote Sensing of Environment, 84, 572-588.

Wu, S.Q., Er, M.J., & Gao, Y. (2001). A fast approach for automatic generation of fuzzy rules by generalized dynamic fuzzy neural networks. IEEE Transactions on Fuzzy Systems, 9, 578-594.

Yoder, B.J., & Pettigrewcrosby, R.E. (1995). Predicting Nitrogen and Chlorophyll Content and Concentrations from Reflectance Spectra (400-2500 nm) at Leaf and Canopy Scales. Remote Sensing of Environment, 53, 199-211.

19

Application of Artificial Intelligence in Environmental Sciences – Forecasting CO_2 Emission in Poland

Alicja Kolasa - Więcek
Opole University of Technology
Faculty of Management, Department of Economics and Regional Research
Poland

1. Introduction

Study on the impact of greenhouse gases emissions on the environment is currently an issue undertaken by scientists and policy makers around the world. The observed increase in the average temperature is often interpreted as a result of normal cyclical changes and long-term phenomenon and global warming is in dispute. In accordance with the precautionary principle efforts are undertaken to stabilize greenhouse gas concentrations in the atmosphere by limiting their anthropogenic emissions and put in place mechanisms to intensify their absorption. During the past 150 years the amount of carbon dioxide in the earth's atmosphere has increased from 280 parts per million to more than 380 parts per million on account of burning of fossil fuels (Srinivasan, 2008). The simulations and forecasts which are being carried out show that the global temperature may increase by 1.6 - 2.0°C in the second half of the 21st century (Timofeev, 2006).

1.1 CO_2 emission in Poland

Poland needs to reduce greenhouse gases emissions by 6%, which means in 2008-2012 the average, annual level must be so lower to compared to 1988 emissions. To attain its objectives, we must limit emissions from all spheres of social life.

In accordance with the European Parliament resolution the European Committee considers that by 2020 the EU will have to reduce greenhouse gas emissions by 15-20%, and for the next 30 years up to 60-80% (compared to 1990).

The main producer of anthropogenic CO_2 in the world is first of all the energy and industry, transport, agriculture and progressive deforestation. The EU directives oblige Poland to maintain specific levels of total national emissions of CO_2, regardless of its source. It is expected that in the coming years, Polish economic development financed from the EU structural and cohesion funds will contribute to the growth of CO_2 emissions.

Particularly important in recent years is the necessity to predict possible scenarios in the greenhouse gases production due to the progressive greenhouse effect. It should be stressed that this is a complex issue because of the diversity and overlapping factors affecting the emission. European Union climate policy is a serious challenge for Poland. To implement this policy in accordance with current recommendations and announced restrictions will constitute a significant burden on the Polish economy. It should be noted that transport, despite the fact that Poland produces some tons of million of CO_2 is not covered by the ETS. Economic development increases the mobility and traffic loads, causing a steady increase in energy demand, which is the main source of coal and fuel oil.

Polish automotive industry is characterized by a strong growth. A dramatic change occurred with the free market reforms in the 90s. Cars in Poland contribute to emission to atmospheric average 30% pollution and in large cities and agglomerations, their share is much higher and may reach 70% to even 90%. According to Polish Climate Policy, the country should focus primarily on the restructuring of economic sectors towards the diversification of fuels, resulting in a reduction of air pollution.

The transport share in greenhouse gas emissions is increasing. The most difficult in this sector is to carry out activities aimed at emission reductions because of its dependence on petroleum fuels and coal (Resources-use, 2008). You cannot expect on easy successes in reducing greenhouse gas emissions without a change in lifestyles and consumption models, management space use, which conditioning mobility and transport absorptivity. It is predicted a permanent intensity of road traffic in Poland. By 2020, EU countries are obliged to reduce greenhouse gas emissions by 20%. In the same year, we are also supposed to reach the level of 20% of energy generated from renewable sources in the total energy production balance, increase energetic effectiveness of the whole European Union by 20% and increase the share of energy coming from renewable sources in transport by 10%. For the Polish, this may mean instability in the sense of danger of power shortages due to more stringent requirements on emissions of CO2 and equally ever-increasing demand for energy.

Difficulty in matching the imposed by the European Commission limits may hit the economy functioning. Hard coal plays a very important role in the Polish energy mix, occupying a large share in electricity generation and primary energy consumption, resulting in high and intensity emissions of CO_2.

High CO_2 emission in Poland to result from the fact that the energy sector is based primarily on coal power plants (table 1). Although overall coal consumption in Poland is falling still the share of fossil fuels in electricity production in Poland is near 92% and is the highest among EU countries.

According to current forecasts, the average emissions in Poland in 2008-2012 should not exceed 400 million tons per year. Due to a radical reduction of emission in the 1990s caused by conversion and modernisation of the economy, the cheapest ways of volume reduction concerning the greenhouse gases emission have already been used. The next reductive actions are associated with high capital expenditure and realisations of such investments frequently exceed financial capabilities of companies. It is a fact that the power industry system in Poland is efficient in 33-35%, compared to market-available power blocks with efficiency reaching 50% (Kolasa-Więcek, 2009).

International programs will aim to eliminate power plants based on traditional resources - coal and petroleum. Coal power plants will be gradually phased out in Poland. More and more energy will be generated from alternative sources. The share of renewable energy in total energy production in Poland in 2008 amounted to 7.24% (Environmental protection, 2009), dominated mainly by biomass and hydropower plant. It is expected to increase the participation of wind energy. Undoubtedly, the direction of fuel sources structure development in Poland will result in the emission of energy-fuel sector in the coming years.

Specification	CO_2 emission
Electricity together:	**310 592,29**
Fuel combustion:	310 341,40
- power industry	187 500,65
- manufacturing and construction	33 724,50
industry	37 381,40
- transport	250,88
Ethereal fuels emission	
Industrial processes:	**19 040,21**
Mineral products	9 147,39
chemical industry	4 276,75
metals producion	4 471,88
Other industrial process	1 144,19
Solvents and other products use	**581,75**
Waste	**309,32**

Table 1. Total CO_2 emission by major sources of emission in 2007 (COS, 2009).

Modern technology can provide Poland with the potential reduction in greenhouse gas emissions, but their development is uncertain. Would be needed life style population changes including technologies that increase energy efficiency in transport and construction. The most important measures have to be taken in improving energy efficiency, its use of low-carbon energy sources and sequestration of CO_2 but it involves a costly investment.
Participation in the emission reduction will have, among others nuclear power plants. It is estimated that in 2020 Poland should have the first nuclear power plant. Much of the traditional coal power plants will end his use period in coming years, and how they will be replaced by is crucial to the country emissivity.
Polish forests are an asset. In industrialized Europe forests occupy a relatively large area in Poland. In recent decades, their surface increasing very slowly but gradually.
There has been observed a theme of making the modeling of CO_2 emissions and spread in many scientific-research institutes in the world, although the modeling in this area is a difficult process even though because of many factors which determine the nature of the phenomenon.

2. Methodology and tools

2.1 ANN in environmental sciences

The character of climatic phenomena is highly complex, with the result that modeling attempts are still taken, which would allow the predictions of high probability. It should be noted that the continuous increase in computing power of modern computers and the development of advanced artificial intelligence tools and statistical tools allow to obtain an application enabling the simulation to gain satisfactory results in modeling.
Present-day, such a far-reaching and widespread interest in neural networks, among both engineers, representatives of science - mathematics, physics and biologists or neurophysiologists stems primarily from research on ways to build more efficient and more reliable information processing equipment, and the nervous system is an unattainable model. There are many successful examples of applications. Just to mention some: electronic systems

diagnosis, biological research interpretation, pattern recognition, speech recognition, medical diagnostics, control theory and optimization issues.

Thanks to the artificial networks it is possibile to solve the tasks, which are struggling to cope with traditional computational techniques. Indeed, neural networks, can be used wherever there are problems with the processing and data analysis, with their prediction, classification and control.

The original inspiration for the artificial networks structure was the construction of natural neurons and neural systems. Artificial neural network consists of a large number of items in parallel information processing. These elements are just neurons, although in relation to the real nerve cells their functions are very simplified.

The relatively new insights in environmental sciences provide computational methods based on the idea of artificial intelligence. They are extremely useful in disposing of the noise measurement data information, emerging as a result of overlapping impact of external and internal effects. Thanks to Artificial Neural Networks it is possible to identify the dominant factors.

Theme of modeling the CO_2 emission and dispersion is taken by many research institutes around the Word (Auffhammer et al., 2006; IPCC, 2000; Nickerson, 2004; Samoilov &Nakutin, 2009; Sarrat et al., 2007; Schmalensee et al., 1998). Modeling in this area is a difficult process because of for instance the multitude of factors which determine the phenomenon nature (Soon et al., 2001). More importantly, aspects that may seem less related to carbon emissions themselves, such as regulation and private sector strength, or the relative percentage of industry compared to agriculture, or a measure of science and technology are worth exploring so that we may discover a new way to combat this environmental problem (Nickerson, 2004). Modeling is but one approach to understanding climate change. To place more confidence in climate modeling by computer, observational capability must advance (Soon et al., 2001). Simulations carried out by scientists show that even with a dramatic reduction of CO_2 emission, the temperature will not decrease for a certain period of time (Alexiadis 2007).

A significant advantage of the neural network as a forward-looking devices is that through a learning process the network can acquire the ability to predict the output signals based on the observations during the training data. The network is able to predict the output signals, even when using researcher it does not know anything about the nature of the relationship between the conditions with conclusions (Tadeusiewicz, 1993). The neural networks advantage is that they can be used wherever there are problems with the mathematical models creation. Network creator does not have to declare a model sought form and may not even be sure whether any relationship that is possible to a mathematical model even exists. Another important advantage of artificial neural networks is the ability to detect and use any nonlinearities that may occur in the data, even in incomplete data or in the presence of so-called "Noise-information." In order to detect overfitting problems and develop a useful and fair modeling exercise, researchers must follow the technical and practical recommendations and guidelines proposed in the literature on computer science (Bishop, 1995).

Actually, it has been shown that a neural network which is properly designed can approach any continuous function to any desired level of accuracy. Thus in this way the technique is more appropriate than traditional methods in order to model and predict phenomena distinguished by a complex behavior.

Artificial intelligence tools are more and more frequently used in solving issues related to environmental sciences due to, to name just a few, high likelihood of results reception and a possibility to find an alternative solution. There should be also mentioned the disadvantages, which are cited. One of them states that there is no economic theory behind an artificial neural Network. Sometimes this method is criticized because it is considered a black-box without any economic foundation (Álvarez-Díaz, 2009). Another complaint is difficulty in analyzing the impact of input variables to output variable, and moreover it is difficult to verify the statistical importance of predictions. Time-consuming and tedious procedure for the design of neural networks is also emphasized. Another shortcoming is fact that the results can strongly vary depending on the determination of some technical parameters. The last one and more important, the great power of the neural networks to replicate data can be also a serious disadvantage. There is a risk that the network merely mimic data and it cannot generalize new observations (Álvarez-Díaz et al., 2009).

2.2 Research metodology

In this paper, the neural analysis has been made with the use of a neural network of the Flexible Bayesian Models on Neural Networks, Gaussian Processes, and Mixtures, operating in the UNIX/Linux environment (Neal, 2004). Properly designed input–output neural network can learn from the data and provide a reasonable estimate of carbon emissions.

Flexible Bayesian models for regression and classification applications are carried out by this software. The base for these models is multilayer perceptron neural networks or Gaussian processes while in the implementation Markov chain Monte Carlo methods are used. Software modules not only support Markov chain sampling but they also support the distribution and may be useful in other applications.

Flexible Bayesian Neural Networks shows that Bayesian methods allow complex neural network models to be used without fear of the "overfitting" that can occur with traditional neural network learning methods. They can safely be used when training data is limited (Neal, 1996). They can be used to model complex relationships between inputs and outputs or to find patterns in data.

The Bayesian approach treats the issue of model complexity very differently and in particular it allows all of the avalible data to be used for "training". Since the evidence can be evaluated using training data, we see that Bayesian method are able to deal with the issue of model complexity , without the need to use cross-validation (Bishop, 1995).

This paper analyses the functional relation between the CO2 emissions and some factors like:

- CO_2 emissions from the energy industry, transport and other industrial processes in general,
- the size of afforestation,
- hard coal consumption,
- cars and tractors burdensome for clean air (COS, 1991 - 2009).

Analyzed factors are not coincidental, they play and will play a significant role in greenhouse gas emissions in coming years. Training set comprise data from the years 1990-2008 obtained from the CSO database. It was built a network with 4 neurons ine the input layer, 8 neurons in the hidden layer and 1 output.

Samples of input signals of training set is shown in the table 2.

Ordinal number	Afforestation	Number of Vehicles	Hard coal consumption	CO_2 emissions from transport	CO_2 emissions
1	9.98	9.51	19.45	9.43	14.02
2	9.98	9.6	19.2	9.55	12.64
3	9.98	9.63	18.42	9.67	13.1
4	9.98	9.65	18.36	9.49	12.27
5	9.98	9.7	16.76	9.68	13.1
6	9.98	9.73	17.47	9.6	10.76
7	9.99	9.79	19.43	9.56	13.19
8	9.99	9.84	17.64	9.71	12.1
9	9.99	9.88	15.61	9.98	9.68
10	10	9.93	13.57	10.31	8.84
11	10	10.02	11.9	10.06	7.35
12	10	10.08	12.15	10	7.65
13	10.01	10.16	11.54	9.99	6.43
14	10.01	10.2	13.06	10.07	7.54
15	10.02	10.28	11.33	10.25	7.56
16	10.02	10.29	11.57	10.44	7.69
17	10.03	10.41	12.81	10.63	8.83
18	10.03	10.56	12.65	10.78	8.69
19	10.04	10.74	12.1	10.82	8.57

Table 2. The input signals of training set

The forecasts show a possible direction for the development emissions level, assuming a continuation of current trends and the slight additional measures to prevent climate change. Modelling also shows the other scenarios - optimistic resulting from e.g. introduction of modern technology reducing the emission and pessimistic, assuming such a parameters like expected growth vehicles and thus increasing emissions from transport or other taking into account the increase in coal consumption.

It was analyzed the situation taking into consideration the expected increase in the number of vehicles with the reduction in transport emissions resulting from e.g the initiation of alternative fuels inter alia biofuels.

To determine the factors most connected with CO_2 emissions and try to find a model describing the relationship between input and output variables the linear regression was used. The above analysis was made using R-Project. R is a modern tool that allows programming, advanced statistical analysis and visualization of research results (Biecek 2008).

3. Results and their interpretation

3.1 Forecasting with FBM

The gained selected (numerical and graphic) parameters of the quality of the network learning, among others, so called recoil index and the trajectory graph of the control values, so called weight hyper-parameters, show proper and relatively optimal course of the process of the network learning. About a balance in the impulses flow through the network, provides the resulting coefficient - 0.503 (Fig. 1), which is within the range of variability 0.2-0.8.

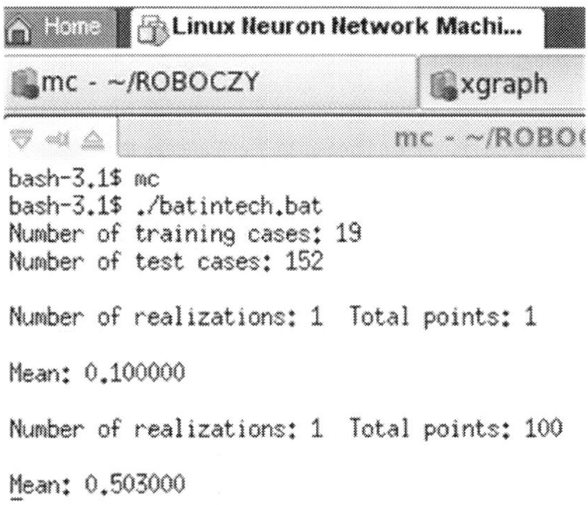

Fig. 1. Obtained coefficients size

The results of modelling allow for making certain remarks. The forecasts show that limiting or increasing analysed factors affects the volume of CO_2 emission. In consequence, along with an rise in the parameters increasing CO_2 emission.

In Figure 2 the different scenarios of CO_2 emissions were presented.

It appears that "coal consumption" is a very important variable. It is the most important variable and primarily decisive about the CO_2 emission in the analyzed cases.

Based on the modeling results on the figure 2 the observed relationships between variables were presented. For this purpose scatter plots were used, which may even visually help us to assess the force and nature of relationships between variables. The diagrams show the observations for three variables. If the points are arranged in an irregular cloud, then there is no relationship between variables (Figure 2a).

If, however, the points are arranged along a straight line or a curve, it can be discerned a connection between variables.

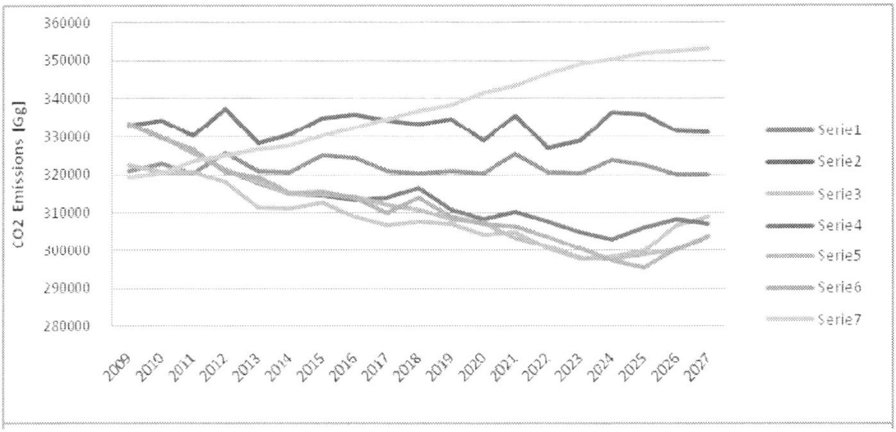

Fig. 2. Forecasting CO_2 emissions taking into account different scenarios: serie 1 – observed trends, serie 2 – CO_2 emissions reduction in transport, Rest parameters with observed trends, serie 3 – reduction hard coal consumption and emissions from transport, serie 4 - reduction hard coal consumption with permanent emissions from transport, 5 – increase of afforestation, 6 - reduction hard coal consumption, reduction emissions from transport from 90 years, permanent number of vehicles, 7 - hard coal consumption increase, emissions from transport and number of vehicles increase.

a)

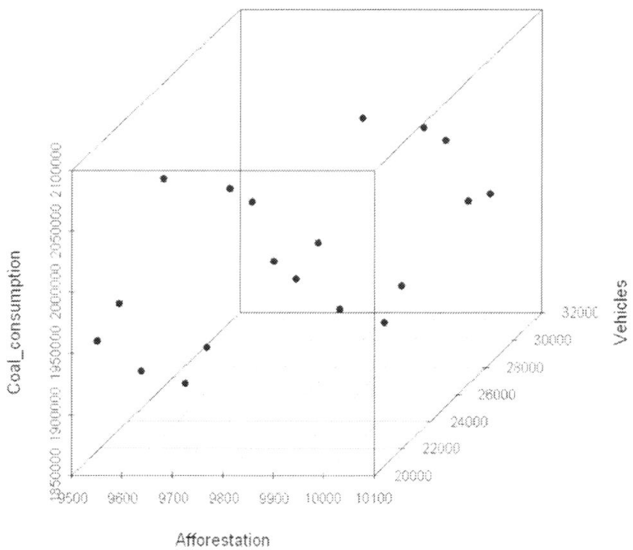

Points contracting perfectly along a straight are very infrequent. Figure 2b is a excellent example that reflects the existence of a negative linear correlation (case of a reduction in coal consumption).

b)

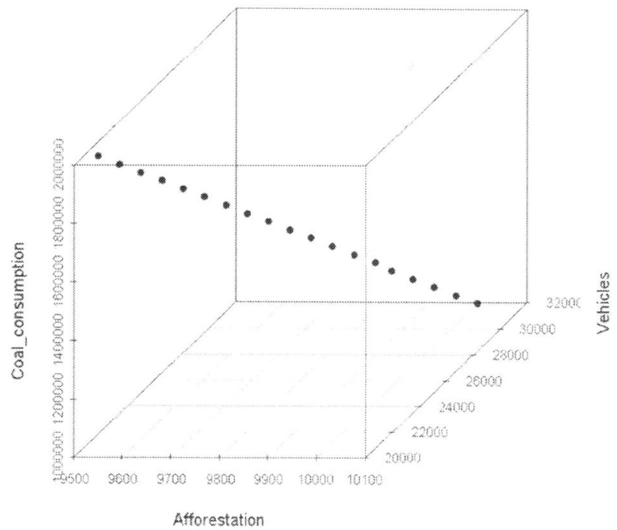

Graph 2c presents a relationship in case when the analyzed parameters are rising. A strong positive correlation between variables was observed. With an increase in the number of vehicles, emissions from transport and coal consumption, CO_2 emissions rise.

c)

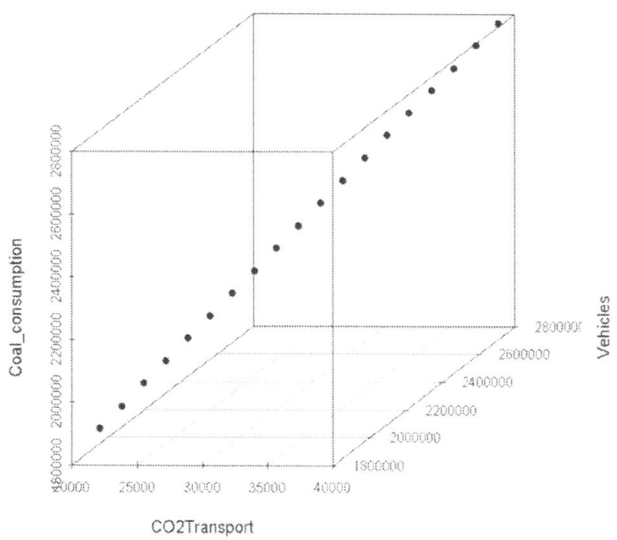

Fig. 2. Scatterplots for chosen parameters

3.1 Modelling using linear regression

The next stage of this study was to define a model describing the relationship between the explanatory variables and the amount of CO_2 emissions. In this case, a linear regression analysis was used. It is a popular and widely used statistical analysis which allows to find the relationship between inputs and outputs. It takes into account the interdependence modeling of the studied traits. This technique is based on estimation of some data from the other. There are known and used many regression techniques. Linear regression assumes that between the input and output variables, there is a linear relationship (Faray, 2002). Using lm () function fit a linear model to the data was conducted (fig. 3).

In case 3a with explanatory variable "vehicles" obtained a negative coefficient, which means that this parameter is not significantly different from zero and can be omitted in the model. Taking into consideration other factors it is a small value.

Coefficient value of R^2 and Adjusted R^2 testifies to fit a linear model. Adjusted R^2 takes into account the number of variables in the model. If the coefficient is closer to 1 the better model fits in the data.

Adjusted R^2 showing the percentage of variance explained by the model is highest.

a)

```
Call:
lm(formula = CO2emision ~ forests + vehicles + coal + CO2transport,
    data = data.co2)

Residuals:
    Min      1Q  Median      3Q     Max
-9549.1 -4044.2  -458.3  3132.5 18598.0

Coefficients:
               Estimate Std. Error t value Pr(>|t|)
(Intercept)  -4.083e+04  5.446e+05  -0.075    0.941
forests       1.813e+01  6.628e+01   0.274    0.788
vehicles     -1.727e+00  3.374e+00  -0.512    0.617
coal          8.728e-02  1.046e-02   8.341  8.4e-07 ***
CO2transport  1.573e+00  1.330e+00   1.183    0.256
---
Signif. codes:  0 '***' 0.001 '**' 0.01 '*' 0.05 '.' 0.1 ' ' 1

Residual standard error: 7348 on 14 degrees of freedom
Multiple R-squared: 0.9324,     Adjusted R-squared: 0.9131
F-statistic: 48.29 on 4 and 14 DF,  p-value: 4.849e-08
```

Statistically non-significant variable was rejected and modeling were carried out again (e.g. 3b).

In case 3b also obtained high coefficients of R^2 and modified R^2.

With three independent variables least statistically significant was variable "forests", which was also omitted and modeling were carried out again (e.g. 3c).

Important parameters were variables: a highly significant - "coal" and a less important - "CO2transpor".

b)

```
Call:
lm(formula = CO2emision ~ forests + coal + CO2transport, data = data.co2

Residuals:
    Min      1Q  Median      3Q     Max
-9725.6 -4084.6  -106.1  2859.0 18445.8

Coefficients:
               Estimate Std. Error t value Pr(>|t|)
(Intercept)   2.032e+05  2.569e+05   0.791    0.441
forests      -1.171e+01  3.076e+01  -0.381    0.709
coal          8.886e-02  9.746e-03   9.118 1.66e-07 ***
CO2transport  1.583e+00  1.297e+00   1.221    0.241
---
Signif. codes:  0 '***' 0.001 '**' 0.01 '*' 0.05 '.' 0.1 ' ' 1

Residual standard error: 7165 on 15 degrees of freedom
Multiple R-squared: 0.9311,     Adjusted R-squared: 0.9174
F-statistic: 67.62 on 3 and 15 DF,  p-value: 6.047e-09
```

c)

```
Call:
lm(formula = CO2emision ~ coal + CO2transport, data = data.co2)

Residuals:
    Min      1Q  Median      3Q     Max
-9870.8 -3614.3   611.5  2393.4 18955.3

Coefficients:
              Estimate Std. Error t value Pr(>|t|)
(Intercept)  1.064e+05  3.750e+04   2.839   0.0119 *
coal         8.975e-02  9.211e-03   9.744 3.94e-08 ***
CO2transport 1.160e+00  6.539e-01   1.774   0.0950 .
---
Signif. codes:  0 '***' 0.001 '**' 0.01 '*' 0.05 '.' 0.1 ' ' 1

Residual standard error: 6971 on 16 degrees of freedom
Multiple R-squared: 0.9305,     Adjusted R-squared: 0.9218
F-statistic: 107.1 on 2 and 16 DF,  p-value: 5.455e-10
```

Fig. 3. The results of fitting the model to data.

With higher results (fig. 3c), the model is as follows:

$$\text{Emisja } CO_2 = 1{,}064e^{+05} + 8{,}975e^{-03} * \text{coal} + 1{,}160e^{-01} * \text{CO2transport} \quad (1)$$

Figures show a graphic interpretation of evaluation model coefficients, which clearly show that the explanatory variable of the highest importance is the coal consumption (variables are arranged along a straight line - e.g. 4a).

a)

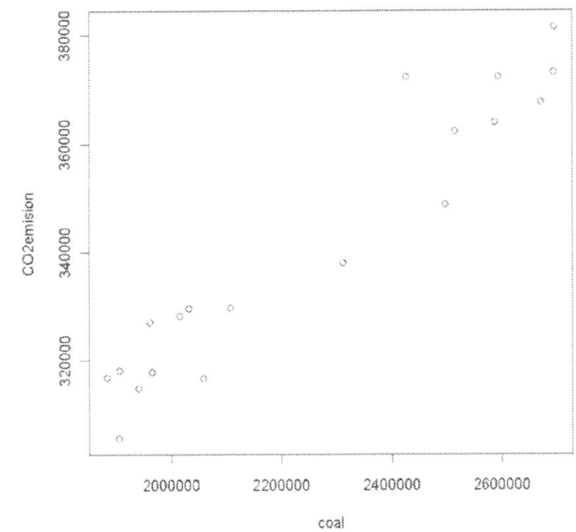

b)

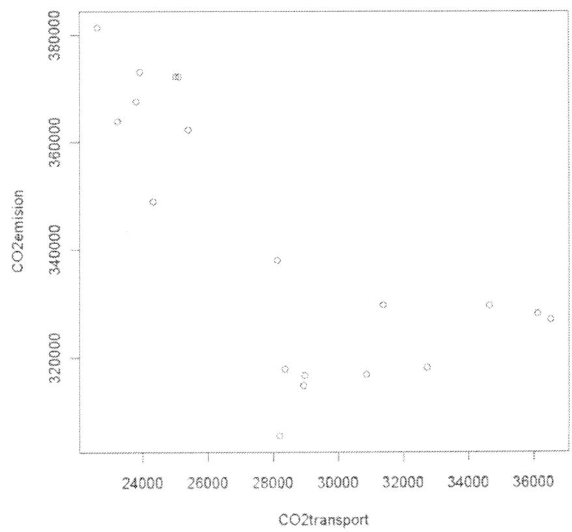

Fig. 4. Scatter diagram showing the emission of CO2 a) depending on the size of coal consumption, b) depending on CO_2 emissions from transport

We can examine the model assumptions, verifying the properties of residues. If the stipulations are achieved, the random noise should have a normal distribution with equal variances. That's why diagnostic graphs were used (fig. 5). This is a good method when the model is adequate.

a) The chart "Residuals vs Fitted"shows that the average value of residuals is close to 0 and the variance is homogeneous. On the horizontal axis shown values are matched by the model and the vertical axis are shown the elements of the residuals of standardized modules.

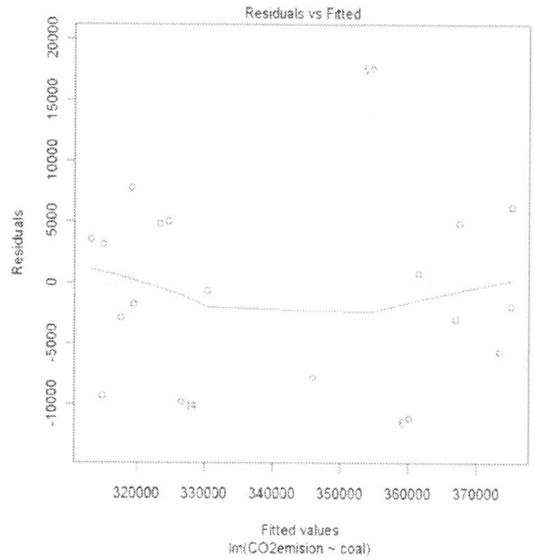

b) Figure "Normal Q-Q" it is a fractile graph for a normal distribution. The horizontal axis shows the values corresponding to the normal distribution quantiles residuals, and the vertical axis for the standardized empirical quantile of residuals. Contracting points along a straight line suggests that the model can be considered adequate and the distortion has a normal distribution.

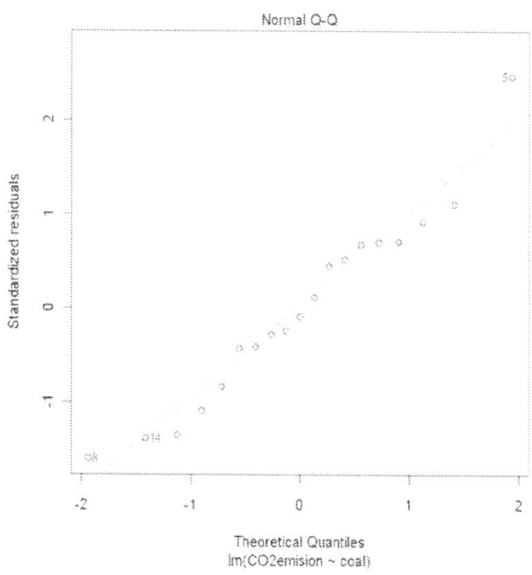

c) Graph "Scale-Location" present, as in the case a) on the horizontal axis shown values are matched by the model and the vertical axis - the elements of the residuals of standardized modules. Results was observed in the form of derogations unevenly spaced points.

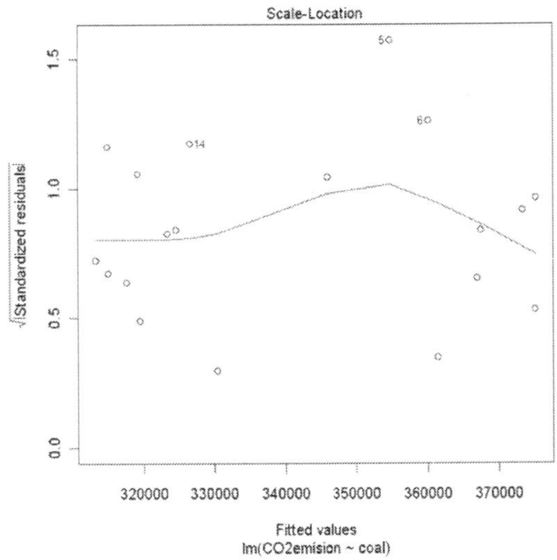

d) Graph "Residuals vs Leverage" takes into account the confidence range. It is very useful chart for detecting abnormal values.

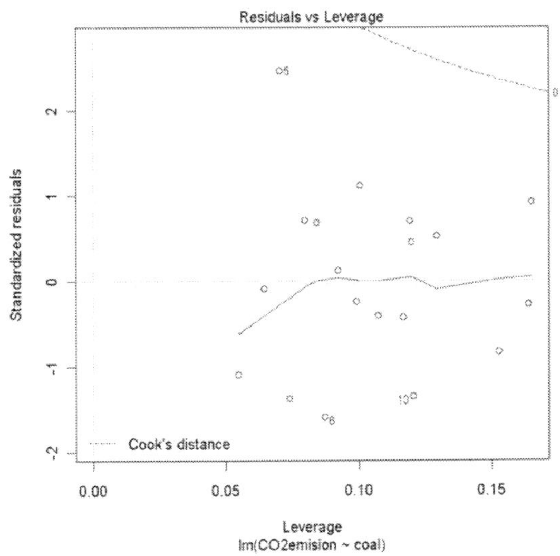

Fig. 4. Diagnostic diagrams for the tested model

4. Conclusion

Phenomena occurring in the natural environment are usually random or stochastic processes. Conventional calculation and statistic methods are sometimes inefficient when solving certain environmental problems. In the recent years, scientists all over the world have been trying to use methods based on artificial neural networks to solve environmental issues. The success of generating forecasts by a neural network is determined by having a representative collection of data which manifest the phenomenon being modelled. This investigation and model allowed to make an analysis of sensitivity in order to calculate the impact of each input parameter of the neural network on the total emission. From the experimental results it is possible to argue that coal consumption has the greatest impact on CO_2 emissions in polish situation.

Taking into consideration all the parameters in the model it is not easy and often impossible. Often, a determining factor is the availability of data.

The resultant match factor Adjusted R^2, provides high-fit model to the data. In the test case linearregression proved to be a good tool for estimating the correlation of the tested variables.

5. References

Alexiadis A. (2007). Global warming and human activity: A model for studying the potential instability of the carbon dioxide/temperature feedback mechanizm, *Ecological Modeling*, Vol. 203, No.3-4,2007, pp. 243-256

Auffhammer M. & Carson R. T. (2006). *Forecasting the Path of China's CO_2 Emissions: Offsetting Kyoto - And Then Some,* Department of Agricultural &, Resource Economics, UCB, CUDARE Working Papers, University of California, Berkeley

Álvarez-Díaz M., Caballero-Miguez, G. & Soliño, M. (2009). The institutional determinants of CO2 emissions: a computational modeling approach using Artificial Neural Networks and Genetic Programming, Environmetrics

Biecek P. (2008). *Guidebook to the R packet,* Publishing House GiS, Wrocław (in polish)

Bishop C. M. (1995). *Neural Networks for pattern Recognition,* Oxford University Press.

Cybenko, G. (1989). Approximation by superposition of a sigmoidal function, *Mathematics of Control, Signals and Systems,* vol. 2, no. 4, pp. 303-314

COS. (1991-2009). Environmental protection, Central Statistical Office, Warsaw, Statistical Publishing Estabilishment

Faraway J. J. (2002). Practical Regression and Anova using R

Haupt S. E., Pasini A. & Marzban C. (2008). Artificial Inteligence Methods in the Environmental Sciences, Springer

IPPC. (1996). Emissions Scenarios, Summary for Policymakers, *A Special Report of IPCC Working Group III, 2000,* Intergovernmental Panel on Climate Change

Kolasa-Więcek A. (2009). Influence of Selected Parameters on CO_2 Emission in Poland - Modelling with the Use of Neural Networks, *Polish Journal of Environmental Studies,* vol. 18, No. 3A, Hard Olsztyn, pp. 149-154,

Neal R. (1996). *Bayesian Learning for Neural Networks,* Springer - Verlag, New York

Neal R. (2004). Flexible Bayesian Models on Neural Networks, Gaussian Processes, and Mixtures v. 2004-11-10, University of Toronto, Toronto

Nickerson B. A. (2004). *Modeling Carbon Dioxide Emissions: Applying Empirical and Economic Analysis to a Global Environmental Issue,* The Ohio State University, National

Undergraduate Research Contest in Agricultural, Environmental and Development Economics

Resources-use and CO_2 Emissions Modelling, (2008) *A raport for the East of England Development Agency,* Cambridge Econometrics, Cambridge

Sarrat C., Noihan J., Dolman A.J., Gerbig C., Ahmadov R., Tolk L.F., Meesters A. G. C. A., Hutjes R. W. A., Ter Maat H. W., Perez-Landa G. & Donier S. (2007). Atmospheric CO2 modeling at the region al scale: an intercompartion of 5 meso-scale atmospheric models, *Biogeosciences Discussions,* vol. 4, pp. 1923-1952

Soon W., Baliunas S., Idso S. B., Kondratyev K. Y. & Posmentier E. S. (2001). Modeling climat effects of antrohropgenic carbon dioxide emissions: unknowns and uncertainties, *Climate Research,* vol. 18, pp. 259-275

Schmalensee R., Stoker T. M. & Judson R. A. (1998). World Carbon Dioxide Emissions: 1950–2050, *The Review of Economics and Statistics,* MIT Press, Vol. 80, No. 1: pp. 15–27

Srinivasan J. (2008). Climate change, Greenhouse gases and aerosols, *Resonance,* Vol. 13, No.12, p. 1146-1155

Tadeusiewicz R. (1993). *Neural Networks,* Warsaw, Academic Publishing House RM, (in polish)

Timofeev N. A. (2006). Greenhouse effect of the atmosphere and its influence on Earth's climate (satellite data), *Phisical Oceanography,* Vol.16, No. 6, pp. 322-336

20

Applying Artificial Neural Network on Modelling Waterbird Diversity in Irrigation Ponds of Taoyuan, Taiwan

Wei-Ta Fang[1], K. Douglas Loh[2], Hone-Jay Chu[3] and Bai-You Cheng[3]
Chung Hua University[1], Texas A&M University[2], National Taiwan University[3]
Taiwan, Republic of China

1. Introduction

Irrigation ponds, or *pi-tang* in Chinese, are defined as an artificial construction made to impound water by constructing a dam or an embankment, or by excavating a pit or dugout. Some ponds at both microhabitat and the landscape scales may be a relevant influence for explaining bird communities due to a habitat effect or more-moderate and complex effects (Froneman et al., 2001). These ponds, regarding as wintering waterbird refuges, represent some of the multi-functional dimensions in the restoration results of agro-ecosystems. Previous studies detected that causes of species diversity are affected by habitat heterogeneity (Forman and Godron, 1986; Forman, 1995; Begon et al., 1996; Francl & Schnell, 2002; Fang et al., 2009). According to habitat selection as bio-choices, irrigation pond patterns associated with various microhabitats provide environmental clues that are used by birds to select stopover sites, such that ponds within the range of avian communities may potentially remain unoccupied or under-occupied if they lack those clues. Therefore, the appropriate microhabitats for a particular species in a guild might not be spatially constant if the habitat status changes the distance to the edge between pond cores to peripheral habitats, i.e., by water-table drawdown, farmland consolidation, or other anthropogenic influences. Pond-species relationships, thus, are connected like a neural network with a non-parametric nature, as clues suggest.

In fact, estimating the avian community is a difficult task as various species may inhabit same patch in a heterogeneous landscape, so taxonomic analysis of avian guilds would be advantageously coupling them here with the development of forecasting techniques based on habitat characteristics. Surprisingly, attempts to estimate entire avian guilds with scientific rigor on such grounds are scarce in the literature, except with a few taxonomic studies (McArthur et al., 1967). Conversely, a wealth of work deals with linear predictions on a regional scale (McArthur et al., 1967; Froneman et al. 2001). In this respect, they proposed theoretical linear-relationship models using a wide range of multivariate techniques, including several methods of multivariate linear discriminant analyses, canonical analyses, and logistic regressions.

Many critical reviews have indicated that these conventional models, usually based on multiple regressions, assume simple linear relationships between variables (Palmer, 1990; Reby et al., 1997). Some authors argued that regression model did not fit non-linear relationships and interactions among variables. Virkkala (2004) stipulated that avian habitat selection is a dynamic and nonlinear process. Based on linear principles, they produce exclusive results since the main processes that determine the level of biodiversity or species abundance are often non-linear. To some extent, these methods are often rather inefficient after variable transformation when the data are non-linearly distributed. Therefore, species-habitat relationships often yield skewed and bimodal data. There are also other complexities associated with fluctuating avian populations and hierarchical decision-making on different scales before a final habitat selection. This highly complex relationship is inherently unpredictable between birds and their microhabitats. However, on the local scale many habitat models for birds have achieved considerable success in predicting habitat selection.

In addition, there is no specific a priori mathematical tool for predicting guild biodiversity, so the techniques used for prediction should also work for non-linear transformation. In ecology, multivariate-based models relating environmental variables to avian communities have been presented by several authors sometimes using non-linear transformations of independent or dependent variables to improve results. Even so, the results are still insufficient, with a low percentage of variance explained. Therefore, additive variables regarding bird and pondscape relationships require that networks be interwoven for detailed studies.

According to aforementioned analyses, this study assesses a non-linear relationship using neural network models instead of linear regression. We developed an approach adopted by Artificial Neural Networks (ANN) to model the relationship between pondscape and waterbird diversity. Study areas with thousands of irrigation ponds are unique geographic features from the original functions of irrigation converted to waterbird refuges. An important advantage of using an artificial neural network model is its non-parametric nature. It is not necessary to transform data to match a certain distribution. ANN models can be non-linear and can model logical expressions such as "and", "or", "not", and "exclusive or" as the pages that follows.

The groundwork for neural networks was laid out in the 1940s in the field of neurophysiology. ANN, which originated about several decades ago (McCulloch & Pitts, 1943), was inspired by a desire to emulate human learning. ANN is highly effective for modeling nonlinear problems. Only recently it was shown that ANN models may efficiently model some non-linear systems in ecology. In recent avian studies, some authors have focused on an approach of ANN, which were developed as an original prediction method according to the principle of the operation of the human neural system (Ozesmi et al., 2006; Fang et al., 2009). The practical implication is that an ANN can accurately predict nest occurrence and breeding success of red-winged blackbird in response to ecological applications (Ozesmi et al., 2006).

Neural networks are determined by the neurons, or units, which are interconnected within the entire dynamic system. In this research, therefore, we attempted to apply this method to relate the structure and diversity of an assemblage of wintering birds to microhabitats. Our model considers pond shape and size, neighboring farmlands, and constructed areas in calculating parameters pertaining to the interactive influences on avian diversity, among them the Shannon-Wiener diversity index (Shannon and Weaver, 1949; Oertli et al., 2002).

2. ANN's methods

In our research, we used multiple logistic regression (MLR) models associated with ANN's models. The multiple logistic regression (MLR) models are identical to a neural network with no hidden units. For neural network hidden units, each hidden unit computed a logistic regression (different for each hidden unit), and the output is therefore a weighted sum of logistic regression outputs. Initially, (ANN) were developed to provide simplified models of biological neural architecture. Each of these domains can be characterized as ones in which (a) multiple hypotheses need to be pursued in parallel, (b) enormous amounts of data need to be processed, and (c) the best current systems are far from equaling human performance.

The error back-propagation (BP) training algorithm has proven to be one of the most useful approaches in training the development of an ANN. This algorithm adjusts the connection weights according to the back-propagated error computed between the observed and the estimated results. This is a supervised learning procedure that attempts to minimize the error between the desired and the predicted outputs.

For this research, we chose a three-layered model with one input layer of three to four neurons (one for each input variable), one hidden layer of two to eight neurons (it is the number which gave the best prediction result), and one output layer of one neuron which was the output variable (see Fig. 1). Each input layer was connected to each neuron in the hidden layer via adjustable weighted links and likewise between the hidden layer and the output layer.

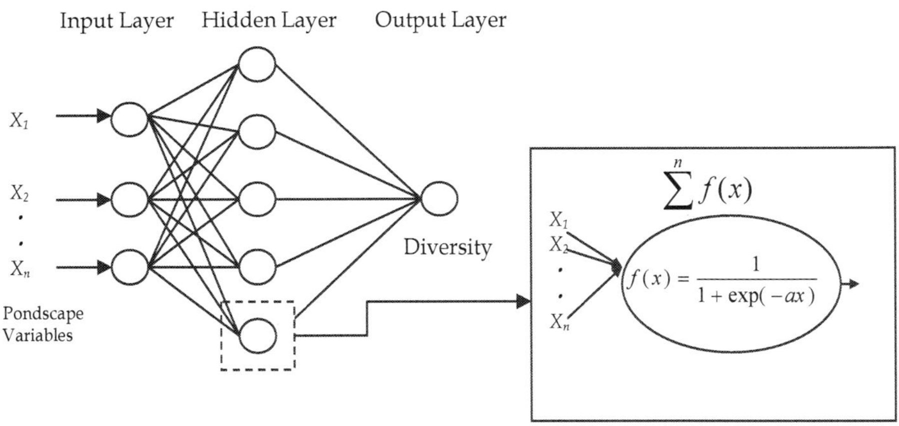

Fig. 1. Structure of neural networks used in this study based on the error back-propagation (BP) training algorithm. Input layer of neurons comprising as many neurons as pondscape variables at the entry of the system; hidden layer of neurons whose number is determined empirically; output layer of neurons with a single neuron (i.e., diversity) corresponding to the single dependent variable.

In the processes of BP training, the input data pattern is presented at the input neurons. These values are propagated through the network from the input to the hidden layer and then from the hidden layer to the output layer. At each stage the values, summed weighting inputs, are multiplied by the individual links on each connection. Then, the output layers are generated by the network based on the input data set. The errors, based on the differences between the "true" output and the "test" output, are fed back through the propagated loops. The individual weights associated with each of the connections to the hidden neurons are adjusted slightly to diminish the error.

Modelling was carried out in two phases to adjust with the training set and then test with the test set to determine the best ANN configuration. First, testing the model to calibrate the model variables. Second, to test the ANN models, we selected at random a training set (80% of the pond records, i.e., 35) and a validation set (20% of the pond records, i.e. 10). For each of the two sets, the model was determined with the training set and then validated with the test set. The quality of the model was judged through the correlation between observed and predicted values in the validation set. The ANN analysis was performed with the computer package, MATLAB 6.1 (MathWorks, Inc., Natick, MA, 2001).

3. Materials and supported methods

3.1 Materials sampled

In general, this study would detect differences between the linear model and non-linear model by logistic regression and ANN in the low-density rural population pondscape areas. There was a necessity to carefully select the predicted area of pondscape as well as environmental gradients between these models. Regarding the scientific rigor, all cases of sampling ponds, waterbirds, and other data related to this study are examined in material details as follows.

We selected ecologically significant Taoyuan Tableland associated irrigation ponds as our study area because one fifth of all the bird species find home on these ponds in Taiwan (Chen, 2000; Fang, 2004a). This tableland, at an area of 757 km^2 in size, comprises an area of 2,898 ha of irrigation ponds on the northwestern portion of Taiwan. Located approximately 30 km from the capital city of Taipei, this rural area was easily converted to urban lands due to the aggregated effects of urbanization and commercialization. Socioeconomic benefits are driving public opinion which is urging the government to approve land-use conversion from farmlands into urban uses. The Taoyuan Tableland lies between the northern border of the Linkou Tableland (23°05'N, 121°17'E) and the southern border of the Hukou Tableland (22°55'N, 121°05'E); it borders the town of Yinge in the east (22°56′N, 121°20′E) and the Taiwan Strait in the west (22°75′N, 120°99'E) (Department of Land Administration, Ministry of the Interior, 2002)(see Fig. 2.). It sits at elevations from sea level to 400 m and is composed of tableland up to 303 m and hills with sloping gradients from 303 to 400 m. It runs in a southeast-to-northwest trend, abutting mountains in the southeastern corner and the shore of the Taiwan Strait at the far end. With a high average humidity of 89%, the tableland is located in a subtropical monsoon region with humid winters and warm summers. January temperatures average 13 °C, and July temperatures average 28 °C. Annual average precipitation ranges from 1,500 to 2,000 mm.

The tableland gradually rose approximately 180,000 years ago. At that time, the Tanshui River had not yet captured the flow from the ancient Shihmen Creek, which directly poured out of the northwestern coast forming alluvial fans. Eventually, foothill faults caused by earthquakes during the same era, resulted in the northern region of Taiwan abruptly dropping by 200 m, and thus, the Taipei basin was born. Since the Taipei area had subsided, the ancient Shihmen Creek which meandered across the Taoyuan Tableland was captured by northward-flowing rivers some 30,000 years ago. The middle streams changed their courses because of the subsidence in the Taipei basin. The resulting Tahan Creek, became the upstream portion of the Tanshui River in the Taipei Basin. Due to blockage of water sources, downstream areas on the Taoyuan Tableland were deficient in water. This caused high flushing and drops in water yields. Historically, it was difficult to withdraw and

supply irrigated surface water from rivers due to the tableland's unique topography, thus, forming an obstacle for the development of agriculture (Huang, 1999; Chen, 2000).
This area has a population density of 2,331 persons/km^2 and its population is increasing at a rate of 2,000~3,000/month. Population pressures have contributed to reductions in historical areas of farmlands and irrigation ponds (Fang, 2001). Losses of farm-pond and farmland habitats have had series effects on a range of avian communities as well as other fauna and flora (Fang and Chang, 2004). On the Taoyuan Tableland, agricultural practices are intensifying, which is reducing the heterogeneity of the existing landform, and adding pollutants, also resulting from industrial practices.

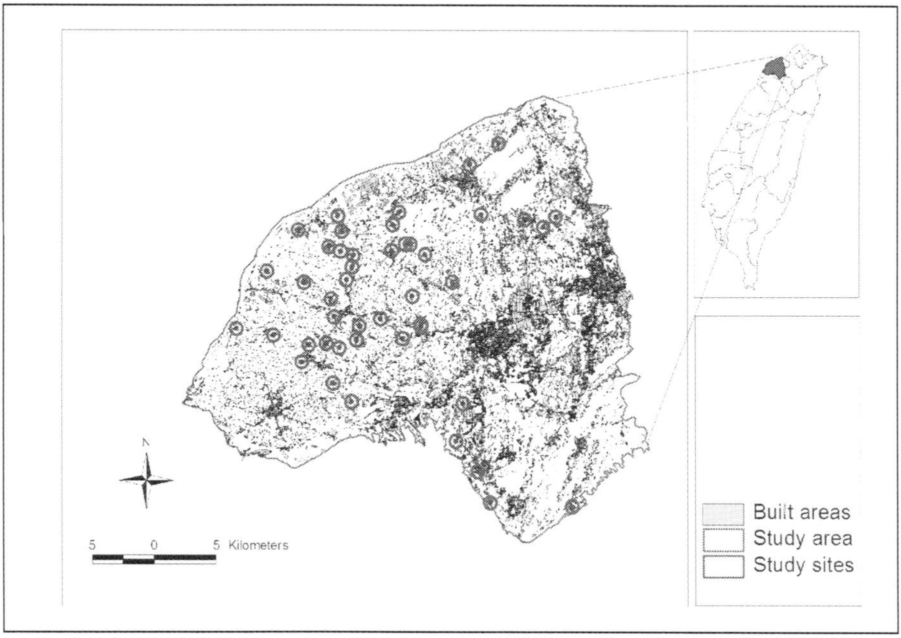

Fig. 2. Location away the city limits more than 2 km of forty-five study ponds in the range of the tableland.

3.2 Pond sampled

The pond complex in the Tableland is typical of the many farm-pond complexes found in the Taoyuan and Hsinchu Counties. The Tableland was first stratified into nine sub-regions, six in the north, five in the south, and thirty-four in the western regions. Data were collected at forty-five study sites in farm ponds in various size gradients (43 individuals > 1 ha; 2 individuals < 1 ha) according to large areas of ponds accounted for 628 individuals (>1 hectare) in Taoyuan Tableland (Fig. 2.). The number of farm-pond sites selected in each region was roughly proportional to the accessible area of each region riding by automobiles. We did not place sampling sites in eastern and southern urbanized high-density areas where the population was relatively intact. This was done because the bird composition of such an urban sites containing a large proportion of generalists would have driven a large proportional bias with the other sites with more specialists, thus making it inappropriate for diversity analysis. Although we did not select sites based on any predetermined definition of the degree of urbanization along a rural-urban gradient (e.g. distance from urban core), the relatively large number of randomly selected survey sites ensured that there was a good representation of sites far away from major urbanized corridors approximately more than 2 km area, and far from natural forest areas in the eastern regions. The farm ponds studied ranged from the slight disturbed farmlands to the fairly natural farmlands. We placed the linear transect routes on areas that were accessible by trails and footpaths around ponds. Therefore, forty sites were situated within table range in western range, and five sites were situated in relatively continuous interlocked ponds in southern range. All pond sites were stratified selected randomly to minimize variability in vegetation structure and composition. Detailed measurements from tree species records on a subset showed them to be structurally very similar areas.

Fig. 3. Avian observers recorded all bird species seen within a 100-ha radius at 564.19-m basal radius of the bird census point at pond edge (photo by Wei-Ta Fang).

3.3 Waterbirds sampled

Avian observers recorded all bird species seen within a 100-ha radius at 564.19-m basal radius of the bird census point at pond edge associated with line transects along pond-edge trails during 30-minute periods (one case of irrigation ponds see Fig. 3.). Sites were visited four times in the winter seasons between November and February. To reduce the effects of bird-observer bias, three to four observers were grouped and rotated between ponds. The observers counted birds that were in any habitats. All counts were conducted between 7:00 a.m. and 10:00 a.m. on days without rainy days when visibility was good (Bookhout, 1996). Foliage-loving species was also recorded followed the point-count method. Avian presence/absence on foliage strata was recorded in each pond at each of the following height intervals: edge ground, wetland grasses (< 0.5 m in height), bushes (> 0.5- 2.5 m in height), trees (> 2.5 m in height). Points were sampled at 10-m internals along edge trails established down each side of each pond. Waterbirds were grouped into microhabitat guilds based on actual observations on the sites. Foliage-loving species were initially classified into four height categories: pond-edge ground, low foliage (< 0.5 m in height), middle foliage (> 0.5- 2.5 m in height), and high foliage (> 2.5 m in height). Species were subsequently classified into two groups: understory (ground and low foliage groups) and canopy (middle and high foliage groups).

We calculated the number of individuals detected of each species at each pond for each month. Then, we calculated mean values of these variables for each study microhabitat across all study ponds in a wintering season.

3.4 Pond metrics calculation

Most pondscape studies imply a comparison with rural or natural habitats and tend to group urban or suburban areas into a simple type (Boothby, 1997). But pondscape associated with farmlands is not alike. They vary greatly in internal and external factors. To find a habitat relationship, the major variables for species diversity in pondscape patches are categorized to meso-scale and micro-scale distribution, such as: (a) matrix heterogeneity (meso-scale), and (b) habitat diversity (micro-scale) in size, shape, isolation from sources, and boundary delineation of disturbances. Variables were selected concerning the main differences in vegetation, the intensity of anthropogenic influences, and their distance from urban limits and ocean edges. In this study, matrix heterogeneity was decided by insensitive farming by consolidation. Habitat diversity indices in area and shape were calculated by FRAGSTAT® according to Taoyuan's Geographic Aerial Map (1:5,000 of scale in digital database form) (Department of Land Administration, Ministry of the Interior, 2002).

These diversity indices were categorized as follows: (1) Largest Pond Index (LPI), (2) Mean Pond Size (MPS), (3) Number of Ponds (NP), (4) Mean Pond Fractal Dimension (MPFD), (5) Mean Shape Index (MSI), (6) Edge Density (ED), and (7) Total Edge (TE). The indices (1)- (3) were categorized as the indices of "area"; and the (4)- (7) were categorized as the indices of "shape" (McGarigal et al, 2002). Disrupted by anthropogenic influences, an isolation index was calculated: (8) the distance to city limit (in m), (9) the ratio of constructed area within a radius of 100 ha from the pond's geometric center (in (m^2)/ha), and (10) the ratio of all road and trail areas within a radius of 100 ha from the pond's geometric center (in (m^2)/ha). A source connectivity index was calculated: (11) the distance to coastline (in m), (12) the ratio of all surrounding pond areas within a radius of 100 ha from the pond's geometric center (in (m^2)/ha), and (13) the ratio of all river and canal system areas within a radius of 100 ha from the pond's geometric center (in (m^2)/ha). Afterwards, the disturbance and buffer zone was measured using the density of drawdown and foliage cover, and windbreak boundaries were delineated by field surveys and an examination of aerial photographs, 1:5,000 of scale (Agricultural and Forestry Aerial Survey Institute, 2003). The composition of the complex landscape matrix mentioned above could modify the degree of effects, probably by increasing or limiting the availability of foraging sources and resting sites for avian communities. All elevation (in m) of ponds and perimeters (in m) of pond edges were measured by Global Position System (GPS)(GarminVista-Etrex, made in Taiwan) and rolling rulers (in m) associated with the calibration of aerial photographs, 1:5,000 of scale (Agricultural and Forest Aerial Survey Institute, 2003). Indices were required to calculate class and landscape levels as follows (McGarigal et al, 2002):

1. Largest Pond Index, LPI.

$$LPI = \frac{\max\limits_{j=1}^{n}(a_{ij})}{A}(100) \tag{1}$$

a_{ij} = maximum pond ij area (in m^2).
A = pond areas (in ha).
Level: CLASS, LANDSCAPE
Units: Percent
Range: 0 < LPI > 100
Description: LPI equals the pond area (m^2) divided by total pond areas, multiplied by 100 (to convert to a percentage).

2. Mean Pond Size, MPS.

MPS is the mean size of ponds (in ha.)

$$MPS = \frac{\sum\limits_{j=1}^{n} a_{ij}}{n_i}\left(\frac{1}{10000}\right) \tag{2}$$

a_{ij} =the area of pond ij (in m^2).
n_i = the number of the pond ij, a single pond size (PS) in this case equal to 1.
Level: CLASS, LANDSCAPE
Units: Ha
Range: MPS > 0, without limit.
Description: MPS equals the pond area (m^2) of all ponds of the corresponding patch type, divided by 10,000 (to convert to ha).

3. Number of Ponds, NP.

$$NP = n_i \tag{3}$$

Level: CLASS, LANDSCAPE
Units: None
Range: NP > 1, without limit.
Description: NP equals the number of ponds of the corresponding patch type (class).

4. Mean Pond Fractal Dimension, MPFD.

$$MPFD = \frac{\sum\limits_{j=1}^{n}\left(\frac{2\ln p_{ij}}{\ln a_{ij}}\right)}{n_i} \tag{4}$$

a_{ij} = the area of pond ij (in m^2).
n_i = the number of the pond ij.

p_{ij} = the perimeter of pond ij (in m).
Level: CLASS, LANDSCAPE
Units: None
Range: 1 < MPFD < 2
Description: MPFD reflects shape complexity across a range of pond size. It equals 2 times the logarithm of pond perimeter (m) divided by the logarithm of pond area (m^2) (Li and Reynolds, 1994). MPFD approaches 1 for shapes with very simple perimeters such as circles or squares, and approaches 2 for shapes with highly convoluted and plane-filling perimeters.

5. Mean Shape Index, MSI.

$$MSI = \frac{\sum_{j=1}^{n} \frac{p_{ij}}{2\sqrt{\pi \times a_{ij}}}}{n_i} \quad (5)$$

a_{ij} = the area of pond ij (in m^2).
n_i = the number of the pond ij.
p_{ij} = the perimeter of pond ij (in m).
Level: CLASS, LANDSCAPE
Units: None
Range: MSI > 1, without limit.
Description: MSI equals the sum of the pond perimeter (m) divided by the square root of pond area (m^2), and divided by the number of ponds. MSI represents the mean shape pattern. If MSI = 1, the pond is circular and increases without limit as pond shape becomes more curvilinear.

6. Edge Density, ED.

$$ED = \frac{\sum_{k=1}^{n} e_{ik}}{A}(10000) \quad (6)$$

e_{ik} = the total parameters between pond$_i$ and landscape$_k$ (in m).
n = the number of the pond; a single pond in this case equal to 1.
A = pond area (in m^2).
Level: CLASS, LANDSCAPE
Units: None
Range: MSI > 1, without limit.
Description: Edge density (in m/ha) equals the pond perimeter (in m) divided by the pond area. Edge density is a measurement of the complexity of the shape of pond.

7. Total Edge, TE.

$$TE = \sum_{k=1}^{n} e_{ik} \quad (7)$$

e_{ik} = the total perimeters between pond$_i$ and landscape$_k$ (in m).
n = the number of the pond; a single pond in this case equal to 1.

Level: CLASS, LANDSCAPE
Units: meters
Range: MSI > 0, without limit.
Description: Total Edge (TE) represents the total pond perimeters in meters.

3.5 Waterbird diversity analyses

There are two traditional bird analyses for entire avian communities and specific avian groups, richness, and diversity. Differences in the characteristics of avian groups and pondscape configuration may vary according to species-area relationships among regions. Therefore, to find differences in the response of species to habitat area and isolation, studies must include multiple analytical approaches to detect which analysis was better based on an entire community, or on a specific group.

Descriptive statistics for entire communities were used as the first stage of statistical avian data processing. The main aim was initial analysis of the distribution of avian communities sooner, such as an average individual value and; or a guild value was described for specific groups later. Afterwards, avian diversity was described in the result of diversity indices for all communities or a single group. To detect species evenness and abundance, we used Shannon-Wiener diversity index (H') (also named for Shannon index or Shannon-Weaver index), which is given a measure of the richness and relative density of a species to calculate diversity (Shannon and Weaver, 1949). This diversity measure conducted by Shannon and Weaver which originally came from information theory and measures the order observed within a particular system. Regarding to my studies, this order was characterized by the number of avian individuals observed for each species in the sampling ponds. The first step was to calculate P_i for each category (i.e., avian species), and then we multiplied this number by the log of the number. The index was computed from the negative sum of these numbers. In short, the Shannon-Wiener index *(H')* is defined as (8):

$$H' = -\sum_{i=1}^{S} P_i \log 2\, P_i \qquad (8)$$

S: avian species richness
Pi: The percentage of the *i* species in avian community

This index reflected bird richness in species and evenness amongst the avian community. The benefits of H' was sensitive by the change in threatened birds by avian study than that of Simpson's diversity index (D)(Dean et al., 2002). If the value of H' is higher, it means that species is abundant, or species distribution is even. However, species diversity is sometimes difficult to see relationships with spatial heterogeneity by limited survey data. Grouping and classification are required as well as for spatial heterogeneity reduction from the analyzed variables. It is the main procedure in this methodology for invoking avian groups with similar attributes of spatial behavior. The main approach in cluster analysis application is based on the idea to represent the grouping structure by avian data classification, based on the similarity in guilds between the species.

4. Results and discussion

The procedure was applied to waterbird assemblage of the Taoyuan Tableland, Taiwan. One variable was selected to describe its structure: Shannon-Wiener's diversity index (H') of the same waterbird guild. Four environmental variables were selected as explanatory variables: pond size (PS), pond shape (MPFD)(see equation (4)), proportion of farmland area in peripherals (%FARM), and proportion of constructed area in peripherals (%BUILD) than that of other variables due to their intensive correlations. Correlations between observed values and values estimated by ANN models of the four dependent variables were moderately significant. The ANN models were developed from 35 sample sites of farm ponds chosen at random and were validated on the 10 remaining sample sites of farm ponds. The role of each variable was evaluated by inputting fictitious configurations of independent variables and by checking the response of the model. The resulting habitat profiles depict the complex influence of each environmental variable on the biological parameters of the assemblage, and the non-linear relationships between dependent and independent variables. The main results and the ANN potential to predict biodiversity and structural characteristics of species assemblages are discussed as follows.

4.1 Logistic modelling

Based on logistic regression and criteria selection, we present three strategic landscape scenarios as follows. The multiple linear regression (MLR) models decided as equation (4) and developed advanced Logit models by equation (9):

$$\text{Logit (Y)} = 1.90 - 3.02\text{PS} + 0.01\text{TE} \tag{9}$$

$$\frac{\ln[1000(TE_{km})]^2}{\ln(10000PS)} = 1.5 \tag{10}$$

$$TE_{km} = PS^{\frac{3}{4}} \tag{11}$$

$$Logit(Y) = \ln\frac{p}{1-p} = 1.90 - 3.02PS + 0.1PS^{\frac{3}{4}} \tag{12}$$

$$Logit(Y) = \ln\frac{p}{1-p} = 1.90 - 3.02(TE_{km})^{\frac{4}{3}} + 0.01TE_{km} \tag{13}$$

where TEkm = total edge (in km), PS = pond size (in ha)

The pond-loss likelihood (p), Logit (Y), PS, and TEkm were calculated as the Table 1. According to Table 1, the strategic landscape scenarios for farm pond adjacent land-uses were divided as: (a) Scenario A: conservative land use, (p =0.25); (b) Scenario B: moderate land use (p = 0.50); (c) Scenario C: intensive land use (p = 0.75) for waterbird refuges:

We used Scenario A for a conservative land use. If the likelihood of pond lossas a lower value is equal to 0.25, all ponds noted as threatened red spots (pond size > 0.996 ha, TEkm > 0.997 km) are required conservatively protected due to their loss likelihood. The base map of waterbird's diversity H' is suggested to designate waterbird refuges in 2 yellow patches (H'>1.5) against pond-loss likelihood overlaid by threatened red spots (Hpool: pond size > 0.996 ha, TEkm > 0.997 km). [Diversity H':0.4~0.6; 0.6~0.8; 0.8~1.0; 1.0~1.5; 1.5~1.741; Distance (km); 12].

Land-use Scenarios	Pond-Loss Likelihood (p)	PS (in ha)	TEkm (in km)	Logit (Y)= ln(p/1-p)
Extremely Conservative	0.05	1.6087	1.4284	-2.9444
Highly Conservative	0.10	1.3609	1.2600	-2.1972
Conservative	0.25	0.9962	0.9971	-1.0986
Moderate	0.50	0.6310	0.7080	0
Intensive	0.75	0.2666	0.3710	1.0986

Table 1. The Pond-loss likelihood rate and Logit functions.

We also used Scenario B for a moderate land use. If the likelihood of pond lossas a moderate value is equal to 0.50, all ponds noted as threatened red spots (pond size > 0.631 ha, TEkm > 0.708 km) are required moderately protected due to their loss likelihood. The base map of waterbird's diversity H' is suggested to designate waterbird refuges in 3 yellow patches (H'>1.5) against pond-loss likelihood overlaid by threatened red spots (Hpool: pond size > 0.631 ha, TEkm > 0.708 km). [Diversity H':0.4~0.6; 0.6~0.8; 0.8~1.0; 1.0~1.5; 1.5~1.741; Distance (km); 12].

Actually, Scenario C was used for an intensive land-use pattern, too (Fig. 4.). If the likelihood of pond loss as a high value is equal to 0.75, all ponds noted as threatened red

Fig. 4. Scenario C was used for an intensive land-use pattern (before ANN's application)

spots (pond size > 0.2666 ha, TEkm > 0.371 km) are required intensively protected due to their loss likelihood. The base map of waterbird's diversity H′ is suggested to designate waterbird refuges in 4 yellow patches (H′>1.5) against pond-loss likelihood overlaid by threatened red spots (Hpool: pond size > 0.2666 ha, TEkm > 0.371 km). [Diversity H′:0.4~0.6; 0.6~0.8; 0.8~1.0; 1.0~1.5; 1.5~1.741; Distance (km); 12].

4.2 ANN's application

On the basis of the results of this study, there were limitations for waterbird's diversity on the linear model simulation. First, the linear relationship is so simple that it could not indicate all non-linear relationship. Second, the pond sites numbers merely ranging from 1 to 45 simply could affect the precision of simulation results of bird distribution.

The diversity of waterbirds was predicted throughout the exercise using the backpropagation (BP) algorithm with a three mutli-layered neural network. The first layer, called the input layer, comprised 4 cells representing each of the environmental variables. The second layer, or hidden layer, is composed of a further set of neurons whose number depends on the best-calculated results without bias. Since BP algorithm was trained by the least mean square method. The least mean square training could reduce the error, or distance between the actual output and the desired output, by adjusting the weights. Training cases were presented sequentially and the weights are adjusted. We determined the number of second-layer neurons through a serious of iterations varied from two, four, and eight neurons. In each case, we calculated the correlation coefficients between true values of H′ and the predicted value of ANN's H′. In our study, a network with one hidden layer of four neurons was selected. It was emphasized in a stable fit and avoided overtraining (see Figs. 5. & 6.).

In this study, the backpropagation (BP) neural network architecture is shown and consists of four layers of neurons connected by weights. We used MATLAB 6.1 (MathWorks, Inc., Natick, MA, 2001) to calculate a refining simulation model for extra values of H′.

The information was captured by the network when input data passed through the hidden layer of neurons to the output layer. The weights connecting from neuron one to neuron four were denoted as wji. Each neuron was calculated its output based on the amount of stimulation it received from the given input vector xi, while xi was the input of neuron i. The net input of a neuron was calculated as the weights of its inputs, and the output of the neuron was based on some sigmoid function which indicated the magnitude of this net input. So the net output uj from a neuron can be indicate as equations (14) and (15) (Fang et al, 2009).

$$u_j = \sum_{i=1}^{p} w_{ji} x_i \tag{14}$$

$$y_j = \varphi(u_j - \theta_j) \tag{15}$$

Where

w_{ji} is the incremental change in the weight from xi to uj

θ_j is a threshold to be passed through by non-linear activation function $\varphi(\cdot)$

x_i is the pondscape ith variable

u_j is the jth neuron from an outgoing signal to the magnitude of all observations

$\varphi(\cdot)$ activation function

y_j is the output of jth neuron in any layer

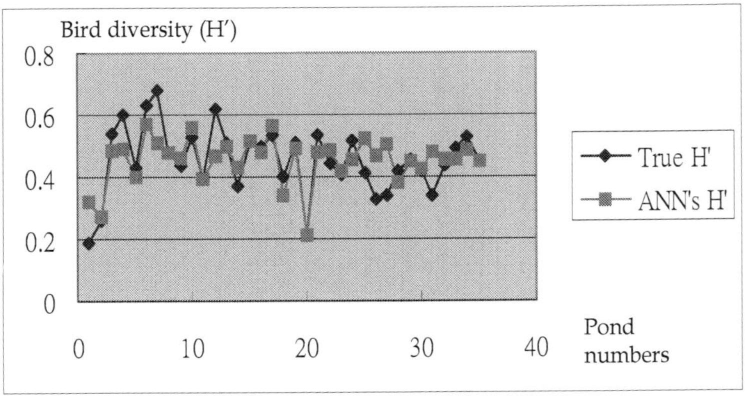

Fig. 5. The correlation trends between true H' and ANN's predicted H' in training sets for four neurons. (correlation coefficient (r) = 0.725537 ≒ 0.722752, n = 35).

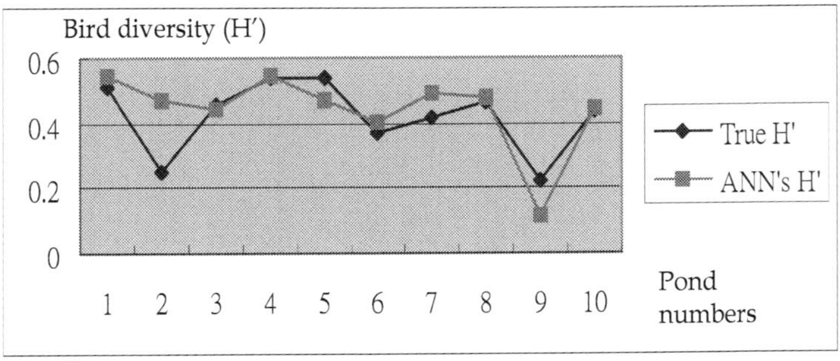

Fig. 6. The correlation trends between true H' and ANN's predicted H' in validated sets fitting for four neurons. (correlation coefficient (r) = 0.722752 ≒ 0.725537, n = 10).

The structure of the neural network used in this study. The input layer comprises 4 cells representing each of the 4-pondscape variables Xi (i =1, 4). The hidden layer comprises 4 neurons which calculate the dot products between its vector of weights wj =[wji, i =1,4] and x = [xi, i=1,4] from MATLAB 6.1.

This research chose continuous sigmoid as basic function:

$$\varphi(v) = \frac{1}{1+\exp(-cv)} \tag{16}$$

where v is the net effect, and c is a constant.

For a given input set, the network produced an output, and this response was compared to the known desired response of each neuron. The weights of the network were then changed to correct or reduce the error between the output of the neuron and desired response, and this process was keeping on. The weights were continually changed until the total error of all training set was reduced below the acceptable sums of errors. The BP algorithm for determining the optimal weights from training sets could be seen as similar to any function approximation technique like least square regression. But BP had an improved function to learn highly complex and non-linear data.

According to BP simulation, the strategic landscape scenarios for farm pond adjacent land-uses were refined as: (1) Scenario A: conservative land use, (p =0.25); (2) Scenario B: moderate land use (p = 0.50); (3) Scenario C: intensive land use (p = 0.75) for waterbird refuges as the pages that follow by Fig. 7. The Scenario B (moderate land use) has simulated to increase one waterbird's refuge (r = 0.72); and the Scenario C (intensive land use) has simulated to increase two waterbird's refuges (r = 0.72) (see Fig. 7.).

Fig. 7. Scenario C was used for an intensive land-use pattern (after ANN's application).

Scenario A was refined by the ANN's model for a conservative land use. If the likelihood of pond loss as a lower value is equal to 0.25, all ponds noted as threatened red spots (pond size > 0.996 ha, TEkm > 0.997 km) are required conservatively protected due to their loss likelihood. The base map of waterbird's diversity H' is suggested to designate waterbird refuges in 2 yellow patches (H'>1.5) against pond-loss likelihood overlaid by threatened red spots (Hpool: pond size > 0.996 ha, TEkm > 0.997 km)[Diversity H': 0.4~0.6; 0.6~0.8; 0.8~1.0; 1.0~1.5; 1.5~1.741; Distance (km); 12] (r = 0.72).

Scenario B was refined by the ANN's model for a moderate land use. If the likelihood of pond loss as a moderate value is equal to 0.50, all ponds noted as threatened red spots (pond size > 0.631 ha, TEkm > 0.708 km) are required moderately protected due to their loss likelihood. The base map of waterbird's diversity H' is suggested to designate waterbird refuges in 4 yellow patches (H'>1.5) against pond-loss likelihood overlaid by threatened red spots (Hpool: pond size > 0.631 ha, TEkm > 0.708 km)[Diversity H': 0.4~0.6; 0.6~0.8; 0.8~1.0; 1.0~1.5; 1.5~1.741; Distance (km); 12] (r = 0.72).

Scenario C was refined by the ANN's model for an intensive land-use pattern (see Fig. 7.). If the likelihood of pond loss as a high value is equal to 0.75, all ponds noted as threatened red spots (pond size > 0.2666 ha, TEkm > 0.371 km) are required intensively protected due to their loss likelihood. The base map of waterbird's diversity H' is suggested to designate waterbird refuges in 6 yellow patches (H'>1.5) against pond-loss likelihood overlaid by threatened red spots (Hpool: pond size > 0.2666 ha, TEkm > 0.371 km)[Diversity H':0.4~0.6; 0.6~0.8; 0.8~1.0; 1.0~1.5; 1.5~1.741; Distance (km); 12] (r = 0.72).

4.3 Discussion

The pondscape configuration was in fact a very relevant factor for avian diversity. However, pond shape (MPFD) was not recognized for its significant influences on waterbird's diversity. The final prediction results for a detailed H' contourmap were satisfactory, testifying then a good prediction of avian diversity which was better with ANN model (r = 0.72) than with linear regression model (r < 0.28), confirming the non-linearity of the relationship between the variables. From an ecological point of view, MPFD, the pond shape and %FARM, the ratio of farmland area, were the most significant variables in non-linear model rather than the linear model.

Some of the most significant findings came from the ANN's model. ANN was detected one of the tools that could resolve prediction problems, and this ANNs property is now well understood. On such finding was that pond shape (i.e., MPFD) to the pondscape might pose a tremendous influence to waterbird's diversity in Taoyuan Tableland. The value from ANN's method provided a good indication of the cumulative influences for the four environmental factors: such as %BUILD, %FARM, PS, and MPFD. The cumulative influences were those that resulted from the anthropogenic influences, and became statistically significant on waterbird's diversity. The above-mentioned environmental factors were selected from correlation analysis associated with linear regression model, and each factor to be detected its impact trend by ANN's model testing. Finally, the impact trends were calculated as the sequences of MPFD, %FARM, PS, and %BUILD, respectively. However, the correlation coefficients (r) of MPFD, %FARM, PS, and %BUILD were not following this sequence. Another significant finding from the extended simulation data may suggest that consolidated area has contributed to a negative influence on the cumulative impacts to decline diversity H′. Therefore, non-consolidated area has become important to design wintering bird refuge due to its domination of the tableland, the refuge structures of regular pond shape, big pond size, high-density green spaces, and low-density housing development seemed to be regarded.

Conservation of avian diversity is influenced greatly by the extent to which intensive anthropogenic practices are applied in the pondscape. The models suggest small and curvilinear ponds together with urban development associated with high-density rural population landscapes will adversely affect waterbird species to a greater magnitude than agricultural practices in low-density rural population landscapes. Extensive agricultural practices associated with ranching enterprises appear to maintain the native plant communities essential for maintaining waterbirds. Considering the tremendous increase in development and intensive agricultural practices applied at the rural-urban fringe, native vegetation will continue to be replaced with human-made construction and introduced woodland species. Therefore, biologists and conservationists should focus their educational programs on maintaining avian species in the rural-urban fringe.

Increased species and structural diversity within these pond units would result in higher ecological values of spatial diversity resulting from the occurrence of habitat and regional scales. At the same time this reduces the need for making microhabitat density measurements to emphasize the "edge-effect" and also, to some extent, compensates for the under-representation of small habitats in the measurement of ecological value. For example, drawdown can be beneficial to shorebirds; foliage building at waterfront can be beneficial to waterfowl. There is clearly some mechanism responsible for the convergence of taxon density and composition across the pond size gradient for the greater part of the species assemblages. According to MacArthur & Wilson (1967), the nature of this mechanism is interesting as the island biogeographic concept predicts that smaller microhabitats should contain fewer species due to the effects of reduced immigration rates. For area-sensitive species, their incidence is expected to increase as pond size increases. In addition, a larger pond is also more likely to contain at least one individual of a species, especially an uncommon or rare one.

5. Conclusion

In Taoyuan Tableland, all ponds are similarly isolated. Within the complex pondscape, ponds are similarly isolated from each other and steppingstone colonization can take place to enable species to establish throughout the complex (Forman, 1995). A population may become move to surrounding ponds, or nearly so, due to stochastic or deterministic mechanisms and steppingstone recolonization might then ensure the persistence of that population among wintering stopovers. This is effectively the colonization effect where functional groups are continuously moving by colonization from nearby neighboring ponds. Because there are many ponds within the tableland and they are close together in space, vulnerable populations are likely to be enhanced by immigrants from multiple neighboring populations during migration. Stable microhabitats are also likely to receive immigrants from several neighboring populations. Migration between farm ponds is thus likely to be high and thus the whole pond complex is likely to be responding as a multiple community. There is likely to be a concentric-ringed gradient in pond systems between waterside species and habitat "islands". We confirmed that, due to similar mechanisms operating in all ponds and the high connectivity between them, farm ponds are very close to the environmental gradients. Given the wide range examining in my study, it is quite possible that the predicted group diversity exist at different positions along this gradient. Therefore, the colonization effect can be helpful to predict waterbird's diversity (H') in surrounding study ponds throughout the values of input pondscape variables by ANN algorithm to determine a detailed regional contour map surrounding by urbanized areas.

6. Acknowledgements

The authors would like to thank the National Science Council of Taiwan, ROC for financially supporting this research under Contract No. NSC 98-2410-H-216-017. The authors also extend their gratitude to Taoyuan Wild Bird Society for their supporting to provide field data.

7. References

Agricultural and Forestry Aerial Survey Institute. (2003). *Aerial Photographs*, 1:5,000 of scale in digital debase forms, Taipei, Taiwan, ROC.

Begon, M; Harper J.L. & Townsend C.R. (1996) *Ecology: Individuals, Populations and Community*, Third Edition, Blackwell Science, ISBN: 0632038012, Oxford, UK.

Bookhout, T.A. (1996) Research and Management Techniques for Wildlife and Habitats. The Wildlife Society, ISBN:093586881, Bethesda, Massachusetts, USA.

Boothby, J. (1997) Pond conservation: towards a delineation of pondscape, Aquatic Conservation-Marine and Freshwater Ecosystems, Vol. 7, No.2, 127-132. *ISSN*:1052-7613.

Chen, C.J. (2000) The Change about Culture Landscape of Irrigation Reservoir and Pond in the Taoyuan Terrace, and the Establishment of Sustainable Environment Waterways, National Science Council, Taipei, Taiwan, ROC. (in Chinese)

Cheng, Q. & Agterberg, F.P. (1995) Multifractal modeling and spatial point processes. *Mathematical Geology* Vol. 27, 831-845, *ISSN* (electronic): 1573-8868.

Dean, W. R. J.; Anderson, M.D.; Milton, S. J. & Anderson, T. A. (2002). Avian assemblages in native Acacia and alien Prosopis drainage line woodland in the Kalahari, South Africa. *Journal of Arid Environments* Vol. 51, 1-19, ISSN:0140-1963.

Department of Land Administration, Ministry of the Interior. (2002) *Taiwan's Geographic Aerial Map*, 1:5,000 of scale in digital database forms, Taipei, Taiwan, ROC. (in Chinese)

Fang, T.-Y. (2001) *The Study of the Spatial Structure Change of Water Land in Taoyuan Terrace*, Master Thesis, Department of Bioenvironmental Systems Engineering, National Taiwan University, Taiwan, ROC. (in Chinese)

Fang, W.-H. (2004a) *Threaten Birds of Taiwan*, Second Edition. Wild Bird Federation Taiwan, ISBN:9867415817, Taipei, Taiwan, ROC. (in Chinese)

Fang, W.-T. (2004b) The ecological drawdown assessment for avian communities in Taoyuan's constructed wetlands. In: *Proceeding of 2004 Annual Symposium of Environmental Education*, Yeh. S.-C. (ed.), pp. 861-869, Chinese Society for Environmental Education, Kaohsiung, Taiwan, ROC. (in Chinese)

Fang, W.-T. & Chang, T.-K. (2004) The scientific exploring of ecoscape-design on constructed wetlands in Taoyuan, In: *The Proceeding of Water Source Management of Taoyuan Main Canal,* Lee, C.-J. (ed.), pp. 345-369, Taoyuan Irrigation Association, Taoyuan, Taiwan, ROC. (in Chinese)

Fang, W.-T.; H. Chu; & B.-Y. Cheng. (2009). Modelling waterbird diversity in irrigation ponds of Taoyuan, Taiwan using an artificial neural network approach. *Paddy and Water Environment* Vol. 7, 209-216, *ISSN*: 1611-2490.

Forman, R.T.T. (1995). *Land Mosaic: The Ecology of Landscape and Regions*, The University of Cambridge, ISBN:9780521474627, Cambridge, UK.

Forman, R.T.T. & Godron, M. (1986). *Landscape Ecology*. John Wiley & Sons, ISBN:0471870374, New York, USA.

Francl, K.E. & Schnell, G.D. (2002). Relationships of human disturbance, bird communities, and plant communities along the land-water interface of a large reservoir. *Environmental Monitoring and Assessment Vol. 73,* 67-93, *ISSN: 0167-6369.*

Froneman. A.; Mangnall. M.J.; Little, R.M. & Crowe, T.M. (2001). Waterbird assemblages and associated habitat characteristics of farm ponds in the Western Cape, South Africa. *Biodiversity and Conservation* Vol. 10, 251-270, *ISSN: 0960-3115.*

Huang, B.-J. (1999). *Assessment and Application of Groundwater Resource in Taoyuan Area,* Master Thesis, Department of Bioenvironmental Systems Engineering, National Taiwan University, Taipei, Taiwan, ROC. (in Chinese)

Li, H. & Reynolds, J.F. (1994). A simulation experiment to quantify spatial heterogeneity in categorical maps. *Ecology* Vol. 75, 2446-2455, ISSN:0012-9658.

MacArthur, R. H. & Wilson, E. O. 1967. *The Theory of Island Biogeography*. Princeton University Press, ISBN:0691088365, Princeton, New Jersey, USA.

McCulloch, W. & Pitts, W. (1943). A logical calculus of ideas immanent in nervous activity. *Bulletin of Mathematical Biophysics* Vol.5, 115-133, *ISSN:* 0007-4985.

McGarigal, K.; Cushman, S.A.; Neel, M.C.; Ene, E. (2002). *FRAGSTATS: Spatial Pattern Analysis Program for Categorical Maps*, Computer software program produced by the authors at the University of Massachusetts, Amherst, Massachusetts, USA.

Oertli, B.; Joye, D.A.; Castella, E.; Juge, R.; Cambin. D. & Lachavanne, J. (2002). Does size matter? The relationship between pond area and biodiversity, *Biological Conservation* Vol. 104, 59-70, ISSN:0006-3207.

Osborne, P.E.; Alonso, J.C. & Bryant, R.G. (2001). Modelling landscape-scale habitat use using GIS and remote sensing: a case study with great bustards, *Journal of Applied Ecology*, Vol. 38, No. 2, 458-471, ISSN:0021-8901.

Ozesmi, U.; Tan, C.O.; Ozesmi. S.L. & Robertson, R. J. (2006). Generalizability of artificial neural network models in ecological applications: Predicting nest occurrence and breeding success of the red-winged blackbird Agelaius phoeniceus, *Ecological Modelling*, Vol. 195, No. 1-2, 94-104, ISSN:0304-3800.

Palmer, M. W. (1990). The estimation of species richness by extrapolation. *Ecology* Vol. 71, 1195-1198, ISSN:0012-9658.

Reby, D.; Lek, S.; Dimopoulos, I.; Joachim, J.; Lauga, J. & Aulagnier, S. (1997). Artificial neural network as a classification method in the behavioral sciences. *Behavioral Processes* Vol. 40, 35-43, *ISSN:0376-6357.*

Shannon, C. E. & Weaver, W. (1949). *The Mathematical Theory of Communication.* University of Illinois Press, *ISBN*:0252725484, Urbana, Illinois, USA.

Virkkala, R. (2004). Bird species dynamics in a managed southern boreal forest in Finland. *Forest Ecology and Management* Vol. 195, 151-163, ISSN:0378-1127.

21

Developing an Artificial Neural Network for Modeling and Prediction of Temporal Structure and Spectral Composition of Environmental Noise in Cities

Antonio J. Torija, Diego P. Ruiz and Ángel Ramos-Ridao
University of Granada
Spain

1. Introduction

Noise pollution in large cities is an ever-growing problem, due to several factors: the increase in demographic density, the increase in the number of per capita devices, appliances and vehicles capable of generating loud noise, and the fact that society is getting used to higher noise levels.

One of the most important factors that help us to explain this fact is the road traffic, since as is generally established, road traffic is the most important and generalized sound source in the urban zones of the developed countries. Generally speaking, this one is also, with difference, the sound source that produces more disturbances and nuisances on the urban residents. However, road traffic is not the only noisy source in urban environments: other noisy sources relating to construction work, commercial activity, recreation, etc. have been found. At the same time, sound spaces where road traffic does not have a direct incidence and in which natural and social sounds predominate, e.g. green areas, can be observed (Torija et al., 2010a).

The European Directive 2002/49/EC on the Assessment and Management of Environmental Noise aims to create a common framework for assessing exposure to environmental noise in all Member States. With the use of indicators and evaluation methods harmonized the results will be grouped into strategic maps. These maps are designed to comprehensively assess noise exposure in a given area, or for overall predictions in that area. In addition, they will be the basis for developing both action plans and strategies in the fight against noise (Directive 2002/49/EC).

For the development of assessment and achievement of the objectives stated in the above mentioned directive, from the European Commission the methods used to predict different emission sources present in urban environments (industrial noise, road traffic, railway traffic and aircraft traffic) are recommended (Commission Recommendation 2003/613/EC). All these methods are based only on the obtaining of the A-weighted energy-equivalent sound pressure level (L_{Aeq}). Nevertheless, any physical characterization of a sound environment calls not only for consideration of the A-weighted sound pressure level (L_{Aeq}), but also requires description of the temporal structure and spectral composition of the sound (Berglund & Nilsson, 2001; Botteldooren et al., 2006). These factors bear great weight in the perception of noise (Viollon & Lavandier, 2000; Berglund & Nilsson, 2001;

Botteldooren et al., 2006) and in its negative impact (specific annoyance) on the population (Berglund et al., 2002; Björk, 2002; Lercher & Schulte-Fortkam, 2003).
The heterogeneous physiognomy of urban environments, together with the characteristics of environmental noise, with their great spatial, temporal and spectral variability, makes the matter of modeling and prediction a very complex and non-linear problem, to which we may apply a powerful tool of data mining —artificial neural networks. These constitute a paradigm of automatic processing that ultimately seek to emulate the biological brain, or at least some of its functions, such as learning (Patra & Panda, 1998). Artificial neural networks (ANNs) are widely used in environmental modeling and prediction (Chelani et al., 2002; Hamed et al., 2004; Maier et al., 2004; Almasri & Kaluarachchi, 2005; Ordieres et al., 2005) as a preference to more conventional statistical techniques (Maier & Dandy, 1998). The reason is that ANNs are non-linear (Chakraborty et al., 1992), relatively insensitive to data noise (Tang et al., 1991; Burke & Ignizio, 1992), they perform reasonably well when limited data are available (Tang et al., 1991; Schizas et al., 1994), and they provide flexibility, accuracy and some amount of fault tolerance in changing environments (Patra & Panda, 1998).

2. Literature review of the application of soft-computing techniques in urban noise field

	Artificial Neural Networks	Fuzzy Techniques	Genetic Algorithms	Hidden Markov Models
Sound Pressure Level Prediction	(Cammarata et al., 1995; Avsar et al., 2004; Genaro et al., 2010)	(Aguilera de Maya, 1997; Caponetto et al., 1997)	(Caponetto et al., 1997)	
Noise Annoyance Prediction	(Zaheeruddin & Garima, 2006)	(Botteldooren & Verkeyn, 2001; Botteldooren & Verkeyn, 2002a,b,c,d,e; Botteldooren et al., 2002a,b; Botteldooren et al., 2003a,b; Botteldooren & Lercher, 2004; Zaheeruddin & Garima, 2006)	(Botteldooren & Verkeyn, 2001; Botteldooren et al., 2002b; Botteldooren et al., 2003b)	
Noise Classification	(Berg, 2002; Couvreur & Laniray, 2004; Betkowsa et al., 2005) (Caponetto et al., 1997)	(Beritelli et al., 2000)		(Couvreur et al., 1998; Gaunard et al., 1998; Ma et a., 2003a,b; Couvreur & Laniray, 2004; Betkowsa et al., 2005;
Urban Traffic Flow Prediction	(Fortuna et al., 2004; Dougherty & Cobbett, 1997; Ledoux, 1997; Dia, 2001; Yin et al., 2002)	(Fortuna et al., 1994; Yin et al., 2002)		

Table 1. Taxonomy of the urban noise vs. soft-computing methods publications (Genaro et al., 2010)

This section deals with a detailed review of publications at the international level that link urban noise with soft-computing techniques. To carry out this review, four soft-computing techniques are considered: Artificial Neural Networks, Fuzzy Techniques, Genetic Algorithms and Hidden Markov Models. In turn, we explore its use in the treatment of the following aspects of environmental noise: Sound Pressure Level Prediction, Noise Annoyance Prediction, Noise Classification and Urban Traffic Flow Prediction. A taxonomy of the found articles is shown in table 1.

2.1 Sound pressure level prediction

Cammaratta et al. (1995) develop a model for predicting noise based on a back-propagation neural network. In this work it was proposed an architecture based on two levels. In the first level, a network LVQ (Learning Vector Quantization) filtered the data, eliminating the data considered erroneous, while in the second tier, the back-propagation neural network predicts the sound pressure level.

Turkish standards allow up to 45 dB in places of study environment. In (Avsar et al., 2004) it is studied whether these standards are met using a multilayer perceptron neural network with noise data of 16 points in a Turkish campus. The neural network is built with seven inputs: position of the measuring point, distance from the source to the point of action, wind speed and direction, air temperature, relative humidity and time of day. The output is the descriptor A-weighted energy-equivalent sound pressure level (L_{Aeq}).

A method based on fuzzy logic for urban noise prediction is briefly described in (Aguilera de Maya, 1997). The results obtained are not accurate enough, however in the section of conclusions it is indicated that the results of the fuzzy model have been contrasted with actual data from measurements made in the prediction scenarios and it has been proved to be highly successful.

Caponetto et al. (1997) put forth a method based on genetic algorithms, which seeks the optimization of fuzzy rules based system for environmental noise prediction. The obtained results demonstrate the success of their method.

In (Genaro et al., 2010) a neural network based model for urban noise prediction is developed. In this paper a selection of 12 street locations with different characteristics of the city of Granada (Spain) is carried out to obtain a representative sample of the complexity of urban streets with presence of road traffic. A set of 289 data vectors, each one with 26 components, was obtained. A total of 25 input variables were used (Torija et al., 2010a), being the only output variable the A-weighted energy-equivalent sound pressure level (L_{Aeq}). The results were compared to those obtained with mathematical models. It was found that the proposed ANN system was able to predict noise with greater accuracy, and thus was an improvement on these models.

2.2 Noise annoyance prediction

With regard to noise annoyance prediction, Zaheeruddin & Garima (2006) propose a neurofuzzy model to predict the annoyance suffered by workers exposed to high noise levels. Once demonstrated that the parameters that most affect workers are noise pollution, type of task and the exposure time to it, a neurofuzzy system is developed.

The most prolific authors who have dealt with techniques based on fuzzy logic modeling of environmental noise are Botteldooren and Verkeyn (Botteldooren & Verkeyn, 2001; Botteldooren & Verkeyn, 2002a,b,c,d,e; Botteldooren et al., 2002a,b; Botteldooren et al., 2003a,b; Botteldooren & Lercher, 2004). Their main field of study is the prediction of the noise annoyance level on people. For this reason, a fuzzy model is used in the majority of its proposals, looking for a set of rules that describe the fuzzy system. It deals with the study creating a fuzzy rules based system that predicts responses from the public about the noise annoyance caused by road and railway traffic noise.

2.3 Noise classification

Couvreur & Laniray (2004) describes an Automatic Noise Recognition System. The system is based on neural networks and Hidden Markov Models and is able to distinguish, from 1000 sound recordings, between two sounds: horn or motorcycle engine. The neural network phase includes a multilayer perceptron ANN, where the coefficients were obtained by supervised training.

Another noise classifier is developed in (Berg, 2002), which recognizes sounds of planes, with the use of neural networks. The neural network is built with a backpropagation architecture with three neurons in the hidden layer.

In (Beritelli et al., 2000) an urban noise classifier based on fuzzy techniques is presented. Considering a set of acoustic characteristics it tries to distinguish among seven categories: bus, car, rail, construction works, people talking, street and factory.

Several works (Gaunard et al., 1998; Couvreur et al., 1998; Ma et a., 2003a,b) develop a Hidden Markov Model based noise classifier system. These publications describe how a Hidden Markov Model can be used to develop a recognition system based on the ambient noise frequency analysis. A preprocessor provides frequency representation in time of the audio signal, which is then used by a classifier. The classifier makes a decision depending on the nature of the noise source, according to the characteristics given by the preprocessor.

Two ways of improving the performance of automatic noise recognition are presented in (Betkowsa et al., 2005). Firstly, it is proposed the minimization of the number of parameters of a Hidden Markov Model based noise classifier, in order to reduce its complexity. Secondly, it seeks to combine the results of different recognition systems, applying the method of combining expert (MoE, Mixture of Experts). It uses neural networks, which are applied to combine the results and make a final decision on the status of the signal.

2.4 Urban traffic flow prediction

There are some works that develop urban traffic flow prediction models. It is necessary annotate here as most mathematical noise prediction models consider traffic flow the most influential variable. Urban traffic flow is predicted in (Fortuna et al., 2004; Dougherty & Cobbett, 1997; Ledoux, 1997; Dia, 2001; Yin et al., 2002).

3. Pursued goal

After review the use of ANN for modeling and prediction of sound levels, we will introduce a new model to predict both temporal structure and spectral composition of the sound pressure level by using artificial neural networks. The process of model developing is made in an inductive way, first selecting the input and output variables and then building an ANN based on an error minimization criterion. The net is then validated using real noise data. An extensive measurement campaign, conducted in the city of Granada (Spain), gives a wide database, which includes the spatial and temporal heterogeneity characteristic of urban agglomerations. With this measurement campaign the short-term information (integration period of 5 minutes) necessary for the input and output variables involved in model development is obtained.

The constructed ANN model allows not only the equivalent sound level to be predicted but also the average temporal and spectral structure of sound. In view of the large impact of temporal and spectral structure on sound perception, the model could achieve both a precise modeling and evaluation of the studied soundscape. The accompanying results given in this chapter show that this prediction model based on ANN along with a perceptual and psychosocial assessment of sound ambient can be a very useful tool for urban soundscapes management becoming an interesting application of Neural Networks for environmental sound modeling.

4. Selection of input and output variables for the development of the model

This section focuses on the selection of input and output variables for the construction of temporal structure and spectral composition of the sound pressure level prediction model.
To accurately describe and assess urban noise, a critical issue is the selection of input variables, conducive to the implementation of a model, which is representative of urban complexity (Torija et al., 2010a). In our opinion, prior to the model construction stage, it is necessary to study the acoustic variables for the characterization of the sound environment, as well as their range of possible values. This is a necessary condition for the development of an urban noise prediction model. For this purpose, as we see in Table 2, a series of 24 input variables was selected.
The input variables for the built of the artificial neural network based model are chosen from a previous existing knowledge in the field, both obtained from our own experience in our experimental work and the used and studied bibliography about environmental acoustics (see references at Torija et al., 2010a).
On the other hand, 30 output variables, the A-weighted equivalent sound pressure level (L_{Aeq}) and no weighted equivalent sound pressure level (L_{eq}), the temporal sound level variance (TSLV) and the crest factor (temporal composition) (Torija et al., 2010b), as well as the sound level for each of the 1/3-octave bands between 31.5-10000 Hz (spectral composition) have been selected.
The energy equivalent sound pressure level (L_{eq}) is a parameter that corresponds to the value of sound pressure level in dB, of a hypothetical steady sound that in a time interval T has the same mean squared sound pressure that the measured sound and whose level varies with time. Its mathematical expression is:

$$L_{eq} = 10 \cdot Log\left(\frac{1}{t_2 - t_1} \cdot \int_{t1}^{t2} \frac{P_i(t)}{P_0^2} dt\right) \tag{1}$$

where:
L_{eq} is the continuous sound level in dB (dB(A) for the descriptor L_{Aeq}), determined in the time interval T, between instants t_1 and t_2.
P_0 is the reference sound pressure (20 µPa).
$P_i(t)$ is the instantaneous sound pressure.
With respect to the descriptor TSLV, let $L_p(t)$ with t in [0 s, 300 s] be the one second measured sound pressure. The standard deviation of the instantaneous sound pressure is noted as σ_L. Furthermore, let us define the energy-equivalent sound pressure level $L_{eq}(T)$ of the sound measured up to time T, as

$$L_{eq}(T) = 10 \cdot \log_{10}\left[\frac{1}{T}\int_0^T 10^{L_{p(t_i)}/10} dT\right] \tag{2}$$

and let us further note the standard deviation of $L_{eq}(T)$ as σ_{eq}. We then define the Temporal Sound Level Variance (TSLV) as

$$TSLV = \sigma_L * \sigma_{eq} \tag{3}$$

With this indicator, the more commonly used standard deviation of the instantaneous (1 s) sound level, σ_L is multiplied or 'weighted' by σ_{eq} (Torija et a., 2010b).
Finally, the Crest Factor (CF) is defined as the ratio between the maximum sound pressure and the RMS value of the sound pressure:

$$CF = \frac{\max_T 10^{L_{p(t_i)/10}}}{10^{L_{eq,T/10}}} \tag{4}$$

We have $L_p(t_i)$ as the instantaneous sound pressure level (one second SPL) and $L_{eq,T}$ as the energy-equivalent sound pressure level in 5-min period. The CF gives the value of sound-pressure impulsiveness within 5-min of measurement (Torija et al., 2010b).

Nº	Input variable
1	Type of day
2	Day period
3	Commercial/leisure environment
4	Type of location
5	Presence of vegetation
6	Statilization time of the sound level
7	Type of traffic flow dynamic
8	Anomalous sound events related to traffic
9	Anomalous sound events no related to traffic
10	Ascendant light vehicles
11	Descendant light vehicles
12	Ascendant heavy vehicles
13	Descendant heavy vehicles
14	Ascendant buses
15	Descendant buses
16	Ascendant motorcycles-mopeds
17	Descendant motorcycles-mopeds
18	Vehicles with siren
19	Average speed
20	Number of upward lanes
21	Number of downward lanes
22	Street geometry
23	Street width
24	Street height

Table 2. Input variables used for the development of the prediction model

5. Data sampling

To carry out this study a representative sample of locations (120 locations) of the city of Granada (Spain) was selected. Locations were selected in such a way that they included the higher variability in the value range of the input variables given in table 2. In the given subset of locations is included all the input variables (street geometry, ascendant or descendant flow, stabilization time etc) in such way that one or more elements of the subset of variables will be noteworthy or with a high change range in at least one location point.
The selection included locations where the main source of environmental noise at the time of measurement was road traffic. Some locations were affected by other noise sources as well. Overall, there were variations in traffic intensity, traffic flow dynamics, geometry of the traffic routes, types of road surface, traffic slope and speed, and situation within the city. Moreover, because urban environments do not necessarily entail the direct incidence of road traffic noise, we also selected settings with other predominant sound sources, such as pedestrian areas, locations with commercial/leisure activities, and squares or urban parks where the soundscape would principally comprise social and natural sounds.
Measurements were obtained following european procedures of reference; all microphones were mounted away from reflecting facades, at a height of 4 m above local ground level (Directive 2002/49/EC). Once all the measurements had been taken, the acoustical descriptors used in this research were calculated, so that from the different selected input variables and with 5 minutes set as the integration time period, the prediction of each one of the used acoustical indicators could be effected.

6. Artificial Neural Network structure

To undertake the goal established in this work, we chose to apply a back-propagation neural network. The ANN based prediction model involves implementation of the Levenberg-Marquardt variant with Bayesian regulation back-propagation. The internal parameters and geometry of the back-propagation neural network were carefully studied (Maier and Dandy, 1998), and the ANN structure affording major precision, minor prediction error, and low computation time was selected.

	ANN Configuration
Input Variables	24
Output Variables	30
Neurons on Hidden Layer	17
Divide Function	dividerand
Learning Function	learngdm
Performance Function	mse
Training Function	trainbr
Transfer Function	tansig + purelin
Mu Parameter	0.005

Table 3. Artificial neural network (ANN) configuration

The structure of the ANN can be seen in Table 3 and Fig. 1. The adaptation learning function is Learngdm and the performance function is MSE. The ANN has 24 input variables, 17 neurons on the hidden layer and 30 output variables. The transfer function is Tangsig (layer 1) + Purelin (layer 2) and the Marquardt adjustment parameter (mu) is 0.005.

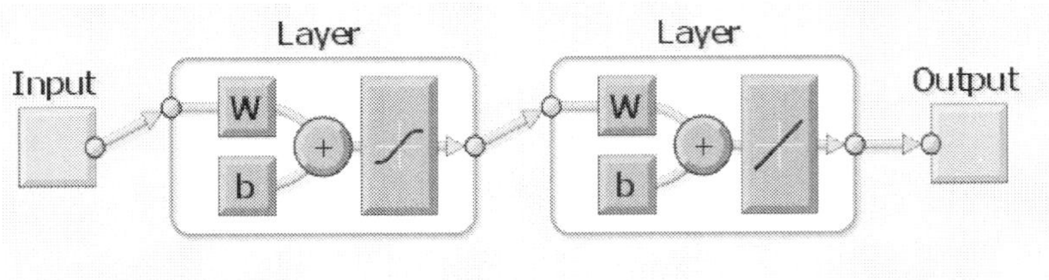

Fig. 1. Artificial neural network (ANN) structure

We have divided the available 543 input records into three data subsets (Training, validation and test) which are different from each other. The training subset contains 400 records (75% of the 543 input records), the validation subset comprises 27 records (5% of the 543 input records) and the test subset includes 116 records (20% of the 543 input records).

7. Results

Once established the structure of the artificial neural network (ANN) and to evaluate the precision of the prediction model, this ANN has been trained and tested 25 times, 5 times for each of the previously established 5 training-validation-test subsets. As we can see in Table 4, the ANN was trained with a number of epochs between 24 (data subset 3) and 51 (data subset 5). The time spent on the completion of the training phase has been between 77.77 sec (data subset 3) and 161.62 sec (data subset 5).

	Subset 1	Subset 2	Subset 3	Subset 4	Subset 5
Epochs	30	26	24	34	51
Training time (sec)	116.29	84.98	77.77	109.33	161.62

Table 4. Number of epochs and training time for the 5 data subsets used

Table 5 shows the mean squared error (MSE) of the 5 training subsets for the ANN based prediction model. As can be seen from the results shown in Table 5, for the case of descriptors L_{Aeq} (between $8.3 \cdot 10^{-5}$ in subset 1 and $1.2 \cdot 10^{-4}$ in subsets 2, 3) and L_{eq} ($1.2 \cdot 10^{-4}$ in subset 1 and $1.5 \cdot 10^{-4}$ in subsets 2, 3, 4 and 5), the value of the mean squared error (MSE) remains relatively stable for all the five data subsets.

Acoustical descriptors	Subset 1	Subset 2	Subset 3	Subset 4	Subset 5
L_{Aeq}	$8.3 \cdot 10^{-5}$	$1.2 \cdot 10^{-4}$	$1.2 \cdot 10^{-4}$	$1.1 \cdot 10^{-4}$	$1.0 \cdot 10^{-4}$
L_{eq}	$1.2 \cdot 10^{-4}$	$1.5 \cdot 10^{-4}$	$1.5 \cdot 10^{-4}$	$1.5 \cdot 10^{-4}$	$1.5 \cdot 10^{-4}$
TSLV	$5.5 \cdot 10^{-4}$	$4.9 \cdot 10^{-4}$	$5.5 \cdot 10^{-4}$	$5.9 \cdot 10^{-4}$	$5.3 \cdot 10^{-4}$
CF	$4.8 \cdot 10^{-4}$	$5.1 \cdot 10^{-4}$	$3.8 \cdot 10^{-4}$	$4.1 \cdot 10^{-4}$	$3.8 \cdot 10^{-4}$
1/3-octave bands (31.5-10000 Hz)	$4.4 \cdot 10^{-4}$	$5.6 \cdot 10^{-4}$	$5.5 \cdot 10^{-4}$	$5.3 \cdot 10^{-4}$	$5.0 \cdot 10^{-4}$

Table 5. Mean squared error (MSE) of the training subsets for the proposed ANN based prediction model

As for the descriptors for the characterization of temporal structure, that is TSLV (between $4.9 \cdot 10^{-4}$ in subset 2 and $5.9 \cdot 10^{-4}$ in subset 4) and CF (between $3.8 \cdot 10^{-4}$ in subsets 3, 5 and $5.1 \cdot 10^{-4}$ in subset 2), the MSE value fluctuates slightly in the five used data subsets. Something very similar happens in the case of output variables related to the spectral composition (1/3-octave bands between 31.5-10000 Hz), where fluctuations in the MSE value between 4.4 ·10^{-4} (subset 1) and 5.6 ·10^{-4} (subset 2) are found.

Acoustical descriptors	Subset 1	Subset 2	Subset 3	Subset 4	Subset 5
L_{Aeq}	2.3 ·10^{-4}	2.3 ·10^{-4}	1.9 ·10^{-4}	1.9 ·10^{-4}	1.8 ·10^{-4}
L_{eq}	1.3 ·10^{-4}	1.5 ·10^{-4}	1.7 ·10^{-4}	1.7 ·10^{-4}	1.8 ·10^{-4}
TSLV	4.0 ·10^{-4}	4.2 ·10^{-4}	5.0 ·10^{-4}	3.8 ·10^{-4}	4.5 ·10^{-4}
CF	5.0 ·10^{-4}	3.5 ·10^{-4}	3.3 ·10^{-4}	3.1 ·10^{-4}	2.9 ·10^{-4}
1/3-octave bands (31.5-10000 Hz)	6.4 ·10^{-4}	8.4 ·10^{-4}	7.2 ·10^{-4}	7.2 ·10^{-4}	7.6 ·10^{-4}

Table 6. Mean squared error (MSE) of the test subsets for the proposed ANN based prediction model

In Table 6 we can observe the MSE value of the 5 test subsets for the ANN based prediction model. In view of the obtained results, the MSE value follows a quite similar pattern to that observed for the case of training subsets (Table 4) with regard to the MSE value found in the different test subsets.

1/3-octave bands [Hz]	Subset 1	Subset 2	Subset 3	Subset 4	Subset 5
31.5	0.79	0.76	0.79	0.80	0.76
40	0.79	0.78	0.80	0.79	0.76
50	0.88	0.87	0.87	0.86	0.86
63	0.86	0.87	0.85	0.86	0.86
80	0.77	0.76	0.78	0.78	0.78
100	0.81	0.79	0.83	0.79	0.81
125	0.84	0.87	0.88	0.88	0.88
160	0.86	0.86	0.87	0.88	0.87
200	0.86	0.86	0.87	0.88	0.87
250	0.88	0.88	0.89	0.91	0.89
315	0.90	0.89	0.90	0.92	0.91
400	0.90	0.89	0.90	0.91	0.91
500	0.88	0.87	0.88	0.89	0.87
630	0.88	0.89	0.89	0.90	0.89
800	0.88	0.89	0.90	0.89	0.92
1000	0.87	0.88	0.88	0.88	0.90
1250	0.88	0.88	0.88	0.88	0.90
1600	0.90	0.89	0.89	0.89	0.89
2000	0.89	0.88	0.90	0.90	0.90
2500	0.88	0.87	0.88	0.89	0.89
3150	0.85	0.83	0.85	0.86	0.85
4000	0.88	0.85	0.87	0.88	0.88
5000	0.84	0.84	0.86	0.87	0.86
6300	0.82	0.80	0.83	0.84	0.83
8000	0.82	0.80	0.82	0.83	0.82
10000	0.81	0.80	0.83	0.84	0.82

Table 7. R^2-value for the 1/3-octave bands (31.5-10000 Hz) of the ANN test subsets

As for descriptors L_{Aeq} and L_{eq} MSE values between 1.8·10^{-4} (subset 5) - 2.3·10^{-4} (subsets 1 and 2) and between 1.3·10^{-4} (subset 1) - 1.8·10^{-4} (subset 5) are found respectively. The variability of the MSE value in the different test subsets for the descriptors TSLV (3.8·10^{-4} in subset 4 and 5.0·10^{-4} in subset 3), CF (2.9·10^{-4} in subset 5 and 5.0·10^{-4} in subset 1) and 1/3-octave bands between 31.5-10000 Hz (6.4·10^{-4} in subset 1 and 8.4·10^{-4} in subset 2) is greater than that observed for the two previous descriptors.

Regarding the R^2-value of the third octave bands for all the used test subset (Table 7), it can be observed that the correlation factor of prediction varies depending on the frequency band considered. We found that the frequency band with a lower correlation factor corresponds to the third octave band of 80 Hz (R^2 = 0.76-0.78). On the other hand, the 1/3-octave band of 315 Hz has the highest value of R^2 factor (R^2 = 0.89-0.92).

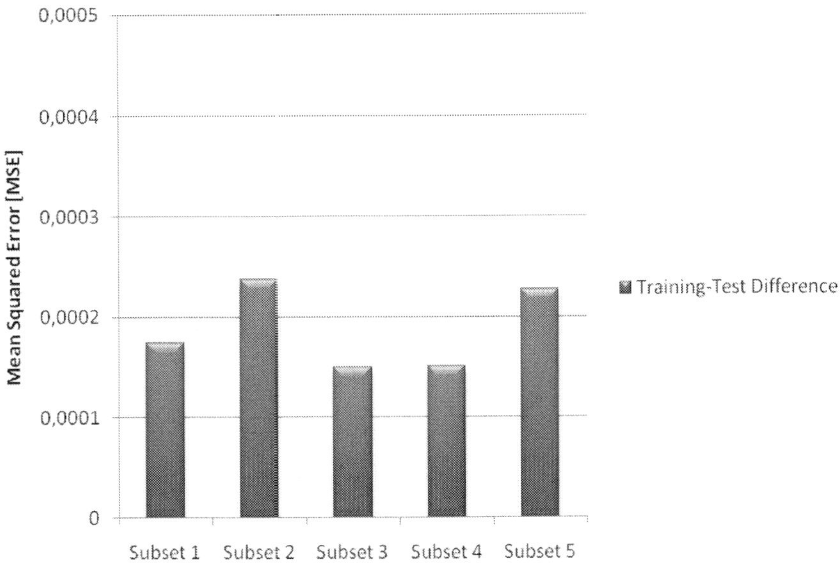

Fig. 2. Mean Squared Error (MSE) differences between training and test subsets

In view of the results shown in Tables 5 and 6, we can check that the magnitude of the MSE value is practically similar between the training and test data subsets. This finding is confirmed by the results reflected in Fig. 2. This figure represents the difference in the MSE value between the training and test subsets for all used data subsets (1-5). According to the Fig. 2, the MSE value decreases slightly from the training to the test subsets in a value between 2.2·10^{-4} and 1.5·10^{-4}.

These results inform us about the great ability of generalization of the developed prediction model, since not only accurately predicts the output variables of the training subsets but also the output variables of the test subsets, which correspond to the blind data for the neural network (not used in the training phase).

In order to certify the good results obtained with the developed ANN based prediction model in Figs. 3-7 (a), are shown as an example the correlation values between measured and estimated by the model output variables for the case of data subset 5. In addition, as an example in Figures 3-7 (b) display the evolution of measured and estimated value of the output variables (L_{Aeq}, L_{eq}, TSLV, CF and 800 Hz sound level) for all records used for the test phase (in the case of the data subset 5).

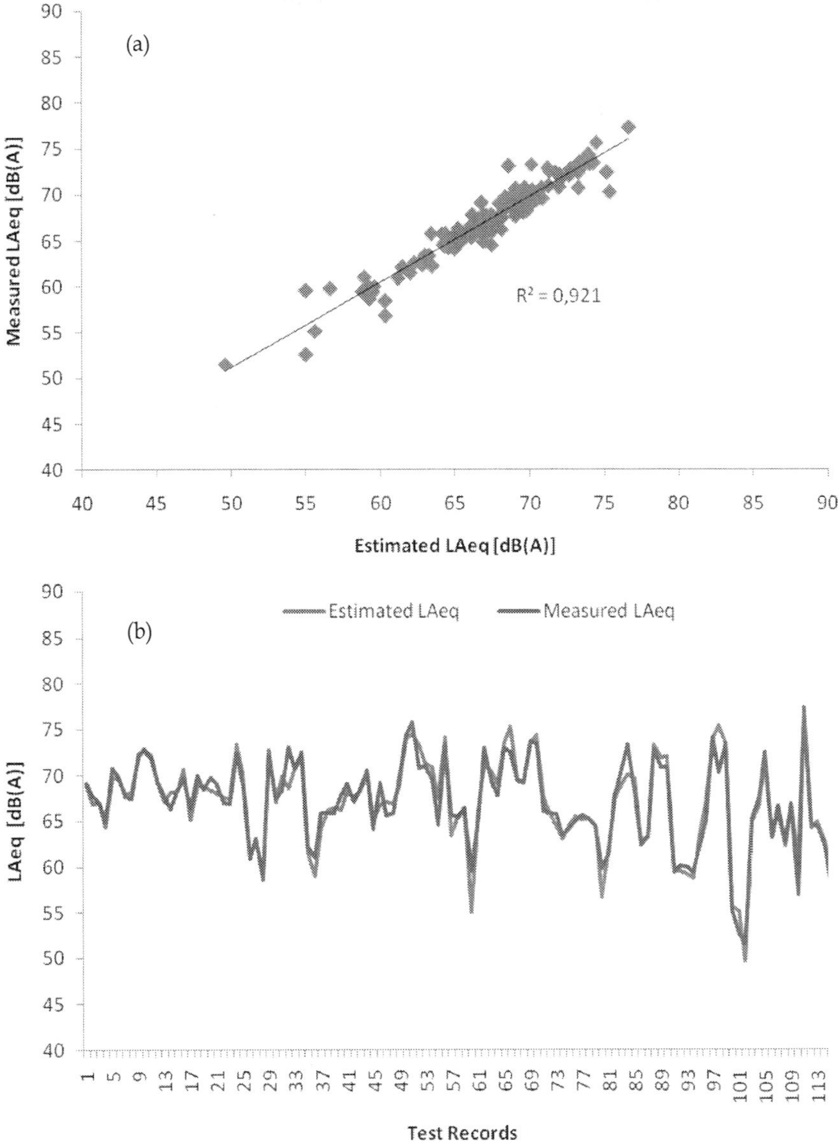

Fig. 3. (a) R^2-value between estimated and measured L_{Aeq} and (b) Evolution of the estimated and measured L_{Aeq} for the used test records (subset 5)

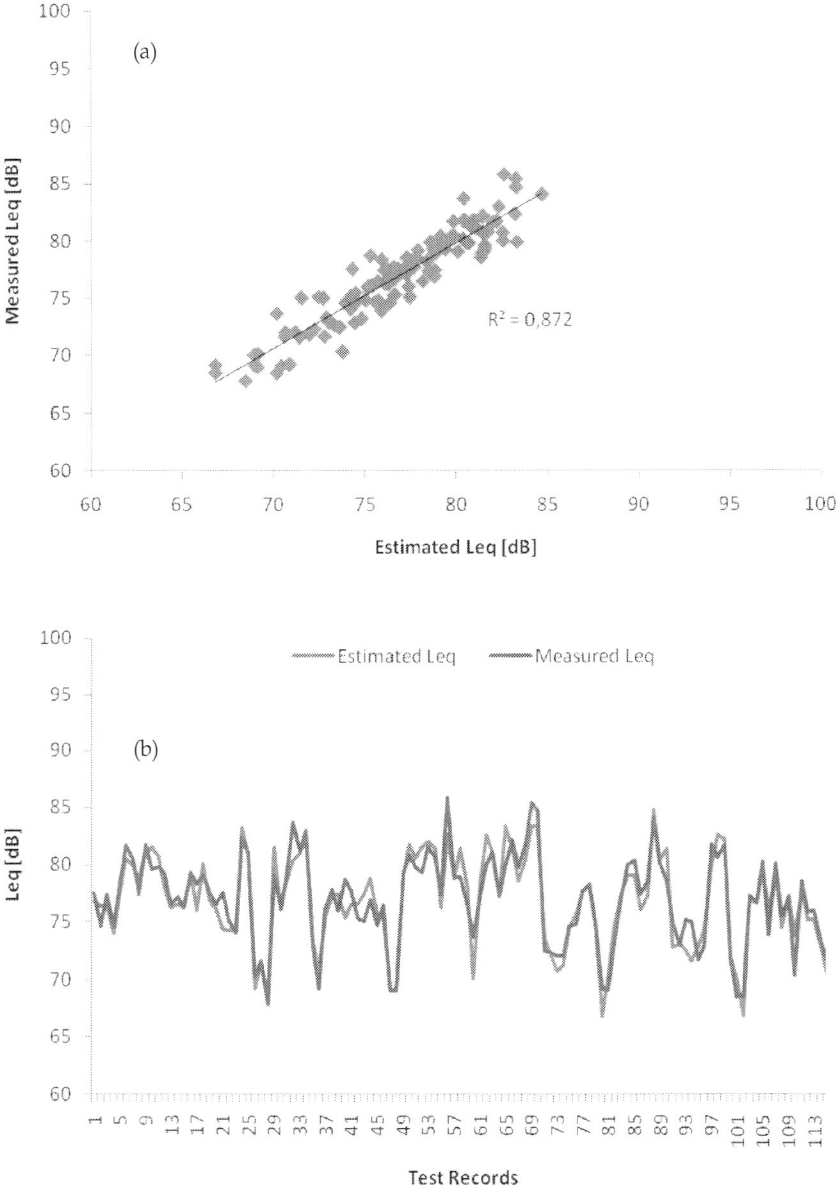

Fig. 4. (a) R^2-value between estimated and measured L_{eq} and (b) Evolution of the estimated and measured L_{eq} for the used test records (subset 5)

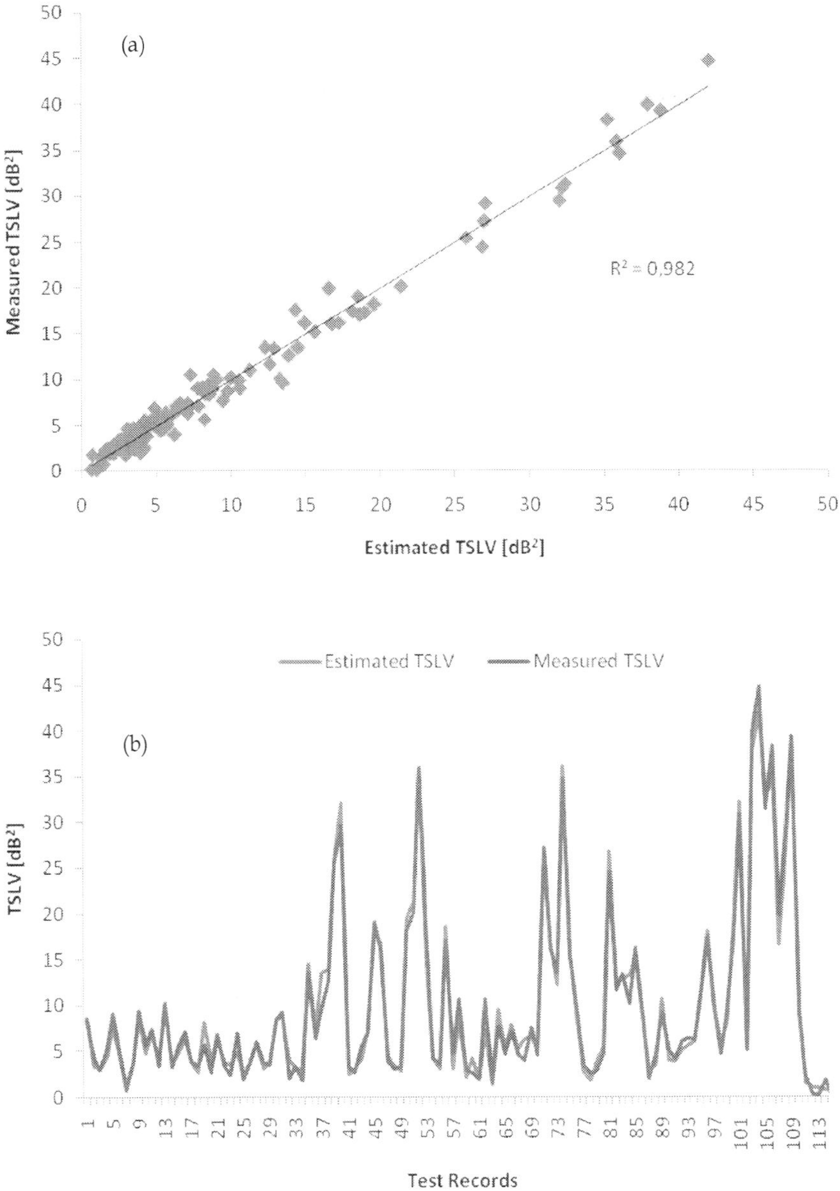

Fig. 5. (a) R^2-value between estimated and measured TSLV and (b) Evolution of the estimated and measured TSLV for the used test records (subset 5)

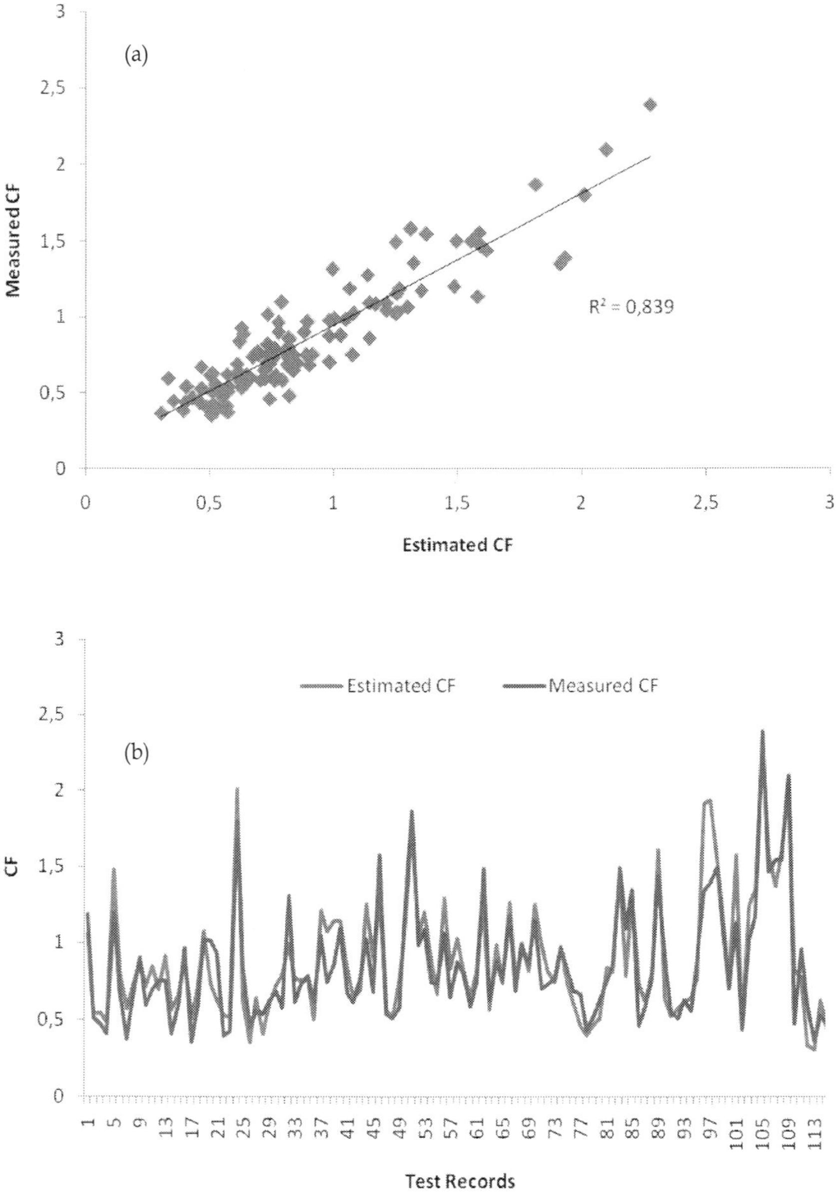

Fig. 6. (a) R^2-value between estimated and measured CF and (b) Evolution of the estimated and measured CF for the used test records (subset 5)

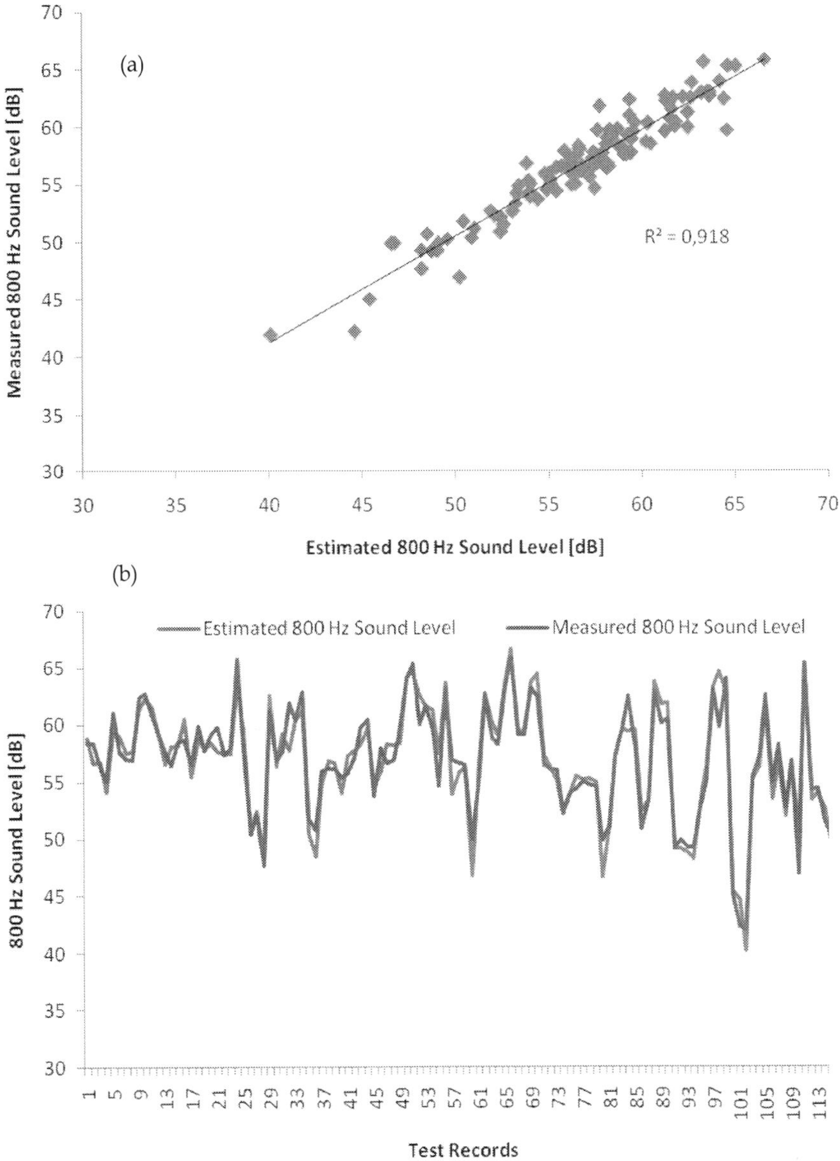

Fig. 7. (a) R^2-value between estimated and measured 800 Hz Sound Level and (b) Evolution of the estimated and measured 800 Hz Sound Level for the used test records (subset 5). *The results with respect to the output variable 800 Hz Sound Level are shown as an example of the ANN behavior to predict the 1/3-octave Sound Level between 31.5-10000 Hz. The correlation value for all the other frequency bands is shown in Table 7.

In view of the obtained results, where the proposed ANN based model achieves prediction with a reasonably low mean squared error (MSE), and shows a great capacity for generalization, we may affirm that the proposed neural network is capable of predicting, with considerable precision and accuracy, both the sound pressure level (A-weighted and not weighted) and the temporal and spectral composition of the different types of situations presented to the network.

8. Discussion and conclusions

It has been widely recognized that noise pollution is one of the most important environmental problems in urban agglomerations (Miedema & Vos, 1998). It is fully assumed and research studies in various countries have shown that noise affects daily activities and causes sleep disturbance as well as a poorer life quality (Lercher, 1996).

Undertake a proper modeling and prediction of environmental noise in urban environments is a challenging task. This is due to several reasons but mainly to the great variability (temporal and spatial) of sound sources. Road traffic is the main source of environmental noise in urban areas, nevertheless, road traffic is not the only noisy source in urban settings; we also encounter noise coming from construction works, commercial activities, recreation, etc. At the same time, we can find urban locations in which road traffic does not have a direct incidence, e.g. green urban areas, in which natural and social sounds predominate. This latter aspect is indicative of the great urban heterogeneity. In this sense, one of the most salient characteristics of urban agglomerations is the great heterogeneity of situations that can arise in them. From the perspective of environmental modelling, this heterogeneity is a serious problem since this situational diversity must be accounted for in any well-designed environmental model. Regarding the characterization of sound environments, something similar occurs because the number of variables that influence both the sound emission and the sound spread is very high (Torija et al., 2010a).

For these reasons, to undertake the problem of noise modelling in cities, it is more effective to fully characterize the sound space of a given urban area. To carry out an adequate characterization of a sound space is necessary to address not only the evaluation of sound pressure level but is also necessary to consider the temporal structure and spectral composition of the sound (Torija et al., 2010b). We choose these variables as defining of the given sound space, going beyond the classical noise level prediction.

Once the problem is established, a critical step is to select the variables that affect the sound space. Based on a deep study of the problem, several variables are selected, together with the output variables we need to define the sound space. The tool selected for performing the modeling, due to the reasons stated above, are neural networks. Due to their well-known characteristics, the use of artificial neural networks to approach the complex problem of modeling and prediction of urban noise seemed highly recommended. In this paper, this hypothesis is certified in view of the obtained results. The developed ANN based prediction model is able to predict, with great accuracy, the short-term level and both temporal and spectral composition of the sound pressure in urban agglomerations. In the cases studied, the proposed model is not only able to learn and predict those records presented during the training phase, but also it is able, with a high success degree, to predict those records used for the testing phase, which inform about its great capacity of generalization. This fact reports that the proposed methodology will not only be very useful for the measured situations/locations, but it may be of great usefulness in any situation/location of other Southern Europe medium-sized cities.

9. Future research work

As future work, there are several proposals that have emerged from this research.
Firstly, it would be of great interest to implement the proposed ANN based prediction model in a GIS tool, so that we could represent the spatial distribution of the obtained results. This will allow obtaining mapping with the value of each one of the different used descriptors, being this information of great value for the urban planner, as for decision making in the management of a sound space.
Secondly it will be very useful to test the model in other cities. Although the methodology describes here is fully applicable to any urban areas, the model should be refined to take into account new sound spaces arising in other cities. This would increase the applicability and generality of the model.
Finally, another aspect of great interest to consider for future work is to use another data mining techniques or new algorithms to improve the above described model. In the latter case, we are considering the use of genetic algorithms to optimize an artificial neural network, in order to evaluate their potential pros and cons regarding the development of an urban noise prediction model. The principal goal would be to analyze the main differences found between the use of backpropagation algorithms and genetic algorithms to carry out the training of an artificial neural network.

10. References

Aguilera de Maya, J.L. (1997). Método de predicción de ruido urbano basado en teoría fuzzy, *Proceedings of the XXVIII Congreso Nacional de Acústica (Tecniacústica)*, Oviedo (Spain).

Almasri, M.N. & Kaluarachchi, J.J. (2005). Modular neural networks to predict the nitrate distribution in ground water using the on-ground nitrogen loading and recharge data. *Environmental Modelling & Software*, Vol. 20, No. 7, pp. 851-871.

Avsar, Y. ; Saral, A. ; Gönüllü, M.T. ; Arslankaya, E. & Kurt, U. (2004). Neural network modelling of outdoor noise levels in a pilot area. *Turkish Journal of Engineering & Environmental Sciences*, Vol. 28, No. 3, pp. 149-155.

Berg, T. (2002). Classification of environmental noise by means of neural networks, *Proceedings of Forum Acusticum*, Sevilla (Spain).

Berglund, T. & Nilsson, M. (2001). An attempt to capture the perceived soundscape, *Proceedings of the International Symposium on Noise Pollution and Health (NOPHER)*, Cambridge (UK).

Berglund, B. ; Hassmén, P. & Preis, A. (2002). Annoyance and spectral constrast are cues for similarity and preference of sounds. *Journal of Sound and Vibration*, Vol. 250, No. 1, pp. 53-64.

Beritelli, F. ; Casale, S. & Ruggeri, G. (2000). New results in fuzzy pattern classification of background noise, *Proceeding of ICSP2000*, pp. 1483-1486.

Betkowsa, A. ; Shinoda, K. & Furui, S. (2005). Model optimization for noise discrimination in home environment, *Proceedings of Symposium on Large-Scale Knowledge Resources (LKR2005)*, pp. 167-170, Tokyo (Japan).

Björk, E.A. (2002). Effects of inter-stimulus interval and duration of sound elements on annoyance. *Acta Acustica United with Acustica*, Vol. 88, No. 1, pp. 104-109.

Botteldooren, D. & Verkeyn, A. (2001). Fuzzy modelling of traffic noise annoyance, *Proceedings of Joint 9th IFSA World Congress and 20th NAFIPS International Conference*, Vol. 2, pp. 1176-1181.

Botteldooren, D. & Verkeyn, A. (2002a). Fuzzy models for accumulation of reported community noise annoyance from combined sources. *Journal of the Acoustical Society of America*, Vol. 112, No. 4, pp. 1496-1508.

Botteldooren, D. & Verkeyn, A. (2002b). An iterative fuzzy model for cognitive processes involved in environment quality judgement, *Proceeding of the 11th IEEE International Conference on Fuzzy Systems*, Hawaii (USA).

Botteldooren, D. & Verkeyn, A. (2002c). Aggregation of specific noise annoyance to a general noise annoyance rating : a fuzzy model, *Proceedings of the 9th International Congress on Sound and Vibration*, Orlando, Florida (USA).

Botteldooren, D. & Verkeyn, A. (2002d). Annoyance prediction with fuzzy rule bases, Proceedings of the 5th International FLINS Conference on Computational Intelligent Systems for Applied Research, Singapore.

Botteldooren, D. & Verkeyn, A. (2002e). The effect of land-use variables in a fuzzy rule based model for noise annoyance, *Proceedings of International Congress and Exposition on Noise Control Engineering*, Dearborn, Michigan (USA).

Botteldooren, D. ; Verkeyn, A. ; Cornelis, C. & De Cock, M. (2002a). On the meaning of noise annoyance modifiers : A fuzzy set theoretical approach. *Acta Acustica United with Acustica*, Vol. 88, No. 2, pp. 239-251.

Botteldooren, D., Verkeyn, A. & Lercher, P. (2002b). Noise annoyance modelling using fuzzy rule based systems. *Noise and Health*, Vol. 4, No. 15, pp. 27-44.

Botteldooren, D. ; Verkeyn, A. ; De Cock, M. & Kerre, E. (2003a). Generating Membership functions for a noise annoyance model from experimental data. *Soft computing in measurement and information acquisition, Studies in Fuzziness and Soft Computing* 127, Springer-Verlag, pp. 51-67.

Botteldooren, D. ; Verkeyn, A. & Lercher, P. (2003b). A fuzzy rule based framework for noise annoyance modelling. *Journal of the Acoustical Society of America*, Vol. 114, No. 3, pp. 1487-1498.

Botteldooren, D. & Lercher, P. (2004). Soft-computing base analysis of the relationship between annoyance and coping with noise and odor. *Journal of the Acoustical Society of America*, Vol. 115, No. 6, pp. 2974-2985.

Botteldooren, D. ; De Coensel, B. & De Muer, T. (2006). The temporal structure of urban soundscapes. *Journal of Sound and Vibration*, Vol. 292, No. 1-2, pp. 105-123.

Burke, L.I. & Ignizio, J.P. (1992). Neural networks and operations research : an overview. *Computer and Operations Research*, Vol. 19, No. 3-4, pp. 179-189.

Cammarata, G. ; Cavalieri, S. & Fichera, A. (1995). A neural network architecture for noise prediction. *Neural Networks*, Vol. 8, No. 6, pp. 963-973.

Caponetto, R. ; Lavorgna, M. ; Martinez, A. & Occhipinti, L. (1997). GAS for fuzzy modeling of noise pollution, *Proceedings of the First International Conference on Konwledge-Based Intelligent Electronic Systems*, pp. 219-223, Adelaide (Australia).

Chakraborty, K. ; Mehrotra, K. ; Mohan, C.K. & Ranka, S. (1992). Forecasting the behavior of multivariate time series using neural networks. *Neural Networks*, Vol. 5, No. 6, pp. 961-970.

Chelani, A.B. ; Chalapati Rao, C.V. ; Phadke, K.M. & Hasan, M.Z. (2002). Prediction of sulphur dioxide concentration using artificial neural networks. *Environmental Modelling & Software*, Vol. 17, No. 2, pp. 159-166.

Commission Recommendation (2003/613/EC) of 6 August 2003 concerning the guidelines on the revised interim computation methods for industrial noise, aircraft noise, road traffic noise and railway noise, and related emission data. Official diary n ° L 212 of 22/08/2003 p. 0049-0064.

Couvreur, C. ; Fontaine, V. ; Gaunard, P. & Mubikangiey, C.G. (1998). Automatic classification of environmental noise events by Hidden Markov Models. *Applied Acoustics*, Vol. 54, No. 3, pp. 187-206.

Couvreur, L. & Laniray, M. (2004). Automatic noise recognition in urban environments based on artificial neural networks and hidden Markov models, *Proceedings of the 33rd International Congress and Exposition on Noise Control Engineering (Inter-noise)*, Prague (Czech Republic).

Dia, H. (2001). An object-oriented neural network approach to short-term traffic forecasting. *European Journal of Operational Research*, Vol. 131, No. 2, pp. 253-261.

Directive 2002/49/EC of the European Parliament and of the Council of 25 June 2002 relating to the assessment and management of environmental noise.

Dougherty, M.S. & Cobbett, M.R. (1997). Short-term inter-urban traffic forecasts using neural networks. *International Journal of Forecasting*, Vol. 13, No. 1, pp. 21-31.

Fortuna, I. ; Occhipinti, L. ; Vinci, C. & Xibilia, M.G. (1994). A neuro-fuzzy model of urban traffic, *Proceedings of the 37th Midwest Symposium on Circuits ans Systems*, Vol. 1, pp. 603-606.

Gaunard, P. ; Mubikangiey, C.G. ; Couvreur, C. & Fontaine, V. (1998). Automatic classification of environmental noise events by Hidden Markov models, *Proceedings of the IEEE International Conference on Acoustics, Speech and Signal Processing*, Vol. 6, pp. 3609-3612.

Genaro, N. ; Torija, A. ; Ramos, A. ; Requena, I. ; Ruiz, D.P. & Zamorano, M. (2010). A neural network based model for urban noise prediction. *Journal of the Acoustical Society of America*, doi:10.1121/1.3473692.

Hamed, M.M.; Khalafallah, M.G. & Hassanien, E.A. (2004). Prediction of wastewater treatment plant performance using artificial neural networks. *Environmental Modelling & Software*, Vol. 19, No. 10, pp. 919-928.

Ledoux, C. (1997). An urban traffic flow model integrating neural network. *Transportation Research Part C : Emerging Technologies*, Vol. 5, No. 5, pp. 287-300.

Lercher, P. (1996). Environmental noise and health : an integrated research perspective. *Environment International*, Vol. 22, No. 1, pp. 117-128.

Lercher, P. & Schulte-fortkamp, B. (2003). The relevance of soundscape research to the assessment of noise annoyance at the community level, *Proceedings of the Eighth International Congress on Noise as a Public Health Problem*, pp. 225-231, Rotterdam (The Netherlands).

Ma, L. ; Smith, D.J. & Miller, B.P. (2003a). Environmental noise classification for context-aware applications, *Proceedings of DEXA (LNCS 2736)*, pp. 360-370.

Ma, L. ; Smith, D.J. & Miller, B.P. (2003b). Context awareness using environmental noise classification, *Proceedings of Eurospeech*, pp. 2237-2240, Geneva (Switzerland).

Maier, H.R. & Dandy, G.C. (1998). The effect of internal parameters and geometry on the performance of back-propagation neural networks : an empirical study. *Environmental Modelling & Software*, Vol. 13, No. 2, pp. 193-209.

Maier, H.R. ; Morgan, N. & Chow, C.W.K. (2004). Use of artificial neural networks for predicting optimal alum doses and treated water quality parameters. *Environmental Modelling & Software*, Vol. 19, No. 5, pp. 485-494.

Miedema, H.M.E. & Vos, H. (1998). Exposure-response relationships for transportation noise. *Journal of the Acoustical Society of America*, Vol. 104, No. 6, pp. 3432-3445.

Ordieres, J.B. ; Vergara, E.P. ; Capuz, R.S. & Salazar, R.E. (2005). Neural network prediction model for fine particulate matter ($PM_{2,5}$) on the US - Mexico border in El Paso (Texas) and ciudad Juarez (Chihuahua). *Entironmental Modelling & Software*, Vol. 20, No. 5, pp. 547-559.

Patra, J.C. & Panda, G. (1998). ANN-based intelligent pressure sensor in noisy environment. *Measurement*, Vol. 23, No. 4, pp. 229-238.

Schizas, C.N. ; Pattichis, C.S. & Michaelides, S.C. (1994). Forecasting minimum temperature with shor time-length data using artificial neural networks. *Neural Network World*, Vol. 4, No. 2, pp. 219-230.

Tang, Z. ; Dealmeida, C. & Fishwick, P.A. (1991). Time series forecasting using neural networks vs Box-Jenkins methodology. *Simulation*, Vol. 57, No. 5, pp. 303-310.

Torija, A.J. ; Genaro, N. ; Ruiz, D.P. ; Ramos-Ridao, A. ; Zamorano, M. & Requena, I. (2010a). Priorization of acoustic variables : environmental decision support for the physical characterization of urban sound environments. *Building and Environment*, Vol. 45, No. 6, pp. 1477-1489.

Torija, A.J. ; Ruiz, D.P. ; De Coensel, B. ; Botteldooren, D. ; Berglund, B. & Ramos-Ridao, A. (2010b). Relationship between road and railway noise annoyance and overall indoor sound exposure. *Transportation Research part D : Transport and Environment*, doi:10.1016/j.trd.2010.07.012.

Viollon, S. & Lavandier, C. (2000). Multidimensional assessment of the acoustic quality of urban environments, *Proceedings of Internoise*, Nice (France).

Yin, H. ; Wong, S.C. ; Xu, J. & Wong, C.K. (2002). Urban traffic flow prediction using a fuzzy-neural approach. *Transportation Research part C : Emerging Technologies*, Vol. 10, No. 2, pp. 85-98.

Zaheeruddin & Garima (2006). A neuro-fuzzy approach for prediction of human work efficiency in noisy environment. *Applied Soft Computing*, Vol. 6, No. 3, pp. 283-294.

Part 6

Application of ANN in Nanotechnology

22

Artificial Neural Networks: Applications in Nanotechnology

Amir Amani[1] and Dariush Mohammadyani[2]
[1]*Department of Medical Nanotechnology, School of Advanced Medical Technologies, Tehran University of Medical Sciences*
[2]*Materials and Energy Research Center (MERC)*
Iran

1. Introduction

Artificial neural networks (ANNs), as techniques that mimic the processing way of information in human brain have emerged as promising methods in dealing with non-linear and complex relations. The ability to learn, tolerance to data noises and capability to model incomplete data have made them unique analyzing approaches in many scientific procedures. When employing neural nets, once the network has been trained, new data in similar domain may be analyzed and predicted avoiding the time- and money- consuming experiments. Taking into account that to solve problems, ANNs may combine the data from literature and experiments, the potential of this approach can be easily estimated in nanoscience and nanotechnology.

Two types of training are commonly employed when using ANNs. While in unsupervised networks, the training procedure is not affected by the output(s) of the network; supervised networks attempt to modify the neurons weights so that the network output(s) becomes as close as possible to the desired output. As application in nanotechnology, supervised associating networks may be considered as alternatives to conventional response surface methodology (RSM). The unsupervised feature-extracting networks are alternatives to principal component analysis (PCA) and are able to map multidimensional data sets onto two-dimensional spaces. Therefore, ANNs not only have attracted the attention of many computer scientists, but also a huge number of successful applications of them is found in the literature, reporting problems solving in various areas of sciences, engineering and business.

Although increasing number of ANNs applications are now observed in diverse scientific fields, nanotechnologists do not generally appear to be interested or fully aware of the potentials of such approaches. Here we have described principles of the ANNs in dealing with certain properties of nano-materials. To present the *'state of the art'*, available publications on nanotechnology and nanoscience which have used the advantages of ANNs have been evaluated. In this chapter, a brief description about importance of nanotechnology has been given. We then have summarized common applications of ANNs and tried to identify various areas in nanoscience and nanotechnology where the successful application of ANNs can be envisaged, followed by the areas of future developments.

2. Importance of nanotechnology

The lecture "There's Plenty of Room at the Bottom" by Richard R. Feynman in 1959 -that it is nowadays considered as one of the classic science talks in twentieth century- is now regarded as the basic idea for nanotechnology (Bhushan, 2004). In this lecture the potentials of nano-sized materials has been considered (Poole Jr. and Owens, 2003) and publishing Encyclopedia Brittanica on a pin head has been predicted (Balaz, 2008). The quote by the American visionary about nanotechnology is also amazing: "Just wait-the next century is going to be incredible. We are about to be able to build things that work on the smallest possible length scales, atom by atom. These little nano-things will revolutionize our industries and our lives" (Smalley, 1999). It is predicted that in near future, nanotechnology will play an important role in our economy and society, as is being observed in computers, cellular/molecular biology and many others fields. Nanotechnology is about to show its significant role in areas such as medicine, materials and manufacturing, energy, information technology, electronics, etc (Bhushan, 2004).

Nanotechnology in Oxford dictionary means: "the branch of technology that deals with dimensions and tolerances of less than 100 nanometers, especially the manipulation of individual atoms and molecules" (Oxford Online Dictionary, 2010). The National Science Foundation, defines nanotechnology as "research and technology development at the atomic, molecular or macromolecular levels, in the length scale of approximately 1-100 nanometer range, to provide a fundamental understanding of phenomena and materials at the nanoscale and to create and use structures, devices and systems that have novel properties and functions because of their small and/or intermediate size" (National Nanotechnology Initiative, 2004).

In order to realize the importance of nanotechnology, analysis of nanotechnology market is probably the first approach. In 2000, the market of microsystems was about 15 billion USD. Considering an annual increase rate of 10-20%, more than 100 billion USD is anticipated as the market size of microsystems for the end of 2010. In 2001, the nanosystems market was about 100 million USD, while the expected market for the integrated nanosystems is about 25 billion USD by the end of 2010. Such notable increase is thought to be due to the extensive impact they may have in their different applications. Certainly, the role of governments in supporting nano-related technologies should be considered, too (Bhushan, 2004). So far, a large variety of nano- devices and structures have been employed in areas such as sensors, actuators, and miniaturized systems and a large market is anticipated for nano/micro electromechanical machines (NEMS/MEMS) in the near future (Bhushan, 2004; Lyshevski, 2001). Development of NEMS and MEMS is necessary to the economy and society, since these electromechanical systems have shown important effects in medicine, manufacturing and fabrication, aerospace and avionics, information technologies, automotives, public safety, etc (Lyshevski, 2001). Bearing in mind the fact that many initiatives and governments have devoted considerable funds for research and development in nanotechnology, and will probably continue to do so, nanotechnology can still be regarded as "intact" area of research and development in both its science and technology aspects.

3. Classification of applications of ANNs

Reviewing the literature, several classes of applications may be identified for ANNs (Mehrotra et al., 1997; Gardner and Dorling, 1998; Kalogirou, 2001; Agatonovic-Kustrin and

Beresford, 2000; Manisha et al., 2008; Achanta et al., 1995). To avoid the common complications raised when attempting to distinguish between such classes, here we review the ANNs applications without scrutinizing the differences suggested for each application class.

ANNs may be used to *recognize* a specific output *pattern* when presenting an input sample (Mehrotra et al., 1997). Employing this ability, ANNs can effectively solve difficult problems such as recognition of sounds, images or videos. Interestingly, this task may be performed with no priori definition for the pattern. In this case, a completely new pattern is identified by the network.

Recognizing the laws underlying the system behavior is the most accurate way for *prediction*. However, finding these laws is not usually easy. Studying the variables together instead of investigating a single variable at a time (i.e. one-factor-at-a-time approach) is usually a suitable option to obtain better knowledge, thus taking better prediction. Perfect prediction is not possible, but reasonable prediction can be obtained by neural networks (Mehrotra et al., 1997; Weigend et al., 1990; Li et al., 1990).

Another application for the ANNs is what usually called as *function approximation*. Computational models are often some functions that map numerical inputs to numerical outputs (Mehrotra et al., 1997). Function approximation is described as constructing a function that with acceptable approximation generates similar outputs from input valuables. This process is done through learning based on available training data. Unlike most statistical techniques, which usually end up in a distinct equation, when using ANNs, mathematical function relating the outputs to the input variables may not be clear (Mehrotra et al., 1997). Tracking the behavior in a moving object can be regarded as a good example for function approximation. Herein one may approximate behavior of the object understudy as a function of time (Mehrotra et al., 1997).

When the goal of a problem is *optimization* of a function, ANNs may be employed as attractive option. For example when attempting to arrange the components on a circuit board to reach the minimum length for the wire while certain parts should be connected to certain others, we are optimizing the components structure. Problems in this category can also be dealt by ANNs (Mehrotra et al., 1997).

4. Application of ANNs in nanotechnology

In this section, we group the applications of ANNs in three classes: applications in nanomaterials, in nanomedicine, and in nanophysics.

4.1 Nanomaterials

The science and technology of nanomaterials consist of subfields which study or develop materials with nanoscale dimension having unique properties (Clarkson et al., 2004). The majority of nanotechnology works include preparation and characterization of nanomaterials.

The first report on application of ANNs in nanomaterials was in 2000 (Lee et al., 2000), where the sensitivity signals of an array was modelled using artificial neural network, and a gas recognition system was implemented for the classification and identification of explosive gases. The properties of multi-dimensional sensor signals obtained from the nine sensors were analyzed using PCA technique, and a gas pattern recognizer was implemented using a multi-layer neural network with an error back propagation (EBP) learning algorithm. As shown in Fig. 1, the network contained an input layer with nine nodes receiving the data from the sensors on the sensor array, a hidden layer with eight neurons, and an output layer with nine nodes. The simulation and experimental results showed that the proposed gas recognition system is capable of identifying explosive gases.

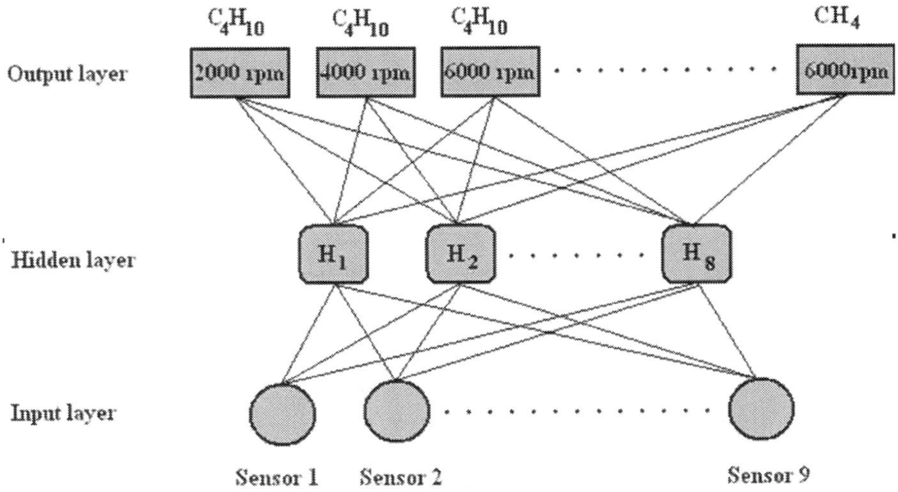

Fig. 1. Schematic of the multi-layer neural network structure for gas recognition system.

Lee et al. (Lee et al., 2001) (Lee et al., 2002) have published two papers on developing recognition systems which can classify and quantify the volatile organic compounds (VOCs). The gas pattern recognizer was implemented using a multi-layer Neural Network with an EBP learning algorithm. The neural network consisted of an input layer (which received data from the sensors on the sensor array), a hidden layer and an output layer. The overall network structure used in this study was similar to the one shown in Fig. 1. The work indicated that the proposed gas recognition system is effective in identifying VOCs.

A three-layer BP-ANNs model (five-input model) was developed to predict purity of $SrTiO_3$ nano-crystals (Qing-li and Quan-xi, 2006). The network used in this study included reaction time, reaction temperature, molar rate of $TiCl_4$ to HCl, NaOH concentration and $SrCl_2$ concentration as input variables and purity of $SrTiO_3$ as the output. It was found that the BP neural network is efficient for predicting the purity of perovskite-type $SrTiO_3$ nano-crystals.

In another study, finite element (FE) simulation and ANNs approach was used (Lee et al., 2007) to describe the elasto-plastic stress–strain behaviour in coated layers using nano-indentation tests. A single-bahaviour model, with one stress-strain behaviour and a layer-behaviour model with separate layers and substrates were used. The loading–unloading data (i.e., force displacement) with changes in yield strength and strain hardening exponents obtained from the FE simulations were employed as training data for the ANN, and the loading–unloading data from the indentation tests were used as the input data. The outputs of the ANNs were the yield strength and strain hardening exponent, which generated the same loading–unloading data as the indentation test did. The layer-behaviour model was shown to be satisfactorily accurate.

Combination of finite-element (FE) simulation and ANNs modelling is becoming an interesting tool in nanomaterials. A study by Haj-Ali (Haj-Ali et al., 2008) reported the use of ANNs models in dealing with nanohardness tests in a wide range of materials with nonlinear behavior. ANNs models were trained with separate FE simulations with nonlinear properties and different geometries. When generating the model, from load-displacement indentation response, only the monotonic loading part was utilized, which is a key difference from classical experiments which normally use the unloading portion. The experimental nanoindentation tests included a silicon substrate with and without a copper film in its nanocrystalline form. Comparing the results from the modelling with those available in the literature, the obtained model was suggested as very efficient with the ability to calibrate and predict the inelastic material properties for depths above 50 nm. The overall resisting force in the study was found to be a continuum response.
Optimal variables for preparation of sol-gel prepared colloids of titania were determined using ANNs in a report by Liau et al (Liau and Dai, 2008). In this work, the inputs are concentration of [NH_3], [H_2O], and reaction temperature; while the outputs are the titania particle size (PS) and particle size distribution (PSD). The relationship of the operating variables (inputs) and PS and PSD (outputs) can be built using the ANN approach. The built ANN model can then represent the input-output relation in the sol-gel processing system and predict PS and PSD in relation to operating conditions. The model was then used to optimize the operating variables in order to obtain desired particle size with narrow particle size distribution. The feasible optimal operating conditions can be determined to fabricate monodispered uniform TiO_2 particles for practical cases.
Preparation of composites of polyphenylene sulfide (PPS) filled with short carbon fibers (SCFs) and sub-micron particles of TiO_2 to study the tribological behaviour of the composite using ANNs has been reported by Jiang et al. (Jiang et al., 2008). The extrusion and injection-molding technique to prepare the particles followed by sliding wear tests to optimize the composition of PPS, suggested 15 vol.% SCF and 5 vol.% TiO_2 as the lowest specific wear rate. More optimal composition was estimated from the ANNs as 15 vol.% SCF and 6 vol.% T_iO_2 chosen input variables in neural network were material compositions (PPS matrix, short carbon fiber, nano-TiO_2 particles and lubricant contents) and testing conditions (sliding speed and applied pressure) while the output variables were specific wear rate and friction coefficient, as well as the range of the experimental values.
In 2009, Madadlou et al. (Madadlou et al., 2009) predicted micelles particle size. The following five variables were used as inputs to networks: pH value of casein solutions, frequency of ultrasonic bath (kHz), frequency of ultrasonic probe (kHz), acoustic power of sonication (W) and time of sonication (min). The output of system was particle size (nm) of re-assembled casein micelles. It was measured with a laser diffraction based particle size analyzer. The size of micelles differed from 203 to 431nm. A feed-forward network having one hidden layer was used in this study. Optimization was performed on number of hidden neurons, epochs and training runs as well as momentum coefficient and step size. They also stated that RSM can be successfully used in optimizing the topology of ANNs but RSM considered as a complicated and time-consuming task. Using this approach results in shortening the time required for optimization and providing the possibility of analyzing the influence of more variables on performance of networks.
Prediction of heat transfer in copper-water nanofluid by ANNs was reported in differentially heated square cavity (Santra et al., 2009). The nanofluid was taken as a non-

Newtonian fluid and the network was trained based on resilient-propagation (RPROP) algorithm. Input and output data were from a numerical simulation. Results of simulation and ANNs model were compared and was reported to be correct in the range of training data. Furthermore, taking into account the considerable longer times required for simulations, the RPROP based ANNs was suggested as competitive alternative in prediction of heat transfer.

In 2009, Shokuhfar et al. (Shokuhfar et al., 2009) studied the effect of different training approaches on the ANNs when dealing with Al_2TiO_5- based ceramics. Herein, addition of micron size talc led to satisfactory stabilizing behaviour. In addition, nano boehmite and colloidal silica managed to improve other physical properties. Subsequently, using BP-ANNs, the effect of temperature and additives percentages on the density of bulk was estimated. Levenberg-Marquardt algorithm was found to have the best estimation and the response surfaces between the variables (additives percentage and temperature) are presented. The model was then suggested to be used in optimizing the sintering process for the particles.

The effect of concentration of MnS on the nano-crystalline $Cd_{1-x}Mn_xS$ size ustilizing feed-forward multilayer perceptron was reported by Jajarmi et al (Jajarmi and Valipour, 2009). The reports pointes out that the generated ANNs model can be considered as applicable method in predicting of the size of nano-crystalline nickel coatings. The grain size of nano-crystalline nickel was also the subject of another study by Rashidi et al (Rashidi et al., 2009). In their study, operation conditions were used as the inputs variables and the grain size of coating was taken as the single output of the model. Good agreement was shown between the predictions of the model and the experimental data. Performing the sensitivity analysis on the model, it was indicated that the current density was the most important factor, while the temperature had the lowest impact on the grain size.

In 2009, Sarkar et al. (Sarkar et al., 2009) used ANNs as tools to study the diameter of electrospun nanofibers. The input variables in this study were concentration of the solution, electrical conductivity, flow rate, and strength of the electric field. The results of the computer model indicated satisfactory viability for the neural network to predict the diameter of the nanofibers. From this study, insights into employing ANNs models in investigating electrospinning processes is determined.

In a series of ANNs models in 2009, Ma et al. (Ma et al., 2009) using back-propagation technique, studied the correlations between processing factors (high-energy planetary ball milling) and the morphology of nanocomposite WC-18at.%MgO powders. Milling speed, diameter of ball and weight ratio of ball-to-powder was investigated on the crystallite and particle size as well as specific surface. The model was shown to be capable of predicting properties of the composite at different milling parameters. Optimization in processing parameters and ball milling conditions was also suggested as another ability of ANNs in such situations.

A report by Corni et al. (Corni et al., 2009) detailed the effect of deposition time and applied potential as well as their interactions on synthesis of nano-composite films of Al_2O_3–polyetheretherketone on stainless steel. The process was performed in non-aqueous colloidal suspensions using electrophoretic deposition. In their study, the numbers of hidden layers, neurons in each layer and epochs were optimized to improve the results from this approach. Furthermore, this work was complemented by the use of Monte Carlo simulation to better study the effect of deposition time and difference of applied potential on the deposition yield of deposition.

In studies by Haciismailoglu et al. and Kucuk et al. (Haciismailoglu et al., 2009; Kucuk et al., 2009), dynamic hysteresis models from measurements in wide frequency range (1-50 kHz) were developed using ANNs by delta-bar-delta learning. They showed computation of hysteresis loops in nano-crystalline cores by ANNs, using dynamic Preisach model to be fast, with no need to so much of computational efforts. Using geometrical dimensions of cores, peak magnetic induction and magnetizing frequency as input parameters, the ANNs was shown to have acceptable estimation capability. The model is fast, and allows the application of standard learning algorithms for the neural network.

In a study by Averett (Averett et al., 2010), ANNs examined the effect of stress ratio, maximum fatigue stress, unreformed modulus, cycles and residual strain from fatigue as input variables on residual strength behaviour and elastic modulus degradation in filaments. The results indicate that ANNs can be used to predict the residual strength and modulus degradation behavior of poly(ethylene terephthalate) and poly(ethylene terephthalate) fibers with vapor grown carbon nanofibers under different loading conditions. In their study, back propagation were used along with momentum and conjugate gradient algorithms. The multilayer perception network was trained to model the mechanical behaviour in single filaments after loading of fatigue.

Catalytic conversion of two substrates namely, ethyl acetate and toluene, using two nanostructures catalysts HZSM-5 and Co-ZSM-5 was investigated by Hosseini et al. (Hosseini et al., 2010). The ANNs model was based on experimental data from wet impregnation prepared catalysts. Good agreement was shown between the results from the model and those of experiments. This study in agreement with other reports shows that the nanostructure catalysts show higher activity than other catalysts because of having higher specific surface area. The model makes it possible to predict how much each variable affects on the conversion efficiency.

Baseri et al. (Baseri et al., 2010) estimated the effect of concentration of liquid phase and the ratio liquid/powder on the mechanical strength of cement as well as both initial and final setting times in hydroxyapatite (HA). They employed back propagation ANNs with variety of inputs. The comparison of the predicted values and the experimental data indicated that the developed model had a satisfactory performance in estimation of the setting times and the mechanical strength in HA bone cement. Also, it was concluded that the prediction accuracy of 3-outputs model is better than those of other 1-output models.

Detailing the dialysis process performance under as a function of different conditions in dialysis has also been reported using ANNs by Godini et al. (Godini et al., 2010). Charged micelles were transferred through neutral and charged membranes and the behaviour of the micelles was studied using ANNs. High interconnections of the parameters as well as problems associated with the available models in tracking the performance of the process made the ANNs as interesting approach to study this case. The mass transfer was analyzed in terms of its amounts and the mechanism in both membranes in different conditions. The report shows that the developed model can deal with the process when manipulating the parameters individually or simultaneously with adequate accuracy.

4.2 Nanomedicine

Nanomedicine has been defined as "medical application of nanotechnology". Nanomedicine includes use of nanomaterials in medical applications, nanoelectronic biosensors, and future

applications of molecular nanotechnology. The main problem in nanomedicine nowadays is the toxicity issues and environmental aspects of nanomaterials (Freitas Jr., 1999).
The factors controlling the nanoemulsion particle size was studied by our group in 2008 (A. Amani, et al., 2008). Oil in water nanoemulsion samples with different percentages of co-surfactant and drug, applying various amount and rate of applied energy were prepared and the particle size was measured. The generated ANNs model demonstrated the ability of ANNs in dealing with such systems. The model indicated that the total energy amount was the dominant factor in influencing the final particle size.
We also (Amani et al., 2010) identified the parameters affecting the stability of nanoemulsions, using ANNs. A nanoemulsion preparation of budesonide containing polysorbate 80, ethanol, medium chain triglycerides and saline solution was designed, and the particle size of samples with various compositions, prepared using different rates and amounts of applied ultrasonic energy, was measured 30 min and 30 days after preparation. Data modelling and assessing were carried out using ANNs. The derived predictive model was validated statistically and then used to determine the effect of different formulation and processing input variables on particle size growth of the nanoemulsion preparation as an indicator of the preparation stability. The results of this study indicated that the data can be satisfactorily modelled using ANNs, while showing a high degree of complexity between the dominant factors affecting the stability of the preparation. The total amount of applied energy and concentration of ethanol were found to be the dominant factors controlling the particle size growth.
In a microfluidic reactor when nanoprecipitating a hydrophobic drug, ANNs was employed to find out the relationships between input parameters and the size of prepared nanoparticles (Ali et al., 2009). In this study saturation levels of drug, flow rates for solvent and antisolvent, angles for the inlet of microreactors and internal diameters were investigated and rate of antisolvent was found to have dominant role on determining final particle size.

4.3 Nanophysics

The subject of nanophysics is physics of systems having some tens of atoms (Joachim and Plevert, 2009). Considerable number of reports has been mentioned the use of ANNs in nanophysics:
In 2006, Kucuk and Derebasi (Kucuk and Derebasi, 2006) using the data from toroidal wound cores developed a mathematical model for core losses. The improved model was used to optimize the parameters for ANNs. Geometrical parameters, frequency of magnetising, resistivity of the soft magnetic materials and magnetic induction were input parameters while power loss and correlation coefficients comprised the output neurons. The correlation coefficients for calculation of power loss can simply be estimated from the ANN and GA genetic algorithm within acceptable error limits. This means that the ANN and GA could help to assess the core performance before manufacture, thereby reduce the material wastage. Studying nanoscale complementary metal-oxide-semiconductor (CMOS) circuits, Djeffal et al. (Djeffal et al., 2007) used ANNs and showed very acceptable comparisons between the results from numerical models and those of ANNs where L, VDS, VGS, tsi, tox, and ID were channel length, drain source voltage, gate source voltage,silicon film thickness, gate oxide thickness and drain current, respectively. Each of these parameters was indexed with one neuron. The activation function used in this ANN structure was the sigmoid

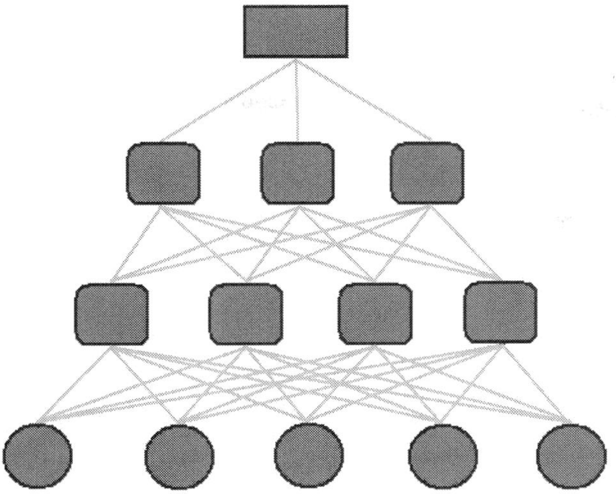

Fig. 2. Neural network consisting of two hidden layers.

function. It is important to denote that the number of input parameters of our ANN model can be extended for other parameters (temperature, band-to-band leakage current, and gate direct tunnelling current and ...). Is this work two hidden layer was used (Fig. 2) and the developed ANNs model indicated to be particularly appropriate as SPICE-like (simulation program with integrated circuit emphasis) tools for simulation of nanoscale CMOS circuits.

Three commercial membranes, based on nanofiltration techniques (ie. NF90, NF270, N30F) were utilized to treat solutions of three different salts in high concentrations (Al-Zoubi et al., 2007). Obtained data were modelled using ANNs and Spiegler–Kedem model. The model determined the reflection coefficients and the of the solute permeability at different levels of salinity. No more than 5% deviation was observed between the predictions by the ANNs and the experimental data. In total, the obtained results indicated that NF90 and NF270 hadhigh rejection at pressures above 5 bar for two salts (ie. Na_2SO_4, and $MgSO_4$), while the rejection for KCl was 30–89%. The third membrane produced lesser rejection for Na_2SO_4 and $MgSO_4$ salts with very low rejection for KCl.

In 2007, Farsi et al. (Farsi and Gobal, 2007) used a four-layer ANNs structure with two hidden to model the performance of a model capacitor. The output variables in this study were power and energy density and utilization to the intrinsic, synthetic and operating characteristics and the inputs included size of crystals (in range of 5-30 nm), lattice length and exchange current density of active material as well as employed cell current. The findings showed that results have a very good agreement with models, developed previously.

Incorporation into SPICE-like tools for simulation of nanoscale circuits has also been by Hayati et al. (Hayati et al., 2010), where ANNs modeled carbon nanotube metal-oxide-semiconductor field-effect transistors (CNT-MOSFETs). The ANNs model needed less computational time compared with other conventional models like non-equilibrium Green's function (NEGF) formalism with having similar accuracy. The ANN model was subsequently imported into HSPICE software as a subcircuit.

One of the most recent uses of ANNs in nanophysics is to generate explicit nonlinear empirical physical formulas (EPFs) in nonlinear electro-optical responses from doped nematic liquid crystals (NLCs) (Yildiz et al., 2010). Layered feed-forward neural network (LFNN) was used due to its ability in nonlinear function approximation. The obtained responses were successfully fitted to the model to predict the new response data. It was then concluded that generally, LFNN may be applied to construct different EPFs in various physical perturbation data such as thermal, molecular and optical conditions in doped NLCs.
ANNs have also been used to determine a relationship between diffuse reflectance spectra in near-infrared region and particle size. Back-propagation artificial neural network (BP-ANN) was utilized in by Khanmohammadi et al. (Khanmohammadi et al., 2010) to estimate the particle size from diffuse reflectance spectra. 44 nano TiO_2 samples were analyzed to validate the applicability of the new method in determining the particle size. It was shown that the BP-ANN caould successfully predict the size of nanoparticles.

5. Conclusion

The high number of reports of researches at nano-levels, manipulting and/or creating novel materials and processes has provided enormous applications in all aspects of human life. Nantechnology has shown its great potential in industrial processes, computers, pharmaceuticals and many other fields. Such a scientific breakthrough, as an inter-disciplinary tool has proved efficient in utilizing various sciecntific approaches such as physics, chemistry and medicine in dealing with a single problem. Surprisingly, the literature review on nanotechnology reports shows no large number. This chapter aims to highlight the need for increased understanding of applications of ANNs in nanotechnology so that these networks can be used even more efficiently in future applications. It should be clarified that here we have only focused on so far reported applications and undoubtedly much more uses can be suggested for ANNs dealing with nano-issues.
Models from ANNs are multifactorial models which can predict, classify, approximate function or recognise patterns in many disciplines. Theoretically, ANNs are able to estimate any function and if used properly, can be used effectively in any discipline, including nanotechnology. Outputs from ANNs models are generated from non-linear combinations of input variables and as shown in this chapter, such models can be effectively employed to deal with experimental data routinely observed in nanotechnology and to find rules governing a process from raw input data.
ANNs are now considered as easy-to-use, while reliable methodology, which is a new emerging technique in the new emerging science "nanotechnology". To see more applications of ANNs in nanotechnology in future, we suggest that researchers in both academic and commercial areas of nanotechnology should be more familiarized with the idea of neural networks. Additionally, forming team groups of experimentalists with those working on neural networks and statistics needs to be promoted. We believe ANNs, as the tools with the ability to handle the nonlinear processes and avoiding the commonly observed noises in experimental data, are fascinating means of working with data observed by nanotechnologists.

6. References

Achanta, A.S.; Kowalski, J.G. & Rhodes, C.T. (1995). Artificial Neural Networks: Implications for Pharmaceutical Science. *Drug Development and Industrial Pharmacy* , Vol. 21, 119-155.

Agatonovic-Kustrin, S. & Beresford, R. (2000). Review: Basic concepts of artificial neural network (ANN) modeling and its application in pharmaceutical research. *Journal of Pharmaceutical and Biomedical Analysis*, Vol. 22, 717–727.

Ahmed, F. (2009). The role of capillary electrophoresis–mass spectrometry to proteome analysis and biomarker discovery. *Journal of Chromatography B* , Vol. 877, 1963–1981.

Ali, H.S.M.; Blagden, N.; York, P.; Amani, A.; Brook, T. (2009). Artificial neural networks modelling the prednisolone nanoprecipitation in microfluidic reactors. *European Journal of Pharmaceutical Sciences*, Vol. 37, 514–522.

Al-Zoubi, H.; Hilal, N.; Darwish, N.A. & Mohammad, A.W. (2007). Rejection and modelling of sulphate and potassium salts by nanofiltration membranes: neural network and Spiegler–Kedem model. *Desalination*, Vol. 206, 42-60.

Amani, A.; York, P.; Chrystyn, H. & Clark, B.J. (2010). Factors Affecting the Stability of Nanoemulsions—Use of Artificial Neural Networks. *Pharmaceutical Research* , Vol. 27, 37-45.

Amani, A.; York, P.; Chrystyn, H.; Clark, B.J. & Do, D.Q. (2008). Determination of factors controlling the particle size in nanoemulsions using Artificial Neural Networks. *European Journal of Pharmaceutical Sciences*, Vol. 35, 42-51.

Averett, R.D.; Realff, M.L.; Jacob, K.I. (2010). Comparative post fatigue residual property predictions of reinforced and unreinforced poly(ethylene terephthalate) fibers using artificial neural networks. *Composites: Part A*, Vol. 41, 331-344.

Averett, R.D.; Realff, M.L.; Jacob, K.I.; (2010). Comparative post fatigue residual property predictions of reinforced and unreinforced poly(ethylene terephthalate) fibers using artificial neural networks. *Composites: Part A*, Vol. 41, 331-344.

Balaz, P. (2008). *Mechanochemistry in Nanoscience and Minerals Engineering*. Springer.

Barciela, R.M.; Garcıa, E.; Fernandez, E. (1999). Modelling primary production in a coastal embayment affected by upwelling using dynamic ecosystem models and artificial neural networks. *Ecological Modelling*, Vol. 120, 199–211.

Baseri, H.; Rabiee, S.M.; Moztarzadeh, F. & Solati-Hashjin, M. (2010). Mechanical strength and setting times estimation of hydroxyapatite cement by using neural network. *Materials and Design*, Vol. 31, 2585–2591.

Battiston, F.M.; Ramseyer, J.P.; Lang, H.P.; Baller, M.K.; Gerber, Ch.; Gimzewski, J.K.; Meyer, E. & Guntherodt, H.J. (2001). A chemical sensor based on a microfabricated cantilever array with simultaneous resonance-frequency and bending readout. *Sensors and Actuators B: Chemical*, Vol. 77, 122-131.

Bhushan, B. (2004). *Springer Hanbook of Nanotechnology*. Springer, Germany.

Clarkson, A.J.; Buckingham, D.A.; Rogers, A.J.; Blackman, A.G. & Clark, C.R. (2004). Nanostructured Ceramics in Medical Devices: Applications and Prospects. *Journal of the Minerals, Metals and Materials Society (JOM)* , Vol. 56, 38–43.

Corni, I.; Cannio, M.; Romagnoli, M. & Boccaccini, A.R. (2009). Application of a neural network approach to the electrophoretic deposition of PEEK–alumina composite coatings. *Materials Research Bulletin*, Vol. 44, 1494–1501.

Djeffal, F.; Chahdi, M.; Benhaya, A. & Hafiane, M.L. (2007). An approach based on neural computation to simulate the nanoscale CMOS circuits: Application to the simulation of CMOS inverter. *Solid-State Electronics*, Vol. 51, 48-56.

Farsi, H. & Gobal, F. (2007). Artificial neural network simulator for supercapacitor performance prediction. *Computational Materials Science*, Vol. 39, 678-683.

Gardner, M.W. & Dorling, S.R. (1998). Artificial Neural Networks (the Multilayer Perceptron)-a Review of Applications in the Atmospheric Science. *Atmospheric Environment*, Vol. 32, 2627-2636.

Godini, H.R.; Ghadrdan, M.; Omidkhah, M.R.; Madaeni, S.S. (2010 (Article in Press)). Part II: Prediction of the dialysis process performance using Artificial Neural Network (ANN). *Desalination*.

Haciismailoglu, M.C.; Kucuk, I. & Derebasi, N. (2009). Prediction of dynamic hysteresis loops of nano-crystalline cores. *Expert Systems with Applications*, Vol. 36, 2225–2227.

Haj-Ali, R.; Kim, H.K.; Koh, S.W.; Saxena, A. & Tummala, R. (2008). Nonlinear constitutive models from nanoindentation tests using artificial neural networks. *International Journal of Plasticity*, Vol. 24, 371-396.

Hayati, M.; Rezaei, A. & Seifi, M. (2010). CNT-MOSFET modeling based on artificial neural network: Application to simulation of nanoscale circuits. *Solid-State Electronics*, Vol. 54, 52–57.

Hosseini, S.A.; Niaei, A.; Salari, D.; Jodaei, A. (2010). Gas Phase Oxidation of Toluene and Ethyl Acetate over Proton and Cobalt Exchanged ZSM-5 Nano Catalysts-Experimental Study and ANN Modeling. *Bulletin of the Korean Chemical Society*, Vol. 31, 808-814.

Hou, T.H.; Su, C.H. & Liu, W.L. (2007). Parameters optimization of a nano-particle wet milling process using the Taguchi method, response surface method and genetic algorithm. *Powder Technology*, Vol. 173, 153–162.

Jain, V. (2009). Magnetic field assisted abrasive based micro-/nano-finishing. *Journal of Materials Processing Technology*, Vol. 209, 6022–6038.

Jajarmi, P. & Valipour, S. (2009). Prediction of the grain size of Cd–Mn–S nanocrystalline structures. *Computational Materials Science*, Vol. 47, 384–387.

Jiang, Z.; Gyurova, L.A.; Schlarb, A.K.; Friedrich, K. & Zhang, Z. (2008). Study on friction and wear behavior of polyphenylene sulfide composites reinforced by short carbon fibers and sub-micro TiO_2 particles. *Composites Science and Technology*, Vol. 68, 734–742.

Joachim, C., Plevert, L. (2009). *Nanoscience, the invisible revolution*. Word Scientific.

Jr., R. F. (1999). *Nanomedicine, Volume I: Basic Capabilities*. Landes Bioscience, USA.

Kalogirou, S. (2001). Artificial neural networks in renewable energy systems applications: a review. *Renewable and Sustainable Energy Revi*, Vol. 5, 373–401.

Kassaee, M.Z.; Ghavami, M.; Cheshmehkani, A.; Majdi, M. & Motamedi, E. (2009). Nano Iron Oxide with the Neural-Network Morphology. *Journal of the Iranian Chemical Society*, Vol. 6, 812-815.

Khanmohammadi, M.; Garmarudi, A.B.; Khoddami, N.; Shabani, K. & Khanlari, M. (2010). A novel technique based on diffuse reflectance near-infrared spectrometry and back-propagation artificial neural network for estimation of particle size in TiO_2 nano particle samples. *Microchemical Journal*, Vol. 95, 337–340.

Kucuk, I. & Derebasi, N. (2006). Prediction of power losses in transformer cores using feed forward neural network and genetic algorithm. *Measurement*, Vol. 39, 605–611.

Kucuk, I.; Haciismailoglu, M.C. & Derebasi, N. (2009). Dynamic hysteresis modelling for nano-crystalline cores. *Expert Systems with Applications*, Vol. 36, 3188-3190.

Lee, D.S.; Jung, H.Y.; Lim, J.W.; Lee, M.; Ban, S.W.; Huh, J.S. & Lee, D.D. (2000). Explosive gas recognition system using thick film sensor array and neural network. *Sensors and Actuators B*, Vol. 71, 90-98.

Lee, D.S.; Jung, J.K.; Lim, J.W.; Huh, J.S. & Lee, D.D. (2001). Recognition of volatile organic compounds Using SnO_2 Sensor Array and Pattern Recognition Analysis. *Sensors and Actuators B*, Vol. 77, 228-236.

Lee, D.S.; Kim, Y.T.; Huh, J.S. & Lee, D.D. (2002). Fabrication and characteristics of SnO_2 gas sensor array for volatile organic compounds recognition. *Thin Solid Films*, 416, 271-278.

Lee, J.M.; Ko, D.C.; Lee, K.S. & Kim, B.M. (2007). Identification of the bulk behavior of coatings by nano-indentation test and FE-analysis and its application to forming analysis of the coated steel sheet. *Journal of Materials Processing Technology*, Vol. 187-188, 309-313.

Li, M.; Mehrotra, K.G.; Mohan, C.K. & Ranka, S. (1990). Sunspot numbers forecasting using neural networks. *Proceeding of the IEEE Symposium on Intelligent Control*, pp. 524-529). IEEE.

Liau, L.C.K. & Dai, W.W. (2008). Process optimization of preparing spherical titania colloids with uniform distribution using artificial neural networks. *Colloids and Surfaces A: Physicochemical and Engineering Aspects*, Vol. 320, 68-73.

Lyshevski, S. (2001). *Nano- and Micro Electromechanical Systems - Fundamentals of Nano- and Microengineering*. CRC Press, USA.

Ma, J.; Zhu, S.G.; Wu, C.X. & Zhang, M.L. (2009). Application of back-propagation neural network technique to high-energy planetary ball milling process for synthesizing nanocomposite WC–MgO powders. *Materials and Design*, Vol. 30, 2867–2874.

Madadlou, A.; Emam-Djomeh, Z.; Mousavi, M.E.; Ehsani, M.; Javanmard, M. & Sheehan, D. (2009). Response surface optimization of an artificial neural network for predicting the size of re-assembled casein micelles. *Computers and Electronics in Agriculture* , Vol. 68, 216-221.

Manisha, P.J.; Rastogi, A.K. & Mohan, B.K. (2008). Critical Review of Applications of Artificial Neural Networks in Groundwater Hydrology. *The 12th International Conference of International Association for Computer Methods and Advances in Geomechanics (IACMAG)*. pp. 2463-2474, Goa, India, IACMAG.

Mehrotra, K.; Mohan, C.K. & Ranka, S. (1997). *Elements of Artificial Neural Networks Complex Adaptive Systems*. MIT Press, USA.

Miller, J.C.; Serrato, R.M.; Represas-Cardenas, J.M. & Kundahl, G.A. (2005). *The Handbook of Nanotechnology - Business, Policy, and Intellectual Property Law*. John Wiley & Sons, New Jersey.

Nabok, A. (2005). *Organic and Inorganic Nanostructures*. ARTECH HOUSE.

NASA. Retrieved from http://www.ipt.arc.nasa. gov/nanotechnology.html.

National Nanotechnology Initiative. (2004). What is Nanotechnology? (2004). Retrieved from: http://www.nano.gov/html/facts/whatIsNano.html

Niemeyer, C.M. & Mirkin, C.A. (2004). *Nanobiotechnology - Concepts, Applications and Perspectives*. Wiley-VCH, Weinheim - Germany.

Nugent, M.A.; Porter, R. & Kenyon, G.T. (2008). Reliable computing with unreliable components: Using separable environments to stabilize long-term information storage. *Physica D*, Vol. 237, 1196–1206.

Olyaee, S.; Ebrahimpour, R.; Hamedi, S. (2010). Modeling and Compensation of Periodic Nonlinearity in Two-mode Interferometer Using Neural Networks. *IETE Journal of Research*, Vol. 56, 102-110.

Oxford Online Dictionary. (2010). Retrieved from http://oxforddictionaries.com/.

Parthiban, T.; Ravi, R. & Kalaiselvi, N. (2007). Exploration of artificial neural network (ANN) to predict the electrochemical characteristics of lithium-ion cells. *Electrochimica Acta*, Vol. 53, 1877–1882.

Poole Jr., C.P. & Owens, F.J. (2003). *Introduction to Nanotehcnology*. John Wiley & Sons, New Jersey.

Qing-li, R.E.N. & Quan-xi, C.A.O. (2006). Predictive model based on artificial neural net for purity of perovskite-type $SrTiO_3$ nanocrystalline. *Transaction of Nonferrous Metals Society of China*, Vol. 16, 865-868.

Rashidi, A.M.; Eivani, A.R. & Amadeh, A. (2009). Application of artificial neural networks to predict the grain size of nano-crystalline nickel coatings. *Computational Materials Science* , Vol. 45, 499–504.

Sakkas, V.A.; Azharul Islam, M.; Stalikas, C. & Albanis, T.A. (2010). Photocatalytic degradation using design of experiments: A review and example of the Congo red degradation. *Journal of Hazardous Materials* ,Vol. 175, 33-44.

Santra, A.K.; Chakraborty, N. & Sen, S. (2009). Prediction of heat transfer due to presence of copper–water nanofluid using resilient-propagation neural network. *International Journal of Thermal Sciences*, Vol. 48, 1311–1318.

Sarkar, K.; Ghalia, M.B.; Wu, Z. & Bose, S.C. (2009). A neural network model for the numerical prediction of the diameter of electro-spun polyethylene oxide nanofibers. *Journal of Materials Processing Technology*, Vol. 209, 3156-3165.

Shirvany, Y.; Hayati, M. & Moradian, R. (2008). Numerical solution of the nonlinear Schrodinger equation by feedforward neural networks. *Communications in Nonlinear Science and Numerical Simulation*, Vol. 13, 2132–2145.

Shokuhfar, A.; Samani, M.N.; Naserifar, N.; Heidary, P. & Naderi, G. (2009). Prediction of physical properties of Al_2TiO_5-based ceramics containing micro and nano size oxide additives by using artificial neural network. *Materialwissenschaft und Werkstofftechnik* , Vol. 40, 169-177.

Shoseyov, O. & Levy, I. (2008). *Nanobiotechnology - BioInspired Devices and Materials of the Future*. Humana Press, New Jersey.

Smalley, R. (1999). *Nanotechnology: The State of Nano-Science and Its Projects for the next Decade*. US Congress Hearings.

Turel, O.; Lee, J.H.; Ma, X.; Likharev, K.K. (2005). Architectures for nanoelectronic implementation of artificial neural networks: new results. *Neurocomputing*, Vol. 64, 271-283.

Weigend, A.S.; Huberman, B.A. & Rumelhart, D.E. (1990). Predicting the future: A connectionist approach. *International Journal of Neural Systems* , Vol. 1, 193-209.

Xu, J.; Zhuo, C.; Han, D.; Tao, J.; Liu, L. & Jiang, S. (2009). Erosion–corrosion behavior of nano-particle-reinforced Ni matrix composite alloying layer by duplex surface treatment in aqueous slurry environment. *Corrosion Science*, Vol. 51, 1055–1068.

Yildiz, N.; San, S.E.; Okutan, M. & Kaya, H. (2010). A novel method to produce nonlinear empirical physical formulas for experimental nonlinear electro-optical responses of doped nematic liquid crystals: Feedforward neural network approach. *Physica B*, Vol. 405, 2049–2056.

Zhang, Q.; Xie, C.; Zhang, S.; Wang, A.; Zhua, B.; Wang, L. & Yang Z. (2005). Identification and pattern recognition analysis of Chinese liquors by doped nano ZnO gas sensor array. *Sensors and Actuators B*, Vol. 110, 370–376.

Zhang, Q.; Zhang, S.; Xie, C.; Fan, C.; Bai, Z. (2008). 'Sensory analysis' of Chinese vinegars using an electronic nose. *Sensors and Actuators B*, Vol. 128, 586–593.

Zhang, S.L.; Zhang, Z.X.; Xin, Z.X.; Pal, K. & Kim, J.K. (2010). Prediction of mechanical properties of polypro pylene/waste ground rubber tire powder treated by bitumen composites via uniform design and artificial neural networks. *Materials & Design*, Vol. 31, 1900-1905.

23

Application of Artificial Neural Networks in Optical Properties of Nanosemiconductors

M. Farzalipour Tabriz[1], P. Salehpour[2] and A. Esmaielzadeh Kandjani[1]

University of Tabriz

[1]Faculty of Mechanical Engineering,

[2]Faculty of Electrical Engineering and Computer,

Iran

1. Introduction

1.1 Nanoscience

Nanoscience is an interdisciplinary field which deals with the unconventional phenomena observed in materials with at least one characteristic dimension in the range of 1-100nm. Nanoscale materials exhibit some novel and/or improved properties over either atoms/molecules or bulk state which is resulted from limited size of their constituent components. There are two main issues discussed in nanomaterials. One of them is high surface to volume ratio for nanomaterials over bulk. In nanomaterials, higher percentage of atoms is located on the surface which leads to high specific surface area, as shown in figure 1.

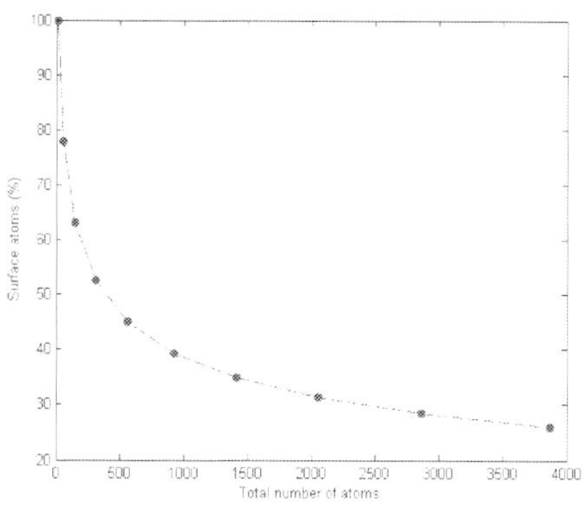

Fig. 1. Variations of the percentage of surface atoms by increasing the total number of atoms in close packed icosahedron clusters (adapted from geometrical model data in (Allpress & Sanders, 1970))

Atoms at the surface have fewer direct neighbors than atoms in the bulk. Therefore, nanomaterials have a large fraction of their atoms at surface with a low average coordination number (which is the number of nearest neighbors), high surface energy and diffusion rates (Jiang et al., 2004). Surface properties are of particular interest in this subject because of their importance in chemistry (Burda et al., 2005) and influence on electronic and optical properties (Puzder et al., 2002). Solid-gas or solid-liquid chemical reactions can be mostly confined to the surface and/or subsurface regions of the solid. The interior atoms in particles are more highly coordinated, form more bonds and therefore are more stable than those at the surface. For this reason, the surface (especially edge and corner) atoms normally exhibit the highest affinity to form bonds with other molecules. This fact is of utmost importance for chemical activity (Burda et al., 2005). Thus, particle size distribution and shape play important role in determining properties of nanomaterials. Another issue is quantum confinement effect which is change of electronic and optical properties of materials when their structural size is sufficiently small - typically 10 nanometers or less (Stucky & Mac Dougall, 1990).

1.2 Nanosemiconductors

Nanocrystalline semiconductors and specially their electrical and optical properties have been studied extensively in recent years (Pal, 1999; Schmitt-Rink et al., 1987). These materials behave differently from bulk semiconductors. With decreasing particle size the band structure of the semiconductor changes; the band gap increases and the edges of bands split into discrete energy levels. Specifically, the phenomenon results from electrons and holes being squeezed into a dimension that approaches a critical quantum measurement, called the exciton Bohr radius. But researchers have also found band gap increase in some nanomaterials having sizes far beyond the quantum confinement regime (Chen et al., 2006). The band gaps have a major influence on the properties of the semiconductors including optical absorption, electrical conductivity and index of refraction. According to the band gap type, semiconductors are normally classified as direct and indirect.

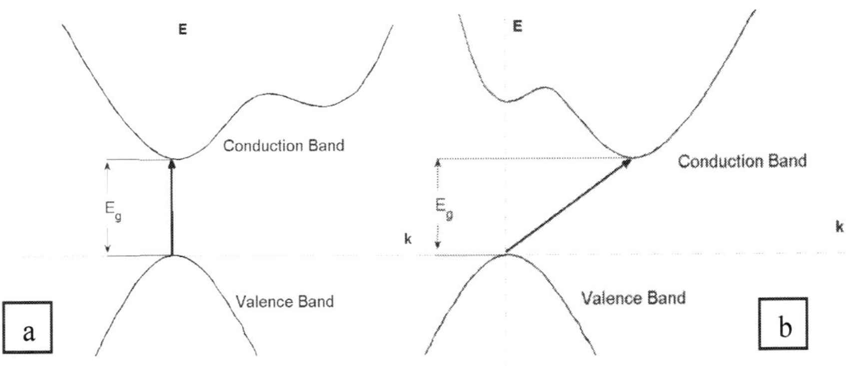

Fig. 2. a) Direct and b) Indirect transition of electrons in semiconductors.

When the carriers transfer between the conduction and valence band, in direct band gap the momentum (or k) is conserved but it's changed for indirect band gap semiconductors. The direct band gap semiconductors are found to be advantageous over indirect band gap semiconductors, as they do not require phonons to satisfy crystal momentum conservation (Sze, 1981).

In semiconductors, the main characteristic of light absorption is slightly different from metals and insulators. This is due to their band structure where the band gap between lowest point of conduction and upper point of valance bands is low enough to allow the transferring of electrons from valance band to conduction band by exciting with energy sources like light, electrical field, etc. Thus, the energy difference between conduction and valance bands (i.e. band-gap) could be detected by considering the energy absorbance of semiconductors (Sze & Ng, 2007).

When a light beam propagates into a media rather than vacuum, based on its photon energy, a portion of light is absorbed, another part is transferred and a small portion could be reflected. The physical meaning of absorbance could be defined as the logarithmic proportion of intensity of propagating light with specified wavelength passed through a sample to the intensity of the light before entering it. The absorbance which is detected via UV-Vis spectroscopy always shows this absorbance which is defined as optical density (Zhang, 2009).

On the other hand, the light absorbance can be expressed by light absorption coefficient $\alpha(h\upsilon)$, which is the relative decrease rate of propagating light intensity $I(h\upsilon)$ passing through a matter along its propagating path (x) (Gaponenko, 1998):

$$\alpha(h\nu) = \frac{1}{h\nu} \cdot \left(\frac{dI(h\nu)}{dx} \right) \tag{1}$$

Absorption coefficients of colloidal suspension (α, cm^{-1}) have been calculated using the following equation:

$$\alpha = 2303 \left(\frac{D.\rho}{C.l} \right) \tag{2}$$

where, D is the optical density of a solution which is measurable by UV-Vis absorbance spectroscopy, ρ is the density of dispersed particles, C is its concentration and l is the optical path (cm). The main interest in calculating $\alpha(h\upsilon)$ is due to its relation with semiconductor's band gap energy. This relation can be expressed as follow:

$$\alpha(h\nu) = A^*(h\nu - E_g)^n \tag{3}$$

where A^* is a constant determined by the index of refraction, and electron and hole effective masses, or

$$\alpha(h\nu) = A \frac{(h\nu - E_g)^n}{h\nu} \tag{4}$$

where E_g is semiconductor's band gap A is a coefficient of the given electronic transition probability and n equals to 0.5 (for direct band gap semiconductors) and 2 (for indirect band gap semiconductors) in allowed direct and indirect transitions (Zhang, 2009).

When a photon with sufficient energy is absorbed with a semiconductor, an electron can be excited from valance band and move to conduction band and subsequently, an electron-hole pair is generated in the semiconductor. In this sense an optical excitation is a two-particle transition, an electron and a hole. Existing two different type particles (i.e. an electron and a hole) makes a Columbus interaction between the electron and hole and thus it is act as a hydrogen atom. This electron-hole is namely known as exciton. Excitons are potentially mobile and, due to producing a positive hole by exciting a negative electron, are neutral charged (Klingshirn, 2005).

Excitons are divided into two general categories, Mott-Wannier excitons and Frenkel excitons. Mott-Wannier excitons have weak electron-hole interactions caused by a small Coulomb attraction due to relatively far distance between constituents. Corresponding binding energies are on the order of 10meV. By contrast, in Frenkel excitons the carriers are close and have strong Coulomb interactions. Corresponding binding energies are on the order of 100meV. Frenkel excitons are commonly seen in organic semiconductors while in nonorganic semiconductors Mott-Wannier excitons are the main detectable excitons (Klingshirn, 2005).

Excitons can be detected in the absorption spectrum of semiconductors as extrema points in absorption or transmission spectra. They generally appear just below the band edge of the semiconductor. This is because the energy of the exciton is lower than the band edge transition by its binding energy.

Although most oxides are good insulators but some of them such as ZnO and TiO_2 are well-known semiconductors. Oxide semiconductors are very interesting materials because they combine easily adjustable electronic properties with relatively high working temperature. Some examples of the oxide semiconductors (with their corresponding band gaps energy) are Cu_2O (2.1 eV), Bi_2O_3 (2.8 eV), TiO_2 (3.2 eV), ZnO (3.4 eV) and SnO_2 (3.7 eV), $BaTiO_3$ (3 eV), $SrTiO_3$ (3.3 eV) and $LiNbO_3$ (4 eV). These materials are employed in a variety of electronic applications, such as positive temperature coefficient thermistors (Goodman, 1963), varistors (i.e., resistors with nonlinear, but symmetric, current-voltage characteristics which are used for the protection of electronic devices and circuits) (Levinson & Philipp, 1975), capacitors of high dielectric constant (Robertson, 2004) and gas sensors (Eranna et al., 2004).

1.3 Zinc oxide

Among the studied metal oxide nanomaterials, zinc oxide is a notable case. Zinc oxide is a II-VI wide band-gap semiconductor, with a direct band gap of 3.37 eV (at room temperature in bulk state) and large exciting band energy (60 meV) (Madelung et al., 1999).

Thermodynamically stable crystalline structure of ZnO under ambient conditions is hexagonal wurtzite (space group $P6_3mc$) with a = 0.32501 nm and c = 0.52071 nm (Kisi & Elcombe, 1989). This structure can also be described as alternating stacking of O and Zn ionic planes along the c axis. Absence of inversion symmetry (center of symmetry) in this crystalline structure is the origin of its piezoelectric and pyroelectric properties (Hübner, 1973).

Wurtzite crystals are dominated by four low Miller index surfaces: the nonpolar $(10\bar{1}0)$ and $(11\bar{2}0)$ surfaces and the positively charged polar zinc terminated (0001)-Zn and the negatively charged oxygen terminated $(000\bar{1})$-O surfaces (Diebold et al., 2004). These polar surfaces results in a normal dipole moment and spontaneous polarization along the c axis as well as a divergence in surface energy which influences the adsorption of existing ions in reaction media which can affect the morphology (Wang, 2005) and properties (Jang et al., 2006) of resulted materials.

X-ray diffraction is one of the most important characterization tools in materials science. X-ray diffraction can be used for characterization of crystalline materials and the

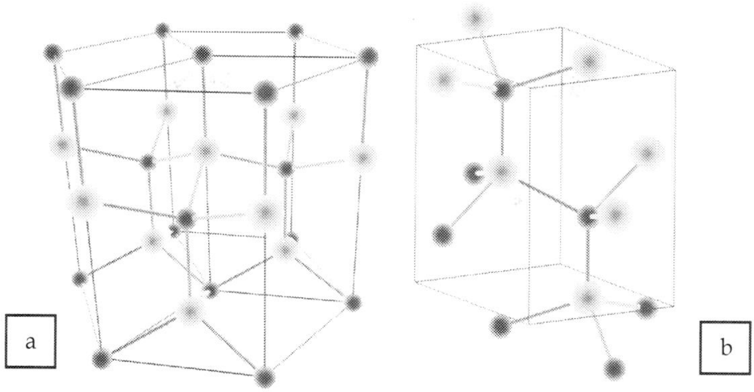

Fig. 3. Stick-and-ball model of a) alternating stacking of O and Zn ionic planes along the c axis, and b) unit cell of wurtzite structure from the results of (Xu & Ching, 1993)

determination of their structure. The diffraction of X-rays by a crystalline solid results in a pattern of sharp Bragg diffractions characteristic of the different d-spacings of a solid. A typical X-Ray diffraction pattern of wurtzite zinc oxide is shown in figure 4.

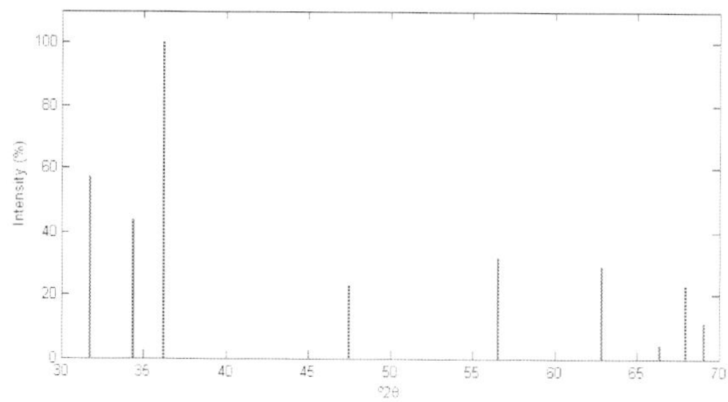

Fig. 4. X-Ray diffraction pattern of wurtzite zinc oxide (JCPDS No.036-1451)

Broadening of these reflections beyond that arising due to instrumental factors is generally attributed to crystallite size effects. The average crystallite sizes of particles can be estimated from the full width at half maximum (FWHM) of the highest X-ray diffraction peaks using the Debye–Scherrer equation (Cullity, 1978):

$$D = \frac{k\lambda}{\beta\cos\theta} \tag{5}$$

where D is the mean crystallite size; k is a grain shape dependent constant (0.89 for spherical particles); λ is the wavelength of the incident beam; θ is the Bragg diffraction peak angle; and β is the full width at half maximum.

Nanocrystalline ZnO is widely used in many applications such as blue light emitting diodes (Tsukazaki et al., 2005), photo detectors (Jun et al., 2009), gas sensors (Xu et al., 2000), photocatalysts (Hariharan, 2006), and field-effect transistors (Arnold et al., 2003). Various chemical methods have been successfully used for synthesizing nanostructured ZnO material, such as hydrothermal (Xu et al., 2004), sol-gel processing (Ristic et al. 2005; Li et al., 2005), chemical bath deposition (Wu et al., 2006) and sonochamical synthesis (Kandjani et al., 2008).

1.4 Design of experiments and chemical synthesis

Increase in the demands for chemical goods with specific desired properties has made controlling of synthesis methods as a challenging scope in production of these goods. As the variables for a synthesis could vary from less than ten to the thousands based on the synthesis route and also the fact that most of synthesis parameters influence each other's effects, controlling and obtaining the situations in which the desired properties could be achieved from synthesis has become one of the most important complexity for many researches (Box & Draper, 2007). Thus, for obtaining optimal properties of the final product a lot of experiments should be conducted in classical method. Although, the simultaneous effects of variables on final properties can't be clearly determined due to exponentially increase in experiments needed for covering all features of the synthesis by increase in the numbers of the variables (Lazic, 2004). Thus, designing a method for decreasing costs and also time schedule for understanding a process has become almost crucial for high-tech systems where costs and speed in achieving the answers has a critical role in getting results and survival in technological competition.

To design an experiment means to choose the optimal experiment design to be used simultaneously for varying all the effective parameters. By designing an experiment one gets more precise data and more complete information on a studied phenomenon with a minimal number of experiments and the lowest possible cost. Two approaches are available for design of experiments; first, classical experimental design (one factor at a time-OFAT) and second, statistically designed experiments (DOE) (Ferreira et al., 2007). The latter which allow the simultaneous study of several control variables, are faster to implement and more cost-effective than traditional uni-variable approach.

There are two different conditions occurs on most of experiments, first-order and second-order models. When a linear function can be used to describe a phenomenon, first-order model is applicable. For data which do not obey simple linear functions or when an optimization is necessary, first-order models are not a suitable so the second-order models are usually used such as Box–Behnken design (BBD), central composite (CCD), and Doehlert (DD) designs. The efficiency of these designs decreases by increase of the variables. The efficiency decrease rate in Doehlert design is much slower than other designs by increasing variables. In the other words, among the mentioned second-order models Doehlert is the most efficient design (Ferreira et al., 2004). The main characteristic of this model could be summarized as (Bezerra et al., 2008):

- Total number of needed experiments are $N = k^2 + k + 1$, where k is the variables number;
- Each variable is studied at a different number of levels;
- The intervals between its levels make a uniform distribution; displacement of the experimental matrix to another experimental region can be achieved using previous adjacent points.

For three variables, DD is represented by a geometrical cuboctahedron, and, depending on how this shape is projected on the plane, it can generate different experimental matrices. Table 1 shows the experimental matrix of DD for a two variables experiment and two different matrices for DD with three-variable. The explanation of how these matrixes obtained is beyond the scope of this chapter.

Two Variables		Three Variables (Type 1)			Three Variables (Type 2)		
X_1	X_2	X_1	X_2	X_3	X_1	X_2	X_3
0	0	0	0	0	0	0	0
1	0	0	-1	0	1	0	0
0.5	0.866	1	0	0	0.5	0.866	0
-0.5	-0.866	-1	0	0	-1	0	0
0.5	-0.866	-0.5	-0.5	0.707	-0.5	-0.866	0
−0.5	0.866	0.5	-0.5	0.707	-0.5	-0.289	-0.817
		0.5	0.5	0.707	0.5	-0.866	0
		-0.5	0.5	0.707	0.5	-0.289	-0.817
		-0.5	-0.5	-0.707	-0.5	0.866	0
		0.5	-0.5	-0.707	0	0.577	-0.817
		0.5	0.5	-0.707	-0.5	0.289	0.817
		-0.5	0.5	-0.707	0	-0.577	0.817

Table 1. Doehlert matrices for two and three variables

1.5 ANN application in nanotechnology

Statistical experimental designs have been widely used in nanoscience and technology to determine the combined effects of variables for the goal of optimizing desired properties but they need a mathematical model to estimate the results in the domain of interest. Unfortunately the underlying relations between the processing parameters and the properties of nanomaterials have not yet been fully understood so usually no analytical model is available as the relation of parameters under investigation and using empirical models often gives inaccurate results. For this purpose using artificial neural network is usually considered a more beneficial approach for modeling these poorly understood datasets of experimental results. Artificial neural networks have been reported to be successfully used for modeling of growth rate (Yo et al., 2009), grain size (Rashidi et al., 2009), particle size (Khanmohammadi et al., 2010), photocatalytic properties (Kandjani et al., 2010), magnetic properties (Mohorianu et al., 2009), oxidation kinetic (Straszko et al., 2008) and emulsion stability (Amani et al., 2010) of nanomaterials and also the effects of parameters in ball milling processing (Ma et al., 2009), sol-gel synthesis (Fan & Liu, 2009), spray reaction synthesis (Zhang et al., 2007) on resulted materials.

1.6 Hydrothermal synthesis

The term "hydrothermal" first was used by British geologist Sir Roderick Murchison in 1840s for describing the action of water at high pressures and temperature on earth crust which leads to natural formation of rocks and minerals. It's now referred to heterogeneous reactions in aqueous solution or mineralization in high temperature and pressure. Hydrothermal process permits dissolution and recrystallization of materials which are not soluble under normal conditions. Thus, hydrothermal can be used in various processes i.e. crystallization (Matthews, 1976), crystal growth (Laudise & Nielsen, 1961), synthesis (Sōmiya & Roy, 2000), decomposition (Jomaa et al., 2003), extraction (Goguel, 1985), etc. Lots of researches in this field have been dedicated to "Hydrothermal synthesis" which usually involves aqueous chemical reactions at temperatures higher than 100°C in a closed system.

This synthesis method in comparison with other conventional chemical methods has higher efficiency and controllability and its products have high purity and good crystalline quality with narrow particle size distributions.

Hydrothermal method has been successfully used for synthesizing a wide variety of nanomaterials with different morphologies which an extensive review can be found in (Byrappa & Adschiri, 2007).

There are a number of parameters which can influence the products of hydrothermal synthesis. Some of the most important variables include temperature, duration and concentration of reactants. The temperature determines the solubility of materials in water and the pressure in closed autoclaves and also influences the diffusion/reaction rate and Gibbs free energy changes for various reactions. Duration of synthesis provides needed time to reach the thermodynamically stable state of phase, size and morphology (in elevated temperature and pressure). Initial concentration of reactants determines the reaction rate and influences the nucleation and growth rate, reaction mechanism and final obtained phase.

One of the models, which can describe formation and growth mechanism of crystalline ZnO from solution, is growth unit model (Li et al., 1999).

Zhong firstly presented the growth unit model in early 1990s (Zhong et al., 1991; Zhong et al., 1994). In this model, growth units are the polyhedral complexes with $(OH)^-$ ligands, in which the cations have the same coordination number as in the oxide crystal lattice. According to this model, the growth units of ZnO crystals are $Zn(OH)_4^{2-}$ complexes which produce zinc oxide by sharing elements as following:

$$Zn\,(OH)_4^{2-} + Zn\,(OH)_4^{2-} \rightarrow Zn_2O(OH)_6^{4-} + H_2O \tag{6}$$

These reactions yield ZnO particles with OH^- ligands on their surfaces. It has been reported that, $Zn(OH)_2$ is predominantly formed at pH 6-9, while wurtzite ZnO is mainly obtained at pH 9-13 (Yamabi & Imai, 2002).

Drying of samples cause to $Zn(OH)_2$ crystals to decompose into ZnO by forced hydrolysis (Matijevic, 1985):

$$Zn\,(OH)_2 \rightarrow ZnO + H_2O \tag{7}$$

2. Materials preparation

Sodium hydroxide, NaOH and zinc acetate, $Zn(O_2CCH_3)_2.2(H_2O)$ were purchased from Merck and were both used without further purification.

Doehlert experimental design was used for investigating the effect of synthesis temperature, synthesis time and initial concentrations of precursors on the properties of synthesized nanopowders. The ratio of the $Zn(Ac)_2$ to NaOH was kept equal to 1/2. The complete experimental design and variables are listed in table 2.

First; aqueous solution of $Zn(Ac)_2$ was added dropwisely to the same amount of NaOH aqueous solution with defined concentration. The obtained solution was poured into 35ml PTFE lined autoclaves (up to 80%Vol). Then the autoclaves were kept at defined temperature. After a defined period of time, autoclaves were cooled to room temperature naturally and the resulted precipitates were filtered and washed with distilled water and ethanol for several times. Finally obtained powders were dried at 50°C for 24 hours.

Sample	Temp. [°C]	Time [hrs]	$Zn(Ac)_2$ [mol]
S1	150	12:00	0.75
S2	190	12:00	0.75
S3	170	17:12	0.75
S4	170	13:44	0.5
S5	110	12:00	0.75
S6	130	6:48	0.75
S7	130	10:18	0.5
S8	170	6:48	0.75
S9	170	10:18	0.5
S10	130	17:12	0.75
S11	150	15:30	0.5
S12	130	13:44	1
S13	150	8:30	1

Table 2. Mulivariate experimental design for present study

3. ANN modeling

In these studies, special software was developed to be able to compute accurate neural network results. This program was written in C++ and tried to be as fast as possible to create more results in shorter time. It is developed under windows operating system. In this program every training function used are implemented strictly to follow the mathematical code of mentioned functions.

The experimental data used for ANN design and training were divided into two separate sets which were used as training and testing data. Considering low number of overall available data due to high cost of experiments for providing them, both sets were used as testing and training. In each time of training one of them were chosen as the training set and the other as the testing set. Following this procedure, all data were affected the overall performance of artificial neural network. Without testing set, artificial neural network may incur overfitting problem. If this phenomena occurs we may add unusual or unnecessary curves in predicted data that will distance us from real behavior of the function and if we use less data for our training we may incur underfitting problem and produced artificial neural network produced won't be the network we need and its prediction ability will be less than what is expected in the testing set. So selecting a good percentage of data as training and testing will enable us to reach better behavior. Experiments has shown that using 75% of data as training set and the remaining parts as testing set will yield most satisfiable result in data under investigation.

The tested data were normalized before usage in artificial neural network training. As it is shown in table 3 for choosing correct normalization range, different sets of normalized input data were used which were 0 - 1, 0 - 2, and -1 - 1. Also it was tried to use unnormalized data to see whether normalization is beneficial or not. The experiments has shown that if normalization is around zero it will have slightly better performance and the data produced are better mapped to real data.

In this study two different classes of artificial neural networks were used. The first class was consisted of multi- layer feed forward backpropagation network and the other class was recurrent networks where each layer uses its own output as one of the inputs of that layer.

Normalization method	No normalization	0 - 2	0 - 1	-1 - 1
Average Mean Squared Error	2e-2	4e-4	3e-4	2e-4

Table 3. Effects of normalization on average Mean Squared Error (MSE) in training the recurrent and feed-forward ANN

As recurrent class tries to use more parameters to define the output and input relationship, the vector space defining their relation will have more dimensions. These added dimensions give the network more power than the same network structure without feedback. The base structure used for computation is three layers artificial neural network. This structure is the most used structure in scientific prediction and modeling. The first layer is input layer and the third layer is the output layer and the second layer is the hidden layer which will do the main job of modeling the relationship between input and output data. Each layer has an activation function which was selected from logarithmic sigmoid, tangent sigmoid and linear function. These functions use following formula respectively:

$$\log sig(n) = \frac{1}{1+e^{-n}} \tag{8}$$

$$\tan sig(n) = \frac{2}{1+e^{-2n}} - 1 \tag{9}$$

$$lin(n) = n \tag{10}$$

Each of the three layers will use one of the functions said. If we want to try different combinations of these function 27 different combinations are used in experiments which involves all of the functions.
It can be seen that all of the neurons in the layer will affect the output. Considering this effect we have to determine the right number of neurons in each layer. Input layer will have the number of factors and the output layer is the number of outputs. For determining the number of hidden layer neurons as it is shown in table 4 we have to try different numbers of neurons and deduce the right number by using best result achieved. Different experiments have shown the 13 neurons for feed-forward network and 9 neurons for recurrent network yield the best result.

Nodes deleted		1	2	3	4	5	6
MSE	Recurrent ANN	3e-4	4e-4	1e-3	1e-3	1e-2	2
	Feed-forward ANN	0.5e-3	1e-3	2e-3	2.1e-3	3.6e-3	4e-3

Table 4. Effects of nodes number on average MSE of training ANNs

4. Results and discussion

4.1 Materials characterization

The XRD patterns of synthesized nanoparticles are shown in figure 5. All peaks are attributed to wurtzite ZnO (JCPDS 036-1451) and no other crystalline phases were detected.

The diffractions from (101) plane sets were chosen for estimating the crystallites size of synthesized particles using equation (5).

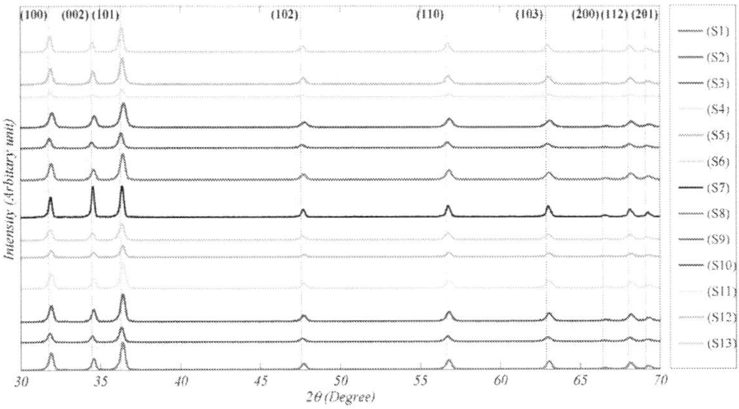

Fig. 5. XRD Patterns of synthesized ZnO nanoparticles

Figure 6 illustrates the UV-Vis spectra of the samples. All samples have an extremum point which is related to generation of exciton in the absorption just below the band edge of the semiconductor. All synthesized particles show a blue shift (Shift to lower wavelengths) in their absorption spectra in comparison with bulk ZnO. The absorption coefficient of the samples was calculated using equation (2). The density of bulk ZnO, nanoparticles concentration and optical path used in this derivation were equal to 5.606 g/cm^3, 3×10^{-4} g/cm^3 and 1 cm, respectively.

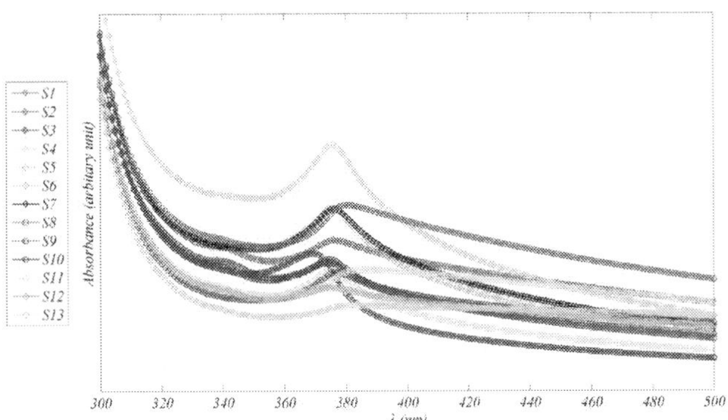

Fig. 6. Absorption spectra of synthesized samples

The exciton band energy was determined by plotting $\left(da/d(h\nu) \right)$ vs. $h\nu$, as shown in figure 7.

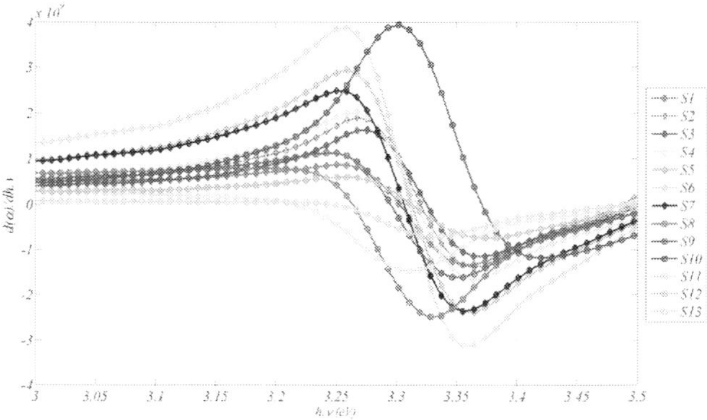

Fig. 7. Transformed absorption spectra of synthesized samples

The band gap energy of the synthesized nanoparticles were calculated using equation (4) and considering the allowed direct transition probability (n=0.5).

4.2 ANN results

4.2.1 Physical explanation using multi- layer feed forward backpropagation network

The ANN results for samples with 0.75 M initial concentration of $Zn(Ac)_2$ are shown in figure 8. The contours are shown below the 3D surfaces of the modeled properties.

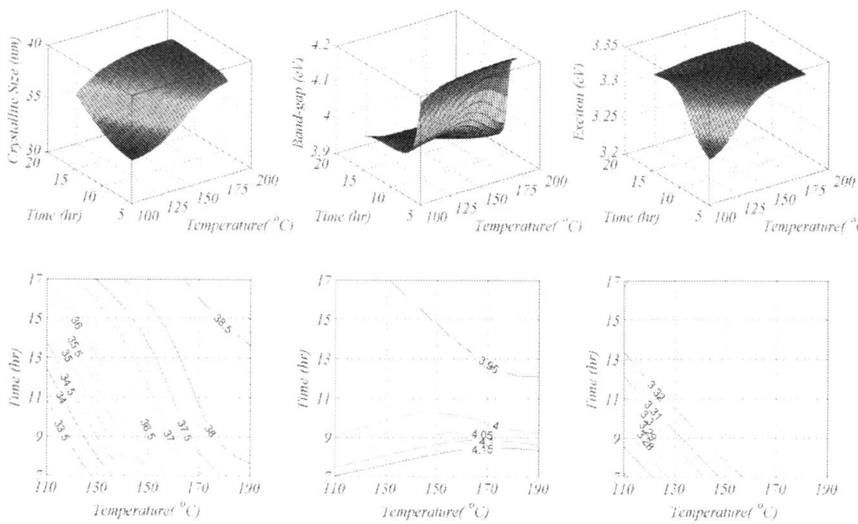

Fig. 8. ANN results for $[Zn(Ac)_2]$=0.75M; a) Crystallite size, b) Band gap energy and c) Exciton energy

As it can be seen in this figure, increasing synthesis time and temperature resulted in bigger crystallite sizes. From thermodynamics point of view, nucleation of new solid phase in aqueous medium has some energy barrier. Temperature can provide the needed energy to overcome this barrier. It also increases solubility of materials in water which can accelerate the rate of materials solution and precipitation in saturated aqueous medium.

Ostwald ripening is the phenomenon of dissolution of unstable phases and their recrystallization in a more stable form. This process involves solution of materials in water and their precipitation in more stable condition.

Plane defects as grain boundaries and particles surfaces are the main forms of high energy defects in materials which can be partially fixed by crystallites and particles growth. Materials with bigger crystallites have less grain boundary per unit volume so they are more stable. Thus, by increasing synthesis time and temperature, Ostwald ripening processes causes an increase in crystallites size.

When the first stable nuclei of ZnO are formed with sub-nano sizes, due to quantum confinement effects these particles have widest band gap (Wang & Herron, 1991). As crystallite size increases band gap will decrease. When the band gap of particles is equal to bulk material, it can be seen that the band gap energies and the exciton energy bands respectively become lower and higher.

Considering these changes, the overall changes in the properties by increase of time and temperature should be similar to what is shown in figure 8. In conclusion, by increase in time and temperature:

- Crystallite size of the obtained ZnO nanoparticles should increase.
- Band gap energy of the obtained ZnO nanoparticles should decrease.
- Exciton energy of the obtained ZnO nanoparticles should increase.

4.2.2 Comparison between recurrent ANN and feed-forward ANN

The ANN models for crystallites size, band-gap and exciton energy of obtained nanoparticles are shown in figures 9, 10 and 11, respectively. As could be seen in these figures, results of models designed by recurrent and feed-forward ANN estimate greatly differ from each other.

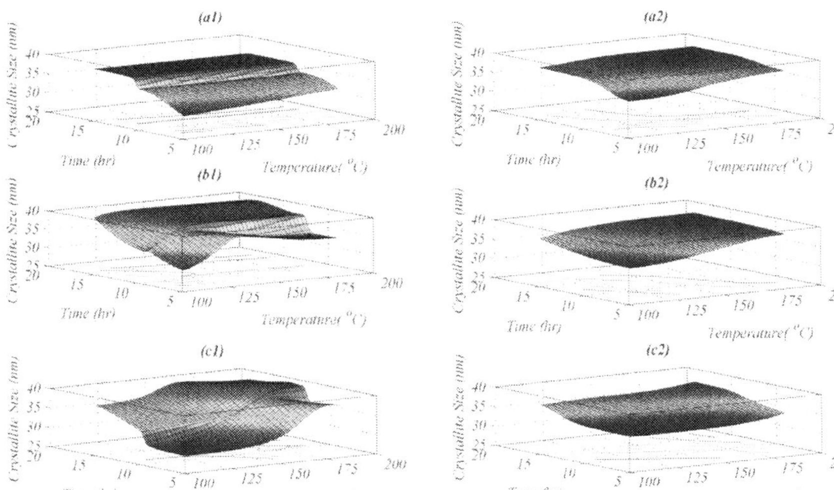

Fig. 9. Crystallite sizes for initial concentration of $Zn(Ac)_2$ equal to a) 0.5, b) 0.75 and c) 1 molar. Right column results are obtained from recurrent and left column from feed-forward ANN.

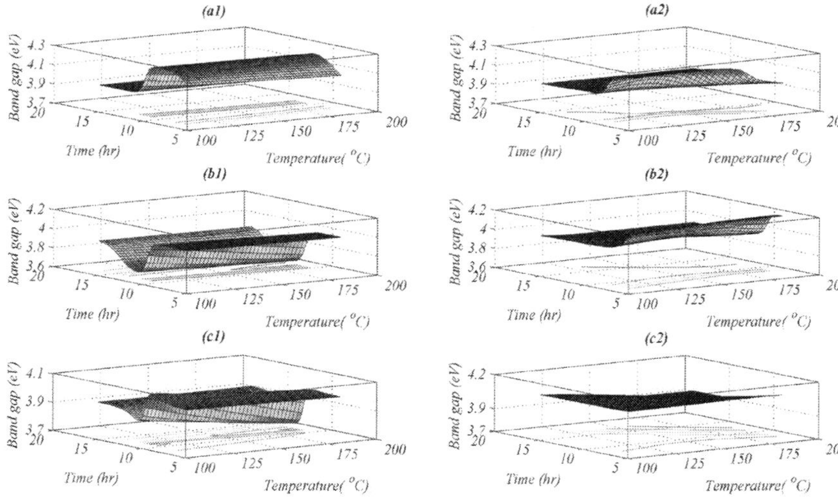

Fig. 10. Band gap energy for initial concentration of $Zn(Ac)_2$ equal to a) 0.5, b) 0.75 and c) 1 molar. Right column results are obtained from recurrent and left column from feed-forward ANN

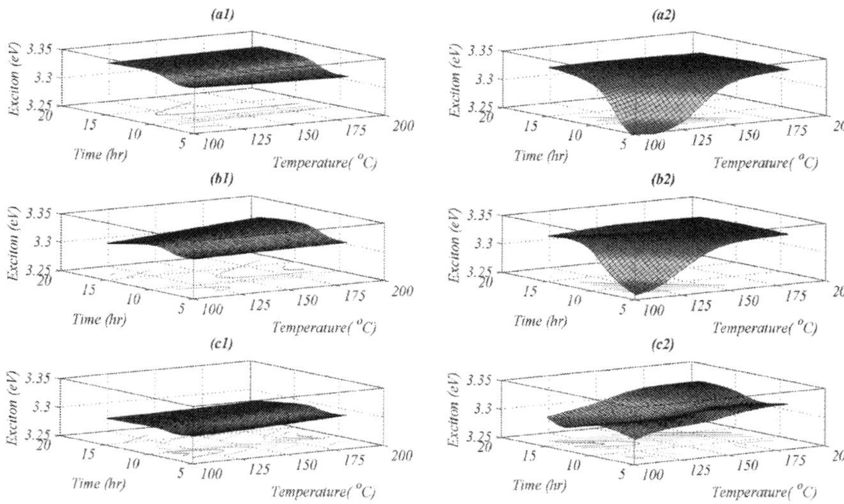

Fig. 11. Exciton energy for initial concentration of $Zn(Ac)_2$ equal to a) 0.5, b) 0.75 and c) 1 molar. Right column results are obtained from recurrent and left column from feed-forward ANN

As it can be seen in figures 9, 10 and 11, the lack of training data in borders of studied domain causes physically incorrect results around central points. This problem can be solved by getting more experimental results in border area.

As it is shown in table 5, the average MSE achieved in recurrent ANN is much better than feed-forward ANN. Although recurrent network has a better fitness, its results are not physically realistic. This is due to introducing unexplainable curvatures in the parts with insufficient experimental points. This kind of variations in curvature could not be happening from physical point of view due to explanations cited in previous sections. As we have little training data for recurrent network considering it has more parameters than feed-forward one, the recurrent network tries to cope with this problem by adding curves in places where it lacks the data needed and it will try to predict this data and it will underfitted regarding real physical models.

Modeled property	Average MSE	
	Recurrent ANN	Feed-forward ANN
Exciton energy	3e-4	3e-3
Band gap energy	2e-4	1e-3
Crystallite size	3e-4	2e-3

Table 5. Comparing the average MSE achieved in recurrent and feed-forward ANN

5. References

Allpress, J.G. & Sanders, J.V. (1970). The Structure and Stability of Small Clusters of Atoms. *Australian Journal of Physics*, Vol. 23, pp. 23-36, ISSN 0004-9506

Amani, A.; York, P.; Chrystyn, H. & Clark, B.J. (2010). Factors Affecting the Stability of Nanoemulsions—Use of Artificial Neural Networks. *Pharmaceutical Research*, Vol. 27, No. 1, pp. 37-45, ISSN 0724-8741

Arnold, M.S.; Avouris, P.; Pan, Z.W. & Wang, Z.L. (2003). Field-Effect Transistors Based on Single Semiconducting Oxide Nanobelts. *The Journal of Physical Chemistry B*, Vol. 107, pp. 659-663, ISSN 1089-5647

Bezerra, M.A.; Santelli, R.E.; Oliveira, E.P.; Villar, L.S. & Escaleira, L.A. (2008). Response Surface Methodology (RSM) as a Tool for Optimization in Analytical Chemistry, *Talanta*, Vol. 76, pp. 965–977, ISSN 0039-9140

Box, G.E.P. & Draper, N.R. (2007). *Response Surfaces, Mixtures, and Ridge Analyses*, 2nd Ed., John Wiley & Sons, Inc., ISBN 978047005357-7, New Jersey, USA

Burda, C.; Chen, X.; Narayanan, R. & El-Sayed M.A. (2005). Chemistry and Properties of Nanocrystals of Different Shapes. *Chemical Reviews*, Vol. 105, pp. 1025-1102, ISSN 0009-2665

Byrappa, K. & Adschiri, T. (2007). Hydrothermal Technology for Nanotechnology. *Progress in Crystal Growth and Characterization of Materials*, Vol. 53, pp. 117-166, ISSN 0960-8974

Chen, C.W.; Chen, K.H.; Shen, C.H.; Ganguly, A.; Chen, L.C.; Wu, J.J.; Wen, H.I. & Pong, W.F. (2006). Anomalous Blueshift in Emission Spectra of ZnO Nanorods with Sizes Beyond Quantum Confinement Regime. *Applied Physics Letters*, Vol. 88, p. 241905, ISSN 0003-6951

Cullity, B.D. (1978). *Elements of X-ray Diffraction*, 2nd Ed., Addison-Wesley, ISBN 978-0201011746, USA

Diebold, U.; Koplitz, L.V. & Dulub, O. (2004). Atomic-Scale Properties of Low-index ZnO Surfaces. *Applied Surface Science*, Vol. 237, pp. 336–342, ISSN 0169-4332

Eranna, G.; Joshi, B.C.; Runthala, D.P. & Gupta, R.P. (2004). Oxide Materials for Development of Integrated Gas Sensors—A Comprehensive Review, *Critical Reviews in Solid State and Materials Sciences*, Vol. 29, pp. 111-188, ISSN 1040-8436

Fan, H. & Liu, L. (2009). Optimizing Design of the Microstructure of Sol-gel Derived $BaTiO_3$ Ceramics by Artificial Neural Networks. *Journal of Electroceramics*, Vol. 22, pp. 291-296, ISSN 1385-3449

Ferreira, S.L.C.; dos-Santos, W.N.L.; Quintella, C.M.; Neto, B.B. & Bosque-Sendra, J.M. (2004). Doehlert Matrix: A Chemometric Tool for Analytical Chemistry—Review. *Talanta*, Vol. 63, pp. 1061–1067, ISSN 0039-9140

Ferreira, S.L.C.; Bruns, R.E.; da-Silva, E.G.P.; dos-Santos, W.N.L.; Quintella, C.M.; David, J.M.; de-Andrade, J.B.; Breitkreitz, M.C.; Jardim, I.C.S.F. & Neto, B.B. (2007). Statistical Designs and Response Surface Techniques for the Optimization of Chromatographic Systems, *Journal of Chromatography A*, Vol. 1158, pp. 2–14, ISSN 0021-9673

Gaponenko, S.V. (1998). *Optical Properties of Semiconductor Nanocrystals*, Cambridge University Press, ISBN 0521582415, Cambridge, UK

Goguel, R. (1985). Hydrothermal Extraction of Potassium, Sodium, Rubidium and Cesium from Rocks by Lithium Hydroxide and Determination at Very Low Natural Levels. *Analytica Chimica Acta*, Vol. 169, pp. 179-193, ISSN 0003-2670

Goodman, G. (1963). Electrical Conduction Anomaly in Samarium-Doped Barium Titanate. *Journal of the American Ceramic Society*, Vol. 46, pp. 48–54, ISSN 0002-7820

Hariharan, C. (2006). Photocatalytic Degradation of Organic Contaminants in Water by ZnO Nanoparticles: Revisited. *Applied Catalysis A: General*, Vol. 304, pp. 55-61, ISSN 0926-860X

Hübner, K. (1973). Piezoelectricity in Zincblende- and Wurtzite-Type Crystals. *Physica Status Solidi (b) - Basic Solid State Physics*, Vol. 57, No. 2, pp. 627–634, ISSN 0370-1972

Jang, E.S.; Won, J.H.; Hwang, S.J. & Choy, J.H. (2006). Fine Tuning of the Face Orientation of ZnO Crystals to Optimize Their Photocatalytic Activity. *Advanced Materials*, Vol. 18, pp. 3309–3312, ISSN 0935-9648

Jiang, Q.; Zhang, S.H. & Li, J.C. (2004). Grain Size-dependent Diffusion Activation Energy in Nanomaterials. *Solid State Communications*, Vol. 130, 581–584, ISSN 0038-1098

Jomaa, S.; Shanableh, A.; Khalil, W. & Trebilco, B. (2003). Hydrothermal Decomposition and Oxidation of the Organic Component of Municipal and Industrial Waste Products. *Advances in Environmental Research*, Vol. 7, pp. 647-653, ISSN 1093-0191

Jun, J.H.; Seong, H.; Cho, K.; Moon, B.M. & Kim, S. (2009). Ultraviolet Photodetectors Based on ZnO Nanoparticles. *Ceramics International*, Vol. 35, pp. 2797-2801, ISSN 0272-8842

Kandjani, A.E.; Tabriz, M.F. & Pourabbas, B. (2008). Sonochemical Synthesis of ZnO Nanoparticles: The Effect of Temperature and Sonication Power. *Materials Research Bulletin*, Vol. 43, pp. 645–654, ISSN 0025-5408

Kandjani, A.E.; Salehpoor, P.; Tabriz, M.F.; Arefian, N.A. & Vaezi, M.R. (2010). Synthesis of Nano-SnO_2 and Neural Network Simulation of its Photocatalytic Properties. *Materials Science-Poland*, Vol. 28, No. 2, pp. 377-391, ISSN 0137–1339

Khanmohammadi, M.; Garmarudi, A.B.; Khoddami, N.; Shabani, K. & Khanlari, M. (2010). A Novel Technique Based on Diffuse Reflectance Near-infrared Spectrometry and Back-propagation Artificial Neural Network for Estimation of Particle Size in TiO_2 Nano Particle Samples. *Microchemical Journal*, Vol. 95, pp. 337–340, ISSN 0026-265X

Kisi, E. H. & Elcombe, M.M. (1989). u Parameters for the Wurtzite Structure of ZnS and ZnO Using Powder Neutron Diffraction. *Acta Crystallographica Section C: Crystal Structure Communications*, Vol. 45, pp. 1867-1870, ISSN 0108-2701

Klingshirn, C. (2005), *Semiconductor Optics*, 2nd Ed., Springer Berlin Heidelberg, ISBN 3540213287, New York, USA

Ko, Y.D.; Moon, P.; Kim, C.E.; Ham, M.H.; Myoung, J.M. & Yun, I. (2009). Modeling and Optimization of the Growth Rate for ZnO Thin Films Using Neural Networks and Genetic Algorithms. *Expert Systems with Applications*, Vol. 36, pp. 4061–4066, ISSN 0957-4174

Laudise, R.A. & Nielsen, J.W. (1961). Hydrothermal Crystal Growth, In: *Solid State Physics*, Vol. 12, Seitz, F. & Turnbull, D. (Eds.), pp. 149-222, Academic Press, ISBN 978-0126077124, New York

Lazic, Z.R. (2004). *Design of Experiments in Chemical Engineering*, John Wiley & Sons, Inc., ISBN 3527311424, Weinheim, USA

Levinson, L.M. & Philipp, H.R. (1975). The Physics of Metal Oxide Varistors. *Journal of Applied Physics*, Vol. 46, pp. 1332-1341, ISSN 0021-8979

Li, W.J.; Shi, E.W.; Zhong, W.Z. & Yin, Z.W. (1999). Growth Mechanism and Growth Habit of Oxide Crystals. *Journal of Crystal Growth*, Vol. 203, pp. 186-196, ISSN 0022-0248

Li, H.; Wang, J.; Liu, H.; Zhang, H. & Li, X. (2005). Zinc Oxide Films Prepared by Sol–gel Method. *Journal of Crystal Growth*, Vol. 275, pp. e943–e946, ISSN 0022-0248

Ma, J.; Zhu, S.G.; Wu, C.X. & Zhang, M.L. (2009). Application of Back-propagation Neural Network Technique to High-energy Planetary Ball Milling Process for Synthesizing Nanocomposite WC-MgO Powders. *Materials & Design*, Vol. 30, pp. 2867-2874, ISSN 0261-3069

Madelung, O.; Rössler, U.; Schulz, M. (1999). Landolt-Börnstein - Group III Condensed Matter: Numerical Data and Functional Relationships in Science and Technology, II-VI and I-VII Compounds; Semimagnetic Compounds, Vol. 41B, Springer-Verlag, ISBN 978-3-540-64964-9, Germany

Matijevic, E. (1985). Production of Monodispersed Colloidal Particles. *Annual Review of Materials Science*, Vol. 15, pp. 483–516, ISSN 0084-6600

Matthews, A. (1976). The Crystallization of Anatase and Rutile from Amorphous Titanium Dioxide under Hydrothermal Conditions. *American Mineralogist*, Vol. 61, pp. 419-424, ISSN 0003-004X

Mohorianu, S.; Lozovan, M. & Rusu, F.-V. (2009). Simulation and Design Method in Advanced Nanomaterials Fine-Tuning for Some Perovskites Type AHE Study. *Romanian Journal of Physics*, Vol. 54, pp. 73–84, ISSN 1221-146X

Pal, A.K. (1999). Size Quantization Effects in Optical and Electrical Properties of II–VI Semiconductor Films in Nanocrystalline Form. *Bulletin of Materials Science*, Vol. 22, No. 3, pp. 341-351, ISSN 0250-4707

Puzder, A.; Williamson, A. J.; Grossman, J.C. & Galli, G. (2002). Surface Control of Optical Properties in Silicon Nanoclusters. *The Journal of Chemical Physics*, Vol. 117, pp. 6721-6729, ISSN 0021-9606

Rashidi, A.M.; Eivani, A.R. & Amadeh, A. (2009). Application of Artificial Neural Networks to Predict the Grain Size of Nano-Crystalline Nickel Coatings. *Computational Materials Science*, Vol. 45, pp. 499-504, ISSN 0927-0256

Ristic, M.; Music, S.; Ivanda, M. & Popovic, S. (2005). Sol–gel Synthesis and Characterization of Nanocrystalline ZnO Powders. *Journal of Alloys and Compounds*, Vol. 397, pp. L1–L4, ISSN 0925-8388

Robertson, J. (2004). High Dielectric Constant Oxides. *The European Physical Journal - Applied Physics*, Vol. 28, pp. 265–291, ISSN 1286-0042

Schmitt-Rink, S.; Miller, D.A.B. & Chemla, D.S. (1987). Theory of the Linear and Nonlinear Optical Properties of Semiconductor Microcrystallites. *Physical Review B*, Vol. 35, pp. 8113-8125, ISSN 1098-0121

Sōmiya, S. & Roy, R. (2000). Hydrothermal Synthesis of Fine Oxide Powders. *Bulletin of Materials Science*, Vol. 23, No. 6, pp. 453–460, ISSN 0250-4707

Straszko, J.; Biedunkiewicz, A. & Strzelczak, A. (2008). Application of Artificial Neural Networks in Oxidation Kinetic Analysis of Nanocomposites. *Polish Journal of Chemical Technology*, Vol. 10, pp. 21-28, ISSN 1509-8117

Stucky, G.D. & Mac Dougall, J.E. (1990). Quantum Confinement and Host/Guest Chemistry: Probing a New Dimension. *Science*, Vol. 247, No. 4943, pp. 669–678, ISSN 0036-8075

Sze, S.M. (1981). *Physics of Semiconductor Devices*, 2nd Ed., John Wiley and Sons, ISBN 0-471-09837-X, Canada

Sze, S. M. & Ng, K.K. (2007). *Physics of Semiconductor Devices*, 3rd Ed., John Wiley & Sons, Inc., ISBN 9780471143239, New Jersey, USA

Tsukazaki, A.; Kubota, M.; Ohtomo, A.; Onuma, T.; Ohtani, K.; Ohno, H.; Chichibu, S.F. & Kawasaki, M. (2005). Blue Light-Emitting Diode Based on ZnO. *Japanese Journal of Applied Physics*, Vol. 44, No. 21, pp. L643–L645, ISSN 0021-4922

Wang, Y. & Herron N.(1991), Nanometer-sized semiconductor clusters: materials synthesis, quantum size effects, and photophysical properties, Journal of Physical Chemistry, Vol. 95, No. 2, pp.525–532, ISSN 1089-5639.

Wang, Z.L. (2005). Self-Assembled Nanoarchitectures of Polar Nanobelts/Nanowires. *Journal of Materials Chemistry*, Vol. 15, pp. 1021–1024, ISSN 0959-9428

Wu, C.; Qiao, X.; Chen, J.; Wang, H.; Tan, F. & Li, S. (2006). A Novel Chemical Route to Prepare ZnO Nanoparticles. *Materials Letters*, Vol. 6, pp. 1828–1832, ISSN 0167-577X

Xu, Y.N. & Ching, W.Y. (1993). Electronic, Optical, and Structural Properties of Some Wurtzite Crystals. *Physical Review B*, Vol. 48, pp. 4335–4351, ISSN 1098-0121

Xu, J.; Pan, Q.; Shun, Y. & Tian, Z. (2000). Grain Size Control and Gas Sensing Properties of ZnO Gas Sensor. *Sensors and Actuators B: Chemical*, Vol. 66, pp. 277-279, ISSN 0925-4005

Xu, H.; Wang, H.; Zhang, Y.; He, W.; Zhu, M.; Wang, B. & Yan, H. (2004). Hydrothermal Synthesis of Zinc Oxide Powders with Controllable Morphology. *Ceramics International*, Vol. 30, pp. 93–97, ISSN 0272-8842

Yamabi, S. & Imai, H. (2002). Growth Conditions for Wurtzite Zinc Oxide Films in Aqueous Solutions. *Journal of materials chemistry*, Vol. 12, pp. 3773-3778, ISSN 0959-9428

Zhang, H.; An, Z.T.; Tang, Q. & Li, W.C. (2007). Optimization Design of Novel Spray Reaction Synthesis of Mesoporous c-ZrO_2 Spherical Particles. *Journal of Computer-Aided Materials Design*, Vol. 14, pp. 309–316, ISSN 0928-1045

Zhang, J.Zh. (2009). *Optical Properties and Spectroscopy of Nanomaterials*, World Scientific Publishing Co. Pte. Ltd., ISBN 9789812836649, Singapore

Zhong, W.; Hua, S. & Shi, E. (1991). The Structure and Morphology of Polar Crystal. *Journal of Synthetic Crystals*, Vol. 20, No. 1, pp. 350-351, ISSN 1000-985X

Zhong, W.; Liu, G. & Shi, E. (1994). Growth Units and Formation Mechanisms of the Crystals under Hydrothermal Conditions. *Science in China Series B: Chemistry*, Vol. 37, No. 11, pp. 1288-1291, ISSN 1674-7291

Part 7

Application of ANN in Science

24

Evolutionary Artificial Neural Networks in Neutron Spectrometry

José Manuel Ortiz-Rodríguez[1,3], Ma. del Rosario Martínez-Blanco[2] and
Héctor René Vega-Carrillo[2]
Unidades Académicas: [1]Ingeniería Eléctrica,
[2]Estudios Nucleares, Universidad Autónoma de Zacatecas.
[3]Depto. de Electrotecnia y Electrónica, Escuela Politécnica Superior, Córdoba España.
México

1. Introduction

1.1 Artificial neural networks

Artificial Neural Networks (ANN), are highly simplified models of the brain processes (Graupe, 2007; Kasabov, 1998). An ANN is a biologically inspired computational model which consists of a large number of simple processing elements called neurons, units, cells, or nodes which are interconnected and operate in parallel (Galushkin, 2007; Lakhmi & Fanelli, 2000). Each neuron is connected to other neurons by means of directed communication links, which constitute the neuronal structure, each with an associated weight (Dreyfus, 2005). The weights represent information being used by the net to solve a problem. Figure 1 shows an abbreviated notation for an individual artificial neuron, which is used in schemes of multiple neurons (Beale et al., 1992). Here the input **p**, a vector of R input elements, is represented by the solid dark vertical bar at the left. The dimensions of **p** are shown below the symbol **p** in the figure as $Rx1$. These inputs post multiply the single-row, $R - column$ matrix **W**. A constant 1 enters the neuron as an input and is multiplied by a bias b. The net input to the transfer function f is n, the sum of the bias b and the product **Wp**. This sum is passed to the transfer function f to get the neuron's output a.

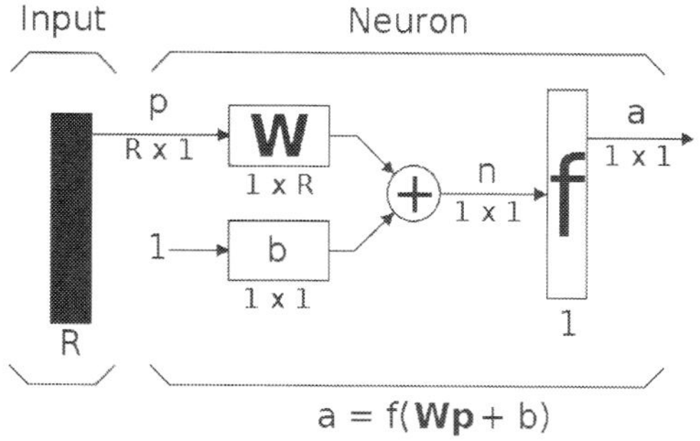

Fig. 1. Abbreviated notation for an individual artificial neuron

Although a single neuron can perform certain simple information-processing functions, a single node is insufficient for many practical problems, and networks with a large number of nodes are frequently used. A single layer of neurons having different transfer functions can be created simply by putting the neuron shown earlier in parallel (Kishan et al., 2000). All the neurons would have the same inputs, and each neuron would create the outputs, however, a layer of neurons is not constrained to have the number of its inputs equal to the number of its neurons, and it is common for the number of inputs to a layer to be different from the number of neurons. To describe networks having multiple layers, it needs to make a distinction between weight matrices that are connected to inputs and weight matrices that are connected between layers. It also needs to identify the source and destination for the weight matrices. Weight matrices connected to inputs are called *input weights* (IW), whereas weight matrices coming from layer outputs are called *layer weights* (LW). Further, superscripts are used to identify the source (second index) and the destination (first index) for the various weights and other elements of the network.
Figure 2 shows an abbreviated notation of a single layer of neurons. As can be seen from this figure, the weight matrix connected to the input vector **p** is labeled as an input weight matrix ($\mathbf{IW}^{1,1}$). The input vector elements enter the network through the weight matrix **W**. The row indices on the elements of matrix **W** indicate the destination neuron of the weight, and the column indices indicate which source is the input for that weight. Thus, the indices in $w_{1,2}$ say that the strength of the signal from the second input element to the first (and only) neuron is $w_{1,2}$. Elements of layer 1, such as its bias, net input, and output have a superscript 1 to say that they are associated with the first layer.

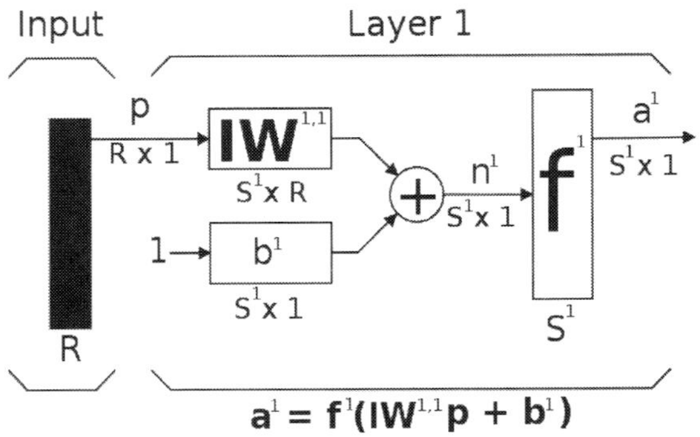

Fig. 2. Abbreviated notation of a single layer of neurons

Multiple-layer networks are quite powerful and can solve more complicated problems than can single-layer nets. A multilayer neural network consists of a combination of neurons or nodes and synaptic connections, which are capable of passing data trough multiple layers (Fausett, 1993). Each layer has a weight matrix **W**, a bias vector **b**, and an output vector **a**. The layers of a multilayer network play different roles, i.e., the x-y-z neural network structure refers to number of neurons in the input, hidden and output layers respectively. Input layers receive input signal or values from an external source, output layer transmit the result of the neural network processing and hidden layer(s) make up the internal layer(s) between input and output node layers (Haykin, 1999). To distinguish between the weight matrices, output vectors, etc., as mentioned previously, the number of the layer is appended as a superscript to the variable of interest.

Figure 3 shows a three-layer network using abbreviated notation. From this figure can be seen that the network has $\mathbf{R}^1$ inputs, $\mathbf{S}^1$ neurons in the first layer, $\mathbf{S}^2$ neurons in the second layer, etc. A constant input 1 is fed to the bias for each neuron. The outputs of each intermediate layer are the inputs to the following layer. Thus layer 2 can be analyzed as a one-layer network with $\mathbf{S}^1$ inputs, $\mathbf{S}^2$ neurons, and an $\mathbf{S}^2 x \mathbf{S}^1$ weight matrix $\mathbf{W}^2$. The input to layer 2 is $\mathbf{a}^1$; the output is $\mathbf{a}^2$. Now that all the vectors and matrices of layer 2 have been identified, it can be treated as a single-layer network on its own. This approach can be taken with any layer of the network.

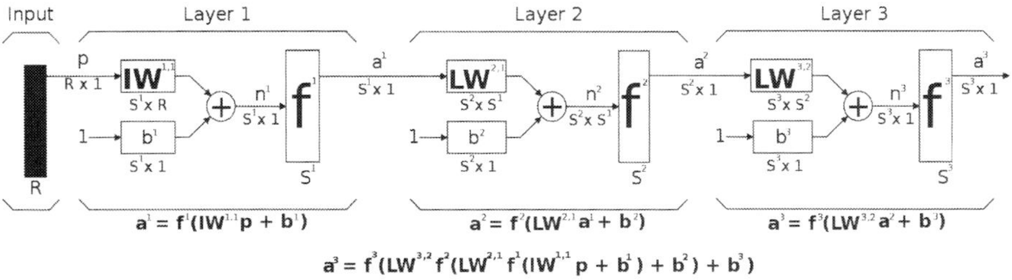

Fig. 3. Three-layer neural network using abbreviated notation

The arrangement of neurons into layers and the connection patterns within and between layers is called the *net architecture* (Jain et al., 1996; Zupan, 1994). According to the absence or presence of feedback connections in a network, two types of architectures are distinguished:

- **Feedforward architecture**. There are no connections back from the output to the input neurons; the network does not keep a memory of its previous output values and the activation states of its neurons; the perceptron-like networks are feedforward types.
- **Feedback architecture**. There are connections from output to input neurons; such a network keeps a memory of its previous states, and the next state depends not only on the input signals but on the previous states of the network; the Hopfield network is of this type.

The central idea of neural networks, where w and b are both adjustable parameters of the neuron, is that such parameters can be adjusted by means of learning or training, so that the network exhibits some desired or interesting behavior (Fausett, 1993; Graupe, 2007; Haykin, 1999; Kasabov, 1998; Kishan et al., 2000; Lakhmi & Fanelli, 2000). Learning is not an individual ability of a single neuron, it is a collective process of the whole neural network and a result of a training procedure. Training is the algorithmic procedure whereby the parameters of the neurons of the network are estimated, in order for the neural network to fulfill, as accurately as possible, the task it has been assigned.
As shows figure 4, an ANN is trained so that a set P of input vectors produces the desired, or at least a consistent, set of target output vectors T, or the network learns about internal characteristics and structures of data from a set P. The set P used for training a network is called *training set* and the elements $\mathbf{p}$ of this set P are called *training examples*. The training process is reflected in changing the connection weights of the network. The default performance function for feedforward networks is the mean square error (*mse*), which is the average squared error between the network outputs a and the target outputs T. During training, the network weights should gradually converge to values such that each input vector $\mathbf{p}$ from the data set training causes a desired output vector $\mathbf{t}$ produced by the network.

Learning occurs if after supplying a training example, a change in at least one synaptic weight takes place. Input vectors and the corresponding target vectors are used to train a network until it can approximate a function, associate input vectors with specific output vectors, or classify input vectors in an appropriate way as defined by the experimenter.

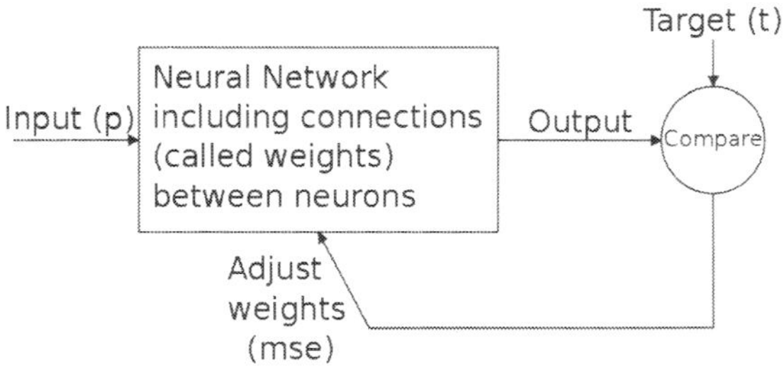

Fig. 4. Training procedure of neural networks

The learning ability of a neural network is achieved through applying a learning or training algorithm. Training algorithms are mainly classified into three groups:

- **Supervised**. This training algorithm has been the most used mainly because the training examples comprise input vectors **p** and the desired target output vectors **t**. Training is performed until the neural network "learns" to associate each input vector **p** to its corresponding and desired output vector **t**.
- **Unsupervised**. Only input vectors **p** are supplied; the neural network learns some internal features of the whole set of all the input vectors presented to it.
- **Reinforcement learning**. Sometimes called reward-penalty learning, is a combination of the above two paradigms; it is based on presenting input vector **p** to a neural network and looking at the output vector calculated by the network. If it is considered "good," then a "reward" is given to the network in the sense that the existing connection weights are increased; otherwise the network is "punished," the connection weights, being considered as "not appropriately set," decrease. Thus reinforcement learning is learning with a critic, as opposed to learning with a teacher.

Several different training algorithms for feedforward networks use the gradient of the performance function to determine how to adjust the weights to minimize performance. The gradient is determined using a technique called Back-Propagation (BP), which involves performing computations backward through the network, which refine one of the principal components of neural networks: the connection weights. The BP computation is derived using the chain rule of calculus (Taylor, 1993). BP was created by generalizing the Widrow-Hoff learning rule to multiple-layer networks and nonlinear differentiable transfer functions (Fausett, 1993; Graupe, 2007; Haykin, 1999; Kasabov, 1998; Kishan et al., 2000; Lakhmi & Fanelli, 2000).

Despite the apparent success of the BP learning algorithm, there are some aspects, which make the algorithm not guaranteed to be universally useful.

- One of the problems of BP is that it can get stuck in a local minimum. This is not too bad if the local minimum turns out to be close to the global minimum, but there is no guarantee that is the case.

- Another problem associated with BP is that the place at which one starts on the error surface (which is determined by the initial weight settings, which are often random) determines whether or not a good or the best solution is found. When a solution is found that performs well on the training set, the network might still perform badly on the overall set of input, if the training set was not representative.
- A last problem is the occurrence of interference. This occurs when a network is supposed to learn similar tasks at the same time. Apart from the fact that smaller networks are unable to learn to many associations, they simply are full after a certain amount of learned associations, there is also the danger of input patterns being so hard to separate, that the network can't find a way to do it.

ANN has been well known for its effectiveness in representing nonlinear process system (Apolloni et al., 2009). The power of neural computation comes from connecting neurons in networks, and the way these nodes are connected, determines how computations proceed, and constitutes an important early design decision by a neural network developer. However, ANN can not solve all problems in the real world. One of the biggest drawbacks in the use of neural networks nowadays is the problem of finding an appropriate structure for a given task, mainly because it is very hard to know beforehand the size and the structure of a neural network one needs to solve a given problem (Ortiz-Rodríguez et al., 2006; Packianather & Drake, 2004; Packianather et al., 2000; Peterson et al., 1995). An ideal structure is a structure that independently of the starting weights of the net, always learns the task, i.e. makes almost no error on the training set and generalizes well.

The problem with neural networks is that a number of parameter have to be set before any training can begin. However, there are no clear rules how to set these parameters. Yet these parameters determine the success of the training. Among the limitation of ANN, the followings should be given added emphasis:

1. **Network architecture**. There is a lack of fixed rule or systematic guideline for optimal ANN architecture design. Since there is no a prior knowledge about the problem complexity, the network architecture was typically set arbitrarily. The network topology was often determined by trial and error. This subjected the network to performance uncertainties since the size of network influence the network performance: too small a network cannot learn well, but too large may lead to overfitting. Thus, algorithms that can find appropriate network architecture are needed. This includes the determination of optimum number of neuron in each layer as well as number of hidden layer needed.
2. **Training algorithm**. The best training algorithm still cannot be singled out for general neural network. Although BP algorithm has been widely used, it does not guarantee the global optimal solution. The training may result in ANN model that is only accurate in the same operating zones as in the training data set but inaccurate in others. Besides, the selection of some parameters in BP training, such as learning rate and momentum, also lacks of systematic guideline.
3. **Training data**. The quality and quantity of training data is an important issue for ANN modeling. Usually, the success of ANN relies heavily on a large amount of data, but this demand more computing time for training. In order to reduce the amount of data whilst maintaining the model quality, the data used must be carefully selected to ensure that they are sufficiently rich. This demands project understanding on the process involved. Additionally, to eliminate noise and outliers, process data may require pre-processing prior to application in neural network model development.

4. **Training set**. Since it is normally impossible to present a network with all possible inputs, we only present it with part of it, the training set. This set has to be chosen in such a way that the network also gives correct output for an input that was not in the training set. If the network also responds well to inputs that were not in the training set, it is said to generalize well. Often an ANN is trained with one set of patterns (the training set) and tested with another (the test set). If the training set was not a good representation of all possible inputs, the network probably will not perform too well on inputs that are not in the training set. Generalization is quite similar to interpolation in mathematics.
5. **Process relationship**. Being black-box method for modeling, ANN is criticized for unable to explain and analysis the relationship between inputs and outputs. This may cause difficulties in interpreting results from the network.

All of these limitations have motivated researchers to generate ideas of merging or hybridizing ANN with other approaches in the search for better performance. Some of the available schemes include expert systems, statistical methods (Ortiz-Rodríguez et al., 2006; Packianather & Drake, 2004), fuzzy logic (Chennakesava, 2008), wavelet transform and as well as Neuro Evolutionary (NE) Approaches (Floreano & Mattiussi, 2008; Leardi, 2003; Melin & Castillo, 2005; Yao, 1993). In this work, the use of NE is considered.

1.2 Neuro Evolution

Neuro Evolution (NE) leverages the strengths of two biologically inspired areas of Artificial Intelligence (AI) (Coppin, 2004; Luger, 2005; Rasskin-Gutman, 2009): Artificial Neural Networks (ANN) and Evolutionary Algorithms (EA) (Gen et al., 2009; Munakata, 2008; Rothlauf, 2006; Whiteson & Stone, 2006). EA are stochastic and adaptive population-based search methods based on the principles of natural evolution. They involve a population of individuals represented in a genotypic form (chromosomes/genotypes), each of which is a potential solution to the problem. Each individual has a fitness score associated with it, and individuals with better fitness scores are better solutions. Between one generation and the next, individuals are selected from which to create offspring by applying mutation and crossover operators. Generally selection is biased towards fitter individuals, and unpromising areas of the search space are abandoned with the loss of poorer performing individuals from the population over time. EA encompass Genetic Algorithms (GA), Evolutionary Programming (EP) and Evolution Strategies (ES) (Affenzeller et al., 2009; Goldberg, 1989; Haupt & Haupt, 2004; Mitchell, 1998; Periaux & Winter, 1995).
Although EA and ANN have in common that they are general search strategies, they vary in their range. EA perform a more global search than ANN with BP. Figure 5, illustrates the convergence of the strategies. BP takes more time to reach the neighborhood of an optimal solution, but then reaches it more precisely. On the other hand, EA investigate the entire search space. Hence, they reach faster the region of optimal solutions, but have difficulties to localize the exact point. This happens, because for the final "fine-tuning" of the solution relies almost entirely on mutation. Combining both strategies seems to be the best thing to do (Floreano & Mattiussi, 2008; Leardi, 2003; Melin & Castillo, 2005; Yao, 1993), and the NE approach outperforms EA as well as ANN in finding a satisfying solution.

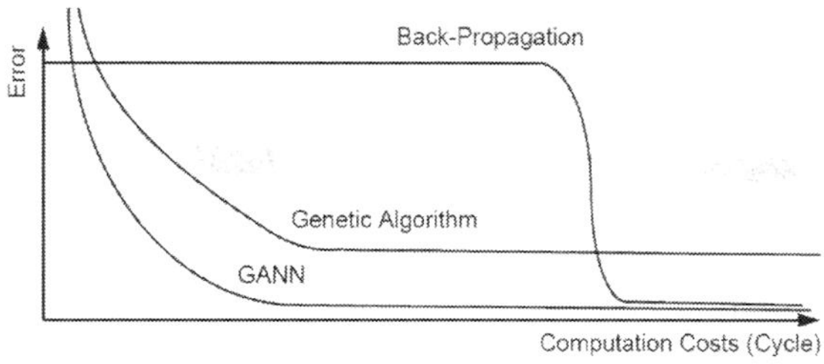

Fig. 5. Convergence of ANN and EA

Because GAs sample many points in the search space simultaneously, they are less susceptible to local minima than single solution methods (BP), and are capable of rapidly locating high payoff regions of high dimensional search spaces. Figure 6, shows a hypothetical fitness landscape to illustrate how a GA operates. The fitness of each individual in the population is represented by its position on the landscape. In a single solution method, such as BP training, if the initial search point (the yellow circle) happens to fall in the neighborhood of a local maxima, the algorithm can become trapped because it has only local information with which to make a next guess and improve the solution. Therefore, it will climb the gradient towards the local maxima. In a GA, although some individuals (the red circles) may reside near local maxima, it is less likely to get trapped because the population provides global information about the landscape. There is a better chance that some individual will be near the global maxima, and the genetic operators allow the GA to move the population in large jumps to focus the search in the most fruitful regions of the landscape.

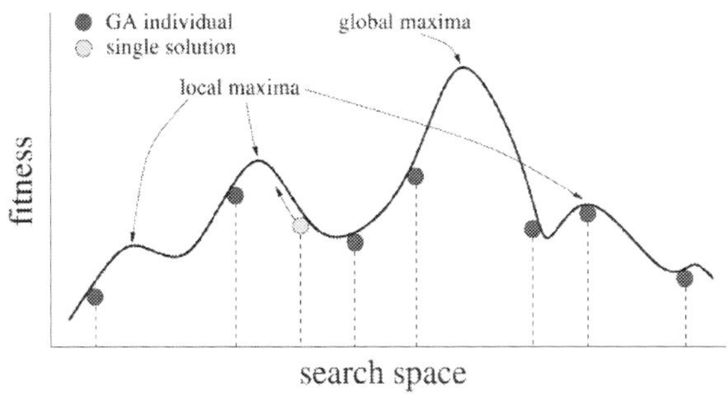

Fig. 6. Fitness landscape which illustrates how a GA operates

As is showed in figure 7, the basic idea of NE is to search the space of neural network policies directly by using a GA. From this figure can be seen that each chromosome is transformed into a neural network phenotype and evaluated on the task. The agent receives input from the environment (observation) and propagates it through its neural network to compute an output signal (action) that affects the environment. At the end of the evaluation, the network is assigned a fitness according to its performance. The networks that perform well on the task are mated to generate new networks.

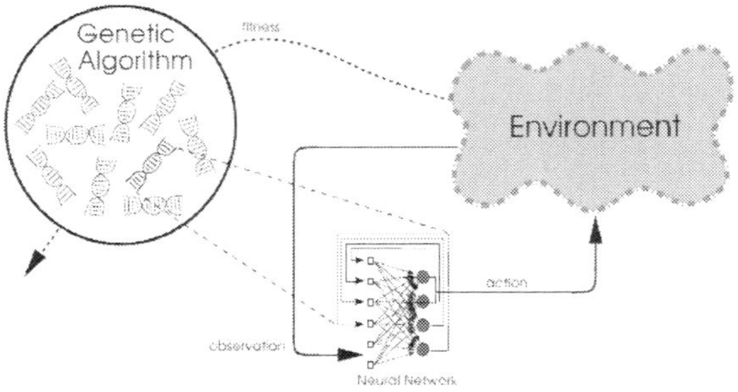

Fig. 7. Neuro Evolution approach

GA were introduced by John Holland in 1975 (Goldberg, 1989), and are a class of stochastic search procedures founded on the principles of natural selection. Unlike conventional search methods that iteratively improve a single solution, a GA maintains a set or population of candidate solutions that sample the search space at multiple points. These solutions are encoded as strings called chromosomes that represent the genotype of the solution. The chromosomes are usually composed of a fixed number of genes that can take on some set of values called alleles.

1.2.1 Genetic algorithms

GA belongs to a class of population-based stochastic search algorithm that are inspired from principles of natural evolution known as EA. Similar to other EA algorithms, GA is based on the principle of "survival of fittest", as in the natural phenomena of genetic inheritance and Darwinian strife for survival. In other words, GA operates on a population of individuals which represent potential solutions to a given problem. Mimicking the biological principles in nature, a single individual of a population usually is affected by other individuals as well as the environment. Normally, the better an individual performs under these competitive conditions the greater is the change for the individual to survive and reproduce. This in turn inherits the good parental genetic information. Hence, after several generations, the bad individual will be eliminated and better individuals are produced.
The most important terms used in the GA, analogous to the terms used to explain the evolutionary processes, are:

- **Gene**. A basic unit, which controls a property of an individual.
- **Chromosome**. A string of genes; it is used to represent an individual, or a possible solution of a problem in the solution space.
- **Population**. A collection of individuals.
- **Operation of crossover or mating**. Substrings of different individuals are taken and new strings (offsprings) are produced.
- **Mutation**. Random change of a gene in a chromosome.
- **Fitness or goodness function**. A criterion which evaluates each individual.
- **Selection**. A procedure for choosing a part of the population that will continue the process of searching for the best solution, while the other part of the population "dies".

Although the evolutionary principle of GA is similar with other EA varieties, its implementation is different. Initially, the evolutionary process of GA starts with the creation of the blind random population defined by the problem statement. This is followed by the series of activity including solutions encoding, fitness evaluation, selection, genetic operator alteration and replacement which are iteratively executed until the stopping criterion is satisfied. Figure 8 outlines a typical evolutionary structure of GA.

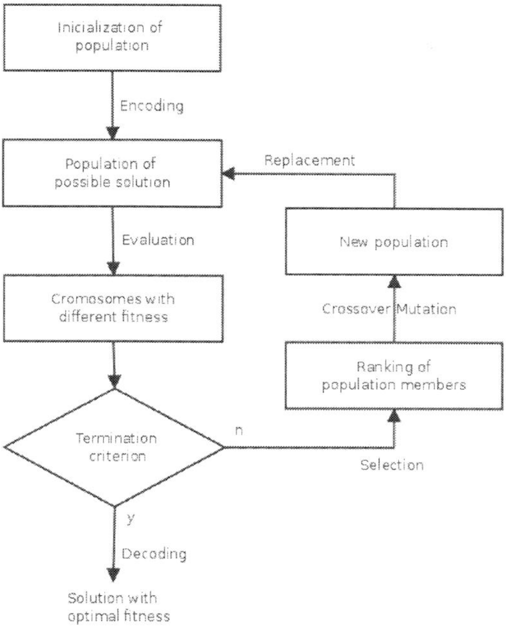

Fig. 8. Evolutionary structure of a GA

As a population-based search algorithm, information exchange among the individual is particularly important for GA. Such mechanisms are achieved by genetic operators, the more common ones are reproduction, crossover and mutation. Following a process analogous to natural evolution, each genotype is transformed into its phenotype and evaluated on a given problem to assess its fitness. Those genotypes with high fitness are then mated using crossover and mutation at low levels to produce new solutions or offspring. Figure 9 illustrates how crossover and mutation work. Crossover produces two offspring from two parents by exchanging chromosomal substrings on either side of a random crossover point, each offspring is a concatenation of contiguous gene segments from both parents. When an offspring is mutated, one of its alleles is randomly changed to a new value. By mating only the most fit individuals, the hope is that the favorable traits of both parents will be transmitted to the offspring resulting in a higher scoring individual, and eventually leading to a solution. In general, GA is applicable to a wide range of problem in learning and optimization. They can deal with complex problems which are multimodal and discontinuous. GA has two prominent features that are different from other search algorithms. First, it is population-based. Second, there is information exchange among individuals in a population.

Primarily, GA was designed to optimally solve sequential decision processes more than to perform function optimization but over the years, it has been used widely in both learning and optimization. For these reasons, GAs are well suited for searching the space of neural networks. Instead of training a network by performing gradient descent on an error surface, the GA samples the space of networks and recombines those that perform best on the task in question.

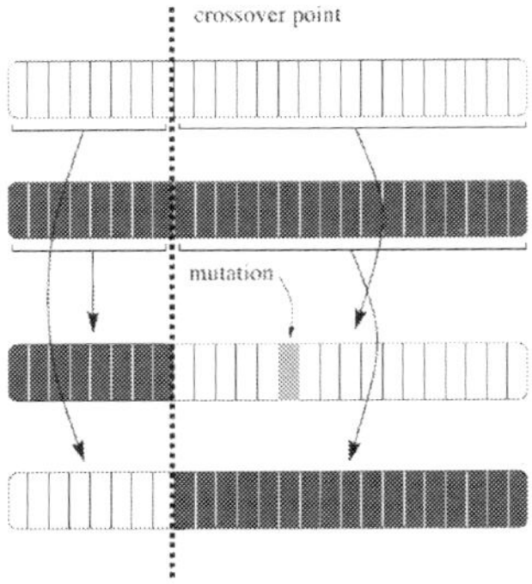

Fig. 9. Crosover and mutation genetic operators

Today neural networks can be trained to solve problems that are difficult for conventional computers or human beings, and have been trained to perform complex functions in various fields, including pattern recognition, identification, classification, speech, vision, and control systems. Recently, the use of ANN technology has been applied with success in the research area of nuclear sciences, mainly in the neutron spectrometry and dosimetry domains.

1.3 Artificial neural networks and neutron spectrometry

Nowadays, neutrons are widely used in many fields of both research and technology (Wielunski et al., 2008b). Reliable determination of neutron doses is still an issue in the field of radiation protection (Lacoste et al., 2007). In recent years, the characterization of ionizing radiation fields in workplaces is one of the challenging activities over the world (Mazrou et al., 2008). The workers subject to these radiations especially those who are submitted to neutron risk have to be well monitored and protected according to relevant national regulations which are more and more restrictive. As a result, there is an increasing demand in the field of radiation protection to quantify these various neutron fields and to determine the radiation doses involved (Mazrou et al., 2008). The dosimetry of neutron radiation is one of the most complicated tasks in radiation protection (Wielunski et al., 2008a), mainly because is a complex technique (Bedogni et al., 2007), and highly neutron energy dependent, and a precise knowledge on neutron spectrometry is highly essential for all dosimetry-related studies as well as many nuclear physics experiments. In consequence, it becomes necessary to develop additional measuring techniques to enhance the actual workers monitoring systems.

The term radiation spectrometry can be used to describe measurements of the intensity of a radiation field with respect to energy, wavelength, momentum, mass, angle of incidence or any other related quantity (Thomas, 2004; Vega-Carrillo et al., 2009a; 2010). The distribution of the intensity with one of these parameters is commonly referred to as the spectrum, i.e., the measurement of neutron energy spectra is the variation of the intensity of these radiations with energy (Vega-Carrillo et al., 2009b).

One of the suitable approaches to improve the knowledge on neutron radiation fields to which individuals are exposed during their work, is based on spectrometric measurements (Brooks & Klein, 2002; McDonald et al., 2002; Thomas, 2004). The measured yield of a neutron source is the convolution of the neutron energy distribution with the response function of the spectrometer summed over the interaction energy range. As is shown in equation 1, which represents the discrete form of the Fredholm's integral equation of the first kind (Vega-Carrillo et al., 2006).

$$C_j = \sum_{i=1}^{N} R_{i,j}\Phi_i - -- > j = 1, 2, ..., m \tag{1}$$

where C_j is j^{th} detector's count rate; $R_{i,j}$ is the jth detector's response to neutrons at the ith energy interval; Φ_i is the neutron fluence within the ith energy interval and m is the number of spheres utilized. Equation 1 is an ill-conditioned problem wich has an infinite amount of solutions

Although there is a wide range of different devices used for neutron spectrometry, the majority of the instruments can be grouped together into a small number of broad categories, each one based on a common underlying technique (Matzke, 2003; McDonald et al., 2002; Thomas, 2004). Among the many available neutron spectrometry techniques, the multisphere or Bonner sphere spectrometer (BSS) system is the most used for radiation protection purposes (El Messaoudi et al., 2004; Lacoste et al., 2004; Vylet, 2002), due to advantageous characteristics as wide energy range (from thermal to GeV neutrons), large variety of active or passive thermal sensors allowing adapting the sensitivity to the specific workplace, good photon discrimination and simple signal management. Disadvantages are the poor energy resolution, which does not allow appreciating fine structures as narrow peaks, the weight, and the need to sequentially irradiate the spheres, requiring, in general, long exposure periods (Bedogni et al., 2007).

The BSS consists of a thermal neutron sensor such as $^6LiI(Eu)$, which is placed at the centre of a number of moderating spheres of different diameter. With the BSS, neutron spectrum can be obtained, however, the derivation of the spectral information is not simple. The unknown neutron spectrum is not given directly as a result of the measurement. The BSS response matrix, the count rates and the neutron spectrum are related trough the equation 1. The most delicate part in the neutron spectrometry based on the BSS, is the unfolding process. The unfolding spectra of the neutrons measured consist on establishing the rate of energy distribution of fluency $\phi(E)$, known as the response matrix, $R_{i,j}$, and the group of carried out measures, C_j. Because the number of unknowns overcome to the number of equations, this is an ill-conditioned system and has an infinite number of solutions. The procedure of selecting the solution that has meaning for the problem type, is part of the unfolding process (Vega-Carrillo et al., 2005; 2006). The spectral information needs to be unfolded from the BSS system detector responses by using a suitable computational code, most of them are based in some of these methods: least square, iterative (Bedogni et al., 2007; Miller, 1993), bayesian and maximum entropy (Reginatto & Zimbal, 2008), and Monte-Carlo (Vega-Carrillo et al., 2007a). The current interest in the neutron spectrometry problem, has stimulated the development of diverse unfolding procedures which try to obtain a better energy resolution through the reconstruction of the spectrum. During the past decades have been carried out intents to develop new neutron spectra unfolding codes like BUNKIUT (Miller, 1993), FRUIT (Bedogni

et al., 2007), MAXED, UMG (Roberts, 2007), etc., to attain improved energy resolution through spectrum unfolding. However, these methods still present the serious drawback of requiring a very expert user for their operation and the necessity to provide an initial guess spectrum for the deconvolution of the spectrum. To overcome these drawbacks, alternative approaches have been studied and proposed, to make an efficient neutron dosimetry, and several unfolding procedures combined with various types of experimental methods have been reported such as Genetic Algorithms (GA) (Freeman et al., 1999; Mukherjee, 2004), and Artificial Neural Networks (ANN) (Vega-Carrillo et al., 2007b; 2005; 2006; 2009a; 2010).
Many of the previous studies in neutron spectrometry and dosimetry by using the ANN approach have found serious drawbacks in the ANN design process itself, mainly in the proper determination of the structural and learning parameters of the networks being designed (Ortiz-Rodríguez et al., 2006). These parameters are significant contributing factors to the ANN performance, however, the optimal selection of these parameters follows in practical use no rules, and their value is at most arguable, mainly because they are generally heuristically chosen by using the trial and error technique, which produces poor artificial neural networks with low generalization capacity and poor performance. For the anterior, the nuclear research community needs approaches that implement ANN models faster than what is currently available. In consequence, more research has been suggested in order to overcome these drawbacks (Bedogni et al., 2007; Vega-Carrillo et al., 2007b; 2006; 2010).
At present, one promising technique to design the structural and learning parameters of ANN is by introducing adaptation of network training using EA. EA seems to be a proper alternative to solve the ANN optimization problem and can be used to assist in the ANN design and training (Ortiz-Rodríguez et al., 2008; 2009b; 2010a). However, as a novel approach in the nuclear sciences area, the lack of information and tools for the analysis of the results obtained whit these new technologies, makes difficult the work in this research area.
The aim of the present work is focused in analyzing the intersection of ANN and GA, analyzing like it is that GA can be used to help in the design processes and training of ANN, i.e., in the optimum selection of the structural and learning parameters of ANN, improving its generalization capacity, in such a way that the neural network designed is able to unfold in an efficient way neutron spectra, starting only from the count rates obtained with a BSS system.
Because the novelty of Evolutionary Artificial Neural Networks (EANN) technology in neutron spectrometry, lack of tools for the analysis is observed. For this reason, an unfolding code based on EANN technology, devoted to the operational workplace neutron monitoring, would be of great help to the radiation protection community. With this purpose, in this work a new computer tool based on EANN technology called "Neutron Spectrometry and Dosimetry based on Evolutionary Artificial Neural Networks" (NSDEann), was developed in a customized front end user capable to unfold neutron spectra and to simultaneously calculate 13 equivalent doses, by using only as input data the count rates coming of a BBS system, in just a few seconds if compared with the time spent with the classical techniques, not being needed a priori information about the spectra being calculated.

2. EANN in neutron spectrometry

EANN technology was used for the modeling and optimization of ANNs capable to solve the neutron spectra unfolding problem, starting from the count rates coming from a BSS with a $^{6}LiI(Eu)$ thermal neutron detector, 7 polyethylene spheres of $0, 2, 3, 5, 8, 10, and, 12$ inches of diameter respectively, and the $UTA4$ response matrix expressed for 31 energy bins (Vega-Carrillo et al., 2009a). In this study, two neutron spectra were produced using a $^{239}PuBe$

neutron source (Vega-Carrillo et al., 2009b). A neutron spectrum was produced by the $^{239}PuBe$ neutron source located at 100 cm of distance, in an open space at 200 cm above floor level, and was measured using the BSS previously described. Then, the same neutron source was inserted in a cylindrical container with water, and the neutron spectrum was measured again. The count rates measured in both cases with the BSS, were utilized to unfold the neutron spectra and to calculate the dosimetric features using four EANN designed for each case, varying some GA and ANN parameters during training stage. To analyze the performance and generalization capability of the evolved networks, a new neutron spectra unfolding code denominated "Neutron Spectrometry and Dosimetry based on Evolutionary Artificial Neural Networks" (NSDEann), was used. Also, the spectra were unfolded with the BUNKIUT code and UTA4 response matrix (Vega-Carrillo et al., 2009a), and compared with that obtained with NSDEann code using a computer tool known as "Neutron Spectrometry and Dosimetry Tool Box" (NSDTB) (Ortiz-Rodríguez et al., 2009a;b; 2010b).
The general idea of combining EA and ANN is illustrated in figure 10. The EANN approach is based on a fundamental cyclic process which consists of:

1. Creating an initial population of genotypes (genetic representations of the ANN).
2. Building neural networks (phenotypes) based on the genotypes.
3. Training and testing the neural networks to determine how fit they are.
4. Comparing the fitness of the networks and keeping the best.
5. Selecting those networks in the population which are better, discarding those which aren't.
6. Refilling the population back to the defined size.
7. Pairing up the genotypes of the neural networks.
8. Mating the genotypes by exchanging genes (features) of the networks.
9. Mutating the genotypes in some random fashion; Then returning back to step (2) and continuing this process until some stopping criteria is reached or manually stops the process.

Through the process described previously, the better networks survive and their features carry forward into future generations and are combined with others to find better and better networks for the problem considered. This genetic search capability is much more effective than random searching, as the genetic process of recombining features vastly improves the speed of identifying highly fit networks.
To train the evolved networks, a data set of 187 neutron spectra, compiled by the International Atomic Energy Agency (IAEA) (IAEA, 2001) was used (Iñiguez & Vega-Carrillo, 2002; Vega-Carrillo et al., 2005; 2006). The ANN genetically evolved were designed by meas of the NeuroGenetic Optimizer (NGO) software (BiocompSystems, 2010). In the use of NGO, there are 10 working steps as follows:

1. **Initial population**. The first step is started from building new population consisted of chromosomes derived from random sampling by having total chromosomes as population size.
2. **Decode**. This step is involved with decoding heredity from chromosomes derived from population in the 1st step by transforming them in hidden neuron in the hidden layer of ANNs.

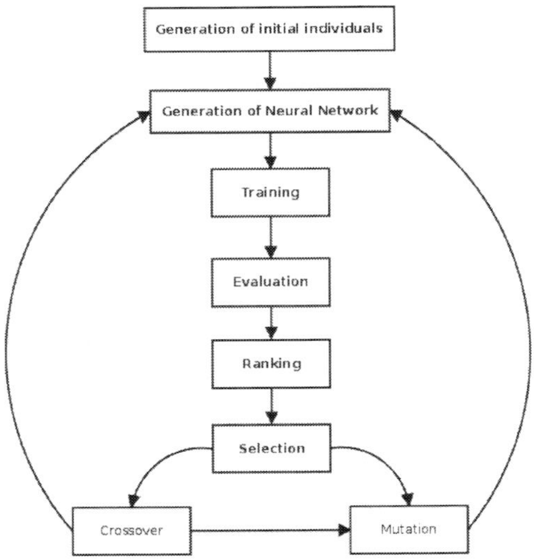

Fig. 10. General approach of Evolutionary ANN

3. **Train Back-propagation Neural Network.** In this step, network for learning would be derived from the past data by assigning numbers of hidden neuron as equal as the value from decoding. Before data could be applied in learning, data must be made into normal design. Afterwards, data must be divided into 2 set, one in training, another in testing. Learning process is the reverse learning process with variance that could be reversed back to adjust weight so that variance may be reduced.

4. **Fitness evaluation.** In this step, calculation is done to find variance of network which considered proper fitness value of heredity by using the Root-Mean-Square Error of Prediction (RMSEP) as objective function. RMSEP is the square root of the sum of the squared differences between the observed and predicted values for all observations in the test set divided by the number of such observations, to estimate the prediction error, as ishowed in the following equation:

$$RMSE = \sqrt{\frac{1}{n-1}\Sigma_{i=1}^{n}(y_i - \widehat{y}_i)^2} \tag{2}$$

where n is the number of trials, y_i is the measured values of each response and $\widehat{y}_i$ is the neural model output.

5. **Stop criteria.** This is the step to check when the design stops working by setting up conditions for numbers of result compilation. If answers in each round are still stable, it should stop working. For examples, stop at 10 rounds of compilation or receiving duplicate answers 5 times in the row. If the stop conditions are real, operation may stop at step 10. On the contrary, for unreal stop conditions, proceed further with step 6.

6. **Selection.** In this step, two chromosomes with the least fitness values are selected from population to be the breeders.

7. **Crossover.** This is the step for crossing species by exchanging genes among selected breeders in Step 6 for offspring.

8. **Mutation**. After deriving at offspring with 2 chromosomes after crossover, mutation would be done by randomly selected position of gene with the possibility of mutation. Then, after randomly selected position, value of gene would have opposite value.
9. **Replacement**. The offspring with fitness value would take place of the suitable chromosome in order to derive at new group of population before going back to 2nd step.
10. **Stop**. After the stop conditions had been verified, the operation of model would stop with only the best network design had been collected for being used for measuring effectiveness of network.

The following steps were carried out for developing four EANN models with NGO:

1. **Identify data by dividing into 2 sets**. Input layer data set, comprised for the count rates coming from polyethylene spheres of BSS and, output layer data set, comprised for neutron spectra unfolded and equivalent doses.
2. **Specifying neuron in the structure of ANNs**. Input layer has 7 neurons, corresponding to spheres of BSS, hidden layer(s) use GAs to specify neurons and, output layer has 44 neurons, first 31 are for the neutron spectra unfolded and the remaining 13 for different equivalent doses (Vega-Carrillo et al., 2010).
3. **Input data classification**. A data set with 187 neutron spectra was used. Training and testing data sets were created by dividing the whole data set, by using a random procedure, into 80% for training and 20% for testing.
4. **Neural Parameters**. In this work, ANNs with supervised learning through BP were chosen, the net architecture was optimized with the application of GAs to find suitable networks. Sigmoid function was employed as transfer function for hidden layer(s) and linear for output layer. The optimizer of the network structure, used all inputs, and searched the neural architecture.
5. **Genetic Parameters**. In this study, as is showed in table 1, in four experimental cases, two configuration parameters of GA were varied by using the trial and error technique: the number of generations run (GR) and population size (PS). However, a major difficulty encountered when using GAs is the parameter setting (Pongcharoen et al., 2007). There exist many forms and variations of GAs and the best choice is problem dependant on the proper selection of the genetic operators. A GA can show good or weak results even when applied on the same problem. More research is needed in order to overcome the drawbacks associated with the optimum selection of GA parameters.

NET	GR	PS	SEL	ROP	MAT	MUT
1	10	60	50%S	CS	TST	RET25%S
2	10	60	50%S	CS	TST	RET25%S
3	5	30	50%S	CS	TST	RET25%S
4	10	30	50%S	CS	TST	RET25%S

Table 1. GA configuration parameters

where GR are the Generations Run, PS is the Population Size, SEL is the Selection technique, 50%S is the top 50% Surviving, ROP is the Refilling of the Population Technique, CS is Cloning the Survivors technique, MAT is the Mating technique, TST is the TailSwap Technique, MUT is the Mutation technique and RET25%S is Random Exchange Technique at a rate of 25%.

6. **Training Parameters**. As can be seen from table 2, by using the trial and eror technique, in first three experiments, the minimum network training passes (MNTP) and the cutoff for network training passes (CNTP) were selected between 200-250 respectively for each network trained. In a similar way, in the last experiment, the same parameters were selected between 50-55. The Limit on Hidden Neurons (LHN) was varied as well, as is showed in table 2. In experiments one and three, each evolved network was trained five and three times respectively and then the results were averaged. In all experiments, the weight initialization was between 0-0.3, and the learning rate and momentum between 0.1-0.4 and 0.1-0.3 respectively. The performance of the EANN is highly dependant on the proper selection of these parameters, however, from the literature reviewed, there is not a methodological criteria for this selection, and more research is needed to overcome this drawback.

NET	MNTP	CNTP	LHN
1	200	250	8
2	200	250	32
3	200	250	256
4	50	55	256

Table 2. EANN training configuration parameters

where MNTP are the minimum network training passes for each network, CNTP are the cutoff for network training passes for each network, and LHN is the the Limit on Hidden Neurons in the design process of the EANN methodology.

After optimum net topologies were determined, was observed that NGO presents several inconveniences when applied in the neutron spectroscopy domain. First problem is due the way the compendium of neutron spectra of IAEA compilation was realized. These spectra are normalized to one and are used to train the different EANNs. This does not represent a problem in the training and testing stages of EANN design, however, after training was done and the neural net is used to solve real experimental problems, this becomes a drawback because the spectra unfolded and doses calculated resulting are normalized to one and this has not physical meaning. Because the anterior, in the solution of real experimental problems a procedure to un normalize the spectra unfolded was needed. Another drawback when NGO is used in the neutron spectrometry domain is that has not the capability to graph in a proper way the spectra and doses calculated. The anterior suggested the necessity to design a customized computer tool to overcome the drawbacks mentioned.

Because the novelty of EANN methodology applied in the neutron spectrometry research and the lack of tools for the analysis of the spectrometric and dosimetric results obtained with NGO, a customized computer code denominated "Neutron Spectrometry and Dosimetry based on Evolutionary Artificial Neural Networks" (NSDEann), showed in figure 11, was designed in a graphical user interface, under the LabVIEW programming environment, which is easy, intuitive, friendly and quick in their use. This code is oriented to be used by the end user in laboratory, experimental and/or research environments, and its aim is to overcome the drawbacks associated with NGO when applied to solve the neutron spectra unfolding problem.

The principle of operation of NSDEann is the following: after executing the main program, a window, as showed in figure 11, will open. To unfold the spectra by using the NSDEann code, the user should execute the following steps:

1. Select a file text with the rate counts measured with the BSS system through the "BSS counts rate" tool. Previously, the end user should be created a file with extension *.txt, with the rate counts arranged in column form. In the case of several measurements, the text file could contain several rate counts in columns tabulation separated. The tool "Select BSS from file" can be used to select one spectra from the file created just adjusting the number of column selection.
2. Store the normalized rate counts in a file text with extension *.txt by means of the button "Save normalized counts". In this step, the program calculates a normalized value of rate counts which has two purposes, normalize the BBS measurements to be used with NGO and to un normalize the spectra and doses calculated.
3. Open the optimum EANN trained with NGO and make a prediction with this configuration, using the normalized rate counts calculated in step two.
4. Store the neutron spectra unfolded and doses calculated by NGO, which are normalized to one, saving this information in a similar way than step one.
5. Open the file with the spectra and doses calculated with NGO by means of the tool "Evolved Spectra&Doses". This tool works similar to described in step one.
6. Click the button "Plot Spectra&Doses" to see the spectrometric and dosimetric information un normalized in the graph and numeric form in the middle and right areas of the main window.
7. The numerical values of the spectra and doses can be stored in a file text using the button "Save Spectra&Doses"

For each spectra, the procedure before described must be repeated.
As described previously, four EANN architectures were designed with NGO for two experimental cases: the neutron spectra of a $^{239}PuBe$ neutron source in water and on air. To compare the several spectra obtained in both experiments and to analyze the performance and generalization capability of the nets designed, the tool known as "Neutron Spectrometry and Dosimetry ToolBox" (NSDTB), was used (Ortiz-Rodríguez et al., 2009a; 2010b). NSDTB code has the capability to analyze spectrometric and dosimetric information obtained with several neutron unfolding techniques as for example: iterative procedures and the approaches based on ANN or EANN, as is the case of the present work.

3. Results

In this work, the EANN technology was analyzed and applied in the neutron spectrometry research area. The spectrometric and dosimetric features of a $^{239}PuBe$ neutron source measured under two different experimental conditions were unfolded by using the NSDEann unfolding code. The results obtained in this work reveals that the hybrid technology of EA-ANN applied in the neutron spectrometry and dosimetry problems, present some drawbacks in the optimum selection of the GA and ANN training parameters. When these parameters were varied before GA execution, in the four experimental cases considered, different network architectures were obtained, as is showed in table 3. As can be seen from this table, a total of 1650 evolutionary network architectures were designed, trained and tested by means of EA, under four different experimental conditions. The accuracy on training and testing, is similar in the four cases considered, being around 97%.
where NET-TOP is the optimum evolved net topology, ATrS is the Accuracy on Training Set, MATtS is the Maximum Accuracy on Test Set, NT are the total number of Networks Trained,

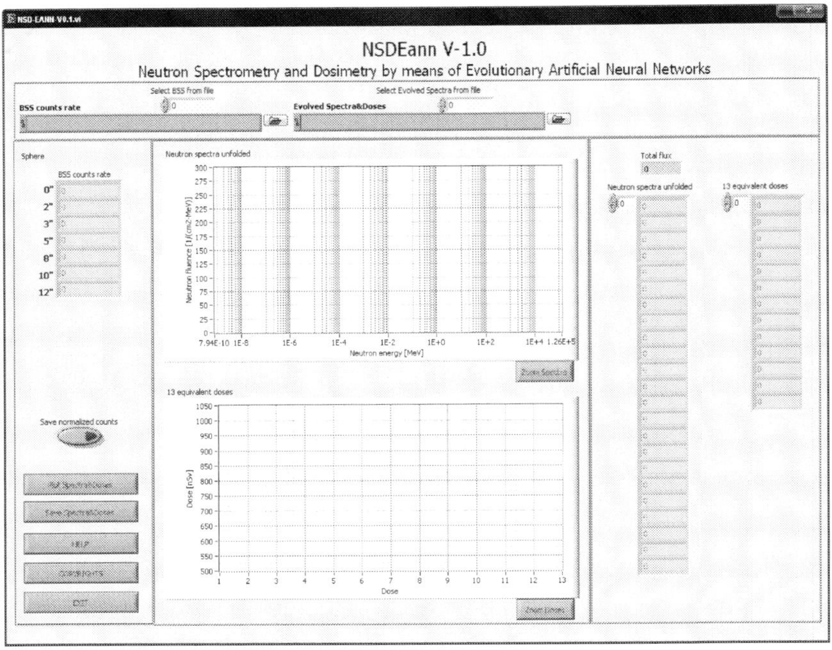

Fig. 11. Main window of NSDEann unfolding code

NET	NET-TOP	ATrS	MATtS	NT	TIME	FOG
1	7-8-44	98.67%	91.89 %	600	06:04:49	9
2	7-19(1)-44	98.00%	94.59%	600	01:54:30	10
3	7-183(14)-123(39)44	100.00%	97.30%	150	04:42:35	4
4	7-66-44	97.33%	94.59%	300	01:16:34	10

Table 3. Evolved network topologies and performance

TIME is the time used by GA to train all net topologies and FOG is the best network Found on Generation.

The accuracy on training and testing reveals that the four network architectures learned well the training and testing data sets, which lets infer that the performance and generalization capability of all networks architectures is good, which was confirmed by using the NSDTB code, as is showed in figure 12. In this figure can be seen the four neutron spectra unfolded with the four network architectures showed in table 3, for a $^{239}PuBe$ neutron source measured at 1m in water. Here, spectra-1 and doses-1 corresponds to the spectra unfolded with the architecture of the NET 1, spectra-2 and doses-2 corresponds to the spectra unfolded with the architecture of the NET 2, etc. From this figure can be seen that although the four EANN with different architectures were used to unfold the neutron spectra of the source before mentioned, by using in all cases the same rate counts measured with the BSS system, the results are similar. By comparing the spectra calculated with the codes NSDEann and BUNKIUT, as is showed in figure 13, can be seen that are alike. The spectra have a peak in the thermal region and between 0.1 and 10 MeV (Vega-Carrillo et al., 2010).

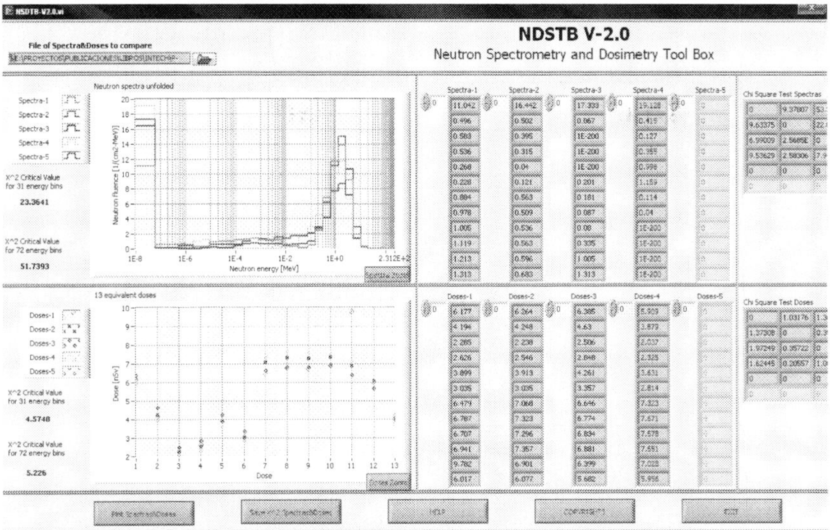

Fig. 12. Neutron spectra unfolded with the NSDEann code for a $^{239}PuBe$ at $1m$ in water

The NSDTB code realizes a chi square statistical test among the spectra analyzed, as is showed at right side of the main window. As can be seen from table 4, Spectra-1 and Doses-1 are statistically compared whit the rest of spectra and doses of row 1, Spectra-2 and Doses-2 are compared with spectra and doses of row 2, etc. This comparison reveals that there are statistical differences between most of the spectra unfolded with the different network topologies, mainly spectra 3 and 4. In the case of the equivalent doses, the test reveals that statistically there are not differences between doses calculated with the four network architectures.

Chi square test compares two groups of data, as in the case of the energy bins that conform the neutron spectra calculated with the several EANN architectures, however, when the energy bins presents high variations in some of the values of the data being compared, as can be appreciated in figures 12 to 15, this test tends to fail. From the analysis realized in the present work, has been observed that the chi square test presents some drawbacks, and a more accurate statistical test is needed.

NET	S1	S2	S3	S4	D1	D2	D3	D4
1	0	9.378	53.355	58.761	0	1.032	1.366	1.346
2	9.634	0	22.043	45.063	1.373	0	0.359	0.145
3	7E+199	3E+199	0	1E+200	1.972	0.357	0	0.945
4	1E+201	3E+200	8E+200	0	1.624	0.206	1.007	0

Table 4. Chi square test of NSDTB code for a $^{239}PuBe$ at $1m$ in water

Figure 13 shows a comparison of the four neutron spectra obtained with the NSDEann code with respect to the neutron spectra calculated using the BUNKIUT code. Here, spectra-1 corresponds to the spectra calculated with the BUNKIUT code and the rest as was explained for figure 12.

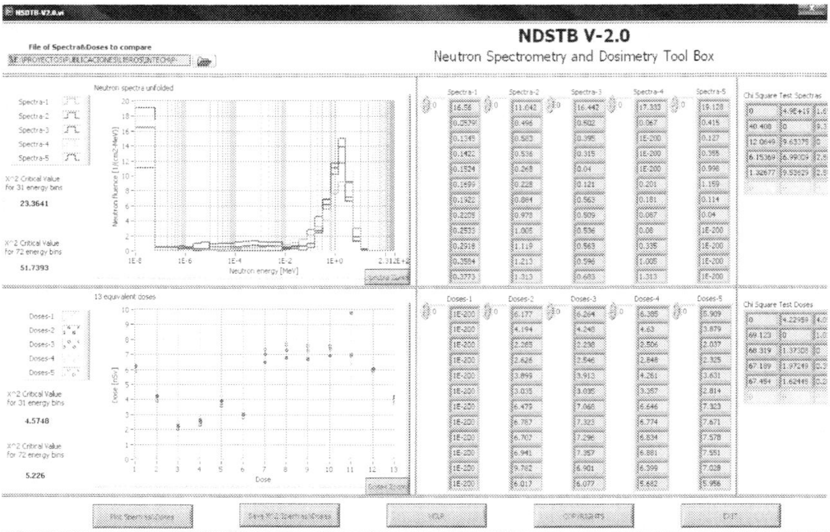

Fig. 13. BUNKIUT-NSDEann comparison of the spectra of a $^{239}PuBe$ at $1m$ in water

In the case of figure 13, the chi square test fails because the high variations of some of the values of the energy bins that compose the several spectra compared, despite the similarity between the shape and features of the spectra, as was explained for figure 12.

Figure 14 shows the neutron spectra unfolded for a $^{239}PuBe$ measured at $1m$ on air. As can be seen from this figure, the spectra are very similar in shape and features, however, the chi square test fails when compare the different spectra, as is showed in table 5.

Table 5 shows the statistical test realized by the NSDTB code. As can be seen, despite the similarities of the spectra, the test fails. A more accurate statistical test for comparing the neutron spectra obtained with several unfolding codes is needed.

NET	S1	S2	S3	S4	D1	D2	D3	D4
1	0	2E+200	5E+201	6E+201	0	0.261	0.153	1.74
2	14.892	0	108.52	98. 579	0.27	0	0.413	0.711
3	7E+198	1E+200	0	5E+200	0.162	0.419	0	1.788
4	5E+201	2E+201	4E+201	0	1.888	0.741	1.893	0

Table 5. Chi square test of NSDTB code for a $^{239}PuBe$ at $1m$ in air

Figure 15 shows a comparison of the four neutron spectra obtained with the NSDEann code with respect to the neutron spectra calculated using the BUNKIUT code for a $^{239}PuBe$ measured at $1m$ on air. Here, spectra-1 corresponds to the spectra calculated with the BUNKIUT code. As can be seen from this figure, the spectra are very similar in shape and features, however, the chi square test fails when compare the different spectra.

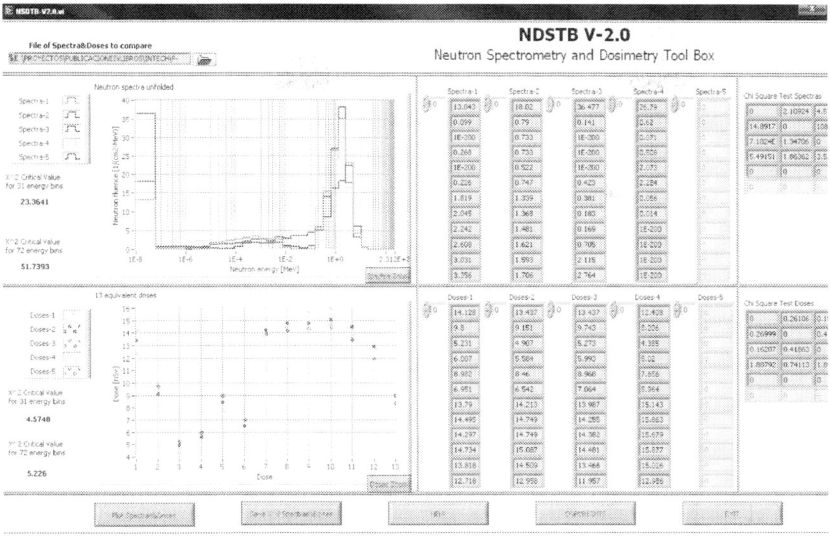

Fig. 14. Nueutron spectra unfolded with the NSDEann code for a $^{239}PuBe$ at $1m$ in air

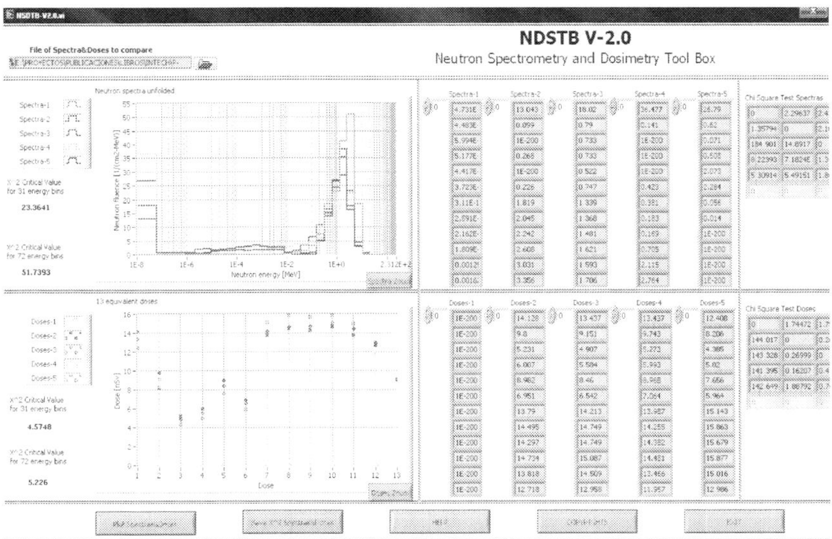

Fig. 15. BUNKIUT-NSDEann comparison of the spectra of a $^{239}PuBe$ at $1m$ in air

4. Conclusions

In this work, the intersection of GA and ANN in the neutron spectrometry research by means of ANN technology was analyzed. The most common and widely used methods of optimization in ANN are classical gradient methods, such as BP. These methods are characterized by a very fast reaching the optimum, yet, they have a considerable disadvantage "converging the algorithm to the closest optimum". So never is known whether the result of the optimization is a local or a global optimum. On the other hand, the genetic search capability in ANN design is much more effective than random searching approaches, as the genetic process of recombining features vastly improves the speed of identifying highly fit networks. It also has a potential advantage over just using personal experience in building neural networks, as new and potentially better solutions may be found through this process than might be found using the nearly unavoidable assumptions made by the user.
Contrary to the classical methods, the Evolutionary Algorithms cope with the global optimum searching quite well, but they are not as precise as the classical methods. Another disadvantage of the EA is a big (sometimes very big) amount of compilations. A major difficulty encountered when using GAs is the parameter setting. There exist many forms and variations of GAs and the best choice is problem dependant. Accordingly, a GA can show a good or weak result even when applied on the same problem. Like other learning paradigms, the performance of GA is dependent on the parameter choice, on the problem representation and on the fitness landscape.
The new ideas and concepts of EA and ANN bring new life into artificial intelligence research applied in the nuclear ciences. However, new problems arise of combining EA and ANN, such as the proper determination of the EA parameters or the need of computer tools to apply this new technology.
Because the novelty of EANN technology in neutron spectrometry and the lack of tools for the analysis, an unfolding code based on EANN technology, called "Neutron Spectrometry and Dosimetry based on Evolutionary Artificial Neural Networks" (NSDEann), was developed in a customized front end user capable to unfold neutron spectra and to simultaneously calculate 13 equivalent doses, by using only as input data the count rates coming of a BBS system, in just a few seconds if compared with the time spent with the classical techniques, not being needed a priori information about the spectra being calculated.
One disadvantage of the NSDEann code is the dependency with NGO software. Because the anterior, a customized and independent code should be of help in the neutron spectrometry field where EANN technology is applied. At present, work is being done in this sense.
When the NSDTB code was used to compare the spectra unfolded with four evolutionary network architectures obtained with the NGO software and analyzed with the NSDEann unfolding code, was observed that the chi square statistical test failed. This is due of high variations in some of the energy bins that compose the neutron spectra. From the analysis realized in the present work, has been observed that the chi square test presents some drawbacks, and a more accurate statistical test for comparing the neutron spectra obtained with several unfolding codes is needed.

5. References

Affenzeller, M., Winkler, S., Wagner, S. & Beham, A. (2009). *Genetic algorithms and genetic programming, modern concepts and practical applications*, CRC Press.
Apolloni, B., Bassis, S. & Marinaro, M. (2009). *New directions in neural networks*, IOS Press.

Beale, M. H., Hagan, M. T. & Demuth, H. B. (1992). *Neural networks toolbox, user's guide*, Mathworks. www.mathworks.com/help/pdf_doc/nnet/nnet.pdf.

Bedogni, R., Domingo, C., Esposito, A. & Fernández, F. (2007). Fruit: an operational tool for multisphere neutron spectrometry in workplaces, *Nuclear Instruments and Methods in Physics Research A* 580: 1301–1309.

BiocompSystems (2010). Biocomp systems.

Brooks, F. D. & Klein, H. (2002). Neutron spectrometry, historical review and present status, *Nuclear Instruments and Methods in Physics Research A* 476: 1–11.

Chennakesava, R. (2008). *Fuzzy logic and neural networks, basic concepts and applications*, New Age International Publishers.

Coppin, B. (2004). *Artificial intelligence illuminated*, Jones and Barttlet Publishers.

Dreyfus, G. (2005). *Neural networks, methodology and applications*, Springer.

El Messaoudi, M., Chouak, A., Lferde, M. & Cherkaoui, R. (2004). Performance of three different unfolding procedures connected to Bonner sphere data, *Radiation Protection Dosimetry* 108(3): 247–253.

Fausett, L. (1993). *Fundamentals of neural networks, architectures, algorithms and applications*, Prentice Hall.

Floreano, D. & Mattiussi, C. (2008). *Bio-inspired artificial intelligence, theories, methods and technologies*, MIT Press.

Freeman, D. W., Edwards, D. R. & Bolon, A. E. (1999). Genetic algorithms, a new technique for solving a neutron spectrum unfolding problem, *Nuclear Instruments and Methods in Physics Research A* 425(3): 549–576.

Galushkin, A. (2007). *Neural networks theory*, Springer.

Gen, M., Green, ., Katai, O., McKay, B., Namatame, A., Sarker, R. A. & Zhang, B. T. (2009). *Intelligent and evolutionary systems*, Springer-Verlag.

Goldberg, D. (1989). *Genetic Algorithms in search, optimization, and machine learning*, Addison Wesley.

Graupe, D. (2007). *Principles of artificial neural networks*, World Scientific.

Haupt, R. L. & Haupt, S. E. (2004). *Practical genetic algorithms*, Wiley.

Haykin, S. (1999). *Neural networks: a comprenssive foundation*, Prentice Hall.

IAEA (2001). Compendium of neutron spectra and detector responses for radiation protection purposes, *Technical Report 403*.

Iñiguez, M. P. & Vega-Carrillo, H. R. (2002). Catalogue to select the initial guess spectrum during unfolding, *Nuclear Instruments and Methods in Physics Research A* 476(1): 270–273.

Jain, A. K., Mao, J. & Mohiuddin, K. M. (1996). Artificial neural networks: a tutorial, *IEEE: Computer* 29(3): 31–44.

Kasabov, N. K. (1998). *Foundations of neural networks, fuzzy systems, and knowledge engineering*, MIT Press.

Kishan, M., Chilukuri, K. & Sanjay, R. (2000). *Elements of artificial neural networks*, The MIT Press.

Lacoste, V., Gressier, V., Pochat, J. L., Fernández, F., Bakali, M. & Bouassoule, T. (2004). Characterization of bonner sphere systems at monoenergetic and thermal neutron fields, *Radiation Protection Dosimetry* 110(1-4): 529–532.

Lacoste, V., Reginatto, M., Asselineau, B. & Muller, H. (2007). Bonner sphere neutron spectrometry at nuclear workplaces in the framework of the evidos project, *Radiation Protection Dosimetry* 125(1-4): 304–308.

Lakhmi, J. & Fanelli, A. M. (2000). *Recent advances in artificial neural networks design and applications*, CRC Press.

Leardi, R. (2003). *Nature-inspired methods in chemometrics: genetic algorithms and artificial neural networks*, Elsevier.

Luger, F. G. (2005). *Artificial Intelligence, structures and strategies for complex problem solving*, Addison-Wesley.

Matzke, M. (2003). Unfolding procedures, *Radiation Protection Dosimetry* 107(1-3): 155–174.

Mazrou, H., Sidahmed, T., Idiri, Z., Lounis-Mokrani, Z., , Bedek, Z. & Allab, M. (2008). Characterization of the CRNA Bonner sphere spectrometer based on 6lii scintillator exposed to an 241ambe neutron source, *Radiation Measurements* 43: 1095–1099.

McDonald, J. C., Siebert, B. R. L. & Alberts, W. G. (2002). Neutron spectrometry for radiation protection purposes, *Nuclear Instruments and Methods in Physics Research A* 476(1-2): 347–352.

Melin, P. & Castillo, O. (2005). *Hybrid intelligent system for pattern recognition using soft computing, an evolutionary approach for neural networks and fuzzy systems*, Springer.

Miller, S. (1993). *AFITBUNKI: a modified iterative code to unfold neutron spectra from Bonner sphere detector data*, Master's thesis.

Mitchell, M. (1998). *An introduction to genetic algorithms*, MIT Press.

Mukherjee, B. (2004). Andi-03: a genetic algorithm tool for the analysis of activation detector data to unfold high-energy neutron spectra, *Radiation Protection Dosimetry* 110(1-4): 249–254.

Munakata, T. (2008). *Fundamentals of the new artificial intelligence, neural, evolutionary, fuzzy and more*, Springer.

Ortiz-Rodríguez, J. M., Martínez-Blanco, M. R., Gallego, E. & Vega-Carrillo, H. R. (2008). Artificial neural networks modeling evolved genetically, a new approach applied in neutron spectrometry and dosimetry research areas, *Proceedings of the Electronics, Robotics and Automotive Mechanics Conference (CERMA'08)*, IEEE Computer Society, Cuernavaca, Mor., México, pp. 387–392.

Ortiz-Rodríguez, J. M., Martínez-Blanco, M. R., Gallego, E. & Vega-Carrillo, H. R. (2009a). A computational tool design for evolutionary artificial neural networks in neutron spectrometry and dosimetry, *Proceedings of the Electronics, Robotics and Automotive Mechanics Conference (CERMA'09)*, IEEE Computer Society, Cuernavaca, Mor., México, pp. 113–118.

Ortiz-Rodríguez, J. M., Martínez-Blanco, M. R., Gallego, E. & Vega-Carrillo, H. R. (2009b). Evolutive artificial neural networks for neutron spectra unfolding, *American Nuclear Society Transactions* 101: 647–648.

Ortiz-Rodríguez, J. M., Martínez-Blanco, M. R., Gallego, E. & Vega-Carrillo, H. R. (2010a). Neutron spectrometry and dosimetry based on a new approach called genetic artificial neural networks, *12th Congress of the International Radiation Protection Association (IRPA12)*, IAEA Procceding Series STI/PUB/1460 1-9, International Atomic Energy Agency, Vienna.

Ortiz-Rodríguez, J. M., Martínez-Blanco, M. R., Gallego, E. & Vega-Carrillo, H. R. (2010b). A neutron spectrometry and dosimetry computer tool based on ann, *12th Congress of the International Radiation Protection Association (IRPA12)*, IAEA Procceding Series STI/PUB/1460 1-9, International Atomic Energy Agency, Vienna.

Ortiz-Rodríguez, J. M., Martínez-Blanco, M. R. & Vega-Carrillo, H. R. (2006). Robust design of artificial neural networks applying the Taguchi methodology and DoE, *Proceedings of the Electronics, Robotics and Automotive Mechanics Conference (CERMA'06)*, IEEE Computer Society, Cuernavaca, Mor., México, pp. 131–136.

Packianather, M. S. & Drake, P. R. (2004). Modeling neural network performance through response surface methodology for classifying wood veneer defects, *Proceedings of the Institution of Mechanical Engineers, Part B* 218(4): 459–466.

Packianather, M. S., Drake, P. R. & H., R. (2000). Optimizing the parameters of multilayered feedforward neural networks through Taguchi design of experiments, *Quality and Reliability Engineering International* 16: 461–473.

Periaux, J. & Winter, G. (1995). *Genetic algorithms in engineering and computer science*, John Wiley & Sons.

Peterson, G. E., St. Clair, D. C., Aylward, S. R. & E., B. W. (1995). Using Taguchi's method of experimental design to control errors in layered perceptrons, *IEEE Transactions on Neural Networks* 6(4): 949–961.

Pongcharoen, P., Chainate, W. & Thapatsuwan, P. (2007). Exploration of genetic parameters and operators through traveling salesman problem, *Science Asia* 33: 215–222.

Rasskin-Gutman, D. (2009). *Chess metaphors, artificial intelligence and the human brain*, The MIT Press.

Reginatto, M. & Zimbal, A. (2008). Bayesian and maximum entropy methods for fusion diagnostic measurements with compact neutron spectrometers, *Review of Scientific Instruments* 79(2): 398–403.

Roberts, N. J. (2007). Investigation of combined unfolding of neutron spectra using the UMG unfolding codes, *Radiation Protection Dosimetry* 126(1-4): 398–403.

Rothlauf, F. (2006). *Representations for Genetic and Evolutionary Algorithms*, Springer.

Taylor, J. G. (1993). *Mathematical approaches to neural networks*, North-Holland Mathematical library.

Thomas, D. J. (2004). Neutron spectrometry for radiation protection, *Radiation Protection Dosimetry* 110(1-4): 141–149.

Vega-Carrillo, H. R., Hernández-Dávila, V. M., Manzanares-Acuña, E., Gallego, E., Lorente, A. & Iñiguez, M. P. (2007b). Artificial neural networks technology for neutron spectrometry and dosimetry, *Radiation Protection Dosimetry* 126(1-4): 408–412.

Vega-Carrillo, H. R., Hernández-Dávila, V. M., Manzanares-Acuña, E., Mercado Sánchez, G. A., Gallego, E., Lorente, A., Perales-Muñoz, W. A. & Robles-Rodríguez, J. A. (2005). Artificial neural networks in neutron dosimetry, *Radiation Protection Dosimetry* 118(3): 251–259.

Vega-Carrillo, H. R., Hernández-Dávila, V. M., Manzanares-Acuña, E., Mercado-Sánchez, G. A., Iñiguez de la Torre, M. P., Barquero, R., Preciado-Flores, S., Méndez-Villafañe, R., Arteaga-Arteaga, T. & Ortiz-Rodríguez, J. M. (2006). Neutron spectrometry using artificial neural networks, *Radiation Measurements* 41: 425–431.

Vega-Carrillo, H. R., Manzanares-Acuña, E., Ortiz-Rodríguez, J. M. & Arteaga-Arteaga, T. (2007a). Neutron spectra re-binning and dose calculation using monte carlo methods, *Revista Mexicana de Física* 53: 1–7.

Vega-Carrillo, H. R., Martínez-Blanco, M. R., Hernández-Dávila, V. M. & Ortiz-Rodríguez, J. M. (2009a). Spectra and dose with ANN of 252Cf, 241AmBe, and 239PuBe, *Journal of Radioanalytical and Nuclear Chemistry* 281: 615–618.

Vega-Carrillo, H. R., Ortiz-Rodríguez, J. M., Hernández-Dávila, V. M., Martínez-Blanco, M. R., Hernández-Almaraz, B., Ortiz-Hernández, A. & Mercado, G. A. (2009b). Different spectra with the same neutron source, *Revista Mexicana de Fśica S* 56(1): 35–39.

Vega-Carrillo, H. R., Ortiz-Rodríguez, J. M., Martínez-Blanco, M. R. & Hernández-Dávila, V. M. (2010). Ann in spectroscopy and neutron dosimetry, *American Institute of Physics Proccedings* 1310: 12–17.

Vylet, V. (2002). Response matrix of an extended Bonner sphere system, *Nuclear Instruments and Methods in Physics Research A* 476: 26–30.

Whiteson, S. & Stone, P. (2006). Evolutionary function approximation for reinforcement learning, *The Journal of Machine Learning Research* 7: 877–917.

Wielunski, M., Wahl, W., EL-Faramawy, N., Ruhm, W., Luszik-Bhadra, M. & Roos, H. (2008a). Development of a Brazilina gamma-neutron dosimeter, *Nuclear Instruments and Methods in Physics Research B* 266(12-13): 3174–3177.

Wielunski, M., Wahl, W., EL-Faramawy, N., Ruhm, W., Luszik-Bhadra, M. & Roos, H. (2008b). Intercomparison exercise Whith MeV neutrons using various electronic personal dosimeters, *Radiation Measurements* 43(2-6): 1063–1067.

Yao, X. (1993). Evolutionary artificial neural networks, *International Journal of Neural Systems* 4(3): 203–222.

Zupan, J. (1994). Introduction to artificial neural network methods: what they are and how to use them, *Acta Chimica Slovenica* 41(3): 327–352.

25

Analysis of Thermal Transient Processes by Means of Neural Network Technique

Rafał Rakoczy and Stanisław Masiuk
Institute of Chemical Engineering and Environmental Protection Process,
West Pomeranian University of Technology
al. Piastów 42, 71-065 Szczecin
Poland

1. Introduction

Particularly in the past decade, a very large effort has been expended in developing numerical methods for solving complex multidimensional problems in area of engineering processes. In the last few years the complex behaviour of biological, chemical and industrial systems has been explained in terms of dynamic analysis and many techniques to obtain predictions have been developed. The dynamic investigations of a various processes have focused attention on the problem of the mathematical description. In principle, this knowledge may be obtained by many computational modelling. As an easier alternative, the experimental data may be used to find out a black-box model or an empirical correlation defining the system behaviour. The limitation of this approach is that it requires assumption of the functional form of the proposed correlation.

The popular approach to analyse the unsteady and steady heat transfer problems is associated with the availability of non-linear empirical modelling methodologies, such as neural networks, inspired by the biological network of neurons in the brain (Hussain, 1999; Ou & Achenie, 2005). Authors (Liau & Chen, 2006) proposed this methodology to model optimal concentrations of reactants for preparing sub-micron silica particles. Different sets of the reactant concentrations were selected within an operating range and were designed to evaluate the PSD data. The relationship between the reactant concentration and resultant PSD can be evaluated by means of the ANN modelling approach. The neural network models can be successfully used to compute PSD of particles with different shapes in highly concentred suspensions from laser diffraction measurements (Nascimento et al., 1997; Guardani et al. 2002). The ANN pattern recognition (ANNPR) approach has also been proposed for fed-batch cultivation processes of *Escherichia coli* (Duan et al., 2006). A novel data mining macro-kinetic approach based on ANN was proposed to develop the macro-kinetic model of oxidation of *p*-xylene to terephthalic acid in a industrial type of continuous stirred tank reactor (Yan, 2007). Authors (Liu & Kim, 2008) used the purely mathematic and mechanical model with ANN to model membrane filtration process. As a tool of modelling, neural network technique has been used by (Jones et al., 1999) to magnetic inverse problem of determining the anisotropy field distribution from experimental transverse susceptibility data. Approximation models such as artificial neural networks (ANNs) are powerful and reliable in predicting the complex conditions such as nonlinear and time-variant biological

processes (Liu et al., 2008). Consequently, this approach has been used to predict hold-up in slurry pipelines (Lahiri & Ghanta, 2008), for mapping the structure of a liquid spray (Heinlein et al., 2007), for analysis of heat and mass transfer (Kahrs & Marquardt, 2007).
The dynamic investigations of the unsteady heat transfer process has focused attention on the problem of the mathematical description. In principle, this knowledge can be obtained by many computational modelling. As an easier alternative, the experimental data may be used to find out a black-box model or an empirical correlation defining the system behaviour. The limitation of this approach is that it requires assumption of the functional form of the proposed correlation. The popular approach to analyse the unsteady and steady heat transfer problems is associated with the availability of non-linear empirical modelling methodologies, such as neural networks, inspired by the biological network of neurons in the brain. The implementation of ANN technique in heat transfer science literature is limited. For the identification or analysis of heat transfer problems a neural network approach has been attempted by authors (Thibault & Grandjean, 1991; Christtofindes, 2001; Alotaibi et al., 2004; Zdaniuk, 2006; Ashforth-Frost et al.,1995 and Yilmaz & Atik,2007). In the relevant thermal scientific literature is most concerned with the performance prediction and control of heat exchangers (Islamoglu, 2003; Diaz et al., 2001; Pacheco-Vega et al. 2001).
In the present work, an attempt has been made to use ANN to model the thermal transient process and the thermal behaviour of reciprocating mixer. We believe that this modelling approach is considerably interesting than the more conventional empirical correlation approach. This encouraged us to investigate the problem which is presented in this chapter.

2. Experimental details

The investigations of the temperature transient processes were made using the experimental set-up shown in Figure 1. The experimental investigations were performed using a vertical cylindrical vessel of 0.248 m in inside diameter and 0.678 m in height. The mixing was varied out with a single perforated plates agitators with the different degree of perforation (ratio of hole-to-solid area of plate) oriented horizontally were reciprocating in a vertical direction. The agitator was always placed at half of the liquid height in the vessel and the diameter is equal to 0.241 m. An electric a.c. motor coupled through a variable gear and V-belt transmission turned a flywheel. A vertical oscillating shaft with a single plate perforated and a hardened steel ring through a sufficiently long crankshaft were articulated eccentrically to the flywheel. This system were used to generate reciprocating movements of agitator. The water was used as the mixed liquid as well as cooling medium. The flow rates of municipal water continuously flowing through the mixer and jacket surrounding internal tubular vessel were established and controlled by means of flow meters. The temporal variations of temperature as a transient thermal processes were measured by using the microprocessor sensors. Therefore, these processes were obtained by means of the thermal-response technique. This method is very flexible and may be applied to large scale systems but it required very sensitivity measuring sensors. The measured electronic signals proportional to the temperature were passed through converter and system of temperature sequential sampling to personal computer where the temperature transient processes may be easily analytically recorded and formed the database including the characteristic quantities of this process. These processes were generated by the thermal disturbance of the cold water stream introducing on the free surface of the mixer vessel by means of centrally mounted perforated distributor. This loading device was protected against premature penetration of cold bulk liquid in the mixer vessel

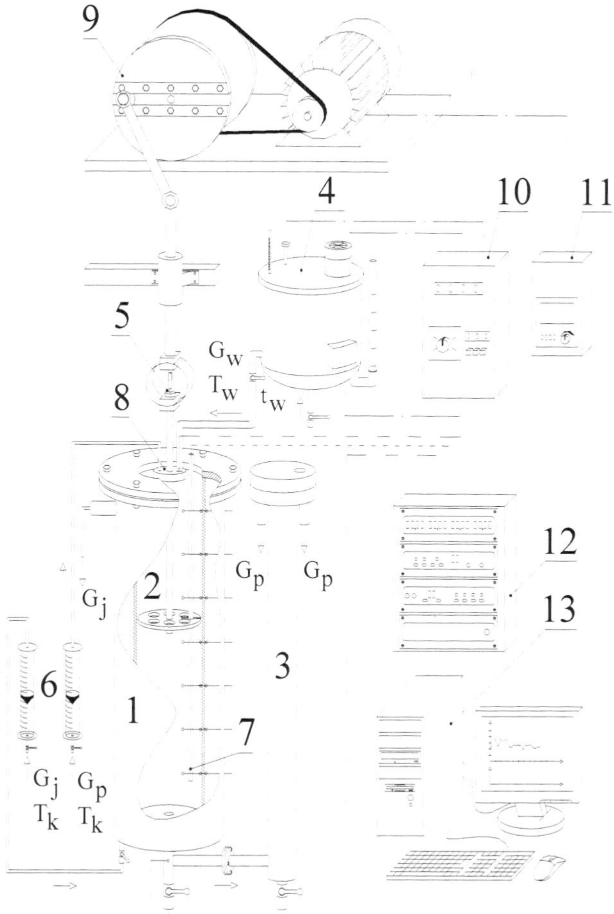

Fig. 1. Experimental set-up: 1 - tubular vessel, 2 - perforated plate agitator, 3 - external overflow, 4 - generator of input temperature signal and hot liquid feeder, 5 - hardened ring with inductive transducer, 6 – flow meters, 7 - temperature sensors, 8 - distributor of cold liquid, 9 - electromechanical eccentric drive, 10 - power cube, 11 - controller of motor speed, 12 - system of temperature sequential sampling, 13 - personal computer

The thermal disturbance as the pulse temperature input signal was the volume of hot liquid described by parameters G_w, T_w and t_w. Before the experimental measurements the mixer bulk was mixed to constant field temperature inside the mixed and flowing water. This field was controlled by the set of movable temperature sensors. Next the hot water was injected to the stream of cold water and the temperature transient process was recorded simultaneously. The transient process was regarded as a complete when the temperature variation in the stream flowing out the mixer vessel did not change with time. Then the transient response curve is asymptotic to the time axis. As mentioned above, experimental studies of the thermal transient processes were conducted in the reciprocating mixer and the databases included the operational parameters, such as: perforation degree of the reciprocating plate agitator - ψ, amplitude of reciprocating motion - Γ, frequency of reciprocating motion - ω, mass flow rate of water in mixer vessel - G_p, mass flow rate in cooling jacket - G_j, mass of hot water introduced into the steam of the water flowing through the mixed vessel - G_w, time duration of the thermal impulse signal - t_w, temperature of hot water - T_w and temperature of the mixed water - T_k are collected in Table 1.

parameter	$\psi\left[m^2 \cdot m^{-2}\right]$	$\Gamma[m]$	$\omega\left[s^{-1}\right]$	$G_p\left[kg \cdot s^{-1}\right]$	$G_j\left[kg \cdot s^{-1}\right]$	$G_w\left[kg \cdot s^{-1}\right]$	$t_w[s]$	$T_w\left[^\circ C\right]$	$T_k\left[^\circ C\right]$
minimal value	0.05	0.01	0.028	0.02778	0.0692	1	5	32.1	3.2
maximal value	0.45	0.14	2.5	0.1667	0.1528	6	120	92.9	10

Table 1. The range of operational parameters

Such programming of the experimental investigations enables to explore many aspects of the unsteady heat transfer realised by using the mixed vessel equipped with the reciprocating agitator. The results of the experiments for the various set of the operational parameters may be graphically presented as a dependence of the output temperature response on the time duration of the temperature variation. Figure 2 illustrates the typical example of transient response curve. The response curves obtained for the different combination of the operational parameters were similar to the typical example of thermal response curve (see Figure 2).

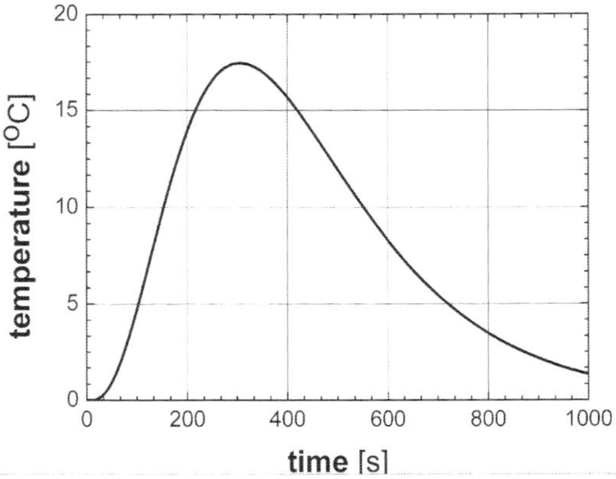

Fig. 2. Typical example of thermal-response curve

The influence of the operational parameters on the transient process may be assessed by the analytically approximated of transient curves or characterized in the more simple way using the specially chosen characteristic quantities of these curves. As follows from the comparison of these thermal transient process for the different sets of operational parameters, it may be found that these thermal-response curves should be defined by means of the five characteristic parameters such as: the time lag of thermal process - t_0, the maximal value of temperature - T_{max}, the time of the achievement of maximal value of temperature - t_{max}, the time duration of thermal process - t_p and the quantity of area between the thermal response of transient process and the time axis - A.
The typical example of thermal response curve with the marked characteristic quantities is graphically presented in Figure 3.

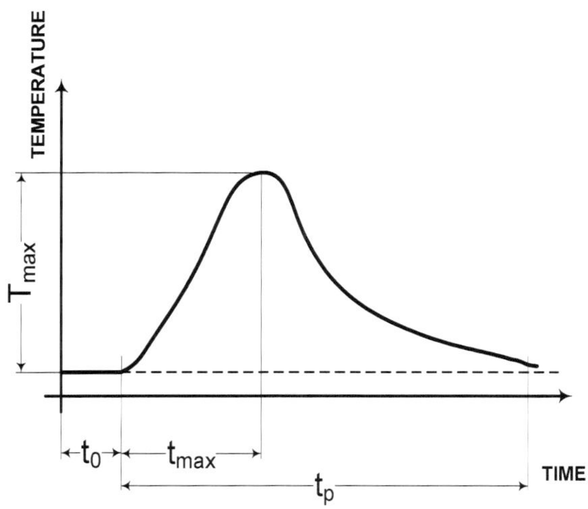

Fig. 3. Typical example of thermal-response curve with the marked characteristic quantities

The series of the 3000 experimental values of the five characteristic quantities were obtained for the various sets of operational parameters. Recent approaches to building mathematical description have been based on the statistical or numerical modelling of experimental database. In the case of the absence of accurate theoretical models, regression methods have been employed to find an approximate functional form that can best describe the relationship between the independent variables and the observed dependent parameters. Artificial neural networks (ANN) are an attempt to predict the effect of changing input data on the dependent variables. Earlier experimental works have reported from the use of the various types of networks to analysis the number of engineering problems. The produce ANN model estimates the five characteristic parameters with respect to the establish values of operational condition. The great advantage of the proposed methodology is that the complex mathematical relationship for the non-linear unsteady heat transfer processes is omitted. Consequently, the computational time required to solve the classical mathematical models is significantly reduced and the description of the dynamic behaviour of thermal transient process with various effects under constantly changing conditions is possible.

3. Results and discussion

3.1 Predictions of operational characteristics value by using the ANN model

The nature of obtained databases is permitted to analyse and describe the experimental results applying the statistical or numerical modelling. In the case of the absence of accurate theoretical models, regression methods should be exploded to find an approximate functional form for description of the relationship between the independent variables and the observed dependent quantities. Artificial neural networks have offered of the splendid attempt to predict the effect of changing input data on the dependent variables. The produce ANN model estimates the power characteristics for the novel construction of static mixer with respect to the establish values of operational parameters. The great advantage of the proposed methodology is that the computational time required to solve the classical mathematical models is significantly reduced and the description of the operational behaviour of the static mixer under constantly changing conditions is possible.

Traditionally, ANN has been used to model complex non-linear systems and appeared to be a good alternative to traditional empirical, phenomenological or statistical correlations. The ANN models are more powerful and can manipulate non-linear input-output relationships more successfully than available literature conventional correlations.

The critical step in building a robust ANN is to create an architecture, which should be as simple as possible and has a fast capacity for learning of the data set. The choice of the input variables is the key to insure complete description of the analysed systems, whereas the experimental data set have a tremendous impact on the reliability and performance of the ANN model. This type of model provides a non-linear mapping between input and output variables and is also useful in providing cross correlation among these variables. The ANN is a very useful tool in rapid predictions such as steady-state or transient process flow sheet simulations, on-line process optimization and visualisation and parameter estimation.

The experimental database are processed using ANN models. The neural network approach was thus carried out by means of the Statistica Neural Network software. The multi layer perceptron (MLP) networks consist of three layers, namely the input layer, the hidden layer and the output layer. For practical application, the RBF network is structured so that it can approximate the five characteristic quantities of thermal-transient curves (transient processes) and estimate the dynamic behaviour of temperature at unsteady heat transfer in the reciprocating mixer. To achieve this, the input layer of the analysed network is formulated so that it contains the input parameters as follows:

$$\bar{x} = \left[\psi \; \Gamma \; \omega \; G_p \; G_j \; G_w \; t_w \; T_w \; T_k \right]^T \tag{1}$$

The neural network output is the estimation of the five characteristic parameters of the thermal-transient processes, which are calculated as a weighted sum of the responses of the hidden layer nodes. Figure 4 presents the structure of the MLP network used to model the thermal-transient processes.

It should be noticed that the training a MLP network is conducted by the minimal deviation between the predicted and the true values of the output variables over the set of the available experimental database. As follows from the realised analysis, the MLP model consisting of 11 nodes in the hidden layers. This number of nodes is caused by the

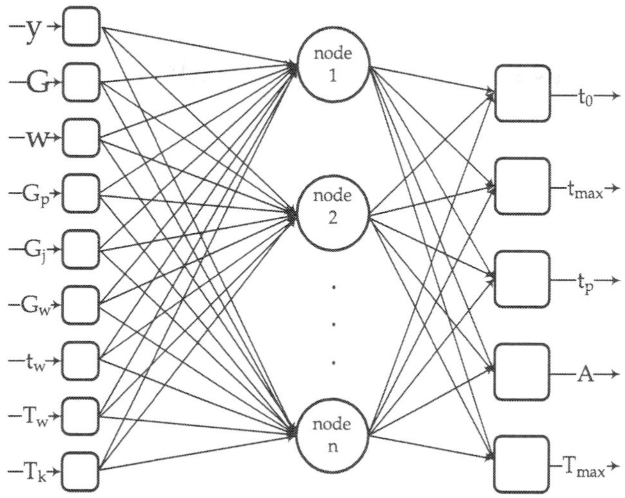

Fig. 4. The MLP neural network architecture for the characteristic quantities of the thermal transient process

complexity of the analysed heat transfer problem and the non-linear relationship between the input vector of the operational parameters and the approximated values of output parameters. As follows from the analysis of the proposed ANN architecture model, the values of qualitative coefficients for the training, validating and testing sets are amount to 0.991136, 0.987181 and 0.989819, respectively. Moreover, the operational parameters (input parameters) may be reorganised from the most to the least important parameter for the proposed architecture of the MLP model as follows:

$$\bar{x} = \left[t_w \; G_p \; \psi \; T_k \; \Gamma \; \omega \; T_w \; G_w \; G_j \right]^T \tag{2}$$

Figure 5 gives the generalization result, by plotting the power characteristics for the novel type of static mixer calculated by using the ANN model as a function of the experimental investigations.

The first conclusion drawn from the inspection of these graphs is that the proposed neural network is predicted the analysed experimental data very well. Therefore, these results suggest that the characteristic parameters for the novel type of static mixer my be successfully approximated by means of the ANN methods.

Moreover, the radial basic function (RBF) network was used to model the thermal-transient curves. Figure 6 presents the values of time duration of thermal-transient process, t_p, obtained from the RBF model and the values measured from experiments. Almost all the results lay in the limits of the ±30% maximal error. As follows form the analysis of the obtained results, the MLP model is shown to be superior to the RBF network approach.

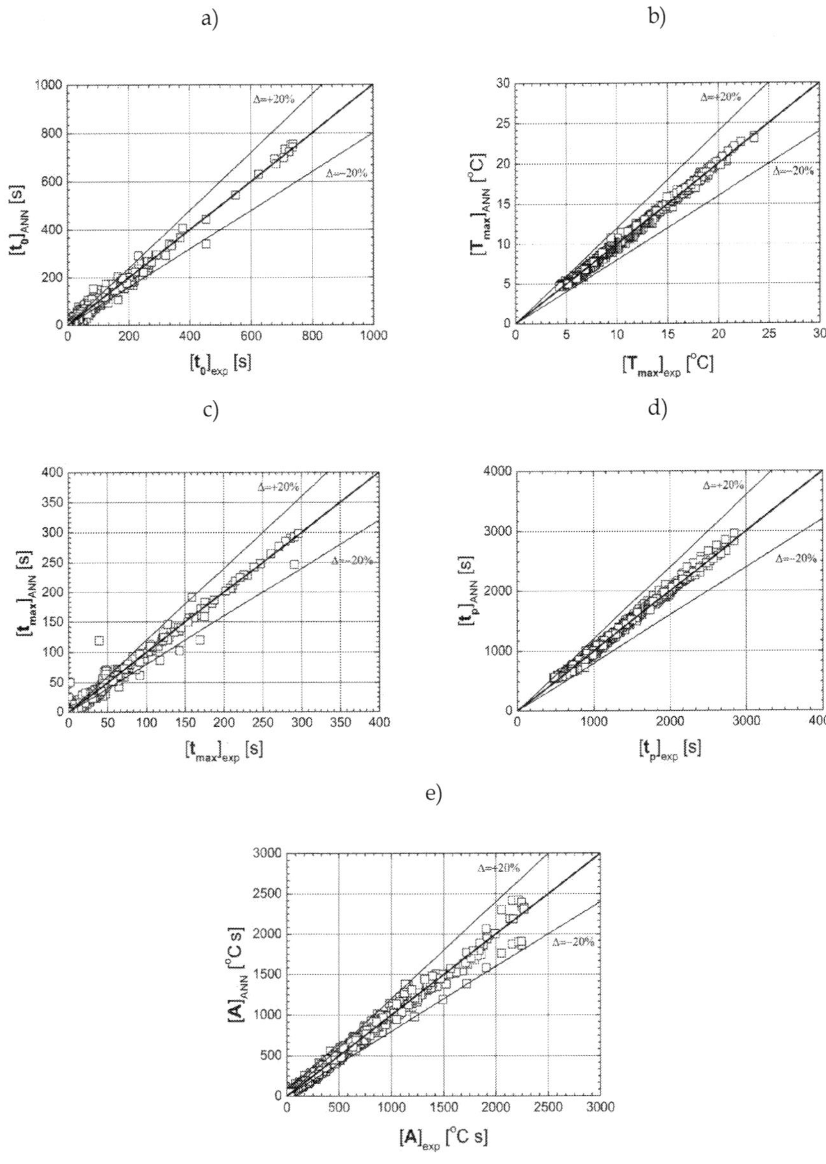

Fig. 5. The graphical comparison of values of characteristic quantities for results obtained experimentally and using ANN model: a) the time lag of thermal process - t_0, b) the maximal value of temperature - T_{max}, c) the time of the achievement of maximal value of temperature - t_{max} d) the time duration of thermal process - t_p and the e) quantity of area between the thermal response of transient process and the time axis - A

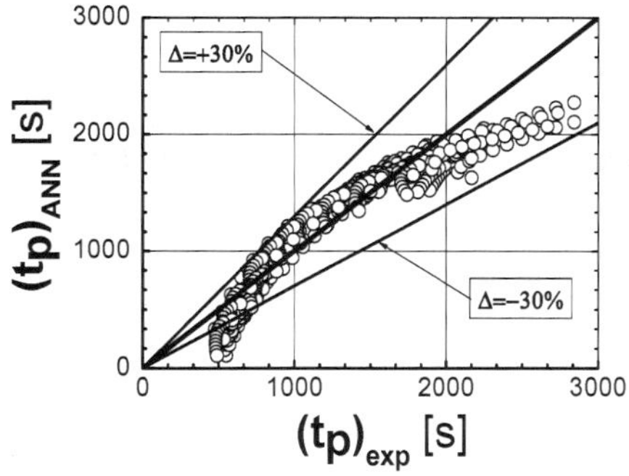

Fig. 6. The graphical comparison of the experimental and predicted values of the time lag of thermal process (t_0) for the RBF network model

3.2 Effects of operational parameters on characteristic quantities of thermal transient process

The practical utility of the results presented here is to illustrate the effects of operational parameters on the characteristic quantities for the realized transient process in the reciprocating mixing system. In recognition this fact, the three-dimensional response surfaces were generated and used to study the liquid properties and operating conditions on characteristic quantities.

Figure 7 illustrate the effect of the selected operational parameters on the time lag of thermal transient process (t_0). As it can be observed in Figure 7, this parameter depends significantly on the operational conditions.

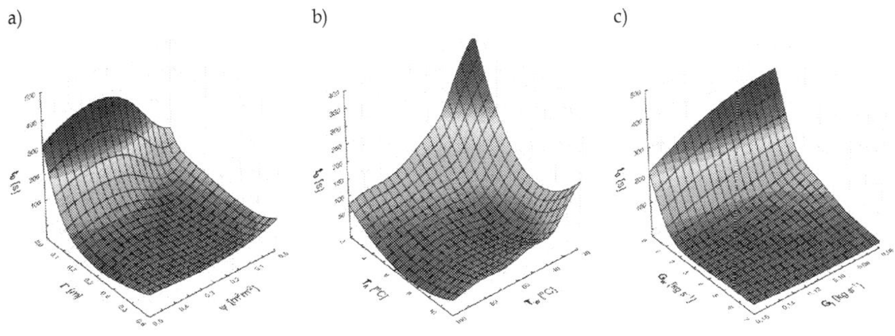

Fig. 7. The effect of selected operational parameters on the time lag of thermal transient process (t_0)

Figure 7a shows the effect of the parameter connected with the reciprocating mixer on on the time lag of thermal transient process (t_0) as an attempt to simulate the effect of changing the perforation degree of the reciprocating plate agitator (ψ) and the amplitude of reciprocating motion (r). It was found that, t_0 values seem to decrease with increasing the amplitude of reciprocating motion of the tested mixer. Moreover, this figure shows that the obtained t_0 values increase with increasing amplitude of reciprocating motion. In this study, the effect of the temperature of hot water (impulse temperature - T_w) appears to be

stronger than the mixed water temperature (T_k) leading to an increase of the time lag of thermal transient process (t_0), as can be seen in Fig.6b. In analyzed reciprocating mixer, the lag time values were found to change with the mass flow rate in cooling jacket (G_j) and mass of hot water introduced into the steam of the water flowing through the mixed vessel (G_w). Therefore, the Figures 7a-c indicate that the time lag of thermal transient process (t_0) is considerably changed with variation of operational conditions.
As follows from the realized simulations, the complicated hydrodynamics in the tested reciprocating mixer may successfully described by means of the ANN technique. The non-linear relationship between the input vector of the operational parameters and the approximated values of output parameters is approximated. The appropriate design, scale-up and optimization of industrial processes is depended on the description of influence of operating conditions on the characteristics parameters of the thermal transient process.
Figures 8a-c shows the effect of operational conditions on the maximal value of temperature (T_{max}). As can be observed in this figure, the maximal value of temperature (T_{max}) seem to increase with increasing the operational parameters $(\Gamma, \psi, T_k, T_w, G_w, G_j)$.

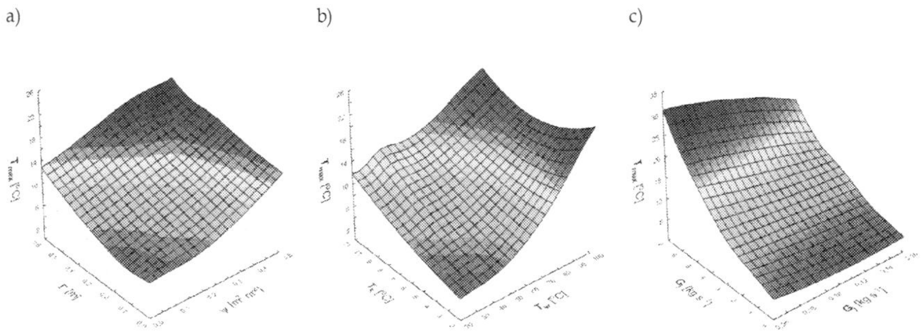

Fig. 8. The effect of selected operational parameters on the maximal value of temperature (T_{max})

Figures 9a-c presents the effect of operational conditions on the time of the achievement of maximal value of temperature (t_{max}), and as can been seen, this parameter appears to

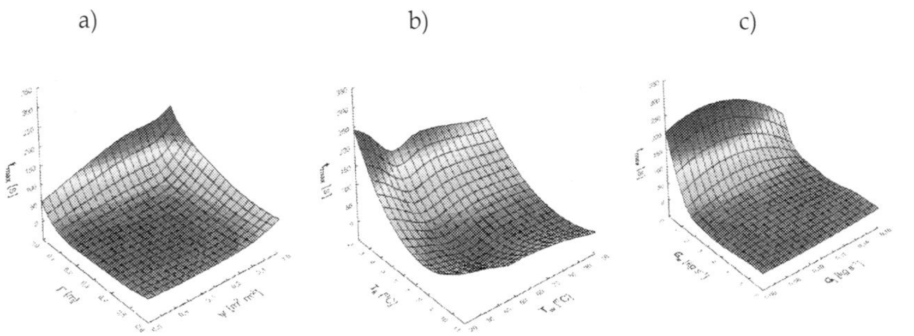

Fig. 9. The effect of selected operational parameters on the time of the achievement of maximal value of temperature (t_{max})

decrease with the changes of operational parameters range, which is in agreement with the realized experimental works.

Figure 10 depict the effect of operational conditions on the time duration of thermal process (t_p). In agreement with the realized experimental investigations, this parameter was found to decrease with the operational conditions. This figure may be used to speculate the effect of mixing device on the mixing time in industrial applications. From practical point of view, this parameter may treated as an important criterion in analysis of the mixing process. Moreover, this magnitude may be used in the selection of the suitable agitator or the mixing manner for the homogenisation process. The most importance of costs of production which should be depends on the time duration of mixing process. The operational costs of the production process are obviously an important element in the economic design. The capital costs will be comprised of the expenditure on the driving units and the employed of suitable mixing device. Longer mixing time will inevitable demand a higher cost of production. In the case of this experimental investigations, the time duration of mixing process progressively decreases with increasing of the operational conditions.

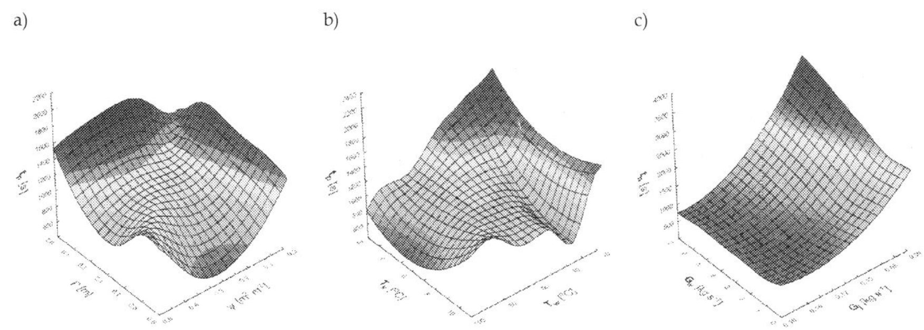

Fig. 10. The effect of selected operational parameters on the time duration of thermal process (t_p)

Figure 11 depicts the effect of operational conditions on the the quantity of area between the thermal response of transient process and the time axis (A).

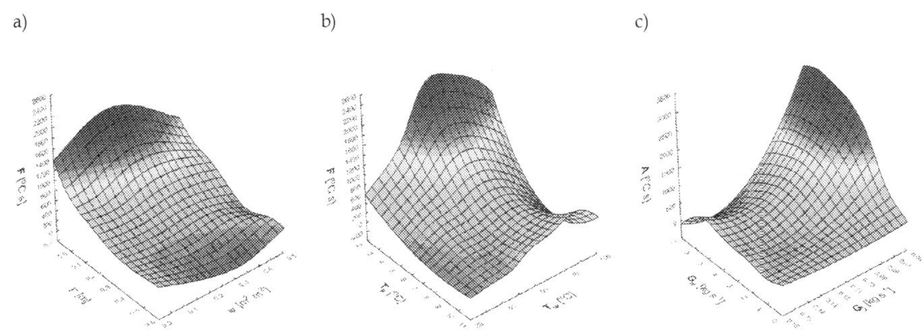

Fig. 11. The effect of selected operational parameters on the quantity of area between the thermal response of transient process and the time axis (A)

It should be noticed that the MLP model successfully captures different thermal-transient curves. Therefore, the unsteady heat transfer processes as given by this ANN model have been developed. According to the realized analysis, the time duration of the thermal impulse signal, t_w, and the mass flow rate of water in mixer vessel, G_p, are mostly influenced on the output parameters of the MLP model (see Equation 2). Therefore, three different cases have been considered: the first one concerns small values of operational parameters (variant I). In the second, the values of these parameters are maximum (variant III). In order to have a accurate analysis of thermal-transient processes, a middle values of operational parameters is obviously required in the ANN model (variant II). A procedure was followed with the time duration of the thermal impulse signal, t_w, and the mass flow rate of water in mixer vessel, G_p, taking values between 5÷120°C and 0.02778÷0.1667 kg·s^{-1}, respectively. The performance of the produced MLP neural network model with respect to the values of operational parameters collected in table 2.

parameter	$\psi\left[m^2\cdot m^{-2}\right]$	$\Gamma[m]$	$\omega\left[s^{-1}\right]$	$G_p\left[kg\cdot s^{-1}\right]$	$G_j\left[kg\cdot s^{-1}\right]$	$G_w\left[kg\cdot s^{-1}\right]$	$t_w[s]$	$T_w\left[^{\circ}C\right]$	$T_k\left[^{\circ}C\right]$
variant I	0.05	0.01	0.028	0.02778 ÷ 0.1667	0.0692	1	5÷ 120	32.1	3.2
variant II	0.255	0.07	1.25		0.0764	3		60,5	6,6
variant III	0.45	0.14	2.5		0.1528	6		92.9	10

Table 2. The set of operational parameters for the analysis of the performance of the produced RBF neural network model

Figures 12 and 13 have been drawn using the successfully produced MLP model of the unsteady heat transfer in the reciprocating mixer to depict the effect of the operational parameters on the five characteristic quantities of thermal-transient curve while t_w and G_p parameters are varied in the established range. Some of the presented figures reveal interesting aspects. These figures show that the values of five characteristic quantities for the selected arbitrary sets of the operational parameters (variant I, II and III) may be predicted by MLP model.

As gives in this figures, the operational parameters affects significantly the values of characteristic quantities. It can be noticed that the differences between the values for the various variants of the operational parameters are significant. The effect of the operational parameters on the characteristics quantities of thermal-transient processes was examined by increasing the operational parameters from the minimal values up to the maximal values (see Table 2) for which the variation of these quantities are observed.

Figures 12 and 13 may be used to obtain the values of the characteristic parameters of thermal-transient process without the complicated analysis of the experimental curve. The dynamic behaviour of the tested reciprocating mixer may be predicted by means of the analysed thermal transient process. The dynamic response of the investigated system may be predicted by means of the five characteristic parameters (see figure 3). The obtained

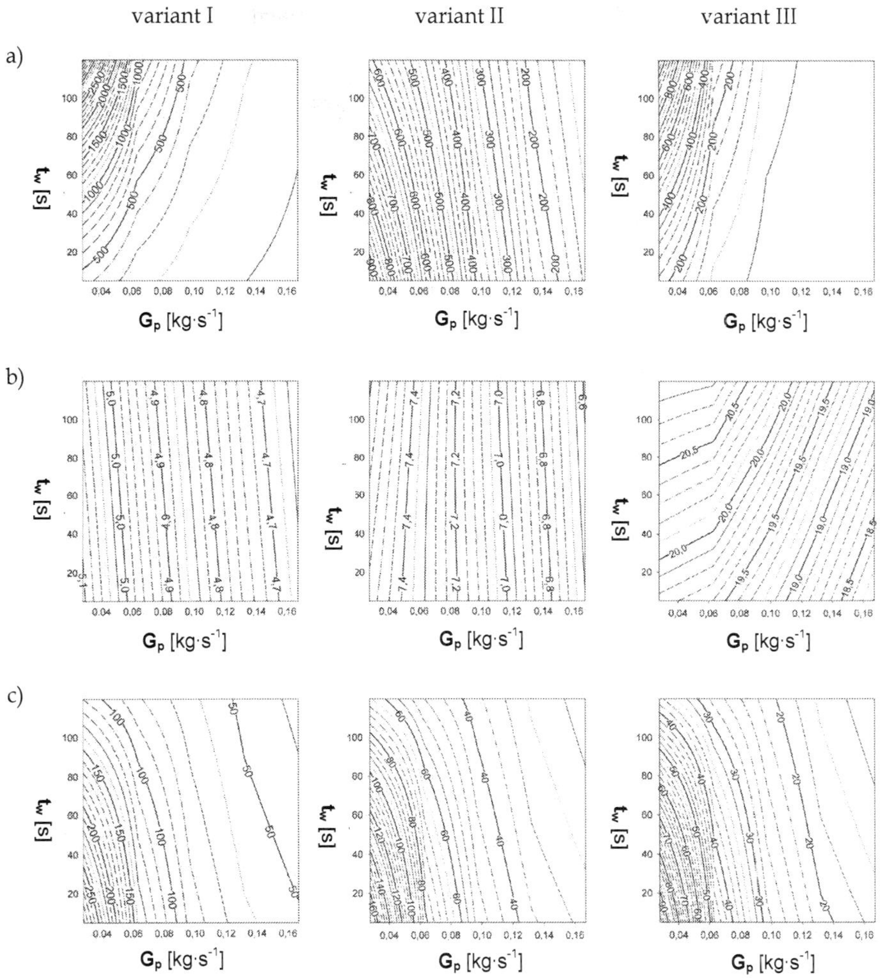

Fig. 12. Predictions of the time lag of thermal process (a), the maximal value of temperature (b) and the time of the achievement of maximal value of temperature (c) depending on the time duration of the thermal impulse signal (t_w) and the mass flow rate of water in mixer vessel (G_p)

results suggest significant influence of the operational conditions (especially the time duration of the thermal impulse signal and the mass flow rate of water in mixer vessel) on the obtained parameters of the thermal response curves. Referring to the graphical presentation of the reliable simulation results, it is observed that the different configuration of operational parameters has been reported to change the turbulences at the mixed liquid leading to a variation of the thermal-transient response curves.

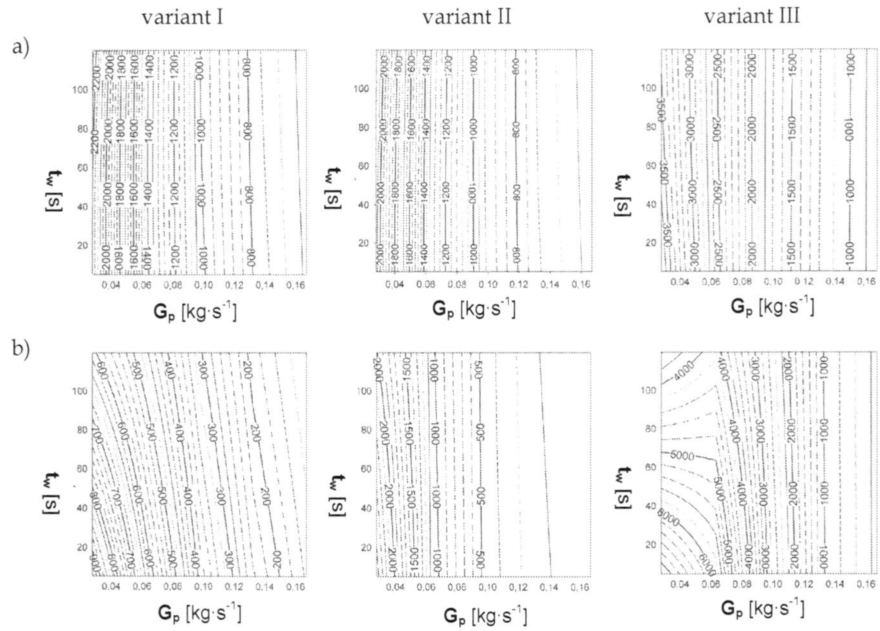

Fig. 13. Predictions of the time duration of thermal process (a) and the quantity of area between the thermal response of transient process and the time axis (b) depending on the time duration of the thermal impulse signal (t_w) and the mass flow rate of water in mixer vessel (G_p)

4. Conclusion

The main aim of this paper is to present the application of artificial neural network (ANN) technique for the development of a mathematical description of thermal-transient processes for a mixer equipped with reciprocating agitator. The proposed ANN model, describing the thermal behavior of this type mixer, is developed and compared with the experimental measurements.

Unsteady heat transfer process prediction of the reciprocating mixer by using MLP model is investigated. The simulation results indicate that the MLP network model can appropriately predict the characteristic quantities of thermal transient processes (the time lag of thermal process, the maximal value of temperature, the time of the achievement of maximal value of temperature, the time duration of thermal process and the quantity of area between the thermal response of transient process and the time axis) by using the set of input operational parameters. The predictions obtained by computational simulation are very good agreement with experimental data. This good agreement leading to the conclusion that ANN technique is a powerful tool for modeling parametrical sensitivity in the dynamic investigations of the heat transfer phenomena for the realized mixing process. Therefore, neural network can be an alternative approach to assessment of the thermal-transient processes without the nonlinear sequential estimation of the shape of transient curves.

5. References

Alotaibi, S., Sen, M., Goodwine, B. & Yang K.T. (2004). Flow-based control of temperature in long ducts. *International Journal of Heat and Mass Transfer* 47, 4995-5009. ISSN 0017-9310

Ashforth-Frost, S., Fontama, V.N., Jambunathan, K. & Hartle, S.L. (1995). The role of neural networks in fluid mechanics and heat transfer, *Proceedings of the IEEE Instrumentation and Measurement Technology Conference 1*, 6-9.

Christofides, P. (2001). Nonlinear and robust control of PDE systems: Methods and applications to transport reaction processes, Birkhäuser, ISBN 978-0-8176-4156-6, Boston.

Diaz, G., Sen, M., Yang, K.T. & McClain R.L. (2001). On-line training of artificial neural networks for control of a heat exchanger test facility, *Proceedings of National Heat Transfer Conf. 1*, 1671-1679.

Duan S., Shi Z., Feng H. & Mao Z. (2006). An on-line adaptive control based on DO/pH measurements and ANN pattern recognition model for fed-batch cultivation, *Biochemical Engineering Journal* 30, 88-96. ISSN 1369-703X

Guardani, R., Nascimento, C.A.O. & Onimaru R.S. (2002). Use of neural networks in the analysis of particle size distribution by laser diffraction: tests with different particle systems, *Powder Technology* 126, 42-50. ISSN 0032-5910

Heinlein, J., Schulye, G., Fritsching, U. & Guardani, R. (2007). Mapping the structure of a liquid spray by means of neural networks. *Chemical Engineering and Processing* 46, 1357-1364. ISSN

Hussain, M.A. (1999). Review of the applications of neural networks in chemical process control-simulation and on line implementation, *Artificial Intelligence in Engineering*, 13, 55-68. ISSN 0952-1976

Islamoglu Y. (2003). A new approach for the prediction of the heat transfer rate of the wire-on-tube type heat exchanger-use of an artificial neural network model. *Applied Thermal Engineering* 23, 243-249. ISSN 1359-4311

Jones, H.V., Duller, A.W.G., Chantrell, R.W., Hoare, A. & Bissell, P.R. (1999). Application of neural networks to the determination of H_K distributions from transverse susceptibility data, *Journal of Magnetism and Magnetic Material* 193, 416-419. ISSN 0304-8853

Kahrs, O. & Marquardt, W. (2007). The validity domain of hybrid models and its applications in process optimization. *Chemical Engineering and Processing* 46, 1054-1066. ISSN 0255-2701

Lahiri, S.K. & Ghanta, K.C. (2008). Development of an artificial neural network correlation for prediction of hold-up of slurry transport in pipelines. *Chemical Engineering Science* 63, 1497-1509. ISSN 0009-2509

Liau, L.C. & Chen, Y.T. (2006). Process optimization of preparing silica particles with uniform distribution in sub-micron sizes using artificial neural networks. *Colloids and Surfaces A: Physicochemical and Engineering Aspects* 286, 138-143. ISNN 0927-7757

Liu, H.L., Yang, F.Ch., Lin, H.Y., Huang, Ch.H., Fang, H.W., Tsai, W.B. & Cheng, Y.Ch. (2008). Artificial neural network to predict the growth of the indigenous Acidthiobacillus thiooxidans. Chemical Engineering Journal 137, 231-237. ISSN 1385-8947

Liu, Q.F. & Kim, S.H. (2008). Evaluation of membrane fouling models based on bench-scale experiments: A comparison between constant flowrate blocking laws and artificial neural network (ANNs) model. *Journal of Membrane Science* 310, 393-401. ISSN 0376-7388

Nascimento, C.A.O., Guardani, R. & Giulietti, M. (1997). Use of neural networks in the analysis of particle size distributions by laser diffraction. Powder Technology 90, 89-94. ISSN 0032-5910

Ou, S. & Achenie, J. (2005). A hybrid neural network model for PEM fuel cells, *Journal of Power Sources*, 104, 319-330. ISSN 0378-7753

Pacheco-Vega, A., Sen, M., Yang, K.T. & McClain R.L. (2001). Neural network analysis of fin tube refrigerating heat exchanger with limited experimental data. *International Journal of Heat and Mass Transfer* 44, 763-770. ISSN 0017-9310

Thibault, J. & Grandjean, B.P.A. (1991). A neural network methodology for heat transfer data analysis. *Journal of Heat and Mass Transfer* 34, 2063-2070. ISSN 0017-9310

Yan, X. (2007). Data mining macrokinetic approach based on ANN and its application to model industrial oxidation of *p*-xylene to terephthalic acid. *Chemical Engineering Science* 62, 2641-2651. ISSN 0009-2509

Yilmaz, S. & Atik K. (2007). Modeling of a mechanical cooling system with variable cooling capacity by using artificial neural network. *Applied Thermal Engineering* 27, 2308-2313. ISSN 1359-4311

Zdaniuk G.J. (2006). Heat transfer and friction in helically-finned tubes using artificial neural networks, Ph.D. dissertation, Mississippi Sate University.

26

Application of Artificial Neural Networks and Hybrid Methods in the Solution of Inverse Problems

Jader Lugon Junior[1,5], Antônio J. da Silva Neto[2],
Luiz Biondi Neto[2], Francisco José da Cunha Pires Soeiro[2],
Cesar Costapinto Santana[3] and Haroldo F. Campos Velho[4]
[1]*Instituto Federal de Educação, Ciência e Tecnologia Fluminense,*
[2]*Universidade do Estado do Rio de Janeiro,*
[3]*Universidade Estadual de Campinas,*
[4]*Instituto Nacional de Pesquisas Espaciais*
[5]*Centro de Tecnologia SENAI-RJ Ambiental*
Brazil

1. Introduction

In this chapter Artificial Neural Networks are presented and used to solve different parameter estimation inverse problems, that is, Gas-liquid Adsorption Mass Transfer, Radiative Transfer Problems, and Simultaneous Heat and Mass Transfer. Besides, results obtained using hybrid methods are also presented, combining the Artificial Neural Network (ANN) method to other inverse problem solutions techniques, such as Simulated Annealing (SA) and Levenberg-Marquardt (LM).

The first problem studied is the radiative transfer phenomenon, modeled with an integro-differential equation known as Boltzmann equation. This equation describes mathematically the interaction of the radiation with the participating medium, i.e., a medium that may absorb, scatter and emit radiation. The inverse radiative transfer problem considered the simultaneous estimation of the absorption and scattering coefficients of a two-layer medium, using measured exit radiation intensities. In this sense, a study is presented regarding the estimation of radiative properties using ANN and hybrid methods combining ANN and LM.

Then, the inverse problem of simultaneous heat and mass transfer modeled by Luikov equations is studied using a hybrid combination of the ANN, LM and SA. Direct and inverse problems are presented, formulated and solved. An ANN was used to generate the initial guess for the LM, another ANN to approximate the gradient needed by LM, and finally the global minimum was searched using the SA. The experimental data used was generated using the solution for the direct problem with the addition of artificial noise.

The gas-liquid interface adsorption isotherm identification is also investigated using the same hybrid approach, that is, the combination of an ANN, LM and SA methods. The bubble and foam fractionation columns system works basically through the injection of a gas at the base of a column containing the solution. The gas bubbles formed in the distributor rise and along this path adsorb the solute, which is extracted in the foam region, formed above the bubble column. The inverse problem approach described allows the determination of the adsorption isotherms needed to solve the mathematical and numerical models developed.

2. Formulation of the direct heat and mass transfer problems

2.1 Radiative transfer

Consider the problem of radiative transfer in a composite medium with two plane-parallel, isotropically scattering, gray layers, with diffusely reflecting boundary surfaces and interface, as shown in Fig. 1. The medium is subjected to external irradiation at both sides with intensity $f_1(\mu)$ at $x=0$ and $f_2(\mu)$ at $x=L_1+L_2$, where μ is the cosine of the polar angle, and L_1 and L_2 represent the thickness of layers 1 and 2, respectively.

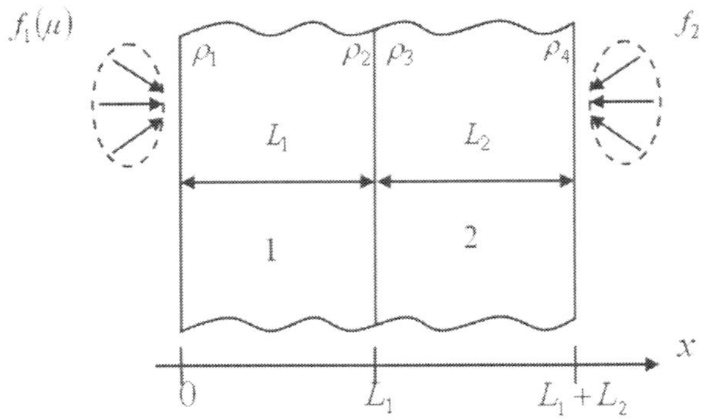

Fig. 1. Two-layer semitransparent medium.

The mathematical formulation of the direct steady-state radiative transfer problem with azymuthal symmetry is given by (Özisik, 1973)

Region 1

$$\mu\frac{\partial I_1(x,\mu)}{\partial x}+\beta_1 I_1(x,\mu)=\frac{\sigma_{s_1}}{2}\int_{-1}^{1} I_1(x,\mu')d\mu' \text{ in } 0<x<L_1,\ -1\le\mu\le 1 \tag{1a}$$

$$I_1(0,\mu)=f_1(\mu)+2\rho_1\int_0^1 I_1(0,-\mu')\mu' d\mu',\ \mu>0 \tag{1b}$$

$$I_1(L_1,\mu)=(1-\rho_3)I_2(L_1,\mu)+2\rho_2\int_0^1 I_1(L_1,\mu')\mu' d\mu',\ \mu<0 \tag{1c}$$

Region 2

$$\mu\frac{\partial I_2(x,\mu)}{\partial x}+\beta_2 I_2(x,\mu)=\frac{\sigma_{s_2}}{2}\int_{-1}^{1} I_2(x,\mu')d\mu' \text{ in } L_1<x<L_1+L_2,\ -1\le\mu\le 1 \tag{2a}$$

$$I_2(L_1,\mu)=(1-\rho_2)I_1(L_1,\mu)+2\rho_3\int_0^1 I_2(L_1,-\mu')\mu'd\mu',\ \mu>0 \tag{2b}$$

$$I_2(L_1+L_2,\mu)=f_2(\mu)+2\rho_4\int_0^1 I_2(L_1+L_2,\mu')\mu'd\mu',\ \mu<0 \tag{2c}$$

where $I_i(x,\mu)$ represents the radiation intensity in layer i, with $i=1 or 2$, β_i, is the total extinction coefficient

$$\beta_i=k_{a_i}+\sigma_{s_i} \tag{3}$$

k_{a_i} is the absorption coefficient, σ_{s_i} is the scattering coefficient, and ρ_j are the diffuse reflectivities, with $j=1,\ldots,4$.

When the geometry, the radiative properties, and the boundary conditions are known, problem (1-2) may be solved yielding the values of the radiation intensities $I_1(x,\mu)$, for $0\le x\le L_1$ and $-1\le\mu\le 1$, and $I_2(x,\mu)$, for $L_1\le x\le L_1+L_2$ and $-1\le\mu\le 1$. This is the direct problem. For the solution of the direct problem we use in the present work a combination of Chandrasekhar's discrete ordinates method (Chandrasekhar, 1960) with the finite difference method (Soeiro and Silva Neto, 2006).

2.2 Drying (simultaneous heat and mass transfer)

In Fig. 2, adapted from Mwithiga and Olwal, 2005, it is represented the drying experiment setup considered in this section. In the approach considered it was introduced the possibility of using a scale to weight the samples, and sensors to measure temperature in the sample, as well as inside the drying chamber.

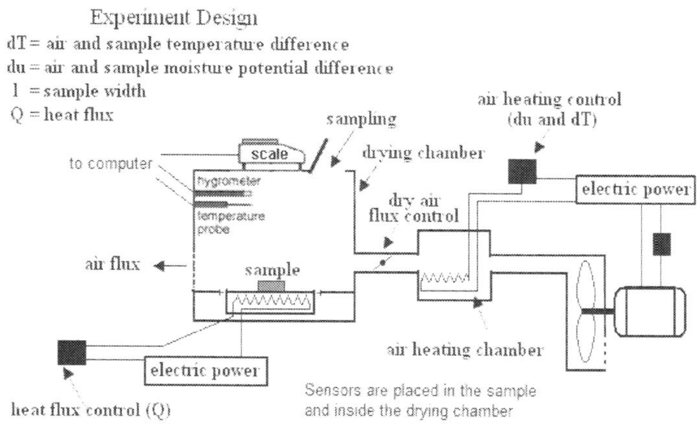

Fig. 2. Drying experiment setup (Adapted from Mwithiga and Olwal, 2005).

In accordance to the schematic representation shown in Fig. 3, consider the problem of simultaneous heat and mass transfer in a one-dimensional porous media in which heat is supplied to the left surface of the porous media, at the same time that dry air flows over the right boundary surface.

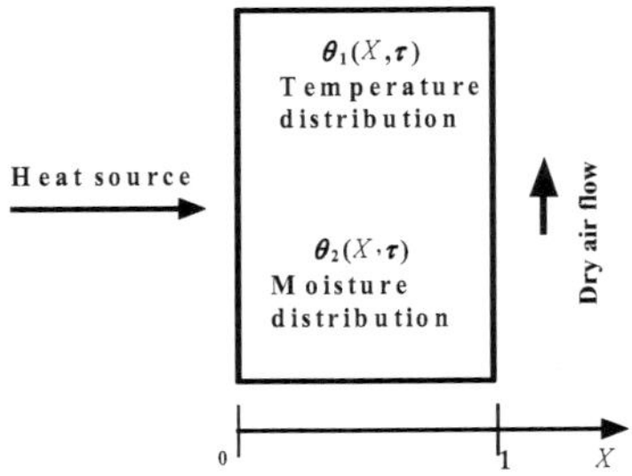

Fig. 3. Drying process schematic representation.

The mathematical formulation used in this work for the direct heat and mass transfer problem considered a constant properties model, and in dimensionless form it is given by (Luikov and Mikhailov, 1965; Mikhailov and Özisik, 1994),

$$\frac{\partial \theta_1(X,\tau)}{\partial \tau} = \alpha \frac{\partial^2 \theta_1}{\partial X^2} - \beta \frac{\partial^2 \theta_2}{\partial X^2}, \quad 0 < X < 1, \quad \tau > 0 \tag{4}$$

$$\frac{\partial \theta_2(X,\tau)}{\partial \tau} = Lu \frac{\partial^2 \theta_2}{\partial X^2} - Lu\, Pn \frac{\partial^2 \theta_1}{\partial X^2}, \quad 0 < X < 1, \quad \tau > 0 \tag{5}$$

subject to the following initial conditions, for $0 \le X \le 1$

$$\theta_1(X,0) = 0 \tag{6}$$

$$\theta_2(X,0) = 0 \tag{7}$$

and to the boundary conditions, for $\tau > 0$

$$\frac{\partial \theta_1(0,\tau)}{\partial X} = -Q \tag{8}$$

$$\frac{\partial \theta_2(0,\tau)}{\partial X} = -Pn\, Q \tag{9}$$

$$\frac{\partial \theta_1(1,\tau)}{\partial X} + Bi_q \theta_1(1,\tau) = Bi_q - (1-\varepsilon) Ko Lu Bi_m \left[1 - \theta_2(1,\tau)\right] = 0 \tag{10}$$

$$\frac{\partial \theta_2(1,\tau)}{\partial X} + Bi_m^* \theta_2(1,\tau) = Bi_m^* - [\theta_1(1,\tau) - 1] \tag{11}$$

where

$$\alpha = 1 + \varepsilon\, Ko\, Lu\, Pn \tag{12}$$

$$\beta = \varepsilon\, Ko\, Lu \tag{13}$$

$$Bi_m^* = Bi_m\left[1-(1-\varepsilon)Pn\,Ko\,Lu\right] \tag{14}$$

and the dimensionless variables are defined as

$$\theta_1(X,\tau)=\frac{T(x,t)-T_0}{T_s-T_0}\text{, temperature} \tag{15}$$

$$\theta_2(X,\tau)=\frac{u_0-u(x,t)}{u_0-u^*}\text{, moisture potential} \tag{16}$$

$$X=\frac{x}{l}\text{, spatial coordinate} \tag{17}$$

$$\tau=\frac{at}{l^2}\text{, time} \tag{18}$$

$$Lu=\frac{a_m}{a}\text{, Luikov number} \tag{19}$$

$$Pn=\delta\frac{T_s-T_0}{u_0-u^*}\text{, Possnov number} \tag{20}$$

$$Ko=\frac{r}{c}\frac{u_0-u^*}{T_s-T_0}\text{, Kossovitch number} \tag{21}$$

$$Bi_q=\frac{hl}{k}\text{, heat Biot} \tag{22}$$

$$Bi_m=\frac{h_m l}{k_m}\text{, mass Biot} \tag{23}$$

$$Q=\frac{ql}{k(T_s-T_0)}\text{, heat flux} \tag{24}$$

When the geometry, the initial and boundary conditions, and the medium properties are known, the system of equations (4-11) can be solved, yielding the temperature and moisture distribution in the media. The finite difference method was used to solve the system (4-11).
Many previous works have studied the drying inverse problem using measurements of temperature and moisture-transfer potential at specific locations of the medium. But to measure the moisture-transfer potential in a certain position is not an easy task, so in this work it is used the average quantity

$$\overline{u}(t)=\frac{1}{l}\int_{x=0}^{x=l}u(x,t)dx \tag{25}$$

or

$$\bar{\theta}_2(\tau) = \int_{X=0}^{X=1} \theta_2(X,\tau)dX \tag{26}$$

Therefore, in order to obtain the average moisture measurements, $\bar{u}(t)$, one have just to weight the sample at each time (Lugon and Silva Neto, 2010, Silva Neto et al., 2010).

2.3 Gas-liquid adsorption

The mechanism of proteins adsorption at gas-liquid interfaces represented in Fig. 4 has been the subject of intensive theoretical and experimental research, because of the potential use of bubble and foam fractionation columns as an economically viable means for surface active compounds recovery from diluted solutions, (Öztürk et al., 1987; Deckwer and Schumpe, 1993; Graham and Phillips, 1979; Santana and Carbonell, 1993a,b; Santana, 1994; Krishna and van Baten, 2003; Haut and Cartage, 2005; Mouza et al., 2005; Lugon, 2005).

The system works basically through the gas injection at the base of a column containing the solution. The gas bubbles formed in the distributor rise and along this path adsorb the solute. In the foam region, formed above the bubble column, the extraction of the material of interest is made (see Fig. 4).

The direct problem related to the gas-liquid interface adsorption of bio-molecules in bubble columns consists essentially in the calculation of the depletion, that is, the reduction of solute concentration with time, when the physico-chemical properties and process parameters are known.

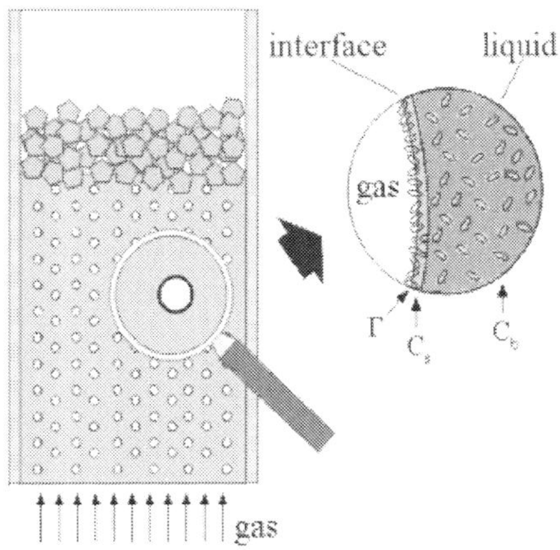

Fig. 4. Gas-liquid adsorption process in a bubble and foam column.

The solute depletion is modeled by

$$\frac{dC_b}{dt} = -\frac{6v_g}{\left(1-\varepsilon_g\right)Hd_b}\Gamma \tag{27}$$

where C_b is the liquid solute concentration (bulk), d_b is the bubble diameter, H is the bubble column height, v_g is the superficial velocity (gas volumetric flow rate divided by the area of the transversal section of the column, A), and Γ is the surface excess concentration of the adsorbed solute.

The symbol ε_g represents the gas volumetric fraction, which can be calculated from the dimensionless correlation of Kumar (Özturk et al., 1987),

$$\varepsilon_g = 0.728U - 0.485U^2 + 0.095U^3 \tag{28}$$

where

$$U = v_g \left[\frac{\rho_l^2}{\gamma\left(\rho_l - \rho_g\right)g} \right]^{\frac{1}{4}} \tag{29}$$

ρ_l is the liquid density, γ is the surface tension, g is the gravity acceleration, and ρ_g is the gas density.

The quantities Γ and C are related through adsorption isotherms such as:

i. Linear isotherm

$$\Gamma = B + KC \tag{30}$$

ii. Langmuir isotherm

$$\Gamma_1 = \frac{1}{\hat{a}} \left[\frac{K_1(T)C}{1 + K_1(T)C} \right] \tag{31}$$

iii. Two-layer isotherm

$$\Gamma_t = \Gamma_1 + \Gamma_2 = \frac{K_1(T)\exp(-\lambda\Gamma_1)C\left[1 + K_2(T)\hat{a}C\right]}{\hat{a}\left[1 + K_1\exp(-\lambda\,\Gamma_1)C\right]} \tag{32}$$

where Γ_1 and Γ_2 are the excess superficial concentration in the first and second adsorption layers respectively (see Fig. 4).

Considering that the superficial velocity, bubble diameter and column cross section are constant along the column,

$$\frac{\partial\Gamma(z,t)}{\partial z} = \frac{(k_l a)d_b\left[C_b(t) - C_s(z,t)\right]}{6v_g} \tag{33}$$

where z represents the spatial coordinate along the column, C_s is the solute concentration next to the bubbles and $(k_l a)$ is the volumetric mass transfer coefficient.

There are several correlations available for the determination of $(k_l a)$ but following the recommendation of Deckwer and Schumpe (1993) we have adopted the correlation of Öztürk et al. (1987) in the solution of the direct problem:

$$Sh = 0,62\,Sc^{0,5}\,Bo^{0,33}\,Ga^{0,29} \left(\frac{v_g}{\sqrt{gd_b}} \right)^{0,68} \left(\frac{\rho_g}{\rho_l} \right)^{0,04} \tag{34}$$

where

$$Sc = \left(\frac{\nu_l}{D_i} \right), \text{ Schmidt number} \tag{35}$$

$$Sh = \frac{(k_l a) d_b^2}{D_i}, \text{ Sherwood number} \tag{36}$$

$$Bo = \frac{\nu_l}{D_i}, \text{ Bond number} \tag{37}$$

$$Ga = \frac{g d_b^3}{\nu_l^2}, \text{ Galilei Number} \tag{38}$$

where D_i is the tensoactive diffusion coefficient and ν_l is the liquid dynamic viscosity. Combining Eqs. (27) and (33) and using an initial condition, such as $C_b = C_{b0}$ when $t = 0$, and a boundary condition, like $\Gamma = 0$ at $z = 0$, the solute concentration can be calculated as a function of time, $C_b(t)$. Santana and Carbonell (1993a,b) developed an analytical solution for the direct problem in the case of a linear adsorption isotherm and the results presented a good agreement with experimental data for BSA (Bovine Serum Albumin).
In order to solve Eq. (27) a second order Runge Kutta method was used, known as the mid point method. Given the physico-chemical and process parameters, as well as the boundary and initial conditions, the solute concentration can be calculated for any time t (Lugon et al., 2009).

3. Formulation of inverse heat and mass transfer problems

The inverse problem is implicitly formulated as a finite dimensional optimization problem (Silva Neto and Soeiro, 2003; Silva Neto and Moura Neto, 2005; Silva Neto and Becceneri, 2009), where one seeks to minimize the cost functional of squared residues between the calculated and experimental values for the observable variable,

$$S(\mathbf{P}) = \left[\mathbf{V}_{calc}(\mathbf{P}) - \mathbf{V}_{meas}(\mathbf{P}) \right]^T \mathbf{W} \left[\mathbf{V}_{calc}(\mathbf{P}) - \mathbf{V}_{meas}(\mathbf{P}) \right] = \mathbf{F}^T \mathbf{F} \tag{39a}$$

where $\mathbf{V}_{meas}$ is the vector of measurements, $\mathbf{V}_{calc}$ is the vector of calculated values, $\mathbf{P}$ is the vector of unknowns, $\mathbf{W}$ is the diagonal matrix whose elements are the inverse of the measurement variances, and the vector of residues $\mathbf{F}$ is given by

$$\mathbf{F} = \mathbf{V}_{calc}(\mathbf{P}) - \mathbf{V}_{meas}(\mathbf{P}) \tag{39b}$$

The inverse problem solution is the vector $\mathbf{P}^*$ which minimizes the norm given by Eq. (39a), that is

$$S(\mathbf{P}^*) = \min_{\mathbf{P}} S(\mathbf{P}) \tag{40}$$

Depending on the direct problem considered, as described in sections 2.1 - 2.3, different measurements are to be taken, that is:

a. Radiative problem

We are interested in obtaining estimates for the vector of unknowns $\mathbf{P}$, given by: σ_{s_1}, k_{a_1}, σ_{s_2} and k_{a_2}. Measured data were used on the emerging radiation intensity acquired at the boundary surfaces $x=0$ and $x=L_1+L_2$, and the interface $x=L_1$, Y_i, with $i=1,2,\ldots,N$, being N the total number of experimental data.

b. Drying problem

Using temperature measurements, T, taken by sensors located inside the medium, and the average of the moisture-transfer potential, $\overline{u}$, during the experiment, we try to estimate the vector of unknowns $\mathbf{P}$, for which a combination of variables was used: Lu (Luikov number), δ (thermogradient coefficient), r/c (relation between latent heat of evaporation and specific heat of the medium), h/k (relation between heat transfer coefficient and thermal conductivity), and h_m/k_m (relation between mass transfer coefficient and mass conductivity).

c. Gas-liquid adsorption problem

Different vectors of unknowns $\mathbf{P}$ are possibly considered, which are associated with different adsorption isotherms: (i) K and B (Linear isotherm); (ii) $K_1(T)$ and $\hat{a}$ (Langmuir isotherm); (iii) $K_1(T)$, $K_2(T)$, λ and $\hat{a}$ (two-layers isotherm). Here the BSA (Bovine Serum Albumin) adsorption phenomenon was modeled using a two-layer isotherm.

4. Solution of the inverse problems with Artificial Neural Networks, simulated annealing and hybrid methods

Instead of going directly to the description of the inverse problem solution methods, we opted for presenting first the approach considered in the analysis of the sensitivity of the observable variables with respect to the unknown parameters to be determined with the inverse problem solution.

4.1 Design of experiments

The sensitivity analysis plays a major role in several aspects related to the formulation and solution of an inverse problem (Dowding et al., 1999; Beck, 1988). Such analysis may be performed with the study of the sensitivity coefficients. Here we use the modified, or scaled, sensitivity coefficients

$$Y_{P_j V(t)} = P_j \frac{\partial V(t)}{\partial P_j}, \quad j=1,2,\ldots,N_p \tag{41}$$

where V is the observable state variable (which can be measured), P_j is a particular unknown of the problem, and N_p is the total number of unknowns considered.

As a general guideline, the sensitivity of the state variable to the parameter we want to determine must be high enough to allow an estimate within reasonable confidence bounds. Moreover, when two or more parameters are simultaneously estimated, their effects on the state variable must be independent (uncorrelated). Therefore, when represented graphically, the sensitivity coefficients should not have the same shape. If they do it means that two or more different parameters affect the observable variable in the same way, being difficult to distinguish their influences separately, which yields to poor estimations.

Another important tool used in the design of experiments is the study of the matrix

$$\mathbf{Y} = \begin{bmatrix} Y_{P_1V_1} & Y_{P_2V_2} & \dots & Y_{P_{N_P}V_1} \\ Y_{P_1V_2} & Y_{P_2V_2} & \dots & Y_{P_{N_P}V_2} \\ \dots & \dots & \dots & \dots \\ Y_{P_1V_m} & Y_{P_2V_m} & \dots & Y_{P_{N_P}V_m} \end{bmatrix} \tag{42}$$

where V_i is a particular measurement of the observable variable, i.e. radiation intensity, concentration, temperature or moisture potential, and m is the total number of measurements. Maximizing the determinant of the matrix $\mathbf{Y}^T\mathbf{Y}$ results in higher sensitivity and uncorrelation (Beck, 1988).

4.2 Artificial Neural Network (ANN)

The multi-layer perceptron (MLP) is a collection of connected processing elements called nodes or neurons, arranged in layers (Haykin, 1999). Signals pass into the input layer nodes, progress forward through the network hidden layers and finally emerge from the output layer (see Fig. 5). Each node i is connected to each node j in its preceding layer through a connection of weight, w_{ij}, and similarly to nodes in the following layer.

In order to solve the inverse problem we use here a multi-layer perceptron (MLP) neural network (Soeiro et al., 2004). In Fig. 5 is given a representation of the MLP with the input and output layers, and one hidden layer for the solution of the inverse problem of determining the vector of unknowns $\mathbf{P}$. By providing $\mathbf{V}_{meas}$ at the input layer we expect that the ANN will provide at the output layer an estimate for $\mathbf{P}$.

Each neuron j, with $j = 1,2,\dots,N_H$, in the hidden layer performs a linear combination of the input values provided at the input layer

$$p_j = \sum_{i=1}^{N} w_{ji}^{(1)} x_i + w_{j0}^{(1)} = \sum_{i=1}^{N} w_{ji}^{(1)} Y_i + w_{j0}^{(1)}, \quad j = 1,2,\dots,N_H \tag{43}$$

where $w_{ji}^{(1)}$, $j = 1,2,\dots,N_H$, $i = 1,2,\dots,N$ are the weights of the connections between the nodes of the input layer and the neurons of the hidden layer, N is the number of nodes in the input layer, and N_H is the number of neurons in the hidden layer.

The weighted sum p_j given by Eq. (43) is viewed as an excitation to neuron j of the hidden layer, which provides in response

$$q_j = f\left(p_j\right), \quad j = 1,2,\dots,N_H \tag{44}$$

where $f(.)$ is an activation function. Various choices for the function $f(.)$ are possible (Haykin, 1999).

Each neuron k, $k = 1,2,\dots,N_{un}$ of the output layer performs a linear combination of the response q_j, $j = 1,2,\dots,N_H$, of the neurons of the hidden layer

$$s_k = \sum_{j=1}^{N_H} w_{kj}^{(2)} q_j + w_{k0}^{(2)}, \qquad k = 1,2,\dots,N_{un} \tag{45}$$

where $w_{kj}^{(2)}$, $k = 1,2,\dots,N_u$, $j = 1,2,\dots,N_H$, are the weights of the connections between the neurons of the hidden layer and the neurons of the output layer, and N_{un} is the number of

neurons in the output layer, which coincides with the number of unknowns of the inverse problem..
The weighted sum s_k given by Eq. (45) is viewed as an excitation to neuron k of the output layer, which provides in response

$$t_k = g(s_k), \qquad k = 1,2,...,N_{un} \tag{46}$$

where $g(.)$ is an activation function. Various choices for the function $g()$ are possible (Haykin, 1999).
Combining Eqs. (43-46) we get

$$t_k = g\left(\sum_{j=1}^{N_H} w_{kj}^{(2)} f\left(\sum_{i=1}^{N} w_{ji}^{(1)} Y_i + w_{j0}^{(1)} \right) + w_{k0}^{(2)} \right) \qquad k = 1,2,...,N_{un} \tag{47}$$

Considering available the experimental data Y_i, $i = 1,2,...,N$, we observe in Eq. (47) that t_k, $k = 1,2,...,N_{un}$, are estimates for the unknowns Z_k, $k = 1,2,...,N_{un}$, obtained by the ANN. But before we can use Eq. (47) we must determine the weight parameters $w^{(1)}$ and $w^{(2)}$.

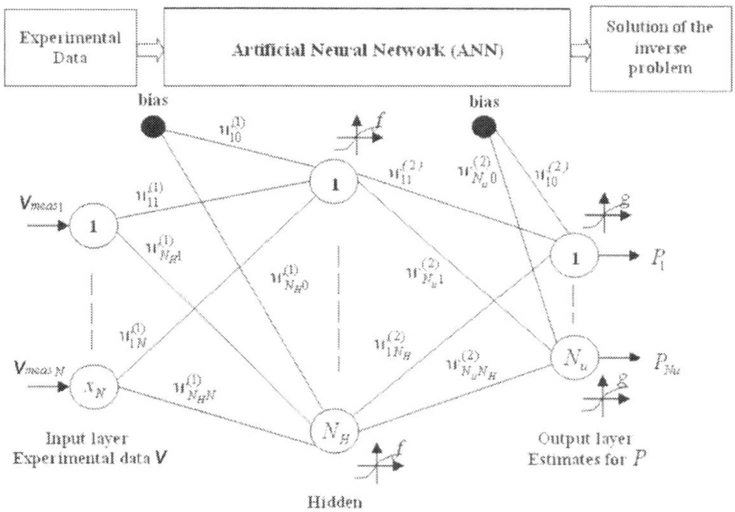

Fig. 5. Multi-layer perceptron network with one hidden layer for the inverse radiative transfer problem.

The determination of the weights $w^{(1)}$ and $w^{(2)}$ is accomplished by presenting a set of patterns (known input $\mathbf{P}_{exact}$ and outputs $\mathbf{V}_{exact}$) and calculating the weights that provides the best match between the calculated values $\mathbf{t}$ and the target values $\mathbf{P}_{exact}$. The patterns used in this supervised training stage of the ANN were generated by calculating the values $\mathbf{V}_{exact}$ from known sets $\mathbf{P}_{exact}$ with the discrete ordinates and finite difference solution (Soeiro and Silva Neto, 2006; Silva Neto and Becceneri, 2009).
For the determination of $w^{(1)}$ and $w^{(2)}$ we used the back propagation algorithm. We start with an initial guess for the weights, $w^{(1)n}$, $w^{(2)n}$, with $n = 0$, and the set of inputs $\mathbf{V}$ is

passed forward through the network yielding trial outputs $\mathbf{t}^{n=0}$ which are compared with the desired outputs $\mathbf{P}_{exact}$ leading to the errors,

$$e_k^n = P_{k\,exact} - t_k^n, \quad k = 1,2,\ldots,N_{un} \tag{48}$$

The weights are then adjusted using the information provided by the output error (Haykin, 1999)

$$w_{kj}^{(2)n+1} = w_{kj}^{(2)n} + \eta^{(2)}\delta_k^{(2)n} q_j^n \tag{49a}$$

$$w_{ji}^{(1)n+1} = w_{ji}^{(1)n} + \eta^{(1)}\delta_j^{(1)n} Y_i \tag{49b}$$

where

$$\delta_k^{(2)n} = e_k^n g'\left(s_k^n\right) \tag{50a}$$

$$\delta_j^{(1)n} = f'\left(p_j^n\right)\sum_{k=1}^{N_u}\delta_k^{(2)n} w_{kj}^{(2)n} \tag{50b}$$

$\eta^{(1)}$ and $\eta^{(2)}$ are the learning rates, which can assume different values for the weights between input-hidden layers (1) and hidden-output layers (2).

The forward and backward sweeps procedure is continued until a convergence criterion related to errors e_k, $k = 1,2,\ldots,N_{un}$, is satisfied.

The presentation of a full set of patterns is denominated epoch. After one epoch is completed the set of patterns is presented again, in a different (random) order. After a number of epochs, once the comparison error is reduced to an acceptable level over the whole training set, the training phase ends and the ANN is established.

4.3 Simulated Annealing method (SA)

Based on statistical mechanics reasoning, applied to a solidification problem, Metropolis et al. (1953) introduced a simple algorithm that can be used to accomplish an efficient simulation of a system of atoms in equilibrium at a given temperature. In each step of the algorithm a small random displacement of an atom is performed and the variation of the energy ΔE is calculated. If $\Delta E<0$ the displacement is accepted, and the configuration with the displaced atom is used as the starting point for the next step. In the case of $\Delta E>0$, the new configuration can be accepted according to Boltzmann probability,

$$P(\Delta E) = \exp\left(-\Delta E / k_B T\right) \tag{51}$$

A uniformly distributed random number p in the interval [0,1] is calculated and compared with $P(\Delta E)$. Metropolis criterion establishes that the new configuration is accepted if $p<P(\Delta E)$, otherwise it is rejected and the previous configuration is used again as a starting point.

Using the objective function $S(\mathbf{P})$, given by Eq. (39a), in place of energy and defining configurations by a set of variables $\{P_i\}, i = 1,2,\ldots,N_p$ where N_p represents the number of unknowns we want to estimate, the Metropolis procedure generates a collection of

configurations of a given optimization problem at some temperature T (Kirkpatric et al., 1983). This temperature is simply a control parameter. The simulated annealing process consists of first "melting" the system being optimized at a high "temperature", then lowering the "temperature" until the system "freezes" and no further change occurs.
The main control parameters of the algorithm implemented ("cooling procedure") are the initial "temperature", T_0, the cooling rate, r_t, number of steps performed through all elements of vector $\mathbf{P}$, N_s, number of times the procedure is repeated before the "temperature" is reduced, N_t, and the number of points of minimum (one for each temperature) that are compared and used as stopping criterion if they all agree within a tolerance ε, N_ε.

4.4 Levenberg-Marquardt method (LM)

The Levenberg-Marquardt is a deterministic local optimizer method based on the gradient (Marquardt, 1963). In order to minimize the functional $S(\mathbf{P})$ we first write

$$\frac{dS}{d\mathbf{P}} = \frac{d}{d\mathbf{P}}(\mathbf{F}^T\mathbf{F}) = 0 \rightarrow \mathbf{J}^T\mathbf{F} = 0 \tag{52}$$

where J is the Jacobian matrix, with the elements $J_{ps} = \partial V_p / \partial P_s$ being $p = 1, 2, ..., M$, and $s = 1, 2, ..., N_p$, where M is the total number of measurements and N_p is the number of unknowns. It is observed that the elements of the Jacobian matrix are related to the scaled sensitivity coefficients presented before.
Using a Taylor's expansion and keeping only the terms up to the first order,

$$\mathbf{F}(\mathbf{P} + \Delta\mathbf{P}) \cong \mathbf{F}(\mathbf{P}) + \mathbf{J}\Delta\mathbf{P} \tag{53}$$

Introducing the above expansion in Eq. (52) results

$$\mathbf{J}^T\mathbf{J}\Delta\mathbf{P} = -\mathbf{J}^T\mathbf{F}(\mathbf{P}) \tag{54}$$

In the Levenberg-Marquardt method a damping factor γ^n is added to the diagonal of matrix $\mathbf{J}^T\mathbf{J}$ in order to help to achieve convergence.
Equation (54) is written in a more convenient form to be used in the iterative procedure,

$$\Delta\mathbf{P}^n = -\left[(\mathbf{J}^n)^T\mathbf{J}^n + \gamma^n\mathbf{I}\right](\mathbf{J}^n)^T\mathbf{F}(\mathbf{P}^n) \tag{55}$$

where $\mathbf{I}$ is the identity matrix and n is the iteration index.
The iterative procedure starts with an estimate for the unknown parameters, $\mathbf{P}^0$, being new estimates obtained with $\mathbf{P}^{n+1} = \mathbf{P}^n + \Delta\mathbf{P}^n$, while the corrections $\Delta\mathbf{P}^n$ are calculated with Eq. (55). Actually in most cases the vector $\Delta\mathbf{P}^n$ is obtained directly from the solution of the linear system of equations (54). This iterative procedure is continued until a convergence criterion such as

$$\left|\Delta P_k^n / P_k^n\right| < \varepsilon, \qquad n = 1, 2, \cdots, N_p \tag{56}$$

is satisfied, where ε is a small number, e.g. 10^{-5}.
The elements of the Jacobian matrix, as well as the right side term of Eq. (54), are calculated at each iteration, using the solution of the direct problem with the estimates for the unknowns obtained in the previous iteration.

In order to calculate the gradient, a central difference approximation was used (Lugon Jr. and Silva Neto, 2010; Silva Neto et al., 2010)

$$\frac{\partial V}{\partial P} = \frac{V(P+\Delta P) - V(P-\Delta P)}{2 \times \Delta P} \tag{57}$$

In the beginning of the process, an ANN trained to solve the direct problem was used to approximate $V(P+\Delta P)$ and $V(P-\Delta P)$. This faster scheme proved to be accurate enough to begin the process. Afterwards, the direct problem solution itself was used in Eq. (57) and although being slower, it offers better results at the final stages of the LM method.

4.5 Hybrid combination of ANN, LM and SA optimizers

Due to the complexity of the design space, if convergence is achieved with a gradient based method it may in fact lead to a local minimum. Therefore, global optimization methods are required in order to reach better approximations for the global minimum. The main disadvantage of these methods is that the number of function evaluations is high, becoming sometimes prohibitive from the computational point of view (Soeiro et al., 2004).

In this chapter different combinations of methods are used for the solution of inverse heat and mass transfer problems, involving in all cases Artificial Neural Networks:

a. when solving radiative inverse problems, it was used a combination of the ANN and LM;
b. when solving adsorption and drying inverse problems, it was used a combination of ANN, LM and SA.

Therefore, in all cases studied ANN was used after the training stage in order to quickly provide an inverse problem solution. This solution was used as an initial guess for the LM.

In order to improve the solution, we have also studied the combination of ANN, LM and SA methods. After using LM, reaching within a few iterations a point of minimum, we run the SA. If the same solution is reached, it is likely that a global minimum was reached, and the iterative procedure is interrupted. If a different solution is obtained it means that the previous one was a local minimum, otherwise we could run again the LM and SA until the global minimum is reached.

5. Test case results

As real data for the three problems considered were not available we simulated the experimental data using

$$V_{p_{meas}} = V_{p_{calc}} + r_p \sigma \ , \ p = 1,2,\ldots,N_p \tag{58}$$

where r_p is a random number in the range $[-1,1]$ and σ simulates the standard deviation of the measurements error.

5.1 Radiative transfer problem

In Table 1 we present the results obtained with the LM method starting with the initial guess: $\sigma_{s_1} = 0.10\ cm^{-1}$, $k_{a_1} = 0.8\ cm^{-1}$, $\sigma_{s_2} = 0.10\ cm^{-1}$ and $k_{a_2} = 0.8\ cm^{-1}$ for the particular case with the exact values for the unknowns $\sigma_{s_1} = 0.45\ cm^{-1}$, $k_{a_1} = 0.05\ cm^{-1}$, $\sigma_{s_2} = 0.45\ cm^{-1}$ and $k_{a_2} = 0.05\ cm^{-1}$ (maximum noise in the experimental data = 8%,

i.e. σ = 0.002 in Eq. (58). Note that LM does not converge with such initial guesses for the unknown parameters.
For the test case presented it is also considered $L_1 = L_2 = 2cm$, $\rho_1 = 0.1$, $\rho_2 = \rho_3 = 0$, $\rho_4 = 0.9$, $f_1 = 1.0$ and $f_2 = 0$, which represents a difficult test case.

Iteration	σ_{s_1} (cm^{-1})	k_{a_1} (cm^{-1})	σ_{s_2} (cm^{-1})	k_{a_2} (cm^{-1})	*Obj. Func. [Eq.(39a)]*
0	0.10	0.8	0.10	0.8	7.439
5	0.52	0.049	2.1E09	0.01	6.86E-01
10	0.45	0.05	5.5E07	3.7E07	1.216

Table 1. Estimates obtained with LM (10 iterations). Noisy data (8%)

In Table 2 are shown the results for the same test case using ANNs, and in Tables 3 and 4 are presented the results obtained when the ANN is used to generate the initial guess for the LM method. Here we used noisy data (maximum 8%), i.e., σ = 0.002 in Eq. (58). The experimental data used for the solution of the inverse problem consisted of a set of 40 radiation intensities measured at different polar angles, 20 intensities measured by external detectors and 20 intensities measured by internal detectors located at the interface between the two-layers, i.e. $x = L_1$. Therefore, there are N = 40 entries in the input layer of the ANN. For the hidden layer we considered $N_H = N = 40$. We used 500 patterns (N_P) and a decreasing number of epochs (N_E) in order to save computational time.
In this work the Neural Network Toolbox of the software MATLAB (Mathworks, Inc.) was used with the following neuron model in the backpropagation network: 40 elements in the input vector, log-sigmoid (logsig) transfer (activation) function between the input layer and the hidden layer (with 40 elements) and a linear transfer function (purelin) in the output layer (with 4 elements in the output vector).

NE	CPU *time(min)*	Estimates (ANN)			
		σ_{s_1} (cm^{-1})	k_{a_1} (cm^{-1})	σ_{s_2} (cm^{-1})	k_{a_2} (cm^{-1})
500	120	0.40	0.01	0.43	0.01
200	48	0.34	0.01	0.33	0.01
100	22	0.35	0.09	0.32	0.09
30	7,5	0.50	0.10	0.60	0.05

Exact values: $\sigma_{s_1} = \sigma_{s_2} = 0.45cm^{-1}$, $k_{a_1} = k_{a_2} = 0.05cm^{-1}$

Table 2. Neural Network solutions for the inverse problem and CPU time considering different number of epochs ($N_H = 40$, $N_P = 500$) and noisy data (8%)

It can be observed from Table 2 that the ANN did not provide good estimates for the unknowns. An improvement can be obtained, but at the expense of a higher CPU time requirement. A different strategy is then adopted with a hybridization ANN-LM. In Table 3 are presented the results obtained with such hybridization in which the former method provides an initial guess for the latter. The solution of the ANN was obtained considering 100 epochs in the training stage of the ANN. An improvement in the results of the inverse problem is then observed.

Noise	ANN estimates				Results (LM)			
	σ_{s_1} (cm^{-1})	k_{a_1} (cm^{-1})	σ_{s_2} (cm^{-1})	k_{a_2} (cm^{-1})	σ_{s_1} (cm^{-1})	k_{a_1} (cm^{-1})	σ_{s_2} (cm^{-1})	k_{a_2} (cm^{-1})
8%	0.35	0.09	0.32	0.09	0.447	0.050	0.455	0.050
4%	0.40	0.03	0.45	0.04	0.450	0.050	0.445	0.049
2%	0.39	0.04	0.42	0.05	0.450	0.049	0.449	0.050
0%	0.37	0.04	0.40	0.05	0.45	0.05	0.45	0.05

Table 3. Combined method results with ANN to obtain estimates for the LM, with noisy data and number of epochs N_E = 100. Exact values $\sigma_{s_1} = 0.450$, $k_{a_1} = 0.05$, $\sigma_{s_2} = 0.450$ and $k_{a_2} = 0.050$

In Table 4 are shown the results obtained using also the hybridization ANN-LM, but now with only 30 epochs in the training stage of the ANN. It can also be observed that very good results are obtained for the inverse problem.

Noise	ANN estimates				Results (ANN-LM)			
	σ_{s_1} (cm^{-1})	k_{a_1} (cm^{-1})	σ_{s_2} (cm^{-1})	k_{a_2} (cm^{-1})	σ_{s_1} (cm^{-1})	k_{a_1} (cm^{-1})	σ_{s_2} (cm^{-1})	k_{a_2} (cm^{-1})
8%	0.50	0.10	0.60	0.05	0.447	0.050	0.455	0.050
4%	0.49	0.01	0.47	0.01	0.450	0.050	0.445	0.049
2%	0.54	0.03	0.53	0.04	0.449	0.050	0.449	0.050
0%	0.51	0.02	0.49	0.04	0.45	0.05	0.450	0.050

Table 4. Combined method results with ANN providing estimates for the LM, with noisy data and number of number of epochs N_E = 100. Exact values $\sigma_{s_1} = 0.450$, $k_{a_1} = 0.05$, $\sigma_{s_2} = 0.450$ and $k_{a_2} = 0.050$

It must be stressed that the solution of the inverse problem with either the LM or ANN methods using only external detectors led to non-unique solutions of the inverse radiative transfer problem. That is the reason why internal detectors located at the interface of the two layers were also considered for the solution of the inverse problem.

5.2 Drying (simultaneous heat and mass transfer)

Much research effort has already been made in order to estimate the Possnov, Kossovitch, heat Biot and mass Biot numbers (Dantas et al., 2003; Huang and Yeh, 2002; Lugon Jr. and Silva Neto, 2004), but it was considered the possibility of optimizing the number and location of temperature sensors, experiment duration, etc. In this work instead, δ, r/c, h/k and h_m/k_m are estimated using an "optimum" experiment (Dowding et al., 1999 and Beck, 1988) for wood drying, and doing so, it was also considered the following process control parameters: heat flux, Q, the medium width, l, the difference between the medium and the air temperatures, $dT = T_s - T_0$, and the difference between the medium and the air moisture potential, $du = u_0 - u^*$.
There is no difference between the sensitivity coefficients for the two sets of variables, that is, the scaled sensitivity coefficients are exactly the same for both vectors $\{Lu, Pn, Ko, Bi_q, Bi_m, \varepsilon\}^T$ and $\{Lu, \delta, r/c, h/k, h_m/k_m, \varepsilon\}^T$,

$$SC_{\delta}(X,\tau)=\delta\frac{\partial V(X,\tau)}{\partial \delta}=Pn\frac{\partial V(X,\tau)}{\partial Pn}=SC_{Pn}(X,\tau) \quad (59a)$$

$$SC_{r/c}(X,\tau)=r/c\frac{\partial V(X,\tau)}{\partial r/c}=Ko\frac{\partial V(X,\tau)}{\partial Ko}=SC_{Ko}(X,\tau) \quad (59b)$$

$$SC_{h/k}(X,\tau)=h/k\frac{\partial V(X,\tau)}{\partial h/k}=Bi_q\frac{\partial V(X,\tau)}{\partial Bi_q}=SC_{Bi_q}(X,\tau) \quad (59c)$$

$$SC_{h_m/k_m}(X,\tau)=h_m/k_m\frac{\partial V(X,\tau)}{\partial h_m/k_m}=Bi_m\frac{\partial V(X,\tau)}{\partial Bi_m}=SC_{Bi_m}(X,\tau) \quad (59d)$$

The reasons for changing the estimated variables are the use of the design of experiment tools and interpretation. Consider the heat and mass Biot numbers for example. If one changes the media width, l, both heat and mass Biot numbers change. The mathematical problem would be different, even though the material is still the same, because one is estimating two different heat and mass Biot numbers. In order to solve this problem, it was decided to estimate the relation between heat transfer coefficient and thermal conductivity, h/k, and the relation between mass transfer coefficient and mass conductivity, h_m/k_m, so that we could change the media width and continue with the same value for both variables to be estimated.

The same idea was used, choosing to estimate the thermogradient coefficient (δ) and the relation between latent heat of evaporation and specific heat of the medium (r/c), instead of the Possnov (Pn) and Kossovitch (Ko) numbers. Doing so, one is able to optimize the experiment considering the difference between the medium and the air temperatures, $dT=T_s-T_0$, and the difference between the moisture-transfer potential between the medium and the air, $du=u_0-u^*$, without affecting the estimated parameters values.

In Fig. 7 is represented the variation of the value of the matrix $\mathbf{Y}^T\mathbf{Y}$ determinant as a function of the temperature differences and moisture potential differences between the medium and the air flowing over it. It is not difficult to understand that one could not build such a graph using a vector of unknown parameters containing Possnov (Pn) and Kossovitch (Ko) numbers. In order to achieve greater sensitivities, while the temperature difference has to be the lowest, the moisture potential difference has to be the highest possible. The solid square represents the chosen designed experiment, considering the existence of practical difficulties that may limit our freedom of choice.

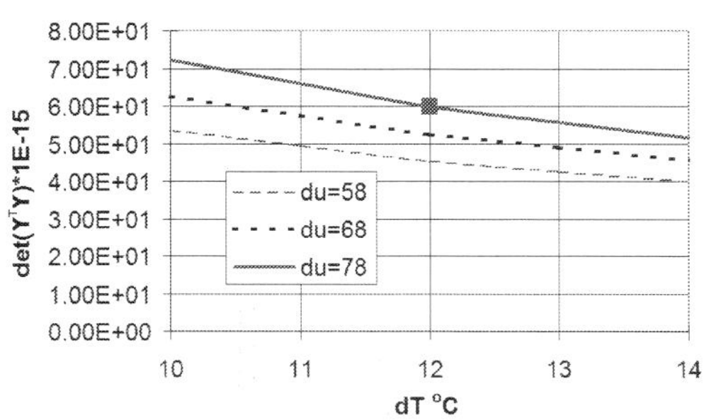

Fig. 7. Determinant of matrix $\mathbf{Y}^T\mathbf{Y}$ as a function of temperature (dT) and moisture potential ($d\overline{u}$) differences.

In Fig. 8 are represented the values of the determinant of matrix $\mathbf{Y}^T\mathbf{Y}$ for different values of the heat flux Q and media thickness l. It is also easy to understand that one could not build such a graph using a vector of unknown parameters containing heat and mass Biot numbers. For practical reasons it was chosen to limit the sample temperature to 130° C. In Fig. 8 the same curve has a continuous-line part and a dashed-line one, when the sample temperature exceeds the limit of 130° C. The solid square shows the chosen designed experiment.

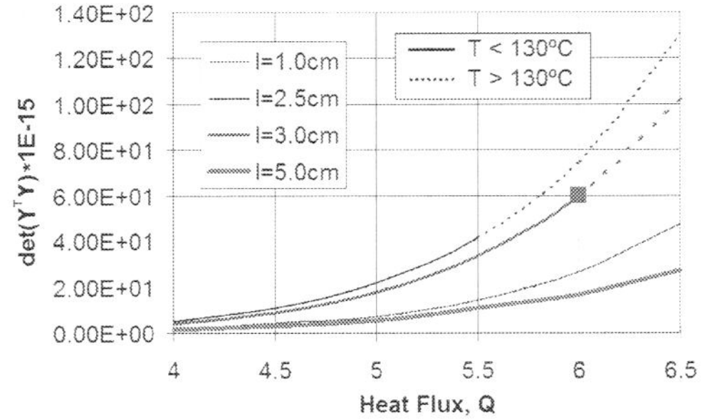

Fig. 8. Determinant of $\mathbf{Y}^T\mathbf{Y}$ matrix for different values of the heat flux Q and medium thickness l.

Considering the previous analysis of the sensitivity graphs and matrix the $\mathbf{Y}^T\mathbf{Y}$ determinant, it was designed the experiment whose geometric and process parameters are shown in Table 5. Since the average moisture potential, $\bar{u}$, is more difficult to measure than the temperature, θ_1, the measurement interval for the average moisture potential, $\Delta\tau_{\bar{u}}$, was considered larger than the interval for the temperature $\Delta\tau_{\theta_1}$.

Geometric or process parameter	Values	Geometric or process parameter	Values
$dT = T_s - T_0$	12 °C	Q	6.0
T_0	24 °C	l	0.03 m
T_s	36 °C	τ_0	0
$du = u_0 - u^*$	78 °M	τ_f	20
u_0	86 °M	$\Delta\tau_{\theta_1}$	0.2
u^*	8 °M	$\Delta\tau_{\bar{u}}$	1
ε	0.2	-	-

τ_0 and τ_f represent the initial and sampling times, respectively.

Table 5. Reference values for the designed experiment.

An experiment was designed to perform the simultaneous estimation of Lu, δ, r/c, h/k and h_m/k_m. In order to study the proposed method, since real experiment data were not available, we generated synthetic data using

$$\theta_{1meas_i} = \theta_{1calc_i}(\vec{P}_{exact}) + \sigma_{\theta_1} r_i\,,\ i = 1,\ 2,\ \ldots,\ M_{\theta_1} \qquad (60a)$$

$$\bar{u}_{meas_i} = \bar{u}_{calc_i}(\vec{P}_{exact}) + \sigma_{\bar{u}} r_i \,, \; i = 1,\, 2,\, \ldots,\, M_{\bar{u}} \tag{60b}$$

where r_i are random numbers in the range [-1,1], M_{θ_1} and $M_{\bar{u}}$ represent the total number of temperature and moisture-transfer potential experimental data, and σ_{θ_1} and $\sigma_{\bar{u}}$ emulates the standard deviation of measurement errors. It was established a standard deviation of $\sigma_{\theta_1} = 0.03$ considering 100 temperature measurements ($\Delta\tau = 0.2$), resulting in a maximum error of 2%, and $\sigma_{\bar{u}} = 0.001$ considering 20 moisture measurements ($\Delta\tau = 1.0$), resulting in a maximum error of 4%.

In Fig. 9 the temperature (θ_1) and moisture potential ($\bar{\theta}_2$) measurements are presented. The continuous line represents the direct problem solution and the squares represent noisy data. In order to show a better representation, only 20 temperature (θ_1) measurements were represented.

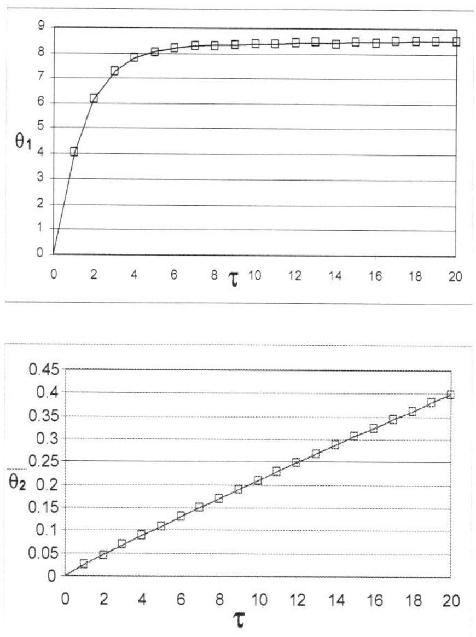

Fig. 9. Temperature (θ_1) and moisture potential ($\bar{\theta}_2$) artificially simulated data.

The results obtained using the methods LM 1 (gradient approximated by FDM - Finite Difference method), LM 2 (gradient approximated by Artificial Neural Networks), ANN, SA and hybrid combinations, for different levels of noise represented by different values of the standard deviation of measurements errors in temperature and average moisture potential, σ_T and $\sigma_{\bar{u}}$, respectively in Eqs. (60a,b) are shown in Table 6.

One observes that when there is no noise, that is, the standard deviation of measurements errors are zero, the LM method was able to estimate all variables very quickly (see test cases 1 and 2). When noise is introduced, the LM is retained by local minima (test cases 3 and 4); the ANN did not reach a good solution, but quickly got close to it (test case 5). The ANN solution was then used as a first guess for the LM method with good performance in test cases 6 and 7. The SA reached a good solution but required the largest CPU time, and finally the combination of all methods was able to reach a good solution, without being retained by local minima, and also without taking too much time, i.e. one sixth of the SA time. The time shown in the eleventh column of Table 6 corresponds to the CPU time on a Pentium IV 2.8 GHz processor (Lugon Jr., 2005; Silva Neto et al., 2010).

Case	Method	σ_{θ_1}	σ_Z	Information	Lu	δ	r/c	h/k	h_m/k_m	Time (s)	S Eq. (39a)
-	-	-	-	Exact values	0.0080	2.0	10.83	34.0	114.0	-	-
1	LM 1 (grad. FDM)	0	0	Initial guess	0.0040	1.50	8.00	20.0	80.0	15	0
				Result $\vec{Z}_{LM\,FDM}$	0.0080	2.00	10.83	34.0	114.0		
2	LM 2 (grad. ANN)	0	0	Initial guess	0.0040	1.50	8.00	25.0	80.0	10	0
				Result $\vec{Z}_{LM\,ANN}$	0.0080	2.00	10.83	34.0	114.0		
3	LM 1 (grad. FDM)	0.03	0.001	Initial guess	0.0040	1.50	8.00	20.0	80.0	15	977
				Result $\vec{Z}_{LM\,FDM}$	0.0076	2.09	10.76	34.1	121.2		
4	LM 2 (grad. ANN)	0.03	0.001	Initial guess	0.0040	1.50	8.00	20.0	80.0	11	897
				Result $\vec{Z}_{LM\,ANN}$	0.0093	1.71	10.73	34.1	95.7		
5	ANN (without initial guess)	0.03	0.001	Result $\vec{Z}_{ANN}$	0.0083	2.10	10.04	35.0	117.1	1	3190
6	LM 1 (grad. FDM)	0.03	0.001	Initial guess $\vec{Z}_{ANN}$	0.0083	2.10	10.04	35.0	117.1	16	974
				Result $\vec{Z}_{LM\,FDM}$	0.0083	1.92	10.75	34.1	110.0		
7	LM 2 (grad. ANN)	0.03	0.001	Initial guess $\vec{Z}_{ANN}$	0.0083	2.10	10.04	35.0	117.1	11	903
				Result $\vec{Z}_{LM\,ANN}$	0.0082	1.79	9.89	35.1	114.5		
8	SA (SA 20,000 evaluations)	0.03	0.001	Initial guess	0.0040	1.50	8.00	25.0	80.0	300	856
				Result $\vec{Z}_{SA}$	0.0094	1.58	9.96	35.0	98.2		
9	ANN-LM 2-SA (SA 2,000 evaluations)	0.03	0.001	Initial guess $\vec{Z}_{ANN}$	0.0083	2.10	10.04	35.0	117.1	47	760
				Result $\vec{Z}_{LM\,ANN}$	0.0082	1.79	9.89	35.1	114.5		
				Result $\vec{Z}_{SA}$	0.0079	2.01	11.00	33.9	113.8		
				Result $\vec{Z}_{LM\,ANN}$	0.0080	2.05	10.93	33.8	113.9		

Table 6. Results obtained using LM 1 (partial derivatives obtained with finite differences), LM 2 (partial derivatives obtained with Artificial Neural Network), ANN, and, and hybrid combinations.

5.3 Gas-liquid adsorption

Recently, the inverse problem of interface adsorption has attracted the attention of an increasing number of researchers (Lugon Jr., 2005; Forssén et al., 2006; Garnier et al., 2007; Voelkel and Strzemiecka, 2007; Ahmad and Guiochon, 2007).

Based on sensitivity analysis we concluded that in order to solve the inverse problem of gas-liquid adsorption, considering the two-layer isotherm given by Eq. (32), it was necessary to design two different experiments. One to estimate $K_2(T)$ and $\hat{a}$, called experiment 1, and another one to estimate λ, called experiment 2. In all cases studied the sensitivity to $K_1(T)$ is low and therefore this parameter was not estimated with the inverse problem solution.

In Fig. 10 are shown the sensitivity coefficients related to the parameters $K_1(T)$, $K_2(T)$, λ and $\hat{a}$ in experiment 1. It is observed that the sensitivity to $K_2(T)$ and $\hat{a}$ for BSA (Bovine

Serum Albumin) are higher than the sensitivity to the other parameters and their shapes are different, indicating that these variable are uncorrelated.

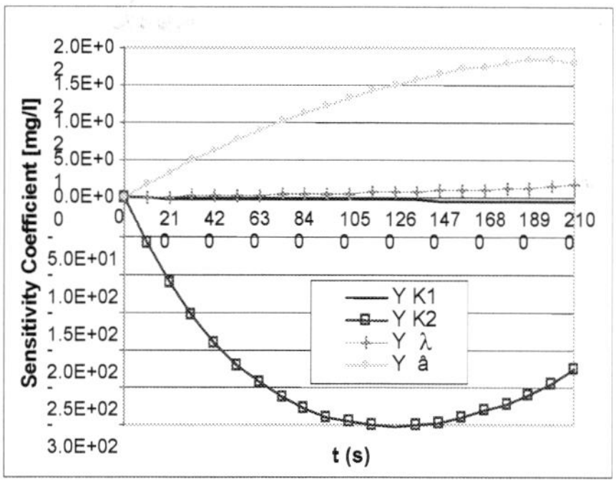

Fig. 10. Scaled sensitivity coefficients for BSA - Experiment 1.

In Fig. 11 are shown the sensitivity coefficients related to the parameters $K_1(T)$, $K_2(T)$, λ and $\hat{a}$ for BSA in experiment 2. It is observed that the sensitivity to λ is higher than the sensitivity to the other parameters.
Another important tool used in the design of experiments is the study of the matrix $\mathbf{Y}^T\mathbf{Y}$, that is, maximizing the determinant of the matrix $\mathbf{Y}^T\mathbf{Y}$ results in higher sensitivity and uncorrelation (Dowding et al., 1999).

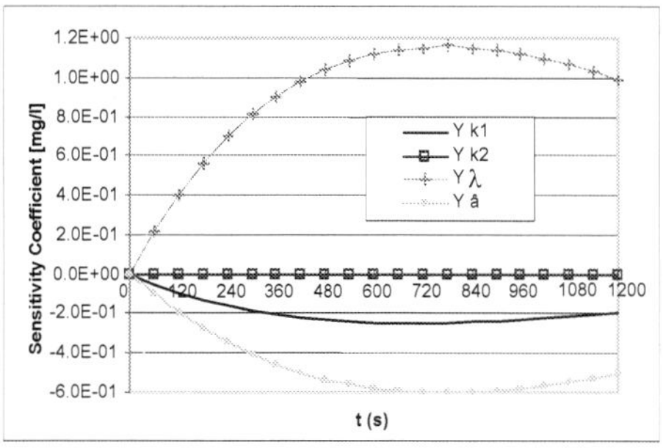

Fig. 11. Scaled sensitivity coefficients for BSA - Experiment 2.

The difference between the two experiments is related to the BSA concentration, being larger in the first experiment (see Table 7).
In Fig. 12 are shown the values of the determinant of the matrix $\mathbf{Y}^T\mathbf{Y}$ for BSA in experiment 1. The designed experiment is marked with a full square. Its choice is justified by the small gain in sensitivity considering the operational difficulties in using a longer column or a higher superficial velocity.
Considering the analysis of the sensitivity graphs and the determinant of the matrix $\mathbf{Y}^T\mathbf{Y}$, two experiments were designed, one to estimate $K_2(T)$ and $\hat{a}$, and another to estimate λ, as shown in Table 7.

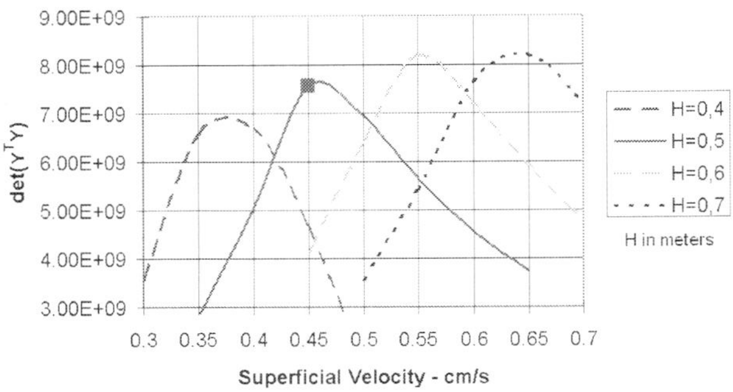

Fig. 12. Matrix $Y^T Y$ determinant for BSA – Experiment 1.

	Units	Experiment	
		1	2
Estimated parameters	-	K_2, $\hat{a}$	$\hat{\lambda}$
Initial solute concentration, C_{b0}	g/m³	1,000	10
Bubble column height, H	m	0.50	0.80
Superficial velocity, v_g	m/s	4.50E-3	1.00E-3
First measurement	s	210	120
time measurement steps	s	210	120
Last measurement	s	2100	1200

Table 7. Reference values for the designed experiment (Lugon, 2005, Lugon et al., 2009).

The results achieved using the ANN, LM 1 (gradient approximated by FDM), LM 2 (gradient approximated by ANN), SA and hybrid combinations, for different standard deviations for the measurements errors, σ, are shown in Tables 8 and 9.

In Table 8 are presented the results obtained for the estimation of $K_2(T)$ and $\hat{a}$, using the designed experiment number 1. Test cases 3-9 used simulated artificial data generated with

Case	Method	σ	Information	k_2	$\hat{a}$	Time (s)	S [mg²/l²] Eq. (39a)
1	LM 1 (grad. FDM)	0	Result $\vec{Z}_{LM\,FDM}$	0.01040	0.322	169	0
2	LM 2 (grad. ANN)	0	Result $\vec{Z}_{LM\,ANN}$	0.01040	0.322	80	0
3	LM 1 (grad. FDM)	10	Result $\vec{Z}_{LM\,FDM}$	0.00790	0.158	170	8.39
4	LM 2 (grad. ANN)	10	Result $\vec{Z}_{LM\,ANN}$	0.00805	0.157	78	8.64
5	RNA	10	Result $\vec{Z}_{ANN}$	0.01101	0.377	1	6.81
6	LM 1 (grad. FDM)	10	Result $\vec{Z}_{LM\,FDM}$	0.01080	0.335	172	6.27
7	LM 2 (grad. ANN)	10	Result $\vec{Z}_{LM\,ANN}$	0.01058	0.314	79	5.68
8	SA (2.000 evaluations)	10	Result $\vec{Z}_{SA}$	0.01050	0.312	6034	4.22
9	ANN-LM-SA SA (200 evaluations)	10	Result $\vec{Z}_{LM\,ANN}$	0.01101	0.377	682	4.16
			Result $\vec{Z}_{LM\,ANN}$	0.01058	0.335		
			Result $\vec{Z}_{SA}$	0.01054	0.314		

The exact values used are: $k_2 = 0.0104 mg/(m^2 wt\%)$ and $\hat{a} = 0.322\, m^2/mg$.

Table 8. Results obtained using ANN, LM 1, LM 2, SA and hybrid combinations for experiment 1.

the direct problem solution corrupted with white gaussian noise with standard deviation $\sigma = 10mg/l$, which corresponds to measurement errors of the order of 4%. While in test cases 1, 2, 3, 4 and 8 the initial guesses are $K_2 = 0.0080mg/(m^2wt\%)$ and $\hat{a} = 0.100m^2/mg$,in test cases 6, 7 and 9 the initial guesses are the estimates obtained with the ANN.
In Table 9 are presented the results obtained for the estimation of λ, using the designed experiment number 2. Test cases 3-9 used simulated artificial data generated with the direct problem solution corrupted with white gaussian noise with standard deviation $\sigma = 0.10mg/l$, which corresponds to measurement errors of the order of 3%. While in test cases numbers 1, 2, 3, 4 and 8 the initial guess is $\lambda = 0.700m^2/mg$, in test cases 6, 7 and 9 the initial guesses are the estimates obtained with the ANN.

Case	Method	σ	Information	λ	Time (s)	S [mg²/l²] Eq. (39a)
1	LM 1 (grad. FDM)	0	Result $\vec{Z}_{LM^{FDM}}$	1.117	40	0
2	LM 2 (grad. ANN)	0	Result $\vec{Z}_{LM^{ANN}}$	1.117	29	0
3	LM 1 (grad. FDM)	0.1	Result $\vec{Z}_{LM^{FDM}}$	1.159	45	7.96
4	LM 2 (grad. ANN)	0.1	Result $\vec{Z}_{LM^{ANN}}$	1.159	30	7.96
5	RNA	0.1	Result $\vec{Z}_{ANN}$	1.432	1	202.9
6	LM 1 (grad. FDM)	0.1	Result $\vec{Z}_{LM^{FDM}}$	1.159	6	7.96
7	LM 2 (grad. ANN)	0.1	Result $\vec{Z}_{LM^{ANN}}$	1.159	4	7.96
8	SA (2.000 evaluations)	0.1	Result $\vec{Z}_{SA}$	1.099	5937	10.12
9	ANN-LM-SA SA (200 evaluations)	0.1	Result $\vec{Z}_{ANN}$	1.432	601	7.92
			Result $\vec{Z}_{LM^{ANN}}$	1.159		
			Result $\vec{Z}_{SA}$	1.156		

The exact value used is: $\lambda = 1.117\, m^2/mg$.

Table 9. Results obtained using ANN, LM 1, LM 2, SA and hybrid combinations for experiment 2.

6. Conclusions

6.1 Radiative transfer

In this case, Artificial Neural Networks (ANN), Levenberg-Marquardt (LM) and hybrid combinations of methods were used to solve the inverse radiative transfer problem. The solution with ANN and LM methods using only external detectors led to non-unique solutions of the inverse radiative transfer problem. It was demonstrated that the hybid combination of ANN-LM obtained better results than using either methods alone.

6.2 Drying (simultaneous heat and mass transfer)

The direct problem of simultaneous heat and mass transfer in porous media modeled with Luikov equations can be solved using the finite difference method, yielding the temperature and moisture distribution in the media, when the geometry, the initial and boundary conditions, and the medium properties are known.
Inverse problem techniques can be useful to estimate the medium properties when they are not known. After the use of an experiment design technique, the hybrid combination ANN-LM-SA resulted in good estimates for the drying inverse problem using artificially generated data.
The design of experiments technique is of great importance for the success of the estimation efforts, while previous works studied the estimation of Lu, Pn, Ko, Bi_q and Bi_m, here is

considered Lu, δ, r/c, h/k and h_m/k_m. The main advantage of such approach is to be able to design an "optimum" experiment using different medium width, l, porous medium and air temperature difference, $T_s - T_0$, and porous medium and air moisture potential difference, $u_0 - u^*$.
The combination of deterministic (LM) and stochastic (ANN and SA) methods achieved good results, reducing the time needed and not being retained by local minima. The use of ANN to obtain the derivatives in the first steps of the LM method reduced the time required for the solution of the inverse problem.

6.3 Gas-liquid adsorption

After the use of an experiment design technique, the hybrid combination ANN-LM-SA resulted in good solutions for the gas-liquid adsorption isotherm inverse problem.
The use of the ANN to obtain the derivatives in the first step of the LM method reduced the time necessary to solve the inverse problem.

7. Acknowledgements

The authors acknowledge the financial support provided by CNPq, *Conselho Nacional de Desenvolvimento Científico e Tecnológico,* FAPERJ, *Fundação Carlos Chagas Filho de Amparo à Pesquisa do Estado do Rio de Janeiro,* and FAPESP, Fundação de Amparo à Pesquisa do Estado de São Paulo.

8. References

Ahmad, T. and Guiochon, G, 2007, Numerical Determination of the Adsorption Isotherms of Tryptophan at Different Temperatures and Mobile Phase Composition, J. of Chromatography A, v. 1142, pp. 148-163.

Beck, J. V., 1988, Combined Parameter and Function Estimation in Heat Transfer with Application to Contact Conductance, J. Heat Transfer, v. 110, pp. 1046-1058.

Chandrasekhar, S, 1960, Radiative Transfer, Dover Publications Inc., New York.

Dantas, L. B., Orlande, H.R.B. and Cotta, R. M., 2003, An Inverse Problem of Parameter Estimation for Heat and Mass Transfer in Capillary Porous Media, Int. J. Heat Mass Transfer, v. 46, pp. 1587-1598.

Deckwer, W. R. and Schumpe, A., 1993, Improved Tools for Bubble Columns Reactor Design and Scale-up, Chem. Eng. Sc., v.48, No., pp. 889-911.

Dowding, K. J., Blackwell, B. F. and Cochran, R. J., 1999, Applications of Sensitivity Coefficients for Heat Conduction Problems, Numerical Heat Transfer, Part B, v. 36, pp. 33-55.

Forssén, P., Arnell, R. and Fornstedt, T., 2006, An Improved Algorithm for Solving Inverse Problems in Liquid Chromatography, Computers and Chemical Engineering, v.30, pp.1381-1391.

Garnier, C., Görner, T., Villiéras, F., De Donato, Ph., Polakovic, M., Bersillon, J. L. and Michot, L. J., 2007, Activated Carbon Surface Heterogeneity Seen by Parallel Probing by Inverse Liquid Chromatography at the Solid/Liquid Interface and by Gas Adsorption Analysis at the Solid/Gas Interface, Carbon, v. 45, pp. 240-247.

Graham, D. E. and Phillips, M. C., 1979, Proteins at Liquid Interfaces, II. Adsorption Isotherms, J. Colloid and Interface Science, v. 70, No. 3, pp. 415-426.

Haut, B. and Cartage, T., 2005, Mathematical Modeling of Gas-liquid Mass Transfer Rate in Bubble Columns Operated in the Heterogeneous Regime, Chem. Eng. Science, v. 60, n. 22, pp. 5937-5944.

Haykin, S., 1999, Neural Networks - A Comprehensive Foundation, Prentice Hall.

Huang, C. H. and Yeh, C. Y., 2002, An Inverse Problem in Simultaneous Estimating the Biot Number of Heat and Moisture Transfer for a Porous Material, Int. J. Heat Mass Transfer, v. 45, pp. 4643-4653.

Kirkpatrick, S., Gellat, Jr., C. D. and Vecchi, M. P., 1983, Optimization by Simulated Annealing, Science, v. 220, pp. 671-680.

Krishna, R. and van Baten, J. M., 2003, Mass Transfer in Bubble Columns, Catalysis Today, v. 79-80, pp. 67-75.

Lugon Jr., J. and Silva Neto, A. J., 2004, Deterministic, Stochastic and Hybrid Solutions for Inverse Problems in Simultaneous Heat and Mass Transfer in Porous Media, Proc. 13th Inverse Problems in Engineering Seminar, pp. 99-106, Cincinatti, USA.

Lugon Jr., J., 2005, Gas-liquid Interface Adsorption and One-dimensional Porous Media Drying Inverse Problems Solution, D.Sc Thesis, Universidade do Estado do Rio de Janeiro (in Portuguese).

Lugon Jr., J, Silva Neto, A. J. and Santana, C. C., 2009, A Hybrid Approach with Artificial Neural Networks, Levenberg-Marquardt and Simulated Annealing Methods for the Solution of Gas-Liquid Adsorption Inverse Problems, Inverse Problems in Science and Engineering, Vol. 17, No. 1, pp.85-96.

Lugon Jr., J and Silva Neto, A. J., 2010, Solution of Porous Media Inverse Drying Problems Using a Combination of Stochastic and Deterministic Methods, Journal of the Brazilian Society of Mechanical Sciences and Engineering, Accepted for publication.

Luikov, A. V. and Mikhailov, Y. A., 1965, Theory of Energy and Mass Transfer, Pergamon Press, Oxford, England.

Marquardt, D. W., 1963, An Algorithm for Least-Squares Estimation of Nonlinear Parameters, J. Soc. Industr. Appl. Math., v. 11, pp. 431-441.

Metropolis, N., Rosenbluth, A. W., Teller, A. H. and Teller, E., 1953, Equation of State Calculations by Fast Computing Machines, J. Chem. Physics, v.21, pp.1087-1092.

Mikhailov, M. D. and Özisik, M. N., 1994, Unified Analysis and Solutions of Heat and Mass Diffusion, Dover Publications, Inc.

Mouza, A. A., Dalakoglou, G. K. and Paras, S. V., 2005, Effect of Liquid Properties on the Performance of Bubble Column Reactors with Fine Pore Spargers, Chem. Eng. Science, v. 60, n. 5, pp. 1465-1475.

Mwithiga, G., and Olwal, J. O., 2005, The drying kinetics of kale (Brassica oleracea) in a convective hot air dryer, J. of Food Engineering, v. 71, No. 4, pp. 373-378.

Özişik, M. N., 1973, Radiation Transfer and Iterations with Conduction and Convection, John Wiley.

Özturk, S. S., Schumpe, A. and Deckwer, W.D., 1987, Organic Liquids in a Bubble Column: Holdups and Mass Transfer Coefficients, AIChE Journal, v. 33, No. 9, pp. 1473-1480.

Santana, C. C. and Carbonell, R. G., 1993a, Waste Minimization by Flotation: Recovery of Proteins and Other Surface-Active Compounds, 3rd Int. Conf. Waste Management, Bahia, Brazil.

Santana, C. C. and Carbonell, R. G., 1993b, Adsorptive Bubble Separation as a Means of Reducing Surface-Active Contaminants in Industrial Wastewaters, Proc. Int. Symp. on Heat and Mass Transfer, Cancun, Mexico, pp. 1-11.

Santana, C. C., 1994, Adsorptive Bubble Separation Process as a Means of Reducing Surface-Active Contaminants in Industrial Wastewaters, Brazilian J. Engineering-Chemistry, v. 5, pp. 7-74.

Silva Neto, A. J. and Becceneri, J. C. (Eds.), 2009, Nature Inspired Computational Intelligence Techniques - Application in Inverse Radiative Transfer Problems, SBMAC, São Carlos, Brazil. (in portuguese).

Silva Neto, A. J., Lugon Jr., J., Soeiro, F. J. C. P., Biondi Neto, L, Santana, C. C., Lobato, F. S. and Steffen Jr., V., 2010, Application of Simulated Annealing and Hybrid Methods in the Solution of Inverse Heat and Mass Transfer Problems, In Simulated Annealing, Theory with Applications, Ed. Chibante, R., Chapter 2, pp. 17-50, ISBN 978-953-307-134-3, Sciyo, Croatia

Silva Neto, A. J. and Moura Neto, F. D., 2005, Inverse Problems: Fundamental Concepts and Applications, EdUERJ, Rio de Janeiro (in Portuguese).

Silva Neto, A. J. and Soeiro, F. J. C. P., 2003, Solution of Implicitly Formulated Inverse Heat Transfer Problems with Hybrid Methods, Mini-Symposium Inverse Problems from Thermal/Fluids and Solid Mechanics Applications - 2nd MIT Conference on Computational Fluid and Solid Mechanics, Cambridge, USA.

Soeiro, F.J.C.P., Soares, P.O. and Silva Neto, A.J., 2004, Solution of Inverse Radiative Transfer Problems with Artificial Neural Networks and Hybrid Methods, Proc. 13th Inverse Problems in Engineering Seminar, pp. 163-169, Cincinnati, USA.

Soeiro, F. J. C. P. and Silva Neto, A. J., 2006, Inverse Radiative Transfer Problems in Two-Layer Participating Media, Proc. III European Conference on Computational Mechanics, Lisbon, Portugal.

Voelkel, A. and Strzemiecka, B., 2007, Characterization of Fillers Used in Abrasive Articles by Means of Inverse Gas Chromatography and Principal Components Analysis, Int. J. of Adhesion and Adhesives, v. 27, pp. 188-194.

27

The Use of Artificial Neural Networks (ANNs) in Aquatic Ecology

Antoni Quetglas, Francesc Ordines and Beatriz Guijarro
Instituto Español de Oceanografía, Centre Oceanogràfic de les Balears
Spain

1. Introduction

Complex network systems are pervasive in life sciences at all levels, from molecules and genes to organisms and ecosystems. All these systems are characterized by being constituted of numerous components or nodes (molecules, genes, cells, tissues, organisms), which are interconnected by many links in an intricate tangle, just as biological neural networks consist of many interacting neurons (Fig. 1). Apart from its structural complexity, complex networks are inherently difficult to understand because interactions are non-linear, distributed non-randomly, and are adaptive, that is, changing continuously in response to the state of the system itself (Strogatz, 2001; Pascual & Dunne, 2006). Understanding the functioning of these systems consisting of a large number of strongly interacting units represents therefore a major endeavour for biologists and ecologists.

As complex networks, ecosystems are non-linear systems constituted by countless interacting pieces, both biotic and abiotic, constituting the entangled web of life. In a world threatened by global environmental problems such as biodiversity loss, climate change, fishing overexploitation or pollution, ecologists are challenged by the need to understand and predict the dynamics of ecosystems as never before. Along with the complexity of ecological systems, ecologists are also faced with a huge amount of information that recent advances in data collection technology such as remote sensing have produced. To cope with the ecosystem complexity and large data sets currently available, ecologists nowadays have the opportunity to use machine-like learning techniques such as the artificial neural networks (ANNs).

As their name implies, ANNs are biologically inspired and were initially intended to mimic the neural activity in the human or animal brains (Garson, 1991; Goh, 1995; Stern, 1996). ANNs models are based on the same learning processes as the animal brain, which gathers information from the environment (input data) and gives an answer (output data) after using learned training algorithms. However, given that the architecture and dynamics of the animal brain is exceedingly complex, even the most elaborated ANN models are mere caricatures of the biological brain. Although the original works on ANNs date back to the forties (McCulloch & Pitts, 1943; Pitts & McCulloch, 1947), they not became really popular until the eighties after the work of the physicist John Hopfield. Hopfield (1982) introduced an oversimplified neural network, comprising a set of fully connected binary units, as a metaphor of neural computation. The most remarkable feature of this model was that it could learn by association and was quiet insensitive to noise. This capacity to recognize previously learned patterns, which was thought to be an exclusive property of brains, is precisely what the Hopfield model does (Solé & Goodwin, 2000).

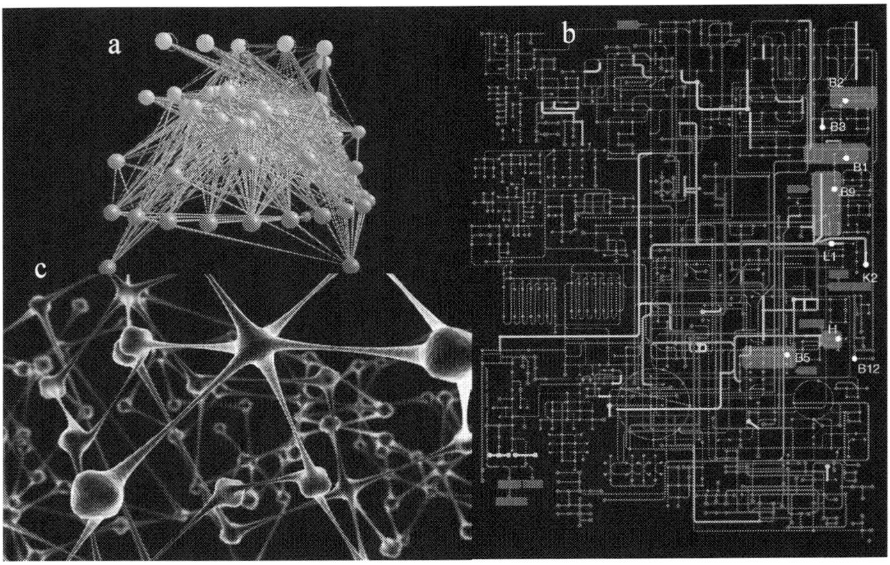

Fig. 1. Examples of complex networks in living systems: a) Caribbean Reef food web. The image is organized vertically, with basal species in the bottom, top predators above and intermediate species in between. b) Metabolic pathways of *H. sapiens* and two bacteria present in the human intestine and considered key commensals in the human intestinal microflora. c) Depiction of highly interconnected neurons in the animal brain.

The first applications of ANNs did not appear until the early 1990s after the publication of the error back-propagation algorithm (Rumelhart et al., 1986). ANNs have enjoyed explosive growth since then and have been successfully applied across a broad range of scientific domains, as shows this book and other previous works (e.g. Bishop, 1995; Sarle, 1997; Picton, 2000). However, a review of the literature reveals only a modest use of these approaches in ecology as compared to other disciplines, which could be related to the lack of the computational background necessary to implement these methods among ecologists (Olden et al., 2008). In spite of these limitations, ecologists have nowadays good comprehensive overviews of ANN applications in ecological sciences, such as the books of Fielding (1999), Lek & Guegan (2000), Lek et al. (2005) and Recknagel (2006). These books adds to an ever-increasing number of papers being published during the last years in many scientific journals, among which is worth highlighting some specialized ones such as Ecological Modelling (www.elsevier.com/locate/ecolmodel) and the recently launched Ecological Informatics (www.elsevier.com/locate/ecolinf).

In this chapter we review the use of ANNs in marine and freshwater ecology, including fisheries science, during the 1990s and 2000s. Such review is restricted to works published in international journals and is not intended to be exhaustive but simply to familiarize the reader with the capabilities and practical applications of ANNs in aquatic ecology. Detailed insights on the methodology are not given because those general aspects of ANNs are already discussed either on other chapters of this book or in other works (e.g. Bishop, 1995; Picton, 2000), and those issues specific to ecological applications have been reviewed elsewhere (e.g. Maier & Dandy, 2000; Lek & Guegan, 2000; Ozesmi et al., 2006).

2. Handling ecological data with ANNs

The characteristics of ecological data are quite different from those data handled by sciences traditionally considered harder than ecology like mathematics or physics. Ecological data are generally bulky, non-linear and highly complex, showing noise, redundancy, internal relations and outliers (Park et al., 2003a). In many cases researchers have rather unbalanced data sets, such as in community or taxonomical studies when data contain both a lot of uncommon, or not present species, and a reduced number of very abundant species. Traditionally, multivariate analyses of ecological data have been done using conventional techniques based on linear principles, such as multiple regression or discriminant analysis. However, relationships between variables in ecology are often non-linear or even unknown, which demands non-linear transformations to improve the results. Despite transformations by logarithmic, power or exponential functions, results are not satisfactory in many cases (Lek et al., 1996b; Brosse et al., 1999). In this respect ANNs constitute a promising alternative approach since they are powerful tools that manage large, complex datasets well, and are especially suitable when relationships between variables are non-linear or unknown (Lek et al., 1996b). This idea that neural networks do not require distributional assumptions is fully shared by ecologists and is generally claimed as the most important advantage of ANNs over classical statistical models. In fact, Maier & Dandy (2000) recommend that the primary focus should be on achieving good results, rather than statistical optimality, as this is one of the features that has attracted water resources modellers to ANNs in the first place. According to Sarle (1997), however, ANNs are subjected to the same assumptions as statistical models, and the explanation is simply that, whereas statisticians are concerned about the implications of those assumptions, many neural network users ignore them.

Formerly, ANNs were compared to "black boxes" because they always give an answer (output) when they are fed with data (input), although the internal processes taking place inside the network were not clearly understood. This prevented knowing the contribution of the independent variables in the prediction process, which is a major concern to ecologists, who are always interested in uncovering the causal relationships driving ecological phenomena (Olden & Jackson, 2002). The "black box" term is no longer a suitable term, since recent advances in the field of environmental sciences have provided a set of techniques to determine the relative importance of each input variable. These techniques include sensitivity analyses (Scardi, 1996; Lek et al., 1996a; Recknagel et al., 1997), input variable relevancies and neural interpretation diagrams (Ozesmi & Ozesmi, 1999), randomization tests of significance (Olden, 2000; Olden & Jackson, 2002), and partial derivatives (Dimopoulos et al., 1999; Reyjol et al., 2001; Gevrey et al., 2006). All these approaches are based on the fact that the contribution of each independent variable depends on the magnitude and direction of the connection weights between neurons (Olden et al., 2008). Good examples of papers dealing with the performance of several of these methods are Olden & Jackson (2002) and Gevrey et al. (2003). Olden & Jackson (2002) reviewed both qualitative and quantitative algorithms, but also described a randomization procedure for testing the statistical significance of the input variables. Gevrey et al. (2003) compared up to seven approaches and found that the partial derivatives method was the most useful in an empirical example predicting the density of brown trout spawning redds using habitat characteristics.

There are many different types of ANNs, which are classified according to their learning process and learning algorithm (Sarle, 1997). In supervised learning, the known target values are given to the ANN during training, after which the network is tested using exclusively the input values. In unsupervised learning, the target values are not provided to

N	Reference	Type of ANN	Dependent variables	Independent variables
1	Xu et al. (2005)	BRBPNN	Algal abundance (1)	Environmental variables (3-5)
2	Park et al. (2003b)	CPN	Fish richness (1)	Environmental variables (34)
3	Jeong et al. (2008a)	TARNN	Algal biomass (1)	Algal biomass (1)
4	Palmer et al. (2009)	GRNN, MLP	Fishing strategies (4)	Fish catches (33, 6)
5	Iglesias et al. (2004)	FNN, MLP	Fish landings (1)	Environmental variables (6)
6	Scardi (1996)	MLP	Algal abuncance (1)	Environmental variables (3, 4)
7	Scardi & Harding (1999)	MLP	Algal abundance (1)	Environmental variables (12)
8	Scardi (2001)	MLP	Algal abundance (1)	Environmental variables (11)
9	Wilson & Recknagel (2001)	MLP	Algal abundance (1)	Environmental variables (4, 5)
10	Recknagel et al. (1997)	MLP	Algal abundance (10)	Environmental variables (7, 10, 11)
11	Ozesmi & Ozesmi (1999)	MLP	Bird nesting probability (1, 3)	Environmental variables (6)
12	Manel et al. (1999)	MLP	Bird occurrence (1)	Environmental variables (32)
13	Fang et al. (2009)	MLP	Bird richness (1)	Environmental variables (4)
14	Dedecker et al. (2005)	MLP	Crustacean density (1)	Environmental variables (24)
15	Mouton et al. (2010)	MLP	Crustacean density (1)	Environmental variables (24)
16	Huse & Gjosaeter (1999)	MLP	Fish abundance (1)	Environmental variables (6)
17	Joy & Death (2004)	MLP	Fish and crustacean occurrence (14)	Environmental variables (31)
18	Dagorn et al. (1997)	MLP	Fish behaviour (1)	Environmental variables (7)
19	Huse & Ottersen (2003)	MLP	Fish density (1)	Environmental variables (10)

N	Reference	Type of ANN	Dependent variables	Independent variables
20	Baran et al. (1996)	MLP	Fish density (1)	Environmental variables (11)
21	Brosse et al. (1999)	MLP	Fish density (1)	Environmental variables (8)
22	Gevrey et al. (2003)	MLP	Fish density (1)	Environmental variables (10)
23	Lae et al. (1999)	MLP	Fish density (1)	Environmental variables
24	Lek et al. (1996b)	MLP	Fish density (1)	Environmental variables (11)
25	Gutierrez-Estrada et al. (2009)	MLP	Fish landings (1)	Environmental variables (18)
26	Olden et al. (2006)	MLP	Fish occurrence (16)	Environmental variables (24)
27	Maravelias et al. (2003)	MLP	Fish occurrence (2)	Environmental variables (5)
28	Mastrorillo et al. (1997)	MLP	Fish occurrence (2)	Environmental variables (10)
29	Olden (2003)	MLP	Fish occurrence (27)	Environmental variables (9)
30	Chen & Hare (2006)	MLP	Fish recruitment (1)	Environmental variables (2)
31	Ibarra et al. (2003)	MLP	Fish richness (1)	Environmental variables (5)
32	Beauchard et al. (2003)	MLP	Invertebrate richness (1)	Environmental variables (7)
33	Dedecker et al. (2004)	MLP	Invertebrates occurrence (1)	Environmental variables (15)
34	Engelhard & Heino (2004)	MLP	Age at maturation (1)	Annual growth layers (3-9)
35	Engelhard et al. (2003)	MLP	Age at maturation (1)	Annual growth layers (3-9)
36	Dreyfus-Leon (1999)	MLP	Fishermen strategies (3, 16)	Fishing variables (9, 20)
37	Newbury et al. (1995)	MLP	Fish density (10)	Frequency image data (51)
38	Power et al. (2005)	MLP	Fishing location (3)	Parasite abundances (5)
39	Haralabous & Georgakarakos (1996)	MLP	Fish identification (3)	School descriptors (25)

N	Reference	Type of ANN	Dependent variables	Independent variables
40	Song et al. (2006)	SOM	Sampling sites; invertebrates assemblages	
41	Jeong et al. (2008b)	SOM	Sampling sites	
42	Brosse et al. (2001)	SOM	Fish assemblages	
43	Hyun et al. (2005)	SOM	Fish assemblages	
44	Zhu et al. (2006)	SOM	Fish genetic structure	
45	Chon et al. (1996)	SOM	Invertebrates assemblages	
46	Cereghino et al. (2001)	SOM	Invertebrates assemblages	
47	Park et al. (2006)	SOM	Invertebrates assemblages	
48	Cho et al. (2009)	SOM	Sampling sites	
49	Hardman-Mountford et al. (2003)	SOM	Sea level variations	
50	Park et al. (2003a)	SOM, MLP	SOM: sampling sites; MLP: invertebrate assemblages	
51	Gevrey et al. (2004)	SOM, MLP	SOM: sampling sites; MLP: diatom assemblages	
52	Tison et al. (2007)	SOM, MLP	SOM: sampling sites; MLP: diatom assemblages	
53	Park et al. (2004)	SOM, ART	Invertebrates assemblages	
54	Chon et al. (2000)	SOM, ART	Invertebrates assemblages	

Table 1. List of papers with applications of ANNs in aquatic ecology: source, type of ANN, dependent variable and independent variables. In the case of MLPs, the numbers into brackets are the number of input neurons (independent variables) or output neurons (dependent variables). In the case of SOMs, the single cell under the dependent and independent variable headers contains the type of data that was patternized by means of the SOM. In those papers (50-53) using unsupervised (SOM) followed by supervised neural networks (MLP), the variable to be predicted by the MLP it is also shown.

the network, which usually performs some kind of dimensionality reduction or clustering. Depending on the existence or not of cycles in the connections between nodes the networks are classified as feedback, or recurrent ANNs, and feed-forward ANNs. Up to now, the most popular ANNs in ecological applications are the multilayer perceptron (MLP) with back-propagation algorithm and the Kohonen network or self-organizing map (SOM), although examples of other family of models have also been applied. In this work, for instance, we have reviewed a total of 54 papers dealing with applications of ANNs in the field of marine and freshwater ecology (Table 1): the MLP and the SOM were used in 39 and 15 cases, respectively, whereas other types of networks (see Section 8) were only used in 7 cases. In later sections, we give a succinct description of these methods and revise their main applications among researchers working on aquatic ecology.

3. Development of ANN models

Several papers have reviewed the use of ANNs in ecological applications and summarized both the main drawbacks in the available works and the main methodological issues that should be considered in the development of new models (Maier & Dandy, 2000; Maier & Dandy, 2001; Ozesmi et al., 2006). Maier & Dandy (2000) analysed different modelling issues of ANNs for the prediction and forecasting of water resources variables by reviewing up to 43 papers published until the end of 1998. One year later, the same authors (Maier & Dandy, 2001) published a systematic approach to the development of ANNs for environmental studies, which was intended to act as a guide for users of feed-forward, back-propagation ANNs. Ozesmi et al. (2006) also analysed different methodological issues in building, training and testing ANNs in ecological applications and made useful suggestions on its use. More recently, Suryanarayana et al. (2008) performed a thorough revision of the use of neural networks in fisheries research; after a brief description of ANNs the authors reviewed their applications in forecasting, classification, distribution and fisheries management since 1978 (97 and 103 papers during 1978-1999 and 2000-2006, respectively). What follows is an extract from all these papers; although they focused on the MLP, most of their recommendations also apply to other types of ANNs.

In general the modelling process is not described clearly, what prevents to assess the optimality of the results and the comparison between models. The major problem was overtraining (over-fitting), which could be avoided by limiting the complexity of the model. To do so, there are some rules of thumb, such as using at least 10 times the number of samples as parameters in the model (Burnham & Anderson, 2002). Another important concern refers to the lack of independent data sets, what makes that some data are used both in the training and testing processes. Given that it is difficult or costly to obtain a sufficient number of replicates in ecological studies, examples with independent test data sets are rather scarce. As an alternative, researchers use different methodologies to create a testing data set such as jack-knife or cross-validation. Finally, the choice of the type of model, its architecture and the internal parameters (e.g. number of hidden layers) are also poorly described in most cases.

In order to avoid all these concerns and to optimize the performance of the models, specialists recommend considering the following methodological issues. First, the input variables should be standardized and, although there is no need to transform data, it is recommended in order to remove trends and heteroscedasticity. Next, appropriate input variables should be determined with the aid of *a priori* knowledge, by using analytical techniques or a stepwise model-building approach. Learn rate and weight range should also be determined since these network parameters influence the performance of the model by affecting the weights. The choice of adequate network geometry involves the optimization of the architecture, the number of hidden layers and number of hidden neurons. Although there are guidelines in the literature to obtain optimal network geometries, for each application it has been done traditionally by a process of trial and error. To compare the performance of models created with the same data set it is recommended the use of criteria such as the Akaike Information Criteria (AIC). Finally, model performance should be assessed using independent data sets to ensure that the results obtained are valid, since the real model test does not involve the training but the testing phase.

N	Reference	Type of ANN	ANN Performance	Type of MSM	MSM Performance
1	Haralabous & Georgakarakos (1996)	MLP	95.92%	DA	89.29%
2	Baran et al. (1996)	MLP	0.92, 0.93	GLM	0.54, 0.69
3	Lek et al. (1996b)	MLP	0.96	MLR	0.47^{1}, 0.72^{2}
4	Brosse et al. (1999)	MLP	66, 97%	MLR	46, 95%
5	Lae et al. (1999)	MLP	0.95, 0.83	MLR	0.62^{1}, 0.81^{2}
6	Gevrey et al. (2003)	MLP	0.75, 0.76	MLR	0.47
7	Ibarra et al. (2003)	MLP	0.55, 0.82	MLR	0.33, 0.72
8	Engelhard et al. (2003)	MLP	66.6%	DA	68.0%
9	Engelhard & Heino (2004)	MLP	0.976	DA	0.985
10	Maravelias et al. (2003)	MLP	83.3, 85.6%	DA	49.5, 83.3%
11	Mastrorillo et al. (1997)	MLP	82.1, 90.1%	DA	62.5, 78.0%
12	Fang et al. (2009)	MLP	0.28	MLR	0.28
13	Gutierrez-Estrada et al. (2009)	MLP	0.98^{t}, 0.92^{s}	MLR, GAM	MLR: 0.69^{t}, 0.70^{s} GAM: 0.87^{t}, 0.86^{s}
14	Jeong et al. (2008a)	TARNN	0.97, 0.98^{t}, 0.94, 0.92^{s}	SARIMA, SES	SARIMA: 0.54^{t}, 0.28^{s} SES: 0.88^{t}, 0.38^{s}
15	Olden et al. (2006)	MLP	66, 91%	MDA, LOG	MDA: 46%, LOG: 83%
16	Power et al. (2005)	MLP	92, 94%	DA, QDA, KKN	DA: 93, 94% QDA: 92, 93% KNN: 94, 96%
17	Lae et al. (1999)	MLP	0.95^{t}, 0.83^{s}	MLR	0.81
18	Scardi (1996)	MLP	0.90, 0.954	MLR	0.27^{3}, 0.74^{4}

Table 2. Performance of ANNs compared to classical multivariate statistical models (MSM) in aquatic ecological applications. The indexes used to calculate the performance are not specified (mainly determination coefficient and percentage of correctly classified instances) but are the same in each reference for comparisons. When available, results are given for the training (t) and testing (s); numbers in superscripts refer to raw (1) *vs.* transformed (2) data, and single (3) *vs.* composite (4) linear model. MLR: multiple linear regression; GLM: generalized linear models; DA: discriminant analysis; GAM: generalized additive models; SARIMA: seasonal auto-regressive integrated moving average; SES: simple exponential smoothing; MDA: multiple discriminant analysis; LOG: logistic regression analysis; QDA: quadratic discriminant analysis; KKN: *k*-nearest neighbour classification.

4. ANNs *vs.* multivariate analyses

Several studies indicate that ANNs are identical or similar to different standard statistical models. Changing some parameters of the network structure, such as the transfer function or the number of hidden nodes, gives rise to existing models. Feed-forward networks with no hidden layer, for instance, are basically generalized linear models, whereas Kohonen SOMs are discrete approximations to principal curves and surfaces (Sarle, 1997). The training and learning phases in neural networks are not different from the parameter estimation phase in conventional statistical models (Maier & Dandy, 2000).

Many of the published works on ANNs in marine and freshwater ecology compare this modelling method with classical multivariate statistical procedures, such as multiple linear regression (MLR) or discriminant analysis (DA). In all cases, these works found that ANNs either clearly outperformed (e.g. Baran et al., 1996; Lek et al., 1996b; Mastrorillo et al., 1997; Brosse et al., 1999) or at least performed as well (e.g. Engelhard et al., 2003; Engelhard & Heino, 2004; Power et al., 2005; Fang et al., 2009) as classical techniques (Table 2). Differences between methods are very important in some applications. Analysing the relationships between density of trout spawning sites and habitat characteristics, for instance, Lek et al. (1996) obtained values of determination coefficients of 0.96 for the MLP and 0.47 (raw data) or 0.72 (transformed data) for the MLR. In a similar study, Gevrey et al. (2003) also found important differences, about 0.77 for MLP and 0.47 for MLR. However, the highest differences were obtained by Jeong et al. (2008a) comparing a type of ANN known as temporal autoregressive recurrent neural network (TARNN) and two model types based on root mean square error (RMSE), seasonal auto-regressive integrated moving average (SARIMA) and simple exponential smoothing (SES).

The work of Manel et al. (1999) exemplifies the concerns raised by most researchers when ANNs were not more performant than linear models. In their analysis of a river bird species distribution, substitute major conclusion was that ANN does not currently have major advantages over logistic regression and DA in the particular case of modelling species distribution, providing these latter methods are correctly applied. They also noted that the best method would depend on the aims of the study. When models are intended to be explanatory, any of the three approaches compared might be suitable, since all produced good overall fit to the data, but when there exist complex or non-linear influences on species distribution, the ANN may well turn out to be advantageous.

In spite of all these considerations, and provided that enough information is available, it is not possible that a multiple regression outperforms an ANN because if a process is inherently linear, an ANN is as effective as a linear model although it may take more data to be properly generalized (Palmer et al., 2009). When ANNs were not found to perform better than linear methods it was most probably due to non-optimal training strategies, ANN architectures or data-limited situations.

Haralabous & Georgakarakos (1996) reported that comparing ANNs and DA is not straightforward, because an ANN can only be tested on a subset of training-free cases, while DA can be acceptably tested on the whole dataset. However, this is not exactly correct because the performance of DA cannot be tested without an independent test set. The accuracy of DA can be inferred according to the underlying statistics, but these inferences rely on several assumptions that are probably not met in real world applications (e.g. multi-normality). Consequently, a proper comparison should take a single subset of the data to train the ANN and DA, and then a separate subset to test both methods (Palmer et al., 2009). However, this would require having a sufficiently large number of cases to obtain enough examples in each subset, which is not usual in environmental sciences where sampling programs are costly.

5. Multilayer perceptron (MLP)

The MLP is a supervised ANN which architecture is defined by highly interconnected neurons (units or nodes) that process information in parallel along three successive layers (Fig. 2). The input layer contains as many neurons as independent variables or descriptors used to predict the dependent variables, which in turn constitute the output layer. The third layer, called the hidden layer, is situated between the input and output layers and its number of layers/neurons is an important parameter since it optimizes the performance of the ANN. Neurons from one layer are interconnected to all neurons of neighbouring layers, but no connections are established within a layer or feedback connection. Training any type of supervised ANN consists in using a training dataset to adjust the connection weights in order to minimize the error between observed and predicted values. Once the connections have been established by training they remain fixed in the hidden layer and the ANN can be used for testing. After the network has been trained it should be able to correctly classify patterns that are different from those used during the training phase.

Since the MLP was first used in ecological studies (Komatsu et al., 1994; Lek et al., 1995), the network has been extensively implemented in diverse fields (Park & Chon, 2007). A good deal of examples (39 cases) of applications in marine and freshwater ecology is shown in Table 1. Most studies used the predictability capabilities of MLPs to infer some dependent variable from a set of environmental variables (29 cases). This dependent variable was generally an index of the quantity of individuals of a certain species (16 cases) such as the abundance, biomass or density or, to a lesser extent, the species occurrence (presence/absence; 7 cases). In other cases the dependent variable referred to community indexes (species richness; 4 cases).

In the overall set of papers the number of input and output neurons ranged between 2-51 and 1-27 respectively. An output layer with a single neuron was by far the most usual network architecture (28 cases), representing this single output the value to be predicted by the MLP for a single species (e.g. abundance, biomass, species richness). In other cases, the MLP was used to predict those values for a set of species. Recknagel et al. (1997), for instance, predicted the abundance of 10 algae species from four different lakes using different sets of environmental variables (7, 10 and 11). Joy & Death (2004) predicted the occurrence of 14 species of fish and crustaceans taking into account up to 31 driving variables. Similarly, Olden (2003) predicted the occurrence of 27 fishes considering 9 physical variables, whereas Olden et al. (2006) used 24 variables to infer the occurrence of 16 fish species.

Other applications in aquatic ecology different from the prediction of species abundances or occurrences are reported in this paragraph. In two cases the MLP has been used to determine the age at maturation of fish species from annual growth layers in scales or otoliths (Engelhard et al., 2003; Engelhard & Heino, 2004). Ozesmi & Ozesmi (1999) predicted the nesting probability of two riverine bird species using 6 environmental variables. The MLP has also been used to identify three different fish species from 25 variables corresponding to the main school descriptors (Haralabous & Georgakarakos, 1996). Power et al. (2005) made use of MLP to classify a marine fish species according to the three different fisheries from which it was harvested using as predictors the abundance of different sets of parasites (3-6). Dreyfus-Leon (1999) built a model to mimic the search behaviour of fishermen with two MLPs to cope with two separate decision-making processes in fishing activities. One MLP (20 input neurons, 16 output neurons) dealt with decisions to stay or move to new fishing grounds and the other one was constructed to finding prey within the fishing areas (9 inputs, 3 outputs).

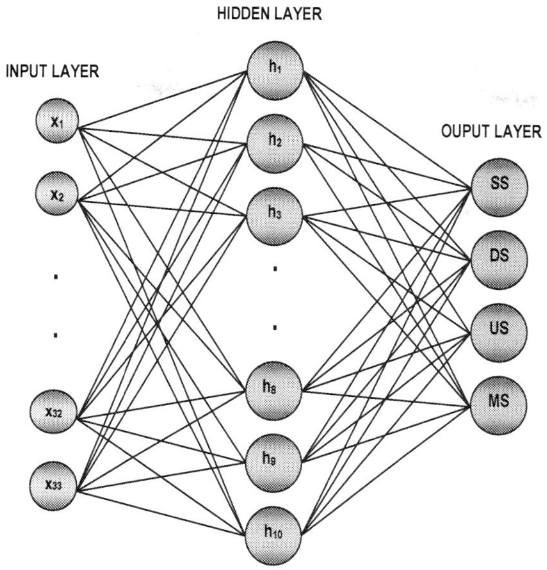

Fig. 2. Scheme of the architecture of a multilayer perceptron (MLP). The example was taken from Palmer et al. (2009), who used the MLP to infer the fishing tactics used by fishermen in their daily trips, taking as predictors the species composition present in the landings statistics. The figure represents a three-layered MLP with 10 neurons in the hidden layer and 33 neurons in the input layer corresponding to the landings of the 33 most important commercial species. The 4 nodes in the output layer are the 4 different fishing tactics to be predicted.

6. Self-organizing map (SOM)

The SOMs, also referred to as Kohonen network, are unsupervised ANNs that approximates the probability density function of the input data to display the data sets in a more comprehensible representation form (Kohonen, 2001). In terms of grouping the input data, the SOM is equivalent to conventional multivariate methods such as principal component analysis; it maps the multidimensional data space of complex data sets on two or a few more dimensions, preserving the existing topology as much as possible (Chon et al., 1996). The description that follows on the SOM functioning is based on the book of Lek et al. (2005). The SOM consists exclusively of two layers, the input and output layers, connected by weights that give the connection intensity; the outputs are usually arranged into two dimensional grids on a hexagonal lattice for better visualization (Fig. 3). When an input vector is sent through the network, each neuron in the network computes the distance between the weight vector and the input vector. Among all the output neurons, the one having the minimum distance between the weight and input vectors is chosen. The weights of both this winner neuron and its neighbouring neurons are then updated using the SOM algorithm to further reduce the distance between the weight and the input vector. The training is usually done in two phases: a rough training for ordering based on a large neighbourhood radius, followed by fine tuning with a small radius. As a result, the network is trained to classify the input vectors according to the weight vectors that are closest to them. Given that there are not still boundaries between clusters in the trained SOM map, it has to be subdivided into different groups according to the similarity of the weight vectors of the neurons. To analyse the contribution of variables to clusters, each input variable calculated during the training process is visualised in each neuron of the trained SOM in grey scale. The resulting clusters can outperform the results obtained using conventional classification methods, although there is the drawback that the size and shape of the map have to be fixed in advance.

Since Chon et al. (1996) first applied the SOM to patterning benthic communities, it has became the most popular unsupervised neural network in aquatic ecology applications for classification and patterning purposes (Park & Chon, 2007). In most cases the SOM has been used to classify sampling sites according to different environmental variables or faunal assemblages from their species composition. Jeong et al. (2008b), for instance, classified the different habitats present in a lagoon from a set of 21 limnological characteristics, whereas Cho

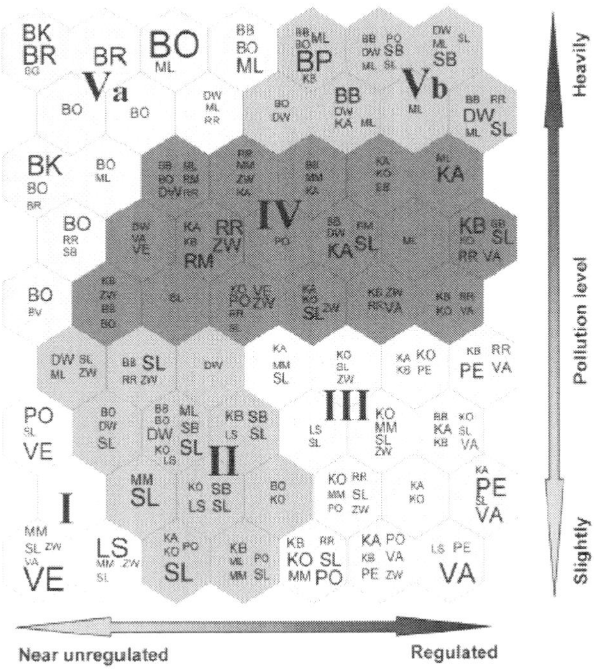

Fig. 3. Example of an output of a two dimensional hexagonal lattice obtained using a self-organizing map (SOM). The figure comes from Park et al. (2003a), who used the SOM to classify sampling sites with different environmental variables. The Latin numbers (I–V) represent different clusters, and the acronyms in the hexagonal units represent different water types. The font size of the acronym is proportional to the number of sampling sites in the water types in the range of 1–18 samples.

et al. (2009) characterized the habitat preferences of a river otter species taking into account several environmental variables. Song et al. (2006) used the SOM with two different objectives: first to define hydro-morphological patterns of the sampling sites based on four environmental variables, and then to reveal temporal changes in the macro-invertebrate communities inhabiting the sites clustered by SOM. Concerning the classification of faunal communities, the SOM has been mainly used to pattern invertebrate (Chon et al., 1996; Cereghino et al., 2001; Park et al., 2006) and fish (Brosse et al., 2001; Hyun et al., 2005) assemblages. In an original paper, Park et al. (2006) used SOM to patternize benthic macro-invertebrate communities in terms of exergy, which is a measure of the free energy of a system and it is used as an ecological indicator. Hyun et al. (2005) used the SOM to pattern temporal variations in long-term fisheries data (1954-2001) according to the 30 commercially most important species; five clusters were identified corresponding to different time periods reflecting environmental and economic forcings on fish catch. Other SOM applications include the study of the genetic population structure of a sturgeon species (Zhu et al., 2006) and the identification of characteristic patterns from sea level differences using a seven-year time series of satellite-derived data (Hardman-Mountford et al., 2003; Fig. 4). Further SOM applications, in combination with other neural network types, are reviewed in the following section.

In most cases, the ecological studies dealing with SOM applications manage complex, large data matrices. The results of all these works agree that the SOM is a powerful tool to extract information from such complex datasets which outperforms conventional approaches used previously in ecology for patterning purposes (e.g. principal component analysis).

7. Combined networks

Although ANNs are mainly used for prediction (e.g. MLP) or classification (e.g. SOM), there are also networks performing both functions at the same time. One example used in some ecological applications is the counter-propagation network (CPN), which consists of unsupervised and supervised learning algorithms to classify input vectors and predict output values. The CPN, which name alludes to the counter-flow of data through the network with data flowing inward from both sides, functions as a statistically optimal self-adapting look-up table (Hecht-Nielsen, 1988). Park et al. (2003b) applied a CPN to predict species richness and diversity index of benthic macro-invertebrate communities using 34 environmental variables. The trained CPN was useful for finding the corresponding values between environmental variables and community indices and displayed a high accuracy in the prediction process.

In some cases, researchers simply use two different networks in sequential steps for classification purposes first, followed by prediction. Chon et al. (2000) analysed patterns of temporal variation in community dynamics of benthic macro-invertebrates by combining two unsupervised ANNs, the adaptive resonance theory (ART) and the SOM. Park et al. (2004) also used the combination of ART and SOM to assess benthic communities in stream ecosystems, first using the SOM to reduce the dimension of the community data and secondly the ART to further classify the groups in different scale. Park et al. (2003a) used the SOM to classify sampling sites using species richness of aquatic insect orders and afterwards applied the MLP to predict the arrangements obtained using a set of environmental variables. Gevrey et al. (2004) used the SOM to classify samples according to their diatom composition, and then MLP to predict these assemblages using environmental characteristics of each sample. Similarly, Tison et al. (2007) classified diatom samples using the SOM and then predicted the community types with different environmental variables through a MLP.

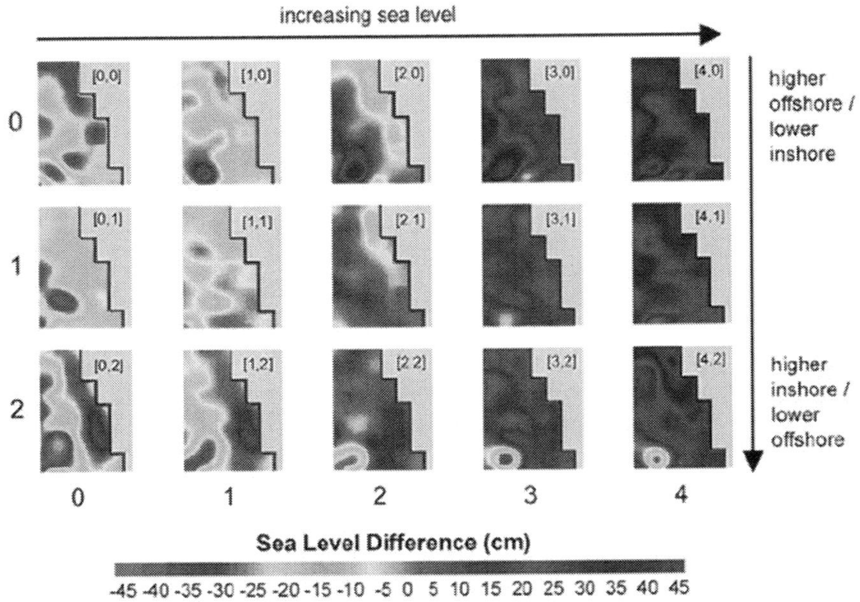

Fig. 4. The SOM of sea level differences obtained by Hardman-Mountford et al. (2003) using remote sensing data. The 15 patterns in a 5 by 3 array, where the land is shown in grey, correspond to different time periods with contrasting oceanographic scenarios.

8. Other types of ANNs

Apart from MLP and SOM there are still very few examples of applications of other types of ANNs in ecological studies. We have only found the use of four different types of networks in our review: functional neural network (FNN), Bayesian regularized back-propagation neural network (BRBPNN), temporal autoregressive recurrent neural network (TARNN) and generalized regression neural network (GRNN).

Iglesias et al. (2004) applied the FNN, a type of network in which the weights of the neurons are substituted by a set of functions, to predict the catches of two pelagic fish species taken as independent variables a set of oceanographic parameters obtained from remote sensors. The results of this study showed that functional networks considerably improved the predictions obtained using MLP. Xu et al. (2005) used the BRBPNN to predict chlorophyll trends in a lake; the advantage of this model is that it can automatically select the regularization parameters and integrate the characteristics of high convergent rate of traditional back-propagation neural networks and prior information of Bayesian statistics. Jeong et al. (2008a) developed a TARNN model to predict time-series changes of phytoplankton dynamics in a regulated river ecosystem. The TARNN algorithms were found to be an alternative solution to overcome the increasing size and structural complexity of the models used in freshwater ecology. Palmer et al. (2009) used the GRNN, together with MLP and DA, to predict fishing tactics from daily landing data. In this application, the GRNN, which is a type of ANN having the same number of neurons as there are cases in the training data set, outperformed both the MLP and DA.

9. Conclusion

The study of the highly complex structure and dynamics of ecological systems demands appropriate powerful tools such as ANNs. This is especially relevant nowadays, when the scientific community handles a lot of bulky databases and has to cope with global environmental threats that require urgent international attention. The purpose of this review is twofold. First, to familiarize ANNs users from other scientific disciplines, such as the ones covered in this book, with the use that ecologists make of these methods. Second, introduce ecologists unfamiliar with the ANNs to the capabilities of these tools and show them the palette of practical applications currently available in the domain of the aquatic ecology. Although the majority of ecologists lack the theoretical and computational background needed to implement these approaches (Fielding, 1999), they can take advantage of the user-friendly software that is being rapidly developed during recent years (Olden et al., 2008). One important drawback is, however, the fact that ANN modelling is a very active research area and the dissemination of useful information for practitioners constitutes one of the greatest challenges facing ANNs users (Maier & Dandy, 2000). By contrast, these approaches are flexible and readily combinable with other methods (Lek et al. 2005; Recknagel 2006), which would allow ecologists to develop models of increasing complexity as requires the analysis of ecological systems.
According to Pascual & Dunne (2006), understanding the ecology and mathematics of ecological networks is central to understanding the fate of biodiversity and ecosystems in response to perturbations. Knowing the network structure is essential to understand the properties of the network and the use of ANNs in ecological models constitutes a first step towards this understanding. We hope our review could awake the interest of ecologists in ANN modelling and maybe to help them with the use of these approaches in their studies on aquatic ecology.

10. Acknowledgements

The image of Figure 1a was produced with FoodWeb3D, written by R.J. Williams and provided by the Pacific Ecoinformatics and Computational Ecology Lab (www.foodwebs.org, Yoon et al., 2004). Figures 1b, 2, 3 and 4 were reproduced with permission. Figure 1c was reproduced with permission from http://technology.desktopnexus.com/wallpaper/48950/.

11. References

Baran, P., Lek, S., Delacoste, M. & Belaud, A. (1996). Stochastic models that predict trout population density or biomass on a mesohabitat scale. *Hydrobiologia*, 337, 1-3, 1-9, ISSN: *0018-8158*

Bishop, C.M. (1995). *Neural networks for pattern recognition,* Clarendon Press, ISBN-10: 0198538642, Oxford

Brosse, S., Giraudel, J.L. & Lek, S. (2001). Utilisation of non-supervised neural networks and principal component analysis to study fish assemblages. *Ecological Modelling*, 146, 1-3, 159-166, ISSN: 0304-3800

Brosse, S., Guegan, J.F., Tourenq, J.N. & Lek, S. (1999). The use of artificial neural networks to assess fish abundance and spatial occupancy in the littoral zone of a mesotrophic lake. *Ecological Modelling*, 120, 2-3, 299-311, ISSN: 0304-3800

Burnham, K.P. & Anderson, D.R. (2002). Model selection and multimodel inference: a practical information-theoretic approach, Springer, ISSN-10: 0387953647, New York

Cereghino, R., Giraudel, J.L. & Compin, A. (2001). Spatial analysis of stream invertebrates distribution in the Adour-Garonne drainage basin (France), using Kohonen self organizing maps. *Ecological Modelling*, 146, 1-3, 167-180, ISSN: 0304-3800

Cho, H.S., Choi, K.H., Lee, S.D. & Park, Y.S. (2009). Characterizing habitat preference of Eurasian river otter (*Lutra lutra*) in streams using a self-organizing map. *Limnology*, 10, 3, 203-213, ISSN: 1439-8621

Chon, T.S., Park, Y.S., Moon, K.H. & Cha, E.Y. (1996). Patternizing communities by using an artificial neural network. *Ecological Modelling*, 90, 1, 69-78, ISSN: 0304-3800

Chon, T.S., Park, Y.S. & Park, J.H. (2000). Determining temporal pattern of community dynamics by using unsupervised learning algorithms. *Ecological Modelling*, 132, 1-2, 151-166, ISSN: 0304-3800

Dimopoulos, I., Chronopoulos, J., Chronopoulou-Sereli, A. & Lek, S. (1999). Neural network models to study relationships between lead concentration in grasses and permanent urban descriptors in Athens city (Greece). *Ecological Modelling*, 120, 2-3, 157-165, ISSN

Dreyfus-Leon, M.J. (1999). Individual-based modelling of fishermen search behaviour with neural networks and reinforcement learning. *Ecological Modelling*, 120, 2-3, 287-297, ISSN: 0304-3800

Engelhard, G.H., Dieckmann, U. & Godo, O.R. (2003). Age at maturation predicted from routine scale measurements in Norwegian spring-spawning herring (*Clupea harengus*) using discriminant and neural network analyses. *ICES Journal of Marine Science*, 60, 2, 304-313, ISSN: 1054-3139

Engelhard, G.H. & Heino, M. (2004). Maturity changes in Norwegian spring-spawning herring before, during, and after a major population collapse. *Fisheries Research*, 66, 2-3, 299-310, ISSN: 0165-7836

Fang, W.T., Chu, H.J. & Cheng, B.Y. (2009). Modeling waterbird diversity in irrigation ponds of Taoyuan, Taiwan using an artificial neural network approach. *Paddy and Water Environment*, 7, 3, 209-216, ISSN: 1611-2490

Fielding, A.H. (1999). Machine learning methods for ecological applications, Klumer Academic Publishers, ISBN-10: 0412841908, Massachusetts

Garson, G.D. (1991). Interpreting neural network connection weights. *Artificial Intelligence Expert*, 6, 47-51, ISSN: *0004-3702*

Gevrey, M., Dimopoulos, I. & Lek, S. (2006). Two-way interaction of input variables in the sensitivity analysis of neural network models. *Ecological Modelling*, 195, 1-2, 43-50, ISSN: 0304-3800

Gevrey, M., Dimopoulos, L. & Lek, S. (2003). Review and comparison of methods to study the contribution of variables in artificial neural network models. *Ecological Modelling*, 160, 3, 249-264, ISSN: 0304-3800

Gevrey, M., Rimet, F., Park, Y.S., Giraudel, J.L., Ector, L. & Lek, S. (2004). Water quality assessment using diatom assemblages and advanced modelling techniques. *Freshwater Biology*, 49, 2, 208-220, ISSN: 0046-5070

Goh, A.T.C. (1995). Back-propagation neural networks for modelling complex systems. *Artificial Intelligence in Engineering*, 9, 143-151, ISSN: 0954-1810

Gutierrez-Estrada, J.C., Yanez, E., Pulido-Calvo, I., Silva, C., Plaza, F. & Borquez, C. (2009). Pacific sardine (*Sardinops sagax*, Jenyns 1842) landings prediction. A neural network ecosystemic approach. *Fisheries Research*, 100, 2, 116-125, ISSN: 0165-7836

Haralabous, J. & Georgakarakos, S. (1996). Artificial neural networks as a tool for species identification of fish schools. *ICES Journal of Marine Science*, 53, 2, 173-180, ISSN: 1054-3139

Hardman-Mountford, N.J., Richardson, A.J., Boyer, D.C., Kreiner, A. & Boyer, H.J. (2003). Relating sardine recruitment in the Northern Benguela to satellite-derived sea surface height using a neural network pattern recognition approach. *Progress in Oceanography*, 59, 2-3, 241-255, ISSN: 0079-6611

Hecht-Nielsen, R. (1988). Applications of counterpropagation networks. *Neural Networks*, 1, 2, 131-139, ISSN: 0893-6080

Hopfield, J.J. (1982). Neural networks and physical systems with emergent collective computational abilities. *Proceedings of the National Academy of Sciences of the United States of America-Biological Sciences*, 79, 8, 2554-2558, ISSN: 0273-1134

Hyun, K., Song, M.Y., Kim, S. & Chon, T.S. (2005). Using an artificial neural network to patternize long-term fisheries data from South Korea. *Aquatic Sciences*, 67, 3, 382-389, ISSN: 1015-1621

Ibarra, A.A., Gevrey, M., Park, Y.S., Lim, P. & Lek, S. (2003). Modelling the factors that influence fish guilds composition using a back-propagation network: Assessment of metrics for indices of biotic integrity. *Ecological Modelling*, 160, 3, 281-290, ISSN: 0304-3800

Iglesias, A., Arcay, B., Cotos, J.M., Taboada, J.A. & Dafonte, C. (2004). A comparison between functional networks and artificial neural networks for the prediction of fishing catches. *Neural Computing and Applications*, 13, 1, 24-31, ISSN: 0941-0643

Jeong, K.S., Kim, D.K., Jung, J.M., Kim, M.C. & Joo, G.J. (2008a). Non-linear autoregressive modelling by temporal recurrent neural networks for the prediction of freshwater phytoplankton dynamics. *Ecological Modelling*, 211, 3-4, 292-300, ISSN: 0304-3800

Jeong, K.S., Kim, D.K., Pattnaik, A., Bhatta, K., Bhandari, B. & Joo, G.J. (2008b). Patterning limnological characteristics of the Chilika lagoon (India) using a self-organizing map. *Limnology*, 9, 3, 231-242, ISSN: 1439-8621

Joy, M.K. & Death, R.G. (2004). Predictive modelling and spatial mapping of freshwater fish and decapod assemblages using GIS and neural networks. *Freshwater Biology*, 49, 8, 1036-1052, ISSN: 0046-5070

Kohonen, T. (2001). *Self-organizing maps*. Springer, ISBN: 3-540-67921-9, New York

Komatsu, T., Aoki, I., Mitani, I. & Ishii, T. (1994). Prediction of the catch of Japanese sardine larvae in Sagami Bay using a neural network. *Fisheries Science*, 60, 4, 385-391, ISSN: 0919-9268

Lae, R., Lek, S. & Moreau, J. (1999). Predicting fish yield of African lakes using neural networks. *Ecological Modelling*, 120, 2-3, 325-335, ISSN: 0304-3800

Lek, S., Belaud, A., Baran, P., Dimopoulos, I. & Delacoste, M. (1996a). Role of some environmental variables in trout abundance models using neural networks. *Aquatic Living Resources*, 9, 1, 23-29, ISSN: 0990-7440

Lek, S., Belaud, A., Dimopoulos, I., Lauga, J. & Moreau, J. (1995). Improved estimation, using neural networks, of the food consumption of fish populations. *Marine and Freshwater Research*, 46, 8, 1229-1236, ISSN: 1323-1650

Lek, S., Delacoste, M., Baran, P., Dimopoulos, I., Lauga, J. & Aulagnier, S. (1996b). Application of neural networks to modelling nonlinear relationships in ecology. *Ecological Modelling*, 90, 1, 39-52, ISSN: 0304-3800

Lek, S. & Guegan, J.F. (2000). *Artificial neural networks: application to ecology and evolution.* Springer, ISSN-10: 3540669213, New York

Lek, S., Scardi, M., Verdonschot, P.F.M., Descy, J.P. & Park, Y.S. (2005). *Modelling community structure in freshwater ecosystems.* Springer, ISBN-10: 3540239405, New York

Letunic, I., Yamada, T., Kanehisa, M. & Bork, P. (2008). iPath: interactive exploration of biochemical pathways and networks. *Trends in Biochemical Sciences*, 33, 3, 101-103, ISSN: 0968-0004

Maier, H.R. & Dandy, G.C. (2000). Neural networks for the prediction and forecasting of water resources variables: a review of modelling issues and applications. *Environmental Modelling & Software*, 15, 1, 101-124, ISSN: 1364-8152

Maier, H.R. & Dandy, G.C. (2001). Neural network based modelling of environmental variables: A systematic approach. *Mathematical and Computer Modelling*, 33, 6-7, 669-682, ISSN: 0895-7177

Manel, S., Dias, J.M. & Ormerod, S.J. (1999). Comparing discriminant analysis, neural networks and logistic regression for predicting species distributions: a case study with a Himalayan river bird. *Ecological Modelling*, 120, 2-3, 337-347, ISSN: 0304-3800

Maravelias, C.D., Haralabous, J. & Papaconstantinou, C. (2003). Predicting demersal fish species distributions in the Mediterranean Sea using artificial neural networks. *Marine Ecology Progress Series*, 255, 249-258, ISSN: 0171-8630

Mastrorillo, S., Lek, S., Dauba, F. & Belaud, A. (1997). The use of artificial neural networks to predict the presence of small-bodied fish in a river. *Freshwater Biology*, 38, 2, 237-246, ISSN: 0046-5070

McCulloch, W.S. & Pitts, W. (1943). A logical calculus of the ideas imminent in nervous activity. *Bulletin of Mathematical Biophysics*, 5, 115-133, ISSN: 0007-4985

Olden, J.D. (2000). An artificial neural network approach for studying phytoplankton succession. *Hydrobiologia*, 436, 1-3, 131-143, ISSN: 0018-8158

Olden, J.D. (2003). A species-specific approach to modeling biological communities and its potential for conservation. *Conservation Biology*, 17, 3, 854-863, ISSN: 0888-8892

Olden, J.D. & Jackson, D.A. (2002). Illuminating the "black box": a randomization approach for understanding variable contributions in artificial neural networks. *Ecological Modelling*, 154, 1-2, 135-150, ISSN: 0304-3800

Olden, J.D., Joy, M.K. & Death, R.G. (2006). Rediscovering the species in community-wide predictive modeling. *Ecological Applications*, 16, 4, 1449-1460, ISSN: 1051-0761

Olden, J.D., Lawler, J.J. & Poff, N.L. (2008). Machine learning methods without tears: A primer for ecologists. *Quarterly Review of Biology*, 83, 2, 171-193, ISSN: 0033-5770

Ozesmi, S.L. & Ozesmi, U. (1999). An artificial neural network approach to spatial habitat modelling with interspecific interaction. *Ecological Modelling*, 116, 1, 15-31, ISSN: 0304-3800

Ozesmi, S.L., Tan, C.O. & Ozesmi, U. (2006). Methodological issues in building, training, and testing artificial neural networks in ecological applications. *Ecological Modelling*, 195, 1-2, 83-93, ISSN: 0304-3800

Palmer, M., Quetglas, A., Guijarro, B., Moranta, J., Ordines, F. & Massuti, E. (2009). Performance of artificial neural networks and discriminant analysis in predicting fishing tactics from multispecific fisheries. *Canadian Journal of Fisheries and Aquatic Sciences*, 66, 224-237, ISSN: 0706-652X

Park, Y.S., Cereghino, R., Compin, A. & Lek, S. (2003b). Applications of artificial neural networks for patterning and predicting aquatic insect species richness in running waters. *Ecological Modelling*, 160, 3, 265-280, ISSN: 0304-3800

Park, Y.S. & Chon, T.S. (2007). Biologically-inspired machine learning implemented to ecological informatics. *Ecological Modelling*, 203, 1-2, 1-7, ISSN: 0304-3800

Park, Y.S., Chon, T.S., Kwak, I.S. & Lek, S. (2004). Hierarchical community classification and assessment of aquatic ecosystems using artificial neural networks. *Science of the Total Environment*, 327, 1-3, 105-122, ISSN: 0048-9697

Park, Y.S., Lek, S., Scardi, M., Verdonschot, P.F.M. & Jorgensen, S.E. (2006). Patterning exergy of benthic macroinvertebrate communities using self-organizing maps. *Ecological Modelling*, 195, 1-2, 105-113, ISSN: 0304-3800

Park, Y.S., Verdonschot, P.F.M., Chon, T.S. & Lek, S. (2003a). Patterning and predicting aquatic macroinvertebrate diversities using artificial neural network. *Water Research*, 37, 8, 1749-1758, ISSN: 0043-1354

Pascual, M. & Dunne, J.A. (2006). From small to large ecological networks in a dynamic world, In *Ecological Networks: Linking Structure to Dynamics in Food Webs*, Pascual M. & Dunne A. (Editors), 3-24, Oxford University Press, ISBN-10: 0195188160, Oxford

Picton, P.D. (2000). *Neural networks.* Palgrave Macmillan, ISBN-10: 033380287X, New York

Pitts, W. & McCulloch, W.S. (1947). How we know universals: the perception of auditory and visual forms. *Bulletin of Mathematical Biophysics*, 9, 3, 127-147, ISSN: 0007-4985

Power, A.M., Balbuena, J.A. & Raga, J.A. (2005). Parasite infracommunities as predictors of harvest location of bogue (*Boops boops* L.): a pilot study using statistical classifiers. *Fisheries Research*, 72, 2-3, 229-239, ISSN: 0165-7836

Recknagel, F. (2006). *Ecological Informatics: scope, techniques and applications*, Springer, ISBN-10: 3540283838, New York

Recknagel, F., French, M., Harkonen, P. & Yabunaka, K. (1997). Artificial neural network approach for modelling and prediction of algal blooms. *Ecological Modelling*, 96, 1-3, 11-28, ISSN: 0304-3800

Reyjol, Y., Lim, P., Belaud, A. & Lek, S. (2001). Modelling of microhabitat used by fish in natural and regulated flows in the river Garonne (France). *Ecological Modelling*, 146, 1-3, 131-142, ISSN: 0304-3800

Rumelhart, D.E., Hinton, G.E. & Williams, R.J. (1986). Learning representations by back-propagating errors. *Nature*, 323, 6088, 533-536, ISSN: 0028-0836

Sarle, W.S. (1997). Neural network FAQ, periodic posting to the Usenet newsgroup comp.ai.neural-nets. Available from ftp.sas.com/pub/neural/FAQ.html

Scardi, M. (1996). Artificial neural networks as empirical models for estimating phytoplankton production. *Marine Ecology Progress Series*, 139, 289-299, ISSN: 0171-8630

Solé, R. & Goodwin, B. (2000). *Signs of life: how complexity pervades biology*, Basic Books, ISBN-10: 0465019285, New York

Song, M.Y., Park, Y.S., Kwak, I.S., Woo, H. & Chon, T.S. (2006). Characterization of benthic macroinvertebrate communities in a restored stream by using self-organizing map. *Ecological Informatics*, 1, 3, 295-305, ISSN: 1574-9541

Stern, H.S. (1996). Neural networks in applied statistics. *Technometrics*, 38, 3, 205-214, ISSN: 0040-1706

Strogatz, S.H. (2001). Exploring complex networks. *Nature*, 410, 6825, 268-276, ISSN: 0028-0836

Suryanarayana, I., Braibanti, A., Rao, R.S., Ramam, V.A., Sudarsan, D. & Rao, G.N. (2008). Neural networks in fisheries research. *Fisheries Research*, 92, 2-3, 115-139, ISSN: 0165-7836

Tison, J., Park, Y.S., Coste, M., Wasson, J.G., Rimet, F., Ector, L. & Delmas, F. (2007). Predicting diatom reference communities at the French hydrosystem scale: a first step towards the definition of the good ecological status. *Ecological Modelling*, 203, 1-2, 99-108, ISSN: 0304-3800

Xu, M., Zeng, G.M., Xu, X.Y., Huang, G.H., Sun, W. & Jiang, X.Y. (2005). Application of bayesian regularized BP neural network model for analysis of aquatic ecological data: a case study of chlorophyll-a prediction in Nanzui water area of Dongting Lake. *Journal of Environmental Sciences-China*, 17, 6, 946-952, ISSN: 10010742

Yoon, I., Williams, R.J., Levine, E., Yoon, S., Dunne, J.A. & Martinez, N.D. (2004). Webs on the Web (WoW): 3D visualization of ecological networks on the WWW for collaborative research and education. Proceedings of the IS&T/SPIE Symposium on Electronic Imaging, Visualization and Data Analysis, 5295: 124-132,

Zhu, B., Zhao, N., Shao, Z.J., Lek, S. & Chang, J.B. (2006). Genetic population structure of Chinese sturgeon (*Acipenser sinensis*) in the Yangtze River revealed by artificial neural network. *Journal of Applied Ichthyology*, 22, 82-88, ISSN: 0175-8659